Major Problems
in California History

DOCUMENTS AND ESSAYS
EDITED BY

SUCHENG CHAN
UNIVERSITY OF CALIFORNIA, SANTA BARBARA

SPENCER C. OLIN
UNIVERSITY OF CALIFORNIA, IRVINE

D0391347

WADSWORTH
CENGAGE Learning

Australia • Brazil • Japan • Korea • Mexico • Singapore • Spain • United Kingdom • United States

WADSWORTH
CENGAGE Learning™

Major Problems in California History
Documents and Essays
Edited by Sucheng Chan, Spencer C. Olin

Editor-in-chief: Jean L. Woy

Senior Associate Editor: Frances Gay

Senior Project Editor: Janet Young

Editorial Assistant: Elizabeth Emmons

Production/Design Coordinator: Jennifer Waddell

Electronic Production Supervisor: Irene V. Cinelli

Director of Manufacturing: Michael O'Dea

Cover deisgn: Alwyn Velásquez, Lapis Design

Cover art: "Monterey," 1955. Courtesy Darwin Musselman

For product information and technology assistance, contact us at **Cengage Learning Customer & Sales Support, 1-800-354-9706**

For permission to use material from this text or product, submit all requests online at **www.cengage.com/permissions** Further permissions questions can be emailed to **permissionrequest@cengage.com**

Library of Congress Control Number: 96-76880

ISBN-13: 978-0-669-27588-9

ISBN-10: 0-669-27588-3

Wadsworth
20 Channel Center Street
Boston, MA 02210
USA

Cengage Learning is a leading provider of customized learning solutions with office locations around the globe, including Singapore, the United Kingdom, Australia, Mexico, Brazil, and Japan. Locate your local office at **www.cengage.com/global**

Cengage Learning products are represented in Canada by Nelson Education, Ltd.

To learn more about Wadsworth, visit **www.cengage.com/wadsworth**

Purchase any of our products at your local college store or at our preferred online store **www.CengageBrain.com**

Printed in the United States of America
3 4 5 6 7   15 14 13 12 11
FD292

Preface

Few other states—indeed, few nations—can match California in its beauty, in the abundance of its natural and human resources, in the size of its economy, and in the complexity of its history, social structure, politics, and culture. In this volume of documents and essays organized chronologically, we have chosen to highlight certain themes: California's demographic and cultural diversity, the social and environmental consequences of its paths of economic development, and the contradictory impulses that have made California such a land of contrasts.

The selections in this anthology showcase some of the most interesting new scholarship in California history. With rare exceptions, earlier works were dominated by a "triumphal narrative." Like the history of the American West of which it is so important a component, California was portrayed mainly as a region of raw opportunities in which individuals freely pursued their own advancement. In recent years, however, the analytical scope of historical inquiry about California has expanded greatly and new themes have increasingly commanded the attention of historians. Numerous studies have been published about ethnic and racial minorities, women, families, water management, technology, urbanization, and the environment. Such studies have shifted scholarly attention away from California and the American West as a frontier of Euro-American expansion to how peoples of different races, ethnicities, classes, and genders have interacted in complex and multifaceted ways as they settled and developed the region and forged linkages to a wider world. In short, California historiography has become less triumphalist and more nuanced and sophisticated. While many of the articles published in the journals specializing in California history—*California History, Southern California Quarterly, Journal of San Diego History,* and *Pacific Historical Review*—continue to focus on the minutiae of specific events, persons, or trends, recent books about California have used the particularities of the state's development to illuminate larger, more universal processes.

The present volume attempts to reflect both kinds of historical scholarship: the documents and essays discuss particular developments; the chapter introductions and head notes place them into broader contexts. Although this book pays more attention to California's social history than to its conventional political history, such topics as politics, public policy, and the state's interaction with national and world events are also covered. Conflict and the discrepancy between ideal and reality are treated throughout the volume.

In the opening chapter, James Houston points out that California has been "a land of two promises, where abundant possibilities and a potential for disaster live side by side," while Carey McWilliams notes how California's extremely independent stance had become, by the late 1940s, a "problem" for the other states in the American West, as well as for California itself. James Gregory, meanwhile, reminds us that the state's demographic diversity is not a recent phenomenon: California had been home to a great variety of Native American tribes whose members spoke many different languages and were the bearers of divergent cultures long before the arrival of immigrants from Europe, Africa, Asia, Latin America, and the lands scattered around the Pacific Ocean. An important point made in Chapter 2 is that the whole notion of the "California Indian" was a Euro-American invention; in reality, there was no single group called "California Indians."

To illustrate other kinds of complexity in California, many chapters in this book examine different kinds of conflict. Chapter 3 looks at how native Californians learned to live under Spanish colonial rule while resisting some of its harsher aspects. The two events that bracket Chapter 4 are Mexican independence from Spain and the war fought between Mexico and the United States—both of them conflicts between nations. Chapter 5 focuses on conflicts over landownership and land use, while Chapter 6 deals with conflicts over the ownership and use of water. Chapters 7 and 10 explore how workers, urban and agricultural, respectively, have struggled against capitalists—manufacturers, railroads, and large corporate farms. Chapter 13 chronicles the protest politics of students, youth, racial minorities, and women during the very years when conservatism triumphed in mainstream California politics under Governor Ronald Reagan. In Chapter 15, environmental concerns are juxtaposed against the views of those who think that government regulations to protect the environment are too expensive and unnecessary.

Taking a slightly different tack, other chapters illustrate the discrepancy between the ideal and reality. Part of Chapter 7 depicts how Euro-American workers succeeded in excluding the Chinese from both their unions and from the shores of the United States even as they fought to acquire greater benefits for themselves. In this instance, the ideal of proletarian solidarity could not overcome the reality of racial antagonism. Chapter 8 shows how male progressive leaders, despite their liberal vision, were ambivalent about women's political participation. Moreover, these leaders thought that only those immigrants who were racially similar to Europeans were acceptable as permanent members of American society. Progressives, both male and female, supported the anti-Japanese movement because, in their eyes, the Japanese were not assimilable and did not belong in the American body politic. Both race and gender, therefore, proved problematic for these reformers. Chapter 9 analyzes why southern California has been so hospitable to the film industry, which has boosted the state's image as a land of dreams, and how, despite its efforts to depict social realism, Hollywood has been more effective in dealing with cultural conflicts at a mythic level. In some instances, two chapters serve as counterpoints to one another. Chapter 14 discusses a new form of capitalism—one based on the storage, processing, control, and distribution of electronic information—that has become one of the most important and most dynamic sectors in the state's economy. One of the essays examines the social impact of this industry, while a number of the documents in the following chapter hint at some of the long-term environmental costs of its spectacular development.

In almost every chapter, different interpretations of or approaches to the same event or topic are provided, especially in the essays. In Chapter 3, for example, Francis F. Guest's sympathetic account of the methods used by Spanish missionaries to subjugate the Indians contrasts sharply with Antonia I. Castañeda's criticism of the same practices. In Chapter 4, Hubert Howe Bancroft's romanticized and somewhat sarcastic description of the *Californios* (Mexican-Californians) differs from the more even-handed treatment by Douglas Monroy. Paul Wallace Gates's defense of Anglo-American settlers in Chapter 5 counterpoises Monroy's chronicle of the losses suffered by the *Californios* as a result of the influx of Americans. Donald Worster and Norris Hundley, Jr., use different conceptual frameworks to discuss water-resource development in Chapter 6. Lary May and Leslie Fishbein, in Chapter 9, focus on the different social functions Hollywood fulfills. In Chapter 10, Cletus E. Daniel gives credit mainly to communist organizers for leading several farmworkers' strikes in the 1930s, while Devra Anne Weber thinks community organizations formed by the Mexican immigrant laborers and the radical tradition that grew out of the Mexican Revolution had far more influence on the mostly Mexicano farmworkers' militant actions. In Chapter 11, Gerald D. Nash's thesis that World War II was an economic watershed for California is juxtaposed against that of Paul Rhode, who argues that while the rapid growth during the war years may seem impressive in the short run, it, in fact, represented less of a decisive break if one takes a longer view.

Several chapters reveal that historical trends need not always be unidirectional, linear, or permanent. Chapter 12, for example, describes the changing social, economic, and political status of Japanese Americans, African Americans, and women during World War II and in the immediate postwar years. For one group, severe losses were followed by modest gains. For the other two, significant progress was ultimately capped by retrenchment.

The book ends on a somber note. Chapter 16 focuses on the disquieting consequences of contemporary economic, social, and political inequality in California. The Los Angeles civil disorders of 1992 raised serious questions about whether Californians still have the creativity to deal with the difficult challenges of living in a complex, fast-paced, trend-setting, multiethnic state.

In the early 1990s, Californians experienced race riots, earthquakes, mudslides, forest fires, and the bankruptcy of Orange County—up to that point one of the wealthiest counties in the nation—one after another in rapid succession. But once the events ended, journalists and television cameras turned their attention to other news. The events themselves, along with the anxieties that were engendered, were quickly forgotten.

Will California's future be filled with abundance or disaster? Most likely, the answer is "both." "One of the great California ironies," wrote James Houston, "is the way its very virtues sometimes seem fated to bring about the state's undoing." Thus, California's seemingly limitless resources have spawned pervasive habits of wastefulness. Its still breathtaking beauty camouflages dirty air, polluted water, and land poisoned by toxic wastes. Different segments of its multiethnic population periodically deal violent blows against one another.

Despite its tarnished image, looking back at the Golden State's history one cannot help but ask, would a California without such extremes and such contradictions still be California? Probably not. Heir to a myriad of social experiments, including some strange or even truly wacky ones, Californians must find solutions for the most pressing problems confronting the state today. They must learn to live within limits and to take the best possible care of the state's still ample natural endowments. And, regardless of their origins, they must learn to share political power, build coalitions, and forge an inclusive social and economic agenda that takes the well-being of *all* Californians, as well as the overall health of California itself, into consideration.

Like the other volumes in this series, *Major Problems in California History* approaches its subject through both primary sources and the interpretations of scholars. We invite readers to examine critical issues through diverse viewpoints and approaches. In each chapter, the documents and head notes introduce the problem or theme, suggest key questions, reflect the temper of the times, and convey the intensity of debate. These documents allow students to immerse themselves in eras gone by, to develop their own perspectives, and to evaluate the explanations of others. The essays reveal how scholars can read documents in multiple ways, choose to examine different aspects of the same problems, and come to different conclusions about what happened. The format of the books in this series enables students to appreciate the complexity not only of history itself but the *writing* of history and to see that people who lived in the past and the issues they confronted may still be meaningful for today's students as they become scholars and citizens.

In the preparation of this anthology, we received invaluable assistance from Douglas C. Sackman and Robert Gedeon. Sackman, a doctoral candidate in history at the University of California, Irvine, specializing in the history of the American West, located a number of documents and essays, helped to conceptualize Chapter 9, and proofread many of the chapters. Gedeon, an undergraduate majoring in English and Russian at the University of California, Santa Barbara, typed a large part of the manuscript into a computer and helped check bibliographic citations.

We are grateful to Thomas G. Paterson, the series editor, and to the various editors at D. C. Heath and at Cengage Learning—James Miller, Sylvia

Mallory, Patricia Wakeley, Margaret Roll, Jean Woy, Frances Gay, Craig Mertens, Janet Young, Beth Emmons, Jennifer Waddell, Jeff Smith, Ruth Jagolinzer, Kim Hastings, and Mary Lang—who shepherded the manuscript through the publication process.

We also thank those colleagues who, in the early stages of the project, shared ideas and approaches for teaching California history, especially Richard Batman, San Francisco State University; John E. Baur, University of California, Santa Barbara; William A. Bullough, California State University, Hayward; Robert W. Cherny, San Francisco State University; David Chipping, California Polytechnic State University, San Luis Obispo; William Deverell, California Institute of Technology; Peter W. Fay, California Institute of Technology; David Fine, California State University, Long Beach; Benjamin F. Gilbert, San Jose State University; Harlan Hague, San Joaquin Delta College; Donald Teruo Hata, Jr., California State University, Dominiquez Hills; R. W. Hazlett, Pomona College; Howard Holter, California State University, Dominiquez Hills; Robert L. Hoover, California Polytechnic State University, San Luis Obispo; William Issel, San Francisco State University; Helen Jaskoski, California State University, Fullerton; J. H. Krause; David W. Lantis; Crane S. Miller, California State Polytechnic University, Pomona; Leigh W. Mintz, California State University, Hayward; Aldon Nilsen, San Jose State University; Gary Peters, California State University, Long Beach; Rick Peterson, San Diego State University; Richard A. Smith, San Jose State University; and Thomas Watts, California State University, Bakersfield.

Not least, we are grateful to the following reviewers for their helpful criticisms and suggestions: Robert A. Becklund, College of Marin; James N. Gregory, University of Washington; Lisbeth Haas, University of California, Santa Cruz; Gloria Ricci Lothrop, California State University, Northridge; Michael Magliari, California State University, Chico; Daniel W. Markwyn, Sonoma State University; Richard E. Oglesby, University of California, Santa Barbara; Nancy Quam Wickham, California State University, Long Beach; Kent Schofield, California State University, San Bernardino; and Michael L. Smith, University of California, Davis.

We dedicate this book to our partners, Mark Juergensmeyer and Rita Olin, who took time out from their own demanding careers to sustain us in multiple ways.

S. C.
S. C. O.

Contents

C H A P T E R   8
California Progressives: The Ambiguities of Political and Moral Reform
Page 194

C H A P T E R   9
Hollywood and the California Dream, 1910s–1930s
Page 227

CHAPTER 14
The Rise of Information Capitalism
Page 391

CHAPTER 15
The Environment and the Quality of Life Since 1960
Page 421

CHAPTER 16
Racial and Class Tensions, 1960s–1990s
Page 452

The Significance of California History

In 1782 an aristocratic French immigrant named Michel-Guillaume Jean de Crèvecoeur inquired: "What, then, is the American, this new man?" For more than two centuries, Americans have sought, inconclusively, to answer that question (although more recently in a manner less gender-specific than that of Crèvecoeur). That is, they have disagreed about the extent to which the American experience is "exceptional" or different from those of peoples and regions elsewhere.

California has similarly been viewed as different—only more so. One of the state's most astute interpreters, Carey McWilliams, once referred to California as "the great exception." Others have pointed out that California has long been a seedbed of experimentation and innovation. "A putty culture— yeasty, swollen, penetrable, unshaped, elastic, impermanent," one skeptical critic described it. "It is America's America," proclaimed the authors of a Time cover story in late 1991, "the symbol of raw hope and brave (even foolish) invention, where ancient traditions and inhibitions are abandoned at the border." Furthermore, its major city, Los Angeles, has often been hailed as a prototype of the sprawling decentralization that has increasingly characterized metropolitan development throughout the nation. What is happening in California today, so the argument goes, will be happening in America tomorrow. Or, to put it another way, California serves as a window on the future, both reflecting and anticipating powerful social forces that will profoundly affect the nation as a whole.

E S S A Y S

James Houston, the author of the first essay, has attempted in all his writings to map what might be called the cultural geography of California. Here he stresses the importance of California's natural resources and geographical location and the relationship between California as a place on the land and as

1

a place in the mind. Houston has also written numerous works of fiction and nonfiction and has taught at the University of California, Santa Cruz. His works include the novel *Continental Drift* (1978) and the nonfiction works *Farewell to Manzanar* (1973, coauthored with his wife, Jeanne Wakatsuki Houston) and *Californians: Searching for the Golden State* (1982).

The second essay is taken from Carey McWilliams's book *California: The Great Exception* (1949). Longtime editor of *The Nation*, McWilliams wrote several controversial books about California, including *Factories in the Field* (1939), an exposé of farm labor conditions, and *North from Mexico* (1948), a pioneering study of Mexican immigration. In this essay, written nearly half a century ago, McWilliams argued prophetically that California's social and economic "maturity" made it impossible any longer for it to function in isolation from the rest of the American West.

Finally, James Gregory, a leading historian of modern California who teaches at the University of Washington, addresses the larger significance of California in both national and global contexts. In examining the state's cultural and political trends, he suggests reasons for California's regional importance, but he also expresses skepticism about California's "special gift for solving the complex problems of pluralism."

The Place Called California

JAMES D. HOUSTON

When you are trying to locate a place, it is usually safe to begin with maps. I always do. But when the subject is California, you have to be careful. Maps of this region have been deceptive from the start. The earliest ones depicted an offshore island, separated from what is now Nevada by a long narrow channel. Some people say these may be the most reliable maps we have—geographically wrong, but psychologically close to the truth.

On my relief map of North America, the place named California lies along the continent's western rim. A broad valley, shaped like a cucumber, occupies its center. Two great rivers water this valley, fed by a dozen tributaries flowing down from the massive range of high peaks that frame its eastern side. To the west, another range borders the valley, a long pattern of folds and ripples rising up from the Pacific Ocean. The two great rivers empty into delta lands that channel the water, via a wide gap in the coastal mountains, toward San Francisco's nearly landlocked and marvelously protected bay. To the north there are more mountains, extending toward Canada, though a political line cuts through them to mark where California ends and Oregon begins, just as another political line cuts through the desert that occupies the southern quarter of the state, a desert that extends deep into Mexico.

Is this, then, what we mean by *the place*—this complex system of ridges and waterways, this mosaic of micro-climates and varied terrains?

From James D. Houston, "From El Dorado to the Pacific Rim: The Place Called California," *California History*, 68, Winter 1989/90: pp. 173–181. Reprinted by permission of the California Historical Society.

Well, yes. But no. Not exactly. Not when the subject is the state of California. It is now almost impossible to separate the place on the map from the legends that have kept it alive in the imagination. And one would not want to keep them separate for very long. The beguiling attraction of California lives right there, in that interplay. Simply consider the Gold Rush, this region's formative event. How can a few thousand pounds of gleaming metal, no matter how native to the mountainsides and riverbeds, be disentangled from the noise and spectacle of the sudden multitude? Without the gold embedded in the landscape, of course, there would have been no Rush. But without the Rush, we would have only greed to remember, and bank accounts. No magic. No world-class legend to tickle the memory and stir the blood.

These two—the place on the continent, and the place in the mind—have never been easy to pry apart because the legends actually came first. The dream, the expectation of something remarkable out there at the farthest edge of the New World, lived in the minds of the earliest explorers before they ever glimpsed the monumental headlands at Point Reyes and Point Conception or dipped their hands into the bottomlands of the luscious coastal valleys—San Fernando, Ojai, Salinas, Santa Clara. It was a far western version of El Dorado that originates in a sixteenth-century novel by Garcí Ordóñez de Montalvo called *The Adventures of Esplandián*. There California is named and described for the first time—a science fiction name, in those days, as unearthly as Lilliput or Brobdingnag. It was a mythical island, very near the gates of the Terrestrial Paradise, inhabited by Amazons, made impregnable by steep cliffs and rocky shores, and in this whole island, "there was no metal but gold."

California was not the first place on earth to get this type of advance billing. Explorations of every kind have been propelled by heady visions and improbable dreams. An intriguing feature of this region's history is the extent to which its array of natural endowments—climate, landscape, and bountiful resources—lived up to some of the visions, fleshed out the hopes for a blessed and promised land.

The rich potential of the valleys and alluvial plains was evident to the first overland travelers. "All the soil is black and loamy," wrote Fray Juan Crespí, chaplain of the Portolá expedition, as they crossed the Los Angeles basin in the summer of 1769, "and is capable of producing every kind of grain and fruit which may be planted."

It proved to be ideal for farming and ranching, and for seventy years or so this appeared to be what the earth of California had to offer—extensive grazing lands for cattle, prime acreage for wine grapes and wheat. It was the discovery of gold that brought the boomtown mentality to an otherwise quietly fertile outpost. When this remote western landscape actually delivered pockets and seams of the fabled ore so many adventurers had dreamed about, the world's imagination suddenly had a new touchstone. Maybe El Dorado existed after all!

"On our poor little maps of California printed in France," wrote the journalist Etienne Derbec in 1850, "the San Joaquin is shown as a river flowing between the California mountains and the sea, a short distance from San Francisco, in the midst of a rich plain which its waters cover with gold dust every year. The editors have even taken the pains to gild that precious plain on their maps."

A few decades later the legend was recharged and reinforced when the landscape delivered up another treasure, dark and sticky, that had been waiting for millenia, locked in subterranean pools and caverns. Fifty or sixty million years ago, when Long Beach was underwater and the central valley was an inland sea, uncountable generations of plankton sifted downward, leaving tiny skeletons to be transmuted into oil. As these ancient deposits were discovered, one by one—the Doheny strike in Los Angeles in 1892, the Lakeview Gusher in the lower San Joaquin in 1910, the phenomenal find at Signal Hill near Long Beach in the early 1920s (in barrels per acre the richest in the world)—fortunes accumulated, both private and corporate, that far surpassed the wealth created by the Mother Lode. The timing, moreover, seems uncanny, because during the same era, while the substrata was releasing its hoard of black gold, California was developing as a world headquarters for the machine that would be a prime consumer: the automobile, with its own by-products, the car culture and the drive-in style of life.

In the early 1980s, seventy years after the Lakeview Gusher darkened the skies above Taft and Maricopa, Kern County alone still ranked 18th among the world's oil-producing regions, delivering more barrels per day than some of the OPEC nations. (And there were more registered vehicles in California than there were people in the seven nearest western states.)

Meanwhile, another resource, another feature of the place itself, the weather, had fueled three new industries. The first was real estate. From the 1870s onward, land developers packaged the climate, telling easterners that California offered "the loveliest skies, the mildest winters, the most healthful region, in the whole United States." The second was cinema. Early filmmakers, looking for a way to put some distance between themselves and New Jersey, where Thomas Edison was trying to control the patents on film-making equipment, crossed the continent to southern California. They found a number of things that encouraged them to stay, including varied terrain, an abundance of light, and over three hundred clear-sky days in any given year, which made it ideal for outdoor and location shooting.

Hollywood and aviation have at least that much in common. In the early days of flying, pilots and designers also found the southern California climate ideal for testing planes, for taking off and landing. Though the *Spirit of St. Louis* departed from New York in 1927 to make the first transAtlantic flight, the plane was designed in San Diego. The demands of World War II gave this fledgling industry size and shape. One thing led to another. Nowadays, in the endlessly sunny deserts north of Los Angeles, while the U.S. Air Force tests its space-age capsules and weaponry, the spirit of aerial adventure lives on in the work of Paul McReady, the aviation renegade who has developed a record-setting series of engineless and human-powered aircraft, the *Gossamer Condor,* the *Gossamer Albatross,* the *Gossamer Penguin.* In 1981 his 198-lb *Solar Challenger* astonished the aviation world when it crossed the English Channel powered solely by the energy of the sun. The plane was designed in Pasadena. It was systematically tested in the dry clear air above Shafter Airport, a few miles south of Bakersfield.

In this way, time and time again, some feature of the place we call California has led to some new opportunity or perception; and these in turn have advanced the reputation and the legend of the place.

Location itself can be described this way. Simply as a physical creation, the thousand-mile coastline, from Crescent City in the far north, to Point Loma in the far south, is one of the world's most widely praised and often visited beauty zones. Because of its numerous blessings, Californians have hugged this coast from the earliest days of European settlement, spreading out around the long necklace of presidio and port and mission towns founded by the Spanish. This is still where most Californians live, work, and play. Some eighty percent of the state's twenty-six million inhabitants reside within a band about forty miles wide, between Santa Rosa and the Mexican border. They eat fruits and vegetables trucked in from the Central Valley; and their water comes from somewhere farther inland and higher up, sources like Hetch Hetchy and Mono Lake. But they work in San Diego, in the L.A. basin, in the extended megalopolis around San Francisco Bay. And the coastline is their principal recreation zone—the beaches, the tidepools, the several dozen surfing spots, the fishing and sailing in offshore waters, the stirring scenery along Highway One, the drop-off cliffs that launch hang-gliders, the trails and hot springs and campsites throughout the many ridges of the long Coast Range.

Because of its location, this coast that shapes the curving outline of the state has also helped to shape its history. By the late 18th century, Spain, England, Russia, and the United States were all eyeing the strategic advantages of California's as-yet-undeveloped ports and harbors, in their long-distance struggle for control of Pacific trade and trading routes. Today, with control of the Pacific still in mind, some thirty percent of the entire U.S. naval fleet is based in San Diego.

It is the look of this coastline, as perceived from the East, that has had such a profound effect on what we might call the region's psychological history. Most travellers to California have come from somewhere east. Because of its place in history, because it was settled late and happens to occupy the continent's farthest edge, the West Coast has been viewed as some final stopping place, the end of the trail, the conclusion of that great thrust and opening outward from Europe that began five hundred years ago. No one has voiced this more deliberately and passionately than the Carmel poet Robinson Jeffers. For him, the meeting of shore and water was not only a scene of wild and holy magnificence, it was the cultural cliff-edge, where lives culminate, where cross-continental destinies are somehow completed. This theme propels his early poem, *Continent's End* (1924):

I gazing at the boundaries of granite and spray,
the established sea-marks, felt behind me
Mountain and plain, the immense breadth of the
continent, before me the mass and doubled
stretch of water.

If El Dorado was this region's first large metaphor, Continent's End was the second. And in recent years a third image has risen into public consciousness, as a way of describing California's place on the map and in the mind. It is the term, *Pacific Rim*. A rim, of course, suggests a circle, and the term itself places this state, not at the outer edge of European expansion, but on a great wheel of peoples who surround the Pacific Basin. It helps to bring into sharper focus some of our ever-changing ethnic, cultural, and economic realities.

Because it faces west, this coast is where most trans-Pacific travellers have landed and where immigrants from Asia have settled. Among the people of Asian and Pacific Island background now in the United States, some forty percent live in California. The Asian presence, such a vital feature of this state's unique cultural mix, is much more than a matter of numbers. It is felt in the architecture, in eating habits, in the popularity of certain ideas and belief systems, such as zen and yoga, in the practice of martial arts and healing arts, and in the evolution of the economy. In 1982, for the first time, United States trade with Atlantic nations was surpassed by its trade with nations across the Pacific. In 1986 the ports of Long Beach and Los Angeles moved 58.6 million tons of cargo, almost triple the tonnage handled by the ports of New York and New Jersey.

The legends of California are always tied to some feature of its varied and abundant landscape. The oil boom launched by the first major strike in the San Joaquin in 1909 and 1910, for example, had a kind of prologue in the 1906 earthquake. Both episodes begin with underground, innate features of the western earth that have helped to shape both history and mythology. While it wrecked a large piece of San Francisco, the famous quake also flattened the old Russian Orthodox chapel at Fort Ross, seventy miles north, and shook loose a wall of the San Juan Bautista Mission, which we now know stands right in the rift zone, eighty miles south. There had been other fearful quakes in California since settlement began, but this was the one that set a city on fire and first drew widespread attention to something geologists have come to view as a principal feature in the physical life of the place, that six hundred mile crease through the landscape, the San Andreas Fault.

In a similar way the prologue to the Gold Rush is the story of the ill-fated Donner Party, who started too late from the Middle West, fell prey to squabbling along the trail, entered the Sierra Nevada range well past the season when it was considered safe to cross, and thus found themselves trapped in the early winter of 1846. One of the most notorious events in the history of the American West—some say it is the basic event—the Donner tragedy provides an unavoidable counterpoint to the legends of fulfillment and abundance. It is a story not only of seekers pushed past their limits, who devour human flesh in order to survive. It is a story from a region where the weather can turn on you in an hour, where the landscape is no longer an ally or bountiful provider, and where nature is an adversary, or perhaps a mentor you can never afford to take for granted.

The lesson of the Donner Party contains a warning not unlike the warnings of John Muir, the great naturalist and patriarch conservationist who began to tramp the Sierra Nevada range some twenty years later. Be attentive to this land and its habits, he said; learn to enjoy it, but never let down your guard.

The power of the high country so filled Muir with awe and wonder that he devoted his life to preserving as much of this far western landscape as he could. He worked to save Yosemite Valley, and succeeded. He fought harder to save Hetch Hetchy Valley, which he claimed was too beautiful to be dammed up and turned into a reservoir, and failed. He founded the Sierra Club, and in his writings he gave voice to an environmental consciousness, a reverence for natural beauty and a respect for the potent and interlocking cycles of the earth, that speaks ever louder as the years go by.

One of the great California ironies is the way its very virtues sometimes seem fated to bring about the state's undoing. This region still draws people at a phenomenal rate, continuing to grow by a thousand or more per day, day after day, year after year, about half by birth and half by in-migration. As the demands on space and resources intensify, one sees examples everywhere of how some cycle of nature is overlooked, or given low priority, in the rush to develop a parcel of real estate, maximize income, or expand a city: in a new subdivision, built across a fault line, half a dozen duplexes are tipped off their foundations by a quake; somewhere along the coast, a fragile slope, over-logged and over-built, is cut away by erosion and four homes go sliding to the bottom; in the lower San Joaquin Valley, over-irrigation coupled with poor drainage fills a hundred thousand acres of cropland with plant-killing salts and minerals, while a spectacular lake in the High Sierra drops fifty feet in fifty years in order to serve a thirsty city three hundred miles south.

The succession of such events, together with the ongoing debates over river use, air quality, the coastal impact of offshore drilling, and so on, are gradually leading us toward a revision of the original California legend. Gradually we are discovering, or rediscovering, that this land is not a cornucopia of limitless reserves, but a well-endowed place with very specific limits that have to be acknowledged and honored. And these limits, too, are fundamental features of the place—weather, tides, wind and water flow, cycles in the soil and in the earth beneath the soil.

The legend dies hard, however, the one with the boomtown voice saying, "Take what you want while the taking is good." And perhaps we can still learn from the native tribes who once flourished in this part of the world. They understood that in order to survive it was important to find a way to live in harmony with the whole environment. If one failed to do so, the penalty could be severe.

Up along the north coast, the Yurok expressed this via a World Renewal dance, described in Theodora Kroeber's retelling of one of their best-known tales: "To a world in balance, the flat earth's rise and fall, as it floats on Underneath Ocean, is almost imperceptible, and nothing is disturbed by it. Doctors know that to keep this balance, the people must dance the World Renewal dances, bringing their feet down strong and hard on the earth. If they are careless about this, it tips up and if it tips more than a very little, there are strange and terrible misplacements."

That is a prologue to the story of *The Inland Whale*, who became stranded in a landlocked lake. Why? The people had grown careless. They allowed the earth to tip too far, so that ocean waters came pouring across the land, carrying all the creatures of the sea. When the earth finally righted itself, and the sea water drained away, a female whale was left behind. Unable to return to her natural habitat, she became a lonely wisdom figure.

In this ancient story, life is a balancing act, and the earth is a delicately hinged support system one must revere and respect. Evidence suggests that some of the early Spanish explorers saw California this way too. Fray Juan Crespí found the landscape itself to be something one approached respectfully and with more than ordinary caution. As diarist and chaplain with the Portolá party, he was the first writer to give us a detailed account of what this region looked like as European settlement began. Making daily entries as the party crept up the coastline from Baja toward San Francisco Bay, Crespí reported at length on the fauna and the flora, the habits of local tribes, and the habits of the land.

At the end of July 1769 they were camped along the banks of the river we now call the Santa Ana, which follows the Riverside Freeway into Anaheim and Garden Grove. In those days it followed a similar course but had a different name, *el río del dulcísimo nombre de Jesús de los Temblores*. On July 28, the padre wrote:

> The bed of the river is well grown with sycamores, alders, willows, and other trees we have not recognized. It is evident from the sand on its banks that in the rainy season it must have great floods which would prevent crossing it. It has a great deal of good land which can easily be irrigated . . . I called this place The Very Sweet Name of Jesus of the Temblors, because we experienced here a horrifying earthquake which was repeated four times during the day. The first, which was the most violent, happened at one in the afternoon, and the last one about four.

Undaunted, the exploration party continued north the next morning, from Santa Ana into what is now the heart of Los Angeles. For the next five days they were periodically shaken by quakes large and small. Though Crespí was alarmed by the tremors, he never failed to comment on the beauties and endowments of the land they passed through, its possibilities for food and shelter, irrigation, timber, and farming. In his diary these concerns, the land's blessings and the unaccountable quivers in the earth, live side by side.

On Tuesday, August 1, they camped just south of where Mission San Gabriel now stands:

At ten in the morning, the earth trembled. The shock was repeated with violence at one in the afternoon, and one hour afterward we experienced another. The soldiers went out this afternoon and brought an antelope, with which animals this country abounds. They are like wild goats, but have horns rather larger than goats. I tasted the meat, and it was not bad.

On Thursday, August 3, the party forded a river they had named for Our Lady of the Angels of Porciuncula (now called Los Angeles), and Crespí described "a large vineyard of wild grapes and an infinity of rose bushes in full bloom." A few miles later they reach a small stream:

The banks were grassy and covered with fragrant herbs and watercress. The water flowed afterward in a deep channel toward the southwest. All the land that we saw this morning seemed admirable to us. We pitched camp near the water. This afternoon we felt new earthquakes, the continuation of which astonishes us. We judge that in the mountains that run to the west of us there are some volcanoes, for there are many signs on the road which stretches between the Porciuncula River and the Spring of the Alders, for the explorers saw some large marshes of a certain substance like pitch; they were boiling and bubbling, and the pitch came out mixed with an abundance of water . . . and there is such an abundance of it that it would serve to caulk many ships.

Imagine Crespí, born on the Spanish isle of Mallorca, seasoned traveller and soldier of the Cross, marching through the richest land he has yet seen, and struck by subterranean powers such as he has felt nowhere else in New Spain. The dark and loamy soil, where grapes and roses evidently grow wild, is rolling and rumbling beneath his sandals. Ahead of him rise the Santa Monica Mountains, which appear to be volcanic; that is, he *hopes* there are volcanoes up ahead, for that would at least explain the rumbles and the percolating tar pits reported by the scouts.

Crespí has no way of knowing that a rift zone lurks thirty miles to the east. He has no access to the theory of Continental Drift, which some two hundred years later will help account for what is going on. He has no way of knowing that the same forces that created that long crease and these subsurface tremors—two great slabs of the earth's crust grinding together—also contributed to the scenic grandeur and the miraculously fertile fields. And yet in his diary of 1769, he manages to catch this condition, this pairing. Be wary in the land of promise, his diary suggests. Be attentive, because this appears to be a land of two promises, where abundant possibilities and a potential for disaster live side by side.

When the subject is California, the place on the continent and the place in the mind are now so closely wedded that we may never again be able to separate the two. And yet from time to time one cannot help wondering what this region seemed to offer, in and of itself, before dreams and legends began to shape our view of it. If we can trust what Crespí saw and recorded, during the weeks when the white explorers were arriving, with the roads and the rifles and the high expectations and the first bits of merchandise, this much was already here—grapes and roses and petroleum and fault lines—co-existing in the landscape.

California as "The Great Exception"

CAREY MCWILLIAMS

In the last hundred years, the gradual emergence of a new center of power in California has had a constantly disturbing effect on inter-state and inter-regional relationships and has brought into being a peculiar relationship, often verging on outright antagonism, between California and the federal government. California happens to occupy a geographically marginal or peripheral relation to the other western states and the nation, a circumstance that aggravates the disturbing effects. In this case, also, the new center of power has emerged so recently, in historical terms, that not enough time has yet elapsed to develop a new pattern of relationships. Developing *outside,* and to a degree independently of, the other western states, and being a more or less self-contained regional unit, California has become a major problem not only to the western states but to the nation.

One measure of California's power is to be found in the social and economic vacuum which, until recent years, existed in the Inter-Mountain West. Historically, there has been no counterforce in this vast area to balance, steady, or check the power of California. . . .

As a chauvinistic westerner, I have participated in any number of projects, during the last two decades, which had as their primary purpose the stimulation of a heightened western regional consciousness. Extensive use was made, in most of these political ventures, of the familiar theme that the West is a colonial dependency of the East. Over a period of time, however, it gradually dawned on me that this theme seemed to strike a more responsive chord in certain parts of the West than in other parts. It appeared to make sense to the people of Montana, Colorado, Wyoming, Utah, and New Mexico; but, for some reason, the Californians always declined the bait. In fact, more than one ambitiously projected "western states conference" has been still-born because of California's lack of interest and enthusiasm. Obviously the Californians do not think of themselves as "colonials" no matter how loudly the theme is proclaimed.

I finally came to the conclusion, therefore, that the theme of the West as a colonial empire had to be taken with a grain of salt. It was unquestionably a sound theme in the Inter-Mountain West, which still carries the visible scars of Eastern exploitation; but one can look in vain for these scars in California. The more I thought about the problem, the more I came to see that California occupies a relation to other parts of the West which is comparable to the relation that the East occupies to the West. The Inter-Mountain West is a colony in a two-fold sense: a colony of the East and a colony of California; whereas California is a colony of the East in only the most limited sense. I then began to see how successful California has been in using the theme of "colonies" and "colonial status" as a smoke-screen to

From Carey McWilliams, *California: The Great Exception.* (New York: Current Books, 1949): pp. 341–347, 362–367.

conceal certain important aspects of its relations with the other western states.

The difficulty with our social vision has been that an all-inclusive phrase like "The West" conceals the discrepancy of power which actually exists between the western states and California. . . . As industrial power is measured nowadays, California is still at a disadvantage by comparison with older and industrially more mature regions but in *intra-regional competition* it is clearly dominant. For many years, California has been in a much stronger financial position than the other western states and has invested large surpluses of capital in various enterprises in these states. *Within the West,* California has long enjoyed a favorable position even with respect to freight rates since the availability of ocean transport has compelled the railroads to give preferential rates to the terminal points on the coast. In relation to eastern manufacturers, therefore, California manufacturers have a favorable rate throughout the entire area extending from the coast as far east as the Rockies. Essentially, California is to the West what New York, for many years, was to the industrial East: a great center of power with lines of influence radiating outward in all directions. But there is this important difference: California, within the West, has no rivals.

In addition to its unique problems, California has all the problems of all the other western states. But since it is socially and economically more mature than these states, with greater power and "the momentum of an early start," it undertook the solution of many of these problems on its own initiative, apart from the other western states, and without the aid of the federal government. In this respect, its marginal position and its exceptional advantages made possible a development-in-isolation which gave the state a greatly enhanced sense of its own power and independence. When California has gone out for anything, a project, federal funds, or whatever, it has usually acted not as one of 11 western states but as a nation demanding what it had the power to take and the record will show that it has been highly successful in these unilateral raids and political maneuvers. As long as the development of the other western states was retarded, California could act in this imperial manner. But today, with the West coming to a new maturity, California is rapidly discovering that its interests are closely related to the interests of the entire region. However, California has yet to develop a full awareness that it has now entered upon a new phase of its development. It is the failure to realize this fact, indeed, which makes up the California problem. . . .

On March 30, 1949, the number of unemployed in California stood at 528,000, an unemployment rate of 14 per cent: twice that of the nation as a whole. One-fifth of the nation's unemployed, for the first quarter of 1949, were to be found in the three west coast states. Calling attention to this fact in a speech in Los Angeles on May 11th, Governor Earl Warren imparted the further bad news that California must prepare to receive "another 10,000,000" migrants in the next quarter century. Faced with the highest unemployment rate in the nation and with the expectation of continued large-scale migration, California, the Governor went on to say, must undertake a rapid development of all available resources and, in particular, must increase the sources of available energy. "California," he said, "has no great coal fields. . . . At the rate of present use, our known oil and gas reserves will last only about 20 years." Where, then, is this additional energy, so vital to the further expansion of California, to be found?

With the exception of federal projects on the Colorado, California's power program is largely intra-state for its river basins are practically all confined within its own borders. Although there is a large undeveloped energy potential within the state, most of the suitable sites for upstream run-of-the-river hydro systems are already fully developed and further expansion is unlikely. The undeveloped potential, therefore, involves river basin developments. But these developments are inseparably connected with water conservation for all purposes, including irrigation, flood control, navigation, salinity control, recreation, municipal uses, and so forth. Since none of the existing private utility systems has the resources to undertake developments of this character, California has been driven, and will continue to be driven, to seek federal support. Federal support, in turn, hinges on the goodwill of the other western states which have few congressmen but many senators.

Even assuming continued federal support, however, California cannot rely upon its own resources; in fact, it is already directly dependent upon one inter-state resource, namely, the Colorado River. Speaking at the State Water Conference in 1945, Leland Olds, of the Federal Power Commission, summed up California's predicament when he said that the state's energy resources will prove inadequate for the full development of a balanced economy if California's program is conceived entirely in intrastate terms. "The fact is," he said, "that unless your water resource program here in California is recognized as an integral part of the larger program which embraces the entire Pacific and intermountain region, your future development may ultimately be restricted by lack of energy resources . . . Your planning cannot safely assume that California will remain self-contained so far as its energy requirements are concerned." Fortunately the West, as a region, has a developed capacity of about 9,000,000 kilowatts of hydro-and-stream electric power; but, with full development of all resources, it can generate an additional 50,000,000 kilowatts of power. It is this power and this water in which California must share if it is to support its present and anticipated population. Failing to recognize this long-range dependency, California continues to act as though it were the only state west of the Rockies. In doing so, it is holding up the development of the West and also imperiling its own and the nation's economy.

By the time the Central Valley Project is completed—assuming that it is completed as planned—the federal government will have an investment in this one California project of two billion dollars: two and one-half times the federal investment in TVA and almost twice as much as the Bureau of Reclamation has invested in all the other western states in the 43 years of its existence. With an investment of this magnitude, the federal government is bound to "intervene" in California affairs and to insist upon the observance, within the state, of nationally approved policies. At the same time, the other western states, now developing similar projects, feel that California has too long received the lion's share of federal subsidy and "view with alarm" California's attempt to monopolize water resources. "If the interests of the nation as a whole are overlooked by the people of California," warned Mr. Harry W. Bashore at the State Water Conference, "I believe I can say without qualification that you will make little progress with Congress in obtaining the funds you so urgently need." But the problem involves more than placating the other Western states: the fact is that California's resources are basically inadequate to support its future population. "Remember," said Mr. Bashore, "that the day is not far distant when the population of your state will be greater than your resources can sustain, if you do not take wise action now. As population increases, wise husbanding of resources is necessary if you wish to escape the ultimate fate of almost every civilization the world has ever known. . . . Likewise the population of California will increase beyond your ability to support them and your own prosperity will decay, unless you give heed in time to developing your resources to their maximum long-term capacity. Piecemeal development, project by project, will not accomplish this. Only an overall plan which is sound will serve this end." In this sense, an overall plan means, of course, a plan for the entire West, not for California alone. . . .

It isn't simply California's superior power which complicates western unity, but the fact that there is little unity within the West on any issue. Assuming that California wanted to cooperate with the other western states and that these states wanted to cooperate with California, the question would still remain: what do these other states cooperate with? with what particular California should they seek to establish some common bond of interest? For the fact is that California has not yet achieved the internal, the organic unity which would make cooperation and better relations with the other western states possible. The California Congressional delegation is more likely than not to be broken up into rival factions on most issues. With which faction should the other western states cooperate? California is a political cauldron; seldom, if ever, is a governor re-elected. California is Northern California vs. Southern California; newcomers vs. carpetbaggers; hinterland vs. metropolitan areas. It is, as the Los Angeles *Daily News* pointed out in an editorial, "an unarticulated collection of factors looking for a common denominator." And the point made by this editorial, namely, that "California hasn't yet the kind of unity it must have if it is to win the assistance and encouragement of other sections and states and of the nation as a whole," comes close to being the essence of the California problem. When the other western states complain, therefore, that "they are sticking together—all except California," they forget that California, as the largest and most mature western state, is suffering acutely from a disease which is common throughout the region, namely: a lack of social and cultural integration.

Reduced to its essentials, *The California Problem* might be described as follows: a large province on the west coast, occupying a marginal geographical position, possessed of a most exceptional environment with its peculiar advantages and no less peculiar problems, with a most unique historical background, gets a head start of two decades over the other western states in its development and, because of a set of exceptional internal dynamics, develops at an entirely different tempo from its sister states of the West. The uniqueness and novelty of the environment, coupled with its amazing versatility, operates as a constant challenge to social and technological inventiveness. Selective forces at work in the process of migration bring to the state a population which is not so much a cross-section as a highly selected sample of the population of the world. The diversity of the state's resources is matched by the constant diversity of its population. Preoccupied with its peculiar problems, isolated from the rest of the nation during two crucial decades in its early history, California develops a remarkable energy and resourcefulness in the solution of its problems without consultation or assistance from the other western states or the federal government.

Over a period of years, therefore, a spirit of great independence and a self-reliance bordering on truculence develops among its people. But the circumstances which have shaped and moulded this far west province have been such that its people have tended to ignore the fact that, despite its marginal position, or precisely because of this position, the state is closely related to and dependent upon a larger region. The discrepancy in power, as between California and the other western states, has strikingly augmented this tendency on the part of the people to think of California as a province apart, sovereign in its own right, a self-contained empire. The very scale by which happenings, events, and developments are measured in the freakish environment of California makes it extremely difficult for Californians *to relate* their problems to those of the other western states. The environment, in other words, tends to distort the perspective of those who dwell within the state. The scale is so much larger; the tempo of events so much faster; and, in California, everything seems to be reversed, to occur out of the natural order of events, to be upside down or lopsided. Even to describe the state accurately is to run the risk of being branded a liar or a lunatic. Add to these considerations the fact that California is still *new,* almost as new as it was in 1848, and one has a pretty good idea of what makes up the California problem.

How is this problem to be resolved? In the first place, events are rapidly resolving it. This west coast "panther with the splendid hide" is being tamed and made to know its master's will by the inescapable logic of events. For great and diverse as its resources are, they are still inadequate to meet the needs of the population of 20,000,000 people that will one day be residing within its border. Forced to seek federal assistance on a large scale, California will be brought face to face with the fact that the federal government must intervene not at one but at many points in its internal affairs. Coming to a new life, the other western states are now arrayed against California on many issues and California will be driven to seek the cooperation of these states whether it likes the idea or not.

But, more potent than events of this character, is the fact that California's destiny, which can be perceived but dimly today, will correct the balance by investing California, willy-nilly, with the role of western leadership. Events of a magnitude too vast even for conjecture are taking place today around the rim of the Pacific: in China, India, the Philippines, Java, Sumatra, French Indo-China, the Soviet Far East. Regardless of how these events work out, one thing is certain: California is destined to occupy in the future, not a marginal, but a central position in world affairs. The ports of the west coast will be the ports through which the expanding trade and commerce of the West will flow to ports throughout the entire vast area of the Pacific. Once the impact of this development really begins to make itself felt, California will come to occupy a new position in the western scheme of things; not that of the Colossus of the West, the Big Bully, the Untamed Panther, but the state which will link western America with the Orient. . . .

The problem of the West, therefore, is to build toward the future; toward the Pacific. There are all too many indications, however, that the development of the West is being predicated on fragmentary information, improvised planning, and the opportunistic promotion of "projects." Confusion and uncertainty prevail at the moment in almost every aspect and phase of this development. . . .

On the state capitol at Sacramento one can read the scroll: "Bring Me Men to Match My Mountains!" This is California's need today: for men and women who can match, in the scale of their imagination and the depth of their insight, the extraordinary diversity, power, and challenge which is implicit in this immense and fabulous province which sprawls along the Pacific like a tawny tiger. California needs men who can see beyond its mountains; men who can see the entire West and who realize that, as with all good things, there comes a time when the gold runs out, when the exception disappears in the rule, and when California "being so caught up, so mastered by the brute blood of the air" must, indeed, put on knowledge with its power and adopt, as an official policy, the same generous open-handedness with which its magic mountains have showered benefits on those lucky people, the Californians.

The Shaping of California History

JAMES N. GREGORY

California is not just another state. . . . The state population now exceeds thirty million, and there are more Californians than there are Canadians, Australians, or Greeks; more Californians than Czechoslovaks and Hungarians combined; more Californians than Swedes, Norwegians, and Danes. Still more striking is the state's share of global economic activity.

From "California" by James N. Gregory. Excerpted with permission of Charles Scribner's Sons, an imprint of Simon & Schuster Macmillan, from *Encyclopedia of American Social History,* Mary Kupiec Cayton, Elliot J. Gorn, and Peter W. Williams, editors. Vol. II, pp. 1121–1134. Copyright © 1993 Charles Scribner's Sons.

California's gross domestic product makes it the seventh largest economy in the world, ranking ahead of Russia and the People's Republic of China and just behind Great Britain and Italy. And if consumption is the measure, the California presence looms still larger. Californians possess more automobiles, VCRs, and personal computers than do residents of any entity except the entire United States and four other countries, each with at least twice California's population. The state holds the same distinction in the consumption of water, petroleum, and chemicals and in the generation of trash. . . .

An outpost on the Pacific, California was . . . a staging ground for the settlement by white Americans of the final third of the continent, the mountain region and the Pacific West—a mission that encouraged California's premature expressions of grandeur and spirit of independence.

Today the mission has changed. The state's function within the national community is no longer peripheral. In the regional restructuring in the late twentieth century, California has emerged as the nation's second financial and cultural center, a rival, though still junior, to the East Coast power corridor. Global economic shifts and the massive internal redistribution of population, industry, and public policy priorities since World War II have turned the United States into a bipolar nation. California is the capital of the newer America that faces west and south, toward Asia and Latin America.

The state's growing authority in world and national affairs rests least of all on formal politics. Although southern California's wealth and celebrity play a large role in national politics and while two of the last four Republican presidents have been southern Californians, it is in the realms of business and media that California's influence is chiefly felt. Key industries—electronics, bioscience, and aerospace—are concentrated there. Moreover, California is the chief port of entry for Far Eastern goods and capital; for that reason the Japanese collaborate with us in the development of this West Coast power center, investing in banking, real estate, and in the all-important high-tech sector.

Media strength is the other source of California's preeminence. First with the advent of Hollywood as the international film capital in the 1920s, then with the addition of television studios in the 1950s, southern California has played a major role in the production of popular entertainment and the consequent shaping of consumer values. In the 1970s and 1980s, Los Angeles made a multibillion-dollar effort to become a high-culture capital with the establishment of new museums (the Getty, the Norton Simon, the Armand Hammer, the Museum of Contemporary Art), symphonic and performing arts centers, and dozens of theater groups. As Mike Davis notes in *City of Quartz,* his penetrating study of Los Angeles in the 1980s, southern California's elite have been engaged in recent years in the kind of wholesale art grab that brought "culture" to Gilded Age New York in the late nineteenth century.

Like Texas and one or two other states, California is really a region unto itself. Geography makes it part of the western United States, but history sets it partially outside the regional culture area called the West. To be sure, it shares with the other states of the Pacific and Mountain time zones a number of characteristics that lend coherence to the region. Its topography—mountains, valleys, deserts—is decidedly western, as are its mostly arid climate and the resulting water distribution problems. Its political economy also followed developmental patterns common to the region: cities, mining, and railroads came first, then agriculture; the federal government owned, and still owns, much of the land and played, and still plays, a critical role in economic development. Furthermore, one can speak of the state's politics as western. Turn-of-the-century sectional and developmental conflict yielded a western "progressive" political system, with weak parties, strong executives, and liberal provisions for voter initiative. Also in the western mode, California has remained a stronghold of the Republican party throughout the twentieth century.

But there are other historical features that California does not share with western states, matters of demography and mythology that advance California's claim to uniqueness. Underpopulation and a system of ethnic relations based on what Patricia Limerick calls the "legacy of conquest" have been, until recently, defining features of the West. Most western states have known minimal diversity, with few African Americans or foreign-born immigrants. What they have had is minority populations of Native Americans or Mexican Americans living in clear subordination to a largely undifferentiated white population. And western regional mythology dwells on that relationship, celebrating the founding dramas of conquest and repopulation with the same callousness that the South shows in its plantation mythology.

California has built its population and its identity quite differently. Rapid growth and escalating ethnic diversity are the keys. Throughout its American history, California has been a population accumulation zone without parallel. For nearly a century and a half the state has sustained a growth rate that doubles its population every two decades. And that has kept the state's demography in motion. Indeed, continuous repopulation is the critical drama of California's history and the source of some of its unique cultural claims. Wave after wave of newcomers from an ever-changing list of places have remade California again and again, each time adding something new while allowing the state to retain its most paradoxical tradition—the tradition of change.

While none of this resembles typical western regional traits, it does accord with population processes that the nation as a whole celebrates but that actually occur only in a few dynamic cities and states. In this and in many other matters, California earns its right to claim a distinction not through difference but through emphasis. As novelist Wallace Stegner put it, California is just like "America only more so . . . the national culture at its most energetic end." . . .

The state's mythology and sense of identity also diverge from the western "conquest" model. Pioneers, cowboys, and other conquest figures do not dominate the symbolic landscape; indeed, California's lore reads like something of an inversion, with pristine nature idealized and a romanticized role reserved for the Franciscan missions of preconquest California. The state's self-concept descends principally from a pair of founding myths that partially obscure California's own very real legacy of conquest. The first is the gold rush, that extraordinary drama of luck and adventure that forever fixed the state's reputation as a land of dreams. The second derives from the invention of southern California in the late nineteenth century and turns on edenic images of the Mediterranean climate, of sun, sand, and citrus, of new and healthful ways of life. All of this, to be sure, is related to the essential western myths of the big land and the fresh start. But California softens and pluralizes the symbolism, moving away from images of tough men in a rugged land and presenting itself instead as gentle and therapeutic.

One thing California does share is the western emphasis on geography. Land, climate, and location are never far from consciousness and more readily than in other regions suggest their powerful impact on human habitation patterns. The incredibly varied topography and the rich array of land-use capacities have made California both comparatively wealthy and sociologically diverse throughout its long history of habitation.

The state's original inhabitants, its Indian peoples, set the pattern for diversity and perhaps also abundance. Before European settlers arrived, California was the most densely settled part of what is now the United States and home to one of the greatest varieties of discrete cultures of any place on earth. Quilted into the complex of valleys, foothills, deserts, riverbanks, and coastal strips were well over one hundred different tribes speaking nearly eighty discrete languages. Only the Mohave and the Yuma of the Colorado River basin practiced agriculture; the rest lived simply but with remarkable stability on the foodstuffs that their small tribal territories provided—seafood for coastal peoples like the Chumash, salmon for the river tribes of the northern areas, acorns a staple nearly everywhere. . . .

For the two centuries from the mid 1500s to the mid 1700s, Spain regarded the western Pacific as its private realm, controlling what little commerce that vast region saw. Then, in the mid-eighteenth century, the monopoly ended as English, French, and Russians sailed into the area, mapping the Pacific and looking for trading possibilities. Concerned particularly about the string of fur-trading posts that the Russians were establishing, Spanish authorities decided it was time to solidify the claim to California. In 1769 a small colonizing expedition set out from Baja California, composed of the usual Spanish frontier complement of soldiers, civilians, and priests, the first two to establish presidios and pueblos, the last to convert the Indians. . . .

Hispanicization of the indigenous population rather than removal and replacement by land-hungry immigrants was the model settlement plan. Franciscan padres were the chief instrument of colonization. Within thirty years of the arrival of the first Mexican settlers, they had established a string of missions from San Diego to San Francisco and had brought the Indians living in the coastal portions of California under their effective control. . . . [T]he Indians became the work force for expanded levels of production, giving up in the process not only their hunting and gathering economy but also much of their culture and all of their freedom. . . .

Paradoxically, Mexico's independence from Spain, gained in 1821, opened California to American economic penetration. Abandoning the restrictive policies set by the Spanish that had strangled economic activity in the province, the new government in Mexico City allowed free access to the ports, began the redistribution of mission lands, and liberalized immigration procedures. This was good news to the shoe and candle manufacturers of New England, who now provided a market for the products made from the great herds of cattle that grazed the California hills. By the mid 1830s the California economy had been completely remade from one based on self-sufficient agriculture controlled by the missions to a privatized ranching economy (still based on Indian labor) geared to the production of hides and tallow for export in Yankee ships.

The trade brought new wealth to the province and also new people, most notably Americans. . . .

America's first Pacific acquisition came about not through negotiation but through war. California was one of the prizes of America's first full-scale expansionist war, fought on Mexican soil in 1846 and 1847. . . . Signatures had not yet been affixed to the Treaty of Guadalupe-Hidalgo when the real act of conquest began. The discovery of gold in early 1848 did for California in five extraordinary years what generations could not do in New Mexico: it completely Americanized it.

The gold rush was . . . the seminal event in the creation of American California—indeed, in the whole later history of the far West. As an economic event, it transformed the meaning and purpose of the frontier West. The old West, the Mississippi Valley, had been a frontier of trappers and farmers whose slowly developing commerce with the rest of the nation depended on river towns and riverboats. The new West that gold-rush California introduced was not really a frontier at all. It was a ready-made enterprise zone of miners and ranchers, followed almost immediately by cities and railroads. . . .

A quarter of a million newcomers poured into California between 1848 and 1853, all but obliterating the existing inhabitants. . . . Outnumbered twenty to one and unaccustomed to the laws, language, and business culture that now governed their lives, the Mexicans struggled to hold on to the land and the way of life that was guaranteed them by treaty. Within a generation, both had been lost as courts, lawyers, bankers, squatters, drought, and recession forced the sale of most of the original ranchos and as the usual manifestations of Yankee racism and religious prejudice undermined their cultural authority. By the 1880s, many of the "Californios," as the Mexican settlers called themselves, were eking out shabby lives in the barrios of southern California. Poor and forgotten, they had become strangers in their own land.

California's remaining Indian populations fared much worse. . . . A twenty-year campaign of slaughter abetted by the spread of disease became a veritable holocaust. Some tribes were completely eliminated, leaving not a single survivor. In 1880 census takers could find only seventeen thousand Indians, just 6 percent of the area's estimated original population of three hundred thousand. . . .

If in its first American generation California was a mining and urban frontier, its second incarnation was as a farming economy, an orientation that became practical after the completion of the transcontinental railroad in 1869. . . .

The railroad turned the state into a second Midwest, encouraging first the production of wheat and then, with the spread of irrigation and the invention of refrigerated cars, a shift to the cultivation of fruits and vegetables. . . . [B]y 1870 the fastest-growing areas were the inland valleys to which the Central Pacific and other promoters were steering immigrants, luring them with a campaign of advertising conducted extensively in heartland states like Iowa and Illinois. By 1890 midwesterners had replaced Northeasterners as California's principal population group and would remain the largest force in the state's population until World War II. . . .

Immigration in this period was almost entirely from Europe and Canada, and mostly from the same European regions that populated the Midwest: Germany, Britain, Ireland, and Scandinavia. After 1880 Italians and Portuguese came to California in substantial numbers, but not many . . . eastern Europeans. . . . Working mostly in agriculture or in the tiny service sectors that their isolated, much harassed communities could support, Chinese, Japanese, Filipinos, Mexicans, and the equally small population of African Americans held on precariously. Like that of the Midwest, California's population was emphatically European American.

Midwesternization entered a second phase around the turn of the century with the invention of southern California. In 1880 the six counties of southern California claimed fewer than fifty thousand residents, only 6 percent of the state's population. By 1930 there were 2.8 million southern Californians, just about half of the state's total. This new population magnet was built out of orange groves, oil, tourism, real estate, and a huge dose of imagination. Railroads again opened the way, pushing competing lines into Los Angeles in 1876 and 1885, thereby setting off an immediate fare war and putting both the Southern Pacific and the Santa Fe into the business of promoting southern California. . . .

Spanish colonial architecture, "Old Spanish Days" parades and fiestas, new streets and towns tagged with Spanish names, new history lessons in the tourist magazines and school texts—after a generation of deliberate Anglicization of form and consciousness, California now reversed course in a carefully constructed campaign to claim a Spanish (but not Mexican) past.

Collaborating with the image makers was the one grounded industry that southern California could claim in its first period of growth. Orange growing became another exercise in Mediterranean romance, a gentlemanly form of agriculture ideally suited to the fantasies of inhabitants of harsher climes, farmers and townsfolk alike. Later there would be a less glamorous blue-collar economy, with oil producing most of the revenues and con-struction most of the jobs and with a growing branch-plant manufacturing sector. But southern California's image as a leisure frontier had been firmly set. The gold in the second California population rush lay in sun and oranges.

Hollywood completed the fantasy. Chasing the sun like everyone else, the infant film industry drifted into Los Angeles in the early years of the twentieth century just as movies were replacing vaudeville as the dominant popular entertainment medium. The young city and the young industry were a perfect match, each thriving on artifice and invention, both products of an era that was rapidly democratizing the pleasures of consumerism.

Hollywood also gave California its first glimpse of its future influence. By the 1920s the film industry had kicked into high gear. Attracting a grow-ing colony of celebrities, writers, and artists, the studios cranked out miles of celluloid to be seen weekly by tens of millions not just in the United States but around the world. The leading edge of American globalism, Hol-lywood's films spread enticing images of American opulence and equally refracted representations of California far and wide. To the older imagery of climate, health, and wealth were added new suggestions of experiment and excess. Replacing Greenwich Village as the symbol of social experi-mentalism, Los Angeles became synonymous with sex, celebrity, hedon-ism, architectural and religious oddities, and wacky politics—in short, with nearly everything new and outrageous. . . .

World War II initiated California's third developmental era. After a century of looking east, California now turned westward, assuming much of the responsibility for America's involvement on the Pacific Rim. No longer peripheral, the state would now become a leading center of both eco-nomic and cultural production, home to some of the critical industries and cultural innovations that Americans have developed since the 1940s.

The federal government was almost entirely responsible for Califor-nia's new role. Federal policy had always to some extent privileged the state, reflecting the nation's interest in maintaining a credible military pres-ence in the Pacific. A naval shipyard alongside San Francisco Bay was the first substantial federal investment in the region in the 1850s, and there would be others. Transportation services were the major nineteenth-century target for federal funds, and California received more than its share for har-bor and river improvements and for railroad building. Federal land recla-mation and water development projects pumped additional millions into the state in the early decades of the twentieth century, as did the Pacific mili-tary buildup that began in earnest in the 1890s. By the end of World War I, California already possessed a substantial military-industrial complex, including shipyards, navy and army bases, and the beginnings of the air-craft industry that was to be so important to its later development.

World War II turned this stream of federal funds into a torrent. Com-mitted to a two-ocean war, Washington poured 10 percent of its entire war budget into California. Some of this went into building and operating the more than one hundred military installations that funneled men and matériel into the Pacific war. Most of the rest went into war production, giving the state a huge new industrial base. The San Francisco Bay Area became the nation's shipbuilding center, while southern California plants turned out more than 200,000 planes. Every bit as important for California in the long run were the federal dollars spent on scientific research, principally for the nuclear program at the University of California and the rocketry research at the California Institute of Technology. . . .

California emerged from the war with a highly diversified economy, perhaps the most modern in the world. A huge military-industrial complex weighted toward the fast-breaking aerospace and electronics industries now complemented the increasingly efficient agricultural economy. Added to these sectors was an educational/business service sector that developed rapidly in the 1950s and 1960s as forward-looking state officials invested massively in schools and universities, building what they hoped would be the finest public education system in the country. All this turned California into a job-creating and population-attracting machine unlike any other in the late twentieth century. Numbers tell the story. The 1940 population of 6.9 million jumped to 15.7 million by 1960, hit 23.7 million by 1980, and raced on past 30 million in 1990. Along the way, somewhere about 1962, California became the nation's most populous state.

California's new economy also brought a new demography, one befitting the increasingly global outlook of both state and nation in the second half of the twentieth century. In these years, California broke completely with the midwestern pattern. Ninety percent white in 1940, California had become an ethnic kaleidoscope by 1990, with 43 percent of its population claiming Asian, African, Latin American, or Native American ancestry.

African Americans had been only a slight presence in California before the war, preferring the industrial North to the unknown West during the great diaspora from the South of the 1910s and 1920s. But after 1942, shipyard jobs primed the pump for a massive migration from the western South. By 1950 California had a population of almost half a million blacks, which spiraled to 1.4 million by 1970. Migration slowed after that and even reversed somewhat in the 1980s, bringing the 1990 black population to just over 2 million (7 percent of the state's population).

Latin[o] American population growth followed a different trajectory. Beginning after the turn of the century and especially during the revolution in their native land that began in 1910, Mexican immigrants initially sought mainly farm and construction labor jobs in southern and central California. The Great Depression of the 1930s brought that cycle of immigration to a close, but a new one began in the 1940s, spurred mostly by urban opportunities. Much of this was legal immigration, since Mexicans enjoyed various loopholes and entitlements under the immigration restriction statutes passed in the 1920s. But an increasing percentage of the postwar flow was undocumented. The state's largest ethnic minority, with an estimated four hundred thousand members in 1940, the Chicano/Latino population grew exponentially, passing the three million mark in 1970, then exploding in the next two decades. In the 1990 census Hispanics numbered 7.7 million, more than one-quarter of the state's population. Although most Hispanics were of Mexican heritage, there were also substantial communities from each of the Central American countries.

The Asian [American] story is different still. Although World War II and its immediate aftermath removed some of the restrictions on Asian immigration, it was not until Congress rewrote immigration law in 1965 that the way was cleared for the extraordinary proliferation of peoples that in the 1970s and 1980s gave new meaning to the term "diversity" in California. One out of every two legal immigrants into the United States in this period came from Asia or the Pacific Islands, and more than half of these immigrants went to California. This new wave was entirely different from the earlier immigration from China, Japan, and the Philippines, which consisted mostly of unskilled laborers. Often well educated and equipped with commercial or technical skills, the new Asian immigrants came from all around the Pacific Rim: from Korea, Taiwan, Hong Kong, the Philippines, Vietnam, Cambodia, and Laos, as well as from India and Pakistan, giving the state a combined Asian population of 2.7 million in 1990, 9 percent of California's total.

Perhaps the most intriguing aspect of the new demography has been the repopulation of California by Native Americans, who now number almost two hundred thousand. Some of this can be credited to the original California peoples, whose numbers have grown steadily throughout the twentieth century. But the largest increase has come from outside the state, as Navajo, Lakota, Cherokee and Choctaw, as well as members of other nations of the interior, have followed the trail of postwar opportunity to California.

The trail ends in Los Angeles, which is to the late twentieth century what New York was to the century before: a crossroads of the world, the Pacific half of the globe in microcosm. Here, spread out in the legendary city of sprawl, are the unmelted millions, dozens of ethnicities and nationalities, no one constituting a majority: one million African Americans, over three million Latin[o] Americans, the largest concentration of Japanese outside Japan, of Koreans outside Korea, and of Vietnamese outside Vietnam, and Chinese from several nations, as well as substantial enclaves of Filipinos and South Asians. Then there are the recent Arab, Iranian, Israeli, and Russian immigrants, as well as the older ethnic communities: the Jewish West Side and the South Side Okie suburbs. The story goes on and on.

Demography is only one of the foundations of the new, plural California of the last half century. Cultural and political trends that have opened debate about the priorities of modern society have made an especially powerful impression in California, creating a cornucopia of cultural experiments and social movements while demonstrating that Californians are divided by place, life-style, and ideology as well as by ethnicity.

Having pushed past San Francisco as the industrial, financial, and population capital of the West, and extended its domination of American media with the addition of radio, television, and record industries, Los Angeles might have been expected to play a leading role in the creation of the cultural products and agendas for the new era. And to some extent it did.

America's great postwar cult of youth broke first in southern California, in the Anaheim orange groves that became Disneyland, on the white sand beaches that launched the surfing craze, in the music and film now targeting the largest generation ever of young consumers.

But media-drenched Los Angeles was too invested in the ways of consumer society to foster the kinds of oppositional subcultures that were to be the most important social innovations of [the] late 20th century. That role, ironically, would fall to San Francisco, a city that only a few years before had been known for its stodgy old wealth and no-nonsense labor unions. By the late 1960s the San Francisco Bay Area had been reinvented as the capital of alternative America, identified near and far with a succession of new social and political movements: Beat poetry in the late 1950s; the Berkeley Free Speech movement in 1964; Haight-Ashbury, hippies, and acid rock a few years later; then the Black Panther Party in nearby Oakland; and in the 1970s the nation's first politically powerful gay and lesbian community. Meanwhile the Bay Area had played a substantial role in the revitalization of the environmental movement and had nurtured into prominence several New Age religious groups.

If these ideas and movements helped change the nation, they affected California even more profoundly, adding to the welter of voices that increasingly complicated the state's political system. What analysts liked to describe as the state's erratic political behavior was really a matter of escalating diversity. The electorate that could make Ronald Reagan governor one moment and Jerry Brown the next, that could maintain both leftists and reactionaries in Congress, that could send former SDS (Students for a Democratic Society) leader Tom Hayden and former John Birch Society members to the same legislature, was no longer one entity. In the postindustrial age, as in the pre-European one, California had become a mosaic of subregions with very different sociopolitical characteristics. Economic function as well as demography underlay the irreconcilable political differences between the conservative techno-burbs of Orange, San Diego, and Santa Clara counties and the experimental university towns scattered about the state; between the privileged coastal communities with their tourist base and growth-control politics and the mountain/lumber zones that resist environmental regulation; between the core urban areas where multiracial populations and public-sector employment promote Great Society liberalism and the agricultural valleys where the social system is white over brown and the politics follow the needs of agribusiness.

And yet out of this mosaic have come some new public policy priorities. One has to do with population and the environment. Prior to World War II the state had unabashedly pushed population growth except during depression cycles, when Asians, Latin[o] Americans, and occasionally other groups were targeted for exclusion. Since the war both boosterism and xenophobia have diminished greatly, replaced, especially since the 1960s, by a politics of overpopulation anxiety that so far has focused more on infrastructural and environmental regulation than on unpopular social groups.

The result has been some of the toughest environmental legislation in the nation. Ambitious air-pollution programs and water-quality standards, successful campaigns to protect endangered species, stop offshore oil drilling, save wilderness areas and wild rivers, and halt nuclear power plants, special agencies to control development along the coast and in the Lake Tahoe basin, local growth-control initiatives and statewide battles over water supplies, state and local recycling programs, a pioneering law regulating the use and labeling of toxic substances—despite opposition on various fronts the public's concern with issues of environmental quality probably counts as one of the few areas of general consensus. That is not to say that anything of real consequence has been resolved. The problems of resource abuse, air pollution, water scarcity, and waste disposal remain, and will, as long as the culture's chief concern is escalating consumption.

The second new pattern in California politics since World War II involved the readjustment of racial hierarchies. This of course has been the great postwar agenda throughout American society, but the California story has some particular twists. The state's moment of conscience came not in the mid 1950s but a decade earlier, when it began to consider the awful consequences of its last brutal exercise in xenophobia.

Pearl Harbor provided the excuse to carry out the agenda that had many times tempted the state's powerful anti-Asian lobby. Pressured by the West Coast press and members of Congress, President Roosevelt authorized the removal and incarceration of the region's entire Japanese population, some 93,000 persons from California, two-thirds of them citizens. Forced to sell or abandon homes, farms, and businesses, the internees spent most of the war in guarded, barbed-wire-enclosed camps in remote spots in the western interior.

California turned a corner in the years following this last xenophobic exercise. After the war, the state began to dismantle its legal apparatus of caste and exclusion. In 1948 the state's supreme court threw out the long-enforced antimiscegenation statute and four years later invalidated the notorious Alien Land Law that kept first-generation Asian immigrants from owning property. Meanwhile, Congress and the U.S. Supreme Court abolished provisions in immigration law that prevented Asians from becoming naturalized citizens. Two changes were evident in these moves: the liberalizing trend that would soon result in the broad civil rights agendas of the late 1950s and the 1960s and a shift in the axis of racial tension from Asian/white to black/white, a change that brought California into line with the rest of the nation.

The rest of the civil rights era followed conventional northern patterns. White Californians readily abandoned de jure racial restrictions but not so readily de facto segregation. It took a decade of legislative battles before the state passed its first law banning racial discrimination in employment in 1959. When that was followed four years later by "fair housing" legislation, the white majority rebelled, passing a 1964 repeal initiative by a two-to-one-margin, only to see the courts overturn the overturners and reinstate the antidiscrimination measure.

The Watts section of Los Angeles exploded in the summer of 1965, leaving thirty-four people dead and initiating a decade and a half of desperate racial conflict in the streets and courts. A rising tide of militancy in the black and later in the Chicano communities was matched by the backlash mood of many whites, particularly when the courts in the 1970s began ordering school boards to initiate desegregation plans. Affirmative action programs raised further resistance. As was the case nearly everywhere, the result was a standoff. The old system of racial caste had been broken, but neither equality nor integration had taken its place. The new system of inequality joined principles of class to the factor of race, privileging middle-class minorities with both occupational and political opportunities but isolating all those who could not make the cut: the working poor, the dependent, the non-English-speaking.

Today, the new social order's ambiguities are heightened by the multiethnic character of California society and by the uneven distribution of problems and opportunities among the different groups. Asian [Americans], African Americans, and Latinos occupy different niches in the social order. Blacks face the greatest economic and social difficulties but have developed the greatest political resources, wielding political influence out of proportion to their numbers at both state and community levels. Asians are in the opposite position: more economically successful (in the aggregate) than other minorities but politically almost voiceless. Latinos fall in the middle, gaining economic standing and slowly emerging as a political force.

Where it will all lead is anything but certain. Along with the rest of America, California entered the 1990s poised to move either forward into a new era of pluralist understanding or backward into familiar cycles of conflict. The recent past offers portents of both. There is on the one hand the example of the University of California at Berkeley, where the undergraduate student population has become a showpiece of colors and cultures and where the inevitable tensions are muted by a nearly consensual desire to make it work. On the other hand there are the ominous signs that Mike Davis reads in the changing polity and cityscape of Los Angeles, where white homeowner associations erect gated "fortress" communities, where billions are spent on the fine arts while poverty proliferates, where English-only ordinances and building codes are used to fight immigrant "invasions," where industry and public officials alike retreat from the central city, where the war on drugs turns into a police war against a whole generation of blacks and Latinos, where a modern metropolis veers toward the grim future foretold in Ridley Scott's film *Blade Runner.*

The events of 29 April–2 May 1992 seem to confirm that nightmarish prediction. After a suburban jury acquitted four white police officers charged with brutality in the videotaped beating of Rodney King, a black motorist, crowds of young blacks, Latinos, and some whites took to the streets in the worst sequence of urban violence that Americans have seen this century.

When it was over, more than 50 people were dead, more than 2,000 were injured, and 12,000 were arrested. South-Central Los Angeles, already the site of escalating poverty and neglect, faced the task of rebuilding some 5,000 stores and structures burned or damaged in the four-day conflagration.

Still many Californians remain optimists, citing the state's transcendent cultural traditions, in particular, its capacity for innovation and change. This notion, itself a feature of the new, global California, operates more on the plane of myth than of fact. Despite the record of cultural creativity, it would be hard to demonstrate that Californians in the aggregate are any more receptive to change than anyone else; what they have developed is a capacity for social diversity and political schizophrenia, for sustaining a range of discrete, even antagonist, subcultures while moving erratically between public policy agendas. It is all nicely postmodern—the many voices, the invented personas and plastic lifestyles, the short attention span—a microburst cultural system capable of continuous surprise.

Whatever its entertainment value, it is hard to believe that mercurial California has any special gift for solving the complex problems of pluralism, let alone the other pressing issues of a globally interdependent age. In the end, like the nation that it aspires to lead, California will try to get by as it has always gotten by: relying on its geographic gifts and economic good fortune to feed the inflated consumer passions of its growing and changing population, hoping that the regime of abundance will last forever, or at least for another generation.

 FURTHER READING

Tomás Almaguer, *Racial Fault Lines: The Historical Origins of White Supremacy in California* (1994)

"California Archives," special issue of *California History* 75 (Spring 1996)

Albert Camarillo, *Chicanos in California: A History of Mexican Americans in California* (1984)

Sucheng Chan, *Asian Californians* (1991)

Daniel Cornfield, ed., *Working People of California* (1995)

David G. Gutierrez, *Walls and Mirrors: Mexican Americans, Mexican Immigrants, and the Politics of Ethnicity* (1995)

Byran O. Jackson and Michael B. Preston, eds., *Racial and Ethnic Politics in California* (1991)

Joan M. Jensen and Gloria Ricci Lothrop, *California Women: A History* (1987)

Rudolph M. Lapp, *Afro-Americans in California* (2nd ed., 1987)

Patricia Nelson Limerick, *The Legacy of Conquest: The Unbroken Past of the American West* (1987)

Carey McWilliams, *California: The Great Exception* (1949; repr. 1976)

Leonard Michaels, David Reid, and Raquel Scherr, eds., *West of the West: Imagining California* (1989; First California Paperback Printing, 1995)

Doyce B. Nunis, Jr., and Gloria Ricci Lothrop, eds., *A Guide to the History of California* (1989)

Paul Ong, Edna Bonacich, and Lucie Cheng, eds., *The New Asian Immigration in Los Angeles and Global Restructuring* (1994)

George H. Phillips, *The Enduring Struggle: Indians in California History* (1981)
James J. Rawls and Walton Bean, *California: An Interpretive History* (1968; 6th ed., 1993)
Richard B. Rice, William A. Bullough, and Richard J. Orsi, *The Elusive Eden: A New History of California* (1988, 2d ed., 1996)
Laurence A. Rickels, *The Case of California* (1991)
William G. Robbins, *Colony and Empire: The Capitalist Transformation of the American West* (1994)
B. Gordon Wheeler, *Black California: A History of African-Americans in the Golden State* (1993)
Richard White, *"It's Your Misfortune and None of My Own": A History of the American West* (1991)

CHAPTER
2

The First Californians

The Indians lived in California long before anyone else. Yet their contributions to California history have been obscured by a widespread misperception that they were passive in the face of Euro-American intrusions in the late eighteenth century. The Indian of California "was too cowardly to be warlike," wrote one historian in 1878. "The best part of his time was spent in dancing and sleeping." This incomplete and distorted view derives largely from reports by Euro-Americans who found the Indian population depleted and demoralized after Spanish colonization. Such a negative stereotype fails to acknowledge the vitality of numerous Indian cultures prior to their conquest, as well as the importance of subsequent developments. The stereotype may also have served to legitimize the harsh and brutal treatment of Indians in the nineteenth century, and it may account for the trivialization of California Indians in history texts of the twentieth century.

Admittedly, the historical record is sparse with regard to pre-Conquest California. Yet such scholars as Lowell John Bean, Sherburne Cook, Alfred Kroeber, Robert Heizer, Jeannette Costo, Rupert Costo, James Rawls, George Harwood Phillips, and Albert Hurtado have worked to put many of the pieces of the Indians' pre-Conquest world back together. It is now generally agreed that the native Californians were hunter-gatherers whose diet was based on large game, abundant plant foods, and rich marine life. Their most important food staple was the acorn, which they ground into meal and then prepared as porridge or bread. According to the Indian division of labor, men were responsible for hunting and fishing, while women gathered plant foods and cooked.

Although they lacked any concept of land ownership, Indians were by no means its passive occupants. By the eighteenth century, they were experimenting with sophisticated techniques of land and resource management and, at least in the southern part of California, practiced limited horticulture and irrigation. In places like the Yosemite Valley, Indians periodically burned the underbrush to assure that oaks, the source of acorns, would not

29

be choked out by fast-growing evergreens. Their knowledge of the environment was detailed and extensive.

California Indians were not a completely homogeneous population bound together in regional confederation or by a common language. Instead, their settlements were little more than seasonal campsites occupied for limited periods of time by more than one hundred small "tribelets," or autonomous and self-governing groups whose populations averaged only 250. Furthermore, these native Californians spoke more than one hundred languages. According to the findings of Alfred Kroeber, the renowned anthropologist, pre-Conquest California was divided into six specialized, regional "culture areas." Of these, four were part of the larger "California culture area." The remaining two, on the eastern side of the Sierra Nevada, shared cultural traits and customs with the Indians of the Great Basin and Colorado River areas. Some of the most populous tribes—the Chumash living in the area between present-day San Luis Obispo and Ventura, for example—lived along the southern California coast. The Indians of this region were among the first that Spanish missionaries tried to convert to Christianity (see Chapter 3).

Because of this impressive diversity, James Rawls, for one, expresses reservations about the very term "California Indian." As he points out, "The concept of the California Indian is a white invention. It was created for the purposes of description and analysis, but it was also useful as a stereotype for whites overwhelmed by the diversity of the peoples encountered in the area." In Rawls's opinion, this situation led to differentiations based less on the inherent features of distinctive Indian cultures than on the nature of the Indian relationships with whites (e.g., "mission" and "gentile" Indians, "tame" and "wild" Indians, and so forth).

By the beginning of Hispanic settlement in 1769, approximately 300,000 native people lived within what became the political unit called California. This chapter describes the Indians at the time of the Hispanics' arrival and their first dealings with the newcomers. The findings of modern historians have, to a large extent, dispelled the negative stereotypes reflected in earlier writings. What contradictions and tensions appear in a comparison of the documents and essays in this chapter? To what extent do cultural assumptions color these accounts?

In Chapter 3, we shall examine both the destruction of much of the Indian population and the process by which some Indians managed to survive their encounter with an essentially hostile white society during the nineteenth century.

D O C U M E N T S

The first document, following Kroeber's notion of California "culture areas," is a map showing the impressive variety of linguistic groups among native Californians. Several photos of Indian artifacts, including flutes, baskets, and bowls follow. The third document is culled from the field notes of anthropologist John P. Harrington, who recorded a great deal of information about the lives and worldview of the Chumash Indians. The account is especially interesting because it shows how the Chumash linked their cosmology to certain local geographic features, such as Point Conception and the Channel Islands. In the fourth document, Pablo Tac, a Luiseño Indian born at the Mission of San Luis Rey in 1822, provides one of the few available native eyewitness reports of life under the Franciscan mission system. This account, written by a Christianized Indian in Rome about 1835 under the supervision of church authorities who were educating him, tells how the arrival of the Spanish brought peace and relief from the constant strife of battle with the Luiseños' Indian enemies. The fifth document is an early ethnographical description by a Spanish priest, Father Geronimo Boscana. Boscana, a missionary in San Juan Capistrano from 1812 to 1816, was one of the few priests to write about the culture of the Indians. Here he describes aspects of Juaneño culture, including the instruction of children, marriage, and the Juaneños' allegedly "idle and lazy" manner of life. The final document is a brief excerpt from a *Sacramento Union* editorial written in 1855. Note the abrupt shift in tone from a regretful concern regarding the plight of the Indians to a resigned certainty about the need for white people eventually to "annihilate" them.

The Three Worlds of the Chumash

The Three Worlds

There is this world in which we live, but there is also one above us and one below us. The world below is the underworld occupied by the dangerous animals, the other world. . . . This world here is the world of mankind, and the world above is the upper world of the supernaturals. . . . Here where we live is the center of our world—it is the biggest island. And there are two giant serpents . . . that hold our world up from below. When they are tired they move, and that causes earthquakes. The world above is sustained by the great Eagle, who by stretching his wings causes the phases of the moon. And the water in the springs and streams of this earth is the urine of the many frogs who live in it.

The Sky People

There is a place in the world above where Sun and Eagle, Morning Star and Snilemun (the Coyote of the Sky—not the Coyote of this world) play peon. There are two sides and two players on each side, and Moon is referee. They play every night for a year, staying up till dawn. The game is played in a special house—not in Sun's house, but in a place where they only play peon. . . . They make the count of six to see which side has won the game. When Snilemun's side comes out ahead there is a rainy year. Sun stakes all kinds of harvest products—acorns, deer, islay, chia, ducks, and geese—and when Snilemun is the winner he cannot wait for the stakes to be distributed, but pulls open the door so that everything falls down into this world. And we humans are involved in that game, for when Sun wins he receives his pay in human lives. He and Snilemun then have a dispute, for Snilemun wants to pay his debt with old people who are no longer of any use. But once in a while Sun wins the argument and a young person may be picked out to die.

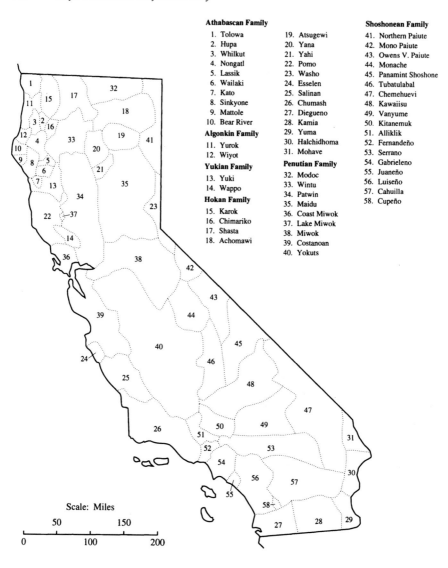

Athabascan Family
1. Tolowa
2. Hupa
3. Whilkut
4. Nongatl
5. Lassik
6. Wailaki
7. Kato
8. Sinkyone
9. Mattole
10. Bear River

Algonkin Family
11. Yurok
12. Wiyot

Yukian Family
13. Yuki
14. Wappo

Hokan Family
15. Karok
16. Chimariko
17. Shasta
18. Achomawi

19. Atsugewi
20. Yana
21. Yahi
22. Pomo
23. Washo
24. Esselen
25. Salinan
26. Chumash
27. Diegueno
28. Kamia
29. Yuma
30. Halchidhoma
31. Mohave

Penutian Family
32. Modoc
33. Wintu
34. Patwin
35. Maidu
36. Coast Miwok
37. Lake Miwok
38. Miwok
39. Costanoan
40. Yokuts

Shoshonean Family
41. Northern Paiute
42. Mono Paiute
43. Owens V. Paiute
44. Monache
45. Panamint Shoshone
46. Tubatulabal
47. Chemehuevi
48. Kawaiisu
49. Vanyume
50. Kitanemuk
51. Alliklik
52. Fernandeño
53. Serrano
54. Gabrieleno
55. Juaneño
56. Luiseño
57. Cahuilla
58. Cupeño

Scale: Miles

50   150

0   100   200

Tribes and Territories of California Indians

Map of Tribal Territories from Robert F. Heizer, ed., *A Collection of Ethnographic Articles on the California Indians*. (Ramona, Calif.: Ballena Press, 1976, p. ii.) Reprinted by permission of Ballena Press.

INDIAN ARTIFACTS: Top Articles from Chamish Indian tribe: stealite olla and comal; serpentine bowl and fragments. Center: Pomo woman weaving basket. Bottom: Articles from Chumash Indian Tribe: stealite canoe effigy; ashphaltum in sandstone bowl with applicator (used to pound tar for canoe).

Top left and right, bottom left and right: Santa Barbara Museum of Natural History, photographs by William Dewey. Center: American Museum of Natural History.

Each one of those beings has a task to perform: Sun lights the day, Morning Star the dawn, and Moon the night. Moon is a single woman. She has a house near that of the Sun. She and Sun and the others never get older; they are always there. Snilemun was like God to the old people. . . . They had great faith in him. Sun is our uncle, but Snilemun is our father— that is why he works for us, giving us food and sparing our lives. He watches over us all the time from the sky. Snilemun has the form of a coyote—a *big* coyote.

And Eagle is up there watching the whole world too. He never moves; he is always in the same spot. When he gets tired of sustaining the upper world, he stretches his wings a little, and this causes the phases of the moon. When there is an eclipse of the moon it is because his wings cover it completely. . . . Sun and Eagle are partners in the peon game, for it was said that both ate people. The place where Eagle lives is surrounded by hills and hills of bleached white bones that can be seen from afar. They are the bones of people of this world that Eagle has eaten. Eagle has neither wife nor family. He is never referred to as a relative, only as wot—he who commands. He is very patient. He is always there in the sky, thinking.

Sun is an *old* man. He is naked, with a feathered banner on his head, and he carries a fire-brand in his hand. The fire-brand is made from the inner bark of a tree that grows only in the sky—not a cottonwood, such as a woman's aprons were once made from, but a tree in the sky with a similar kind of inner bark. The brand is made from a bundle of that fiber, tightly rolled so that it doesn't burn too quickly. Sun uses his thumbnail as a measure to adjust the height of the fire-brand. In the early morning he carries his firebrand at a certain height, and then lowers it one measure at a time to adjust the heat. On very hot days he lowers it a measure or two more. Sun has three resting places on his trail around the world. At about ten o'clock he reaches the first place and rests there a while. At midday he rests longer. At about three o'clock he reaches his third resting spot, where there is a spring. When he reaches the west he takes his fire-brand and returns home very quickly, going around far to the south.

Sun is a widower. He lives alone with his pets and his two daughters, who have never married. They have aprons made of live rattlesnakes like one of the dangerous animal's daughters. The snakes have woven their tails together voluntarily at the top of the aprons so that they seem deliberately made that way. Sun's house is very big, and it is full of all kinds of animals—bears, lions, elk, deer, wolves, rattlesnakes, birds—all of them tame. The house is made of quartz crystal, a kind of crystal that people once used to inlay around the edges of wooden bowls.

When Sun returns home in the evening he takes along whatever people he wants. If they are big he tucks them under his belt, but if they are babies he tucks them under the feathered headband on his head. He arrives home in time for supper, and at first when he enters the house there is a dense fog. He throws the adults down in the doorway and then takes the babies from his feathered headband and throws them down too. And when the fog clears away, there stands Sun with his firebrand. He and his two daughters just pass the people through the fire two or three times and then eat them half-cooked. And they don't drink water like we do, but blood. Every day Sun carries people from this world off this way—every day.

The Dangerous Animals

The dangerous animals are creatures of the other world that come out soon after nightfall and travel all around. The old people used to say that you should bathe early before they return from going around the world, for later the water is steaming because they bathe in it. The haphap is a dangerous animal—he has the form of a man, but he is very dangerous and very devilish. When he inhales he draws trees and rocks and everything toward himself and swallows them. Ququ, lewelew, yowoyow, and the . . . lame devil whose leg is broken and who goes hopping around the world—all have human form also. Ququ and lewelew have bodies covered with pus, and their facial skin is loose. The yowoyow is similar. He lives at a certain place down near Ventura, and the people there see his smoke rising some times. And the people around here believe in La Llorona, the maxulaw or mamismis, that cries up in the trees like a newborn baby. Once a man saw one: it looks like a cat, but with skin like leather or rawhide. When you hear it someone is going to die. It is strange that you don't see La Llorona anymore. And the xolxol are big animals covered with feathers, and the feathers make a noise when they move. . . .

The Sea People

The swordfish are men. They have no wives or children or anything. When they catch a whale they throw it out of the water. They just toss it—and you know how big a whale is. . . . In the old days otter hunters used to see the siren. Once a party of otter hunters was way down by San Diego and saw the siren down there. She has beautiful hair and the body of a woman. She was so hungry that she came close to the boat, and they tossed her a biscuit and she indicated where the otters were.

The Flood

Maqutikok, Spotted Woodpecker, was the only one saved in the flood. He was Sun's nephew. . . . It kept raining and the water kept rising higher and higher until even the mountains were covered. All the people drowned except Maqutikok, who found refuge on top of a tree that was the tallest in the world. The water kept rising until it touched his feet, and the bird cried out, "Help me, Uncle, I am drowning, pity me!" Sun's two daughters heard him and told their father that his kinsman was calling for help. "He is stiff from cold and hunger," they said. Sun held his fire-brand down low and the water began to subside. Maqutikok was warmed by the heat. Then Sun tossed him two acorns. They fell in the water near the tree and Maqutikok picked them up and swallowed them. Then Sun threw two more acorns down and the bird ate them and was content. That is why he likes acorns so much—they are still his food. And after the water was gone only Maqutikok remained. . . . There are rocks in the mountains that are the exact shape of human arms and hands: they are the remains of the people who died in the flood. Those first people . . . who became animals after the Flood were very tall. They used to wade across the channel without needing boats, taking chia and acorns and other things to the islanders in carrying nets. . . . People had found bones on Santa Rosa Island and at Mikiw which were human, but which were yards long.

The Making of Man

After the flood Snilemun (the Coyote of the Sky), Sun, Moon, Morning Star, and Eagle (the great eagle that knows what is to be) were discussing how they were going to make man, and Eagle and Snilemun kept arguing about whether or not the new people should have hands like Snilemun. Coyote announced that there would be people in this world and they should all be in his image since he had the finest hands. Lizard was there also, but he just listened night after night and said nothing. At last Snilemun won the argument, and it was agreed that people were to have hands just like his. The next day they all gathered around a beautiful table-like rock that was there in the sky, a very fine white rock that was perfectly symmetrical and flat on top, and of such fine texture that whatever touched it left an exact impression. Snilemun was just about to stamp his hand down on the rock when Lizard, who had been standing silently just behind, quickly reached out and pressed a perfect hand-print into the rock himself. Snilemun was enraged and wanted to kill Lizard, but Lizard ran down into a deep crevice and so escaped. And Eagle and Sun approved of Lizard's actions, so what could Snilemun do? They say that the mark is still impressed on that rock in the sky. If Lizard had not done what he did, we might have hands like a coyote today.

The Origin of Death

. . . Coyote wanted to make people with hands like his but . . . Lizard wanted them to look like his hands instead, and Lizard won the argument. And later during the same conference Coyote proposed throwing man into a lake when he got old and making him young again. But the matavenado [Jerusalem cricket] said no, the earth will get too full of people and there will be no room to stand. So Coyote lost out in this proposition also. The matavenado is therefore also talked to and killed by the Ventureño, who tell it that it caused death.

Elements

This earth was on top of the waters of the ocean, and . . . there were three elements concerning which we must be cautious—wind, rain, and fire. The rainbow is the shadow of these three colors. The white is wind, the red is fire, and the blue is rain. The wind was sometimes called . . . "breath of the world." And whenever there was lightning the old men would say, "Now beware, that is an element from the hand of a power that caused us to see this world." . . . Thunder was the wind. All the winds get together up above. And sometimes there are whirlwinds so strong that they take the water and convert it into hail.

The Sun

. . . The sun is the beauty of the world—it is born in the east, giving the world beautiful light. . . . The morning and evening stars were the wives of the sun, for before sunrise the morning star comes first, then the dawn, and then the sun. The sun goes to rest in this hole (of the sand dollar) and leaves its rays outside while it rests inside. The sun was like a man. Whenever the dawn of morning comes be careful not to be misguided, for that is the breath of the sun who is a man. . . . Dawn is the sigh of the sun. . . .

The Soul

. . . This world is merely a great flat winnowing tray. Some men move up and some down. And there is much chaff mixed through it all. The dead go west and are born again in this world. It is all a circle, an eddy within the abyss. . . . The soul stayed around the old living place for five days after death, and that is why . . . it was fed . . . every night. But the soul of someone who was cremated went west with the flames and did not stay around for five days like the others. The soul of a drowned person always stayed in the sea, wandering, and never reached the land in the west or was born again. The soul of a baby that died before or after birth went west also, but it never reached the place that souls of adults did. . . . The soul is eternal. The soul went to the west and at the end of twelve years it would return and live here reincarnated, born again. . . . Those were pure spirits. They never slept. They were constantly on guard, watching and waiting for the spirits that were coming. Some spirits would go about the world, observing the nature of all others during those twelve years they inhabited another sphere, far in the west, very far from here. People would place food on the grave of a newly-buried person. They would celebrate for five days. They would cook meals early and at about four o'clock in the afternoon they would sit down to mourn and to scatter food. They scattered it with their hands, they scattered it to the four winds. . . . The "white people are a reincarnation of the souls that had gone west. They had a different color, were reincarnated in a lighter color, and spoke a different language. The color and language of whites and Indians are different, but the noble principles of the soul are the same. For this world is a single congregation. . . .

Reincarnation

. . . Sun sees everything. . . . Those who die . . . they follow the sun. Every day they enter the portal of the sun. All over the world they die when the time comes for them to do so. He who dies will resurrect with the same feelings in his heart, but different in one respect—color. . . . The sun rises from the east and goes to the west, and all the spirits follow him. They leave their bodies. The sun reaches the door and enters, and the souls enter too. When it is time for the sun to fulfill his duty he emerges, for he lights the abysses with his eye, and all who are in the dark resurrect. . . .

The Soul's Journey to Šimilaqša

Three days after a person has been buried the soul comes up out of the grave in the evening. Between the third and fifth day it wanders about the world visiting the places it used to frequent in life. On the fifth day after death the soul returns to the grave to oversee the destruction of its property before leaving for Šimilaqša. The soul goes first to Point Conception, which is a wild and stormy place. It was called humqaq, and there was no village there. In ancient times no one ever went near humqaq. They only went near there to make sacrifices at a great ceremonial enclosure. There is a place at humqaq below the cliff that can only be reached by rope, and there is a pool of water there like a basin, into which fresh water continually drips. And there in the stone can be seen the footprints of women and children. There the spirit of the dead bathes and paints itself. Then it sees a light to the westward and goes toward it through the air, and thus reaches the land of Šimilaqša.

Sometimes in the evening people at La Quemada . . . village would see a soul passing by on its way to Point Conception. Sometimes these were the souls of people who had died, but sometimes they were souls that had temporarily left the body. The people of La Quemada would motion with their hands at the soul and tell it to return, to go back east, and they would clap their hands. Sometimes the soul would respond and turn back, but other times it would simply swerve a little from its course and continue on to Šimilaqša. When the people of La Quemada saw the soul it shone like a light, and it left a blue trail behind it. The disease from which the person had died was seen as a fiery ball at its side. When the soul turned back, as it sometimes did, anyone at La Quemada who might have recognized it would hurry to the village where the man whose soul it was lived, and if the sick man then drank a lot of toloache [jimson weed], he might recover and not die. . . . A short time after the soul passed La Quemada the people there would hear a report like a distant cannon shot, and know that that was the sound of the closing of the gate of Šimilaqša as the soul entered. . . .

There were three lands in the world to the west. . . . When the soul leaves Point Conception and crosses the sea, it first reaches the Land of Widows. When the women there get old their friends dip them in a spring and when they awake they are young again. And they never eat, though they have all kinds of food there. They merely take a handful of food and smell it and throw it away, and as soon as they do so it turns to feces. And when they are thirsty they just smell the water and their thirst is quenched. Once past the Land of Widows the soul comes to a deep ravine through which it must pass. The road is all cut up and consists of deep, fine earth as a result of so many souls passing over it. In the ravine are two huge stones that continually part and clash together, part and clash together, so that any person who got caught between them would be crushed. Any living person who attempted to pass would be killed, but souls pass through unharmed.

Once past the clashing rocks the soul comes to a place where there are two gigantic ravens perched on each side of the trail, and who each peck out an eye as the soul goes by. But there are many poppies growing there in the ravine and the soul quickly picks two of these and inserts them in each eye-socket and so is able to see again immediately. When the soul finally gets to Šimilaqša it is given eyes made of blue abalone. After leaving the ravine the soul comes to La Tonadora, the woman who stings with her tail. She kills any living person who comes by, but merely annoys the soul who passes safely.

Just beyond this woman lies a body of water that separates this world from the next, with a bridge that the soul must cross to reach Šimilaqša. The souls of murderers and poisoners and other evil people never reach the bridge, but are turned to stone from the neck down. They remain there on the near shore forever, moving their eyes and watching other souls pass. When the pole begins to fall the soul starts quickly across, but when it reaches the middle two huge monsters rise from the water on either side and give a loud cry, attempting to frighten it so that it falls into the water. If the soul belongs to someone who had no spirit helper or who did not know about the old religion and did not drink toloache—someone who merely lived in ignorance—it falls into the water and the lower part of the body changes to that of a frog, turtle, snake, or fish. The water is full of these beings, who are thus undergoing punishment. When they are hungry they crawl out of the water and wander through the hills nearby looking for cacomites [edible bulbs] to eat. The old people used to say that someone who drank toloache always passed the pole safely for they were strong of spirit.

Once the soul has crossed the bridge it is safe in Šimilaqša. There are two roads leading from the bridge—one goes straight ahead and the other goes to the left. . . . Souls live in Šimilaqša forever and never get old. It is packed full of souls. They harvest islay [*Prunus ilicifolia*], sweet islay, and there is no end of it. Every kind of food is there in abundance. When children die they take the same route as adults. The ravens peck out their eyes, but they have no other troubles on the journey. They pass the bridge easily, for the monsters that try to frighten other souls do not appear.

Pablo Tac Approves of His Tribe's Conversion, 1835

After the Jesuit Fathers of California had been barred from the mission, there came the Fathers of the Orders of St. Francis and of St. Dominic, the first for Alta California, the second for Baja California. California is one, divided into two parts, that is to say, Baja California and Alta California, thus called by the Señor Don Cortez, who was the first who discovered it. Baja California extends from the Mission of San Lucas to the Mission of San Diego, Alta California from the Mission of San Diego up to Monte Rey.

It is known from history that the first of the missionaries who came to California were the Jesuit Fathers, and the first among them was Father Salvaterra Juan, renowned in the history of California for his works of piety.

The Dominicans came to Baja California, and the Franciscans came to Alta California. The Franciscan Fathers of whom I speak are called Padres Fernandinos in Mexico, because their college or convent is called the Convent of San Fernando Rey de España. These Fathers came to Alta California, and one of them came to our country which we call Quechla, and because of this we called ourselves Quechnajuichom, that is to say, inhabitants of Quechla, when we were at peace, because always there was war, always strife day and night with those who spoke in another language.

It seems that our enemies were those that now are called Diegueños by the Spanish, and Quichamcauichom by us, which means "those of the South." Before going to war they used to paint themselves in order to be terrible to the enemy, and they would surprise the enemy either when he was sleeping or when the men were leaving the house, the women remaining alone; and they would kill the women, old people and children. This done, they burned the camp, fleeing to their homes.

The weapons were bows, arrows and certain swords of wood and lances of wood in our language called *uacatom*. The bows were made of strong wood that could not easily be broken. In length they reached to the shoulders of the man, one finger and a half thick in the middle, three fingers broad. The arrows were of reed, thick as a finger, four hands long. At the tip a little stick one and a half hands long was inserted. The feathering was of three feathers of any bird. The sword was four hands long, three fingers broad, and it began to curve at the third hand. The lance was eight hands long, four fingers thick, and it had a sharp point. To carry the arrows they had at the back of the shoulders a skin of coyote or other animal. The swords were thrown at the enemy, or the head of the enemy was struck off. The swords when they were thrown carried more than five hundred paces of a big man.

With these arms, which we still have, they used to go to war. The life of that time was very miserable, because there was always strife. The god who was adored at that time was the sun and the fire. Thus we lived among the woods until merciful God freed us of these miseries through Father Antonio Peyri, a Catalan, who arrived in our country in the afternoon with seven Spanish soldiers.

When the missionary arrived in our country with a small troop, our captain and also the others were astonished, seeing them from afar, but they did not run away or seize arms to kill them, but having sat down, they watched them. But when they drew near, then the captain got up (for he was seated with the others) and met them. They halted, and the missionary then began to speak, the captain saying perhaps in his language "hichsom iva haluon, pulùchajam cham quinai." "What is it that you seek here? Get out of our country!" But they did not understand him, and they answered him in Spanish, and the captain began with signs, and the Fernandino, understanding him, gave him gifts and in this manner made him his friend. The captain, turning to his people (as I suppose) found the whites all right, and so they let them sleep here. There was not then a stone house, but all were camps (as they say). This was that happy day in which we saw white people, by us called Sosabitom. O merciful God, why didst Thou leave us for many centuries, years, months and days in utter darkness after Thou camest to the world? Blessed be Thou from this day through future centuries.

Father Geronimo Boscana Describes the San Juan Capistrano Indians, 1832

My having resolved to write this history, fabulous in itself, or in its subject matter, but true as far as these Indians are concerned, has been primarily with the aim of being able to fulfill to some degree my duties as Apostolic Missionary, having their fulfillment ever present and near at hand, as well as also of leaving to those who come after me instruction and lights in order that they may be guided without such labor as it has cost me, trying in every way, using all possible means, to gain knowledge of the belief, usages, and customs which these natives had in their gentile state. And by the mercy of God, through labor and cunning during a period of more than ten years [marginal annotation: from 1812 to 1822], I have been able to investigate to a moral certainty everything that is related in the present book.

Since I am of the persuasion that if we are ignorant of the belief held by the Indians, of their usages and customs, it is very difficult to take them out of the error in which they live and to give them to understand the true religion, and to teach them the true way to their salvation. I confess that it is difficult to be able to penetrate their secrets, because the signification of their usages and customs is not known to all of them. This [signification] is only for the chiefs and certain satraps, who performed the work of priests, and [certain] criers, and when these taught it to their sons (and that only to those who were to succeed them), it was always with the admonition that they should not divulge it to anyone, for if they told or divulged it, they would have many misfortunes, and would die, etc., instilling into them much dread and fear; and for that reason so little is known about their affairs, since those few who know and understand keep it to themselves.

Since these Indians did not use writing, letters, or any characters, nor do they use them, all their knowledge is by tradition, which they preserve in songs for the dances which they held at their great feasts. But since these songs have their form or are in a language distinct from that which is spoken at the present time, no one, except those mentioned above, understands the meaning of the song and dance; the others sing and dance but without knowing either what they are saying or what they are doing. I imagine that such songs are in a primitive language, and they preserve them in their feasts, and these songs and dances contain all their religion, usages and customs, and for this reason these songs are not used or sung except in their feasts. . . .

One of the matters in which the Ancients experienced the greatest difficulty and which gave them considerable care was the bringing up of the

children, because on this being good or bad depends the goodness or bad-
ness of the child. Since these Indians did not know either the mechanic arts,
or the liberal ones, nor did they need them because of the manner of life
which they led, but only those necessary for their own preservation, they
therefore were not able to teach their children anything useful to rid them
of their idleness. They merely instructed them in the handling of the bow
and arrow, and this in order that they might learn to hunt for food and
defend themselves from their enemies.

Although these Indians were ignorant of the true path, and the beginning of wisdom is the fear of the true God, and this fear the beginning of
the instruction of children, nevertheless the instructions which the parents
gave their children had their moral virtues, for the parents and grandparents
took care very earnestly that their children be well brought up and good
[children], because if one of them turned out perverse, although they
quickly removed him from their midst, they were disgraced. And for this
reason from the time they were small they admonished them (and this by
showing them beforehand many misfortunes and punishments, if they did
not follow carefully what was being taught them), telling them they should
not be thieves, or liars, that they should not injure people, should not fight
with one another, and should not use bad words, and above all that they
should not make fun of the old people, but should respect and fear them;
and that if they did not give heed to these instructions which their parents
gave them, even though they might kill him [the perverse child], the God
Chinigchinix would punish him much. And this was the daily harangue.
These Indians did not punish the faults of their children, they merely gave
them certain admonishments to correct them, but in reality very few
offenses were committed and the reason was the much fear and great dread
which they felt. . . .

One of the things necessary for the conservation of the life of man was
company, for which reason God ordained that man should have woman,
with whose company he should pursue two ends, one, the intercourse, of
which he was capable, and the other, that from the union of the two would
be born children who would follow in the propagation and increase of the
race. Although it has been an ancient custom among all nations to give the
women to their husbands, it has not been everywhere in the same manner
or with the same ceremonies, and for that reason I shall set forth those
which these Indians employed.

The general custom which they employed for seeking a woman for the
purpose of marriage was that the man who wanted to be married went for
several days to and fro about the house of the woman that he desired, but
without entering it, waiting for an occasion to speak to her, and when he
found her all alone he told her: *I want to marry you*, or *We should get married.* There were others who sent a third [party] to talk to her in private, and
if the girl said yes, she notified her parents, and if they agreed, the bridegroom was notified that he could come into the house and talk with them
and with the girl. There were also certain ones whose marriage was fixed
up by the old people, and it was that after the parents of the girl had been

notified these same old people notified her telling her: you have to marry such a one, and you will live well, and you will have many things, for he knows how to kill deer, cottontail rabbits—and [telling her] other similar things.

The first time that the bridegroom entered the house of the bride he brought his little present, now a deer skin, otter skin or seeds, or shell beads, in fact, whatever he could, and from that day on he was considered bridegroom of the house, tending to the bringing of something to eat, for he ate and in most cases also slept there, but without cohabiting with the bride, or having the least indecency with her either in words or actions, and they were very scrupulous about this.

During this period, which we may call the period of betrothal, the obligations of the bridegroom were to bring wood to the house every day, and to hunt cottontail rabbits, groundsquirrels, mice, etc., to eat. And the girl had the obligation of working at the chores and duties of the house. The first thing that she did was that at the first streak of dawn she arose, went to the water and bathed herself, brought water for the house, sprinkled it, swept it, and this with much promptness and care; then she prepared the food of various kinds of mush, pinoles or of whatever they had, and [did] the other chores of the house, and she had to do all of it alone, without the help of anybody. Sometimes also the parents of the bridegroom went to eat [there]. . . .

The instructions which the parents gave to their daughter before they parted were very good ones, for they told her that she should always remember that she was the daughter of some good parents, and that therefore she should not disgrace them, that she should serve her husband well whom Chinigchinix had given to her, that she should not be with another man, for even though she were executed they would remain disgraced, and other similar things, and at the end they added: and if your husband does not treat you well, let us know, and you shall return to our house.

There were others who went themselves straight to ask the parents for the girl, and if they yielded her, gave them a present of shell beads or something else (which I consider to be like a promise or pledge). These notified their daughter telling her: Daughter, you are to marry such a one, for we have already given you to him. And the poor girl, whether it were her pleasure or against her will, or however it might be, had to marry the man who asked for her.

There were also certain ones who were given in marriage from the time they were small [children], and it was in this way: The children being of tender age, the fathers and mothers on both sides being together, either with a feast or without one, would say: These 2 little children are to be married, and without further ceremony they were already married, and from that time on the 2 little children played together, ate, and slept together, and the 2 houses were one and the same for both of them; until on reaching competent age they gave their feast . . . and they cohabited together. The marriages celebrated thus were mostly those of relatives by affinity, for among them relationship by affinity was not held to be an impediment. In the year

1821 at this Mission I married in the face of the church a couple whose marriage had been contracted since the time they were children, for the girl must have been about 6 months old, and the boy about 2 years old when their parents already married them. . . .

The mode of living or of life which these Indians had is not of great moment, for they led an idle and lazy life, more like that of brutes than that of rational beings, and being ignorant of the arts, they had no employment and profit with which to busy themselves for using up their time, for they did not cultivate the ground or sow any kind of seed, inasmuch as they subsisted on the wild seeds of various plants which the earth produces, and on the fruits of trees, and on game; and therefore their tasks and labors were confined to the making of bows and arrows (nor did all of them do this, for the youths did not wish to work at anything, but the old men and the poor men), the hunting of deer, cottontail rabbits, groundsquirrels, rats, etc., in order to eat and dress, if going about in their bare skins, as they used to go, can be called dress. For the clothing of the men consisted generally of nothing but their naked skins, but some of them put a deer skin or coyote skin over their shoulders, after the fashion of a cape. The women prepared from the skins of cottontails and jackrabbits a kind of cloak after the fashion of a choir-cope; this they made as follows: they kept twisting the skins, making a cord or string of them, long, and about an inch thick; this cord they sewed together turn on turn making the cape, as I said. In front of their private parts they [the women] wore certain little nets, or a kind of fringe made of grass which reached nearly to their knees; and nothing else except the decorations of shells and bones in their ears and on their necks.

Their way of spending their time was in playing games, taking trips about, sleeping and dancing. The whole life of the men was confined to this, except the old men and the poor men, who also busied themselves in making certain household utensils; or again instruments for working the bows and arrows, such as little saws, punches or awls, and other similar things (the little saws they made from the shoulder blades of deer; and the borers of punches from their shin bones, as well as from the bones of fish); in making nets for various uses: now for fishing; or again those which they use for carrying their utensils, the women the babies; for catching quails; and for other uses.

Among the women the mode of life followed was very different, for they in addition to making the household utensils had to seek all the things necessary for a livelihood, which are the wild seeds of the country; after gathering them [they had] to clean them, to grind them or toast them for making their pinoles and various kinds of mush, which were the foods on which they subsisted. It was pitiful and caused compassion to see a poor woman with the baby on her shoulders about the country, suffering cold, and again heat, hunting certain herbs or seeds; [to see her] arrive home without finding either fire or water, and most times not even wood; [to see her] clean them, grind them and cook them, and after they were prepared [to behold] her idler coming now from the game or dance, or getting up from sleep, [to watch him] consume [the fruits of] the toil and fatigue of the poor woman, while if he ate everything up, she had to go without food, not being able to say a word. The women in their gentile condition were worse off than slaves, for one cannot realize the subjection in which they found themselves; it was sufficient [reason] if her husband became angry with her either because she answered harshly or because she did not have what he wanted, for him to leave her, or to slay her, and most times the quarrels came from the husband gambling away the utensils of the poor woman. But thank God, since the light of the faith entered these lands, since the holy gospel has been preached, the women have gained the Christian liberty which Jesus Christ won for us through his passion and death.

A *Sacramento Union* Editorial Ponders the Indians' Fate, 1855

The accounts from the North indicate the commencement of a war of extermination against the Indians. The latter commenced the attack on the Klamath; but who can determine their provocation or the amount of destitution suffered before the hostile blow was struck.

The intrusion of the white man upon the Indians' hunting grounds has driven off the game and destroyed their fisheries. The consequence is, the Indians suffer every winter for sustenance. Hunger and starvation follows [*sic*] them wherever they go. Is it, then, a matter of wonder that they become desperate and resort to stealing and killing? They are driven to steal or starve, and the Indian mode is to kill and then plunder.

The policy of our Government towards the Indians in this State is most miserable. Had reasonable care been exercised to see that they were provided with something to eat and wear in this State, no necessity would have presented itself for an indiscriminate slaughter of the race.

The fate of the Indian is fixed. He must be annihilated by the advance of the white man; by the diseases, and, to them, the evils of civilization. But the work should not have been commenced at so early a day by the deadly rifle.

To show how the matter is viewed on the Klamath, we copy the following from the Crescent City *Herald*. The people look upon it there as a war of extermination, and are killing all grown up males. A writer from Trinidad, under date of January 22d, says:

> I shall start the two Indians that came down with me to-night, and hope they may reach Crescent City in safety, although I think it exceedingly doubtful, as the whites are shooting them whenever an opportunity offers; for this reason I start them in the night, hoping they may be out of danger ere morning. On the Klamath the Indians have killed six white men, and I understand some stock. From the Salmon down the whites are in arms, with determination, I believe, if possible, to destroy all the grown up males, notwithstanding this meets with the opposition of some few who have favorite Indians amongst them. I doubt whether this discrimination should be made, as some who have been considered good have proved the most treacherous. I understand that the ferry of Mr. Boyce, as also that of

Mr. Simms, has been cut away. Messrs. Norton and Beard have moved their families from Elk Camp to Trinidad; they were the only white females in that section that were exposed to the savages. I have no doubt there will be warm times on the Klamath for some weeks, as the Indians are numerous, well armed and determined to fight.

 E S S A Y S

In the first essay, Arthur McEvoy of Northwestern University describes how the insulation of California's Indian tribes from outside influences enabled them to develop in their own special ways. Of particular interest to McEvoy are the intimate familiarity of these indigenous peoples with the ecology of their food resources and their impressive ability to manage "their environment in order to enhance its stability and productivity."

The second essay is drawn from a prize-winning book by Albert Hurtado of Arizona State University, *Indian Survival on the California Frontier* (1988). In this selection, Hurtado discusses the Indian families in California and compares them to their Hispanic counterparts. As he notes, despite the inability of white settlers to consider Indians as family members, family ties, in fact, "bound native people to each other, to their communities, and to the land." Hurtado helps us understand both how kinship and marriage functioned in California Indian society of the eighteenth and early nineteenth centuries and how Hispanic cultural traditions impinged on the Indian family after 1769.

California Indians as Capable Resource Managers

ARTHUR F. MCEVOY

Indian society in California was distinctive in its high density of population, its insularity, and the remarkable complexity of its hunting and gathering economy. While groups in the northwestern and southern coastal regions shared many ethnographic traits with tribes to the north and east of them, respectively, in general the mountains, desert, and ocean that isolated California from the rest of the world physically also insulated its aboriginal cultures from outside influence, enabling them to flourish in their own ways. At the heart of these people's adaptation to their peculiar environment, which contained an extremely variegated, if thinly spread, supply of edible plants and animals, was an economy based on painstaking, seasonal, and broadly diffused effort rather than on special skills or concentration on any particular resource. Aboriginal society in California was sedentary, technologically unsophisticated, relatively free from conflict either with nature or with neighbors, and, to a degree remarkable among North American Indians, free from privation.

Arthur F. McEvoy, from *The Fisherman's Problem: Ecology and the Law in California Fisheries, 1850–1980.* (Cambridge, England: Cambridge University Press, 1986), pp. 26–32. Copyright © 1986 by Arthur F. McEvoy. Reprinted by permission of Cambridge University Press and the author, Professor of Law, History, and Environmental Studies at University of Wisconsin-Madison.

The most critical resources were those the Indians processed and stored for use during the lean months of the winter and early spring (viz., acorns, large game, and fish). Because the addition of easily caught salmon did nothing to diminish their access to other staples, it is no surprise that the most populous tribes in central California were those along the Sacramento and San Joaquin Rivers. The Wintuan-speaking Patwin, Nomlaki, and Wintu groups living along the Sacramento from the delta to its headwaters together made up the largest coherent linguistic group in northern California and, according to Kroeber, were "[among] the most important in the development and diffusion of customs." At the southern limit of the salmon, a line between Monterey Bay and the bend in the San Joaquin River, the Plains Miwok, Yokuts, and Monache people of the San Joaquin Valley also took great quantities of the fish.

The Southern California Bight, between Point Conception and San Pedro Bay, and the islands offshore supported the only maritime cultures in aboriginal California, those of the Chumash and the Gabrielino. Here the coast faces to the south, protected from the prevailing winds that bring fog and high surf to more northerly areas. The rocks and cliffs that divide land from sea to the north and south here give way to sandy, gently sloping beaches. The water is calm and visibility high; the large, verdant Channel Islands loom just offshore. Their geographical situation, combined with the exceptional fertility of the Santa Barbara Channel, drew these people out onto the ocean. Here, too, adequate timber and natural petroleum seeps, not available either to the north or the south, provided planks and caulking for seaworthy canoes. These facilitated trade with the islands and fisheries for sea mammals and for many of the finfish that became commercially important after 1850. An arid hinterland inhibited food production away from the coast and further encouraged the maritime adaptation, which was unique to the area.

The ability to draw on the productivity of the Channel waters, as well as a fertile coastal strip and abundant shellfish resources, permitted human populations to bloom along this part of the coast. The Chumash aggregated into villages of as many as a thousand people each along their stretch of the coast. Wealth and concentrated numbers led in turn to a flowering of culture. The Spanish reckoned the Chumash superior to all other California tribes with which they had contact. With their neighbors, the Gabrielino, the Chumash share the recognition of modern anthropologists as "the wealthiest, most populous, and most powerful ethnic nationality in aboriginal southern California."

Like all hunter-gatherers, California Indians were intimately familiar with the ecology of their food resources and actively manipulated their environment in order to enhance its stability and productivity. Fishery use was qualitatively different among the Yurok and other Lower Klamath culture area peoples and so merits individual treatment. Throughout the region, many groups used artificial fires, for example, with considerable skill to encourage the growth of plants upon which they and the birds and mammals they hunted depended for forage. According to Henry T. Lewis, there were probably few areas in California with any appreciable Indian population whose physical aspect was unaffected by it. In general, the nearly universal use of fire by preagricultural peoples to manipulate their environments by itself calls into question the widely assumed ecological passivity of such peoples.

The Indians seem to have harvested as much from their environment as it could predictably yield. Comparing Sherburne Cook's estimates of the population of central California tribes with his own indices of the productivity of acorns, game stocks, and fisheries in each of their territories, Martin A. Baumhoff found that a linear function of resource productivity accurately predicted the populations of groups in both fertile and barren areas. He concluded that each group's population was in equilibrium with the carrying capacity of its local environment. All groups traded food with each other, to some extent, and were apparently accustomed to supplying emergency rations to neighboring villages in temporary need. There was some, but not much, ability to secure a surplus beyond the community's needs in a moderately severe winter.

Carrying capacity is a function not only of the inherent productivity of a habitat but also of a people's strategies for production. It is a social measure as well as a strictly biological one. That hunting and gathering economies such as those in aboriginal California operated at relatively low population densities did not relieve them of their need to husband their resources if they were to sustain their ways of life. One way in which the California Indians did so was to spread their productive effort over a wide range of resources, each in its season. If a particular crop failed or if salmon or game were scarce in any season, there were usually other foods to fall back on. Central California Indians developed their fishing technology and devoted their time to fishing only to the point at which salmon provided a predictable share of their subsistence in conjunction with the other foodstuffs available to them. The overall fertility of the California environment meant that hunting and gathering could support large numbers of people; meanwhile, the Indians' broad subsistence base contributed to the great stability of their economies.

Although they also took more overt measures to limit their demand for food, one effect of this diffusion was to limit the Indians' use of fish or any other single resource to within prudent bounds. Avoiding the risk of crop failure was thus the standard by which the Indians limited their harvest and kept it safely below the long-term maximum yield that any particular resource could sustain. For southern coastal groups, this was the reason for limiting their shellfish collecting to a small part of their seasonal round. Despite their advanced fishing methods, they continued to rely chiefly on a diversified economy, with acorns the main staple. One study concluded that the maritime capability was itself a response to the overuse of the shellfish upon which the Chumash and Gabrielino relied more heavily and from an earlier time. It made their basically diffuse economies more efficient and more secure but did not supplant them. To have intensified their fishing or any other of their harvests, say, by developing an agricultural specialization, would have at once increased the Indians' exposure to risk and diverted labor away from other pursuits, thereby bringing an initial drop in overall productivity. The Indians, who were secure but who had stretched their economy to its limit, had no incentive to do this.

Of prime importance to the California Indians was the practical concern of maintaining the security of life as they knew it. A more specialized economy held no inherent attraction for them as long as their own methods continued to support them in good style, just as it does not for hunter-gatherers surviving in the late twentieth century. But their complex economic strategy did not emerge and did not endure simply as a matter of chance. They developed it, over time and no doubt at some cost, and maintained it deliberately. Because they used all the resources their habitats would yield safely to their productive system, California hunter-gatherers faced the fundamentally political problems of regulating the harvest and distributing natural resources no less than later Californians with different kinds of economies. For them, as for their successors, resource management was a function of social and political institutions.

Perhaps most basic among the social tools with which California Indians limited their demand for food was population control. The Indians' lack of technological sophistication does not fully explain their apparent ability to live within their ecological means because they could always have tried to feed more people with the same economy. Yet, they did not. Malthusian "positive" checks on population—war, famine, and the like—do not seem to have been significant to the lives of aboriginal Californians. Infanticide, abortion, taboos on intercourse during lactation, meaningful social roles for celibates, and other deliberate controls on human fertility, however, do. The Pomo apparently resorted to a number of tactics, from contraception to geronticide, to protect their relatively dense population from exposure to the risk of famine. Scattered evidence survives of systematic removal of twins, defective infants, or infants of deceased mothers among other California groups, particularly those with fertile habitats and dense populations such as the Yurok and the coastal Chumash. Deliberate, socially sanctioned regulation of their numbers, in response to perceived conditions in individual families, in the community, and in the environment, was crucial to the Indians' ability to balance their demand for food with the capacity of their habitats to produce it.

More directly, California Indian communities limited access to their resources by assigning rights to them. Individual communities claimed exclusive use of all important food-producing resources and denied them to outsiders except under carefully controlled conditions. In general, the more concentrated or critical a resource, the more explicitly the Indians articulated rights to it. Individual "ownership" was far more common in the Klamath River area, where salmon was of overwhelming importance, than anywhere else in California. Northwestern coastal groups lay claim to specific stretches of beach adjoining their villages and defended them against trespass. In central and southern California, where staples were more varied and dispersed, native groups commonly vested their ownership in the community at large. Individuals and households might claim sole use of a particular oak tree or fishing spot for a season, but for the most part important hunting, fishing, and gathering locations belonged in common to the whole community. Well-defined rights to resources not only limited their use but permitted tribes to monitor the effect of their harvesting at specific sites over time and to adjust their use accordingly.

Although individuals sometimes held property of a sort, it was certainly not absolute and resembled a form of trusteeship rather than property in fee simple under Anglo-American common law. Individuals had no right to alienate resources that were crucial to their community's well-being. Nor was shared property left to suffer "the tragedy of the commons." Tribes and villages administered the harvest of communally owned resources according to carefully prescribed and closely supervised procedures, usually in a ceremonial or ritual context. The world-renewal religion of northwestern California was the most complex such ritual system. In central California, the Kuksu religion of the Patwin, Maidu, and Pomo also contained strong elements of world renewal. In both areas, secular and administrative functions entwined with spiritual ones. Shamans, whose social role was to mediate between the community and the spiritual forces that infused the natural world, organized the harvest of key resources, supervised their distribution, and appeased their spirits so as to ensure the continued prosperity and well-being of the group.

Central California communities could harvest neither acorns, fish, nor game until the local shaman performed the appropriate first-fruit rites, which might take several days. Acorn harvests were crucial to central and southern California Indian economies and were most carefully hedged about with ritual. Salmon also received the ceremonial protection of the Kuksu religion, although these rites were perfunctory as compared with those in the northwest. In southern California, civil authorities directed the harvest, storage, and distribution of acorns and presumably shellfish as well, although again not without the assistance of shamans who observed first-fruit rites for them. Individual tribes always invited their neighbors to attend their ceremonies and used the occasion to trade with them and exchange gifts. Trade and reciprocity, integrated within a ceremonial context, relieved competition for scarce resources and helped maintain good relations between neighboring groups.

The ritual organization of production and exchange articulated and reaffirmed to the Indians their interdependence with each other and with the natural world. According to Harold Driver, a belief in active, watchful, and potentially vengeful animal spirits was "probably universal" among North American Indians. The Indians had to use them carefully and propitiate them for their sacrifice if they were to rely on their continued abundance. Animism was the way in which the Indians, like most hunter-gatherers, expressed their awareness of the fact that their lives and those of their food resources were ecologically intertwined. It was the job of the shamans to mediate between the two camps: to interpret for their communities the will of the natural world and to ensure that the former used its resources in prudent ways. This is no more or less than what modern scientific resource agencies with their staffs of ecologists do, although they do so from the standpoint of a profoundly different world view.

There is no reason to suppose that the communion between Indian society and the world around it was perfect. As one Sacramento Valley native put it, "Everything in the world talks, just as we are now, the trees, the rocks, everything. But we cannot understand them, just as the white people do not understand Indians." There is also no reason to suppose that the balance they maintained among environment, production, and ideology at the time of contact with Westerners was not something that developed over a long period of time and with occasional mistakes. We have indirect evidence of some of the mistakes, but the history of the process is lost. It does seem clear, however, that the balance they eventually struck was an enduring and prosperous one. California Indians managed their fisheries and other resources by strategically gearing their productive effort to the ecological realities of the world as they understood them, so as at once to lead comfortable lives, to distribute wealth equitably, and to sustain their resources and their economies over the long run.

Indian and Hispanic Family Patterns Compared

ALBERT L. HURTADO

If settlement by families had been the sole criterion of a civilized territory, California would have been one of the most civilized places in the trans-Mississippi West before the turn of the eighteenth century. With three hundred thousand native people, California was one of the most heavily populated places in North America. But it was not common . . . to think of Indians as family members. White frontiersmen saw them as primitive tribal folk, lacking the sentimental domestic affections that marked Victorian society. Yet family ties bound native people to each other, to their communities, and to the land. Family bonds defined social, political, and economic relationships in native culture and were of paramount importance to Indian personal and corporate life. Tragically, the arrival of family-oriented people from other cultures threatened the network of kinship that had supported native society and survival for untold generations. . . .

The Indian family fit into an elaborate set of social relationships that varied by tribe and locality. To help create order out of this complexity, anthropologists have described general culture areas with similar ways of life and value systems. The interior contained the central and northwestern culture areas. Taking up the central valley and adjacent country, the central culture area included the Nisenan, Maidu, Konkow, Miwok, Yokuts, and other tribes. The northwestern culture area included the Tolowa, Yurok, Karok, Hupa, Shasta, Chimariko, Hupa [*sic*], Whilkut, and other tribes that lived in the rugged Klamath and Cascade mountains and on the adjacent coast. In both areas several *rancherías* (villages) acknowledging a single chief formed a tribelet, and several tribelets constituted a tribe. Tribelets included as few as three rancherías and as many as thirty and held up to 1,000 people, although 250 was about the average. The conjugal couple and their children formed the basic household unit, which was sometimes augmented by aged relatives and unmarried siblings.

Indian families, however, were not merely a series of nuclear units but were knit into a complex set of associations that comprised native society. For most California Indians, kinship defined the individual's place within the community and family associations suffused every aspect of life. Elites, commoners, poor, and sometimes slaves inherited their status, although it was possible to better one's position by a propitious marriage or by gaining wealth. Because northwestern tribes in particular emphasized acquisitiveness, most marriages in this culture area occurred within economic and social ranks, tending to stabilize economic and power relationships.

Chiefs (who were occasionally women) were usually from wealthy families and inherited their positions. Principally they administered economic affairs, governed hunting and gathering on tribelet lands, and assured that food and other goods were fairly distributed. They arranged for public feasting and ceremonial food exchanges with neighboring people. Since secure links with other groups provided insurance against occasional food shortages, a chief would frequently marry several elite women from other rancherías. Diplomatic polygyny provided kinship links, which maintained prosperity and limited the warfare that could result from poaching or blood feuds. In the event of war, kinship considerations helped to determine who would be attacked, as well as the duration and intensity of conflict.

Kinship was important to the daily lives of ordinary people. Families controlled particular hunting and gathering areas; individuals accumulated, shared, or traded resources according to familial associations. In the northwest, where wealth was so important, the owner of a resource could rent, sell, or convey usufructory rights to another family as part of a bride-price to secure an especially desirable marriage alliance. Conversely, the theft of such resources could result in the enslavement of a culpable person who was unable to repay the victim. Northwesterners had a highly developed system of laws that required compensation for any transgression from petty theft to murder. Malefactors and their families, therefore, lost both wealth and status. Throughout California, kinship determined the nature of trading and ordinarily removed the profit motive from the transactions. Marriage and kinship influenced the social structure of each ranchería, depending on tribal customs. Communities were composed of extended residence groups that were linked by familial ties. The Yokuts supplemented blood relations with moieties that connected them to a special totem animal such as the eagle or coyote. Children belonged to their father's moiety and were forbidden to kill their totem animal. If someone else killed the totem, the moiety had to purchase and bury the carcass. Since a wide range of commonly hunted animals were moiety totems, this arrangement tended to redistribute wealth and regulate hunting. Moreover, totemic affiliations affected blood ties because an individual had to marry someone from another moiety.

Given the significance and complexity of kin and moiety relationships, marriage was an extremely important institution, governed according to strict rules. Unions were prohibited if a couple was related within three to five generations, depending on tribal affiliation. Consequently, men had to look for eligible wives outside their tribelet, and women had to leave their home communities when they married. Because kinship was so important, the departing women formed important new links for their families and communities, strengthening the system of reciprocity that girded native California. The bride-price symbolized women's place in this scheme. The groom gave his parents-in-law a gift to demonstrate his worth, acknowledge the status of the bride's family, and compensate them for the loss of her services. If the family approved, they made a complementary gift, although one of lesser value, to the groom. In the northwest, the value of the bride-price was more important than elsewhere, but it did not signify that the wife was a chattel. No husband could sell his spouse; an unhappy wife could divorce her husband, although social pressure militated against it. Even so, men were considered the family heads, descent was usually through the male line, and residence was at the husband's ranchería. . . .

California's native household economy was based on hunting and gathering according to a sexual division of labor. Men hunted, fished, and—after the advent of white settlement—raided livestock herds. Abundant deer, antelope, and elk furnished meat, while bountiful salmon runs provided another excellent source of protein. Fish and sea mammals were important foods to the northwesterners who lived near the ocean, and their skillful boatmen constructed graceful redwood dugout canoes. These boats were also useful for transportation in the rugged northern country, where rivers were the main highways. Obviously, the first object of work was to sustain life, but California Indians were able to accumulate surpluses that enabled them to live beyond the mere subsistence level. Through trade, Indians could acquire wealth in the form of such highly prized trade objects as white deerskins and huge obsidian blades, or woodpecker scalps and dentalium beads that served as money.

As important as the male activities were, women did more work and provided the plant foods that comprised the bulk of the Indian diet. The acorn was a staple food, and although men assisted in gathering acorns, women ground them to flour and leached the tannic acid from the meal. In season, women collected grass seeds, roots, pine nuts, berries, and other foods, prepared them, and stored the surplus against lean times. Basket making was also a female task, and elaborate twined pieces, sometimes adorned with precarious feathers and shell beads, were esteemed items of trade. All California tribes prized hard-working, productive women.

By bearing children—their most important contribution to Indian society—women created the human resources necessary to sustain their communities. When populations suffered significant reductions, the lack of fertile women meant that the capacity to recover was limited. The complicated rules that regulated marriage and kinship were another consideration. The experience of Ishi, a Yahi man who lived in what is now Tehama County, provides a poignant illustration of this point. After most of the Yahi were killed during the gold rush era, a small remnant hid out on Deer Creek, where a steep canyon afforded them protection. Yahi's band included an old man, a young man, Ishi's mother, and a young woman who was either Ishi's sister or a cousin too closely related for him to marry. When the other young man died, Ishi and his kinswomen were the last potential Yahi parents, but only an incestuous relationship could preserve their tribe. To the end they were true to their cultural values. There were no children; everyone but Ishi died on Deer Creek. He lived to tell his tale to anthropologists who took him to a San Francisco museum, where he, too, died a few years later. The Yahis were not unique. Under ordinary conditions the Indian family was flexible, productive, and viable, but when placed under demographic stress it proved highly vulnerable.

When Spanish settlers began to arrive in California in 1769, they brought with them family customs that were well adapted to frontier circumstances. American conditions, especially the lack of Iberian women, modified the ideal Hispanic family in several ways and, as we shall see, impinged on Indian family traditions, with baleful consequences for the latter.

The family was the solid foundation of Spanish-American society. The husband was a patriarch who theoretically controlled all the family's important business. While he went out into the world, his wife took charge of the household, managing child rearing and domestic activities. During most of the colonial era the role of the family was to serve social and economic ends rather than to exemplify romantic love. Especially among the wealthy classes, parents often tried to arrange marriages that would enhance family fortunes, and young couples usually sought their parents' permission to marry. Parental consent, however, was not at first required by Spanish law or the Catholic Church, which upheld the right of individuals to marry freely. The Church oversaw the moral aspects of marriage and sexuality and often performed marriages against the wishes of disapproving parents. In New Spain during the sixteenth and seventeenth centuries, the Church frequently assented to unions that crossed class boundaries. Indeed, by 1776 the Spanish crown was so concerned about liberalized marriage practices that it required parental consent for minors and justified parental disapproval if a proposed marriage would offend family honor or threaten the state.

Frontier priests seemed unwilling to undermine prevailing social norms and the economic motives of powerful families. In the archives of the Archdiocese of Santa Fe, for example, there are no cases of clerics overriding parental objections to cross-class marriages. Isolated and exposed on a distant frontier, New Mexican churchmen chose not to subvert the family arrangements and class distinctions that underpinned social order. Nevertheless, as in New Spain, many couples opted for marriages based on mutual romantic love, regardless of parental or Church sanctions, as society became more secular and less concerned with old conceptions of family honor.

Despite long-term changes in connubial habits, distinctive traditions remained evident in the Hispanic family. As among Indians, important families were allied through marriage and such unions were ordinarily considered a matter of duty for the partners. Masculine passion was reserved for prostitutes and mistresses, if they could be afforded. On the other hand, Hispanic culture supposed that wives should be little interested in sexual relations, engaging in sex only for procreation and reserving their love for their children. Brides were supposed to approach the marriage bed with their maidenheads intact, so families strove to protect the virginity of daughters and sisters and the honor of wives—and thus their husbands—by confining them to the home, out of the reach of virile males.

With few exceptions, men were the household's primary economic providers, although women's economic contribution in the form of maintenance, food preparation, and child rearing were by no means inconsiderable. It was expensive to maintain the ideal Hispanic family, and poor people simply could not afford to rigorously confine women's activities to the home. Among the lower classes women baked, sewed, and acted as herbal healers (*curanderas*). As a rule, men and women tried to marry as high above their own class as circumstances might permit. The bride's family usually paid a dowry to the husband, but in colonial Peru wealthy *conquistadores* sometimes reversed this procedure so that they could marry women of higher rank than themselves. Regardless of the riches he obtained in the New World, only marriage into the upper classes would confer the highest possible status to the Hispanic frontiersman. In America there were comparatively few Iberian women, so Spaniards took Indian concubines and wives. Moreover, even after a marriage with a suitable Spanish woman had been consummated, rustic husbands were sometimes reluctant to give up their native consorts, so philandering was a part of daily life. These habits were well established by the time the Spanish entered California.

The family that evolved in Hispanic America was not merely a frontier replica of an Iberian model. The Mexican family also reflects the values and traditions of Aztec society, which held the collective family, female chastity, industry, and obedience in high esteem. Thus, the Mexican-American family is an amalgam of European and Indian institutions.

 ### FURTHER READING

James Bard, Edward D. Castillo, and Karen Nissen, *A Bibliography of California Indians: Archaeology, Ethnology, Indian History* (1977)

Lowell John Bean and Thomas C. Blackburn, eds., *Native Californians: A Theoretical Retrospective* (1976)

Lowell John Bean and Katherine S. Saubel, *Temalpakh: Cahuila Indian Knowledge and Usage of Plants* (1972)

Lowell John Bean and Sylvia Brakke Vane, *California Indians: Primary Resources* (1977)

Thomas C. Blackburn, ed., *December's Child: A Book of Chumash Oral Narratives Collected by John P. Harrington* (1975)

Robert F. Heizer, *The Indians of California: A Critical Bibliography* (1976)

Robert F. Heizer, ed., *Handbook of North American Indians: California* (1978)

Robert F. Heizer and Albert B. Elasser, *The Natural World of the California Indians* (1980)

Robert F. Heizer and M. A. Whipple, eds., *The California Indians: A Source Book* (1st ed., 1951; 2nd ed., 1971)

Albert L. Hurtado, *Indian Survival on the California Frontier* (1988)

Alfred L. Kroeber, *Handbook of the Indians of California* (1925)

Alfred L. Kroeber, *Yurok Myths* (1976)

Theodora Kroeber, *The Inland Whale: Nine Stories Retold from California Indian Legends* (1959)

Henry T. Lewis, ed., *Patterns of Indian Burning in California* (1973)

Malcolm Margolin, ed., *The Way We Lived: California Indian Reminiscences, Stories and Songs* (1981)

Stephen Power, *Tribes of California* (1877; repr. 1976)

James J. Rawls, *Indians of California: The Changing Image* (1984)

David Hurst Thomas, ed., *Archaeological and Historical Perspectives on the Spanish Borderlands West* (1989)

The Spanish Impact on the Indians, 1769–1821

More than two centuries elapsed from the discovery of California by Europeans to the colonizing efforts that Spanish Franciscan missionaries began
in 1769. Upon their arrival in what they called Alta (or Upper) California
in the 1760s, Spanish colonists encountered a fragmented indigenous population ill suited to resist conquest. Indeed, considering their dispersed situation and their less developed technology (when compared with the Spanish),
it is remarkable that so many of these small Indian tribelets managed to
retain their native way of life to any meaningful degree in the face of overwhelming external pressures.

The Spanish, in turn, had long contemplated occupation of Alta California, but had been preoccupied with other imperial concerns. Despite glowing
reports from various explorers of the late sixteenth and early seventeenth
centuries—such as the Portuguese Juan Rodriguez Cabrillo (sailing under
the Spanish flag), the Englishman Sir Francis Drake, another Portuguese,
Sebastian Rodriguez Cermeño, and the Spaniard Sebastian Vizcaíno—there
was for many years little interest in a remote region that appeared to lack
enough mineral resources to justify the expense and difficulty of conquest.
Indeed, it was not the expectation of wealth that finally prompted the Spanish advance into California. It was, rather, the growing fear that others—
the Russians, in particular—would soon claim that area for themselves.
Such unwelcome occupation would threaten Spain's interests in the rest of
its world empire.

Imperial activism finally replaced long-standing disinterest when, in
January 1768, the Spanish monarch Charles III ordered the viceroy to repel
any Russian intrusions. Moreover, José de Gálvez, the king's visitador-
general sent to investigate colonial affairs in Mexico, had become increasingly disturbed about Spanish weakness on the northern frontier in the face
of Indian violence and rebellion. The energetic and determined Gálvez ultimately became convinced that it was necessary to occupy Alta California. To
that end, in 1769 he organized an historic expedition into the region. Later,
he entrusted the new missions established there to a group of Franciscan

priests from Baja (or Lower) California, under the leadership of Father Junipero Serra.

A challenge for students of California history is to analyze and evaluate the impact on the indigenous population of the Spanish imperial system and its three basic institutions: the presidio, or military post, where soldiers were stationed; the mission, which fulfilled the religious aim of conquest; and the pueblo, or town, which as the civil leg of the tripod was designed to attract civilian colonists. Spain's major goal with respect to the indigenous population can be stated simply: the Indian was to become both Spanish and Catholic. In the process, the social, cultural, and religious characteristics that distinguished Indians from Spanish were to be obliterated. We may inquire, therefore, whether the Spanish system, when compared with rival patterns of colonization (such as that of the British in North America), was basically humane and positive or whether it should be judged more harshly. To what extent did its espoused aims correspond with its actual practices? To what extent did the California missions resemble slave plantations, where freedom was exchanged for protection by the Spanish crown?

D O C U M E N T S

Historical accounts differ markedly about whether the Spanish imperial system had a positive or negative effect on Indians, in part because of reliance on different kinds of sources and in part because of competing interpretive positions. How observers fitted into that imperial system often affected their attitudes toward it. One such observer, a Franciscan priest named Father Luis Jayme, provides a window into both the religious and sexual relations between the Indians and Spanish in October 1772. Consider how his position as a priest shaped his interpretation of the incident in question. The second document is a letter from Father Junipero Serra, who participated in the Gálvez expedition of 1769 and who from then until his death in 1784 served as the vigorous Father-president of the missions in Alta California. In this letter, written to the Viceroy of New Spain in December 1775, Serra describes an Indian attack on the San Diego mission in the previous month, an attack that killed its senior Franciscan missionary (the same Father Jayme who authored the first document). Interestingly, Serra imagines himself in the position of the killed missionary and expresses his ideas about what should be done if he were ever to experience a similar fate.

In Chapter 2 we learned, from several Franciscan eyewitness accounts of mission life, of the triumph of Christianity over "brutish pagans" who, according to observers such as Father Boscana, were "idle and lazy." That point of view was shared by the author of the third document, Captain Alejandro Malaspina, commander of Spain's most ambitious scientific exploratory expeditions. In this account, Malaspina briefly describes the mission of San Carlos, founded by Gaspar de Portolá in 1770, and what he believes to have been the positive influence of the Spanish priests on the Indians. Other eyewitness recollections, such as those provided in the fourth document, present a very different picture. There are numerous examples of native resistance to the Franciscan system, including a sensational assassination of a Father Andrés Quintana, described in this document by a neophyte, Lorenzo Asisara, who was a Santa Cruz Indian. Interviewed in July 1877 as part of a larger oral history project, Asisara provides an assessment of California's colonial past from a nonmissionary perspective.

Father Luis Jayme Criticizes the Behavior of Spanish Soldiers, 1772

With reference to the Indians, I wish to say that great progress would be made if there was anything to eat and the soldiers would set a good example. We cannot give them anything to eat because what Don Pedro has given is not enough to last half a year for the Indians from the Californias who are here. Thus little progress will be made under present conditions. As for the example to be set by the soldiers, no doubt some of them are good exemplars and deserve to be treated accordingly, but very many of them deserve to be hanged on account of the continuous outrages which they are committing in seizing and raping the women. There is not a single mission where all the gentiles have not been scandalized, and even on the roads, so I have been told. Surely, as the gentiles themselves state, they are committing a thousand evils, particularly those of a sexual nature. The fathers have petitioned Don Pedro concerning these points, but he has paid very little attention to them. He has punished some, but as soon as they promised him that they would work at the presidio, he turned them loose. That is what he did last year, but now he does not even punish them or say anything to them on this point. I suppose that some ministers will write you, each concerning his own mission, and therefore I shall not tell you about the cases which have occurred at other missions. I shall speak only of Mission San Diego.

At one of these Indian villages near this mission of San Diego, which said village is very large, and which is on the road that goes to Monterey, the gentiles therein many times have been on the point of coming here to kill us all, and the reason for this is that some soldiers went there and raped their women, and other soldiers who were carrying the mail to Monterey turned their animals into their fields and they ate up their crops. Three other Indian villages about a league or a league and a half from here have reported the some thing to me several times. For this reason on several occasions when Father Francisco Dumetz or I have gone to see these Indian villages, as soon as they saw us they fled from their villages and fled to the woods or other remote places, and the only ones who remained in the villages were some men and some very old women. The Christians here have told me that many of the gentiles of the aforesaid villages leave their huts and the crops which they gather from the lands around their villages, and go to the woods and experience hunger. They do this so that the soldiers will not rape their women as they have already done so many times in the past.

No wonder the Indians here were bad when the mission was first founded. To begin with, they did not know why they [the Spaniards] had come, unless they intended to take their lands away from them. Now they all want to be Christians because they know that there is a God who created the heavens and earth and all things, that there is a Hell, and Glory, that they have souls, etc., but when the mission was first founded they did not know these things; instead, they thought they were like animals, and when the vessels came at first, they saw that most of the crews died; they were very loathe to pray, and they did not want to be Christians at all; instead, they said that it was bad to become a Christian and then they would die immediately. No wonder they said so when they saw how most of the sailors and California Indians died, but now, thanks be to the Lord, God has converted them from Sauls to Pauls. They all know the natural law, which, so I am informed, they have observed as well or better than many Christians elsewhere. They do not have any idols; they do not go on drinking sprees; they do not marry relatives; and they have but one wife. The married men sleep with their wives only. The bachelors sleep together, and apart from the women and married couples. If a man plays with any woman who is not his wife, he is scolded and punished by his captains. Concerning those from the Californias I have heard it said that they are given to sexual vices, but among those here I have not been able to discover a single fault of that nature. Some of the first adults whom we baptized, when we pointed out to them that it was wrong to have sexual intercourse with a woman to whom they were not married, told me that they already knew that, and that among them it was considered to be very bad, and so they do not do so at all. "The soldiers," they told me, "are Christians and, although they know that God will punish them in Hell, do so, having sexual intercourse with our wives. We," they said, "although we did not know that God would punish us for that in Hell, considered it to be very bad, and we did not do it, and even less now that we know that God will punish us if we do so." When I heard this, I burst into tears to see how these gentiles were setting an example for us Christians.

Father Junipero Serra Reports the Destruction of the San Diego Mission, 1775

Hail Jesus, Mary, Joseph!
Most Excellent Lord.
My most revered and most excellent Sir:

As we are in the vale of tears, not all the news I have to relate can be pleasant. And so I make no excuses for announcing to Your Excellency the tragic news I have just received of the total destruction of the San Diego Mission, and of the death of the senior of its two religious ministers, called Father Fray Luis Jayme, at the hand of the rebellious gentiles and of the Christian neophytes. All this happened, November 5th, about one or two o'clock at night. The gentiles came together from forty rancherías, according to information given me, and set fire to the church, after sacking it. Then they went on to the storehouse, the house where the Fathers lived, the soldiers' barracks, and all the rest of the buildings.

They killed a carpenter from Guadalaxara and a blacksmith from Tepic. They wounded with their arrows the four soldiers, who alone were on guard at the said mission. Even though two of them were badly wounded, they have already recovered.

The other religious, whose name is Father Fray Vicente Fuster, over and above the fright he got, received no further injuries than a wound in the shoulder, caused by a stone. He suffered pain from it for several days. On the morning following that sad night, he withdrew, in company with the handful still surviving, to the presidio. They carried on the shoulders of those Christian Indians who had remained loyal the dead, and the badly wounded. From there he writes to me asking me to tell him what he is to do.

This news I received the day before yesterday, at about nine o'clock at night, when the Captain Commandant, Don Fernando, came bringing it and the mail.

Yesterday, with the best part of the morning taken up with the Office for the Dead, the high Mass, and low Masses for the repose of the deceased Father's soul, and the afternoon, with Don Fernando's second visit and his departure, all I could do was to finish reading the letters. He told us that he was leaving in the afternoon, and I proposed to him that a religious go with him. But he answered that he would travel very fast, and nothing would hold him back; that probably he would not even get off his horse at the various missions en route. I then asked him if, later, they could provide an escort for a religious to go down there. His answer was no, because of the few soldiers that were left behind.

On this account, I gave up, as out of the question, my plans to go down there. . . .

I might suggest again to Your Excellency what I proposed in one of my earlier letters: that in conquests of this kind the place where soldiers are most important is in the missions. The presidios, in many places, may be most suitable and very necessary; but for the situation here, I describe only what is before my eyes.

The San Diego Mission is about two leagues from the presidio, but it is in such a position that, throughout the day, they can see the mission from the presidio; and the gunshot that is fired each morning at dawn in the presidio, to change the watchword of the night guard, can generally be heard in the Mission. Yet while the mission was all on fire, the flames leaping up to a great height from one or two o'clock in the morning until dawn, and during all that time shooting was going on, they saw and heard nothing at the presidio; and the wind, they say, was favorable.

Although there were only two men who fired shots during all that time, many lives were saved which would have been lost without the said defense. And now, after the Father has been killed, the Mission burned, its many and valuable furnishings destroyed, together with the sacred vessels, its paintings, its baptismal, marriage and funeral records, and all the furnishings for the sacristy, the house, and the farm implements—now, the forces of both presidios come together to set things right. . . .

Most Excellent Lord, one of the most important requests I made of the Most Illustrious Inspector General, at the beginning of these conquests was: if ever the Indians, whether they be gentile or Christian, killed me, they should be forgiven. The same request I make of Your Excellency. It has been my own fault I did not make this request before. To see a formal statement drawn up by Your Excellency to that effect, in so far as it concerns me, and the other religious who at present are subject to me or will be in the future, would be for me a special consolation during the time Our Lord God will be pleased to add to my advancing years.

While the missionary is alive, let the soldiers guard him, and watch over him, like the pupils of God's very eyes. That is as it should be. Nor do I disdain such a favor for myself. But after the missionary has been killed, what can be gained by campaigns?

Some will say to frighten them and prevent them from killing others.

What I say is that, in order to prevent them from killing others, keep better guard over them than they did over the one who has been killed; and, as to the murderer, let him live, in order that he should be saved—which is the very purpose of our coming here, and the reason which justifies it. Give him to understand, after a moderate amount of punishment, that he is being pardoned in accordance with our law, which commands us to forgive injuries; and let us prepare him, not for death, but for eternal life. . . .

From this Mission, totally dependent on Your
Excellency, of San Carlos de Monterey, December 15, 1775.
　　　Most Excellent Lord,
　　　Kissing the hand of Your Excellency,
　　　　　Your most affectionate and devoted servant and
　　　　　chaplain, who holds you in the highest affection,
　　　　　　　　Fray Junípero Serra

Captain Alejandro Malaspina Praises the Beneficial Impact of Spanish Missions, 1792

Near the banks of the Carmel [River] and the seashore, and about two leagues from the presidio, is the mission of San Carlos [Borromeo]. Its buildings are a moderate-sized church, the hospice for the religious with accompanying offices, one storeroom for the shipments and farm tools and another for the grain, a small house for the corporal and four or five soldiers assigned to the mission guard and for other necessary uses. It was founded in 1770. It is administered by three apostolic missionaries of Propaganda Fide of the College of San Fernando de México. One of these is the president of all the missions of New California, named Fray Fermín de Lasuén. These religious deserve the praise and acquired the affection of all members of the expedition of the corvettes *Descubierta and Atrevida* because of their modesty, piety, austerity of customs, diligence in providing for the spiritual good of the natives, and their graciousness of conduct. They deserved from us of the schooners no lesser indication of the greatest esteem, and we found very clear evidence of the appreciation shown to this small congregation of virtuous men by those of the unfortunate expedition of Mr. La Pérouse.

With flattery and presents they attract the savage Indians and persuade them to adhere to life in society and to receive instruction for a knowledge of the Catholic faith, the cultivation of land, and the arts necessary for making the instruments most needed for farming.

In proof of this it will not be out of place to cite an example that gives evidence of the zeal and tenderness of the father president [Lasuén] and of the inclination of the savages.

The leader of one of these pagan tribes, as respected for his valor as he was loved by his people for the natural talents he possessed, was at death's door. He had shown esteem for the father president, and I don't know whether or not he had done him some kindness. When the latter learned of the sad situation of the former on a stormy night of constant rain, despite his dwelling place being some leagues away, he went there for the purpose of persuading him not to depart this world without embracing the Catholic faith and purifying himself with holy baptism. After great difficulty he arrived at last to talk with him, and having made known to him the reason for his trip and of the ardent desire that he had that a person whom he loved would not be lost forever, but rather, by trying to persuade him of the truth of what he was telling him and subjecting him to the ceremonies required by Christianity, he would obtain the reward that is promised to those who duly profess it. Then the pagan, being convinced, said to the father president: "I believe what you tell me and I will do what you direct because I find that no other interest but what you tell me can have motivated you to leave the comforts of your home to travel a number of leagues on a stormy night; I am convinced of your good will and I place myself in your hands."

Lorenzo Asisara Narrates the Assassination of a Priest by Santa Cruz Indians, 1812

The following story which I shall convey was told to me by my dear father in 1818. He was a neophyte of the Mission of Santa Cruz. He was one of the original founders of that mission. He was an Indian from the ranchería of *Asar* on the *Jarro* coast, up beyond Santa Cruz. He was one of the first neophytes baptized at the founding, being about 20 years of age. He was called Venancio Asar, and was the gardener of the Mission of Santa Cruz.

My father was a witness to the happenings which follow. He was one of the conspirators who planned to kill Father [Andrés] Quintana. When the conspirators were planning to kill Father Quintana, they gathered in the house of Julian the gardener (the one who made the pretense of being ill). The man who worked inside the plaza of the mission, named Donato, was punished by Father Quintana with a whip with wire. With each blow it cut his buttocks. Then the same man, Donato, wanted vengeance. He was the one who organized a gathering of 14 men, among them were the cook and the pages serving the Father. The cook was named Antonio, the eldest page named Lino, the others named Vicente and Miguel Antonio. All of them gathered in the house of Julian to plan how they could avoid the cruel punishments of Father Quintana. One man present, Lino, who was more capable and wiser than the others, said, "The first thing we should do today is to see that the Padre no longer punishes the people in that manner. We aren't animals. He [Quintana] says in his sermons that God does not command these [punishments]—but only examples and doctrine. Tell me now, what shall we do with the Padre? We cannot chase him away, nor accuse him before the judge, because we do not know who commands him to do with us as he does." To this, Andrés, father of Lino the page, answered, "Let's kill the Padre without anyone being aware, not the servants, nor anyone, except us that are here present." (This Lino was pure-blooded Indian, but as white as a Spaniard and man of natural abilities.) And then Julian the gardener said, "What shall we do in order to kill him?" His wife responded, "You, who are always getting sick—only this way can it be possible—think if it is good this way." Lino approved the plan and asked that all present also approve it. "In that case, we shall do it tomorrow night." That was Saturday. It should be noted that the Padre wished all the people to gather in the plaza on the following Sunday in order to test the whip that he had made with pieces of wire to see if it was to his liking.

All of the conspirators present at the meeting concurred that it should be done as Lino had recommended.

On the evening of Saturday at about six o'clock [October 12] of 1812, they went to tell the Padre that the gardener was dying. The Indians were already posted between two trees on both sides so that they could grab Father when he passed. The Padre arrived at the house of Julian, who pretended to be in agony. The Padre helped him, thinking he was really sick and about to die. When the Padre was returning to his house, he passed close to where the Indians were posted. They didn't have the courage to grab him and they allowed him to pass. The moribund gardener was behind him, but the Padre arrived at his house. Within an hour the wife of Julian arrived [again] to tell him [the Father] that her husband was dying. With this news the Padre returned to the orchard, the woman following behind crying and lamenting. He saw that the sick man was dying. The Padre took the man's hand in order to take his pulse. He felt the pulse and could find nothing amiss. The pulse showed there was nothing wrong with Julian. Not knowing what it could be, the Padre returned to pray for him. It was night when the Padre left. Julian arose and washed away the sacraments [oil] that he [the Padre] had administered, and he followed behind to join the others and see what his companions had done. Upon arriving at the place where they were stationed, Lino lifted his head and looked in all directions to see if they were coming out to grab the Father. The Father passed and they didn't take him. The Father arrived at his house.

Later, when the Father was at his table dining, the conspirators had already gathered at the house of the alleged sick man to ascertain why they hadn't seized Father Quintana. Julian complained that the Padre had placed herbs in his ears, and because of them, now he was really going to die. Then the wife of Julian said, "Yes, you all did not carry through with your promised plans; I am going to accuse you all, and I will not go back to the house." They all answered her, "All right, now, in this trip go and speak to the Father." The woman again left to fetch Father Quintana, who was at supper. He got up immediately and went where he found the supposedly sick man. This time he took with him three pages, two who walked ahead lighting his way with lanterns and behind him followed his Mayordomo Lino. The other two were Vicente and Miguel Antonio. The Father arrived at the gardener's house and found him unconscious. He couldn't speak. The Father prayed the last orations without administering the oils, and said to the wife, "Now your husband is prepared to live or die. Don't come to look for me again." Then the Father left with his pages to return to his house. Julian followed him. Arriving at the place where the two trees were (since the Father was not paying attention to his surroundings, but only in the path in front of him), Lino grabbed him from behind saying these words, "Stop here, Father, you must speak for a moment." When the other two pages who carried the lanterns turned around and saw the other men come out to attack the Father, they fled with their lanterns. The Father said to Lino, "Oh, my Son, what are you going to do to me?" Lino answered, "Your assassins will tell you."

"What have I done to you children, for which you would kill me?"

"Because you have made a *cuarta de hierro* [a horse whip tipped with iron] . . . ," Andrés answered him. Then the Father retorted, "Oh, children, leave me, so that I can go from here now, at this moment." Andrés asked him why he had made this *cuarta de hierro*. Quintana said that it was only for transgressors. Then someone shouted, "Well, you are in the hands of those evil ones, make your peace with God." Many of those present (seeing the Father in his affliction) cried and pitied his fate, but could do nothing to help him because they were themselves compromised. He pleaded much, promising to leave the mission immediately if they would only let him.

"Now you won't be going to any part of the earth from here, Father, you are going to heaven." This was the last plea of the Father. Some of them, not having been able to lay hands on Father, reprimanded the others because they talked too much, demanding that they kill him immediately. They then covered the Father's mouth with his own cape to strangle him. They had his arms tightly secured. After the Father had been strangled, they took a testicle [*grano de los companonez*] so that it would not be suspected that he had been beaten, and in a moment Padre expired. Then Lino and the others took him to his house and put him in his bed.

When the two little pages, Vicente and Miguel Antonio, arrived at the house, the former wanted to tell the guard, but the other dissuaded him by saying, "No, they, the soldiers, will also kill your mother, father, all of the others and yourself and me. Let them, the conspirators, do what they want." The two hid themselves. After the Indians had put the Father in his bed, Lino looked for the two pages, and he found them hidden. They undressed the body of Father Quintana and placed him in the bed as if he were going to sleep. All of the conspirators, including Julian's wife, were present. Andrés asked Lino for the keys to the storeroom. He handed them over saying, "What do you want?" And they said silver and beads. Among the group there were three Indians from the Santa Clara mission. These proposed that they investigate to see how much money there was. Lino opened the box and showed them the accumulated gold and silver. The three Indians from Santa Clara took as much as they could carry to their mission. (I don't know what they have done with that money.) The others took their portions as they saw fit.

Then they asked for the keys to the convent or the nunnery. Lino gave the keys to the *jayunte,* or barracks of the single men, to one of them in order to free them and gather them together below the orchard with the unmarried women. They gathered in the orchard so that neither the people in the plaza nor in the ranchería nor in the guardhouse would hear them. The single men left and without a sound gathered in the orchard at the same place where the Father was assassinated. There was a man there cautioning them not to make any noise, that they were going to have a good time. After a short time the young unmarried women arrived in order to spend the night there. The young people of both sexes got together and had their pleasure. At midnight Lino, being in the Padre's living room with one of the girls from the single women's dormitory, entered the Father's room in order to see if he was really dead. He found him reviving. He was already on the point of arising. Lino went to look for his accomplices to tell them that the Padre was coming to. The Indians returned and they crushed the Father's other testicle. This last act put an end to the life of Father Quintana. Donato, the one who had been whipped, walked around the room with the plural results of his operation in hand saying, "I shall bury these in the outdoor privy."

Donato told Lino that they should close the treasure chest with these words, "Close the trunk with the colored silver (that is the name that the Indians gave to gold) and let's see where we shall bury it." The eight men carried it down to the orchard and buried it secretly without the others knowing.

At about two o'clock in the morning, the young girls returned to their convent and the single men to their *jayunte* without making any noise. The assassins gathered once more after everything had occurred in order to hear the plans of Lino and Donato. Some wanted to flee, and others asked, "What for? No one except us knows." Lino asked them what they wanted to take to their houses, sugar, *panocha* [a sugar loaf], honey, or any other things, and suggested that they lay down to sleep for a while. Finally everything was ready. Donato proposed to return to where the Father was to check on him. They found him not only lifeless, but completely cold and stiff. Lino then showed them the new whip that the Padre was planning to use for the first time the next day, assuring them that he [Father Quintana] would not use it. He sent them to their houses to rest, remaining in the house with the keys. He asked them to be very careful. He arranged the room and the Bible in the manner in which the Father was accustomed to doing before retiring, telling them that he was not going to toll the bells in the morning until the Mayordomo and Corporal of the guard came and he had talked to them. All went through the orchard very silently.

This same morning (Sunday), the bells should have been rung at about eight o'clock. At that hour the people from the villa de Branciforte began to arrive in order to attend the mass. The Mayordomo, Carlos Castro, saw that the bells were not being rung and went to ask Lino, who was the first assistant of the Father, in order to ask why the Padre had not ordered him [to toll the bells]. Lino was in the outer room feigning innocence and answered the Mayordomo that he couldn't tell him anything about the Father because he was still inside sleeping or praying, and that the Mayordomo should wait until he should speak to him first. The Mayordomo returned home. Soon the Corporal of the guard arrived and Lino told him the same as to the Mayordomo. The Mayordomo returned to join in the conservation [*sic*]. They decided to wait a little while longer. Finally Lino told them that in their presence he would knock on the door of the room, observing, "If he is angry with me, you will stand up for me." And so he did, calling to the Father. As he didn't hear noise inside, the Mayordomo and Corporal asked Lino to knock again, but he refused. They then left, encharging him to call the Father again because the hour was growing late. All of the servants were busy at their jobs as always, in order not to cause any suspicion. The Mayordomo returned after ten o'clock and asked Lino to call the Padre to see what was wrong. Lino, with the keys in his pocket, knocked at the door. Finally the Mayordomo insisted that Lino enter the room, but Lino refused. At this moment, the Corporal, who was old Nazario Galindo, arrived. Lino (although he had the key to the door in his pocket) said, "Well, I am going to see if I can get the door open," and he pretended to look for a key to open the door. He returned with a ring of keys but he didn't find one that opened the lock. The Mayordomo and the Corporal left to talk to some men who were there. Later, Lino took the key that opened the door, saying it was for the kitchen. He opened another door that opened into the plaza (the key opened three doors), and through there he entered. Then he opened the main door from inside in front of which the others waited. Lino came out screaming and crying, and carrying on in an uncontrolled manner saying that the Padre was dead. They asked him if he was certain and he responded, "As this light that illuminates us. By God, I'm going to toll the bells." The three entered, the Corporal, the Mayordomo, and Lino. He didn't allow anyone else to enter. The Corporal and the Mayordomo and the other people wrote to the other missions and to Monterey to Father Marcelino Marquinez. (This Marquinez was an expert horseman and a good friend.) The poor elderly neophytes, and many other Indians who never suspected that the Father was killed, thought that he had died suddenly. They cried bitterly. Lino was roaring inside the Father's house like a bear.

The Fathers from Santa Clara and from other missions came and they held the Father's funeral, all believing that he had died a natural death, but not before examining the corpse in the entrance room, and had opened the stomach in order to be certain that the Padre had not been poisoned. Officials, sergeants, and many others participated in these acts but nothing was discovered. Finally, by chance, one of those present noted that the testicles were missing, and they were convinced that this had been the cause of death. Through modesty they did not reveal the fact and buried the body with everyone convinced that the death had been a natural one.

A number of years after the death, Emiliana, the wife of Lino, and Maria Tata, the wife of the cook Antonio, became mutually jealous. They were both seamstresses and they were at work. This was around August at the time of the lentil harvest. Carlos Castro was with his men working in the cornfields. Shortly before eleven o'clock he returned to his house for the meal. He was a man who understood well the language of the Indians. Returning from the cornfields, he passed behind one of the plaza walls near where these women were sewing and heard one tell the other that she was secretly eating *panocha*. Castro stopped and heard the second woman reply to the first, "How is it that you have so much money?" The first replied, "You also have it, because your husband killed the Father." Then the second accused the husband of the first woman of the same crime. The war of words continued, and Castro was convinced that Father Quintana had been assassinated, and he went to tell Father Roman Olbés, who was the missionary at Santa Cruz, what he had heard. Father Ramon went to tell Padre Marquinez. The latter sent one of his pages to the orchard to warn Julian and his accomplices that they were going to be caught. At noon, at about the time of the midday meal, Father Olbés spoke to Lino and asked him to send for his wife to come there and also to cut some pieces of cloth. Emiliana arrived, and Father Olbés placed her in a room where there was clothing and gave her some scissors with which to cut some pieces, telling her, "you will eat here." Then he sent a page to bring Maria Tata to take some dirty clothing out of the church to wash. The Mayordomo was observing the maneuverings of the Father. He made Maria Tata stay to eat there. He placed her in another room in order to cut some suits for the pages. The Mayordomo and the two fathers went to eat. After the meal, and when the two women had also eaten, Father Olbés said to Emiliana, "Do you know who eats a lot of white sugar?" She answered that it was Maria Tata, "because her husband killed Father Quintana." The Father made her return to the room and called for Maria Tata. The father asked her, "Tell me if you know who it was that killed Padre Quintana; tell me the truth so that nothing will happen to you." Lino and Antonio often took their meals in the kitchen. Maria Tata replied, "Lino, Father." Father Olbés then sent them to their houses to rest, offering them a present. Then the Father sent for the Corporal Nazario Galindo to arrest the assassins. They began with the orchard workers and the cook, without telling them why they were under arrest. Antonio was the first prisoner. Put in jail, they asked him who his accomplice was. He said who his accomplice was and the man was arrested, and they asked each one the name of their respective accomplices. In this way, they were all arrested, except Lino, who was looked upon as a valiant man of great strength. He was taken through the deceit of his own Compadre Carlos Castro, who handed him a knife to pare some black and white mares in order to make a hakamore for the animal of the Father. Suspiciously, Lino said to Castro, "Compadre, why are you deceiving me? I know that you are going to arrest me." There were already two soldiers hidden behind the corral.

"Here, take your knife, Compadre, that which I thought is already done. I am going to pay for it—and if I had wanted to, I could have finished off the soldiers, the Mayordomos, and any others that might have been around on the same night that I killed the Father."

The result of all this was that the accused were sent to San Francisco, and among them was my father. There they were judged, and those who killed the Father were sentenced to receive *novenano* (nine days in succession) of fifty lashes for each one, and to serve in public works in San Diego. The rest, including my father, were freed because they had served as witnesses, and it was not proven that they had taken part in the assassination.

All returned after many years to their mission.

The Spanish Padres were very cruel toward the Indians. They abused them very much, they had bad food, bad clothing, and they made them work like slaves. I also was subjected to that cruel life. The Padres did not practice what they preached in the pulpit. The Same Father Olbés for all his cruelties, was once stoned by the Indians.

San Andres Ranch/Santa Cruz
Jurisdiction of Watsonville
July 10, 1877
Lorenzo Asisara
(rubric)

 E S S A Y S

Francis F. Guest, a Catholic priest and scholar, begins the first essay by examining possible explanations for the ways in which Franciscan missionaries dealt with the high mortality rate among Indian neophytes. By considering the larger context of social conditions in eighteenth-century Europe, where death was a common feature of everyday life, he argues that Americans of the late twentieth century can understand missionaries' attitudes without at the same time completely exonerating them from responsibility for what happened to California's indigenous population. As institutions, Guest acknowledges, the missions "were an important cause of death among the converted Indians." Yet, according to his point of view, it is important not to impose twentieth-century cultural and ethnocentric norms on eighteenth-century behavior.

In the second essay, Antonia Castañeda, who teaches at the University of Texas, Austin, examines the treatment of Indian women in Alta California by Spanish soldiers during colonization. Using gender as a category of analysis, Castañeda takes a very different approach than that of Guest and reaches a very different conclusion. In describing the sexual and political devaluation of Amerindian women by Spaniards of the late eighteenth century, she does not (unlike Guest) hesitate to judge the Spanish imperial system according to her own twentieth-century values and prefers to emphasize ultimate outcome over original motivation.

Cultural Perspectives on Death and
Whipping in the Missions

FRANCIS F. GUEST, O.F.M.

As every graduate student of California history knows who has ever enjoyed the dubious distinction of assembling statistics on the death rate at the missions, the number of deaths at a given mission in a given year usually exceeded the number of births. The reasons customarily given for this unfortunate situation are commonly known and need not be repeated here. The aboriginal peoples of California had little or no immunity to diseases of European origin. The question we wish to raise in this context, however, is this: How could Franciscan priests, dedicated to the missionary service of the Church and the ideals of St. Francis of Assisi, conscientiously continue their work when they knew that, as they expressed the tragic truth themselves, the shadow of the Spaniard was the death of the Indian? How could they do it? . . .

To find an answer to these questions, let us turn our attention to social conditions as they were in Latin Europe in the late eighteenth century. . . .

In Spanish cities and towns unhygienic conditions prevailed. Competent physicians were scarce, even in populous centers. And infant mortality was extraordinarily high. . . .

[T]ravelers in eighteenth-century Spain paint a rather grim picture of health conditions. In 1754–1757 a plague of locusts afflicted Portugal and southern Spain, the result being famine in the provinces of Andalucía, Murcia, and Valencia. Joseph Townsend, the English scholar and traveler, says of Spain, ". . . few countries have sustained such losses by epidemical diseases, few have been so often ravaged by pestilential fevers." And with respect to Spanish physicians, he says: "In point of honour, no class of citizens meets with less respect than the physicians . . ." Speaking of the epidemic of yellow fever in southern Spain in the year 1800, Domínguez Ortiz says it carried off 12% of the people of Cádiz, a probable 19% of those of Sevilla, and one third the population of Jerez. . . . A military traveler in Spain in the 1830s speaks of whole villages being depopulated by intermittent fevers. . . .

Judging from the evidence here presented, one concludes that death, in the eighteenth century, came often to Spanish cities and towns and stayed long. The people of Spain were much closer to death in the late eighteenth century than they are today. They were familiar with its face. They were also accustomed to the early approach of old age. The Spanish padres who served in the California missions were habituated, then, from early childhood on, to rubbing elbows with death. Of the 123 Franciscans who crossed the ocean from Spain to labor in the California mission field, 93 were brought up in small towns located in rural areas, where disease was frequent, food supplies limited, medical service inadequate, and only the more

From Francis F. Guest, O. F. M., "Cultural Perspectives on California Mission Life," *Southern California Quarterly,* 65, Spring 1983. Reprinted by permission of the Historical Society of Southern California.

rugged survived. . . . The Franciscan missionaries of Hispanic California, 1769–1848, saw death and the death rate at the missions with different eyes than those of late twentieth-century Americans.

This is not to say, of course, that the missionaries were so inured to death as to be indifferent to the mortality rate among the missionized Indians. In their annual and biennial reports they kept a meticulous record of baptisms, deaths, and marriages at the missions. . . .

It is not surprising that the medicines so industriously acquired and administered by the padres and others to the Indians were without adequate effect. . . .

Indeed, Father Narciso Durán was of the opinion that it might be better for the padres not to attempt to administer medicines and other remedies to neophytes who had been taken ill. He pointed out that if a Spaniard administered medicine or even so much as a bowl of chicken broth to a sick Indian, and the Indian should die, the bereaved relatives would blame the Spaniard for the loss of their kinsman. And the result would be alienation of these same Indians. . . .

One does not wish to present all this evidence as an apologia for the Spanish missionaries, excusing them of all blame for the high rate of mortality among the neophytes. . . . [T]he missions themselves, as institutions, were an important cause of death among the converted Indians. One merely wishes to point out that the impression of the Spanish missionaries as callous and indifferent witnesses to the presence of so many fatalities among the Indians is one that should normally be revised in the light of social and health conditions as they were in France and Spain in the eighteenth century. . . .

A second . . . [fact] that needs to be seen in cultural perspective is . . . the whipping of delinquent Indians by the padres of the California missions. We find the same dilemma here as we did in the case of the death rate at the missions. As members of the clergy, the Franciscans were dedicated to the spiritual ideals of the Gospels. As Franciscans, they were pledged to follow in the footsteps of St. Francis of Assisi. On the one hand, there is abundant evidence that the missionaries, in their correspondence, repeatedly expressed their love for the Indians. And they often underwent sacrifices for their neophytes and protected them against the abuse and exploitation to which they were often exposed at the hands of some of the soldiers and townsmen. And yet, on the other hand, there is incontrovertible testimony that delinquent Indians were whipped, sometimes excessively, by the padres. How does one explain this obvious anomaly? How does one reconcile the cross the missionaries carried in one hand with the whip they bore in the other? . . .

To answer these questions, one must remember that the Franciscan presence in Alta California was not only a European presence; it was also a Spanish presence. And it was a Catholic presence dating from the late eighteenth century. Let us do here what we did with the high mortality rate at the missions—study Spanish conditions as they were when the padres who labored in California left Spain for the New World.

Reading about the use of the whip in the Spanish past, we find, first of all, that boys of the lower and middle classes in Spanish elementary and secondary schools were accustomed to severe punishments for not having studied and learned their lessons. They memorized the declension of Latin nouns and the conjugation of Latin verbs to the accompaniment of shouts, reproofs, cuffs, and whippings. All this was part of the Spanish way of life and neither the boys nor their parents thought anything of it. In California mission documents, then, it is not surprising to find a missionary observing that "in an average school a person would receive more punishment for not knowing his lesson than he would receive here for living in concubinage."

We find, secondly, that during the eighteenth century in some churches and chapels in Spain, laymen would come for evening penitential services once or twice a week throughout the year. To begin the ceremony, the religious in choir would chant the appropriate psalms. Then the lights would be put out, both the religious and the laymen would kneel and bare their backs, and all present, while more psalms were chanted, would apply the discipline. The discipline was a whip made of rope, the strands of which were thickened at the ends with knots. Joseph Townsend, the British scholar and traveler . . . , testifies that the whipping at these penitential services went on for a period of twenty minutes. It was not unusual for the penitents to discipline themselves with such vigor and fervor as to draw blood. . . .

[W]hipping played a significant role in Spanish culture in the eighteenth and early nineteenth centuries. It was part of the domestic, social, and religious life of the people. Children were whipped at home and in the schools. Criminals were flogged in prisons. Servants were beaten by their masters. Indian house boys and ranch hands in Mexican California were whipped by their employers much as they had been by the padres at the missions. Among clergy, religious, and lay people self-flagellation was practiced by the devout for religious reasons. . . .

Now then, let us apply this information on the role of whipping in Spanish culture to the punishment of delinquent Indians at the California missions. According to Father Fermín Francisco de Lasuén, a missionary could impose no more than twenty-one strokes of the whip on a given Indian delinquent, striking his bare back with a rope, a lariat, or a pliable reed or cane. According to Lasuén, anything that might draw blood or cause a bruise was to be avoided. But, allowing five seconds for each stroke of the whip, one can deliver twenty-one strokes to a given person in slightly less than two minutes. A number of missionaries raised the permissible punishment to twenty-five strokes, which would have taken slightly more than two minutes to deliver. It will be remembered, however, that once or twice a week throughout the year in Spain there were lay people and religious who were accustomed to flagellate themselves for twenty minutes at a time. Even when one raises the number of strokes to fifty, as a few of the missionaries did in punishing given Indians, the chastisement seems limited when compared with what pious Spaniards customarily inflicted upon themselves every week in their spiritual exercises. . . .

Now let us turn to the question "Why did the missionized Indians submit to these whippings so patiently?"

In the eighteenth century it was customary for religious throughout Latin Europe and Latin America to take the discipline regularly, some more severely and rigorously than others and usually in private rather than in public. In the statutes for the apostolic missionary colleges of the Franciscan Order one reads as follows: "And as regards the use of the discipline, fasting at times other than those prescribed by the Rule, the chapter of faults, and other austerities and practices conducive to observance of the Rule, of monastic life, and of regular discipline, let the friars conform to the General Constitutions of the Order." In the Province of Cataluña in Spain the friars were accustomed to take the discipline every day except for Sundays and for festival days of the first and second class. . . .

[M]ay it not reasonably be inferred that this extraordinary spiritual phenomenon, this self-flagellation, was probably the principal reason why the missionized Indians submitted so patiently to the whippings imposed upon them for their bad behavior? Why did they allow the padre to whip them? Was it not because they knew that he whipped himself much harder and more often than he did them? One may well ask how many of the Indians would have remained at the missions to be beaten for their misdoings if it had not been for the fidelity of the missionaries in their practice of taking the discipline.

[T]he padre's religion made the cross the crux of this mysterious cultural encounter in which converted Indians, in punishment for their defects, received whippings at the hands of ecclesiastics. It was devotion to the cross of Christ that led to self-flagellation by the missionaries. And it was the self-flagellation of the missionaries that seemingly did more than anything else to induce the Indians to accept with some measure of resignation the physical punishments imposed upon them by the force of Spanish custom. . . .

Without the aid of the cultural perspectives outlined above, an American reader might easily be led to describe the Franciscan missionaries as callous and brutal in the way they punished delinquent Indians. Actually, there were some occasions when missionaries were undiscerning and unfeeling in this matter. . . . But to proceed from a page of statistics on whipping to the conclusion that the missionaries were insensitive, harsh, and pitiless is to take more than just a long step. It is to take a leap of considerable distance, even a leap in the dark. . . . Judging by the standards of contemporary American society, one feels inclined to condemn the physical punishments imposed upon delinquent Indians—whippings, shackles, the stocks—as severe, much too severe. One must not fail to devote due attention, however, to the subjective order, the order of thought, the order of conscience. How did these practitioners of physical punishment see themselves? How did they judge their own conduct? Father Fermín Francisco de Lasuén, second Father President of the California missions, leaves one with the impression, in his correspondence, that in these penal practices he saw nothing objectionable, nothing to be indignant or alarmed about, nothing with which to reproach his conscience. Father Estevan Tapis, the third Father President, points out that the Indians from the forest came freely and gladly to the mission, observed everything that went on, including the punishments, received instruction, and asked for baptism when they knew they were free to return to the wilderness if they wished. The non-Christian Indian visitors knew the converted Indians were corrected gently at first and then, when gentleness finally proved ineffective, received some form of punishment. If the non-Christians had been scandalized, repelled, and alienated by these punishments, would they have asked for baptism and entered the ranks of the neophytes? These are facts that challenge our respect. It is certain that the whipping of delinquent Indians was an error in judgment on the part of the missionaries. It is not at all certain that it was necessarily an exercise in brutality. Argumentative though these lines may seem to be, their purpose is not to disinfect mission history. It is to make some kind of sense out of it. . . .

The Spanish missionaries in California followed the dictates of Spanish culture, the California Indians those of their own aboriginal culture. Each culture, the Spanish and the aboriginal, was complete, distinct, and unique. Each consisted of many minute parts, all closely interrelated, all functionally organized into a kind of living social organism. Each had its own configuration, its own *Weltanschauung,* its own world view, its own spirit. . . .

[T]he Franciscan missionaries in Hispanic California . . . made numerous errors both in planning and in implementing their methods of evangelization. The mission, with its fields, crops, granaries, workshops, and church, effected an almost complete separation of recently converted Indians from their aboriginal culture. The missionaries performed a kind of surgical operation on Indian society, cutting off one member after another and placing each one in a totally different society with totally different cultural norms and practices. Furthermore, the unconverted Indians, in the eyes of the missionaries, were heathens, victims of barbarism, of superstition, of error, and they were to be removed from these unfortunate circumstances as soon as possible and Christianized. And finally, they were not only to be Christianized, they were to be Hispanicized, absorbed into Hispanic culture, embodied into the Spanish empire as useful vassals of the Crown. The contrast between Catholic missionization of today, both in doctrine and in practice, and the Spanish missionary program of two hundred years ago is like the difference between day and night. . . .

The Spaniards, by custom, by the weight and force of three hundred years of precedent, were impelled almost irresistibly in the direction they took in their approach to the Indians. It was not reasonably possible for them to have been other, in their missionary policies and methods, than they were. Hence if we Americans today had been Spanish missionaries in California two hundred years ago, we would have found ourselves driven by the force of custom to follow much the same path as that taken by the friars themselves, at least the better ones. . . .

The culture of the Spanish was markedly different from that of contemporary Americans. Their concept of humanism and of humanity belonged to another place and another age. Their definition of what was cruel and unusual in punishment differed greatly from that of contemporary

American schools, courts, and legislators. The spirituality of the padres, as had been explained, was physically demanding. When an Indian submitted to a whipping, he knew that the stripes imposed upon him on this one occasion paled into insignificance when compared with those that the padre inflicted upon himself regularly at least three times a week. And even when he was compelled to wear hobbles or sit in the stocks, the discomfort he suffered was minor in comparison with what the padre freely took upon himself faithfully and often.

To sum up, the solution to the question whether or not mission administration was brutal lies in the use of the discipline, curious and unwonted as that instrument of physical penance may seem to present-day Americans. It lies in the Spanish concept of physical penance as it was in the period of Baroque Catholicism. It lies in the religious devotion of the Spanish to the passion of Christ. And it lies in the conviction of rugged Spaniards that physical punishment, carefully measured and controlled, was good for the character of those who misbehaved.

Now then, was mission administration brutal or not? Let us answer the question briefly. If judged from the standpoint of contemporary American life, mission administration was quite obviously brutal. But if judged from the standpoint of the padres and the other Californios, it quite obviously was not. The two sets of standards differ. To appeal to the subjective order, what seems brutal to Americans of today was not conceived of as brutal by the missionaries and the other Hispanic people of early California. One cannot judge eighteenth-century people by twentieth-century standards. . . . One cannot use Indian standards by which to judge the Indians and then use American standards of today by which to judge the Spanish missionaries of Hispanic California. One cannot absolve the Indians of savagery and then accuse the missionaries of it.

Spanish Violence Against Amerindian Women

ANTONIA I. CASTAÑEDA

In the morning, six or seven soldiers would set out together . . . and go to the distant rancherías [*villages*] even many leagues away. When both men and women at the sight of them would take off running . . . the soldiers, adept as they are at lassoing cows and mules, would lasso Indian women—who then became prey for their unbridled lust. Several Indian men who tried to defend the women were shot to death.

Junipero Serra, 1773

In words reminiscent of sixteenth-century chroniclers Bernal Díaz del Castillo and Bartolomé de las Casas, the father president of the California missions, Junipero Serra, described the depredations of the soldiers against Indian women in his reports to Viceroy Antonio María Bucareli and the father guardian of the College of San Fernando, Rafaél Verger. Sexual assaults against native women began shortly after the founding of the presidio and mission at Monterey in June 1770, wrote Serra, and continued throughout the length of California. The founding of each new mission and presidio brought new reports of sexual violence.

The despicable actions of the soldiers, Serra told Bucareli in 1773, were severely retarding the spiritual and material conquest of California. The native people were resisting missionization. Some were becoming warlike and hostile because of the soldiers' repeated outrages against the women. The assaults resulted in Amerindian attacks, which the soldiers countered with unauthorized reprisals, thereby further straining the capacity of the small military force to staff the presidios and guard the missions. Instead of pacification and order, the soldiers provoked greater conflict and thus jeopardized the position of the church in this region.

Serra was particularly alarmed about occurrences at Mission San Gabriel. "Since the district is the most promising of all the missions," he wrote to Father Verger, "this mission gives me the greatest cause for anxiety; the secular arm down there was guilty of the most heinous crimes, killing the men to take their wives." Father Serra related that on October 10, 1771, within a month of its having been founded, a large group of Indians suddenly attacked two soldiers who were on horseback and tried to kill the one who had outraged a woman. The soldiers retaliated. "A few days later," Serra continued, "as he went out to gather the herd of cattle . . . and [it] seems more likely to get himself a woman, a soldier, along with some others, killed the principal Chief of the gentiles; they cut off his head and brought it in triumph back to the mission."

The incident prompted the Amerindians of the coast and the sierra, mortal enemies until that time, to convene a council to make peace with each other and join forces to eliminate the Spaniards. The council planned to attack the mission on October 16, but changed the plan after a new contingent of troops arrived at the mission. Despite this narrowly averted disaster, the soldiers assigned to Mission San Gabriel continued their outrages.

The soldiers' behavior not only generated violence on the part of the native people as well as resistance to missionization, argued Serra; it also took its toll on the missionaries, some of whom refused to remain at their mission sites. In his 1773 memorial to Bucareli, Serra lamented the loss of one of the missionaries, who could not cope with the soldiers' disorders at San Gabriel. The priest was sick at heart, Serra stated: "He took to his bed, when he saw with his own eyes a soldier actually committing deeds of shame with an Indian who had come to the mission, and even the children who came to the mission were not safe from their baseness."

Conditions at other missions were no better. Mission San Luis Obispo also lost a priest because of the assaults on Indian women. After spending two years as the sole missionary at San Luis, Father Domingo Juncosa asked for and received permission to return to Mexico because he was "shocked at the scandalous conduct of the soldiers" and could not work under such abominable conditions. Even before San Luis Obispo was founded in the early fall of 1772, Tichos women had cause to fear. The most notorious molesters of non-Christian women were among the thirteen soldiers sent on a bear hunt to this area during the previous winter of starvation at Monterey.

The establishment of new missions subjected the women of each new area to sexual assaults. Referring to the founding of the mission at San Juan Capistrano, Serra wrote that "it seems all the sad experiences that we went through at the beginning have come to life again. The soldiers, without any restraint or shame, have behaved like brutes toward Indian women." From this mission also, the priests reported to Serra that the soldier-guards went at night to the nearby villages to assault the women and that hiding the women did not restrain the brutes, who beat the men to force them to reveal where the women were hidden. Non-Christian Indians in the vicinity of the missions were simply not safe. They were at the mercy of soldiers with horses and guns.

In 1773, a case of rape was reported at San Luis Rey, one at San Diego, and two cases at Monterey the following year. Serra expressed his fears and concern to Governor Felipe de Neve, who was considering establishing a new presidio in the channel of Santa Barbara. Serra told Neve that he took it for granted that the insulting and scandalous conduct of the soldiers "would be the same as we had experienced in other places which were connected with presidios. Perhaps this one would be worse."

Native women and their communities were profoundly affected by the sexual attacks and attendant violence. California Amerindians were peaceable, non-aggressive people who highly valued harmonious relationships. Physical violence and the infliction of bodily harm on one another were virtually unknown. Women did not fear men. Rape rarely, if ever, occurred. If someone stole from another or caused another's death, societal norms required that the offending party make reparations to the individual and/or the family. Appropriate channels to rectify a wrong without resorting to violence existed.

Animosity, when it did surface, was often worked out ritualistically— for example, through verbal battles in the form of war songs, or song fights that lasted eight days, or encounters in which the adversaries threw stones across a river at each other with no intent actually to hit or physically injure the other party. Even among farming groups such as the Colorado River people, who practiced warfare and took women and children captive, female captives were never sexually molested. The Yumas believed that intimate contact with enemy women caused sickness.

Thus, neither the women nor their people were prepared for the onslaught of aggression and violence the soldiers unleashed against them. They were horrified and terrified. One source reported that women of the San Gabriel and other southern missions raped by the soldiers were considered contaminated and obliged to undergo an extensive purification, which included a long course of sweating, the drinking of herbs, and other forms of purging. This practice was consistent with the people's belief that sickness was caused by enemies. . . .

It is clear that the sexual exploitation of native women and related violence seriously threatened the political and military objectives of the colonial enterprise in California. Repeated attacks against women and summary reprisals against men who dared to interfere undermined the efforts of the priests to attract Amerindians to the missions and to Christianity. They also thwarted whatever attempts the military authorities might make to elicit political or military allegiance from the native peoples.

From the missionaries' point of view, the attacks had more immediate, deleterious consequences for the spiritual conquest of California, because such actions belied significant principles of the Catholic moral theology they were trying to inculcate. As the primary agents of Christianization/ Hispanicization, the missionaries argued that they could not teach and Amerindians could not learn and obey the moral strictures against rape, abduction, fornication, adultery, and all forms of sexual impurity while the soldiers persisted in their licentiousness and immorality. Their actions repudiated the very morality the friars were to inculcate.

Early conflict between ecclesiastical and civil-military officials over deployment and discipline of the mission escort soon gave rise to constant bitter disputes centering on the question of authority and jurisdiction over the Indians in California. The conflict over control of the Indians revolved around the issue of their segregation from the non-Indian population. Rooted in the early conquest and consequent development of colonial Indian policy, the issue has been extensively discussed by other historians. The concern here is to examine it specifically from the point of view of sex/gender and to define a context for explaining why, despite strenuous efforts by church and state alike, there was little success in arresting the attacks on Indian women.

Serra, for his part, blamed the military commanders and, once appointed, the governor. They were, he said, lax in enforcing military discipline and unconcerned about the moral fiber of their troops. They failed to punish immoral soldiers who assaulted native women, were flagrantly incontinent, or took Amerindian women as concubines. In California, he stated, secular authorities not only condoned the soldiers' assaults on Indian women but interfered with the missionaries' efforts to counter the abuse, and thereby exceeded their authority with respect to Amerindians. . . .

In eighteenth-century California, the status of Amerindian women—as members of non-Christian, indigenous groups under military conquest on Spain's northernmost outpost of empire—made them twice subject to assault with impunity: they were the spoils of conquest, and they were Indian. In the mentality of the age, these two conditions firmly established the inferiority of the Amerindian woman and became the basis for devaluing her person beyond the devaluation based on sex that accrued to all women irrespective of their sociopolitical (race, class) status. The ferocity and longevity of the sexual assaults against the Amerindian woman are rooted in the devaluation of her person conditioned by the weaving together of the strands of the same ideological thread that demeaned her on interrelated counts: her sociopolitical status, her sex, and her gender.

From their earliest contact with Amerindian peoples, Europeans established categories of opposition, or otherness, within which they defined themselves as superior and Amerindians as inferior. These categories were derived from the Aristotelian theory that some beings are inferior by nature, and therefore should be dominated by their superiors for their own welfare, and from the medieval Spanish concept of "purity of blood," which was based on religion and which informed the sense of national unity forged during the reconquest. These ideas—which were fundamentally political concepts that separated human beings into opposing, hierarchical subject-object categories—prevailed during the era of first contact with Amerindians and the early conquests of the Americas.

By the late eighteenth century, a different political concept—racial origin—defined place and social value in the stratified social order of colonial New Spain. Race was inextricably linked to social origin and had long been a symbol for significant cleavages in society; it was one primary basis for valuation—and devaluation—of human beings. In the contemporary ideology and society, Amerindian women were thus devalued on the basis of their social and racial origins, which placed them at the bottom of the social scale, and as members of a conquered group.

Two aspects of the devaluation of Amerindian women are especially noteworthy. First and foremost, it is a political devaluation. That is, it is rooted in and driven by political considerations and acts: by war, conquest, and the imposition of alien sociopolitical and economic structures of one group over another. Second, the devaluation rationalized by conquest cuts across sex. At this level, women and men of the conquered group are equally devalued and objectified by the conquering group. Amerindian women and men were both regarded as inferior social beings, whose inferiority justified the original conquest and continued to make them justifiably exploitable and expendable in the eyes of the conqueror. The obverse, of course, also holds in this equation: women and men of the conquering group share the characterization and privileges of their group. In this instance, the primary opposition is defined by sociopolitical status, not sex.

Although the ideological symbols of sociopolitical devaluation changed over time—from religion to socioracial origins to social class—the changing symbols intersected with a sex/gender ideology that has remained remarkably constant from the fifteenth to the twentieth century. As the term implies, the sex/gender ideology defines two categories of opposition—sex and gender—within which women are categorized as superior or inferior in relation to others.

With respect to sex stratification, women are placed in opposition and in an inferior position to men, on the assumption that in the divine order of nature the male sex of the species is superior to the female. In this conception, the ascribed inferiority of females to males is biologically constructed.

The opposition centering on gender revolves around sexual morality and sexual conduct. This opposition creates a level of superior-inferior or good-bad stratification based on social and political value-centered concepts of women's sexuality. This dichotomization provides a very specific, socially constructed, "sexual morality" category for valuing or devaluing women.

Rooted in the corollary patriarchal concepts of woman as the possession of man and of woman's productive capacity as the most important source of her value, this ideology makes woman a pivotal element in the property structure and institutionalizes her importance to the society in the provisions of partible and bilateral inheritance. It also places woman's value, also termed her "honor," in her sexual accessibility—in her virginity while single and, once wed, in the fidelity of her sexual services to the husband to ensure a legitimate heir.

Within this construct, women are placed in opposition to one another at two extremes of a social and moral spectrum defined by sexuality and accessibility. The good woman embodies all the sexual virtues or attributes essential to the maintenance of the patriarchal social structure: sexual purity, virginity, chastity, and fidelity. Historically, the norms of sexual morality and sexual conduct that patriarchal society established for women of the ruling class have been the norms against which all other women have been judged. These norms are fundamentally rooted in questions of the acquisition and transference of economic and political power, and of women's relationship to that power base.

Since the linchpins of these ideological constructs are property, legitimacy, and inheritance, a woman excluded from this property/inheritance structure for sociopolitical reasons (religion, conquest, slavery, race, class), or for reasons based on sexual immorality (any form of sexual misconduct), is consequently excluded from the corresponding concepts and structures of social legitimacy. A woman so excluded cannot produce legitimate heirs because she is not a legitimate social or sexual being.

The woman who is defined out of social legitimacy because of the abrogation of her primary value to patriarchal society, that of producing heirs, is therefore without value, without honor. She becomes the other, the bad woman, the embodiment of a corrupted, inferior, unusable sex: immoral, without virtue, loose. She is common property, sexually available to any man that comes along.

A woman (women) thus devalued may not lay claim to the rights and protections the society affords to the woman who does have sociopolitical and sexual value. In colonial New Spain, as in most Western societies until the very recent period, the woman so demeaned, so objectified, could be raped, beaten, worked like a beast of burden, or otherwise abused with impunity.

The soldiers, priests, and settlers who effected the conquest and colonization of Alta California in the last third of the eighteenth century perceived and acted toward Amerindians in a manner consistent with the ideology and history of conquest—regarding them as inferior, devalued, disposable beings against whom violence was not only permissible but often necessary. For, despite the Laws of the Indies, the contradictions in the ideology and corresponding historical relations of conquest were great from the very beginning. These contradictions were generally exacerbated, rather than resolved, across time, space, and the expansion to new frontiers.

From the very beginning, the papal bulls and scholarly (ideological) debates that affirmed the essential humanity of Amerindians and initiated the legislation to effect their conversion and protection sanctioned violence and exploitation under certain conditions. Loopholes in the royal statutes that were technically intended to protect Amerindians and guarantee their rights, but more specifically protected the crown's interest in Indian land and labor, had permitted virulent exploitation of Indians since the laws were first passed.

More contemporary military and civil laws, such as those enacted by Neve, Fages, and Borica, carried severe penalties for illegal contact with or maltreatment of Indians; but these laws were especially contradictory because they were intended to curb certain kinds of violence by soldiers who were trained to kill Indians and who were sent to California to effect the temporal (military) conquest of this region. Thus, violence against Amerindians was permissible when it advanced the particular interests of the Spanish Conquest, but punishable when it did not. Since the sexual violence that occurred in this region was but the most contemporary manifestation of a national history that included the violation of enemy women as a legitimate expression of aggression during conquest, it would seem that sexual violence became a punishable offense only when it was the source of military or political problems.

Finally, perhaps the greatest contradictions were those of the greatest champion of Amerindian rights—the Catholic church. On the one hand, Catholic clergy sought to remove Amerindians from contact with Spaniards, in order to protect them from the exploitation and violence of conquistadores, soldiers, and colonists; on the other hand, Jesuits, Franciscans, and other religious orders relied heavily on corporal punishment in their programs to Christianize and Hispanicize native people. While proclaiming the humanity of Amerindians, missionaries on the frontier daily acted upon a fundamental belief in the inferiority of the Indian. Their actions belied their words.

Accordingly, in his lengthy memorial of June 19, 1801, refuting the charges of excessive cruelty to Amerindians leveled against the Franciscans by one of their own, Father President Fermín Francisco de Lasuén disputed the use of extreme cruelty in the missions of the New California. Force was used only when absolutely necessary, stated Lasuén; and it was at times necessary because the native peoples of California were "untamed savages . . . people of vicious and ferocious habits who know no law but force, no superior but their own free will, and no reason but caprice." Of the use of force against neophyte women, Lasuén wrote that women in the mission were flogged, placed in the stocks, or shackled only because they deserved it. But, he quickly added, their right to privacy was always respected—they were flogged inside the women's dormitory, called the *monjero* (nunnery). Flogging the women in private, he further argued, was part of the civilizing process because it "instilled into them the modesty, delicacy, and virtue belonging to their sex."

A key element in the missionaries' program of conversion to Christianity included the restructuring of relations between the sexes to reflect gender stratification and the corollary values and structures of the patriarchal family: subservience of women to men, monogamy, marriage without divorce, and a severely repressive code of sexual norms.

In view of the fact that ideologies, structures, and institutions of conquest imposed here were rooted in two and a half centuries of colonial rule, the sexual and other violence toward Amerindian women in California can best be understood as ideologically justified violence institutionalized in the structures and relations of conquest initiated in the fifteenth century. In California as elsewhere, sexual violence functioned as an institutionalized mechanism for ensuring subordination and compliance. It was one instrument of sociopolitical terrorism and control—first of women and then of the group under conquest.

 F U R T H E R   R E A D I N G

Robert Archibald, *The Economic Aspects of the California Missions* (1978)

Robert Archibald, "Indian Labor at the California Missions: Slavery or Salvation?" *Journal of San Diego History* XXIV (Spring 1978): 172–82

John Francis Bannon, "The Mission as a Frontier Institution: Sixty Years of Interest and Research," *Western Historical Quarterly* X (July 1979): 303–22

Leon G. Campbell, "The Spanish Presidio in Alta California during the Mission Period, 1769–1848," *Journal of the West* XVI (October 1977): 63–77

Edward D. Castillo, ed., *Native American Perspectives on the Hispanic Colonization of Alta California* (1991)

Edward D. Castillo and Doyce B. Nunis, Jr., "California Mission Indians: Two Perspectives," *California History* 70 (Summer 1991): 206–15, 236–38

Sherburne F. Cook, *The Conflict between the California Indian and White Civilization* (1976)

Sherburne F. Cook, *The Population of the Californian Indians, 1769–1970* (1976)

Rupert Costo and Jeannette Henry Costo, eds., *The Missions of California: A Legacy of Genocide* (1987)

Maynard J. Geiger, *The Life and Times of Fray Junipero Serra, O.F.M.; or, The Man Who Never Turned Back, 1713–1784, A Biography* (1959)

Francis F. Guest, "An Examination of the Thesis of S. F. Cook on the Forced Conversion of Indians in the California Missions," *Southern California Quarterly* LXI (Spring 1979): 1–78

Robert L. Hoover, "The Death of Yoscolo," *Pacific Historical Review* LI (August 1987): 312–14

Albert L. Hurtado, *Indian Survival on the California Frontier* (1988)

Robert H. Jackson and Edward D. Castillo, *Indians, Franciscans, and Spanish Colonization: The Impact of the Mission System on California Indians* (1995)

Colin M. MacLachlan, *Spain's Empire in the New World* (1988)

George Harwood Phillips, *Chiefs and Challengers: Indian Resistance and Cooperation in Southern California* (1975)

George Harwood Phillips, *Indians and Intruders in Central California, 1769–1849* (1993)

Irving Berdine Richmond, *California Under Spain and Mexico, 1535–1847* (1965)

James A. Sandos, "Levantamiento! The 1824 Chumash Uprising Reconsidered," *Southern California Quarterly* LXVII (Summer 1985): 109–33

James A. Sandos, "Junipero Serra's Canonization and the Historical Record," *American Historical Review* 93 (December 1988): 1253–69

David Hurst Thomas, *The Spanish Borderlands in Pan-American Perspective* (1991)

Antonine Tibersar, O.F.M., trans. and ed., *Writings of Junipero Serra,* 3 vols. (1955)

David J. Weber, *The Spanish Frontier in North America* (1992)

Richard S. Whitehead, "Alta California's Four Fortresses," *Southern California Quarterly* LXV (Spring 1983): 67–94

CHAPTER
4

Mexican California:
A Study in Contrasts

In seeking to understand what Douglas Monroy has called "the making of Mexican culture in frontier California" (see this chapter's second essay), it is important to focus on the complicated interplay among Indian, Spanish, Mexican, and Anglo cultures during the first half of the nineteenth century. It is important, as well, to remember that throughout the Wars of Independence in Latin America (from 1808 to the birth of the Mexican Republic in 1821), California was a marginal bystander, isolated from Mexico and its rebellion. Such separation encouraged the growth of California sectionalism rather than identification with Mexico and its liberatory aspirations. Nonetheless, when Pablo Vicente de Solá, the last Spanish governor of Alta California, learned of the Mexican revolutionaries' success, he was persuaded by his advisors to declare California a part of the new Mexican empire. In September 1822 the Mexican flag thus replaced the Spanish one at Monterey, then the capital of Alta California.

During the early years of the Mexican Republic, mestizo (or mixed-blood) migrants from the interior of Mexico joined with retired frontier Spanish soldiers to settle in towns near the California missions. The 1820s and 1830s were a period of social and political turbulence during which the mission system ended. This historic transition involved a process called "secularization," or conversion of the missions into ordinary parish churches. As historian Lisbeth Haas recently has reminded us in Conquests and Historical Identities in California, 1769–1936 *(1995), it also involved a related process of "emancipation," or the release of Indian neophytes from close supervision by friars. Together, secularization and emancipation made possible the rise of a vast network of private* ranchos *(ranches used mostly to raise cattle), which eventually covered much of southern California.*

As Monroy points out, the rise of these ranchos "profoundly influenced the course of California history." The Californios *(or Mexican-Californians) prospered greatly from secularization by taking over enormous amounts of former mission lands and mission assets, thereafter constructing a hierarchical, seigneurial system in which they functioned as virtual lords. For the*

Indians, many of whom became menial laborers on the new ranchos, it was, in contrast, an extremely painful and disruptive experience. In other words, whatever positive effects emancipation may have had for the Indians were severely compromised.

One knowledgeable student of that era, Lawrence Jelinek of Loyola Marymount University, has observed in Harvest Empire: A History of California Agriculture *(1982) that "secularization represented not a democratization of land holding for Indian or settler, but the shift of land monopoly from a religious elite to a secular elite." The new* ranchero *elite was itself to be displaced during the 1840s and 1850s through a process of "Americanization," culminating in the Treaty of Guadalupe Hidalgo of 1848, when California became part of the United States.*

There is little doubt that the secularization of the missions and emancipation of the Indians led to a different kind of society, one in which the Mexican administrative and ranchero elite played the dominant role. But it is difficult to summarize the impact of Mexican rule on the social, economic, and legal structure of California. What was daily life like? How did the Indians fare under secularization? Look for evidence of many different points of view in the documents. Did contemporaries experience California as a happy-go-lucky "lotos-land" during this period, or did they perceive problems? To what extent is the message shaped by each speaker's background? The two essays that follow the documents also offer widely differing perspectives; it is tempting to speculate on why each historian wrote as he did.

 D O C U M E N T S

It was not until some years after Mexico gained its independence that the Mexican government addressed the issue of the secularization of missions in Baja and Alta California. In May 1833 a commission of the Mexican chamber of deputies issued a report on the subject, recommending a law that was formally adopted several months later. Portions of that report are included here as the first document. It is followed by a narrative account dictated by Angustias de la Guerra Ord, an upper-class California woman. She was the daughter of Comandante de la Guerra and the wife of Manuel Jimeno Casarin, a leading military and, later, civil official during the 1830s and 1840s. Ord describes the process of secularization from the point of view of a well-placed *Californio*.

The third document is drawn from Richard Henry Dana's *Two Years Before the Mast* (1840), considered by many to be California's first literary classic. Formerly a Harvard undergraduate, Dana signed on the brig *Pilgrim* in 1834 as a common sailor and made the arduous voyage around Cape Horn to California, later recording his observations about the region. The nostalgic, romantic reminiscence of daily life during the so-called pastoral period by Guadalupe Vallejo, whose uncle, General Mariano Guadalupe Vallejo, was for a long time military leader of California, is this chapter's fourth document. The fifth document is selected from a group of letters published in April 1847, one year after the outbreak of the Mexican-American War, as a special supplement to the Philadelphia *North American and United States Gazette*. These letters, signed by "W.G." (who was actually William Robert Garner, a resident of Monterey from 1824 to 1846), contain the most complete description of the customs and life of Californians to reach the broader American public prior to the discovery of gold in 1848.

Several key articles from the Treaty of Guadalupe Hidalgo, which established most of the current boundary between the United States and Mexico, are reproduced as the final document. The treaty's eighth and ninth articles, in particular, were intended by their framers to protect fully the civil and property rights of Mexicans and Indians who remained in the conquered region and who were now residents of the United States. Yet later on these provisions were often interpreted in ways that violated the original intent. After the Mexican-American War, Yankees asserted their own style of domination, arguing that the treaty made California a "white man's country."

A Mexican Commission Urges the Secularization of the California Missions, 1833

The commission of the district and territories in order to recommend to this respectable chamber the project of law on secularization of the missions of both Californias . . . decreed in the year 1813 [*sic;* 1833] the secularization of the missions, ordered the administration and management of the property to be wrenched from the hands of the religious people and deposited with the civil authorities in order that by a just and proper distribution those to whom it belonged by so many titles should enter into the enjoyment of it. What then should be expected of a government truly parental and philanthropic in which we enjoy so satisfactorily the social pleasures?

This government with respect even to the Californias, in order to take the extended view which is exacted by a policy for all those governed, hears from the commission of wise men which is formed for that purpose the projects for the organization of that country, and from them arises the initiative which is about to be discussed. The missionaries, whether Jesuits, Fernandinos, or Dominicans, at the beginning labor with the evangelical spirit. Their toils and apostolic labors are recompensed with seasoned fruits of conversion; they overrun the deserts, they penetrate the forests, they domesticate those savage beings, they mitigate their ferocious customs, and raise them to a certain grade in civil life. Without fear it might be augured that they would be those who without doubt would dissipate ignorance, combat errors and prejudices to the point where they planted there the holy law of Nature which is the foundation of the others. But how soon did they come to submerge those unfortunate beings in a chaos a thousand times more horrible than the other from which they had emerged! Administration of the property turns them aside from their vocation and far from persuading the weak, opposing the rebels and conducting all towards happiness, they continue the conquest like their predecessors, and the natives see renewed in themselves the days of horror and mourning in the punishment and severity which they suffer from those who profess the adorable religion which inspires sweetness and preaches humanity and meekness. This despotic monklike government, once independence was gained, increases the misfortune of the Californias, since the missionaries, being in the greater part Spaniards and refusing to take the oath of independence, make them feel all the evils which afflict subordinates when the mandarins, mad and infuriated, have to turn loose their prey which for so long a time has increased their boundless ambition.

Such misfortunes are in part alleviated by the undertakings of the government, in the greater part the law of colonization which has just been discussed will remedy them. . . .

[T]he commission offers for the deliberation of the chamber the following articles:

Art. 1. The government will proceed to secularize the missions of Upper and Lower California.

2. In each one of these missions a parish will be established served by a parish priest of the secular clergy with a salary of 2000 up to 2500 *pesos* annually according to the judgment of the government.

3. These parish priests shall not collect nor receive any fee for marriages, baptisms, burials, or under any other name whatever. In respect to fees for pomp they can receive those which are expressly set out in the schedule which will be formed with this object in view by the bishop of that diocese as soon as possible and which shall be approved by the supreme government.

4. The churches which have served in each mission with their sacred vessels, ornaments and other equipment which each one has today, are destined for the parishes, and in addition the rooms next to the church itself, which in the judgment of the government may be thought necessary for the most decorous use of the parish itself.

5. For each parish the government will order a cemetery to be constructed outside the town.

6. Five hundred *pesos* annually are assigned to sustain the worship and the servants of each parish.

7. The most appropriate of the buildings belonging to each mission shall be assigned for the habitation of the parish priest, adding to it ground not to exceed 200 *varas* square, and the others shall be assigned especially for the town house, the school of first letters, public establishments and workshops.

8. In order to provide at once and effectively for the spiritual needs of both Californias there is to be established in the capital of Upper California a vicar who shall extend his jurisdiction over both territories, and the bishop will confer on him the corresponding powers with all the amplitude possible.

9. For the endowment of this vicar 3000 *pesos* shall be assigned, all business to be performed by him without exacting under any pretext whatever, not even for paper, any fee.

10. If for any reason the parish priest of the capital or of any other parish of those districts should act in this capacity as vicar 1500 *pesos* annually will be assigned to him beyond his salary as curate.

11. No custom whatever, which obliges the inhabitants of the Californias to make gifts for no matter how pious the object, shall be introduced even if it is said to be necessary, and neither time nor the

willingness of the citizens themselves can give such any force or virtue whatever.

12. The government will effectively take care that the bishop contributes on his part to fulfill the objects of this law.

13. When the new parish priests have been appointed the supreme government will furnish them gratuitously their transport by sea together with their families and besides for their journey by land, it shall allow each one from 400 to 800 *pesos* according to the distance and the number of family which he takes.

14. The government will pay the expenses of transporting the missionaries who return, and that they may perform their journey by land in a comfortable manner to their college or convent it shall give each one 200 to 300 *pesos,* and in its judgment whatever may be necessary to leave the republic for those who reject the oath of independence.

15. The supreme government will pay the expenses contemplated under this law out of the products of real property, the capital and the rents which are now set aside as the Pious Fund of the missions of California.

The committee room of the chamber of deputies,
Mexico, May 9, 1833
Berriel—Losano—Anaya

Angustias de la Guerra Ord Defends the Virtue of Mission Priests, 1878

Genl. Figueroa continued to govern the land with great ability and acquired wide respect. He always maintained, as I said before, good relations with the Diputacion and the other civil officers. His health worsened each day and he anxiously awaited his relief, but it did not come. He finally succumbed to a cerebral attack in August of 1835, and was widely mourned. Though at that time I resided in Monterey, I had come to Santa Barbara to see my parents, and was here when Figueroa died.

His body was embalmed, and honors were rendered to his remains in Monterey according to his rank. Before his death he had directed that his body he interred at Santa Barbara Mission. This was done, the body being brought from Monterey in a ship to Santa Barbara. Captain Muñoz represented the Army and my husband, Jimeno, represented the Ayuntamiento. I do not remember whether any representatives of the Diputacion came. Here he was deposited in a niche in the vault of the Mission by Padres Narciso Durán and Antonio Jimeno, who were the pastors of the Mission, which I believe was then secularized, but was preserved with all its privileges. This was not true of San Miguel which in 1833 was very rich. Padre Juan Cabot showed me all of its warehouses. They were full of goods, grain, etc., and also had a goodly sum of money belonging to the Mission. When I returned there in 1835 I found not even a glass in which to drink water and had to drink from a cup I had brought myself. All of the assets of the Mission, herds, etc., had disappeared.

It has been said by some that before the secularization of the Missions when the padres saw that it was coming upon them, they decided to turn as much of the herds into cash as possible. That to this end extraordinary slaughterings were had, under orders of the missionaries, under contracts with individuals on a half-share basis. That they killed many thousands of cattle, of which they retained only the hides. So great was the slaughter that the authorities became alarmed lest the country be left without neat [*sic*] cattle if limits were not put on it, and that the Jefe Político took steps to stop this destruction of animals.

My father had been Síndico for the missionaries for many years past, under appointment from the College of San Fernando and had in his hands the *sínodos* of the padres. Later when the Missions in the north were turned over to the Guadalupans, he remained as Síndico of the Fernandinos and continued as such until his death. All the padres came to him for their *sínodos* and never took money even to give alms (and the major part of what each owned was involved in this) without his views and advice. They all looked on him as their best friend and loved him like a brother.

On my part, I had two brothers-in-law who were missionaries who loved me as my own brothers.

If there had been dishonest killing of herds to get money before the Missions were secularized, I would have known of it. My father would have had knowledge of all of it. I had no hesitancy in saying that this charge is false, like many others which have been made to the prejudice of the good name of our priests, who were living examples of virtue and who lived for the good of their neophytes.

Surely, the Missions at certain times of the year had slaughterings on a grand scale for hides and tallow with which they purchased from the ships materials in which to dress their neophytes. They also used the meat. They made jerky of it to feed the same Indians during the winter.

I am informed that the Mission of San Gabriel (which they say had about 100,000 neat [*sic*] cattle) had made contracts with some residents of Los Angeles and also of San Diego (in fact it was said that the herds of the Mission reached to San Diego) to kill on shares a great quantity of cattle because they could not confine the cattle within the lands of the Mission. The killers were to take a half of the hides of the cattle they slaughtered and to deliver the other half to the Mission. I do not know whether these contracts were made prior to the death of Padre José Sánchez. I do not remember if the killing began before his death, but the massacre was after his death. I heard it said that more than 30,000 cattle were killed there and there were fears that there might be cholera or some other epidemic because of so much meat rotting in the fields.

The same was done at San Luis Rey, which was also a Mission very rich in herds. I do not believe that any other Missions held killings on a grand scale (there was the usual one each year) and if there had been I would have known of it.

Much has been said of the Missions having large amounts of coins. Special mention has been made of San Gabriel having huge deposits of money. I don't know where such great quantities of money could come from, because their transactions with traders were always goods for goods. There was but little money in the country. Even the ships had scarcely enough to pay their taxes. Many of them took money loaned here for this. No doubt the Missions had some money but it must have been in moderate sums. It may be that some of the Missions in the north which trafficked with the Russians had more opportunities to get cash, but I doubt if even there they received much, because when the Russians bought wheat they paid partly in cash and partly in goods.

The missionary padres whom I knew in my time almost all died here. The only ones who in my time left the country were Ripoll and Altimira, who according to what they wrote themselves, carried money sufficient to pay their passage. Padre Luis Martínez was put out and the money he carried came from my father's house; it had been put there as his *sínodos*. Padre José Viader took his *sínodos* from my father's house when he went.

Padre Antonio Peyri, founder of the Mission of San Luis Rey, on the day of his departure took with him $3,000 as his *sínodos* for his administration. He wrote the Commanding General, who transcribed a paragraph to my father. He also took with him 2 or 3 little Indians to Rome and established them there to be educated for the priesthood. Only one of them survived and he became a priest of great capacity and virtue in Rome. Naturally he paid the travel expenses of his companions from the $3,000.

Those who died in California in my time were Padre José Señán at San Buenaventura. I was very little.

Padre Antonio Jayme at Santa Barbara.

Padre Uría—in my father's house. He was a very generous man; in fact, at his death he had nothing left of his *sínodos*.

Padre Buenaventura Fortuny—in the house of Don José Antonio Aguirre at Santa Barbara. He left no *sínodo* at his death because when he received even one peso of it, he sought permission of the *Síndico* to give it to the poor.

Padre Vicente Francisco de Sarría—was found in 1835 almost dead at the Mission of San Antonio.

I heard it said that he had died of hunger, because he had nothing with which to buy food, because the administrator did not supply him, whether for ignorance or other reason. He was buried at the Mission.

Padre Luis Gil de Taboada—died at San Luis Obispo before the Mission was secularized.

Padre Ramón Abella—died at Mission Santa Inés in 1842. As he was very old my father sent him from here from his *sínodos* what he needed. I believe he had nothing left at his death.

Padre Marcos Antonio de Vitoria—was truly an angel—he was childlike. He died at Santa Inés. I wasn't here but I believe he left nothing at his death.

Richard Henry Dana, Jr., Criticizes the Mexicans in California, 1834

Vessels began to come into the ports to trade with the missions and receive hides in return; and thus began the great trade of California. Nearly all the cattle in the country belonged to the missions, and they employed their Indians—who became, in fact, their serfs—in tending their vast herds. In the year 1793, when Vancouver visited San Diego, the missions had obtained great wealth and power. . . . On the expulsion of the Jesuits from the Spanish dominions, the missions passed into the hands of the Franciscans, though without any essential change in their management. Ever since the independence of Mexico, the missions had been going down; until, at last, a law was passed, stripping them of their possessions, and confining the priests to their spiritual duties, at the same time declaring all the Indians free and independent rancheros. The change in the condition of the Indians was . . . only nominal; they are virtually serfs, as much as they ever were. But in the missions the change was complete. The priests now have no power, except in their religious character, and the great possessions of the missions are given over to be preyed upon by the harpies of the civil power, who are sent there in the capacity of *administradores,* to settle up the concerns; and who usually end, in a few years, by making themselves fortunes, and leaving their stewardships worse than they found them. The dynasty of the priests was much more acceptable to the people of the country, and, indeed, to everyone concerned with the country, by trade or otherwise, than that of the *administradores.* The priests were connected permanently to one mission, and felt the necessity of keeping up its credit. Accordingly, the debts of the missions were regularly paid, and the people were, in the main, well treated, and attached to those who had spent their whole lives among them. But the *administradores* are strangers sent from Mexico, having no interest in the country, not identified in any way with their charge, and, for the most part, men of desperate fortunes—brokendown politicians and soldiers—whose only object is to retrieve their condition in as short a time as possible. The change had been made but a few short years before our arrival upon the coast, yet, in that short time, the trade was much diminished, credit impaired, and the venerable missions were going rapidly to decay. . . .

The government of the country is an arbitrary democracy, having no common law, and nothing that we should call a judiciary. Their only laws are made and unmade at the caprice of the legislature, and are as variable as the legislature itself. They pass through the form of sending representatives to the congress at Mexico, but as it takes several months to go and return, and there is very little communication between the capital and this distant province, a member usually stays there as permanent member. . . .

As for justice, they know little law but will and fear. A Yankee, who had been naturalized and become a Catholic, and had married in the country, was sitting in his house at the Pueblo de los Angeles, with his wife and children, when a Mexican with whom he had had a difficulty entered the house and stabbed him to the heart before them all. The murderer was seized by some Yankees who had settled there, and kept in confinement until a statement of the whole affair could be sent to the governor general. The governor general refused to do anything about it, and the countrymen of the murdered man, seeing no prospect of justice being administered, . . . proceeded to try the man according to the forms in their own country. A judge and jury were appointed, and he was tried, convicted, sentenced to be shot, and carried out before the town blind-folded. The names of all the men were then put into a hat, and each one pledging himself to perform his duty, twelve names were drawn out, and the men took their stations with their rifles, and, firing at the word, laid him dead. He was decently buried, and the place was restored quietly to the proper authorities. . . .

When a crime has been committed by Indians, justice, or rather vengeance, is not so tardy. One Sunday afternoon while I was at San Diego, an Indian was sitting on his horse when another, with whom he had had some difficulty, came up to him, drew a long knife, and plunged it directly into the horse's heart. The Indian sprang from his falling horse, drew out the knife, and plunged it into the other Indian's breast, over his shoulder, and laid him dead. The fellow was seized at once, clapped into the *calabozo,* and kept there until an answer could be received from Monterey. A few weeks afterward I saw the poor wretch, sitting on the bare ground, in front of the *calabozo,* with his feet chained to a stake, and handcuffs about his wrists. I knew there was very little hope for him. Although the deed was done in hot blood, the horse on which he was sitting being his own, and a favorite with him, yet he was an Indian, and that was enough. In about a week after I saw him, I heard that he had been shot. These few instances will serve to give one a notion of the distribution of justice in California.

In their domestic relations, these people are not better than in their public. The men are thriftless, proud, extravagant, and very much given to gaming; and the women have but little education, and a good deal of beauty, and their morality, of course, is none of the best; yet the instances of infidelity are much less frequent than one would at first suppose. . . . [T]he jealousy of their husbands is extreme, and their revenge deadly and almost certain. A few inches of cold steel has been the punishment of many an unwary man, who has been guilty, perhaps, of nothing more than indiscretion. . . . With the unmarried women, too, great watchfulness is used. The main object of the parents is to marry their daughters well, and to this a fair name is necessary. . . .

Of the poor Indians very little care is taken. The priests, indeed, at the missions are said to keep them very strictly, and some rules are usually made by the alcaldes to punish their misconduct; yet it all amounts to but little. . . . Intemperance, too, is a common vice among the Indians. The Mexicans, on the contrary, are abstemious, and I do not remember ever having seen a Mexican intoxicated.

Such are the people who inhabit a country embracing four or five hundred miles of seacoast, with several good harbors; with fine forests in the north; the waters filled with fish, and the plains covered with thousands of herds of cattle; blessed with a climate than which there can be no better in the world; free from all manner of diseases, whether epidemic or endemic; and with a soil in which corn yields from seventy to eighty fold. In the hands of an enterprising people, what a country this might be.

Guadalupe Vallejo Reminisces About the Ranchero Period

Our social life still tends to keep alive a spirit of love for the simple, homely, outdoor life of our Spanish ancestors on this coast, and we try, as best we may, to honor the founders of our ancient families, and the saints and heroes of our history, since the days when Father Junipero planted the cross at Monterey.

The leading features of old Spanish life at the Missions, and on the large ranches of the last century, have been described in many books of travel, and with many contradictions. I shall confine myself to those details and illustrations of the past that no modern writer can possibly obtain except vaguely, from hearsay, since they exist in no manuscript, but only in the memories of a generation that is fast passing away. My mother has told me much, and I am still more indebted to my illustrious uncle, General Vallejo, of Sonoma, many of whose recollections are incorporated in this article.

When I was a child there were fewer than fifty Spanish families in the region about the bay of San Francisco, and these were closely connected by ties of blood or intermarriage. My father and his brother, the late General Vallejo, saw, and were part of, the most important events in the history of Spanish California, the revolution and the conquest. My grandfather, Don Ygnacio Vallejo, was equally prominent in his day, in the exploration and settlement of the province. The traditions and records of the family thus cover the entire period of the annals of early California, from San Diego to Sonoma. . . .

The Jesuit Missions established in Lower California, at Loreto and other places, were followed by Franciscan Missions in Alta California, with presidios for the soldiers, adjacent pueblos, or towns, and the granting of large tracts of land to settlers. By 1782 there were nine flourishing Missions in Alta California—San Francisco, Santa Clara, San Carlos, San Antonio, San Luis Obispo, San Buenaventura, San Gabriel, San Juan, and San Diego. Governor Fajés added Santa Barbara and Purissima, and by 1790 there were more than 7000 Indian converts in the various Missions. By 1800 about forty Franciscan fathers were at work in Alta California, six of whom had been among the pioneers of twenty and twenty-five years before, and they had established seven new Missions—San José, San Miguel, Soledad, San Fernando, Santa Cruz, San Juan Bautista, and San Luis Rey. . . . In 1773 Father Palou had reported that all the Missions, taken together, owned two hundred and four head of cattle and a few sheep, goats, and mules. In 1776 the regular five years' supplies sent from Mexico to the Missions were as follows: 107 blankets, 480 yards striped sackcloth, 389 yards blue baize, 10 pounds blue maguey cloth, 4 reams paper, 5 bales red pepper, 10 arrobas of tasajo (dried beef), beads, chocolate, lard, lentils, rice, flour, and four barrels of Castilian wine. By 1800 all this was changed: the flocks and herds of cattle of California contained 187,000 animals, of which 153,000 were in the Mission pastures, and large areas of land had been brought under cultivation, so that the Missions supplied the presidios and foreign ships.

No one need suppose that the Spanish pioneers of California suffered many hardships or privations, although it was a new country. They came slowly, and were prepared to become settlers. All that was necessary for the maintenance and enjoyment of life according to the simple and healthful standards of those days was brought with them. They had seeds, trees, vines, cattle, household goods, and servants, and in a few years their orchards yielded abundantly and their gardens were full of vegetables. Poultry was raised by the Indians, and sold very cheaply; a fat capon cost only twelve and a half cents. Beef and mutton were to be had for the killing, and wild game was very abundant. At many of the Missions there were large flocks of tame pigeons. At the Mission San José the fathers' doves consumed a cental of wheat daily, besides what they gathered in the village. The doves were of many colors, and they made a beautiful appearance on the red tiles of the church and the tops of the dark garden walls. . . .

Family life among the old Spanish pioneers was an affair of dignity and ceremony, but it did not lack in affection. Children were brought up with great respect for their elders. It was the privilege of any elderly person to correct young people by words, or even by whipping them, and it was never told that any one thus chastised made a complaint. Each one of the old families taught their children the history of the family, and reverence towards religion. A few books, some in manuscript, were treasured in the household, but children were not allowed to read novels until they were grown. They saw little of other children, except their near relatives, but they had many enjoyments unknown to children now, and they grew up with remarkable strength and healthfulness.

In these days of trade, bustle, and confusion, when many thousands of people live in the California valleys, which formerly were occupied by only a few Spanish families, the quiet and happy domestic life of the past seems like a dream. We, who loved it, often speak of those days, and especially of the duties of the large Spanish households, where so many dependents were to be cared for, and everything was done in a simple and primitive way. . . .

It is necessary, for the truth of the account, to mention the evil behavior of many Americans before, as well as after the conquest. At the Mission San José there is a small creek, and two very large sycamores once grew at the Spanish ford, so that it was called *la aliso*. A squatter named Fallon, who lived near the crossing, cut down these for firewood, though there were many trees in the cañon. The Spanish people begged him to leave them, for the shade and beauty, but he did not care for that. This was a little thing, but much that happened was after such pattern, or far worse.

In those times one of the leading American squatters came to my father, Don J. J. Vallejo, and said: "There is a large piece of your land where the cattle run loose, and your vaqueros have gone to the gold mines. I will fence the field for you at my expense if you will give me half." He liked the idea, and assented, but when the tract was inclosed the American had it entered as government land in his own name, and kept all of it. In many similar cases American settlers in their dealings with the rancheros took advantage of laws which they understood, but which were new to the Spaniards, and so robbed the latter of their lands. Notes and bonds were considered unnecessary by a Spanish gentleman in a business transaction, as his word was always sufficient security.

William Robert Garner Promotes the American Annexation of California, 1847

February 24, 1847—In the name of wonder, what is the meaning of all this fuss and bustle about us here in California; or in what is it going to result? Will this country be annexed to the United States of America, or will it not? Some doubts appear to remain, and the question is undecided. Seven-eighths of the inhabitants of California this day believe with me, that it is as easy for the American flag to come down in the city of Washington, as it is that it should ever come down in California; but then we only believe so because we, like most other people, are apt to believe what we wish to be the case; the more especially, as we have good reason to dread the consequences, should the Mexicans ever regain their sovereignty here, which almost all in California are ready to say, *and do say,* God forbid.

There is another strong reason why the U. [*sic*] States is in the present case bound to perform what she has undertaken. She has said, I must have California. The words were hardly spoken before we the inhabitants of California heard them, and on hearing them could not refrain from demonstrating our joy, in the hope of being by her freed from the rapacity and caprices of a few individuals who held us in bondage. Should she now abandon us, that joy would be turned into bitter lamentation; because it will not for one moment be supposed by any who are acquainted with the vindictive spirit of our former masters, that they would hesitate or make any scruple about assassinating all those individuals who had expressed the slightest wish to shake off the fetters with which they have been bound for the last twelve years.

Nothing can prevent this disaster but the retention of California by the United States, and the prompt establishment of settled government under her sanction, and a strict execution of law. Such is the daily and hourly wish of all those persons who hold property. Those who have nothing are the only persons from whom any future dissensions may be expected. But as California has afforded to every man who wished to acquire it, a means of supporting himself and family in an independent manner, those who do not do so may be considered, with a very few exceptions, as a set of worthless men, whose only desire is to support themselves by plundering and cheating the industrious.

As plunder and fraud will not be permitted under the government of the United States with impunity, the result will be one of two things. By a strict execution of justice these delinquents will fall under the iron hand of the law, or they will have to become what they never have been, *honest and industrious citizens.*

The Californians are naturally very docile. Generally speaking, they are very apt to act on the impulse of the moment, without any heed to the future; but the reason is, they have never been taught to look forward for their own benefit. They have been brought up under the government and tuition of vicious and corrupt men, and nothing but example will make them see their folly. Precept will not do it; but as soon as one, two, or three of the worst malefactors have undergone capital punishment, the whole country will be at peace.

Selected Articles from the Treaty of Guadalupe Hidalgo, 1848

Of Peace, Friendship, Limits, and Settlement, between the United States of America, and the Mexican Republic, concluded at Guadalupe Hidalgo, on the Second Day of February, with Amendments by the American Senate, March 10th, 1848, and by the Mexican Senate, May 25th, 1848.

The Treaty

In the name of Almighty God:

The United States of America and the United Mexican States, animated by a sincere desire to put an end to the calamities of the war which unhappily exists between the two republics, and to establish on a solid basis relations of peace and friendship, which shall confer reciprocal benefits on the citizens of both, and assure the concord, harmony, and mutual confidence wherein the two people should live as good neighbours, have, for that purpose, appointed their respective plenipotentiaries . . . who, after a reciprocal communication of their respective powers, have, under the protection of Almighty God, the author of peace, arranged, agreed upon, and signed the following treaty of peace, friendship, limits, and settlement, between the United States of America and the Mexican republic.

Art. I.—There shall be a firm and universal peace between the United States of America and the Mexican republic, and between their respective countries, territories, cities, towns, and people, without exception of places or persons.

Art. II.—Immediately on the signature of this treaty, a convention shall be entered into between a commissioner or commissioners appointed by the general-in-chief of the forces of the United States, and such as may be appointed by the Mexican government, to the end that a provisional suspension of hostilities shall take place; and that in the places occupied by the said forces, constitutional order may be re-established, as regards the political, administrative, and judicial branches, so far as this shall be permitted by the circumstances of military occupation. . . .

Art. VIII.—Mexicans now established in territories previously belonging to Mexico, and which remain, for the future, within the limits of the United States, as defined by the present treaty, shall be free to continue where they now reside, or to remove, at any time, to the Mexican republic, retaining the property which they possess in the said territories, or disposing thereof, and removing the proceeds wherever they please, without their being subjected, on this account, to any contribution, or tax, or charge, whatever.

Those who shall prefer to remain in said territories, may either retain the title and rights of Mexican citizens, or acquire those of citizens of the United States. But they shall be under the obligation to make their selection within one year from the date of exchange of ratifications of this treaty; and those who shall remain in the said territories, after the expiration of that year, without having declared their intention to retain the character of Mexicans, shall be considered to have elected to become citizens of the United States.

In the said territories, property of every kind, now belonging to Mexicans not established there, shall be inviolably respected. The present owners, the heirs of these, and all Mexicans who may hereafter acquire said property by contract, shall enjoy, with respect to it, guaranties equally ample as if the same belonged to citizens of the United States.

Art. IX.—The Mexicans who, in the territories aforesaid, shall not preserve the character of citizens of the Mexican republic, conformably with what is stipulated in the preceding article, shall be incorporated into the union of the United States, and admitted as soon as possible, according to the principles of the federal constitution, to the enjoyment of all the rights of citizens of the United States. In the mean time, they shall be maintained and protected in the enjoyment of their liberty, their property, and the civil rights now vested in them according to the Mexican laws. With respect to political rights, their condition shall be on an equality with that of the inhabitants of the other territories of the United States, and at least equally good as that of the inhabitants of Louisiana and the Floridas, when these provinces, by transfer from the French republic and the crown of Spain, became territories of the United States.

The same most ample guaranty shall be enjoyed by all ecclesiastics and religious corporations or communities, as well in the discharge of the offices of their ministry as in the enjoyment of their property of every kind, whether individual or corporate. This guaranty shall embrace all temples, houses, and edifices dedicated to the Roman Catholic worship, as well as all property destined to its support, or to that of schools, hospitals, and other foundations for charitable or beneficent purposes. No property of this nature shall be considered as having become the property of the American government, or as subject to be by it disposed of, or diverted to other uses.

Finally, the relations and communication between the Catholics living in the territories aforesaid, and their respective ecclesiastical authorities, shall be open, free, and exempt from all hindrance whatever, even although such authorities should reside within the limits of the Mexican republic, as defined by this treaty; and this freedom shall continue, so long as a new demarkation of ecclesiastical districts shall not have been made, conformably with the laws of the Roman Catholic church.

 E S S A Y S

In the nineteenth century, the writing of California history was done largely by talented amateurs, the most important of whom was Hubert Howe Bancroft. Bancroft, a wealthy San Francisco bookseller, began in the 1850s avidly to collect pamphlets, documents, manuscripts, and books relating to California and the Pacific Coast. By the early 1870s his collection had grown to more than 10,000 items. Deciding to write a multivolume history based on his massive collection, he hired a group of research assistants and began work in 1871. Bancroft's series ultimately reached thirty-nine volumes, including *California Pastoral, 1769–1848* (1888), from which the first essay is drawn. From this account, and others like it, the popular conception of life in Mexican California has been derived, romanticized as the "pastoral era," or, in Bancroft's term, "lotos-land society."

In a new and bold reinterpretation of the rancho era and the settlement of southern California by Mexicans and then by Anglos, Douglas Monroy, who teaches at The Colorado College, in the second essay stresses the dramatic encounters of conflicting, even antithetical, cultures and worldviews. Drawn from his prize-winning book, *Thrown Among Strangers: The Making of Mexican Culture in Frontier California* (1990), Monroy argues, contrary to Bancroft, that the situation of Mexicans in California must be understood in terms of their continuing relationship with the native inhabitants. In doing so, Monroy examines what the mission system bequeathed to the history of Mexicans before and after the Mexican-American War of 1846–1848.

Mexican California as "Lotos-Land"

HUBERT HOWE BANCROFT

The theory of the mission system was to make the savages work out their own salvation, and that of the priests also. In fact, whatever work was to be done it was foreordained that the natives should do it. Work was a necessity of civilization. Souls to save was a necessity of the church. Servants to raise cattle and till the land was ever an indispensable factor in missionary economy, [*sic*] Here were all the elements for a new church militant, a new heaven and a new earth. . . .

Pity the poor Spanish man who does not like to work! The motto of the Zacatecas padres, as indeed of many more modern churchmen, was "Divertirse hoy que ya mañana es otro dia." This California country, about as well any could, suited the Mexican settler, with his inherent indolence, relieved only by slow, spasmodic energy. With the richest of soil around him, which to the scratching of the wooden plough would yield sixty and a hundred to one, he disdained tillage, partly because this labor had been turned over to Indian serfs, partly because there was no market for cereals. The plodding tasks and narrow confines of the farm were not for him. More suited to the chivalric instincts of the Mexican, coming to him honestly in his Spanish blood, was general domination over animals, with lordly command of men and horses to aid him in controlling vast herds and flocks. It pleased him to have at his bidding a suite of dusky retainers, drawn from wandering tribes; for the settlers served one another only as friends and brethren, connected as they often were by consanguinity in greater or smaller decree.

With few inhabitants, and a vast extent of country, land was of little value, and could be occupied as fancy dictated, the stock-raiser extending his range beyond original limits whenever the communal tract round the pueblo became too narrow for a rising ambition. Cattle, indeed, roamed in a half-wild state upon the plains, and wiry-limbed, swift horses, of larger size and longer neck than the Mexican prototype, were subordinated at times by nomadic rancheros. Cattle formed a ready recourse with which to obtain from flitting trading vessels such comforts and luxuries as growing taste suggested. The annual rodeo constituted the stock-taking period, when additions to the herds were counted and branded, old marks inspected, and stragglers from adjoining ranges restored to claimants. The occasion became a rural festival, from the necessary congregation of neighbors for mutual aid and supervision of interests. Wives and sisters lent their charms to the meeting, and animation to the scene, by inspiring the horsemen to more dashing feats, either in rounding up the herds, or during the sports that formed the appropriate finale to the event.

These were the equestrian days of California. The saddle was the second and life-long cradle of the race. The men in walking grew awkward, as indicated by the uneven gait, attended by the jingling of the immense spurs at the heels. Riding began in early childhood. The boy, mounted by a friendly hand, sped away in exhilarating race, whirling the lariat at whatsoever attracted his fancy, and speedily acquiring skill for veritable game. The saddle became an object of dearest pride, elaborate with stamped leather and glittering adornments, which extended from the high pommel to the clumsy wooden stirrup, partly hidden by the leather cover that shielded the foot. The bridle was of braided rawhide, with a large and cruel bit. Little was thought of long horseback journeys and camping under the open sky, with the saddle for a pillow and blankets for a cover. The horse might be exchanged from among the bands roaming in all directions. Even the women preferred riding to driving in the clumsy, springless carretas, with frames of rawhide, and sections of logs for wheels. Wagon roads did not exist. When women rode, they would generally be seated in front of their cavalier, shaded by his huge sombrero.

The Californian ever aspired to gallantry; with a graceful figure, when mounted, he was well favored. Latin peoples are more demonstrative in their manners than Anglo-Saxons, more picturesque in their politeness. The common people are more cordial, and the better bred young men more gallant. To French politeness Spaniards add chivalrous courtesy. With only a lasso for a weapon, he ranked not as a soldier, but was not the less venturesome and dashing in facing wild herds, in bearding the grizzly, in mounting and taming the wild horse. Frank and good-natured, polite and ever punctilious, he proved a good friend and admirable host, until checked somewhat in certain directions by the rebuff and deception on the part of blunt and grasping foreigners. Spoiled partly by bountiful nature, he yielded his best efforts to profitless pursuits, heedless of the morrow. Moved by impulses which soon evaporated, his energy was both unsustained and misdirected, and he fell a ready prey to unscrupulous schemers. He lived for the enjoyment of the hour, in reverie or sport, rejoicing in bull-fighting and bear-baiting, eager for the chase as for the fandango, and sustaining the flagging excitement with gambling, winning or losing with an imperturbability little in accord with his otherwise movable nature; yet he gambled for excitement, while the foreigner, who freely gave vent to his feelings in round oaths or ejaculations, was impelled mainly by avarice.

Sunday morning was spent, where possible, in devotion, with senses quickened to loftier feelings by the solemnity of the place, the illuminated splendor of the altar, the beauty of the chant, the awe-imposing ritual. This duty was quite irksome, however, involving as it did so great a restraint. After service, amends were made, the remainder of the day being passed in active games or social entertainments. The load of sins removed by penance or confession, the soul was ready to take on a fresh load of iniquity, to be as easily removed another day. And when in winter time the sun hurried the day along, and night slackened its pace, then lovers met. The old-fashioned rule in Spain was that a kiss was equivalent to betrothal; but there were here many kisses for every betrothal, and many betrothals for every marriage, and sometimes a marriage without a priest. The guitar and violin were in constant use, the players being always ready for dance and song, the simple music being usually marked by a plaintive strain. The singing was frequently improvised, especially in honor of guests, or in sarcastic play upon men and events.

Lazy some of them might be, and were; day after day, at morning and at night, lazily they told their rosary, lazily attended mass, and lazily ate and slept. They were as sleepy, and indolent, and amorous, as if they fed exclusively on mandrakes. But the languor of ennui was not common with them. They could do nothing easily and not tire of it. Theirs was that abnormity wherein rest was the natural condition.

Supremest happiness was theirs; the happiness that knows no want, that harbors no unattainable longing, no desires that might not be gratified, the happiness of ignorance, of absence of pain. Nor might it truthfully be said of them that theirs was only a negative happiness. Was it not happiness to breathe the intoxicating air, to revel in health and plenty, to bask in the sunshine and fatten on luscious fruits, to enjoy all of God's best gifts uncursed, in their Eden to possess their souls in peace? And of the doings of the outer world, of past ages, of progress—these are not happiness; does not knowledge bring with it vastly more pain than pleasure? Yet sadness they were not wholly free from; a shade of melancholy is characteristic of their features. But what of that? Does not the serenest joy often spring from quiet hearts, and sad thoughts find expression in sweetest song?

There were not lacking verse-makers among them, though in poetry no attempt was made to achieve the upper regions of Parnassus, their half-fledged muse being apparently content to flutter round the mountains bare.

Like their language, the Spanish are poetic, rhythmic people; yet stern, majestic, and with a melancholy tone. In their softer moods they are touchingly sweet and tender, but when roused their tongue is terrible.

The empirical law of human nature, which asserts that youth is impetuous and old age cautious, finds in the Hispano-Californians an exception; the young men were impetuous, and the old men scarcely less so. A life-long experience failed to generate circumspection.

Though bursting with conditions favorable to wealth, there was comparatively little wealth in the land. Gold lay scattered in the streams and imbedded in the crevices of the Sierra foothills, and the valleys were fat with grain-producing soil. Yet there lacked the applied labor that should turn these resources into tangible riches. Some, nevertheless, acquired what might be called wealth in those days, though not by voluntarily saving part of their earnings, but because they could not spend their accumulations. They did not love money. Any time they would pour out a gallon of it for a pint of pleasure; but the trouble was too often that there was nothing to buy. . . .

The products of these engendering conditions were of the most material and practical kind, such as were wealth and wealth producing. As they were not largely exchanged for money, silk, foreign wine, and tobacco, not sunk or squandered in these things, they were left to increase, which they did rapidly. All were productive consumers as well as productive laborers. Little was lost or squandered in luxuries or pleasures. Luxury and pleasure there were an abundance of, but they were of such a character as not to be dependent upon money or wealth. . . .

In conclusion, we may sum up our Lotos-land society in this wise: ignorant, lazy, religious, the religion being more for women, children, and Indians than for European men—though Coronel speaks of pausing in the midst of a fandango or rodeo to pray; and all went to church, though they gambled freely afterwards. It was common for heads of families and all circumspect persons to wear sanctimonious faces in the presence of the young, refraining from the mention of wickedness lest they should be contaminated. Morals at first were quite pure; later they became very bad, syphilis being quite common among all classes and both sexes.

They were a frank, amiable, social, hospitable people, and honest enough where it did not require too great an exertion to pay their debts. No obligations of any kind weighed very heavily upon them. They were an emotional race; their qualities of mind and heart floated on the surface; they not only possessed feeling but they showed it.

They were not a strong community in any sense, either morally, physically, or politically; hence it was that as the savages faded before the superior Mexicans, so faded the Mexicans before the superior Americans. Great was their opportunity, exceedingly great at first if they had chosen to build up a large and prosperous commonwealth; and later no less marvelous, had they possessed the ability to make avail of the progress and performance of others. Many were defrauded of their stock and lands; many quickly squandered the money realized from a sudden increase in values. They were foolish, improvident, incapable; at the same time they were grossly sinned against by the people of the United States. There was a class of lawyers, the vilest of human kind, whose lives were devoted to a study of the cunning and duplicity necessary to defraud these simple-minded patriarchs. Nevertheless, as I have said, it would be difficult to find in any age or place, a community that got more out of life, and with less trouble, with less wear and wickedness, than the people of Pastoral California.

The Making of Mexican Culture in Frontier California

DOUGLAS MONROY

Certain attributes a culture takes on as it journeys through history can be explained, as Horkheimer says, simply as the "habitual forms of the individual's adjustment to the social situation." Although the gente de razón confronted circumstances partly of their own making, it is important to remember that their estimation of the Indians derived not only from their daily contact with the natives but also from their position as the socially ascendant people of the region. . . .

In the same manner that missionization entailed more than bringing heathens to Christianity, more prevailed in these relations between rancheros and Indian laborers than work. For the gente de razón, a class in search of social standing and elite self-definition, the conception of the Indian as their opposite played a central role in the formation of their social personalities. On a frontier where brutal appetites seemed to reign, Californios lacked the benefit of the formal and at least mildly scholarly education that enabled the priests to reassure themselves of their rational nature. They had no positive role models for eminence. Whereas the priests concerned themselves with the heathenism of the Indians and not their physical features, now race came to be an operative force in demarcating the peoples of California. To be de razón meant not to be like Indians, who drank to excess, had sex, worked at a pace bound to nature, had a demonic religion, and were generally "wild." But in fact the gente de razón were

Excerpted from Douglas Monroy *Thrown Among Strangers: The Making of Mexican Culture in Frontier California.* Copyright © 1990 by The Regents of the University of California. Reprinted by permission of the University of California Press and the author.

mestizos who also drank, had sex (with Indians, no less), were not known for dedication to hard work, and, between the Holy Trinity, the saints, and the revered Virgin of Guadalupe, had something of a pantheistic religion. This bind, of which the gente de razón were vaguely aware, kept them searching endlessly for meaningful distinctions between "us" and "them." "They" served not only as a work force but also as a contrast to "us." Violence against Indians allowed the gente de razón not only to obliterate threatening similarities but also to realize the forbidden fantasy of wild and unrestrained brutality against an other. Racial ideology was replacing reason and the alleged lack thereof as the divider of the peoples of nineteenth-century California.

The Indians, whose service as the degraded other was expanding, did not wear many clothes. "In those times," affirmed Juana Machada, "female Indians did not clothe themselves except for a cover of rabbit skins that covered their shameful parts." Indeed the Indians were *sin vergüenza*—without shame—in matters of the body. The rancheros, by contrast, dressed thoroughly and lavishly. The *chaleco,* a men's silk or calico jacket, and the short-sleeved gowns of the women continue to symbolize Californio elegance. The rancheros produced neither for the sake of producing nor to accumulate wealth: they traded hides and tallow with the Yankees and British, particularly after the liberalization of trade policy in 1828, for luxury goods. Their expensive clothing indicated their seigneurial status most apparently. Rich waistcoats, gilt-laced velveteen pantaloons, brightly colored sashes, and necklaces and earrings for the hatless and long-haired women sought to establish the prestige and social leadership of the wealthy gente de razón. After 1840 they even had available to them European fashions. Social status was the goal of their productive efforts, and they were not indolent in pursuing it; they diligently endeavored to elevate themselves to grandeur and aristocracy.

The mirror facilitated this way of appearing. The mirrors unloaded from the trade vessels not only allowed the Californios to assure themselves of their sartorial distinctiveness but enabled and encouraged a new awareness of self born of preoccupation with one's image. Dressing in front of a mirror, family members could decorate themselves in a way they imagined would inspire authority and awe.

The horse expressed the gentility of the Californio elites. "Californians are excellent horseback riders," noted the Russian Khlebnikov: "From childhood they begin to ride horses and grow up to be skillful horsemen. They deftly throw the lasso over the horns of bulls and heads of horses. . . . Children also go around with lassos and become trained in this practice from youth, throwing the loop over pigs, chickens and, from sheer mischief, often on horses." Yet another European impressed with the apparent lack of Californio productive ambition sneered in 1861 about the remnants of ranchero society: "The only thing they appear to excel in is riding." Sir George Simpson agreed with the negative estimation of California equestrian culture: "With such painted and gilded horsemen, anything like industry is, of course, out of the question; and accordingly they spend their time from morning until night in billiard-playing and horse-racing, aggravating the evil of idleness by ruinously heavy bets." Simpson's statement reveals something about what his own culture perceived as appropriate activity as well as what the rancheros valued. Racing indeed produced trouble for the Californios . . . in the Yankee period. "The Spanish Californians are passionately fond of horse-racing, and the extravagant bets which they make upon them contribute not a little to their ruin," concurred the French traveler Duflot de Mofras. An elite ranchero did not simply idle about but rode a *caballo*, showing the common folk and the Indians his *gachupín*.

In their own estimation they were honorable men, not idlers. Elites referred to one another as *mi valedor*, "my defender"; the idea of the self-interested individual had not yet come to California. They sought personal riches, to be sure, but maintained a sense of reciprocity and obligation, at least with respect to other gente de razón. These were vecinos—neighbors, not citizens. . . . Vecinos lived in relation to other vecinos. They were not independent citizens who lived in relation to a state. All people in such cultures feel an interconnectedness and a restraint that is absent in liberal society. . . . The amount of *honor* one had made a reputation, not the amount of money. (Of course, material wealth gave one the wherewithall to act graciously, honorably, and generously.) An acquisitive person who acted without regard for other gente de razón was aberrant. Indians (allegedly) and Yankees acted that way toward their own people.

Fealty to the true church was a central aspect of being de razón. The reciting of prayers helped strengthen ties among family members. Family patriarchs asserted their appropriate leadership role by enforcing proper attention to church ritual. They led their wives and children in the morning devotions and evening rosary. Church attendance was obligatory on Sundays and holy days. Education meant learning church doctrine; de razón elites made confession and received the sacraments regularly. Much of their extensive social lives revolved around mass and church fiestas. Religion was a serious matter for the elites. It underpinned their status, provided the rationale for the control of women and children, and kept the elites confident that, even on this frontier, they remained de razón.

These family fathers locked up their unmarried daughters at night. José del Carmen Lugo remembered how "the boys [slept] in the outside porches, exposed to the weather, and the girls in a locked room, of which the parents kept the key, if there was any key, which was not a common thing." Locks primarily functioned to regulate sexuality, maintain sexual propriety, and control and protect girls. Liberal social relations did not take hold in the elite families with respect to marriage. "These [marriage] arrangements," Carlos Híjar recalled of the 1830s, "took place only between the fathers of the children, and they tried to keep them from learning of their plans." Parents may well have considered the wishes of their children and probably headed off disastrous liaisons with marriage bargains when they noticed dangerous flirtations at the Californios' frequent fiestas. Lust and love could not be permitted to inspire de razón social relationships. After all, passion could not be allowed to run its subversive course with so much property at stake. Instinct enslaved the lower classes and Indians; and love, a rather fleeting emotion anyway, could not provide a stable basis for a marriage. To the gente de razón it seemed better that paternal reason should prevail. . . .

While their rule went largely unchallenged, the patresfamilias did not arbitrarily lord it over de razón women, at least in the ideal culture. Women had legal protections against abuse. Men could be punished for maltreating their wives and pressured to marry or fined for "ruining" a woman; in 1821 the authorities "condemned [a soldier] to two years' work in shackles for rape of a child." The many instances of such punishments indicate that such violations happened regularly, that the culture considered them deviant, and that the perpetrators were castigated, however inconsistently. The civil law enforced sexual morality. Living together without benefit of marriage got the man and woman sentenced to hard labor, banished, and subject to public humiliations. . . .

The ascendant frontier culture, through the civil law, made sure that . . . couple[s] lived like reasonable humans rather than *bestias,* animal or aboriginal humans. . . .

Regard for others expressed itself most famously in the Californios' legendary hospitality. According to José del Carmen Lugo, "The traveler could go from one end of California to the other without it costing him anything in money, excepting the gifts he might wish to make to the Indian servants at the missions or on the ranchos." Being respectable—and having Indians about to labor generously—enabled one to partake in the abundance of the region. Said Salvador Vallejo, "Formerly our cattle roamed by thousands, yet not one was stolen, for the unwritten law of the land granted to the weary traveler the privilege of killing cattle whenever he wanted beef, so long as he placed the hide where the owner could easily find it." . . . [F]oreign travelers corroborate these tales. "The virtue of hospitality knows no bounds," declaimed George Simpson. "They literally vie with each other in devoting their time, their homes, and their means to the entertainment of a stranger." . . . "Every rancher's house was open to everybody, free," marveled an Anglo traveler in 1841. . . . In this historical and cultural context a man increased in social standing if he gave away, rather than hoarded, his wealth.

These gente de razón acted from neither foolishness nor pure generosity. They acquitted themselves admirably within the context of their aspiring seigneurial culture. A spirit, in this instance one of social ascendance and caste solidarity, animated this material graciousness. A human being, in this case a don, "does not act so as to safeguard his individual interest in the possession of material goods," Carl Polanyi points out. "He acts so as to safeguard his social standing, his social claims, his social interests." The gente de razón earnestly endeavored to be successful; they were not simple idlers. But success derived not from producing and accumulating; rather, the rancheros valued material goods only insofar as they allowed genteel openhandedness—a sure mark of seigneurial status. The bestowal of some of their surplus through ritualized generosity safeguarded the social standing of the elite gente de razón. This gracious form of disaccumulation became part of their individual and collective characters. . . .

In order for them to exercise this seigneurialism, the elites could not sequester themselves. Their epic and illustrious fiestas allowed them to display their affluence and demonstrate their generosity by redistributing some of their bounty to those of lower status. As distinct as they sought to make themselves from others, the gente de razón did not recoil from social mixing, at least in the years of their emergence as a class. This is not to say that the gente de razón danced and chatted with the rest of the people. Richard Henry Dana noted that "there is always a private entertainment within the house for particular friends." Surely, when everyone assembled in the yard of a ranchero, or in the plaza, the boundaries between gente de razón and servants and laborers remained. But the few elites could not make a whole fiesta, and they could reassert their superior position on the social ladder through community celebrations. . . . It is likely that caste distinctions were sufficiently evident, even at aguardiente-laced fiestas, that the gente de razón did not need to sharpen them further by means of complete segregation.

The apparent democratic sociability of . . . weddings hid their class nature and function. Socioeconomic factors determined marriages. Intermarriage was rare in the Mexican era. Gloria Miranda notes that "in the Spanish era Santa Barbara officers and enlisted men stationed at Los Angeles frequently married daughters of soldiers or inválidos rather than wed women from the pueblo's lower strata." The wedding celebrations included everyone; the ceremony, however, "produced an elite social-political group who perpetuated their newly acquired privileged standing in the community by way of continued intermarriage among themselves." By 1840 careful intragroup marriage prevailed among the increasingly seigneurial gente de razón: recall that "poor, handsome, and brave" Manuel Garfias had to be elevated to landed status by his old commander Micheltorena before he could marry Luisa Ábila. There came to be much at stake in Californio weddings. Love could too easily interfere with the weighty matters of status and land. . . .

[I]n nineteenth-century California, . . . there was more food than there were people there. . . . If Indians or lower-caste persons were hungry, it was easier to give them a cow from the profuse grazing lands than to intensify the sorts of conflict that raged between the haves and the have-nots in places of scarcity. Anyway, a cow's worth was in its hide and tallow, since no value could be realized on the meat in those days before packinghouses and refrigeration. When, for whatever reasons, the rancheros slaughtered cows, they customarily distributed the meat. (The packs of dogs present on every rancho and in every pueblo consumed the offal.) The ranchero laborers received from their patrón a ration of beef, butter, corn, beans, garbanzos, squash, and chile; they also grew some of these victuals on small plots of their own. Beef, which was extremely tough, tortillas, and beans were the most common donations, which the laborers ate from *cajetas de barro,* or clay dishes. The poor had a regimen of meat and more meat, but at least they ate.

And they drank—the employed ones to excess, and the unemployed ones to destruction. "Intemperance, too," Dana noted, uncharacteristically understating the matter, "is a common vice among the Indians." Misery and degradation existed alongside the plenty and festiveness. Indian social organization continued to unravel, and Indian drunkenness and vice did not abate. Many of these Indians were permanently unemployed, a ready pool of itinerant labor, although inefficient and lethargic. Convicted Indians inevitably wound up in a chain gang, pressed into service for petty misdemeanors and drunkenness. As early as 1836 the ayuntamiento of Los Angeles authorized the use of arrested drunken Indians to clean the irrigation ditch. Thus, the law turned the decaying Indians into the city public-works force through the penal system. That the Indians, ever more apparently sin razón, should do all the work was public policy, too.

Those attached to the ranchos labored like peones, not free workers. They lived on their patrón's land in houses made of tules or sticks stuck vertically in mud and then thatched. Some inhabited the *indiada,* or quarters, near the main casa, and others lived in the thatched huts of the rancherías by the water holes and corrals where the herds were. They awoke at daybreak, sometimes joining the patrón in morning prayers, and then got to work. "Throughout all California," observed Dr. John Marsh, visiting in 1836, "the Indians are the principal laborers; without them the business of the country could hardly be carried on." Commented Juan Bandini in 1828, soon to become a ranchero, "Riding on horseback and lounging lazily is the gamut of their days and the women bear all the responsibility of the house."

"While the men are employed in attending to the herds of cattle and horses, and engaged in their other amusements," noted an Anglo traveler of the 1840s, "the women (I speak of the middle classes on the ranchos) superintend and perform most of the drudgery appertaining to housekeeping, and the cultivation of the gardens." "These beautiful creatures," Bandini wrote in 1828, "are without doubt more active and industrious than the men." The patrona worked hard setting the host of Indian women attached to the rancho to work sweeping, sewing, cooking, washing, and gardening. The de razón women supervised the milking of cows and the making of cheese to ensure that the milk was clean and strained. Making bread, candles, and soap and cutting wood for cooking was their responsibility, as was the planting and tending of small gardens. The embroidery of clothes took much of their time. Some few of the girls from prominent families learned to read at the home of one of their mothers, and certainly they mastered the social graces, but what little formal education existed in Spanish and Mexican California was for the boys. The tediousness of the interminable work both of the Indias and the patrona is striking. Both had exhausting jobs: the disinclined Indias were responsible for most of the work but could not comprehend de razón ways and tastes, and the patrona had to coax household production from her muddling charges. A ranchero patriarch fondly, if not wishfully, recalled that the women "were virtuous, industrious, and constantly devoted to the needs of their families, which were never neglected." . . .

This Indian labor produced not only the subsistence of rancho California, but a fundamental part of its seigneurial social relations and ideology as well. The gente de razón built on this base their remarkably new seigneurial status. There was some fusion of Indian and de razón cultures. Material goods and alcohol, together with the supply of food after the disruption of the ecosystem, drew the Indians, gentile and nominal Christians, into the rancho productive and cultural system. Of course, the fusion went only one way—the gente de razón adopted only a few Indian herbal medicines. It would be fascinating to know what sort of relationships prevailed when members of the pueblo married Indians, but the historical record is silent about this matter. It does not appear, however, that any Indian ways came into Hispanic California culture through intermarriage. The Indians served only the old soldier families' efforts to achieve their elevated social position. Perceptions and the reality of relations between the two groups were dissonant. The patrona of the influential Vallejo family declared:

> All our servants are very much attached to us. They do not ask for money, nor do they have a fixed wage; we give them all they need, and if they are ill we care for them like members of the family. If they have children we stand as godparents and see to their education. If they wish to go to a distant place to visit a relative, we give them animals and escorts for the journey; in a word, we treat our servants rather as friends than as servants.

An Anglo traveler with an aversion to the grammatical period observed in 1834 that the stock was "herded by the indians, who cost them but a trifle more than they eat, in fact they always contrived to keep the poor indian in debt, or at least to make the poor devil think so, they were seldom paid more than two or three bullock hides per month or six dollars in goods, this they always drank in Arguadiente [sic] on Sunday."

As incongruous as these two views of the same relationship may seem, they are not contradictory. Yes, the Indian servants were very much attached to the gente de razón, but not because of affection. Rather, after the unraveling of their old way of life and the thorough intrusion on their lands the Indians had no choice but to bind themselves to the ranchos. Fiestas, cloth goods, and aguardiente smoothed over the grimy bond. In this personal and seigneurial relationship the patrón took care of his charges' fractured needs for subsistence and conviviality. There was no place for a fixed wage, a concept foreign to the Indians anyway. An easy familiarity between the two peoples may well have characterized much of their day-to-day relationship, given their powerful mutual dependence, in spite of the vast difference in social position. Indian laborers drank to excess, paid no apparent attention to their health, and did not try to advance from their lowly condition, not because they suffered deracination, but because they remained, like children, sin razón. This situation not only suited the labor needs of the gente de razón but made them feel more confident about their socially ascendant and reasonable selves as well.

FURTHER READING

Robert A. Alvarez, Jr., *Familia: Migration and Adaptation in Baja and Alta California, 1800–1975* (1987)

Hubert Howe Bancroft, *California Pastoral, 1769–1848* (1888)

Antonio Rios-Bustamante and Pedro Castillo, *An Illustrated History of Mexican Los Angeles, 1781–1985* (1986)

Albert Camarillo, *Chicanos in a Changing Society: From Mexican Pueblos to American Barrios in Santa Barbara and Southern California, 1848–1930* (1979)

Robert G. Cleland, *The Cattle on a Thousand Hills* (1951)

Robert G. Cleland, *This Reckless Breed of Men: Trappers and Fur Traders of the Southwest* (1952)

Richard Henry Dana, *Two Years Before the Mast: A Personal Narrative of Life at Sea* (1840)

Ferol Egan, *Frémont, Explorer for a Restless Nation* (1977)

Juan Gomez-Quinones, *Roots of Chicano Politics, 1600–1940* (1994)

Richard Griswold del Castillo, *The Los Angeles Barrio, 1850–1890: A Social History* (1979)

Richard Griswold del Castillo, *The Treaty of Guadalupe Hidalgo: A Legacy of Conflict* (1990)

Lisbeth Haas, *Conquests and Historical Identities in California, 1769–1936* (1995)

Harlan Hague and David J. Langum, *Thomas O. Larkin: A Life of Patriotism and Profit in Old California* (1990)

John A. Hawgood, "The Pattern of Yankee Infiltration in Mexican Alta California, 1821–1846," *Pacific Historical Review* XXVII (February 1958): 27–38

Cecil Alan Hutchinson, *Frontier Settlement in Mexican California: The Híjar-Padres Colony and Its Origins, 1769–1835* (1969)

David J. Langum, *Law and Community on the Mexican California Frontier: Anglo-American Expatriates and the Clash of Legal Traditionism 1821–1846* (1987)

Douglas Monroy, *Thrown Among Strangers: The Making of Mexican Culture in Frontier California* (1990)

Leonard Pitt, *The Decline of the Californios: A Social History of the Spanish-Speaking Californians, 1846–1890* (1966)

David J. Weber, *The Mexican Frontier, 1821–1846: The American Southwest under Mexico* (1982)

David J. Weber, ed., *Foreigners in Their Native Land: Historical Roots of the Mexican Americans* (1973)

Conflicts over Land in a New State, 1850s–1870s

As a result of war with Mexico (1846–1848), Americans took control of the region known as Alta California. This military conquest crowned a half century of growing interest in that region on the part of American merchants, whalers, hunters, and trappers. Before 1800 Americans engaged in a lucrative sea otter trade off California's coast. By the 1820s, when both the sea otter and fur seal were virtually eliminated, commercial interest shifted to an extensive trade in cowhides and tallow. This commerce drew increasing attention to an area as yet unfamiliar to most Americans. The first organized party with intentions to settle in California crossed the Rockies in 1841. Although such migrations became more frequent, Americans living in California by the mid-1840s numbered fewer than one thousand.

By then, however, California's tremendous commercial potential was evident to many national leaders, among them President James K. Polk, who joined others in boldly envisioning the entire Pacific Coast as an essential component of a larger commercial empire. Shortly after taking office in 1845, he actively pursued the acquisition of California, the subsequent occupation of which met surprisingly little resistance from the inhabitants. Eventual capture of Monterey and Los Angeles assured American control. With the signing of the Treaty of Guadalupe Hidalgo in 1848 (see Chapter 4), which ended the war with Mexico, and with the influx of tens of thousands of American citizens during the gold rush, the stage was set for California statehood in 1850.

The discovery of gold by John Marshall in March 1848 fundamentally transformed the pastoral economy of the Mexican period into a much more complex and diversified one, opening up Mexican California to massive Yankee inroads. According to Michael Smith, who has carefully studied the role of the scientific community in the environmental history of nineteenth-century California, Anglo-Americans brought with them "Bibles and gunpowder, microbes and plows, whiskey, cattle, steam engines, courts, and a relentless vision of conquest—of man over nature and man over other men." By midcentury the population of the region had grown dramatically, as *nearly 100,000 eager gold-seekers arrived from other parts of the United States, Latin America, Europe, China, and Australia. Many of those gold-seekers stayed on as settlers after the rich veins in northern California played out in the late 1850s, making California one of the most ethnically and racially diverse regions in the world.*

The newcomers replaced Mexican with American political structures in a wide-open frontier society in which political activity was reserved for a very few people and in which legal institutions were weak and ineffective. Ethnic and racial conflict characterized social relations in the mining districts and also in many urban areas, where the racial division of the labor force was often an important feature of working-class life and union organization (see Chapter 7).

Not surprisingly, newcomers soon discovered, to their dismay, that huge portions of the best land were already taken by a small number of Spanish-speaking California *landholders through grants from the Spanish crown or the Mexican government. In 1850 the census reported that there were only 872 farms in California, with an average size of 4,465 acres. The new immigrants therefore often found themselves in conflict with existing residents over the use of available land.*

As mentioned briefly in Chapter 4, the 1848 Treaty of Guadalupe Hidalgo promised the Californios *American citizenship and the "free enjoyment of their liberty and property." But neither promise was fulfilled. Land and cattle, relatively inexpensive commodities when the treaty was signed, acquired great value as a result of the gold rush. In the early years of the gold rush, not only were the Anglo-Americans flooding into the region successful in banishing* Californios *from the mines (along with Chileans, Sonorans from Mexico, and Chinese), but they also began occupying the large ranchos and cultivating the land. As these defiant "squatters" laid claim to rancho lands, Congress passed the California Land Act of 1851 to adjudicate land grant disputes. An intense historiographical debate over the impact of this land act is addressed in two of this chapter's essays. At issue is whether the immigrants' "land grab" was justified.*

The acrimonious and often violent clash of rights and interests over land resulted in the passing of the large Mexican ranchos into the hands of wealthy Americans or immigrants. Because of these enormous land grants, California began its history as a state with land monopoly, never experiencing the customary frontier phase of land development. And, after 1860, the federal and state governments began to sell land to private individuals, while the railroads were granted nearly 11,500,000 acres by the federal government to help finance the construction of the first transcontinental railroad. The immense holdings thus acquired by such people as William Chapman, Henry Miller, Charles Lux, and James Irvine completely thwarted the aspirations of many other settlers, a situation first publicly decried by social critic Henry George. In an 1871 booklet, George argued that the early agricultural development of the state resulted in large-scale farming units worked by wage laborers, rather than in extensive owner-operated family farms. In no other American state were monopolistic landholding patterns and, eventually, large-scale agriculture (what would later be called "agribusiness") so pronounced. In California, the family farm never had a chance. George and other social critics denounced this situation in the Jeffersonian belief that an egalitarian, democratic society could not exist without widespread landownership.

A question that engages historians today is the origin and impact of large-scale land ownership, hence economic power, in the early days of California as a state. Who laid claim to the land, and what was the authority for their claims? Was it the enormous Spanish and Mexican land grants, the actions of the U.S. government, or the aggressiveness and rapacity of the more powerful Anglo-American immigrants that shaped landownership patterns? Did women, Asians, and other immigrants of modest means control any of the wealth created?

D O C U M E N T S

The documents in this chapter include three compelling accounts of life in gold rush California. One, by a former army lieutenant named E. Gould Buffum, who participated in the subjugation of California during the Mexican War and then stayed on to engage in gold mining, prophetically recognizes the economic and strategic importance of California to the United States. The second document offers a glimpse of women's life in "the diggings" during the 1850s. It is drawn from one of twenty-three remarkable letters written in 1851–1852 by Louisa Clapp under the pen name of "Dame Shirley" (and thus known as the Shirley Letters). The California-born philosopher and historian Josiah Royce later declared those letters to be "the best account of an early mining camp that is known to me."

The forty-niners included not only women but many foreigners. Among the latter, the Chinese stood out the most due to their different appearance and unfamiliar mining method. J. D. Borthwick, a Scottish journalist and artist who spent three years in California in the early 1850s, provides a brief glimpse of Chinese gold miners in the third document. Unfortunately, no account written by a Chinese miner has yet been found in U.S. historical archives.

From the 1850s through the 1880s, members of the California State Agricultural Society consistently espoused a thoroughly Jeffersonian vision regarding the use of land, adamantly denouncing land monopoly. One advocate of such traditional agrarian values was Dr. John F. Morse, who, with rhetorical exuberance, addressed a meeting of that society held in Sacramento in September 1865, arguing that family farming was being denied its rightful place in California. A portion of his remarks appears as the fourth document. Similarly, Henry George rejected the euphoric boosterism so common among the new state's promoters. Born in Philadelphia in 1839, George came to San Francisco in 1857, where as a newspaper reporter he developed a growing concern over the process of land monopolization in California, which he believed fostered acquisitive speculation and foreclosed participation by small farmers. The final document is drawn from his 1871 booklet, *Our Land and Land Policy,* in which he refers to the Mexican grants as a "curse."

E. Gould Buffum Exults in Gold's Discovery, 1850

With the discovery of the gold mines, a new era in the history of California commences. This event has already changed a comparative wilderness into a flourishing State, and is destined to affect the commercial and political relations of the world. Between California as she was at the period of the cession to the United States and as she is at this time, there is no similitude. In two short years her mineral resources have been developed, and she has at once emerged from obscurity into a cynosure upon which nations are gazing with wondrous eyes. Her mountains and valleys, but recently the hunting grounds of naked savages, are now peopled with a hundred thousand civilized men; her magnificent harbours crowded with ships from far distant ports; her rivers and bays navigated by steamboats; her warehouses filled with the products of almost every clime, and her population energetic, hopeful, and prosperous. . . .

Prior to the discovery of the *placers* the country was thinly peopled, the inhabitants being mostly native Californians, Mexicans, and Indians. . . . California, with her delicious climate, her inexhaustible resources, and important geographical position, might to this day have remained an almost unknown region, visited occasionally by a trading vessel with an assorted cargo, to be exchanged for hides, had not a mysterious Providence ordained the discovery of the golden sands of the Rio Americano. This event at once gave a tremendous impetus to commerce and emigration, and may be said to mark an important era in the history of the world. . . .

Never in the history of the world was there such a favourable opportunity as now presents itself in the gold region of California for a profitable investment of capital; and the following are some of the modes in which it may be applied. . . . [T]he beds of the tributaries to the two great rivers that flow from the Sierra Nevada are richer in gold than their banks have yet proved to be. There are many points, at each one of which the river can easily be turned from its channel by a proper application of machinery. Dams are then to be erected and pumps employed in keeping the beds dry. Powerful steam machines are to be set in operation for the purpose of tearing up the rocks, and separating the gold from them. The hills and plains are also to be wrought. Shafts are to be sunk in the mountain sides, and huge excavators are to bring to the surface the golden earth, and immense machines, worked by steam power, made to wash it. The earth, which had been previously washed in the common rockers, is to be re-washed in a more scientifically constructed apparatus, and the minute particles of gold, which escape in the common mode of washing, and which are invisible to the naked eye, are to be separated by a chemical process.

As yet no actual mining operations have been commenced in the gold region of California, for the two reasons, that they require a combination of labour and capital, and that the gold-washings have thus far proved so profitable as to make them most desirable. But there is a greater field for actual mining operations in California than was ever presented in the richest districts of Peru and Mexico. The gold-washings, which have thus far enriched thousands, are but the scum that has been washed from the beds of the ore. I would not wish to say one word to increase the gold mania, which has gone out from California, and has attracted from the whole world thousands of men who were not at all fitted to endure the hardships consequent upon a life in her mountainous regions, or the severe labour which was necessary to extract gold from the earth. It is to be hoped that this mania, however, has now given way to the "sober second thought," and that men have learned to listen to facts, and take the means to profit by them in the most proper manner. I should not consider myself as acting in accordance with duty, were I to assume the responsibility of publishing to the world an account of the gold mines of California, did I not, like the witness upon the stand, "tell the truth, the whole truth, and nothing but the truth."

Louisa Clapp Pokes Fun at Her Experience as a Gold "Mineress," 1851

Nothing of importance has happened since I last wrote you, except that I have become a *mineress;* that is, if . . . having washed a pan of dirt with my own hands, and procured therefrom three dollars and twenty-five cents in gold dust (which I shall inclose in this letter), will entitle me to the name. I can truly say, with the blacksmith's apprentice at the close of his first day's work at the anvil, that "I am sorry I learned the trade;" for I wet my feet, tore my dress, spoilt a pair of new gloves, nearly froze my fingers, got an awful headache, took cold and lost a valuable breastpin, in this my labor of love. After such melancholy self-sacrifice on my part, I trust you will duly prize my gift. I can assure you that it is the last golden handiwork you will ever receive from "Dame Shirley."

Apropos, of lady gold-washers in general—it is a common habit with people residing in towns in the vicinity of the "Diggings," to make up pleasure parties to those places. Each woman of the company will exhibit on her return, at least twenty dollars of the *oro,* which she will gravely inform you she has just "panned out" from a single basinful of the soil. This, of course, gives strangers a very erroneous idea of the average richness of auriferous dirt. I myself thought, (now don't laugh,) that one had but to saunter gracefully along romantic streamlets, on sunny afternoons, with a parasol and white kid gloves, perhaps, and to stop now and then to admire the scenery, and carelessly rinse out of a small panful of yellow sand (without detriment to the white kids, however, so easy did I fancy the whole process to be), in order to fill one's workbag with the most beautiful and rare specimens of the precious mineral. Since I have been here, I have discovered my mistake, and also the secret of the brilliant success of former gold-washeresses.

The miners are in the habit of flattering the vanity of their fair visitors, by scattering a handful of "salt" (which, strange to say, is *exactly* the color of gold dust, and has the remarkable property of often bringing to light very curious clumps of the ore) through the dirt before the dainty fingers touch it; and the dear creatures go home with their treasures, firmly believing that mining is the prettiest pastime in the world.

I had no idea of permitting such a costly joke to be played upon me; so I said but little of my desire to "go through the motions" of gold washing, until one day, when, as I passed a deep hole in which several men were at work, my companion requested the owner to fill a small pan, which I had in my hand, with dirt from the bedrock. This request was, of course, granted, and, the treasure having been conveyed to the edge of the river, I succeeded, after much awkward maneuvering on my own part, and considerable assistance from friend H., an experienced miner, in gathering together the above specified sum. All the diggers of our acquaintance say that it is an excellent "prospect," even to come from the bedrock, where, naturally, the richest dirt is found. To be sure, there are now and then "lucky strikes"; such, for instance, as that mentioned in a former letter, where a person took out of a single basinful of soil, two hundred and fifty-six dollars. But such luck is as rare as the winning of a hundred thousand dollar prize in a lottery. We are acquainted with many here whose gains have *never* amounted to more than "wages"; that is, from six to eight dollars a day. And a "claim" which yields a man a steady income of ten dollars *per diem*, is considered as very valuable.

J. D. Borthwick Observes Chinese Gold Miners, 1851

A whole bevy of Chinamen had recently made their appearance on the creek. Their camp, consisting of a dozen or so of small tents and brush-houses, was near our cabin on the side of the hill—too near to be pleasant, for they kept up a continual chattering all night, which was rather tiresome till we got used to it.

They are an industrious set of people, no doubt, but are certainly not calculated for gold-digging. They do not work with the same force and vigour as American or European miners, but handle their tools like so many women, as if they were afraid of hurting themselves. The Americans call it "scratching," which was a very expressive term for their style of digging. They did not venture to assert equal rights so far as to take up any claim which other miners would think it worth while to work; but in such places as yielded them a dollar to two a-day they were allowed to scratch away unmolested. Had they happened to strike a rich lead, they would have been driven off their claim immediately. They were very averse to working in the water, and for four or five hours in the heat of the day they assembled under the shade of a tree, where they sat fanning themselves, drinking tea, and saying "too muchee hot."

On the whole, they seemed a harmless, inoffensive people; but one day, as we were going to dinner, we heard an unusual hullabaloo going on where the Chinamen were at work; and on reaching the place we found the whole tribe of Celestials divided into two equal parties, drawn up against each other in battle array, brandishing picks and shovels, lifting stones as if to hurl them at their adversaries' heads, and every man chattering and gesticulating in the most frantic manner. The miners collected on the ground to see the "muss," and cheered the Chinamen on to more active hostilities. But after taunting and threatening each other in this way for about an hour, during which time, although the excitement seemed to be continually increasing, not a blow was struck or a stone thrown, the two parties suddenly, and without any apparent cause, fraternised, and moved off together to their tents. What all the row was about, or why peace was so suddenly proclaimed, was of course a mystery to us outside barbarians; and the tame and unsatisfactory termination of such warlike demonstrations was a great disappointment, as we had been every moment expecting that the ball would open, and hoped to see a general engagement. . . . [A]t all events, discretion seemed to form a very large component of Celestial valour.

John F. Morse Supports Traditional Agrarian Values, 1865

Eighteen years of the citizenship of the United States has effected a million time more in the settlement, the opening and portrayal of the natural resources of California and the northern Pacific coast than all the three hundred and thirteen years of Spanish kings, viceroys, and missionary societies. We say, the citizenship of the Union. We do not mean mere Anglo-Saxon energy, but the universal citizenship, native and adopted; which, under the influence of our Government, from the stimulus of free and enlightened institutions, becomes a weird unity of strength in demonstrating the national force to which we have alluded. . . .

This astonishing contrast seeks a solution only at the hands of the nation; and the nation, with its eyes fixed upon the God-inspired maxim of every State—"Liberty, Equality, Fraternity"—answers steadily and forever the questions in these magic words: *"E Pluribus Unum."* There's an atmosphere in the national liberality and quality that so soon as breathed by the individual, transmutes the alien blood of a German, Frenchman, or Irishman, into the same instrumentality of daring and patriotism and independence which inspired the primal declaration of freedom, and set free and emancipate[d] the furtive genius of American character. Under the influence of this atmosphere there are no born or inherent privileged classes; no obstructed or closed avenues to wealth, to fame, or rank. . . .

Here is the sublime secret of our national greatness and prosperity. From this source springs an agriculture as comprehensive, as substantial, as prolific, as exhaustless as the soil upon which the nation is founded. Not an agriculture owned and dispensed by kings and princes, by dukes and lords, by ruling classes, leased and sub-leased until the poor toiler is reduced to a harvest of husks and a bed of straw; but an agriculture almost as free as air, and as rich as rain and sun, light and energy can make it. There is no government in the world so well adapted to the science and power of agriculture as a republic, and no Government can live, become mighty, and expect to endure, without agricultural abundance. The United States, through the genius of the people, formed a government infinitely calculated to inspire a stupendous husbandry—it sowed the seeds of an unparalleled agriculture, and as a sublime and glorious result, it never rests from the pleasurable labor of harvesting homes. Homes that are the fountains of national strength; homes of hospitality and plenty; homes of loyalty and of deathless attachment; and homes which are, in proportion as they are free and diffused, the best conservators of manly vigor, energy, endurance, intelligence, beauty, honesty, chastity, and virtue. Upon this kind of agriculture, more than any other department of governmental reliance, depends the progress, the power, and endurance of the Federal Union. Free and untrammelled agricultural homes, cultivated and kept in order by the men who own the soil, are the sources of the most indestructible national wealth. And in our country there is but one thing that can militate against this great national desideratum. That is the tendency to a monopoly of soil, the holding of more land than can be properly managed, and the introduction of lease-ridden estates. Oppressive monopoly in anything is a curse to society and dishonor toward God and man. But if monopoly must exist, let it live anywhere rather than in the husbandry of our country.

There are no monopolists so arrogant, so dictatorial, so dangerous to the peace and perpetuity of the State, as the overgrown, monopolizing, political nabobs of the soil. Moderately large farms, well tilled, constitute the true glory and security of a nation or state. Contiguity of small farms awaken and maintain an emulation in agriculture which converts valleys, hillsides, and prairies into those wonderful garden fields of beauty and plenty that never fail to enrapture the eye and delight the heart of needy and ennobled humanity. This is the kind of agriculture we want in California, from the partial development of which our State has taken a stride in progress in eighteen years unknown to any half-century of previous historical knowledge. This is the agriculture which yields abundance, and from which springs those exertions of genius and of art through which manufactures originate and thrive, and in the joint power of these resources of wealth is generated the most powerful and enduring commerce of the world. The farms and farmers of California have been a godsend to this coast. What the silent and noiseless sun and seasons have done to eliminate the promises of agriculture, these farmers have, with equal patience and modesty, done to evoke the permanent attachments, to inspire manufactures, and to lay the foundation of that commerce which in one half-century will surpass any interest of national or international intercourse and trade ever recognized by man. But for the agriculture of California we could not have borne the crisis of adversity through which we have been compelled to pass. . . . We will not underrate the mineral and metallic resources of California, but we will say that in comparison to the benefactions which agriculture confers upon a State, they are irregular, unreliable, and capricious. A premium upon the products of the soil, come from whence it may, leaves an equivalent with the producer, whilst a premium upon gold and silver, which is our exclusive circulating medium, we have seen has too often absorbed and removed, not only the product and our currency capital, but the producer also.

God preserve and prosper the farmers of our country! With them abides the true magic of our common prosperity and courage.

Henry George Censures Land Monopoly, 1871

In all the new States of the Union land monopolisation has gone on at an alarming rate, but in none of them so fast as in California, and in none of them, perhaps, are its evil effects so manifest.

California is the greatest land State in the Union, both in extent (for Texas owns her own land) and in the amount of land still credited to the Government in Department reports. With an area of 188,981 square miles, or, in round numbers, 121,000,000 acres, she has a population of less than 600,000—that is to say, with an area twenty-four times as large as Massachusetts, she has a population not half as great. Of this population not one third is engaged in agriculture, and the amount of land under cultivation does not exceed 2,500,000 acres. Surely land should here be cheap, and the immigrant should come with the certainty of getting a homestead at Government price! But this is not so. Of the 100,000,000 acres of public land which, according to the last report of the Department, yet remain in California (which of course includes all the mountains and sterile plains), some 20,000,000 acres are withheld from settlement by railroad reservations, and millions of acres more are held under unsettled Mexican grants, or by individuals under the possessory laws of the State, without color of title. Though here or there, if he knew where to find it, there may be a little piece of Government land left, the notorious fact is that the immigrant coming to the State to-day [*sic*] must, as a general thing, pay their price to the middlemen before he can begin to cultivate the soil. Although the population of California, all told—miners, city residents, Chinamen and Diggers—does not amount to three to the square mile; although the arable land of the State has hardly been scratched (and with all her mountains and dry plains California has an arable surface greater than the entire area of Ohio), it is already so far monopolised that a large part of the farming is done by renters, or by men who cultivate their thousands of acres in a single field. For the land of California is already to a great extent monopolised by a few individuals, who hold thousands and hundreds of thousands of acres apiece. Across many of these vast estates a strong horse cannot gallop in a day, and one may travel for miles and miles over fertile ground where no plough has ever struck, but which is all owned, and on which no settler can come to make himself a home, unless he pay such tribute as the lord of the domain chooses to exact.

Nor is there any State in the Union in which settlers in good faith have been so persecuted, so robbed, as in California. Men have grown rich, and men still make a regular business of blackmailing settlers upon public land, or of appropriating their homes, and this by the power of the law and in the name of justice. Land grabbers have had it pretty much their own way in California—they have moulded the policy of the general Government; have dictated the legislation of the State; have run the land offices and used the courts. . . .

California has had one curse which the other states have not had—the Mexican grants. The Mexican land policy was a good one for a sparsely settled pastoral country, such as California before the American occupation. To every citizen who would settle on it, a town lot was given; to every citizen who wanted it, a cattle range was granted. By the terms of the cession of California to the United States it was provided that these rights should be recognized.

It would have been better, far better, if the American Government had agreed to permit these grant-holders to retain a certain definite amount of land around their improvements, and compounded for the rest of the grants called for by the payment of a certain sum per acre, turning it into the public domain. This would have been best, not only for the future population of California, but for the grant-holders themselves as the event has proved.

Or if means had been taken for a summary and definite settlement of these claims, the evils entailed by them would have been infinitesimal compared with what have resulted. For it is not the extent of the grants (and all told the *bona fide* ones call for probably nine or ten million acres of the best land of California) which has wrought the mischief, so much as their unsettled condition—not the treaty with Mexico, but our own subsequent policy.

It is difficult in a brief space to give anything like an adequate idea of the villainies for which these grants have been made the cover. If the history of the Mexican grants of California is ever written, it will be a history of greed, of perjury, of corruption, of spoliation and high-handed robbery, for which it will be difficult to find a parallel.

The Mexican grants were vague, running merely for so many leagues within certain natural boundaries, or between other grants, though they were generally marked out in rough fashion. It is the indefiniteness which has given such an opportunity for rascality, and has made them such a curse to California, and which, at the same time, has prevented in nearly all cases their original owners from reaping from them any commensurate benefit. Between the Commission which first passed upon the validity of the grants and final patent, a thousand places were found where the grant could be tied up, and where, indeed, after twenty-three years of litigation the majority of them still rest. Ignorant of the language, of the customs, of the laws of the new rulers of their country, without the slightest idea of technical subtleties and legal delays, mere children as to business—the native grant-holders were completely at the mercy of shrewd lawyers and sharp speculators, and at a very early day nearly all the grants passed into other hands.

E S S A Y S

In the first essay, JoAnn Levy, a Los Angeles author specializing in California and western history, challenges the prevailing assumption that "gold-rush California . . . was almost exclusively a male domain." Among the important primary materials upon which Levy relied for this revisionist interpretation are the Shirley Letters (see the second document in this chapter).

The influx of some 100,000 gold-seekers led to numerous conflicts over the ownership and use of land. Most scholars have written sympathetically about the plight of the *Californios*, who saw their ranchos being taken over by American settlers. Only one scholar—Paul Wallace Gates, Professor Emeritus of History at Cornell University—has come to the defense of these settlers, arguing that it was, in fact, "the struggles of the squatters in California for their rights against the Mexican claimants," as well as "the efforts of settlers to find the elusive free government land" and the "failure to break up the great estates left by the Mexican government," that led to the search for solutions to the perceived problem of land monopoly. In this chapter's second essay, Gates argues *against* the prevailing view that the Land Act of 1851 was nothing more than institutionalized theft. Although many historians have criticized Gates for presenting an idealized picture of the family farm and small farmers, for moralizing about allegedly selfish and socially pernicious large land speculators, and for underestimating the importance of agriculture's changing nature, his work is absolutely essential to understanding the relationship between nineteenth-century land policy and twentieth-century corporate farming in California.

In the third essay, Douglas Monroy (whose work also appears in Chapter 4) analyzes the struggles that took place when Anglo-Americans sought to impose their will on *Californios* in a newly conquered region. Borrowing the term "bonanza capitalism" from Hubert Howe Bancroft, Monroy focuses on conflicting cultural assumptions regarding land tenure and land law in a highly acquisitive era. Among other things, he differs from Paul Gates in arguing that the Land Act of 1851 "wreaked havoc on the rancheros' claims," effectively abrogating specific provisions of the Treaty of Guadalupe Hidalgo (see Chapter 4) and setting the stage for "the commodification of the land" with the advent of the Anglo-Americans.

Women in the Gold Rush

JOANN LEVY

If Concord, Massachusetts is remembered for the "shot heard 'round the world," Sutter's Mill, in the foothills of California's Sierra Nevada, is remembered for the "shout heard 'round the world"—"Eureka!" As that cry reverberated across the globe in 1848 (and echoed into the 1850s), a flood of humanity converged on the land of golden opportunity. This human tide irrevocably changed the West, opening up the frontier as no other force in the nation's history has, before or since.

One of the most common assumptions about gold-rush-era California is that it was almost exclusively a male domain—and that such women as could be found there were prostitutes. As recently as 1983, a California historian asserted that "it was, literally, mankind which participated in the gold rush, for woman kind, at least of the 'proper' variety, was almost totally absent."

A careful study of surviving diaries, memoirs, newspapers, and census records from the period refutes this longstanding misperception, revealing

---

This article is reprinted from (7) pages of the February 1992 issue of *American History Illustrated* with the permission of Cowles History Group, Inc. Copyright American History Illustrated magazine.

that the vast wave of migration to California included thousands of "respectable" women—and numerous children, too.

Many of these adventurous women accompanied or followed their husbands, fathers, or brothers to the golden land; others arrived entirely on their own. Once in California, enterprising women engaged in almost every occupation and inhabited every level of society. They mined for gold, raised families, earned substantial sums by their domestic and entrepreneurial labors, and stayed on to help settle the land—contributing a facet of gold-rush history that until now has been largely overlooked or forgotten.

In actuality, so-called respectable women outnumbered prostitutes in California, even in 1850, by four to one. While 25 percent [*sic;* 20 percent, because a ratio of four to one when converted into a fraction equals one in *five*] represents a large number, even if not in this instance a "respectable" one, it is far from a majority.

Before they could avail themselves of the opportunities afforded by the gold rush, woman argonauts, like their male counterparts, had to undertake and survive the arduous journey to California. Many travelers chose the Cape Horn route, braving gale, storm, and shipwreck on a voyage that consumed from five to seven months; others shortened the ocean journey by making the difficult crossing of the Isthmus of Panama via small boat and mule. In 1849, more than twenty thousand gold-seekers arrived at San Francisco by sea, and nearly twenty-five thousand more followed in 1850. Many journals and letters mention the presence of women on these routes, which travelers generally regarded as being safer for families than the even more daunting overland crossings.

Despite the hardships and dangers involved, thousands of other wealth-seekers trekked overland by wagon or on foot, crossing plains, deserts, and forbidding mountain ranges while carrying with them—and then often abandoning for survival's sake—their worldly possessions. Trail-journal entries suggest that of the twenty-five thousand people traveling overland in 1849, at least three thousand were women and fifteen hundred children. Forty-four thousand people crossed the plains the following year, and, given California's census of 1850, about ten percent of these may be assumed to have been female. News of hardship, starvation, and cholera stemmed the tide of overland emigrants in 1851 to little more than a thousand, but in 1852 an estimated fifty thousand again surged across the continent. By July 13, 1852, the Fort Kearny register had tallied for that year alone the passage of more than seven thousand women and eight thousand children.

"The country was so level that we could see long trains of white-topped wagons for many miles," recorded one woman of her experiences on the eastern segment of the overland trail. "And, when we drew nearer to the vast multitude, and saw them in all manner of vehicles and conveyances, on horseback and on foot, all eagerly driving and hurrying forward, I thought in my excitement, that if one-tenth of these teams and these people got [there] ahead of us, there would be nothing left for us in California worth picking up."

On June 28, 1849, the "Buckeye Rovers," a company of young men heading from Ohio to California's gold fields, camped near Independence Rock on the overland trail. One of the group, John Banks, wrote in his diary that night of seeing "an Irish woman and a daughter without any relatives on the way for gold. It is said she owns a fine farm in Missouri." Two weeks later, on the banks of the Green River, their paths converged again: "Last night the Irish woman and daughter were selling liquor near us. . . . Fifty cents a pint, quite moderate."

Some distance beyond the Green River, near the Humboldt River, a woman named Margaret Frink recorded in her journal for August 12, 1850: "Among the crowds on foot, a negro woman came tramping along through the heat and dust, carrying a cast iron bake oven on her head, with her provisions and blanket piled on top—all she possessed in the world—bravely pushing on for California."

Frink and her husband had begun their westward trek in Indiana. Along the way they stopped at the home of a Mr. and Mrs. McKinney near St. Joseph, Missouri. "Mrs. McKinney," wrote Margaret in her diary, "told me of the wonderful tales of the abundance of gold that she had heard; 'that they kept flour-scoops to scoop the gold out of the barrels that they kept it in, and that you could soon get all that you needed for the rest of your life. And as for a woman, if she could cook at all, she could get $16.00 per week for each man that she cooked for, and the only cooking required to be done was just to boil meat and potatoes and serve them in a big chip of wood, instead of a plate, and the boarder furnished the provisions.' I began at once to figure up in my mind how many men I could cook for, if there should be no better way of making money."

These vivid images of independent and determined women are strikingly at odds with the stereotypical picture of the long-suffering and sad-eyed pioneer wife peering wearily westward while a creaking covered wagon carries her ever farther from the comforts of home. Perhaps more startling is the departure from the perception of the gold rush as an exclusively male adventure.

All travelers endured hardships en route to California, but the lure of gold enticed and beckoned like a rainbow's promise. Upon reaching the golden ground, numbers of women, as eager as any male red-shirted miner, grubbed in the dirt and creekbeds for the glittering ore. Gold fever raged in epidemic proportions, and women were not immune.

The journal of schoolteacher Lucena Parsons, married but a year, reveals her infection's daily progress. On May 30, 1851, Parsons confessed to "a great desire to see the gold diggings"; she accompanied the men and watched them mine for gold. On May 31, she wrote: "This morning the gold fever raged so high that I went again with the rest but got very little gold. . . ." On June 2, "again went to the canion [sic] to find that bewitching ore"; and June 3, "a general turn out to the mines . . . we made 10 dollars to day." On June 4, she went again "and did very well."

Elizabeth Gunn, who had sailed around the Horn with four young children to join her prospecting husband in Sonora, observed to her family back

East that "a Frenchman and his wife live in the nearest tent, and they dig gold together. She dresses exactly like her husband—red shirt and pants and hat."

The editor of the *Alta California* reported a similar sighting: "We saw last April, a French woman, standing in Angel's Creek, dipping and pouring water into the washer, which her husband was rocking. She wore short boots, white duck pantaloons, a red flannel shirt, with a black leather belt and a Panama hat. Day after day she could be seen working quietly and steadily, performing her share of the gold digging labor. . . ."

Many of the women who tried mining, however, found the prize unworthy of the effort it required. Eliza Farnham, famed for attempting to deliver one hundred marriageable women to California, wrote that she "washed one panful of earth, under a burning noon-day sun . . . and must frankly confess, that the small particle of gold, which lies this day safely folded in a bit of tissue paper . . . did not in the least excite the desire to continue the search."

Louisa Clapp, wife of a doctor at Rich Bar, concurred, writing to her sister in the East: "I have become a *mineress;* that is, if the [*sic*] having washed a pan of dirt with my own hands, and procured therefrom three dollars and twenty-five cents in gold dust . . . will entitle me to the name. I can truly say, with the blacksmith's apprentice at the close of his first day's work at the anvil, that 'I am sorry I learned the trade'; for I wet my feet, tore my dress, spoilt a pair of new gloves, nearly froze my fingers, got an awful headache, took cold and lost a valuable breastpin, in this my labor of love."

Mary Ballou, at the mining camp of Negro Bar, wrote her son Selden, left behind in New Hampshire, that she "washed out about a Dollars [*sic*] worth of gold dust . . . so you see that I am doing a little mining in this gold region but I think it harder to rock the cradle to wash out gold than it is to rock the cradle for Babies in the States."

The labor was indeed discouraging, and most gold-rushing women found it easier—and more profitable—to market their domestic skills in exchange for the glittering metal. As Margaret Frink had heard, if "a woman could cook at all," she could earn her living. Boasted one fiercely independent woman: "I have made about $18,000 worth of pies—about one third of this has been clear profit. One year I dragged my own wood off the mountain and chopped it, and I have never had so much as a child take a step for me in this country. $11,000 I baked in one little iron skillet, a considerable portion by a campfire, without the shelter of a tree from the broiling sun. . . ."

Forty-niner Sarah Royce, who journeyed overland to California with her husband and three-year-old daughter, met a woman at Weaverville who "evidently felt that her prospect of making money was very enviable." The woman received one hundred dollars a month to cook three meals a day, was provided an assistant, and did no dishwashing.

In San Francisco, Chastina Rix supplemented the family income by ironing. In one week she noted that she had ironed sixty shirts, thirty-five starched and twenty-five plain, plus "hosts of other clothes & I have made twelve dollars by my labor." Her husband Alfred wrote to his friends in the East that Chastina "is making money faster than half the farmers in Peacham. She has just bought her another silk dress & lots of toggery & cravats & gloves for me and all the nice things & has quite a fund at interest at 3 per cent a month."

Laundresses were in especially high demand in the gold fields: during the early days of the rush some desperate miners shipped their laundry to the Sandwich [Hawaiian] Islands and even to China, waiting as long as six months for its return. Abby Mansur, at the Horseshoe Bar camp, wrote to her sister in New England about a neighbor who earned from fifteen to twenty dollars a month washing, "so you can see that women stand as good a chance as men[;] if it was not for my heart I could make a great deal but I am not stout enough to do it."

Whether washing or cooking, mining or ironing, women at work in frontier California toiled arduously. No labor, however, seemed more intimidating than keeping a boarding house. In 1850, about one out of every hundred persons gainfully employed in California ran some sort of hotel. Many were women, and none attested more eloquently to the labor involved than forty-niner Mary Jane Megquier, who had crossed the Isthmus from Winthrop, Maine to run a San Francisco boarding house.

I should like to give you an account of my work if I could do it justice," Megquier wrote. "I get up and make the coffee, then I make the biscuit, then I fry the potatoes[,] then broil three pounds of steak, and as much liver, while the [hired] woman is sweeping, and setting the table, at eight the bell rings and they are eating until nine. I do not sit until they are nearly all done . . . after breakfast I bake six loaves of bread (not very big) then four pies, or a pudding then we have lamb, for which we have paid nine dollars a quarter, beef, pork, baked, turnips, beets, potatoes, radishes, sallad [*sic*], and that everlasting soup, every day, dine at two, for tea we have hash, cold meat[,] bread and butter[,] sauce and some kind of cake and I have cooked every mouthful that has been eaten excepting one day and a half that we were on a steamboat excursion. I make six beds every day and do the washing and ironing[.] [Y]ou must think that I am very busy and when I dance all night I am obliged to trot all day and if I had not the constitution of six horses I should [have] been dead long ago but I am going to give up in the fall whether or no, as I am sick and tired of work." . . .

The first prostitutes to gold-rush California sailed from Valparaiso, Chile, where news of the gold discovery arrived in August 1848 via the Chilean brig *J.R.S.* Many of these women not only married argonauts, but enjoyed the luxury of choosing among their suitors.

Other Latin women, however, fared poorly. Hundreds, through indenture arrangements, were destined for fandango houses, the poor man's brothels. José Fernandez, the first alcalde at San Jose under American rule, wrote: "They did not pay passage on the ships, but when they reached San Francisco the captains sold them to the highest bidder. There were men who, as soon as any ship arrived from Mexican ports with a load of women, took two or three small boats, or a launch, went on board the ship, paid to the captain the passage of ten or twelve unfortunates and took them immediately to their cantinas, where the newcomers were forced to prostitute themselves for half a year, during which the proprietors took the bulk of their earnings."

China, like Chile, received news of California's gold discovery in 1848. By 1854, San Francisco's burgeoning Chinatown included hundreds of Chinese girls imported for prostitution. Typically, agents took arriving Chinese girls to a basement in Chinatown where they were stripped for examination and purchase. Depending on age, beauty, and the prevailing market, they sold from $300 to $3,000.

American women were not exempt from similar exploitation, albeit more subtly executed. In late 1849 and early 1850, several prostitutes in the East received passage to California by signing contracts as domestics. Some unethical agencies subsequently adopted the ploy of advertising that "servants" were wanted in California and receiving exceptional wages. A number of girls innocently responded to these procurement fronts that masqueraded as employment offices.

France similarly pounced on the fortuitous discovery at Sutter's Mill. Recruiting agents, as well as the French government, assisted the emigration of French women, who arrived in California literally by the boatload. Testified one eyewitness: "They have done the wildest kinds of business you can imagine in San Francisco, such as auctioning off women in the public square." . . .

A knowledgeable Frenchman noted that his countrywomen profitably hired themselves out to stand at gaming tables. . . .

"To sit with you near the bar or at a card table, a girl charges one ounce ($16) an evening. She had to do nothing save honor the table with her presence. This holds true for the girls selling cigars, when they sit with you. . . .

"Nearly all these women at home were streetwalkers of the cheapest sort. But out here, for only a few minutes, they ask a hundred times as much as they were used to getting in Paris. A whole night costs from $200 to $400."

Providing theatrical entertainment for lonesome miners offered a less notorious but equally profitable means of amassing California gold. Everywhere forty-niners could be found, from San Francisco's gilt-decorated theaters to the rough boards of a mining camp stage lit by candles stuck in whiskey bottles, actresses, dancers, singers, and musicians performed before appreciative audiences.

The pay varied as much as the venue. In Grass Valley, a black woman presented public piano concerts, charging fifty cents admission. The miners of Downieville bestowed $500 in gold on a young female vocalist who made them homesick by sweetly singing old familiar ballads. A Swiss organ-girl, by playing in gambling halls, accumulated $4,000 in about six months. A Frenchwoman who played the violin at San Francisco's Alhambra gambling hall earned two ounces of gold daily, about $32.

In 1850, three French actresses opened at San Francisco's Adelphi Theatre. A critic observed that two of them "have been on the stage for a long time (I was about to write too long a time), and . . . have never definitely arrived." The women succeeded despite the quality of the performances, for the critic noted that they "have not done badly from a financial point of view, as they now own the building, the lot, and the scenery."

Renowned female performers willing to try their fortunes in far-off California achieved enormous success. Soprano Catherine Hayes, a tall blonde woman of imposing appearance, introduced costumed operatic presentations to the San Francisco stage and was rumored to have departed from the golden state with an estimated quarter-million dollars. Lola Montez cleared $16,000 a week for performing her titillating spider dance.

California's free and open society also permitted women to pursue a variety of other employments normally deemed unacceptable for their gender. The editor of the *Alta California* welcomed a female doctor with a cheerfully delivered jibe: "So few ladies in San Francisco that the new M.D. may attend them all. . . . No circumlocutions necessary. . . . Simply, as woman to woman: 'Saw my leg off!'" . . .

By the end of 1853, a contemporary historian estimated California's female population at more than sixty thousand, plus about half that many children. In San Francisco alone, women numbered about eight thousand.

By that time, energy and gold had transformed San Francisco from a city of tents into a booming metropolis. No longer a hamlet, the city reflected the changes taking place throughout the newly admitted state. Its people were no longer simply transient miners. Men were bankers and businessmen, lawyers and doctors, farmers and manufacturers. They intended to stay.

So did women, as California pioneer Mallie Stafford later recalled. "Very few, if any, in those [first] days contemplated permanently settling in the country. . . . But as time wore on . . . they came to love the strange new country . . . and found that they were wedded to the new home, its very customs, the freedom of its lovely hills and valleys."

Thus tens of thousands of women, through choice, chance, or circumstance, found themselves in California during the "great adventure." And, after the gold fever eventually subsided, many of them remained to help settle the land. Although they are today a neglected part of gold-rush history, the "forgotten forty-niners" were there when history was being made—and they helped to make it.

Early California Land Policy Defended

PAUL WALLACE GATES

The California Land Act of March 3, 1851, seemed to mark the final step in transferring to the courts full responsibility for adjudicating claims to land granted by foreign governments in territory later acquired by the United States. It was framed by members of Congress who were familiar with the errors of the past in the adjudication of land claims in Missouri, Illinois, Louisiana, and Florida, particularly the use of influence at various government levels to secure confirmation of doubtful or incomplete grants, and with the crushing burden Congress had carried in considering the thousands of private land claims presented to it. The growing complexity of public affairs and the increasing tendency of Congress to intrude into matters of transportation, education, overseas shipping, rivers and harbors improvements, agriculture, and industry were absorbing the time of members of Congress who could no longer give the detailed attention of the past to private land claims or to the great number of private financial claims that were deluging it.

The California Land Act of 1851, and a similar measure passed in 1855 to transfer to the newly established Court of Claims responsibility for passing upon the many claims growing out of government activities, were both products of conservative coalitions of Whigs and Democrats and were intended to free Congress of the minutia that had absorbed an unconscionable amount of attention by members. Neither bill was a partisan measure nor was the Land Act by any stretch of the imagination an agrarian measure. Unlike so much of the land legislation of the time, it contained no loopholes through which stultification of its provisions could be achieved. Yet this same Act has been the object of more misunderstanding by contemporaries and by historians than almost any legislation affecting public lands. This early distortion was doubtless somewhat responsible for the partial withdrawal by Congress from its transfer of authority to the courts by the enactment of eleven special interest measures which in turn led to intensive lobbying in Washington for numerous other private acts of a similar character.

In the easygoing days of Mexican California tracts had been granted for cattle ranchos ranging from 4,428 to 133,000 acres, and small residence lots were assigned in what became San Gabriel, San Francisco, and San Jose. The process of conveying public lands was speeded up after the adoption of the secularization law of 1833 and the recovery of the mission lands. In the last three years of Mexican control 288 grants were made. Among the persons most favored with numerous grants were members of the Abila, Bernal, Carrillo, Castro, de la Guerra, Higuero, Pacheco, Peralta, Pico, Sánchez, and Vallejo families [.]

Excerpted from Paul Wallace Gates, "The California Land Act of 1851," *California Historical Quarterly,* 50, December 1971: pp. 395–398, 404–405. Reprinted by permission of the California Historical Society.

Just before American control was established, the basis was laid for numerous fraudulent claims; other claims were rushed through before the usual requirements to make them legal could be satisfied. In the last seven months of his service as governor, Pío Pico hastily approved 56 "eleventh hour" grants of one league or more totaling 1,756,000 acres. Under Mexican law most of these grants were not complete titles and could be denounced and made invalid because they had not been approved by the assembly, had not been improved and made into operating ranchos, or had been conveyed to others. When California was transferred to the United States by the treaty of Guadalupe Hidalgo, residents were allowed to become American citizens or to retain their Mexican citizenship. In either event they were promised that property of every kind "shall be inviolably respected . . . exactly as if the same belonged to citizens of the United States."

Mexican rights were to be interpreted according to Mexican law, not American, and questions of title in equity proceedings were to be judged by Anglo-Saxon law as interpreted by courts holding property rights in the highest regard. No additional rights were to be created in the judicial process but neither were any rights to be diminished.

American control of California and the discovery of gold created a demand for land, the most desirable of which was in private land claims in the coastal valleys and along the San Joaquin and Sacramento Rivers. Containing nearly 15,000,000 acres, these claims had been scarcely saleable prior to 1846, bringing at the most only a few cents an acre. Now, with the inrush of population, the need for land for crops and for cities, and the likelihood of swiftly rising prices, there was a scramble for land that sent prices to levels that promised large returns to speculators. Efforts were made to provide documentation for incomplete claims, new claims were fabricated, and occupancy concessions were transformed into full possessory claims by the alchemy of sworn testimony. Only by the most intensive investigation of the handwriting, the seals, the quality of the ink and paper on which concessions were made, and the closest examination of the parole testimony was it possible to separate the most cunningly contrived claims from those which were valid.

It was desirable that early action be taken to examine the title of the grants claimed to have been made by the Spanish and Mexican governments in California to segregate them from the public land, that the latter might be opened to settlers. Not one of the land claims had been surveyed, and in most instances boundaries were entirely non-existent. Unfortunately, other questions intervened, including the admission of California into the Union, the status of slavery in the territory acquired from Mexico, the slave trade in the District of Columbia, the recovery of fugitive slaves in the North, railroad land grants, and the donation of swamp lands to the state. These questions all had higher priority, and, until the Compromise of 1850 was finally achieved, the California land claims had to wait. Nearly five years passed after California was conquered, and three years elapsed after it became a part of the United States, before Congress got around to providing for the adjudication of the land claims. By that time almost a hundred thousand people were roaming over California looking for gold or for land on which to settle. During this long delay the government archives of California were open to interference and falsification by the insertation [*sic*] of antedated documents and tampering with previously filed documents. . . .

The California Land Act of 1851, therefore, marked a major step forward in the adjudication of land claims, for it placed full authority for their final determination in the courts. A Commission of three members appointed by the president was to hear testimony and to study the documents presented by the claimants, and a law agent "skilled in the Spanish and English languages . . . and learned in the law" was to "superintend [*i.e.,* defend] the interests of the United States in the premises. . . ." After due deliberation the Commission was to confirm or reject the claims. From the decision of the Commission either side could appeal to the district court. Here new evidence could be presented, and the district attorney could contest the Commission's decision if he doubted the authenticity of the documents presented, the integrity of the witnesses, or the interpretation of Spanish and Mexican law. If the district attorney was completely satisfied, he could recommend approval of the decisions of the Land Commission or the district court favorable to the claimants and litigation concerning ownership would then halt. Both the government and the claimants had the right of appeal from the decision of the district judge to the Supreme Court, though no new evidence was to be submitted there.

A factor seriously delaying the final settlement of many claims was the careless manner in which owners had handled their titles. Frequently the papers had been lost or destroyed, all requirements for a complete title under Mexican law had not been completed, or claimants delayed in submitting their claims and then they tried to change their original but vaguely defined boundaries to include valuable improvements made by later settlers. Many claims were so devoid of improvements or signs of ownership that immigrants swept over them, selecting sites and building homes without any knowledge that they were on private claims. It was to take years before the last claims were confirmed. By that time some owners or their heirs either had lost their rights through tax delinquency, mortgage foreclosures, or intra-family litigation, or the titles had been fragmented into so many parts as to make division and sale of the land difficult. . . .

The Act of 1851 was not "in reality a violation of the Treaty of Guadalupe Hidalgo," nor was it "an instrument of evil" or a "devil's instrument." There was no such thing as "needless persecution of the grant holders" by the Attorney General and the courts, and it was not the Land Acts which "stripped" from California rancheros their property. Neither were the claimants "considered guilty until they had proved them innocent." Bancroft's "spoilation of the grant-holders" is sheer nonsense, and his insistence that "it would have been infinitely better to confirm promptly all the claims, both valid and fraudulent," is evidence of the unreasoned and unjust condemnation of the land law which so long characterized elite California opinion.

Such irrational denunciation of the Land Act of 1851 and of the subsequent history of adjudication under it reveals an astonishing failure to appreciate the careful protection Anglo-Saxon-American law has given private property.

Land and the Conflict of Legal Cultures

DOUGLAS MONROY

The war and the formal transference of sovereignty had a profound effect on Hispanic society in California. After all, Americans had waged war against Mexicans. Americans inside and outside the government coveted the wealth of California. The Gold Rush only further encouraged Anglo-American visions of bonanza capitalism. They considered the territory to be their just reward for bringing liberty and prosperity to the once-slumbering northern lands of troubled Mexico. "When I came," recalled one of the city's first businessmen, "Los Angeles was a sleepy, ambitionless adobe village with very little promise for the future. . . . We possessed however, even in that distant day, one asset, intangible it is true, but as valuable as it was intangible—the spirit popularly called 'Western,' but which, after all, was largely the pith of transferred Eastern enterprise." The editor of the *Semi-Weekly News* opined in 1868, "As we stand on the bank of the river and gaze over the fine fields with their teeming population, we cannot but wonder at the goodness of God and the power of man to redeem and civilize a country. A few years ago, the vast tract of land we now so much admire, was only a little Rancho, uninhabited save by a few vaqueros." America, for those of the enterprising spirit and the accumulationist bent, represented a place not merely to live in but also to get rich in. This new, far western region was to be no exception.

America needed open land to maintain its vision of individual liberty and thus its uniqueness. Without it its eastern cities would crowd with unemployed, who might turn to demagogues and mob action for redress. Then the nation with the special mission would become like authoritarian Europe, where in the revolutions of 1848 the unemployed rabble took to the streets. With land available in the West, though, resourceless people could move there and set themselves up as independent freeholders. "How many Countrymen of mine," wrote Alex Forbes to Abel Stearns about California, "who are jostling one another for room at home, might live happily in those fertile but uncultivated plains you describe!" Open land, in other words, guaranteed not only prosperity but also social mobility, and, in turn, political stability and liberty.

This compelling idea never came to much for the underclasses. The urban unemployed had neither the agricultural skills nor the material wherewithal to establish themselves as farmers in the West. (For this reason, the Homestead Act of 1862, which embodied this concept, largely failed.) Moreover, the liberty to speculate in real estate usually meant that all the good land was monopolized. Those who controlled capital at the start often ended up with all the wealth, while army soldiers, recruited from the underclass, pacified the natives, who resisted the appropriation of the lands. But these notions did motivate people in the state and the culture as a whole to acquire lands. Bancroft describes what I have termed *bonanza capitalism:* "The fever was raging in Washington as well as Sacramento. It was not of 500 or 1,000 rancheros, living on stock-farms owned by themselves and their fathers, and of little value by American standards, that the senate was thinking, but of a marvellous land of gold-mines, great towns, and limitless prospects; not of a quiet, pastoral people, but a horde of speculators, hungry for gold and power and land." In California, pastoral dons with Indian vaqueros inhabited huge tracts of land on which they did not do much other than supply hides and tallow, feed themselves, and maintain their seigneurial life-style.

The Californios soon found themselves and their ways placed outside the new Anglo-American laws. The conflict between Spanish law, based in Roman law, and United States law, based in English common law, derived not only from juridical philosophy. When one culture, assuming that its own laws ensure justice and social tranquility, imposes them on another culture, the latter sees that very same legal structure as the mechanism that excludes its people from justice and the material rewards of the newly dominant society. The law, in other words, has been for many the means not of justice but of oppression. In 1850, for example, the California legislature passed a bill establishing the so-called foreign miners' tax so that the state could pay off its debts by regaining some of the wealth that "foreigners" (obviously a vague and relative term at this moment in California history) took out in gold. It also provided physical protection from attack for "foreigners" once they had paid the monthly fee of twenty dollars for a license. Those at whom the lawmakers aimed this legislation perceived it as a discriminatory and arbitrary action and objected strenuously—usually privately but sometimes publicly. The act had the effect of giving license to American miners to eject Mexican (including Californio), Chinese, and Chilean miners through mob action. The reason for this expulsion goes beyond xenophobia. One Californio miner, the most renowned citizen of Hispanic Los Angeles, Antonio Coronel, recalled that "the reason for most of the antipathy against the Spanish race was that the greater portion was composed of Sonorans who were men accustomed to prospecting and who consequently achieved quicker, richer results—such as the Californios had already attained by having arrived first and acquiring understanding of this same art." T. Butler King railed that "more than fifteen thousand foreigners, mostly Mexicans and Chilenos, came in *armed bands* into the mining district, bidding defiance to all the opposition, and finally carrying out of the country some twenty millions of dollars' worth of gold dust." King knew for whom this gold was destined: "[It] belongs *by purchase* to the people of the United States." (The United States formally paid Mexico $15 million for California, Arizona, New Mexico, and much of Colorado, Utah, and Nevada.) "If not excluded by law," thundered King, "they will return and recommence the work of plunder." The legal formality of payment enabled King to put Mexicans outside, and his culture inside, any norms, as laws, regarding "plunder."

Coronel described how, in anticipation of such legislation, "one Sunday, notices appeared in writing in Los Pinos and in several places, that anyone who was not an American citizen must abandon the place within twenty-four hours and that he who did not comply would be obliged to by force. This was supported by a gathering of armed men, ready to make that warning effective." Such armed groups, "the major part under the influence of liquor," terrorized "foreigners"; in one case a mob falsely accused two unfortunates of theft, tied their arms behind their backs, loaded them on a cart, and publicly hanged them. After many others had fled or been chased out, merchants who had initially favored the act found that the gold the "foreigners" were alleged to have removed they actually spent in their stores. The odious act was repealed only a year after passage, though the consequences of expelling nearly everyone except white Americans from the goldfields of the north continued. "Daily, though," Coronel continued, "the weakest were dislodged from the digging by the strongest." The law never protected miners of color; it only supported efforts to exclude everyone from economic opportunities except the conquerors. The ultimate result, in other words, was the expulsion of non-Americans—Mexicans and Chinese especially were singled out—from the mining opportunities of California through apparently state-sanctioned mass violence against people of color. The Mexicans ejected from the goldfields either headed south, where they merged with their compatriots in the so-called cow counties, or crossed the new border into Mexico. They carried with them, along with the few belongings with which they escaped, a profound hatred and fear of Yankees.

Different notions of land tenure produced the most consequential disputes between Californios and Anglos. Let us recall the mechanism by which Californios received grants and their notion of what entitled one to land. Such markers as a "bullocks head on a bluff," a "clump of trees," and so on described the boundaries of the old grants, such as the Lugos' Rancho San Antonio. The validity of the land tenure of such ranchos derived as much from occupancy and tradition as from written documents. Entitlement (granted sometimes to women as well as men under Spanish law) to the land came from living, working, and maintaining, if not extending, the royal domains of the Spanish king. In the Mexican period, when most of the land was granted, the conniving Californios acquired the former mission lands in spite of the desire of many liberal Mexican officials to encourage small freeholds. The governors did sign legal deeds to the Californios converting the land into private property. Vague boundaries, however, still predominated. This situation framed the Californio rancheros' encounter with United States land law and indeed with the whole culture of Anglo land tenure.

The Land Act of 1851 wreaked havoc on the rancheros' claims. It created a three-person commission to which all titles of the Spanish and Mexican eras had to be submitted for validation. The problems for the rancheros lay less in any biases against them on the part of the commissioners than in the biases of the law itself. The commission proceeded from the assumption that all titles were invalid until proved otherwise. This policy put an enormous burden on the Californios, who did not understand the workings of a system based on common law or even the language in which it was implemented. Claims often rested on long-forgotten or misplaced written deeds. Usually the courts did not allow the recollections of eyewitnesses to entitlement; but even when they did, claims could be thrown out on technicalities, and there were successful court challenges to boundaries established only by custom. Even a claim that was perfectly in order could cost a Californio a good deal of land. Except for merchants, Californios had little cash on hand and had to sell land and cattle, or mortgage land, to pay legal fees. That the hearings took place in San Francisco only increased the difficulties of the cow-county rancheros. The Land Act effectively dispossessed Californios of approximately 40 percent of their lands held before 1846. In the contradictory American tradition of liberty, speculators with cash and shrewdness, not small farmers usually, grabbed the lands.

Article 9 of the Treaty of Guadalupe-Hidalgo declared that Mexicans "shall be maintained and protected in the free enjoyment of their liberty and property." Secretary of State James Buchanan said to those nervous about the protections Mexicans would have for their property, "It is our glory that no human power exists in this country which can deprive one individual of his property without his consent and transfer it to another." The massive alienation of Californio lands, and their transfer to others, obviously fell outside the letter and spirit of the treaty and American respect for private property.

A number of factors produced this ruination of many of the ranchos. One was greed. Americans fought the Mexican War to get some of Mexico. Once the Americans won the war, they were not about to allow Mexicans to remain on land they believed now belonged to them. They saw it as their manifest destiny to bring progress and civilization to this land held by indolent Catholics of a different and inferior race. Many came west as forty-niners, and they generally found disappointment in the goldfields; only a few struck it rich. These Americans, believing they had a right, as the yeomanry of a noble democratic tradition, to a farm and to prosperity, looked to acquire farms in bounteous California from the Californios, who indeed monopolized the best tillage with relatively unproductive cattle ranches. Particularly in the north, they squatted on lands they knew were in difficult litigation, compounding the troubles of the rancheros. Out of this situation the lawyers and speculators got much of the land in the areas that had drawn the most immigrants. The earnest efforts of frustrated democratic fortune seekers to gain a freehold proved only slightly more fruitful than their labor in the mines and goldfields. This greed for land, inflamed by the lawyers, would catch up to the rancheros in the south, though there their own profligate ways led in part to their undoing. . . .

To say the least, Anglo-American land law did not work for the Californios in the way that Secretary Buchanan extolled. "The practical working of the law was oppressive and ruinous," stated Bancroft. "They were virtually robbed by the government which was bound to protect them." The accuracy of his description of the efforts of the Land Act of 1851 and his condemnation of it do not replace the need to analyze why the law worked as it did. Having discussed the motive of greed, we need to follow through with a fuller analysis of the conflict of legal cultures. In so doing, we will better understand, in particular, the land and labor situation and other legal matters affecting Hispanic and Indian peoples and, in general, the way that the legal system reflected and illuminated, and framed and affected, Anglo ascendancy in their newly won Southwest. The history of the Mexican War and the transfer of territory and wealth did not end with the signing of the Treaty of Guadalupe-Hidalgo. Because the legal system figured so prominently in this phase, it is important to analyze that factor thoroughly.

 ## FURTHER READING

Charles Bateson, *Gold Fleet for California: Forty-Niners from Australia and New Zealand* (1964)

Edwin A. Beilharz and Carlos U. Lopez, *We Were 49ers! Chilean Accounts of the California Gold Rush* (1976)

John Walton Caughey, *Gold Is the Cornerstone* (1948; repr. as *The California Gold Rush,* 1975)

Ping Chiu, *Chinese Labor in California, 1850–1880,* chapter 2: "In the Mines, 1849–1880" (1967)

David V. DuFault, "The Chinese in the Mining Camps of California, 1848–1870," *Historical Society of Southern California Quarterly* XLI (June 1959): 155–70

Paul Wallace Gates, *Land and Law in California: Essays on Land Policies* (1991)

Theodore Grivas, *Military Governments in California, 1846–1850* (1963)

Neal Harlow, *California Conquered: The Annexation of a Mexican Province, 1846–1850* (1982)

Robert F. Heizer, ed., *The Destruction of the California Indians: A Collection of Documents from the Period 1847 to 1865* (1974; reprinted edition, paperback 1993)

J. S. Holliday, *The World Rushed In: The California Gold Rush Experience* (1981)

James M. Jensen, "Cattle Drives from the Ranchos to the Gold Fields of California," *Arizona and the West* II (Winter 1960): 341–52

David Alan Johnson, *Founding the Far West: California, Oregon, and Nevada, 1840–1890* (1992)

Robert L. Kelley, *Gold vs. Grain: The Hydraulic Mining Controversy in California's Sacramento Valley* (1954)

JoAnn Levy, *They Saw the Elephant: Women in the California Gold Rush* (1990)

Roger W. Lotchin, *San Francisco, 1846–1856: From Hamlet to City* (1974)

Laurie F. Maffly-Kipp, *Religion and Society in Frontier California* (1994)

Ralph Mann, *After the Gold Rush: Society in Grass Valley and Nevada City, California, 1849–1870* (1982)

Jay Monaghan, *Chile, Peru, and the California Gold Rush of 1849* (1973)

R. H. Morefield, "Mexicans in the California Mines, 1848–1853," *California Historical Society Quarterly* XXXV (March 1956): 37–46

Keith A. Murray, *The Modocs and Their War* (1959; paperback 1976)

Rodman W. Paul, *California Gold* (1947)

Rodman W. Paul, *Mining Frontiers of the Far West, 1848–1880* (1963)

Richard H. Peterson, *Manifest Destiny in the Mines: A Cultural Interpretation of Anti-Mexican Nativism in California, 1848–1853* (1975)

Donald Pisani, "Land Monopoly in Nineteenth-Century California," *Agricultural History* 65 (Fall 1991): 15–37

James J. Rawls, "Gold Diggers: Indian Miners in the California Gold Rush," *California Historical Quarterly* LV (Spring 1976): 28–45

William W. Robinson, *Land in California: The Story of Mission Lands, Ranchos, Squatters, Mining Claims, Railroad Grants, Land Scrip, Homesteads* (1948)

M. Colette Standart, "The Sonoran Migration to California, 1848–1856," *Southern California Quarterly* LVIII (Fall 1976): 333–58

Kevin Starr, *Americans and the California Dream, 1850–1915* (1973)

John Umbeck, "The California Gold Rush: A Study of Emerging Property Rights," *Explorations in Economic History* XIV (July 1977): 197–226

CHAPTER

6

Disputes over Water, 1880s–1910s

From the very beginning, Californians were aware of their state's tremendous agricultural potential. In the early 1850s, the state senate's Committee on Agriculture strongly recommended that farming be supported as the most significant industry. In the years following, farming replaced mining as the state's premier industry; by 1860 California had become the nation's leading barley producer and ranked high in the production of wheat. Members of a new landed elite also used enormous tracts of rancho land for cattle raising and feed grains. A flourishing sheep industry developed as well to provide wool for soldiers' uniforms and blankets during the Civil War.

This so-called pastoral and wheat boom era of 1850 to 1890 was soon overshadowed by the cultivation of specialty crops—fruits, vegetables, and nuts of all kinds—although California continued to be an important producer of wheat and other grains. From the farmers' viewpoint, as Donald Worster has demonstrated convincingly in Rivers of Empire: Water, Aridity, and the Growth of the American West (1985), deficient rainfall was the state's major natural imperfection. But many flowing streams could be diverted for agricultural purposes so as to overcome, it was hoped, the problem of aridity. Further, the prospect of irrigation, so important to California's subsequent agricultural success, offered renewed hope to those who opposed monopoly in land. "Thus was born the theory of deliverance through irrigation," observes Worster. However, early irrigation projects aimed at promoting small-scale farming actually ended up strengthening the power of large-scale agribusiness.

Indeed, the high capital expense of irrigation and of its offspring, citrus cultivation, sharply restricted most agricultural opportunities to wealthy investors. Citrus, like irrigation, served as an option, therefore, not for small farmers but only for large capitalists. In 1871, for example, a group of wealthy San Francisco entrepreneurs formed a corporation to sell real estate and then to construct a system of canals for irrigation and water power designed to increase the value of that land. This San Joaquin and King's River Canal and Irrigation Company would serve as a prototype for the

136

continuing power of big capital in California land use and agricultural production. In short, a new form of corporate agriculture, rather than Jeffersonian agrarian ideals and practices, became the norm in agricultural California.

Efforts to develop the state's water resources also drew Californians into the early environmental movement. During the nineteenth century, individuals such as the artist George Catlin, the philosopher Henry David Thoreau, and the landscape architect Frederick Law Olmsted began to articulate a need to conserve nature. It was not until the turn of the century, however, that sporadic advocacy for conservation turned into a social movement. Gifford Pinchot, the chief of the U.S. Forest Service, who coined the term conservation, played a leading role in bringing the issue of natural-resource management to public attention. The utilitarian impulse of the conservationists—that is, their desire to control and manage nature for the benefit of humankind—soon clashed with the ideas of preservationists, who wanted to leave nature alone as a wilderness.

These two divergent viewpoints manifested themselves clearly in the struggle over the Hetch Hetchy Valley in California. The city of San Francisco wanted to build a dam across the Tuolumne River to create a reservoir to hold water for the city dwellers' consumption. But preservationists like John Muir led the fight to stop the project. San Francisco won this battle, and the beautiful Hetch Hetchy Valley remains inundated to this day.

Conservationists and preservationists continue to put forth much the same arguments today as did the city of San Francisco and John Muir. Some historians, however, focus on an underlying issue. In the two essays in this chapter, they ask whether California water policy represents centralized control by a landed elite motivated by greed or whether it is a system that has developed incrementally through the political competition of many diverse groups. In reading the documents in this chapter, look for evidence of both positions.

 D O C U M E N T S

In 1886 the California Supreme Court resolved decades of legal uncertainty regarding water rights by its decision in the case of *Lux* v. *Haggin*, a portion of which is reproduced here as the first document. At issue were two competing legal doctrines—"riparian" rights (which gave landowners along waterways the sole right to divert water and deprived owners of land not contiguous to waterways of that same right) and "prior appropriation" rights (which gave the first user of water the right to divert it and to sell that right to others). Two giant landholders—the widely despised Miller and Lux Land and Cattle Company and the firm of James B. Haggin and Lloyd Tevis—went head-to-head in legal battle, with the court, by a bare majority, holding in favor of the riparian rights of Miller and Lux.

The second document also addresses the importance of water in California's agricultural development. The control of water generated intense rivalries between cattlemen and citrus growers, culminating in the Wright Act (or the Irrigation District Act) of 1887, passage of which may be accounted for in part by the unpopularity of the *Lux* v. *Haggin* decision. This act enabled agricultural communities to organize as official governing units for the purpose of

constructing and operating much-needed irrigation systems. Because it authorized districts to issue bonds, and because it did not measure voting power by
the acreage owned (for fear that large landowners would dominate), the Wright
Act became the model for other western states. Moreover, it was ruled constitutional by the U.S. Supreme Court in 1897 and, according to one expert, was
"California's major nineteenth-century contribution to irrigation law."

The federal Reclamation Act of 1902, brief selections from which appear
as the third document, provided federal funds for the building of irrigation
projects in the arid West. Designed to attack land monopoly and to promote
the family farm, the act restricted the amount of federally subsidized water
that any one landowner could purchase (enough water to irrigate 160 acres, or
320 acres for a married couple). In California this acreage limitation was
resisted by large Central Valley landowners, but the U.S. Supreme Court in
1958 unanimously upheld its constitutionality. Not until 1982 were large landholders successful in increasing the limit to 960 acres.

The fourth document comes from the writings of John Muir, a Scottish
immigrant who grew up in Wisconsin and who, after an accident that almost
blinded him, walked much of the way from the Midwest to California. He first
laid eyes on the Yosemite Valley in 1868 and fell in love with the entire Sierra
Nevada range. He founded the Sierra Club in 1892 and became the nation's
best-known spokesperson for wilderness preservation. Horrified that the
breathtaking Hetch Hetchy Valley (which Muir thought rivaled the Yosemite
Valley in beauty) might be turned into a reservoir, he led the fight to stop the
dam's construction. His failure in this endeavor probably contributed to his
death in 1914. In the selection included here, note the awestruck way in which
Muir spoke about the beauty of Hetch Hetchy; the preservation of nature was,
to him, akin to religious worship.

Robert Underwood Johnson, author of the fifth document, was a friend of
Muir's. After the two took a long hike through Yosemite Valley in 1889, Johnson became one of Muir's chief allies in the fight to preserve sections of the
Sierra Nevada range. As an associate editor of *Century Magazine,* Johnson
advanced the preservationist cause and, along with Muir, played a key role in
securing congressional approval for the creation of Yosemite National Park in
1890. His writings on behalf of Hetch Hetchy were couched in more mundane
terms than Muir's. In the document reprinted here, he states explicitly that "we
hold human life more sacred than scenery . . . if San Francisco could not otherwise obtain an abundant water supply, we should be willing to dedicate to
that purpose not only Hetch-Hetchy, but even the incomparable Yosemite
itself." But, he argued, other sources of water were available; hence, the Hetch
Hetchy should not be despoiled in the manner proposed.

Lux v. *Haggin* Establishes the "California Doctrine," 1886

It is apparent that in deciding whether a use was public the legislature was
not limited by the mere *number* of persons to be immediately benefited as
opposed to those from whom property is to be taken. It must happen that a
public use (as of a particular wagon or railroad) will rarely be directly
enjoyed by all the denizens of the state, or of a county or city, and rarely
that all within the smallest political subdivision can, as a fact, immediately
enjoy every public use. Nor need the enjoyment of a public use be *uncon-*

ditional. A citizen of a municipality to which water has been brought, by a person or corporation, which, as agent of the government, has exercised the power of eminent domain, can demand water only on payment of the established rate, and on compliance with reasonable rules and regulations. And while the court will hold the use private where it appears that the government or public *cannot* have any interest in it, the legislature, in determining the expediency of declaring a use public, may no doubt properly take into the consideration all the advantages to follow from such action; as the advancement of agriculture, the encouragement of mining and the arts, and the general, though indirect, benefits derived to the people at large from the dedication.

It may be that, under the physical conditions existing in some portions of the state, irrigation is not, theoretically, a "natural want," in the sense that living creatures cannot exist without it; but its importance as a means of producing food from the soil makes it less necessary, in a scarcely appreciable degree, from the use of water by drinking it. The government would seem to have not only a distant and consequential, but a direct, interest in the use; therefore a public use. . . .

The main purpose of the statutes is to provide a mode by which the state, or its agent, may conduct water to arable lands where irrigation is a necessity, on payment of due compensation to those from whom the water is diverted. The same agent of the state may take water to more than one farming neighborhood. It must always be borne in mind that under the Codes no man, or set of men, can take another's property for his own *exclusive* use. . . .

From what is said above no inference is to be drawn as to the exact limits, in every respect, of the legislative power to declare a use public. We are only called on to say that sections of the Codes which provide for taking water from riparian proprietors (on due compensation) to supply "farming neighborhoods" are constitutional and valid. Whether, in any supposable instance, the public has such interest in a use which can be directly enjoyed only by an individual for his profit, and without any concomitant duty from him to the public, as that the government may be justified in employing the eminent domain power for the use, as for a public use, is a question somewhat startling, but which is not involved in the decision of the present action. In case further legislation shall be deemed expedient for the distribution of waters to public uses, we leave its validity to be determined after its enactment, if its invalidity shall then be asserted.

The Civil Code authorizes any person, for purposes useful to himself alone, or for the benefit of himself and others, to divert the waters of a stream, the rights of riparian proprietors *not being affected.* The claim of respondent is that, under the provisions of the Code, any person may divert all the waters of a stream from the lower lands, conduct them to a distant place beyond the water shed, and, whatever the additional loss by seepage and evaporation caused by a change of the channel, apply them either to his own purposes or sell them to others, the only conditions being that he shall appropriate them in the manner prescribed by the Code, and that they shall be used for an object beneficial to somebody. . . .

The citizens of the state have never been prohibited from entering upon the public lands of the state. The courts have always recognized a right in the prior possessor of lands of the state as against those subsequently intruding upon such possession. The same principle would protect a prior appropriator of water against a subsequent appropriator from the same stream. It is not important here to inquire whether, as against a subsequent appropriation of water, a prior appropriator of land through which the stream may run, would have the better right. It is enough to say that, as between two persons, both mere occupants of land or water on the state lands, the courts have determined controversies. The implied permission by the general government to private persons to enter upon its lands has been assumed to have been given by the state with reference to the lands of the state; and the state, for the maintenance of peace and good order, has protected the citizen in the acquisition and enjoyment on its lands of certain property rights obtained through possession—perhaps the mode by which all property was originally acquired. In view of these facts, we feel justified in saying that it was the legislative intent to exclude as well the state as the United States from the protection which is extended to riparian proprietors by section 1422 of the Civil Code.

The Wright Act Asserts Community Water Rights, 1887, 1889

An Act to provide for the organization and government of irrigation districts and to provide for the acquisition of water and other property, and for the distribution of water thereby for irrigation purposes.

The people of the State of California, represented in senate and assembly, do enact as follows:

Section 1. Whenever fifty or a majority of freeholders owning lands susceptible to one mode of irrigation from a common source, and by the same system of works, desire to provide for the irrigation of the same, they may propose the organization of an irrigation district under the provisions of this act, and when so organized such district shall have the powers conferred or that may hereafter be conferred by law upon such irrigation district.

Sec. 2. A petition shall first be presented to the board of supervisors of the county in which the lands or the greatest portion thereof is situated, signed by the required number of freeholders of such proposed district, which petition shall set forth and particularly describe the proposed boundaries of such district, and shall pray that the same may be organized under the provisions of this act. The petitioners must accompany the petition with a good and sufficient bond, to be approved by the said board of supervisors, in double the amount of the probable cost of organizing such district, conditioned that the bondsmen will pay all said cost in case said organization shall not be effected. Such petition shall be presented at a regular meeting of the said board, and shall be published for at least two weeks before the time at which the same is to be presented, in some newspaper printed and published in the county where said petition is presented, together with a notice stating the time of the meeting at which the same will be presented. When such petition is presented, the said board of supervisors shall hear the same, and may adjourn such hearing from time to time, not exceeding four weeks in all; and on the final hearing may make such changes in the proposed boundaries as they may find to be proper, and shall establish and define such boundaries. . . . Such notice shall require the electors to cast ballots which shall contain the words, "Irrigation district—Yes;" or, "Irrigation district—No," or words equivalent thereto; and also the names of persons to be voted for to fill the various elective offices hereinafter prescribed. No person shall be entitled to vote at any election held under the provisions of this act unless he shall possess all the qualifications required of electors under the general election laws of this State. . . .

[1889 Amendment]:

An Act supplemental to an act entitled "An act to provide for the organization and government of irrigation districts, and to provide for the acquisition of water and other property, and for the distribution of water thereby for irrigation purposes," approved March seventeenth, eighteen hundred and eighty-seven, and to provide for the examination, approval, and confirmation of proceedings for the issue and sale of bonds issued under the provisions of said act.

The people of the State of California, represented in senate and assembly, do enact as follows:

Section 1. The board of directors of an irrigation district . . . may commence a special proceeding, in and by which the proceedings of said board and of said district providing for and authorizing the issue and sale of the bonds of said district, whether said bonds or any of them have or have not then been sold, may be judicially examined, approved, and confirmed.

Sec. 2. The board of directors of the irrigation district shall file in the superior court of the county in which the lands of the district or some portion thereof are situated a petition praying, in effect, that the proceedings aforesaid may be examined, approved, and confirmed by the court. The petition shall state the facts showing the proceedings had for the issue and sale of said bonds, and shall state generally that the irrigation district was duly organized, and that the first board of directors was duly elected; but the petition need not state the facts showing such organization of the district, or the election of said first board of directors.

Congress Acts: Selections from the Reclamation Act of 1902

Be it enacted by the Senate and House of Representatives of the United States of America in Congress assembled, That all moneys received from the sale and disposal of public lands in Arizona, California, Colorado, Idaho, Kansas, Montana, Nebraska, Nevada, New Mexico, North Dakota, Oklahoma, Oregon, South Dakota, Utah, Washington, and Wyoming, beginning with the fiscal year ending June thirtieth, nineteen hundred and one, including the surplus of fees and commissions in excess of allowances to registers and receivers, and excepting the five per centum of the proceeds of the sales of public lands in the above States set aside by law for educational and other purposes, shall be, and the same are hereby, reserved, set aside, and appropriated as a special fund in the Treasury to be known as the "reclamation fund," to be used in the examination and survey for and the construction and maintenance of irrigation works for the storage, diversion, and development of waters for the reclamation of arid and semiarid lands in the said States and Territories, and for the payment of all other expenditures provided for in this Act. . . .

Sec. 2. That the Secretary of the Interior is hereby authorized and directed to make examinations and surveys for, and to locate and construct, as herein provided, irrigation works for the storage, diversion, and development of waters including artesian wells, and to report to Congress at the beginning of each regular session as to the results of such examinations and surveys, giving estimates of cost of all contemplated works, the quantity and location of the lands which can be irrigated therefrom, and all facts relative to the practicability of each irrigation project; also the cost of works in process of construction as well as of those which have been completed. . . .

No right to the use of water for land in private ownership shall be sold for a tract exceeding one hundred and sixty acres to any one landowner, and no such sale shall be made to any landowner unless he be an actual bona fide resident on such land, or occupant thereof residing in the neighborhood of said land, and no such right shall permanently attach until all payments therefor are made. The annual installments shall be paid to the receiver of the local land office of the district in which the land is situated, and a failure to make any two payments when due shall render the entry subject to cancellation, with the forfeiture of all rights under this Act, as well as of any moneys already paid thereon. All moneys received from the above sources shall be paid into the reclamation fund. Registers and receivers shall be allowed the usual commissions on all moneys paid for lands entered under this Act.

Sec. 6. That the Secretary of the Interior is hereby authorized and directed to use the reclamation fund for the operation and maintenance of all reservoirs and irrigation works constructed under the provisions of this Act: *Provided,* That when the payments required by this Act are made for the major portion of the lands irrigated from the waters of any of the works herein provided for, then the management and operation of such irrigation works shall pass to the owners of the lands irrigated thereby, to be maintained at their expense under such form of organization and under such rules and regulations as may be acceptable to the Secretary of the Interior.

John Muir Admires the Hetch Hetchy Valley, 1908

It is impossible to overestimate the value of wild mountains and mountain temples as places for people to grow in, recreation grounds for soul and body. They are the greatest of our natural resources, God's best gifts, but none, however high and holy, is beyond reach of the spoiler. In these ravaging money-mad days monopolizing San Francisco capitalists are now doing their best to destroy the Yosemjte Park, the most wonderful of all our great mountain national parks. Beginning on the Tuolumne side, they are trying with a lot of sinful ingenuity to get the Government's permission to dam and destroy the Hetch-Hetchy Valley for a reservoir, simply that comparatively private gain may be made out of universal public loss, while of course the Sierra Club is doing all it can to save the valley. . . .

As long as the busy public in general knew little or nothing about the Hetch-Hetchy Valley, the few cunning drivers of the damming scheme, working in darkness like moles in a low-lying meadow, seemed confident of success; but when light was turned on and the truth became manifest that next to Yosemite, Hetch-Hetchy is the most wonderful and most important feature of the great park, that damming it would destroy it, render it inaccessible, and block the way through the wonderful Tuolumne Cañon to the grand central campground in the upper Tuolumne Valley, thousands from near and far came to our help—mountaineers, nature-lovers, naturalists. Most of our thousand club members wrote to the President or Secretary protesting against the destructive reservoir scheme while other sources of city water as pure or purer than the Hetch-Hetchy were available; so also did the Oregon and Washington mountaineering clubs and the Appalachian of Boston and public-spirited citizens everywhere. And the President, recognizing the need of beauty as well as bread and water in the life of the nation, far from favoring the destruction of any of our country's natural wonder parks and temples, is trying amid a host of other cares to save them all. . . .

After my first visit, in the autumn of 1871, I have always called it the Tuolumne Yosemite, for it is a wonderfully exact counterpart of the great Yosemite, not only in its crystal river and sublime rocks and waterfalls, but in the gardens, groves, and meadows of its flowery parklike floor. The floor of Yosemite is about 4,000 feet above the sea, the Hetch-Hetchy floor about 3,700; the walls of both are of gray granite, rise abruptly out of the flowery grass and groves, are sculptured in the same style, and in both every rock is a glacial monument.

Standing boldly out from the south wall is a strikingly picturesque rock called "Kolana" by the Indians, the outermost of a group 2,300 feet high corresponding with the Cathedral Rocks of Yosemite both in relative position and form. On the opposite side of the valley facing Kolana there is a counterpart of the El Capitan of Yosemite rising sheer and plain to a height of 1,800 feet, and over its massive brow flows a stream which makes the most graceful fall I have ever seen. From the edge of the cliff it is perfectly free in the air for a thousand feet, then breaks up into a ragged sheet of cascades among the boulders of an earthquake talus. It is in all its glory in June, when the snow is melting fast, but fades and vanishes toward the end of summer. The only fall I know with which it may fairly be compared is the Yosemite Bridal Veil; but it excels even that favorite fall both in height and fineness of fairy airy beauty and behavior. . . .

So fine a fall might well seem sufficient to glorify any valley; but here as in Yosemite Nature seems in no wise moderate, for a short distance to the eastward of Tueeulala booms and thunders the great Hetch-Hetchy fall, Wapama, so near that you have both of them in full view from the same standpoint. It is the counterpart of the Yosemite Fall, but has a much greater volume of water, is about 1,700 feet in height, and appears to be nearly vertical though considerably inclined, and is dashed into huge out-bounding bosses of foam on the projecting shelves and knobs of its jagged gorge. . . . There is also a chain of magnificent cascades at the head of the valley on a stream that comes in from the northeast, mostly silvery plumes, like the one between the Vernal and Nevada falls of Yosemite, half-sliding, half-leaping, on bare glacier-polished granite, covered with crisp clashing spray into which the sunbeams pour with glorious effect. And besides all these a few small streams come over the walls here and there, leaping from ledge to ledge with birdlike song and watering many a hidden cliff-garden and fernery, but they are much too unshowy to be noticed in so grand a place. . . .

The floor of the valley is about three and a half miles long and from a fourth to half a mile wide. The lower portion is mostly a level meadow about a mile long with the trees restricted to the sides, and partially sepa-rated from the upper forested portion by a low bar of glacier-polished gran-ite, across which the river breaks in rapids.

The principal trees are the yellow and sugar pines, Sabine pine, incense cedar, Douglas spruce, silver fir, the California and gold-cup oaks, Balm of Gilead poplar, Nuttall's flowering dogwood, alder, maple, laurel, tumion, etc. . . . The shrubs forming conspicuous flowery clumps and tangles are manzanita, azalea, spiraea, brier-rose, ceanothus, calycanthus, philadel-phus, wild cherry, etc.; with abundance of showy and fragrant herbaceous plants growing about them, or out in the open in beds by themselves— lilies, Mariposa tulips, brodiaeas, orchids—several species of each—iris, spraguea, draperia, collomia, collinsia, castilleia, nemophila, larkspur, columbine, goldenrods, sunflowers, and mints of many species, honey-suckle, etc., etc. Many fine ferns dwell here, also; . . . therefore that Hetch-Hetchy Valley, far from being a plain common rockbound meadow, as many who have not seen it seem to suppose, is a grand landscape garden, one of Nature's rarest and most precious mountain mansions. . . .

Strange to say, this is the mountain temple that is now in danger of being dammed and made into a reservoir to help supply San Francisco with water and light. This use of the valley, so destructive and foreign to its proper park use, has long been planned and prayed for, and is still being prayed for by the San Francisco board of supervisors, not because water as pure and abundant cannot be got from adjacent sources outside the park—

for it can—but seemingly only because of the comparative cheapness of the dam required. . . .

That any one would try to destroy such a place seemed impossible, but sad experience shows that there are people good enough and bad enough for anything. The proponents of the dam scheme bring forward a lot of bad arguments to prove that the only righteous thing for Hetch-Hetchy is its destruction. These arguments are curiously like those of the devil devised for the destruction of the first garden—so much of the very best Eden fruit going to waste, so much of the best Tuolumne water. Very few of their statements are even partly true, and all are misleading. Thus, Hetch-Hetchy, they say, is "a low-lying meadow."

On the contrary, it is a high-lying natural landscape garden.

"It is a common minor feature, like thousands of others."

On the contrary, it is a very uncommon feature, after Yosemite, the rarest and in many ways the most important in the park.

"Damming and submerging it 175 feet deep would enhance its beauty by forming a crystal clear lake."

Landscape gardens, places of recreation and worship, are never made beautiful by destroying and burying them. The beautiful lake forsooth would be only an eyesore, a dismal blot on the landscape, like many others to be seen in the Sierra. . . .

These temple destroyers, devotees of ravaging commercialism, seem to have a perfect contempt for Nature, and instead of lifting their eyes to the mountains, lift them to dams and town skyscrapers.

Dam Hetch-Hetchy! As well dam for water-tanks the people's cathedrals and churches, for no holier temple has ever been consecrated by the heart of man.

Robert Underwood Johnson Decries Paying Too High a Price for Water, 1909

The Secretary of the Interior, for reasons which doubtless appear to him good and sufficient, and with the approval of the President, has made over to the city of San Francisco, on certain conditions, as a reservoir for its water supply the wonderful Hetch-Hetchy Valley, one of the most beautiful gorges of the Sierra, which, as a part of the Yosemite National Park, was set aside in 1890 by reason of its scenery for the recreation and use of all people. This action has, on the face of it, the authority of a congressional provision (of February 15, 1901) by which the Secretary of the Interior may grant water privileges in the three National Parks of California, *"if not incompatible with the public interest."* Whether the United States Supreme Court would hold that such authority extends to the destruction of so large an extent of the original purpose of the reserve may yet be the subject of adjudication.

In a matter relating to public lands the presumption is in favor of any course taken by President Roosevelt, Secretary Garfield, and Forester Pinchot. As our readers know, we have vigorously supported their enlightened services to the cause of forest conservation, as we have the services of preceding administrations. It was in this magazine that the movement for the creation of the Yosemite National Park first took public form in 1890, and the chief reason urged upon the Public Lands Committee for making the reservation—and we know whereof we speak—was to rescue from private invasion and for public use the rare beauty of the Hetch-Hetchy and of the Cañon of the Tuolumne River, which flows through it. We therefore have particular regret that we do not find satisfactory the reasons officially given for the Administration's extraordinary step, which, logically, would place the great natural scenery of the country at the service of any neighboring city which should consider its appropriation necessary or even desirable.

Let us say at once that we hold human life more sacred than scenery, than even great natural wonderlands, vastly as they contribute to save life and promote happiness; and if that were the issue, if San Francisco could not otherwise obtain an abundant water supply, we should be willing to dedicate to that purpose not only Hetch-Hetchy, but even the incomparable Yosemite itself. But this is not the contention of Secretary Garfield in the official document granting the request. The Administration's position is not that the step is a last resort, that no other source is adequate, but that Hetch-Hetchy affords the most abundant and cheapest available supply of pure water. Even this is stoutly denied by the opponents of the scheme, who contend, moreover, that a dozen other adequate systems may be found. Eminent and disinterested engineers have declared the present supply excellent and capable of ample development, as the water companies claim, and since the city fixes the water rates, and at need may condemn and acquire these sources at reasonable cost, there would seem to be no dangerous "monopoly." Indeed, the permission to dam the beautiful valley into a lake is conditional upon the previous exhaustion by the city of the resources of Lake Eleanor, which is also in the National Park. Other conditions are attached and compensations agreed upon which are believed by the Secretary to be safeguards of the public interests, with the important omission, however, to provide safeguards against the destruction of the scenery; but the fact remains that of this great reservation, which is as large as the State of Rhode Island, the northern third—for the watershed of the valley even above the Tuolumne Meadows must go with the valley itself—is to be withdrawn from the use of the people of the whole United States and given to the city of San Francisco. This involves a new principle and a dangerous precedent, and is a tremendous price for the nation to pay for San Francisco's water, and the burden of proof that it is *necessary* is upon those who advocated the grant. It is not enough that it should be thought merely *desirable*.

It is idle to attempt to discredit such defenders of the public's previous rights in the valley as John Muir and many other members of the SIERRA CLUB and other like organizations by calling them "sentimentalists" and "poets." Cant of this sort on the part of the people who have not developed beyond the pseudo-"practical" stage is one of the retarding influences of American civilization and brings us back to the materialistic declaration that "Good is only good to eat." Most of those who oppose the grant live in San Francisco and vicinity and are deeply interested in the future of that redoubtable city; but they know the growing vogue of the few camping-grounds of the health-giving park, into which, in the torrid and dusty summer, the people of the lowlands swarm in "the pursuit of happiness"; they know the exceptional beauty of the Hetch-Hetchy, only surpassed in the Sierra by the neighboring Yosemite and by the distant and not easily accessible King's River Cañon; they know, also—to meet on its own ground the argument of cheapness—the money value of California's great natural attractions and that once to destroy the beautiful valley floor by flooding will be to render it irrecoverable.

There is one ground of hope that the danger may be averted. By the time it can be demonstrated that Lake Eleanor is not adequate, it is likely to be generally recognized that a pure water supply need not depend upon mountain resources, but may be obtained by filtration from streams of less pure quality. Meantime the citizens of San Francisco, who (alone of Californians!) are to vote upon the question, will do well to exhaust every other possibility of meeting their needs before giving their consent to the ruin of one of their imperial State's greatest natural treasures. We are confident that this issue would be the one most approved by the officials at Washington, who, from conscientious motives, have given assent to local official demands.

 E S S A Y S

The classic "hydraulic civilizations" of ancient Mesopotamia and Egypt were societies organized around the centralized control of large-scale waterworks. In *Rivers of Empire: Water, Aridity, and the Growth of the American West* (1985), Donald Worster of the University of Kansas applies the notions of Karl Marx and Karl Wittfogel (who in *Oriental Despotism* argued that large-scale irrigation was possible only in a tightly ordered society) to describe California as a modern variant of the classic hydraulic complex. In his view, water policy in California and the American West represents both the creation and the captive of "a coercive, monolithic, and hierarchical system, ruled by a power elite based on the ownership of capital and expertise." He also stresses the role of a Leviathan capitalist state whose motive force is "the rational, calculating, unlimited accumulation of private wealth."

In seeking to explain the use, control, and manipulation of water by Californians, Norris Hundley, Jr., professor of history at UCLA and managing editor of the *Pacific Historical Review,* refutes Worster's interpretation. Hundley argues, to the contrary, that the so-called "[water] establishment has never been a monolith driven by a single purpose or vision, save the idea that water (and nature generally) exists to serve humankind." In the essay included here, drawn from his highly regarded book *The Great Thirst: Californians and Water, 1770s–1990s* (1992), he emphasizes instead the importance of political culture and advances a pluralistic interpretation in which many discrete and diverse groups compete to achieve their own specific goals.

The Capitalist Control of Water Use

DONALD WORSTER

Only fragments remain today of . . . [the] intricate Old World hydraulic complexes. . . . Today, most of the systems lie in ruins, buried in "the lone and level sands" like Shelley's statue of Ozymandias, all but vanished on the ground and visible only from the air. Water may still gurgle through a stone-embanked Chinese ditch dug over a thousand years ago, and village farmers in Madras may still wait for the annual monsoon to fill a tank hollowed out by a legendary maharajah, but fragments do not make systems. Where water control is carried out comprehensively these days, it is by means of modern technology—electric pumps that can lift an entire river over a mountain range or mammoth concrete dams that create artificial lakes over a hundred miles long. The early hydraulic societies, organized along agrarian state lines, have now all disappeared along with the apparatus they operated. In their place stand the new modern hydraulic societies, the most developed of them sprawling in the arid American West, and these societies express the reigning mind of the marketplace men, the technological wizards, and the ubiquitous state planners.

Karl Wittfogel refused to gather up his ideas about water and power and make an imaginative leap with them into that water modernity. Doing so would have required him to examine critically his new home, the United States, and he was not prepared for that inquiry. In fact, his split with the Marxists had made him an increasingly stubborn apologist for America and other western capitalist countries as promoters of freedom and progress. On several occasions he inspected the newest achievements in water engineering and always came away complacent about modern hydraulics. He insisted that the approach to social organization behind them differed from both the archaic despotisms and their recent communist descendants. In 1946, he and his wife, Esther Goldfrank, visited the Tennessee Valley Authority works, which were among the most ambitious water-control enterprises in the world. Fifteen years later the Wittfogels toured the Snowy Mountains irrigation scheme in Australia. "What I have been saying about traditional China," he wrote, "is not valid for multicentered societies." Those new "free world" projects could not be despotic because private property was now the norm, and there was no single, overpowering state in control; rather, there was in cases like the United States and Australia a balance among many countervailing forces. One found not a "ruling" but a "controlled" bureaucracy. So once more Wittfogel had to scrap his original ecological argument about history. It was not, after all, the interaction of nature and technology that had made Egypt what it was, but prior social "organization." And for some reason social organization in the old desert empires had been despotic, while in the modern western countries it was open and democratic.

A few of Wittfogel's critics have completely overlooked the distinction he made between capitalist and command economies and have mistakenly accused him of branding all irrigation regimes as tyrannical. They sometimes seize on the American West as an exception to what they take to be his grim generalizations. For instance, Lon Fuller, a Harvard law professor who grew up in the Imperial Valley of California and rosily remembers that world as just and communal, has lambasted Wittfogel for casting a shadow over all irrigation. But in the course of his rambling critique of the Oriental-despotism argument, he actually ends up restating Wittfogel's own discriminations. He accepts completely the idea that water control may have led to despotism in early hydraulic societies, adding only that their problem was they "took on too difficult a social task too soon." With the invention of the marketplace, however, more benign mechanisms for sorting out conflicting interests came into being. Now we have the invisible hand of rational self-interest, Fuller believes, to resolve water disputes peacefully and achieve a fair distribution of benefits. We don't even need the courts, for individuals can now solve their own conflicts without external interference, regaining the autonomy they once enjoyed in developing river resources. All of this progress has been made possible, so Fuller implies, by the rise of capitalism. Its emergence has dispersed concentrated power, put negotiation and contract in the place of repressive authority, and assured that democracy will flourish in the desert.

Unfortunately, it just isn't so. Another, closer look at modern examples of water control, as in the American West, does not support either Fuller's or Wittfogel's comforting notion of progressive liberation of humans from their tools of desert conquest. Quite to the contrary: capitalism has created over the past hundred years a new, distinctive type of hydraulic society, one that demonstrates once more how the domination of nature can lead to the domination of some people over others. Recognizing this, certain important questions must be addressed. What does this latest mode of water control have in common with its predecessors? What are its unique qualities and tendencies? How has it approached that essential substance of life, water? What path of cultural evolution has brought it to its present condition of mastery over the drylands? What inner and outer forces have driven it to achieve mastery? In what ways has that ecological domination expressed in the new water systems shaped the social order of places like the American West, creating new structures of power there, reconcentrating wealth and authority? . . .

This . . . latest mode of water control . . . is one created by the modern capitalist state. In this mode there are two roughly equivalent centers of power: a private sector of agriculturists and a public sector made up of bureaucratic planners and elected representatives. Neither group is autonomous. Both need each other, reinforce each other's values, compete for the upper hand without lasting success, and finally agree to work together to achieve a control over nature that is unprecedentedly thorough.

The agriculturists who constitute the private sector have become in recent times too rich and well organized, when compared with the archaic peasant class, to be cowed into submission by any state. Instead of serving in an involuntary corvée, they pay taxes to the state, often complaining of the high, extortionate rates, or they succeed in compelling others to pay the taxes for them to build and maintain their waterworks. In the world's labor markets they hire an anonymous human army, which they use to turn the arid spaces into green fields. In the West, those workers have come from Mexico, China, Japan, the Philippines, and India, as well as Oklahoma, Texas, and Mississippi. Those hired field hands, not their landowning employers, are the men and women who have constituted the wage-based answer to the corvée, sweating every bit as much as the Egyptian fellahin did. They also have felt the lash of an overseer or the club of a policeman, but they have had no land or village of their own to which they could escape when the season was ended. Consequently, they have been perpetual movers, with a tent or automobile in some cases serving as their only home, a city welfare office their only off-season means of support. With these wage employees, the modern domination of water becomes most vividly and unmistakably translated into hierarchy. Those who rule in that situation are not only those who hire and pay but also all those who take part in designing and controlling the hydraulic means of production. Workers serve as instruments of environmental manipulation; rivers, in turn, become means of control over workers.

The other power center emerging from this mode is the state, which furnishes as it did in archaic times the capital for big-scale engineering and the technical know-how to make it run smoothly. One of the most familiar laws of power is that he who has the capital commands. In the American West, the federal government through its Bureau of Reclamation has put up most of the capital. It therefore exerts enormous leverage over local destinies. When that same government also came to supply most of the hydraulic expertise, it gathered into its hands another means of control, one that has taken on increasing significance as the scale and complexity of water manipulation has grown. Furthermore, the state has asserted, through its various levels and agencies, the authority to settle conflicting claims, to decide which users can tap public resources, and to define what projects are worth undertaking. There is no pharaoh in that arrangement of power—no single despotic ruler who personifies human control over the environment. In the new mode, power becomes faceless and impersonal, so much so in fact that many are unaware it exists.

The most fundamental characteristic of the latest irrigation mode is its behavior toward nature and the underlying attitudes on which it is based. Water in the capitalist state has no intrinsic value, no integrity that must be respected. Water is no longer valued as a divinely appointed means for survival, for producing and reproducing human life, as it was in local subsistence communities. Nor is water an awe-inspiring, animistic ally in a quest for political empire, as it was in the agrarian states. It has now become a commodity that is bought and sold and used to make other commodities that can be bought and sold and carried to the marketplace. It is, in other words, purely and abstractly a commercial instrument. All mystery disappears from its depths, all gods depart, all contemplation of its flow ceases. It becomes so many "acre-feet" banked in an account, so many "kilowatt-hours" of generating capacity to be spent, so many bales of cotton or car-loads of oranges to be traded around the globe. And in that new language of market calculation lies an assertion of ultimate power over nature—of a domination that is absolute, total, and free from all restraint.

The behavior that follows making water into a commodity is aggres-sively manipulative beyond any previous historical experience. Science and technology are given a place of honor in the capitalist state and put to work devising ways to extract from every river whatever cash it can produce. Where nature seemingly puts limits on human wealth, engineering pre-sumes to bring unlimited plenty. Even in the desert, where men and women confront scarcity in its oldest form—not the deprivation of a particular industrial resource, which is always a cultural contrivance, but the lack of a basic biological necessity—every form of growth is considered possible. Undaunted by any deficiency, unwilling to concede any landscape as unprofitable, planners and schemers assure that there is water in the driest rocks, requiring only a few spoken commands to make it gush forth with-out end. That collective drive to make the bleakest, most sterile desert pro-duce more and more of everything comes from aggregating individual drives to maximize personal acquisitiveness without stint or hindrance. It is an ideology shared wholeheartedly by agriculturists and water bureaucrats, providing the bond that unites their potentially rival centers of power into a formidable alliance. . . .

It would be too simple to say that the 1886 decision in *Lux* v. *Haggin* fastened on the state a riparian system of water rights. Nowhere was the law more complicated, more filled with compromise, than here. In contrast to Colorado, where prior appropriation under state ownership and regulation was the rule, California threw together a ramshackle system that came to be known as the "California doctrine." The state adopted the riparian principle but accepted appropriation rights derived from the federal government, which in its Mining Act of 1866 had conceded such rights on the public domain. Where an individual had bought state land or a Mexican grant, the water rights were declared to be riparian; where he had claimed water from the public domain before 1866, he had a right of prior appropriation that could be exercised or sold as personal property. All grants after 1866, state or federal, came under the riparian rule, which in California meant that the appropriator could divert only as much water as riparian owners allowed. Whenever they decided to use the river, the appropriator had to relinquish, no matter how long he had irrigated, no matter how established his orchards and gardens, no matter whether his farm died. In Colorado and the seven states that followed its lead (Wyoming, Montana, Idaho, Nevada, Utah, Ari-zona, and New Mexico), the right to appropriate was a right to "beneficial use" of water only—a right, that is, to take as much water as was needed for a legitimate purpose, a purpose that was in the public interest, that would earn money and add to the state's prosperity. But in California, until 1928, the riparian owner was restricted only in relation to other riparian owners (by the idea of "correlative" or "coequal" rights, which made all those owners equals). Against an appropriator, on the other hand, he could make extravagant demands on the river and use its water with stubborn inefficiency and waste. He could not, however, insist that the stream flow undisturbed by his porch, affording an amenity to enjoy, nor could he protect it as the handiwork of God. Both would have been indeed unreasonable and wasteful. The western law of waters, as with natural resources generally, insisted in every state that instrumental values must always prevail.

Although it was a messy fusion of riparian and appropriationist thinking, the California doctrine was emphatically clear in one particular: it put the irrigator without stream frontage at a disadvantage—potentially a fatal disadvantage for his fortunes. For that reason, irrigators felt compelled to find a way to undo the court's ruling, and the best immediate chance for that, they decided, was to pass a law authorizing the formation of irrigation districts around the state. A Modesto lawyer, C. C. Wright, was elected to the legislature on a promise to do just that, and one year after his election, he delivered. The Irrigation District Act became law in late February 1887. Put briefly, the law permitted agricultural communities to organize as official governing units to construct and operate collectively the irrigation works they needed. It went further than the similar Utah district act of 1865. When fifty freeholders (or a majority in an area) petitioned the state to form such a district, an election was held. Two-thirds of the voters living in the designated area had to approve of the idea. The act did not measure voting power by the acreage owned, for it was feared that a few large landowners might thereby sabotage the community will. Once approved, the district elected officers, and they were given broad authority. They could take by the power of eminent domain any land they needed for an irrigation canal; they could make contracts to build works and tax property in the district or sell bonds to pay for them; and most important perhaps, they could condemn all individual water rights, including riparian, and purchase them in the name of the district. The Wright Act was, according to Thomas Malone, "California's major nineteenth century contribution to irrigation law." It also snatched victory from the strong, blunt fingers of Henry Miller.

In the formation and financing of an irrigation district, a big rancher like Miller had but a single vote. His lands could be taxed, his water rights condemned, and his river control broken by a rabble of little farmers. It was one thing to cooperate with a Haggin, quite another to be tied down by the Lilliputians and have to go along with their schemes. Soon Miller was back in court, fighting for his dominion, along with other large landowners in the state. All the way to the Untied States Supreme Court they went—and lost. In the case of *Bradley* v. *Fallbrook Irrigation District* (1897), brought by a nonresident landowner against a new district, the highest court ruled that the Wright Act was constitutional. It was permissible, the opinion read, to take private property for public uses, and irrigation development was such a public use, one that no individual should be allowed to thwart. Unlike the confrontation between Haggin and Miller, this battle had been unmistakably fought between the Minnie Austins around Fresno and San Bernardino and the power elite of Nob Hill. If California were to be redeemed from concentrated wealth, if irrigation were to be the means of that redemption, giving to the ordinary men and women of the state control over rural life, then, so the hope went, it would be the effect of the Wright Act.

Shortly after the act was passed, the United States census revealed that California now led the nation in irrigated acreage. There were 1,004,233 acres being watered in the state, and the average size of an irrigated farm was 73 acres, more than twice the size of those in Utah. Each of those California acres produced a market value of $19 per year, the highest return in the country. But it also had to be said that California had far more potential for hydraulic engineering than its people had yet realized. According to one of the state's leading civil engineers, C. E. Grunsky, "Irrigation is not general throughout the State." In contrast to Utah, where almost every farm was irrigated, California had only one in four farm units under the ditch. Elwood Mead, who came to the state to conduct a general survey of irrigation progress, blamed the slow progress on prejudicial attitudes that still favored the cattlemen and wheat kings.

> Men pride themselves [here] on great undertakings and on doing whatever they undertake on a large scale. . . . The owner of a range herd was more than a money-maker, he was practically monarch of all he surveyed. The cowboy on horseback was an aristocrat; the irrigator on foot, working through the hot summer days in the mud of irrigated fields, was a groveling wretch. In cowboy land the irrigation ditch has always been regarded with disfavor because it is the badge and symbol of a despised occupation. The same feeling, but in a less degree, has prevailed in the wheat-growing districts of California, and for much the same reason.

Given the widespread criticism of Henry Miller and the riparian landowners, it is difficult to credit Mead's explanation completely. Haggin had demonstrated that irrigation too could be a large undertaking, perfectly in tune with the most passionate enthusiasm for grandeur. The stagnation in irrigation development that was apparent by the 1890s had another cause than prejudice: there were simply not enough Haggins around able or willing to furnish the capital needed.

Almost everything that could be done to rivers with limited funds, with local capital, had been done by the last decade of the century. What was required next, if the state was to escape from its plateau of water development, was to find the money to buy more advanced engineering. The Wright Act sought only to overcome the obstacle presented by riparian priority; it did not put more money in the pockets of the small farmers living far off from rivers. Its authorization of bond sales helped, but not much, for bonds had to be repaid, with interest. Some districts quickly discovered that they had more bonds than they could repay, and yet not enough to complete the works they wanted. What use was it, they began to wonder, to hold elections and obtain water rights if the district had no money? State Engineer William Hammond Hall, itching as much as any district officer to extend the mastery over nature, stated the problem and then suggested a solution:

"The great majority of the streams in California," he wrote, "are of such a character that the work of the farmers can avail nothing. There must be strong associations and large capital." From the vantage of the 1890s, corporate power looked like the only way to get off the plateau, but that would mean falling back into the hands of the moguls.

After several decades of colonization, court decisions, crop experimentation, and ideological sparring, California found itself mired in a dilemma. The redemption of the desert could not go forward without help from concentrated capital. The redemption of society, however, depended on liberation from that same capital. It was God's wish that nature's desolation be turned into a garden. It was also His wish that the garden be ruled by men and women of modest means. Unfortunately, He had not said how both could be done.

American Political Culture and Water Use

NORRIS HUNDLEY, JR.

As an individualistic, freedom-loving people, Americans from the outset of their republic shared a fundamental distrust of government reflected in their Constitution which separated authority among the several branches on the principle that liberty is best preserved when governmental powers war with one another. Agreed on that essential, Americans also from the beginning differed on how far the distrust of government should go. Those coalescing around Thomas Jefferson and then Andrew Jackson, and who by the second quarter of the nineteenth century labeled themselves Democrats, believed that at the national level the least government was the best government and that authority should be overwhelmingly concentrated locally. They vigorously opposed a strong activist central authority that used the public funds of all to benefit a few through such means as internal improvements (canals, roads, river and harbor projects), tariffs, monopolies, and land grants. At best this was a misuse of the people's money; at worst it invited corruption. Those sharing these views included by mid-century many who distrusted an activist government for special reasons of their own—southern Democrats fearful of attempts to contain and root out slavery; and ethnic minorities, especially Irish Catholics of the northern cities, concerned that a powerful government might proscribe their fondness for whiskey, their religion, and their parochial schools. Localism and laissez-faire were the Democrats' political shibboleths.

In contrast to this strong antiactivist government position emerged another faction sympathetic to the ideas of Alexander Hamilton and whose members by the time of the California gold rush made their political home in the Whig party. Their heartland was the Northeast, especially Yankee New England where their Puritan legacy left them convinced that they were

Excerpted from Norris Hundley, Jr., *The Great Thirst: Californians and Water, 1770s–1990s.* Copyright © 1992 by The Regents of the Univesity of California. Reprinted by permission of the University of California Press and the author.

as much God's religious agents as political vehicles for creating a morally and economically strong America. On economic issues, in particular, they attracted kindred spirits elsewhere, including many in the upper and lower South. Henry Clay of Kentucky summarized their national program in the pre-Civil War years in his "American System." Its premise was that a government safely checked by the Constitution and by regular elections could promote a strong national economy through internal improvements, a tariff keeping out foreign goods and allowing domestic factories to develop, and in general intervening with large-scale and centrally designed plans encouraging development of the country. Such goals, in the Whig view, required an educated leadership, a belief reinforced by the traditional New England emphasis on learning but at variance with the Democratic notion that anyone was capable of running the nation.

Though the Whig party collapsed during the intense North-South debate over slavery, its philosophy reemerged in 1854 in the Republican party, essentially a Whig party without southerners and more Yankee in sentiment because of the realignment. The Civil War crisis and the splitting of the Democratic party along North/South lines propelled into power the Republicans who quickly implemented their nationalist agenda: internal improvements, tariffs, a national banking system and uniform currency. With the war's end, rancor over Radical Reconstruction, political corruption, immigration policy, and other issues brought a resurgence of Democratic strength and, except for brief periods of strong Republican ascendancy, a return to policies emphasizing nonactivist government, localism, and laissez-faire.

The Whig/Republican and Democratic political cultures with their contrasting views of the role of government arrived in California with the hordes following the discovery of gold in 1848. Since most newcomers were Democrats (southerners and ethnic minorities, especially Irish Catholics, from northern working-class neighborhoods), their views prevailed throughout much of the latter half of the nineteenth century. Thus, in California as in the nation's capital, distaste for activist government, preference for local decision making, and emphasis on individual enterprise became the norm except for those less frequent occasions of effective Republican control. When the newcomers' enthusiasm for wealth and laissez-faire encountered California's environmental realities—gold, aridity, great fertile valleys—the consequences were profound for the state, the West, and the nation. . . .

The public's initial disappointment with *Lux* v. *Haggin* focused overwhelmingly on the court's continued recognition of riparianism, a doctrine (thanks to Haggin's wondrous ability to obfuscate his intentions) seen as destructive of California's potential for small irrigated farms. A flurry of bills was introduced in the legislature to limit or abolish riparian rights, but within only months the public began to see that the appropriation doctrine was not a panacea either and that the real enemy was monopoly whether by riparians or appropriators. Snoopy newspaper reporters examined county records and found that a relatively small number of people had filed appropriation claims on nearly all California's rivers and often for several times more water than was available. Thus, abolishing riparian rights would merely surrender the field to another set of monopolists and their attorneys. "Private ownership and control of the waters of the state," declared the *Stockton Daily Independent*, "is far more to be dreaded than the objectionable law of riparian rights."

Once alerted to what they perceived as the real evil, small and would-be farmers rallied around the ideas of C. C. Wright, a lawyer from the Central Valley town of Modesto who advanced a popular solution: provide the public with power to take water and land, by means of condemnation, from the huge estates and to create community-controlled *irrigation districts*. His proposal won him immediate election to the legislature where in 1887 he secured unanimous approval of the Wright Act.

The new law represented an effort to foster community values, promote small family farms, and curb the monopolistic excesses produced by the rampant individualism of California's pioneer capitalists. It also reflected the prevailing Jeffersonian emphasis on localism and laissez-faire, and this ultimately contributed mightily to its undoing. The act authorized the residents of an area to form local districts, elect a board of directors, issue bonds and raise revenue, purchase (including the authority to invoke condemnation if required) land and water rights, and distribute water. Except in a few closely circumscribed particulars, the state had no control over these functions. As Wright himself put it, the legislature had now "created a special government for the one purpose of developing and administering the irrigation water for the benefit of the people." It was a "special government" modeled on the swampland district, but as that district had been radically localized in the Green Act.

The small and would-be farmers who championed the Wright Act believed that the local and democratically controlled district represented the most effective weapon against speculators and large landholders. All local residents (whether landowners or not) who were eligible to vote in state elections could cast ballots on district issues. In addition, all were taxed on the value of their property (town lots and buildings as well as rural land), not on whether they received irrigation water. The tax burden, it was thought, would force those holding land for speculative purposes or for the growing of wheat to sell at reasonable prices in small tracts to irrigationists. The new law also reflected the belief that an entire community had a stake in an irrigation enterprise, and everyone—farmers as well as those providing them goods and services—would share in any agricultural success. Also clearly evident was the element of coercion. Once a district had been created with a two-thirds vote of the electorate, even the most reluctant property owner had to go along.

In some ways, the irrigation district was reminiscent of Hispanic institutions. Unlike the situation under either riparian or appropriation law, the water right resided in the district, not with individuals or private corporations. In times of shortage, all users would share equally in the reduced flow, thus serving to reinforce what was essentially a community enterprise. Also as in pre-American California, irrigation districts derived their authority from above—in this case, the legislature—but there was a significant difference: Sacramento had neither Spain's generations of experience derived from living in water-scarce environments nor that country's centralized administration for dealing with aridity. This lack of experience and an overall plan proved a decisive flaw. There were those, including the Grangers and the state engineer, who argued vigorously for more comprehensive solutions directed from Sacramento, but the popular passion for localism and laissez-faire prompted the legislature not only to roundly reject such ideas but also to abolish the office of state engineer.

At first many Californians viewed the Wright Act as the hoped-for panacea. It prompted creation of numerous irrigation districts and increases in irrigated acreage in the late 1880s and 1890s. Waves of landless and small landholders rushed to take advantage of the new law. As early as 1889 California led the nation in irrigated agriculture with nearly 14,000 farmers irrigating a million acres, most of them between Stockton and Bakersfield. Many of these farmers had earlier secured land around the Central Valley's periphery, where there were flowing water courses emerging from the high country, while others had obtained acreage from some of the large landowners, including the railroad. Still others had found ways to circumvent the monopolistic grasp of the large landholders. In the 1890s with the appearance of the modern pump, some turned to groundwater, which was subject to no legal restraint and still remains largely unfettered. And there were those who simply gambled, clandestinely diverting water from a stream in the hope that earlier riparians or appropriators would either not notice or ignore them.

As early as 1857 in *Crandall* v. *Woods,* the state supreme court had allowed many to turn the gamble into a firm right through a device known as "adverse prescription." If irrigators could maintain their unauthorized diversions for at least five years without legal challenge, the right to the water was theirs. It was a loophole that provided many latecomers with legitimate access to water, but attempts to take advantage of the law in this way frequently led to extensive litigation that the poor could ill afford to pursue. Nonetheless, through such means and the Wright Act's encouragement, the irrigated lands increased in the decade after 1889 by some 50 percent to nearly 1.5 million acres at century's end. Much of this was devoted to specialized farming—nuts, vineyards, vegetables, fruit orchards—where small plots yielded impressive returns. Indeed, some 64 percent of the value of all California crops derived from such commodities. At the same time, farm sizes decreased, especially in those areas where irrigation had expanded most rapidly. In Fresno County, for example, the average farm in 1900 was half the size it had been twenty years earlier and in Los Angeles County, 40 percent smaller.

The gains were more illusory than real. The Wright Act proved a limited success at best. The state's irrigated acres expanded, but not as greatly as expected—1.5 million irrigated acres out of a total of 28 million acres of farmland was hardly an impressive figure—and much of that occurred on the large estates. While the size of the average farm declined, the drop was not dramatic: from 426 to 397 acres between 1880 and 1900. Moreover, most of the agricultural land (62 percent of it) remained in large ownerships exceeding a thousand acres. Wheat, while gradually giving way to the specialty crops encouraged by the railroad and refrigerator car, still dominated in many places. Especially disconcerting was the high rate of failure of the irrigation districts, with most surviving only a few years. In the Sacramento Valley, for example, only one of the seven districts created there enjoyed even partial success.

Irrigation districts faced formidable barriers. Opposition from the large landowners, particularly in the form of court challenges, proved costly and time consuming. Heavy reliance on the courts necessarily followed from the Wright Act's decision to localize authority rather than to establish a statewide administrative agency that could issue rulings without necessitating the use of lawyers and expensive lawsuits. Also contributing to the high rate of failure was extraordinarily expensive court-ordered compensation for condemned land and water rights, severe drought in 1889, depression in 1893, ignorance about irrigation farming techniques, and fraudulent schemes of speculators seeking to profit from land sales in areas where the water supply could not support irrigation. Such obstacles made it extremely difficult to sell the bonds needed to cover the cost of irrigation works, a task made impossible when the interest rate that districts could pay—and the Wright Act restricted the rate to 5 percent—was below what investors could obtain elsewhere. There were no limits on the size of a bond issue, however, and when buyers were available, a district's indebtedness often soared beyond reason, encouraging fraud and waste.

Despite such setbacks, the district idea began spreading to other states where it enjoyed remarkable success because of changes made on the basis of the California experience. Thus, it joined such other California inventions adopted elsewhere as the appropriation doctrine, the California doctrine, and hydraulicking. By the 1890s in California, however, the irrigation district concept, which had been introduced with such enthusiasm only a few years earlier, was viewed as largely a failure. . . .

Modern California has attracted numerous critics, many with plans for setting aright all that they perceive is askew. The state's environmental problems seem peculiarly capable of stimulating an extraordinary reawakening of the utopian, deeply romantic thinking about society and nature that flourished in such earlier eras as those of the Transcendentalists and communal-utopian theorists of the Age of Jackson in the 1830s and 1840s, or the advocates of the communal movements of the 1960s and 1970s. Donald Worster, in a fascinating and provocative account of water-resource development, sees contemporary California and the West as the creation and creature of "a coercive, monolithic, and hierarchical system ruled by a power elite based on the ownership of capital and expertise." His "elite" are the water brokers—agribusiness and government agencies, especially the Reclamation Bureau—whose minions "impose their outlook and their demands on nature, as they do on the individual and the small human community." Change, he believes, is possible only through "redesigning the West as a network of more or less discrete, self-contained watershed settlements"—hundreds of small communities "not participating to any great extent in the national or world marketplace, concentrating instead on producing food and fiber for local use." These communities, he predicts, would somehow result in "a more open, free, and democratic" people who would see a river as "a reflection of their own liberated minds, running free and easy."

The message seems to be that people can free themselves from their bureaucratic masters by dismantling elaborate hydraulic systems, retreating to small communities not needing such systems, and in the process of liberating rivers and nature generally also liberate themselves. This is a message that others have advocated, including Peter Berg and Raymond Dasmann who more than a decade ago called for "reinhabiting" California through the "massive redistribution of land to create smaller farms." To them such action required joining "a biotic community and ceasing to be its exploiter." Success, they concluded, also required the establishment of a new and "separate state" consisting of "watershed governments appropriate to maintaining local life-places."

This vision has a certain appeal, but it seems out of touch with modern urban society and a world (increasing by some 250,000 persons daily or 90 million annually) where production only for local needs—even if limited to California and the West—appears a practical impossibility if not undesirable. It shares much (albeit with an important caveat or two) with the Jeffersonian dream of the yeoman farmer, with the hoped-for edens of the nineteenth-century irrigation crusaders, and with the aspirations of those who fought for the Reclamation Act. It forgets that many people's vision of hell is life on a farm or in a small town. Worster implicitly acknowledges the utopian character of his own vision by admitting that its implementation would result in profit losses, the tearing down of much (how much is unclear) of the present infrastructure for moving and storing water, and the redistribution of people to other regions—a requirement that would surely necessitate coercive, not to say totalitarian, measures incongruent with a more "open" and "free" society. . . .

Modern California, with its booming economy (fourth among the nations of the world if measured separately) and its number one ranking nationally in population, agriculture, and industry, dominates the American West and much of the nation like a colossus and exercises great influence not only in Washington (perhaps best measured by its ability to attract more federal dollars—40 percent more—than any other state) but also in foreign capitals. An engine contributing mightily to these achievements has been the passion of Californians to capture the water of other regions as reflected in the thousands of miles of aqueducts crisscrossing the state and extending to the border where they tap into the scarce supplies of much of the American West. To outsiders, California is the feared water hustler *nonpareil*, while to those within the state, there have been (and remain) a host of water seekers of varying strength and influence struggling with one another over increasingly limited supplies. Some of these internecine conflicts are better known than others. The "north" against the "south" stands deceptively at the grossest level of generalization. The variations on [this] theme, however, can be multiplied many times: Los Angeles versus Owens Valley-Mono Basin, San Francisco versus Hetch Hetchy and the preservationists, Army Corps of Engineers against the Reclamation Bureau, Metropolitan Water District of Southern California versus Imperial Valley, Pacific Gas and Electric against the Interior Department, Los Angeles versus the San Fernando Valley cities, the state Water Resources Control Board against the Reclamation Bureau, the California Farm Bureau Federation versus the state Department of Water Resources, and so on in increasing number and complexity. . . .

Note that the battles have sometimes been between and among those groups traditionally identified as providing "water leaders" or as being part of a so-called "water establishment," "water industry," and "water lobby"— that is, those whose collective actions have straitjacketed the state's rivers and given California its reputation as a water imperialist. This "establishment," however, has never been a monolith driven by a single purpose or vision, save the idea that water (and nature generally) exists to serve humankind. Rather, . . . it has consisted of many discrete groups, both in and outside the state, each with its own (frequently changing) agenda that has sometimes led to conflict (for example, the California Farm Bureau Federation's opposition to the Peripheral Canal), at other times to footdragging (the Metropolitan Water District's last minute and reluctant support of the State Water Project), and on still other occasions to compromises and alliances resulting in a major undertaking (the joining of the Imperial Valley, Reclamation Bureau, and Los Angeles on behalf of the Boulder Canyon Project). The alliances have often been fleeting but their frequency and composition have been such as to create in California the world's largest and most complex hydraulic system. The success of that system in promoting growth has ironically intensified internal competition for water, especially between urban and agricultural interests, and made less likely those city-farm alliances that produced the monumental projects of the past.

 F U R T H E R   R E A D I N G

Kendrick A. Clements, "Politics and the Park: San Francisco's Fight for Hetch Hetchy, 1908–1913," *Pacific Historical Review* XLVIII (May 1979): 185–216
Michael P. Cohen, *The Pathless Way: John Muir and American Wilderness* (1984)
Sheridan Downey, *They Would Rule the Valley* (1947)
Norris C. Hundley, Jr., *Water and the West: The Colorado River Compact and the Politics of Water in the American West* (1975)
Norris C. Hundley, Jr., *The Great Thirst: Californians and Water, 1770s–1990s* (1992)
Lawrence J. Jelinek, *Harvest Empire: A History of California Agriculture* (1979; 2nd ed., 1982)

Holway R. Jones, *John Muir and the Sierra Club: The Fight for Yosemite* (1965)

William L. Kahrl, *Water and Power: The Conflict over Los Angeles' Water Supply in the Owens Valley* (1982)

Robert L. Kelley, *Battling the Inland Sea: American Political Culture, Public Policy, and the Sacramento Valley, 1850–1986* (1989)

Douglas R. Littlefield, "Water Rights during the California Gold Rush," *Western Historical Quarterly* XIV (October 1983): 415–34

Donald Pisani, *From Family Farm to Agribusiness: The Irrigation Crusade in California and the West* (1984)

Donald Pisani, *To Reclaim a Divided West: Water, Law, and Public Policy, 1848–1902* (1992)

Marc Reisner, *Cadillac Desert: The American West and Its Disappearing Water* (1986)

Elmo R. Richardson, "The Struggle for the Valley: California's Hetch Hetchy Controversy, 1905–1913," *California Historical Society Quarterly* XXXVIII (September 1959): 249–58

Alfred Runte, *Yosemite: The Embattled Wilderness* (1990)

Ann Foley Scheuring, ed., *A Guidebook to California Agriculture* (1983)

Michael L. Smith, *Pacific Visions: California Scientists and the Environment, 1850–1915* (1987)

Paul S. Taylor, "Excess Land Law: Pressure versus Principle," *California Law Review* XLVII (August 1959): 499–541

Paul S. Taylor, "Excess Land Law: Calculated Circumvention," *California Law Review* LII (December 1964): 978–1014

John Walton, *Western Times and Water Wars: State, Culture, and Rebellion in California* (1992)

Donald Worster, *Rivers of Empire: Water, Aridity, and the Growth of the American West* (1985)

David Wyatt, *The Fall into Eden: Landscape and Imagination in California* (1986; paperback edition, 1990)

Big Business and Urban Labor,

1860s–1930s

Propelled by a major innovation, the "corporate" form of business enter-prise, California's economy developed rapidly in the post–Civil War era. In those decades, representatives of California's new business class sought to achieve a degree of control over public policy by lobbying politicians and party bosses and by pressing for special state assistance in the form of grants, loans, and laws favorable to corporate interests. Politicians, in turn, sought contacts with representatives of large corporations because they provided lucrative "fees" for services rendered. This private relationship between cor-porations and the state government was perhaps most pronounced in trans-portation, where railroad owners secured many benefits from the legislature. In short, both the state and the federal governments became partners of California's railroad entrepreneurs.

This corporate power, especially that of railroads, generated intense political opposition. Those same railroads, however, greatly stimulated eco-nomic growth in California by reducing transportation costs and creating wider markets for the state's agricultural and industrial producers. Indeed, some recent scholars believe that it is important to challenge the long-standing, largely negative, view of the railroads as "The Octopus," to use novelist Frank Norris's descriptive term. One such scholar, Richard Orsi of California State University, Hayward, has suggested that we need "to see the actions of the [railroad] companies more positively and more clearly within a broader context of social, economic, and political change" and to reevalu-ate them "as legitimate businesses responding to changing commercial opportunities and dangers." But many Californians of the late nineteenth century had not successfully reconciled the earlier ideal of a competitive eco-nomic system with the modern reality of a consolidated corporate one. In particular, they felt that the political process had not been responsive to the aspirations and needs of a majority of the people.

As California became more urban and industrial toward the end of the nineteenth century, it experienced widespread poverty, a growth of rigid class divisions, and sporadic conflict between workers and employers. An increasing number of urban workers unionized (rural workers failed to organize successfully until the 1960s) and immediately encountered adamant resistance. Despite the fact that "big business" and "small business" disagreed about many issues, both segments of capital were in complete agreement about unions: they were to be resisted and, where possible, squelched. Workers, in the meantime, suffered from fragmentation and disunity.

Nonetheless, as early as the 1850s, a nascent labor movement had arisen among San Francisco's carpenters, shipyard workers, typesetters, tradesmen, and others, as spontaneous strikes erupted in the city and also in the mining districts. During the 1860s and 1870s, such union activism spread from San Francisco to emerging urban areas such as Oakland and Los Angeles.

A serious economic depression in the late 1870s caused rising unemployment among urban workers and also negatively affected the state's agricultural sector. Many California farmers joined the national Grange movement at that time. Urban workers were even more militant. California's first large-scale advocate for organized labor, the Workingmen's Party of California (WPC), became active in 1877. Headed by a volatile Irish orator named Denis Kearney, it targeted corporate privilege and Chinese immigrants as primary causes of the state's economic problems. The party's chief accomplishment was its successful advocacy of the federal Chinese Exclusion Act of 1882. White workers regarded the Chinese as their "indispensable enemy" and used unions to promote anti-Asian legislation while relying on anti-Chinese sentiments to consolidate their unions. In this manner, unionism and "anticoolieism" merged as one, a merger that would endure for decades.

In general, only a small minority of California workers were union members at the turn of the century, leaving employers essentially free to establish the terms of "the labor process." In the relatively prosperous years of the early twentieth century, however, new unions sprang up in San Francisco in a number of occupations and rapidly grew in number of members and in strength. Los Angeles, on the other hand, became the nation's leading center of the "open shop," as owners stubbornly refused to make agreements requiring union membership of their employees.

In this chapter, the documents offer many different statements for and against the big corporations, especially railroads, for and against labor unions, for and against the Chinese. These voices create a clamor that may be hard to interpret in terms of the larger view of California history, but each perspective deserves serious consideration. The two essays also offer two different perspectives, one centered on the unions and the other on the railroads. What was the basis for the power of each? How did the struggles between them contribute to a final resolution, if there was one? How did the power of each become legitimized?

 ## D O C U M E N T S

Henry George, the journalist and social critic, developed valuable insights about economic and social developments in California. The first document contains portions of a long article he wrote in 1868 for a leading literary journal, *The Overland Monthly.* There he expressed serious—some would say prophetic—reservations about the impact of the impending completion of the first transcontinental railroad. In the second and third documents, Leland Stanford and Collis P. Huntington, two members of the so-called Big Four who had established the Central Pacific Railroad Company to build the western segment of the transcontinental railroad, express their candid and provocative views about railroads and political influence. The next document contains sections from the 1901 classic novel *The Octopus* by Frank Norris. Based in part on a highly fictionalized account of the Mussel Slough massacre of 1880, in which farmers battled agents of the railroad, Norris's anticorporate portrayal has been echoed, until recently, by most historians.

The fifth document contains brief but fiery excerpts from speeches by Denis Kearney in 1877, as well as the platform of the Workingmen's Party of California, which sought to represent the interests of urban workers.

Henryk Sienkiewicz, author of the sixth document, came to California with a small group of immigrants from Poland in 1876 to establish a utopian community in Anaheim. The venture failed, but during his two-year sojourn in California Sienkiewicz wrote many sketches about California life. A segment of one, recording his observations of Chinese workers, is given here. His statement "In the conflict between capital and labor the Chinese have tipped the scales decisively in favor of capital" sums up why white workers were so opposed to the Chinese presence.

The last document comes from a 1902 brochure published by the American Federation of Labor. Samuel Gompers, president of the AFL, is often listed as the author of this brochure, but it is not clear whether he, in fact, penned it. In any case, the words reveal clearly the fears that Euro-American workers harbored with regard to Chinese competition. The brochure was used to persuade Congress to extend, once again, the Chinese Exclusion Act first passed in 1882. The AFL chose immigration exclusion over another possible alternative: removing Chinese competition by *including* them in the labor movement.

Henry George Expresses Skepticism About Railroads, 1868

Upon the plains this season railroad building is progressing with a rapidity never before known. The two companies, in their struggle for the enormous bounty offered by the Government, are shortening the distance between the lines of rail at the rate of from seven to nine miles a day—almost as fast as the ox teams which furnished the primitive method of conveyance across the continent could travel. Possibly by the middle of next spring, and certainly, we are told, before mid-summer comes again, this "greatest work of the age" will be completed, and an unbroken track stretch from the Atlantic to the Pacific.

Though, as a piece of engineering, the building of this road may not deserve the superlative terms in which, with American proneness to exaggeration, it is frequently spoken of, yet, when the full effects of its completion are considered, it seems the "greatest work of the age," indeed. Even the Suez Canal, which will almost change the front of Europe and divert the course of the commerce of half the world, is, in this view, not to be compared with it. For this railroad will not merely open a new route across the continent; it will be the means of converting a wilderness into a populous empire in less time than many of the cathedrals and palaces of Europe were building, and in unlocking treasure vaults which will flood the world with precious metals. The country west of the longitude of Omaha, all of which will be directly or indirectly affected by the construction of the railroad, (for other roads must soon follow the first) is the largest and richest portion of the United States. Throughout the greater part of this vast domain gold and silver are scattered in inexhaustible profusion, and it contains besides, in limitless quantities, every valuable mineral known to man, and includes every variety of soil and climate. . . .

What is the railroad to do for *us*?—this railroad that we have looked for, hoped for, prayed for so long?

Much as the matter has been thought about and talked about; many as have been the speeches made and the newspaper articles written on the subject, there are probably but a few of us who really comprehend all it will do. We are so used to the California of the stagecoach, widely separated from the rest of the world, that we can hardly realize what the California of the railroad will be—the California netted, with iron tracks, and almost as near in point of time to Chicago and St. Louis, as Virginia City was to San Francisco when the Washoe excitement first commenced, or as Red Bluff is now.

The sharpest sense of Americans—the keen sense of gain, which certainly does not lose its keenness in our bracing air—is the first to realize what is coming with our railroad. All over the State, land is appreciating— fortunes are being made in a day by buying and parceling out Spanish ranches; the Government surveyors and registrars are busy; speculators are grappling the public domain by the hundred of thousand of acres; while for miles in every direction around San Francisco, ground is being laid off into homestead lots. The spirit of speculation, doubles, trebles, quadruples the past growth of the city in its calculations, and then discounts the result, confident that there still remains a margin. And it is not far wrong. The new era will be one of great material prosperity, if material prosperity means more people, more houses, more farms and mines, more factories and ships. . . .

The new era into which our State is about entering—or, perhaps, to speak more correctly, has already entered—is without doubt an era of steady, rapid and substantial growth; of great addition to population and immense increase in the totals of the Assessor's lists. Yet we cannot hope to escape the great law of compensation which exacts some loss for every gain. And as there are but a few of us who, could we retrace our lives, retaining the knowledge we have gained, would pass from childhood into youth, or from youth into manhood, with unmixed feelings, so we imagine that if the genius of California, whom we picture on the shield of our State, were really a sentient being, she would not look forward now entirely without regret. The California of the new era will be greater, richer, more powerful than the California of the past; but will she be still the same California whom her adopted children, gathered from all climes, love better than their own mother lands; from which all who have lived within her bounds are proud to hail; to which all who have known her long to return? She will have more people; but among those people will there be so large a proportion of full, true men? She will have more wealth; but will it be so evenly distributed? She will have more luxury and refinement and culture; but will she have such general comfort, so little squalor and misery; so little of the grinding, hopeless poverty that chills and cramps the souls of men, and converts them into brutes?

Amid all our rejoicing and all our gratulation let us see clearly whither we are tending. Increase in population and in wealth past a certain point means simply an approximation to the condition of older countries—the Eastern States and Europe. Would the average Californian prefer to "take his chances" in New York or Massachusetts, or in California as it is and has been? Is England, with her population of twenty millions to an area not more than one-third that of our State, and a wealth which per inhabitant is six or seven times that of California, a better country than California to live in? Probably, if one were born a duke or a factory lord, or to any place among the upper ten thousand; but if one were born among the lower millions—how then?

And so the California of the future—the California of the new era—will be a better country for some classes than the California of the present; and so too, it must be a worse country for others. . . .

The truth is, that the completion of the railroad and the consequent great increase of business and population, will not be a benefit to all of us, but only to a portion. As a general rule (liable of course to exceptions) those who *have* it will make wealthier; for those who *have not*, it will make it more difficult to get. Those who have lands, mines, established businesses, special abilities of certain kinds, will become richer for it and find increased opportunities; those who have only their own labor will become poorer, and find it harder to get ahead—first, because it will take more capital to buy land or to get into business; and second, because as competition reduces the wages of labor, this capital will be harder for them to obtain.

Leland Stanford Extols the Public Benefits of Railroad Construction, 1887

The Pacific Railroad has accomplished all the good, both local and national, that was predicted by its most enthusiastic supporters. It has demonstrated the possibility of the construction of a transcontinental road; it has proved to the financial world that the great interior abounds in resources; it has made it possible for the construction of other transcontinental roads, with numerous branches and feeders; it has shown how the national domain can be utilized; it has encouraged the development of the natural resources of California, and shown that its products of fruits and wines can be transported to the Atlantic States by rail. It was the first enterprise anywhere in the world which made possible the habitation of regions of country far remote from navigable waters, and has added untold millions of wealth to the nation. It has performed the public service so faithfully and expeditiously as almost to annihilate the distance between the Pacific and the Atlantic, and bring the whole country into close and intimate political, social, and commercial relations. It has performed the government service in transportation of mails, materials, and supplies, to the complete satisfaction of all Government officers having charge of such business.

While the company has been spending all its energies in furnishing to the Government and the people every possible facility at the lowest possible rate for transportation, Congress has at times, through a misapprehension of the facts, appeared exacting and unjust. . . .

It was supposed when the company accepted the terms [of the Thurman Act of 1878] and entered into the contracts with the Government that the United States would take into consideration the circumstances under which the road was constructed, the difficulties encountered in its construction, and the great benefits accruing to the Government by its increased facilities in mail service and transportation, and allow it a like compensation to that formerly paid for the service when performed by teams and pack animals. The company, instead of receiving four millions per annum, which would have been its reasonable compensation, has, in fact, received not more than one-eighth of that amount.

Collis P. Huntington Shows Contempt
for Congress, 1887

Q. As a matter of fact, has not the Central Pacific Company frequently had legal assistance both from members of Congress and from members of the State and Territorial legislatures?

A. I know very little of what has been done west of the Missouri River.

Q. Then we will confine ourselves to what you know.

A. I do not think there would be any objection to employing a man to attend to a case in court because he was a member of the Senate or the House.

Q. Even though, at the time, there was a measure pending before the legislature in which the Central Pacific Company had a large pecuniary interest?

A. I should have no hesitation in employing the best man I could find, whether he was a member of Congress or not. . . . I always like to get the best men to do any particular thing that I have to do. . . .

Q. Do I understand the testimony heretofore given by you correctly— that the larger portion of the funds which appear on the vouchers over your signature were applied to legal expenses and expended through payments by you . . . for the purpose of explaining these matters to Congress?

A. I would not be prepared to say that a majority was. We had many things to do. We had a great many things in the Departments to attend to. . . .

Q. Without limiting you to members of Congress, my question is whether the unexplained vouchers were for expenditures, the majority of which were incurred for the purposes such as you have detailed?

A. I could not divide and subdivide them at this distance of time from other transactions; but I have no doubt that they were paid out for legal and proper purposes, such as would be sanctioned by the strictest rules of morality. . . . Most of the money was expended no doubt to prevent Congress and the Departments from robbing us of our property. . . .

. . . I will explain what the difference is between having the Central Pacific road built so that a whole army can be transported comfortably across the continent in six days, and the condition of things before the road was built. . . . We went to work and built the road, and the Government said it would give us so much if we built it. We complied in every particular with the contract, and because some light-weight, narrow-minded politician thought he could make something by maligning us, he went upon the house-top and cried aloud. . . . I spent twenty-five of the best years of my life in building the road across the high, dry, arid plains of the continent, and am abused for it by a portion of the press and by light-weight politicians who know little and care less about what we have done for the country.

Frank Norris Excoriates the Railroad as "The Octopus," 1901

By now . . . it was dark. Presley hurried forward. He came to the line fence of the Quien Sabe ranch. Everything was very still. The stars were all out. There was not a sound other than the *de Profundis,* still sounding from very far away. At long intervals the great earth sighed dreamily in its sleep. All about, the feeling of absolute peace and quiet and security and untroubled happiness and content seemed descending from the stars like a benediction. The beauty of his poem, its idyl, came to him like a caress; that alone had been lacking. It was that, perhaps, which had left it hitherto incomplete. At last he was to grasp his song in all its entity.

But suddenly there was an interruption. Presley had climbed the fence at the limit of the Quien Sabe ranch. Beyond was Los Muertos, but between the two ran the railroad. He had only time to jump back upon the embankment when, with a quivering of all the earth, a locomotive, single, unattached, shot by him with a roar, filling the air with the reek of hot oil, vomiting smoke and sparks; its enormous eye, Cyclopean, red, throwing a glare far in advance, shooting by in a sudden crash of confused thunder; filling the night with the terrific clamour of its iron hoofs.

Abruptly Presley remembered. This must be the crack passenger engine of which Dyke had told him, the one delayed by the accident on the Bakersfield division and for whose passage the track had been opened all the way to Fresno.

Before Presley could recover from the shock of the irruption, while the earth was still vibrating, the rails still humming, the engine was far away, flinging the echo of its frantic gallop over all the valley. For a brief instant it roared with a hollow diapason on the Long Trestle over Broderson Creek, then plunged into a cutting farther on, the quivering glare of its fires losing itself in the night, its thunder abruptly diminishing to a subdued and distant humming. All at once this ceased. The engine was gone.

But the moment the noise of the engine lapsed, Presley—about to start forward again—was conscious of a confusion of lamentable sounds that rose into the night from out the engine's wake. Prolonged cries of agony, sobbing wails of infinite pain, heart-rending, pitiful.

The noises came from a little distance. He ran down the track, crossing the culvert, over the irrigating ditch, and at the head of the long reach of track—between the culvert and the Long Trestle—paused abruptly, held immovable at the sight of the ground and rails all about him.

In some way, the herd of sheep—Vanamee's herd—had found a breach in the wire fence by the right of way and had wandered out upon the tracks. A band had been crossing just at the moment of the engine's passage. The pathos of it was beyond expression. It was a slaughter, a massacre of innocents. The iron monster had charged full into the midst, merciless, inexorable. To the right and left, all the width of the right of way, the little bodies had been flung; backs were snapped against the fence posts; brains knocked out. Caught in the barbs of the wire, wedged in, the bodies hung suspended. Under foot it was terrible. The black blood, winking in the starlight, seeped down into the clinkers between the ties with a prolonged sucking murmur.

Presley turned away, horror-struck, sick at heart, overwhelmed with a quick burst of irresistible compassion for this brute agony he could not relieve. The sweetness was gone from the evening, the sense of peace, of security, and placid contentment was stricken from the landscape. The hideous ruin in the engine's path drove all thought of his poem from his mind. The inspiration vanished like a mist. The *de Profundis* had ceased to ring.

He hurried on across the Los Muertos ranch, almost running, even putting his hands over his ears till he was out of hearing distance of that all but human distress. Not until he was beyond earshot did he pause, looking back, listening. The night had shut down again. For a moment the silence was profound, unbroken.

Then, faint and prolonged, across the levels of the ranch, he heard the engine whistling for Bonneville. Again and again, at rapid intervals in its flying course, it whistled for road crossings, for sharp curves, for trestles; ominous notes, hoarse, bellowing, ringing with the accents of menace and defiance; and abruptly Presley saw again, in his imagination, the galloping monster, the terror of steel and steam, with its single eye, Cyclopean, red, shooting from horizon to horizon; but saw it now as the symbol of a vast power, huge, terrible, flinging the echo of its thunder over all the reaches of the valley, leaving blood and destruction in its path; the leviathan, with tentacles of steel clutching into the soil, the soulless Force, the iron-hearted Power, the monster, the Colossus, the Octopus. . . .

How long must it go on? How long must we suffer? Where is the end; what is the end? How long must the iron-hearted monster feed on our life's blood? How long must this terror of steam and steel ride upon our necks? Will you never be satisfied, will you never relent, you, our masters, you, our lords, you, our kings, you, our task-masters, you, our Pharaohs. Will you never listen to that command *'Let My people go?'* Oh, that cry ringing down the ages. Hear it, hear it. It is the voice of the Lord God speaking in His prophets. Hear it, hear it—'Let My people go!' Rameses heard it in his pylons at Thebes, Caesar heard it on the Palatine, the Bourbon Louis heard it at Versailles, Charles Stuart heard it at Whitehall, the white Czar heard it in the Kremlin—*'Let My people go.'* It is the cry of the nations, the great voice of the centuries; everywhere it is raised. The voice of God is the voice of the People. The people cry out 'Let us, the People, God's people, go.' You, our masters, you, our kings, you, our tyrants, don't you hear us? Don't you hear God speaking in us? Will you never let us go? How long at length will you abuse our patience? How long will you drive us? How long will you harass us? Will nothing daunt you? Does nothing check you? Do you not know that to ignore our cry too long is to wake the Red Terror? Rameses refused to listen to it and perished miserably. Caesar refused to listen and was stabbed in the Senate House. The Bourbon Louis refused to listen and died on the guillotine; Charles Stuart refused to listen and died on the block; the white Czar refused to listen and was blown up in his own capital. Will you let it come to that? Will you drive us to it? We who boast of our land and freedom, we who live in the country of liberty?

Go on as you have begun and it *will* come to that. Turn a deaf ear to that cry of 'Let My people go' too long and another cry will be raised that you cannot choose but hear, a cry that you cannot shut out. It will be the cry of the man on the street, the *'à la Bastille'* that wakes the Red Terror and unleashes Revolution. Harassed, plundered, exasperated, desperate, the people will turn at last as they have turned so many, many times before. You, our lords, you, our task-masters, you, our kings; you have caught your Samson, you have made his strength your own. You have shorn his head; you have put out his eyes; you have set him to turn your millstones, to grind the grist for your mills; you have made him a shame and a mock. Take care, oh, as you love your lives, take care, lest some day calling upon the Lord his God he reach not out his arms for the pillars of your temples. . . .

They own us, these task-masters of ours; they own our homes, they own our legislatures. We cannot escape from them. There is no redress. We are told we can defeat them by the ballot-box. They own the ballot-box. We are told that we must look to the courts for redress; they own the courts. We know them for what they are—ruffians in politics, ruffians in finance, ruffians in law, ruffians in trade, bribers, swindlers, and tricksters. No outrage too great to daunt them, no petty larceny too small to shame them; despoiling a government treasury of a million dollars, yet picking the pockets of a farm hand of the price of a loaf of bread.

They swindle a nation of a hundred million and call it Financiering; they levy a blackmail and call it Commerce; they corrupt a legislature and call it Politics; they bribe a judge and call it Law; they hire blacklegs to carry out their plans and call it Organization; they prostitute the honour of a State and call it Competition.

And this is America. We fought Lexington to free ourselves; we fought Gettysburg to free others. Yet the yoke remains; we have only shifted it to the other shoulder. We talk of liberty—oh, the farce of it, oh, the folly of it! We tell ourselves and teach our children that we have achieved liberty, that we no longer need to fight for it. Why, the fight is just beginning and so long as our conception of liberty remains as it is to-day, it will continue.

For we conceive of Liberty in the statues we raise to her as a beautiful woman, crowned, victorious, in bright armour and white robes, a light in her uplifted hand—a serene, calm, conquering goddess. Oh, the farce of it, oh the folly of it! Liberty is *not* a crowned goddess, beautiful, in spotless garments, victorious, supreme. Liberty is the Man In [*sic*] the Street, a terrible figure, rushing through powder smoke, fouled with the mud and ordure of the gutter, bloody, rampant, brutal, yelling curses, in one hand a smoking rifle, in the other, a blazing torch.

Freedom is *not* given free to any who ask; Liberty is not born of the gods. She is a child of the People, born in the very height and heat of battle, born from death, stained with blood, grimed with powder. And she grows to be not a goddess, but a Fury, a fearful figure, slaying friend and foe alike, raging, insatiable, merciless, the Red Terror.

Denis Kearney Organizes the Workingmen's Party of California, 1877

Kearney, considering the time propitious for the organization of another political party, called a meeting for October 5, 1877. About 150 persons were present, and these took part in the formation of the Workingmen's Party of California. Kearney was chosen president, J. G. Day, vice-president, and H. L. Knight, secretary. The meeting adopted as the platform of the new party the following set of principles, which had been drawn up by H. L. Knight:

The object of this Association is to unite all poor and working men and their friends into one political party, for the purpose of defending themselves against the dangerous encroachments of capital on the happiness of our people and the liberties of our country.

We propose to wrest the government from the hands of the rich and place it in those of the people, where it properly belongs.

We propose to rid the country of cheap Chinese labor as soon as possible, and by all the means in our power, because it tends still more to degrade labor and aggrandize capital.

We propose to destroy land monopoly in our state by such laws as will make it impossible.

We propose to destroy the great money power of the rich by a system of taxation that will make great wealth impossible in the future.

We propose to provide decently for the poor and unfortunate, the weak, the helpless, and especially the young, because the country is rich enough to do so, and religion, humanity, and patriotism demand that we should do so.

We propose to elect none but competent workingmen and their friends to any office whatever. The rich have ruled us until they have ruined us. We will now take our own affairs in our own hands. The republic must and shall be preserved and only workingmen will do it. Our shoddy aristocrats want an emperor and a standing army to shoot down the people.

For these purposes, we propose to organize ourselves into the Workingmen's Party of California, and to pledge and enroll therein all who are willing to join us in accomplishing these ends.

When we have 10,000 members, we shall have the sympathy and support of 20,000 other workingmen.

The party will then wait upon all who employ Chinese and ask for their discharge, and it will mark as public enemies those who refuse to comply with their request.

This party will exhaust all peaceable means of attaining its ends, but it will not be denied justice when it has the power to enforce it. It will encourage no riot or outrage, but it will not volunteer to repress, or put down, or arrest, or prosecute the hungry and impatient who manifest their hatred of the Chinamen by a crusade against "John" or those who employ him. Let those who raise the storm by their selfishness, suppress it themselves. If they dare raise the devil, let them meet him face to face. We will not help them. . . .

A few nights later, Kearney addressed a meeting at the corner of Stockton and Greene streets.

When we issue a call [he said], we want you to act promptly. We want to know the man who will discharge any workingmen who turn out to attend these meetings. We will brand him so that every workingman in this city shall know him. . . . But I tell you, and I want Stanford and the press to understand, that if I give an order to hang Crocker, it will be done. . . . The dignity of labor must be sustained, even if we have to kill every wretch that opposes it.

Henryk Sienkiewicz Appraises Chinese Labor in California, 1880

Let us now look at the kind of work the Chinese perform in California. A single word describes it accurately: everything. A significant proportion of them has turned to agriculture. The whole of San Francisco is situated on arid dunes and sandy hills, and yet whoever goes to the outskirts of the city will perceive at the ends of unfinished streets, on the hills, valleys, and slopes, on the roadsides, in fact, everywhere, small vegetable gardens encircling the city with one belt of greenness. The ant-like labor of the Chinese has transformed the sterile sand into the most fertile black earth. How and when this was accomplished they alone can tell, but suffice it to say that all the fruits and vegetables, raspberries and strawberries, under the care of Chinese gardeners grow to a fabulous size. I have seen strawberries as large as small pears, heads of cabbage four times the size of European heads, and pumpkins the size of our wash tubs. . . .

[T]he whole of San Francisco lives on the fruits and vegetables bought from the Chinese. Every morning you see their loaded wagons headed toward the markets in the center of town or stopping in front of private homes. It may even be said that in all of California this branch of industry has passed exclusively into the hands of the Chinese. . . .

A large number of Chinese likewise work for white farmers, especially in the orchards. . . . In the vicinity of San Francisco and in Alameda County along the railroad are whole orchards of apple trees, pear trees, peach trees, and almond trees; here and there fields comprising scores of acres are covered with red currant bushes; near Sacramento are extensive hop-gardens. The work on these fields and in these orchards is done almost exclusively by hired Chinese. . . .

In the cultivation of grain in northern California the Chinese cannot compete with the whites. For plowing, harrowing, and harvesting, the white worker, being twice as strong, is much more in demand, for he works faster and with greater energy. Where there are no whites, however, Chinese are used even for these jobs.

In southern California where vineyards abound, there, too, very few Chinese are employed. In this area Mexican and Indian laborers, who are as strong as the Yankees and who work as cheaply as the Chinese, are easily obtainable. . . .

[I]n the cities . . . [t]hey are engaged in business; in the factories they serve as laborers; they are hired by the owners of handicraft shops; in the hotels they perform all the more menial tasks; in private homes they are responsible for orderliness and cleanliness. In restaurants and on the railroads they serve as cooks and waiters. Practically all of the laundries in town are in their hands and it must be admitted that they do the laundry neatly, quickly, and cheaply. They serve as nurses for children. In a private home the Chinaman fulfils [*sic*] all of the duties of a maid; he puts things away, sweeps the floors, makes the beds, cooks the meals, washes the dishes, and does the shopping in town; he is a quiet, sober, industrious, gentle, and obedient servant, and he costs much less than a white servant. Ever since the Chinese have become numerous in California, all prices have declined considerably. Everything from the cigars wrapped by Chinese hands to items of food—everything now costs less because the cost of labor is less. . . .

Taking these things into consideration, one might deem the Chinese a blessing to California were it not for the keen competition they create for the white working-class. . . . A white man . . . requires more food and better living quarters instead of suffocating with a score of others in one hole. Finally, a white worker usually has a family, wife and children, whereas the Chinaman is alone. . . . The result is that if the Chinese are a blessing at all it is only for the wealthy classes who need servants and workers. In the conflict between capital and labor the Chinese have tipped the scales decisively in favor of capital. Even though white workers should offer their services more cheaply, some employers would prefer Chinese . . . as workers who are not fellow citizens but half-slaves, quiet, obedient, and docile . . . and as they become more numerous, they begin to create dangerous competition for small business, small farmers, and small industries.

The American Federation of Labor Opposes Chinese Immigration, 1902

[The] ability [of the Chinese] to subsist and thrive under conditions which would mean starvation and suicide to the cheapest laborer of Europe secures to them an advantage which baffles the statesman and economist to overcome, how much less the chances of the laborers pitted in competition against them.

For many years it was impossible to get white persons to do the menial labor usually performed by Chinese. It was Chinamen's labor, and not fit for white. In the agricultural districts a species of tramp has been created, known as the blanket man. White agricultural laborers seldom find permanent employment; the Chinese are preferred. During harvest time the white man is forced to wander from ranch to ranch and find employment here and there for short periods of time, with the privilege of sleeping in the barns or haystacks. He is looked upon as a vagabond, unfit to associate with his employer or to eat from the same table with him. The negro slave of the South was housed and fed, but the white trash of California is placed beneath the Chinese.

The white domestic servant was expected to live in the room originally built for John [what Chinese were often called in nineteenth-century California—*Ed.*], generally situated in the cellar and void of all comforts; frequently unpainted or unpapered, containing a bedstead and a chair; anything was good enough for John, and the white girl had to be satisfied as well. Is it any wonder that self-respecting girls refused to take service under those conditions? And what is true of agricultural laborers and domestics equally applies to the trades in which Chinese were largely employed. Absolute servility was expected from those who took the place of the Chinaman, and it will take years to obliterate these traces of inferiority and re-establish the proper relations of employer and employee. . . .

American labor should not be exposed to the destructive competition of aliens who do not, will not, and cannot take up the burdens of American citizenship, whose presence is an economic blight and a patriotic danger. It has been urged that the Chinese are unskilled and that they create wealth in field, mine, and forest, which ultimately redounds to the benefit of the white skilled workingman. The Chinese are skilled, and are capable of almost any skilled employment. They have invaded the cigar, shoe, broom, chemical, clothing, fruit canning, match making, woolen manufacturing industries, and have displaced more than 4,000 white men in these several employments in the city of San Francisco. As common laborers they have throughout California displaced tens of thousands of men. But this country is not concerned, even in a coldly economic sense, with the production of wealth. The United States has now a greater per capita of working energy than any other land. If it is stimulated by a non-assimilative and non-consuming race, there is grave danger of over-production and stagnation. The home market should grow with the population. But the Chinese, living on the most meager food, having no families to support, inured to deprivation, and hoarding their wages for use in their native land, whither they invariably return, cannot in any sense be regarded as consumers. Their earnings do not circulate, nor are they reinvested—contrary to those economic laws which make for the prosperity of nations. . . .

It was estimated by the Commissioner of Labor that there were a million idle men in the United States in 1886. Certainly the 76,000 Chinese in California at that time stood for 76,000 white men waiting for employment. . . . If the United States increases in population at the rate of 12 per cent per decade, it will have nearly 230,000,000 of people in one hundred years. Our inventive genius and the constant improvements being made in machinery will greatly increase our per capita productive capacity. If it be our only aim to increase our wealth so as to hold our own in the markets of the world, are we not, without the aid of Chinese coolies, capable of doing it, and at the same time preserve the character of our population and insure the perpetuity of our institutions? It is not wealth at any cost that sound public policy requires, but that the country be developed with equal pace and with a desirable population, which stands not only for industry, but for citizenship. . . .

[T]his is not alone a race, labor and political question. It is one which involves our civilization and interests the people of the world. The benefactors, scholars, soldiers, and statesmen—the patriots and martyrs of mankind—have builded [*sic*] our modern fabric firmly upon the foundation of religion, law, science, and art. It has been rescued from barbarism and protected against the incursions of barbarians. Civilization in Europe has been frequently attacked and imperiled by the barbaric hordes of Asia. . . . But a peaceful invasion is more dangerous than a warlike attack. We can meet and defend ourselves against an open foe, but an insidious foe, under our generous laws, would be in possession of the citadel before we were aware. The free immigration of Chinese would be, for all purposes, an invasion of Asiatic barbarians.

E S S A Y S

As labor historian Michael Kazin of American University points out, the completion of the transcontinental railroad in 1869 "thrust California into a burgeoning national economy." Yet for many years only the state's extractive industries could successfully compete in eastern markets, while its manufacturing industries were limited to regional markets until World War II. From about 1870 to 1940, then, California's manufacturing and service industries employed relatively few workers compared to larger firms elsewhere in the nation. Nonetheless, during those years a mature labor movement emerged in the San Francisco Bay Area and the Los Angeles basin. Kazin, in the first essay, describes that movement's characteristics, stressing the role played by ethnicity and race in the formation of California's working class.

A recent study by William Deverell of the California Institute of Technology—*Railroad Crossing: Californians and the Railroad, 1850–1910* (1994)—is representative of a revisionist scholarship that seeks to temper long-standing assertions about railroad domination in California. In the second essay, Deverell contends that the Pullman strike of 1894 "shattered the traditional form and shape of anti-railroad thought and behavior in California," producing "a degree of railroad antagonism not before seen in the state's history." That single event, which many were convinced was a prelude to violent revolution, helped determine patterns and directions for California's economy and politics in the early twentieth century, when progressive reformers utilized the railroad issue for their own political purposes.

The Rise of the Labor Movement in California

MICHAEL KAZIN

From 1870 to 1940, California left its glorious isolation on the fringe of European settlement and became both an economic giant and a significant political region from which firebrands like Denis Kearney, Hiram Johnson, and Upton Sinclair emerged to shake the nation. In 1870, the state was still a frontier boasting only one true city. Except for a few scattered flour, sugar, and lumber mills, manufacturing in California was then limited to San Francisco and its immediate environs.

The completion of the transcontinental railroad rapidly changed that environment. The railroad thrust California into a burgeoning national economy and attracted entrepreneurs in large-scale farming, food processing, petroleum and other extractive industries who created new markets through aggressive sales techniques and, later, the happy coincidence of a rage for automobiles. By 1940, California led the nation in the production of most crops, was the center of the international film industry, and the foremost manufacturer of ships and aircraft frames—for both commercial and military purposes. An ever-increasing flow of migrants from all classes and races came to share in the bounty such a diversified economy made possible.

However, until World War II, California's economic growth did not significantly alter the size and types of businesses most prominent in the state's urban areas. Extractive industries long remained the only ones that could compete in markets east of the continental divide. Cost, distance, and the slow development of power sources limited most California manufacturers to supplying consumer goods to a regional population. . . . Factories, canneries, and sawmills in the state tended to be small concerns employing fewer than a hundred workers and were quite vulnerable to strikes and boycotts. The same was true for service industries—from laundries to restaurants to department stores—that employed the single largest sector of the state's nonagricultural workforce. . . .

The years from 1870 to 1940 also saw the California labor movement grow to maturity. During the Gilded Age, skilled workers organized themselves into trade unions which withstood the blows of open-shop employers and two severe depressions. In the Progressive era, the labor movement attained great influence for a time before being humbled in the aftermath of World War I. During the 1930s, unions regained strength, albeit with a loss of political independence, and tripled their membership in less than a decade.

Throughout this period, the character of the labor movement in the San Francisco Bay area and the Los Angeles basin, where a majority of wage-earners lived, shaped their counterparts elsewhere in California. . . .

Three major characteristics emerge from the labor history of what were California's two largest cities. First, with little opposition, urban federations of skilled craftsmen dominated the labor movement until the 1930s. White women, agricultural workers of all races, and menial laborers in the cities sometimes acted on their own, but the objectives and accomplishments of their isolated struggles were limited in almost every case by the ideological and institutional hegemony of craft unionists.

Key to this supremacy was the sustained influence of strong, citywide central labor federations in both San Francisco and Los Angeles. . . . "City centrals" sponsored and financed whatever labor newspapers existed, and because of their inclusive, representative nature, they could forcefully bring working-class demands to the attention of state and municipal officials. . . . [They were] the place where strategy was made and influence generated for the labor movement as a whole. Inevitably, their leaders came from the largest and economically most powerful unions in each city— usually teamsters, sailors, carpenters, metal workers, and longshoremen.

Second, these dominant groups incorporated much of the critique and rhetoric of the political left rather than opposing it as did the national AFL leadership. . . . [Labor had the] ability to adapt the ideas of Marxists and egalitarian utopians like Henry George to its own trade unionist ends. The most successful unionists routinely spoke to workers and the general public in a language filled with allusions to "class struggle" and "monopoly rule." Yet only a small minority had a desire, much less a strategy, for overthrowing the capitalist system. Their aim instead was to increase the power of trade unions in every area of society as a counterweight to organized corporate might. . . .

Third, the California labor movement pursued its aims as much through political activity as by exerting its muscle at the workplace. Unionists unstintingly yoked their fortunes to candidates, parties, and legal reforms that promised to make the government more responsive to working-class concerns. . . . [U]ntil World War I white workers in California's urban centers often had a "labor party" for which to vote. From the scanty evidence collected thus far, it seems they gave that party at least a plurality of their votes, although none of the chosen vehicles was a frequent winner or dedicated itself to social change once in office. When they could not mount an independent ticket, most union leaders aligned themselves with one of the major parties and, in return, received nominations, and appointments for themselves, and legislation to benefit their members.

Political involvement flowed naturally from the labor movement's claim to be the representative of all *white* working-class Californians. That the campaign for Asian exclusion required continuous pressure on officeholders in both Sacramento and Washington, D.C., contributed to this self-image, but it was not the sole influence. Craft unionists regularly participated in municipal campaigns in which the issue of Chinese and Japanese immigration played only a minor role. When they entered local races—both to advance their careers and as spokesmen for class-identified causes—labor leaders usually did so with the expectation they would win. . . .

Thus, the most salient feature of California urban labor was . . . [the] ability of existing unions to direct working-class discontent to their own ends. The most influential labor leaders proved themselves to be both ecumenical towards political factions within their own ranks and fierce opponents of management at times of industrial conflict. This combination allowed California unionists to avoid bitter internal quarrels that, in other parts of the nation, often split the movement into irreconcilable parts. . . .

What explains the unrivaled supremacy of craft unionists who utilized both economic leverage and electoral coalitions in their search for power? Three interrelated factors seem to have been crucial. First, California was a society in which ethnic divisions among whites were *politically* inconsequential. In the San Francisco Bay area, the two major population groups were Caucasians from the "old immigration" (especially Irish, Germans, and Scandinavians) and Asians (predominately Chinese with a small number of Japanese). In Los Angeles, native-born whites and Mexicans predominated.

The impact of this demographic composition was profound. Workplace hierarchies based on nationality seldom sprouted among whites—in sharp contrast to the steel mills, meat-packing plants, and textile factories of the East, where craftsmen, semi-skilled machine operators, and laborers often spoke different languages and rarely made common cause across a gulf of cultures. In California, white workers bonded together across religious lines, as well as those between immigrants and native-born. They united both *for* positive goals such as high wages and local political power and *against* the supposed threat of Asian labor. For Californians, "the working class" was a racially specific term which enabled white wage-earners to perceive themselves as an embattled majority.

In Los Angeles, Mexicans did not weaken the ethnic unity among whites because, until the 1930s, they seldom worked in the same industries as Anglos and were segregated into menial occupations when they did. Moreover, most lived in a *barrio* apart from the rapidly expanding city which surrounded it. . . . Until World War II, Mexicans, Asians, and Afro-Americans usually entered the majority's consciousness only as voiceless "hands" who dwelled at the bottom of society.

A second reason . . . was the existence of a labor market segmented, in this "middle period" of the state's history, between rural laborers and urban craftsmen. Only one insignificant industry employed *primarily* unskilled workers. That was, of course, agriculture—what Carey McWilliams termed California's "peculiar institution" because of the dominance of huge farms employing nonwhite migrant workers who lived in a style reminiscent of the slave South. All other major industries were urban ones which, except for wartime shipbuilding, resisted the concentration of ownership which had taken hold in the manufacture of durable goods east of the Mississippi River.

Urban industries that employed the most manual workers—such as transportation and the maritime trades, construction, metal manufacturing, and the production of consumer goods such as garments and coffee—were either strongholds of unionism (in San Francisco) or continual battle-grounds between union organizers and open-shop managers (in Los Angeles). . . .

A third reason . . . was the utter lack of deference which characterized white workers' approach to political activity. Since the gold rush, white workers had projected an angry egalitarianism that was constantly renewed as each new generation sought to explain the gulf between California's material abundance and the slim reward earned by most of the population. The absence of a hereditary governing class in the Far West made these glaring inequalities of wealth seem all the more onerous and encouraged the search for political solutions. Workers could not break the economic power of Leland Stanford or Harrison Gray Otis, but they could vote. In response, the California legislature, long before the New Deal, passed scores of measures advocated by organized labor. . . .

The history of urban labor in California from 1870 to 1940 can be separated into three eras—each of which represents a stage in labor's ongoing engagement with political ideas and political power. Despite the different fortunes of the movement in Los Angeles and San Francisco, the aims of working-class activists and the associations formed to achieve them remained essentially the same in both cities throughout the entire period.

From 1870 to 1898, the ideological and organizational contours of the labor movement were established. Workers experimented with a wide range of collective forms—independent parties, radical sects, producer cooperatives, union federations, and craft-based locals—before settling upon a durable amalgam of "business unionism" infused with prodigious political ambitions. . . .

The effects of a nationwide depression—exacerbated by a severe drought and the arrival of cheap eastern goods on the new transcontinental railroad—and the failure of either major party to halt Chinese immigration persuaded many wage-earners to break with their old political loyalties. The Workingmen's party [*sic*] of California (WPC) captured the labor vote in the late 1870s and then self-destructed, leaving an assortment of radical groups to pick up the pieces.

The WPC also filled a vacuum left by the collapse of craft unions that had been created in the 1860s, and it sparked a labor revival. For all the attention paid to Denis Kearney's demagogic oratory and the controversies that swirled around the party's role in writing the new state constitution of 1879, the WPC's functional role is often neglected. The party served as an invaluable bridge to more stable and popular unions. Its sweeping victory in San Francisco and Los Angeles municipal elections demonstrated the appeal to white workers of a platform that attacked both Chinese immigration and a monopolized economy. . . . The party's major shortcoming, in the view of labor activists, was its domination by opportunists like Kearney and those animated by racial hatred alone. Shorn of those failings, it provided an excellent model for those who wanted to fuse political mobilization with a spirited call for the redress of economic grievances. During the 1880s, skilled workers in California's urban centers reestablished their unions, most of which are still operating, on this broad new basis. . . .

[The] common thread . . . [among various labor groups was the call] for the melioration and/or replacement of the capitalist order. White workers were articulating a desire for full participation in the economic realm which they already possessed in the political sphere. They sought democratic control of and fair compensation from their society, not its destruction. . . .

All over the state, union men ran for office on a program that included the eight-hour day, public ownership of utilities, police neutrality during strikes, and the permanent exclusion of Chinese labor. . . .

Unarguably, California labor's most successful political campaign during the Gilded Age was the one waged against the Chinese, culminating in the federal Exclusion Act of 1882. Using boycotts, union labels, and the unifying agency of "city centrals," white workers and the politicians whom they championed developed a sense of mastery that endured into the next century. "Much of the present strength of the California labor movement is due to the sense of common interests and the habit of united action which were acquired in this great campaign," wrote prounion economist Lucile Eaves in 1910. In one of the cruelest ironies of California's past, unions increased their membership and social power at the expense of workers from another race.

Union power was consolidated and extended during the quarter-century from 1898 to 1922, which began with the economic boom touched off by the Spanish-American war and ended in the recession-wracked aftermath of World War I. During this period, San Francisco emerged as the quintessential union town: the closed shop prevailed in construction, transportation, and the bulk of manufacturing industries as well as an array of service trades, such as white-owned steam laundries and most restaurants and bars. Los Angeles provided a contrasting study in weakness. Except for a flurry of organizing in 1910 and 1911, unions in the southern metropolis made little headway against the disciplined and well-financed juggernaut of the Merchants and Manufacturers Association headed by Harrison Gray Otis and F. J. Zeehandelaar. . . .

During the Progressive era, white workers in California took as prominent a part in the anti-Japanese campaign of their time as had their predecessors to whom Chinese were the major villain. This time, however, union officials initiated the campaign, and no freelance orator-politicians emerged to challenge their control. . . .

[Union leaders] managed the anti-Japanese campaign as they did strikes and boycotts against employers—as one of several priorities that had to be balanced to further the ends of organized labor as a whole. In 1913, Olaf Tveitmoe, in his capacity as president of the labor-financed Asiatic Exclusion League, even called for a temporary halt to anti-Japanese activities, lest they jeopardize the success of the upcoming Panama-Pacific International Exposition that had hired thousands of union construction workers.

This pragmatic stance also characterized the relationship of many mainstream unionists towards the organized left, specifically the Industrial Workers of the World and the Socialist party. Both groups had significant numbers of supporters in the state. . . .

Besides potential competitors on their left, California unionists also had to confront the far more serious challenge of progressivism. Every union in the state supported measures, such as the public ownership of utilities and initiative, referendum, and recall, which were also dear to the hearts of Hiram Johnson and his associates in the Lincoln-Roosevelt League. But working-class activists, in addition, advocated state-financed health insurance and a strict anti-injunction law, both of which made all but the most radical progressives recoil. During the legislative sessions of 1911 and 1913, union lobbyists worked closely with Johnson's "insurgent" majority to pass the state's first effective workmen's compensation act, an eight-hour law for women and children, and a number of other bills. In gratitude, working-class voters swung decisively to progressive Republicans in elections for the rest of the decade. At the state level, the AFL became a valued ally in Johnson's battles with conservatives in his own party. . . .

The decade of the 1930s is remembered as a time when millions of workers, with the aid of the federal government, challenged the major industrial corporations in the nation and won recognition for their unions. This upsurge was nowhere as impressive as in California. Longshoremen, warehousemen, farm laborers, retail clerks, and the mélange of trades in the motion picture industry led the way with well-publicized organizing campaigns and massive strikes that inspired other wage-earners to follow their example. Radicals, especially members of the Communist party, played a critical role as motivators, educators, and handlers of detail. By the time the United States entered World War II, San Francisco had regained its reputation as a union town, and Los Angeles had finally shed its image as a paradise for open-shop employers. Almost 200,000 workers, including men and women of *all* races, joined freshly minted affiliates of either the AFL or the CIO. Of the state's major industries, only agriculture and banking were still able to operate free from organized workers and union contracts.

The rank-and-file movement of the 1930s, which was the engine of labor's California revival, severed organizational connections that had endured for a half century, but it marked less of a *political* departure than most observers realized at the time. The San Francisco general strike of 1934, which grew out of a walkout by maritime workers up and down the West Coast, did touch off a whirlwind of activity, affecting practically every manual occupation in the state. Harry Bridges, who advanced in three years from spokesman of a radical faction on the San Francisco waterfront to head of the International Longshoremen's and Warehousemen's Union (ILWU) and director of the California CIO, symbolized to supporters and enemies alike a "syndicalist renaissance" that seemed to threaten the perpetuation of the social order.

However, once the initial flush of organizing fervor had cooled, the new industrial unionists revealed goals no different from those espoused by craft workers in earlier periods. Agricultural laborers—whether under the leadership of a "revolutionary" union formed by the Communist party (the Cannery and Agricultural Workers Industrial Union) in the early 1930s or a more stable affiliate of the CIO (the United Cannery, Agricultural, Packing, and Allied Workers of America) later in the decade—were beaten, shot, and Red-baited. But at each point, they demanded only higher rates for the crops they picked, better treatment from supervisors, and recognition for their union. On the docks of San Francisco and San Pedro, longshoremen sometimes refused to load cargo destined for Mussolini's war in Ethiopia and Japan's invading armies in China. However, the daily struggle to gain a secure income and control over the hiring process was the real work of the union that Bridges headed. . . .

Thus, from 1870 to 1940, California labor had evolved from a lily-white social movement composed of struggling craft unions, leftist sects, and working-class reform groups into a multi-racial formation dominated by large industrial unions. Organized labor had won a legitimate place in the state's political and economic life, one that all but isolated devotees of the far right accepted.

The Southern Pacific Railroad Survives the Pullman Strike of 1894

WILLIAM DEVERELL

After the excitement of the [1879] constitutional convention and the Mussel Slough murders faded, the 1880s witnessed a period of relative quiet between the railroad corporation and its various opponents. Antagonism to the railroad did not disappear by any means, but it seldom reached a comparable level of influence or notoriety. In the political arena, both major parties continued to adopt planks decrying the monopolistic actions of the

Excerpted from William Deverell, *Railroad Crossing: Californians and the Railroad, 1850–1910*. Copyright © 1993 by The Regents of the University of California. Reprinted by permission of the University of California Press and the author.

Southern Pacific and that corporation's concomitant influence in the halls of government. Democratic victories in the 1880 and 1882 elections brought reform elements to the fore. Efforts to enact change, however, proved difficult. As California writer Rockwell Hunt grandly lamented long ago, "sincere efforts at reform seemed like the beating of the feeble waves of a mill pond against Gibralter."

The publication of the infamous Colton letters in 1883 accentuated the railroad corporation's troubles. These exchanges between Collis Huntington and David D. Colton, an important railroad official (the fifth of the "Big Five," or the "Half" of the "Big Four and a Half"), detailed lobbying and political efforts of the Central Pacific during years of rapid consolidation and growth in the 1870s. The letters were made public after Colton's death in the course of legal proceedings begun by Mrs. Colton to recoup assets from the Big Four. They not only divulged Colton's own shady derrings-do as a financial officer in the corporation but also revealed questionable behavior—including hints of bribery, influence peddling, and corporate meddling—at all levels of government. Newspapers and political figures responded all across the state, as well as in Washington, with collective "I told you so" declarations of outrage.

The Southern Pacific had further trouble when it challenged California's tax system. As part of the legacy of the new constitution of 1879, railroad capital had been taxed differently from capital held by other corporations or individuals. In the early 1880s, the Central Pacific went to court with constitutional challenges to the state taxing system and also withheld its tax payments. The courts initially decided against the corporation; it was not until the relevant cases reached the California Supreme Court that the railroad's position was upheld. The controversy did not stop there, however, as angry Californians, Governor George Stoneman among them, blasted the Central Pacific's cheek as well as the state's timid response to such corporate aggressiveness.

Despite these events, the relationship between the railroad corporation and the people of California eased in the 1880s—partly because the company relaxed its monopolistic grip on transcontinental freight and passenger traffic, at least in southern California. The Atchison, Topeka & Santa Fe Railroad broke through the S.P. barrier first in southern California, arriving in that region in 1885. The resulting (if temporary) rate war between the two transportation giants helped spawn and sustain a population and growth boom. "You would have thought all the United States and a part of Canada were on the move," remembered one railroad employee. By the fall of 1886, newcomers to Los Angeles had to line up for rooms to rent, as tourists and immigrants alike discovered the "semi-tropic" paradise of the southland. "The town is just bursting with tourists," wrote one Angeleno in the fall of 1886; "for the last five days they have come in excursions nine or ten sleepers full at a lick. Every thing is full to over flowing and people who live here are just coining money." Prosperous times no doubt helped lessen railroad antagonism; the Atchison, Topeka & Santa Fe, in particular, was hailed as the savior of southern California. . . .

Also during the 1880s, the state's agricultural prosperity gradually returned. California's farm output increased as more settlers arrived and expanded the range of regional market crops. Irrigation brought water to the desert interior; California's agricultural bounty grew to include a wider variety of vegetables, nuts, wines, and citrus fruits. Such growth relied upon the railroad; and, as in the Los Angeles real estate boom, it is reasonable to suppose that economic expansion went hand in hand with a relaxation of railroad antagonism.

But the 1890s brought major changes and new problems. A nationwide depression rocked California, and, as had happened before, the disruption seemed again to rekindle fierce railroad opposition. In depressed times, one could mount almost any political stump, to the right as well as the left, and blast the railroad for a variety of logical, tried-and-true reasons: the company's officials made too much money; the railroad charged too much; inequities between workers and management were too extraordinary; the Southern Pacific hired the wrong workers. In short, the common refrain surfaced: the railway corporation kept California and Californians down. Besides these hardly dormant seeds of discontent, very different types of antagonism appeared: the strident anti-monopoly campaigns of the People's Party populists, the reformist whispers of the major parties, the utopian pleas of organizations like Bellamy Nationalist clubs, and the increasingly militant voice of labor unionism. The 1890s came to be a staging ground for determining California's twentieth-century relationship with the railroad and the railroad corporation. Eruptions of the 1890s would force Californians to rework that unsolved equation describing the state of affairs existing between the multitentacled railroad and the state's political economy.

One such eruption, the Pullman strike of 1894, shattered the traditional form and shape of anti-railroad thought and behavior in California. The strike produced a degree of railroad antagonism not before seen in the state's history. The sheer scale of the strike, not to mention its real potential for violence, marked a departure from the various anti-railroad political movements of the 1870s and early 1880s, where expressions of discontent had been largely reserved for varieties of platforms and campaigns. What is more, the Pullman strike arrived in California ostensibly through the efforts of workers, particularly those affiliated with the American Railway Union. Not since the days of Denis Kearney and the assembled crowds of unemployed workers in San Francisco had a worker-centered affair so captured the attention of the state or so provoked the concerns of the rail corporation. The strike in California was in reality far more than a workers' boycott; the Pullman strike signaled the arrival of an especially turbulent period in the state's complex relationship with the gigantic Southern Pacific. With the exception of affairs in Chicago itself, where the strike originated, the Pullman boycott had as great an impact on California as anywhere else in the entire nation. . . .

The Pullman strike began in May of 1894 in the "model" industrial town of Pullman on the outskirts of Chicago. Among other duties, workers at Pullman manufactured the luxurious private railcars that insulated well-to-do travelers on railroad journeys throughout the nation. Faced with a considerable wage cut that spring, the Pullman employees initiated a strike. After failing to attract support from more conventional labor unions (generally not about to support unskilled laborers, railroad or otherwise), these laborers appealed to a newly formed labor organization, the American Railway Union (ARU), in a bid for solidarity. Begun in 1893, the innovative ARU admitted railroad workers of all skill levels, thus departing from the hierarchical example of the various railroad brotherhoods. Directed by its founder and president, Eugene V. Debs, the egalitarian union agreed to support the striking workers. The support would be more than token: in late June, Debs ordered all ARU members to boycott trains pulling Pullman cars. . . .

Los Angeles railroad workers formed the first California local of the American Railway Union in the fall of 1893. By the time the Pullman strike broke out seven months later, the ARU in southern California had an estimated one thousand members. Other powerful ARU chapters operated in the railroad cities of Oakland and Sacramento. Although open to all railroad employees, the ARU membership was drawn primarily from the ranks of low-skilled workers; the elite railroad brotherhoods (firemen, brakemen, and engineers) shunned the union and rejected its experiment in labor egalitarianism.

The strike rumbled through California like a massive earthquake. The railroad, which had so effectively "sped up" life in post–Gold Rush California, was now the agent of shutdown, almost pushing the state back in time because of strike-induced inertia. In late June, acting on orders from Eugene Debs in Chicago, rail workers in Oakland refused to make up trains carrying Pullman cars. The boycott spread quickly to other rail centers in Los Angeles (where Atchison, Topeka & Santa Fe was boycotted as well), Sacramento, and the California interior. When the railroad companies began to fire workers for not making up complete trains, the boycott turned into a general strike; "we were compelled to fight the Southern Pacific itself," the president of the ARU in Oakland declared. That proved to be a momentous transition: by July 1, rail traffic in the state was paralyzed: overland trains did not run at all, local trains ran only intermittently. "The California roads are all tied up and the railroad company is having its death struggle," Sacramento ARU leader Henry Knox wrote exultantly to Debs. . . .

Strike leaders made sure to disavow violence, surmising correctly that any public support for the boycott would be jeopardized if strikers committed violent acts. Initially, the only apparent violence was symbolic (though ominous): nonstrikers and strikebreakers hanged in effigy. Yet the threat of more potent action permeated the tense atmosphere, which supporters and detractors alike were quick to call a war—even though it was not yet clear what constituted loyalty to one side or the other. Responding to a truculent message from Southern Pacific official Alban N. Towne, the Oakland chapter of the ARU published a communiqué modeled after the

Declaration of Independence, stating that the corporation's intransigence "can be interpreted only in one way, namely: a declaration of war." The union further stated that "Mr. Towne is an employe of a corporation which claims that every man who is not with them is a scoundrel, . . . a black sheep and an anarchist."

The conduct of the strike itself, despite the best efforts of ARU leaders, was laced with violence. Strikers yanked nonstrikers and scabs from railcars, men fought in the railroad yards, railroad tools found new uses as weapons. One nonstriking engineer at Oakland refused to move several empty Pullmans, for fear "of having my head caved in with a coupling pin" by strikers. Worried citizens fearing armed rebellion called in turn for repressive, violent, and speedy action against railroad employees.

The Southern Pacific, though clearly caught offguard by the magnitude and initial success of the boycott, adopted an unyielding stance from the start. In private and public statements, corporation officials displayed their unwillingness to waver on what they saw as principle and, more important, precedent. In their view, the strikers were operating in violation of good faith; since they had as yet no stated grievance with the Southern Pacific, their actions were an inexcusable inconvenience to the public. The strike had nothing to do with affairs in California, officials believed. Once the people of the state voiced their displeasure, the strike would melt away in the glare of popular disapproval. In the meantime, the corporation could try to enhance its image by chipping away at public tolerance for both trade unionism and, equally important, anti-railroad sentiment in general. The strike was certainly no blessing to the Southern Pacific, but it was an opportunity.

Southern Pacific official Henry E. Huntington declared that the railroad would not violate its contract with the Pullman Company or willingly enter into a labor dispute in which it was not directly concerned. In private correspondence, Huntington urged other Southern Pacific executives to discover the hidden opportunities the strike offered. "We are going to break this strike," he wrote to his uncle [Collis Huntington] in early July. "This is the first strike we have ever had here and as we are making history, [I] think we ought not to take a step backward and make such concessions that we will hereafter regret them." In other words, inconvenience and daily losses of $200,000 aside, the corporation should seize the initiative and mold the public relations capital the strike offered.

The Pullman boycott simultaneously offered railroad officials an unprecedented opportunity for aggressive in-house action. Troubled by the influence of the ARU over his employees, the president of the Southern Pacific saw the dispute as a way to begin wiping the slate clean. "When this strike is over," Collis Huntington wrote to his nephew, "I think we should get men on our own line who do not belong to any union, and follow this policy persistently until we do not have a union man on our line." Huntington advised his nephew to look into the possibilities of importing huge numbers of African American workers from the South, much the same way as the railroad had delivered Chinese by the thousands to construction camps in the 1860s: "I think we should almost immediately commence getting some colored people from the South for our yard men all over our lines, doing it in a quiet way, putting a few here and a few there until the change is made." Huntington's motives were twofold. He had indeed established worthy credentials as a supporter of black educational and vocational training, particularly through ties to Booker T. Washington. But there were more "practical" concerns as well, made all the more pressing by the Pullman stalemate. The rail magnate apparently believed that African American employees would not "have that desire to destroy capital that white laborers do, who belong to the Communists and anarchists of our country."

The Southern Pacific's refusal to run trains without Pullmans attached amounted to a colossal mistake in corporate judgment. Backed by an influential anti-railroad San Francisco press, large numbers of Californians simply refused to blame the striking employees for the blockade. After all, the strikers insisted that they had no complaint with the Southern Pacific and that they would run trains if the Pullman cars were cut free. Ever suspicious of the railroad's actions, the public appeared to side with the strikers. As the San Francisco *Call* pointed out, the Southern Pacific's decision to hold back trains "was done in the interests of Pullman, so that by inconveniencing the public in a most distressing way sympathy may be withheld from the strikers." . . .

These first waves of public opinion, which seemingly supported the strikers, ought properly to be interpreted as negative reaction to the Southern Pacific rather than positive support of the ARU and its goals. The Southern Pacific's notoriety and supposedly dastardly role in state history plainly made it a far more viable public enemy than the ARU made a public friend. . . .

The Pullman strike, in California and across the United States, terrified those who were convinced that it represented nothing less than the first salvo of terrible revolution. Ignoring ARU disclaimers (which reiterated the strike's narrow objective—namely, redress for Pullman employees), fearful Californians insisted that the strike threatened the very foundations of the republic. Expressions of solidarity from other labor organizations, as well as critical support from the Populist Party, heightened fears that the strike was the first blow in a conspiracy to overthrow American institutions. A guardsman who had taken place in the Sacramento farce described the strike in terms no less momentous than those of U.S. Attorney [George] Denis: "Never before, in the history of the country, with the exception of the Civil War, was the United States ever menaced by a movement so fraught with danger and terror as this. It had become something of far greater importance than a mere quarrel between railroad corporations and their employees over a matter of wages; it amounted to an armed rebellion against the laws of the United States."

Conservatives feared that the situation in California would eventually erupt much the same way it had in Chicago and elsewhere back East. Certainly anti-strike newspapers (particularly the *Post* in San Francisco, the *Times* in Los Angeles, and the *Record-Union* in Sacramento) did their utmost to convince Californians that a Debs-inspired revolution would soon reach the West if the strike was not swiftly put down. Debs himself was viciously lampooned, in cartoons and in print, as a violently unstable anarchist, madly preaching class warfare. Even the message from the state's pulpits suggested that class revolution lay just around the corner unless cooler and more Christian heads prevailed.

Public sympathy for the strike, though fleeting, nonetheless indicates the degree to which the Southern Pacific was hated in California: a largely—sometimes rabidly—nonunion state backing a railroad strike pushed for by radical labor unionists operating at the orders of a non-Californian. But the realization that the state could not long tolerate the dangerous machinations of Debs and allied labor unions, despite the common enemy in the Southern Pacific, had long lain just beneath the strike surface. Such worries had initially been drowned out by the enthusiasm of apparently potent antagonism toward the Southern Pacific. . . .

As the strike wore on, other voices called for arbitration, often with undisguised frustration at the strike's disruption of commerce and travel. The San Francisco *Call,* a staunchly pro-strike paper, began to back down after the debacle in Sacramento. "It is, we believe, within the power of the business men of this city, professional men of high standing, conscientious men whose counsels carry commanding convictions, to induce the Southern Pacific Company to adopt a policy that will leave the Railway Union without an excuse for further interference in our local affairs." . . .

[Some] saw the strike as nothing but the dangerous ferment of the mob. "I would yield much to the honest wageworker [and] would advise the Company to do so," wrote Collis P. Huntington, "but will yield nothing to the mob which is wantonly destroying our property and seriously injuring the business of our patrons." One concerned Oakland citizen echoed Huntington's prejudices in a letter to the Oakland *Tribune:* "I would much prefer to live under the most despotic of despotic despots than under mob rule."

The strikers lost much of their initial support when they began to embrace just what conservatives feared: the explicit language of radicalism. At some point in the strike, varying from community to community, ARU leaders (as well as, especially in the Bay Area, their Populist advisers) faced increasing difficulties in moderating those who promulgated a more general "capital versus labor" dichotomy. And given the fear and threat of violence that had permeated the strike from the start, many people now regarded the striking workers as revolutionaries out to reorder society by force.

A railroad switchman, speaking before a crowded Metropolitan Hall audience in San Francisco on July 6, declared that the original goal of the ARU fight had been lost sight of: the struggle now pitted labor and capital against one another. Arthur McEwen, noted anti-railroad activist and journalist, wrote a long article in the San Francisco *Examiner* two days later beneath the incendiary headline "The Gigantic Struggle Between Capital and Labor." Such sensationalism may have sold newspapers, but it likely did not help keep the thin thread of community strike support intact. . . .

Such rhetoric . . . startle[d] the public out of its temporary indulgence of the striking railroad employees and their labor union allies. The diminution of support for the strike drove a wedge down the center of the formerly more cohesive anti-railroad forces in the state's political arenas; what had been a tenuous coalition united in anti-railroad action fractured over the question of which direction the strike ought to take following the boycott; what did it mean to society at large?

An interesting illustration of this fracture could be found in the pages of the San Francisco *Examiner,* where William Randolph Hearst guided the paper's virulent anti-railroad editorial policy. Affiliated with the *Examiner* or on Hearst's staff were several men who caused the Southern Pacific no end of torment in the latter years of the century, including editor T. T. Williams, satirist Ambrose Bierce, and railroad-bashing Arthur McEwen. Yet the Pullman strike obliterated the fiction of common anti-railroad positions shared by the three men. While McEwen wrote ostensibly in support of revolution, Bierce rose to the support of Collis Huntington. Of the strike, Bierce wrote that "there can be no doubt whatever that the object sought by these otherwise ludicrously and hideously senseless proceedings is the absolute and final subjugation of every interest and every will to the interest of the labor class and the will of its leaders. That may or may not be reform—it is indubitably revolution, and if it come, must come by the sword. From the point of view of reason and right Mr. Huntington's argument seems to me impregnable at every point to dissent or depreciation."

Events of mid-July convinced many a Californian that perhaps Bierce was right. "Pacified" by the presence of federal troops, strikers permitted Sacramento train operations to resume on July 11. But only minutes after leaving the depot, the first train out of the city since the strike crashed. Bolts had been pried from the rails on a small trestle two miles outside of town, and the train careened into a shallow ditch. The wreck killed the locomotive's engineer and four soldiers. The resulting furor completed the cycle of dwindling public support for the strike. "By this outrageous crime the strikers lost more than they ever could hope to regain," wrote a perceptive observer from the state militia. "Public opinion and press, which had largely supported them, now, when they saw what such support resulted in, turned against them. The public recognized that a strike that carried with it destruction of property and life must not be tolerated. Even the regular had sympathized with them in their struggle against the thieving monopoly—the railroad. But now, woe to the striker who would rub up against a regular." The act not only vindicated the worst fears of those who had long predicted the outbreak of violence but terrified many who perhaps otherwise would have supported the strikers. Train-wrecking terrorism was not likely to mobilize much grass-roots support: the sheer randomness of the act, its "anytime, anywhere, anyone" destructiveness colored the entire strike black. No longer was the strike's violence contained within the prescribed boundaries of rail yards and depots. The sabotage was, a guardsman wrote, the "most cold-blooded train wreck and murder ever perpetuated in the West."

This violent denouement ended any chance for the strikers to garner additional support from the nonstriking constituency. Equally if not more important, the violent act contributed to the Democratic Party's ultimate rejection of alliance with the strikers and supporters on a railroad reform bandwagon. Just as the train fell off the tracks, so too fell the substantive issue of redressing the railroad's place in California society. The Pullman strike had for an instant seemed to put the question on a track headed toward the major political parties, but it stopped well short of that destination.

One way to gauge the Democratic Party's disfavor with the strike (beyond noting that a Democratic president, Grover Cleveland, had ordered U.S. troops into the Pullman fray) is to examine the views of Stephen Mallory White, California's Democratic standard-bearer in the U.S. Senate. White vehemently and unapologetically opposed the form the strike took; the affair was, in his view, "without reason and had nothing to commend it whatever." Though he was "disposed to criticize the railroad as much as anyone" (White was too shrewd a politician not to emphasize his anti-railroad credentials), White found the actions of California's ARU members "so revolting to my ideas of right, so contrary to acceptable principles regarding the ownership of property and the privilege to attend to one's own affairs, that I cannot bring myself to countenance it for a single moment." After a friend wrote him that people in Los Angeles supported the strikers, provided no violence was committed, White wrote:

> I sympathize with labor people for they usually get the worst of it and I will do anything at any time to alleviate their sufferings; but if I have to submit to tyranny, the last form of oppression which I will choose, is that which results from the mob. No strike based upon the absurdities of this one can be carried on without violence, and in this case every crime between murder and arson has been committed wherever the strike prevailed.

White regarded the strike as little better than revolution, and he welcomed the arrival of troops in Los Angeles (and said so in a letter to President Grover Cleveland). Like many who opposed the strike, White equated the strikers with revolutionaries, anarchists, and the "dangerous classes."

White defended the decision to put U.S. troops into the field against the strikers. "When we have to choose between a lot of irresponsible anarchists, who are tearing up trains, imperiling the lives of innocent people, and ruining those who are trying to get their material to market, and the law-abiding portion of the community, I shall certainly join hands with the latter. . . . I am sure that our wives [and] children slept better because of the presence of troops in Los Angeles, whose only mission was to prevent outrage and crime."

The Democratic stance was summed up in a later article in the *Overland Monthly* by John P. Irish, San Francisco editor and influential Democrat. Entitled "California and the Railroad," Irish's essay amounted to little more than a polemical attack on those anti-railroad forces that threatened to stretch dissent too far. In a sense, the essay was an answer to Henry George's prophetic "What the Railroad Will Bring Us," published in the same journal thirty years earlier. . . . Irish sketched out his party's stance toward the railroad, expressing little tolerance of those who crossed the arbitrary line dividing legitimate from illegitimate opposition. Cleverly manipulating language, Irish blurred the distinction between railroad technology and railroad corporation. Those who harbored resentment of the Southern Pacific failed to take into account all the good that the railroad had done in thirty years. "The Californian who is not a railroad man," Irish belligerently declared, "and who does not wish to see a track laid in the service of each thirty-mile strip of our dazzling rich soil, should take his pack-mule and go into the wilderness." Progress, the future, the new century, and the railroad all went together. Railroad antagonists might as well slip back in time.

By the middle of July in Los Angeles, the Pullman strike had dissolved, with "strikers falling over each other to get back to work." In northern California, the presence and prodding of U.S. troops helped convince strikers in Oakland and Sacramento to end their occupation of depots and yards. The dissolution of the strike in those places was not without violence; in mid-July, soldiers fired upon and killed several strikers in Sacramento. In Oakland, infantry and cavalry units charged strikers, "using bayonets to good effect," according to a relieved Henry Huntington. . . .

"The fight is won," Henry Huntington wrote to his uncle on July 21. For the railroad corporation, the strike had proved to be an expensive and unsettling disruption of normal operations. Yet it was not without its benefits. For one, the corporation could proceed with its hidden agenda to stamp out unionization in the ranks. Huntington assured his uncle that the company would henceforth refuse to hire any ARU members, although such blatant discrimination would have to remain secret. To do otherwise "would make us liable as the law states that we shall not discriminate against any order, but our Superintendents are privately informed that they must not under any circumstances employ any man that is a member of the A.R.U."

Corporate leaders also realized that the completion of the strike presented them with the chance to massage California's collective memory of the strike for corporate and political ends. In other words, the legacy of the strike could both be manufactured and manipulated. The railroad corporation had been in the public relations business too long not to realize the opportunity. "If the people of the State use this terrible experience that they have had as a lesson and heed it properly," Collis Huntington advised his nephew, "it can be worked to the benefit of the State and every interest therein." By August, with affairs quieted down and the strike a clear failure, Collis Huntington could brag that the company had weathered the storm of the strike by subtly guiding the actions of the strikers: "Sometimes in dealing with mobs you have to join them and then lead them, which is often better than to try to drive them." . . .

[T]he railroad corporation and its conservative allies not only had weathered the Pullman strike but had clearly benefited from it. The Southern Pacific had survived the potentially perilous days of the strike, witnessed the turning of public opinion in the wake of violence and feared revolution, and gained an all-important ally: the legal and military punch of the federal government. Never again would the power and presence of the railroad corporation be challenged to the degree that it was in the summer of 1894. As Eugene Debs himself wrote, the strike had "shocked the country and jarred the world." California and Californians felt that earthquake more than most places.

 F U R T H E R   R E A D I N G

James L. Brown, *The Mussel Slough Tragedy* (1958)

Mary Roberts Coolidge, *Chinese Immigration* (1909)

Ira B. Cross, *A History of the Labor Movement in California* (1935)

William F. Deverell, *Railroad Crossing: Californians and the Railroad, 1850–1910* (1994)

Robert M. Fogelson, *The Fragmented Metropolis: Los Angeles, 1850–1930* (1967)

William B. Fredericks, *Henry E. Huntington and the Creation of Southern California* (1992)

Robert Gottlieb and Irene Wolt, *Thinking Big: The Story of the Los Angeles Times, Its Publishers, and Their Influence on Southern California* (1977)

Don Graham, *The Fiction of Frank Norris: The Aesthetic Context* (1978)

Michael Kazin, *Barons of Labor: The San Francisco Building Trades and Urban Power in the Progressive Era* (1987)

Robert E. L. Knight, *Industrial Relations in the San Francisco Bay Area, 1900–1918* (1960)

George Kraus, *High Road to Promontory: Building the Central Pacific Across the High Sierra* (1969)

John A. Larimore, "Legal Questions Arising from the Mussel Slough Land Dispute," *Southern California Quarterly* LVIII (Spring 1976): 75–94

Oscar Lewis, *The Big Four* (1938)

Ward McAfee, *California's Railroad Era, 1850–1911* (1973)

Gwendolyn Mink, *Old Labor and New Immigrants in American Political Development: Union, Party, and State, 1875–1920* (1986)

Gerald D. Nash, "The California Railroad Commission, 1876–1911," *Southern California Quarterly* XLIV (December 1962): 287–306

Spencer C. Olin, *California Politics, 1846–1920: The Emerging Corporate State* (1981)

Paul M. Ong, "The Central Pacific and Exploitation of Chinese Labor," *Journal of Ethnic Studies* XIII (Summer 1985): 119–24

Louis B. Perry and Richard S. Perry, *A History of the Los Angeles Labor Movement, 1911–1941* (1963)

"Railroads in California and the Far West," special edition of *California History* 52 (Spring 1991)

Elmer C. Sandmeyer, *The Anti-Chinese Movement in California* (1939)

Alexander P. Saxton, "The Army of Canton in the High Sierra," *Pacific Historical Review* XXXV (May 1966): 141–52

Alexander P. Saxton, *The Indispensable Enemy: Labor and the Anti-Chinese Movement in California* (1971)

David F. Selvin, *A Place in the Sun: A History of California Labor* (1982)
Neil Larry Shumsky, *The Evolution of Political Protest and the Workingmen's Party of California* (1991)
Grace Heilman Stimson, *Rise of the Labor Movement in Los Angeles* (1955)
R. Hal Williams, *The Democratic Party and California Politics, 1880–1896* (1973)
Bill Yenne, *Southern Pacific* (1985)

C H A P T E R
8

California Progressives:
The Ambiguities of Political
and Moral Reform

California progressivism was by no means a unified phenomenon; rather, it comprised a large number of efforts that sought, among other things, to use the legislative process to ameliorate problems brought on by rapid industrialization, urbanization, and immigration. During the first decade of the twentieth century, criticism of the railroad machine continued to stimulate political agitation in California. Yet class antagonisms and divisive factionalism prevented a unified opposition from agriculture, industry, and labor. Instead, avers George Mowry, author of a major study of California progressivism, leadership "was seized by a group of supreme individualists, well educated and bound together by a particularistic code of morality, and more than the normal dash, perhaps, of a sense of indignation and a desire for power." These largely middle-class professional men and women were initially not concerned with battling the Southern Pacific Railroad Company, preferring to engage in municipal reforms particularly in San Francisco and Los Angeles.

Beginning about 1910, however, they developed a common concern that the growing power of capital and labor would generate class conflict to the serious detriment of the middle class. These primarily urban, high-status, Protestant reformers thus sought to prevent special interest groups from controlling the state for those groups' own allegedly selfish purposes. Instead, with what now appears to be astonishing naiveté, they argued that legislation should more properly result from careful deliberation among honest men and women seeking the general welfare while maintaining strict neutrality with respect to competing organizations and groups.

This stance of neutrality was more enduring as rhetoric than as public policy, for once in power progressives were confronted with difficult practical choices. It became immediately necessary for them to develop specific programs to benefit or control various groups, but this process tended to erode their sources of support. For these obvious reasons, the hoped-for "classless" politics of 1910 and thereafter proved to be largely chimerical. As William Deverell and Tom Sitton have recently pointed out in California Progressivism Revisited *(1994), "Ironies abound: progressives disdained 'class politics' but were presumably forced to engage in them, if only out of motives of self-preservation. . . ."*

Ironically, the organized special interest groups so earnestly opposed by the reformers tended to fill the political vacuum created when the party system was virtually demolished by progressive legislation. In subsequent years, California's political parties have rarely managed to advance or to enact coherent programs of public policy. Instead, legislation has tended to derive from well-financed, well-organized special interests such as oil, real estate, agribusiness, and organized labor.

The California progressives may have destroyed effective party organizations, but they provided the electorate with the tools of "direct democracy." These new instruments—the initiative, referendum, recall, and nonpartisan political primaries—were to be used to "return the government to the people." Although most reformers genuinely believed that such measures would permit the "incorruptible" people to purify politics and thereby improve the quality of government, they were overly optimistic about the long-term consequences of their efforts. As it has turned out, for example, the initiative has not been an effective means of enacting new legislation. Moreover, initiative measures have originated not with "the people" but rather with well-financed interest groups.

In their efforts to move beyond Mowry's narrow focus on the leadership of California progressivism, younger scholars, Deverell and Sitton included, are examining a much broader array of issues, such as the social bases of political reform, the contributions of organized labor and of women, and the role of cultural values. They are challenging existing interpretations, such as those that focus too single-mindedly on the battle between the Republican party and the Southern Pacific Railroad Company. The meanings and contributions of the so-called Progressive Era in California are therefore still very much in dispute.

How progressives dealt with gender, ethnicity, and race is especially interesting. Although progressive men supported the suffrage campaign that succeeded in giving California women the vote in 1911, they were ambivalent about the role women later claimed in politics. Women progressives, perhaps as a response to this male ambivalence, carved out a special role for themselves as educators of the growing number of European immigrants stepping ashore in the United States. With the anticipated opening of the Panama Canal, women progressives in California argued they must prepare to deal with the increased influx into Pacific Coast ports. Until immigrants learned American civic and domestic virtues—virtues that women progressives thought they were especially qualified to inculcate—the newcomers constituted a "menace" to American society and civilization.

But there was one group of immigrants that neither male nor female progressives were willing to tolerate—the Japanese. Their numbers in California continued to increase despite a so-called Gentlemen's Agreement made in 1907, in which the Japanese government agreed to stop issuing passports to Japanese laborers who aspired to go to the United States. The number of Japanese male immigrants did decline after that, but the number of female Japanese immigrants increased. To make California less attractive to the Japanese, the state legislature, with the support of Governor Hiram Johnson, passed an Alien Land Act in 1913 to make it illegal for "aliens *ineligible to* [sic] *citizenship"—a code phrase for Japanese—to buy farm land or to lease it for more than three years.*

In short, though the progressives were willing to admit certain groups into the American body politic if they changed their ways, they failed to transcend the racism of the times. In the words of Roger Daniels, a leading authority in Japanese American history, the progressives did not hesitate to "draw the color line."

 # D O C U M E N T S

Students of the Progressive period in California history are indebted to Franklin Hichborn, legislative correspondent for the *Sacramento Bee,* for his detailed reports about the state legislature beginning in 1909. Although Hichborn was strongly biased in favor of progressivism, his eyewitness accounts are nonetheless valuable primary material. From this chapter's first document, in which he praises the new progressive governor, Hiram W. Johnson, we can learn a great deal about the underlying assumptions regarding the democratic process shared by Hichborn and his fellow progressives.

One such political activist was Dr. John Randolph Haynes of Los Angeles, who as early as 1898 had organized the Direct Legislation League and had drafted the initiative, referendum, and recall provisions of the Los Angeles charter of 1903. On the eve of the 1911 election in which these constitutional proposals were to be voted upon statewide, Haynes appeared before the Commonwealth Club of San Francisco to present his arguments in favor of the amendment, excerpts from which are found in the second document.

In the third document, Chester H. Rowell, editor of the *Fresno Bee,* explains that progressives were opposed to Japanese immigrants not because they came from an inferior race but simply because they were different. In the parlance of the times, they were "unassimilable." As guardians of the frontier between "the white man's and the brown man's world," Californians, according to Rowell, could not afford to allow the Japanese to breach the natural racial divide at the continent's edge.

In the fourth, fifth, and sixth documents, progressive women leaders discuss why women should be involved in politics. Carrie Chapman Catt, who worked indefatigably in suffrage campaigns in several states, points out in the fourth document the multiple ways in which public policy impacts the home and vice versa.

Like Catt, Katherine Philips Edson was an effective organizer. One of her first statewide crusades was to get legislation passed to regulate the purity of milk. After campaigning for Hiram Johnson in the 1910 gubernatorial election and for women's suffrage in 1911, she was appointed by Johnson as a deputy inspector in the state Bureau of Labor Statistics in 1912. In that capacity, she lobbied successfully for a minimum-wage law for female and child labor. This 1913 law created an Industrial Welfare Commission, on which she also served. In the fifth document, she explains the significance of such protective legislation and women's influence in getting it passed. As a result of her strong concern for the well-being of workers, however, she opposed Japanese immigration because the Japanese "drove white labor" as well as "small white merchants" out.

Mary S. Gibson, author of the sixth document, was likewise concerned about women's welfare and the problems posed by immigrants. A schoolteacher in Los Angeles, she worked in various charities and helped found an orphanage. Appointed to the Commission on Immigration and Housing by Governor Hiram Johnson, she became a leader in the Americanization movement, especially in programs to educate immigrant women.

Franklin Hichborn Praises Reform Governor Hiram W. Johnson, 1911

[On] January 3, 1911, Hiram W. Johnson was inaugurated Governor of California. . . .

Governor-elect Johnson, earnest of purpose, resolute and with a definite policy—as a plain American gentleman—walked to the Capitol unattended by military escort; entered the Assembly chamber with the retiring Governor, and took the oath of office.

Johnson had something to say, and, in his inaugural address, said it.

The Governor didn't tell his hearers that California has a glorious climate. He took it for granted that Californians are proud of California. But he recognized that before Californians may come into their own, before the best development of the State can be realized, California must be politically and industrially free.

To this live issue—the issue of the campaign through which he had just passed—Johnson devoted his inaugural address. Not a man or woman in the packed assembly chamber failed to realize that Johnson assumed office with a definite plan of action, and a determined purpose to press that plan to realization.

And after all, "the Johnson policies," the term by which the recommendations contained in this inaugural message soon became known, were nothing more nor less than the reforms for which the citizens of California had long been contending, and which were pledged in the State platforms of the Republican and Democratic parties.

The address was based on the assumption that The People of California are competent to govern themselves. Heretofore, California politicians have politely conceded that Californians possess this degree of intelligence, and have taken care that as little opportunity as possible for the exercise of such intelligence should be given.

Johnson not only admitted the intelligence of The People, but on this intelligence he based his hope of the development, prosperity and well-being of the State. That the purpose of The People shall be given its freest expression, he held that the government of the State must be made responsive to The People. The first step toward this desired end he held was to eliminate every private interest from the government, and to make the public service of the State responsive to The People alone.

That this condition might prevail, he contended that the government must be brought closer to The People through direct legislation.

To this end, Governor Johnson urged Constitutional Amendments which shall give The People power to initiate laws—the Initiative; power of veto upon laws which may be enacted by the Legislature—the Referendum; power to remove from elective office the incompetent or the corrupt—the Recall.

He urged further that by legislative enactment the Australian Ballot be restored to its original simplicity and effectiveness, that men may be selected for office because of their personal worth, rather than their political affiliations; that the imperfections of the Direct Primary law of 1909 be corrected; that The People be given the machinery to compel from the Legislature recognition of their selections, by popular vote, to represent the State in the Federal Senate.

There was no half-way course advocated in Johnson's first word to the Legislature; no hesitancy about accepting the logical conclusion, after accepting his major premise that The People of California are intelligent enough to govern themselves.

If The People are intelligent enough to govern themselves, they are intelligent enough to recall from office an official who has shown himself incompetent or corrupt. Nor did the Governor exclude the Judiciary from this provision. If The People have the intelligence to select Judges, he argued, they have the intelligence to remove from the bench that Judge who, in their judgment, has, on trial, demonstrated his unfitness or his unworth.

Johnson's recommendation regarding the nomination by popular vote of United States Senators was based on the same principle. If The People are to be given any voice at all in the election of Federal Senators there is logically no half-way point. Either The People are competent to name their United States Senators or they are not. Johnson held them to be competent.

He accordingly recommended that legislation be enacted to provide that candidates for the United States Senate be nominated at the primaries as State officials are nominated, that the names of the nominees for United States Senator as made by the several parties be placed on the election ballot so that The People at the finals may vote for them the same as for the candidates for any State office; that a form of contract be provided by which candidates for the Legislature may be bound in the event of their election, to abide by The People's choice in naming the Senator, as is done in Oregon.

There was no questioning the logic of Johnson's position. Admit with him that The People are competent to govern themselves, and one must go in full sympathy with his policies from the beginning to the end of his message.

From the moment of the delivery of that message, there was a new alignment in the Legislature of the State of California. In unmistakable terms, Governor Johnson had made the Initiative, the Referendum, the Recall, Restoration of the Australian Ballot, Direct Vote for United States Senator, Effective Railroad Regulation—all the reforms, in a word, to which both parties stood pledged, and for which The People were clamoring—

"administration policies." And "administration policies" in no partisan sense. Johnson left no room for partisanship.

"It is in no partisan spirit that I addressed you," he said in concluding; "it is in no partisan spirit that I appeal to you to aid. Democrats and Republicans alike are citizens, and equal patriotism is in each. Your aid, your comfort, your highest resolve and endeavor, I bespeak, not as Republicans or Democrats, but as representatives of all the people of all classes and political affiliations, as patriots indeed, for the advancement and progress and righteousness and uplift of California. And may God in His mercy grant us the strength and the courage to do the right."

The "bracer" which the Legislature needed had been furnished. The Senator or Assemblyman who had more belief in direct legislation than in his own conviction that direct legislation is based on sound principle, and who was ready to accept any compromise which the machine was willing to offer, found himself confronted with the alternative of following with the administration or running with the "machine." That member who insisted that United States Senators should be elected by direct vote, but hesitated about adopting its equivalent, the Oregon plan, saw there were but two sides; he must either stand with those who advocated popular election of United States Senators, or with those who opposed.

Johnson's message wiped out partisan lines. In the Legislature of 1911, there were to be no Republican policies nor Democratic policies, only "administration policies." Those Democrats and those Republicans who continued faithful to the spirit as well as the letter of the platform of their respective party, must of necessity support the "administration measures."

And those who failed to support such measures would find themselves outside the pale of both parties. It was evident that some changes of attitude had to be made, or certain of the old guard would find themselves without a party.

And there were many such changes. Men of the character of those whom machine managers send to the Legislature were prepared to desert the machine for the "winner," just as they will desert the Progressives should the Reactionaries secure control again.

But even without this shifty crew, the Progressives had a good working majority in both Senate and Assembly. This majority included the Progressive Democrats as well as the Progressive Republicans. Governor Johnson had made it clear that neither party had a monopoly of the progressive movement; the reforms which he advocated in his message had been pledged in the platforms of both parties. The reputable element of both parties united to uphold the Governor in his recommendation that their platform pledges be observed.

John Randolph Haynes Advocates
Direct Legislation, 1911

This amendment should be adopted by the people of California on the tenth day of October, next. The movement for direct popular government is not something by itself; it does not stand alone. It is part of a world-wide movement. The nations and peoples of the earth are rushing towards democracy at a pace that astounds the conservative mind and fills the heart of the radical with joy. Despotisms are giving way to constitutional monarchies; witness Russia, Turkey, Persia, and even China. Constitutional monarchies are giving way to republics; witness France and Portugal; Spain and Italy seem almost ready to follow suit. Republics are giving way in turn to democracies; witness Switzerland and the commonwealths of our own republic. England, nominally a constitutional monarchy, appears almost to have overleaped the intervening stage of a republic, and, under the forms and stage dress of royalty, is taking on many of the characteristics of a pure democracy. . . .

In our own republic of America we find the same evolution in progress. Eight States through the adoption of the initiative and referendum now reserve to the people the right to take the control of affairs out of the hands of their servants at such times and in such matters as they may see fit. Popular rule through the introduction of the initiative and referendum became an actuality in South Dakota in 1898, in Oregon in 1902, in Montana, 1906; in Oklahoma, 1907; Maine and Missouri, 1908; Arkansas and Colorado, 1910. Besides these eight States in which popular rule is in actual operation, the question has been submitted to the people and carried in three other States, Utah, North Dakota, and Arizona, but is not yet in operation. In six [*sic*] other States both party platforms promise the people an opportunity to vote upon the adoption of these measures of direct government; Wisconsin, Illinois, Kansas, and our own California. In still six other States, Ohio, Minnesota, Wyoming, Idaho, Washington, and Iowa, one of the two dominant parties has pledged itself to introduce the same measure. Municipalities are following the states in the adoption of direct government. Two hundred American cities have adopted the initiative and referendum.

Direct Legislation Is Not New

The measures are frequently spoken of as new, untried and experimental in character. Such is not the case. Both the initiative and referendum are older than our Federal Constitution. The people of Georgia as early as 1777 held the power to initiate constitutional amendments. For more than three hundred years the towns of New England have governed themselves under a system of pure democracy, differing little in principle from the legislation system coming into use in States and cities throughout the nation. The general court of Massachusetts in 1778 submitted to the people a constitution for a referendum vote. All of our States, Delaware excepted, submit their constitutions and constitutional amendments to the people; and in many States other measures concerning education, taxation, etc., are submitted to the referendary vote.

The amendment should be adopted in California for the following reasons:

A. Experience shows us that the happiness, wisdom and prosperity of a people bear a definite ratio to the extent of their power and participation in the business of government. Compare the conditions existing in Russia, for example, with those in Switzerland; one, an autocracy and the other a pure democracy.

B. The act of law making operates in the case of the individual voter as a great educator. Twenty per cent more newspapers are published in Switzerland in proportion to the population than in the United States. The Swiss voter feels that he personally bears the responsibility for the right conduct of his government. Hence his sense of responsibility is markedly developed.

C. The people are conservative and do not enact many, nor ultra radical laws. Switzerland and its political subdivisions enact fewer laws than any other political communities in the world. In the first quarter century after the adoption of the initiative in the Canton of Zurich, recourse was had to it in but three cases. In 1902 the people of Oregon, by a vote of ten to one, adopted a direct legislation amendment and since that time have voted upon sixty-four laws and constitutional amendments. They have by a vote varying greatly in the size of the majority adopted thirty and rejected thirty-four of the measures proposed. Maine voted upon and rejected three measures last election. South Dakota rejected woman's suffrage and Washington adopted it. On the fifteenth of November, last, San Francisco voted upon thirty-eight proposed charter amendments; adopted eighteen and rejected twenty. In looking over these amendments I must confess that they seem to have made very few mistakes in judgment. The people of Los Angeles have had the power to directly legislate for eight years and have had only one initiative election during that time and the measures submitted to the people at general elections have been few and have been voted upon with rare discrimination.

Do the People Vote Intelligently Upon Measures?

D. They are better fitted to vote upon measures, the text of which is sent to them three months before election with arguments pro and con; than they are to vote for a long array of office holders of whom they know little or nothing. Surely they are better fitted to express an intelligent opinion on a few measures after three months' consideration, than a legislative body is to act upon two or three thousand measures during a session of sixty days.

Do the People Vote Upon Measures?

E. A surprisingly large number do so and the percentage increases with succeeding elections. In Maine, a few months ago, in the first election in which the people voted upon measures, fifty per cent of those voting for Governor voted upon the measures submitted. In Missouri sixty per cent of the people voted upon measures submitted. In San Francisco the vote cast upon measures exceeded forty-five thousand out of a total registration of sixty-three thousand; and in Oregon, where direct legislation has been longest in working order, the percentage varies from 61 to 87 per cent of the vote cast for candidates.

F. A writer in the March issue of the *Political Science Quarterly,* George Haynes of Worcester, Mass., in an article treating on "People's Rule in Oregon," although approaching his subject in a frankly unfriendly attitude, nevertheless feels called upon to admit that upon the whole, the people and people's rule have made good in Oregon. Referring to the election of last autumn, he says: "As the smoke of the contest clears away, it is evident that 'people's rule' has strengthened its position." In the first place slavish adherence to national party lines must have been very largely destroyed in an election where a State normally Republican by a 25,000 majority chose a Democratic Governor by a plurality of 6,000. In the second place, the conditions of the campaign were such that it "would have been difficult for any Oregon voter to have remained totally ignorant of the principal points involved in the more important measures on which he was to vote." In the third place, the conditions of the campaign brought out a very heavy vote. The State contains about 135,000 registered voters. The vote on these measures referred directly to the people for settlement reached the extraordinary total of 120,248. He concludes thus: "Considering the immense complexity of the task which was set before them, it must be acknowledged that the Oregon voters stood the test remarkably well." . . . There has been a vitality, a genuineness in Oregon politics sharply in contrast with the State campaigns in many of the eastern States. . . .

Bribery of the people's representatives by special interests is the great demoralizing factor in our unchecked representative system of government. The majority of the electorate are honest, and desire good government. If you wish to have a truly representative government, and an honest and efficient one, give to the honest majority the power to directly legislate and to veto the acts of their representatives. It is much easier to bribe a few representatives than to bribe the majority of the many electors.

Chester H. Rowell Analyzes the Problem of Japanese Immigration in California, 1914

Injustice has been the only American way of meeting a race problem. We dealt unjustly by the Indian, and he died. We deal unjustly with the Negro, and he submits. If Japanese ever come in sufficient numbers to constitute a race problem, we shall deal unjustly with them—and they will neither die nor submit. This is the bigness of the problem, seen in the telescope of the imagination, and is the whole reason for the emotional intensity of California's agitation over a situation whose present practical dimensions are relatively insignificant. Californians are vividly conscious of their position as the warders of the Western mark. They hold not merely a political and geographic, but a racial, frontier—the border between the white man's and the brown man's world. To a keen sense of this trust, the possible crisis takes on the significance of a new Thermopylae. Psychologically, this is the Japanese problem in California, and no view of the situation would be just to California if it omitted a sympathetic appreciation of this state of mind, and of its possible ultimate justification.

It is equally necessary to recognize that the question has a psychological aspect on the Japanese side also. At this very moment, while this is being written, twenty thousand people are surging through the streets of Tokyo, clamoring for war with America, all because the California legislature is considering a measure which is already the unprotested law of the United States, by three separate Federal statutes, which is the law of five states, and has been immemorial law in Japan itself. Even a mob would not be so irrational on merely practical provocation. It is the whole revulsion of the brown man's race pride against the white man's race exclusiveness, concentrated for the moment on an otherwise inconsequential act of the white man's outpost province. It is a mutual state of emotional hyperesthesia. . . .

Statistically, the quality of the Japanese immigrants is good. They bring in more money per capita than any but the English and German immigrants; they have less illiteracy than the immigrants from Southern Europe; they are nearly all of vigorous age and in good health; they do not become dependents nor provide many serious criminals: they are intelligent, energetic, and self-reliant, well able to take care of themselves. If white immigrants of equal quality were available, they would be welcomed enthusiastically in unlimited numbers. The opposition to the Japanese is wholly racial. . . .

From the superficial American standpoint, the Japanese are probably less popular than the Chinese whom they displaced. They are less docile and less fitted to that status of human mules which the American wishes the Oriental to occupy. . . .

They are a polite, vivacious, and delightfully likable people. And the bitterest anti-Japanese agitator in California has never once suggested that they are an inferior race. They are of a different and physically unassimilable race; that is all. . . .

That the two chief races of mankind shall stay each on its own side of the Pacific, there to conduct in peace and friendship the commerce of goods and ideas, and of the things of the spirit, but without general interpenetration of populations, or commingling of blood—that is precisely the greatest thing in the world.

Carrie Chapman Catt Argues That Home and Government Are Related, 1907

It is sometimes thought that politics deals with matters difficult to understand, and quite apart from affairs of the home; that while politics touches business, which is man's sphere in all directions, it nowhere touches the home, woman's sphere. Instead, the home is a very important consideration of politics, and is a source of much labor on the part of our "public servants." It would be impossible to maintain the immense machinery of government we do were it not for money. Consequently, that is the first consideration. It is obtained by taxation. A direct tax is laid upon the home; and an indirect tax upon nearly every furnishing of the home; upon nearly every utensil used within the home; upon nearly every article of clothing worn by occupants of the home; upon nearly every article of food consumed in the home, and upon nearly every dose of medicine taken in the home. . . . Indeed, so large a tax is paid through the various avenues of "home consumption," that if it were possible to suddenly remove the home without the pale of government it would find its chief source of support gone. . . .

But not alone in the collection of its annual income does the government—the people—touch the home. Law not infrequently controls what the occupants of the home shall both eat and wear. The children are vaccinated by law, quarantined by law, educated from particular school books and particular methods by law. The health of the family is preserved by law, or endangered by the neglect of the "servants." Even the relative amount of work necessary to keep a home in proper cleanliness depends upon the condition of the streets which are cared for by law. Law determines the disposal of ashes, garbage and litter from the house. Indeed, there is no end to the connections of the home and the government. If the "Queen of the Home" is to be taxed upon nearly all she eats, wears or uses in order to maintain a government; and if this government is to regulate her water supply, her gas supply, her health, her conduct, her comfort; and since the government consists only of officers who act as servants of the people, and the "Queen of the Home" is one of the people, does it not follow by all the logic of common sense and all the sentiment of justice, that she should act as one of the rulers of our land? Aye. Then seat the "Queen of the Home" upon the throne of government beside the "King of Business," and let them rule together. Put upon their brows the diadem of royalty and into their two right hands the same wands of authority.

Katherine Philips Edson Boasts of Women's Influence on State Legislation, 1913

Now, what was woman's particular influence upon legislation? Women are supposed to have a moral influence on legislation. I know that is expected of us, and I think we made good. The bill we women were supposed to be greatly interested in, and in which we were, is the red-light abatement act. . . .

This measure is very revolutionary, but I think that it is an experiment worth the trial. Speaking about the influence of the women particularly, when the time came to get that bill out of committee, all the committeemen were besieged with thousands of letters. It was done by the women of the W. C. T. U. [Women's Christian Temperance Union]—and they deserve credit for it because it was well done. When the time came for voting, I don't think any legislator had less than five hundred letters from constituents saying he had to vote for it. It was pitiable to see men get up and say: "I am entirely out of harmony with this bill, but my constituents say they wish me to do so, and therefore I vote aye." . . .

We have lots of law on the subject of prostitution . . . but this is . . . the first time in the history of the world that the punishment for prostitution has been taken away from the woman and put on property, and for that reason we think it is worth the trial.

Before I attended this session of the legislature, I never realized how strongly men felt on this question. The discussion on this and the health certificate for marriage brought it out, and when the question arose of making the age of consent eighteen instead of sixteen, the discussion was behind closed doors. The wives of some of the Senators and Assemblymen told us the discussion was positively unfit for us to hear.

Which all goes to show that what Bernard Shaw said is true, that many men are afraid of votes for women because they know that if women get power they will impose on men the same standards of sexual morality that men have imposed on women. Now, that is just exactly what we are going to do. If those standards are wrong for men, they are wrong for women. I don't know any better way to find out which is right than by enforcing the same standard for both.

The age of consent was raised to eighteen years and we have equal guardianship of our own children. We women have been fighting for that ten years and could not get it, and yet at this session there was not a man who voted against it. . . .

The bills of largest interest to me were those of great industrial importance—the minimum wage law, the extension of the eight hour law and many of the industrial bills having to do with the sanitation of work shops. My interest in those has been developed by my work in the Bureau of Labor.

The minimum wage legislation we feel proud of, and we believe we have the best bill in the United States. We have a law which is very advanced, from the economic standpoint. It gives the wage commission power, after an investigation lasting about a year, to fix wages if it deems it necessary. This commission may call into existence wage boards of employees and employers who may recommend to the commission standards of work, hours of work and the amount of the minimum wage. However, the commission is not under obligations to accept these. The commission itself has the fixing of the wages. The whole thing is, we have a flexible law in California that will give us an opportunity to go into a careful experiment and see if it is or is not the proper thing. . . .

We have been criticised because we have been anxious to extend the eight hour law. The only extensions made were apartment houses, public lodging houses and places of amusement, and student nurses in hospitals; and upon that part of the bill the battle raged. It was one of the most interesting fights in the whole session. The hospitals were there in force with their very powerful lobby. The women who were to be protected by the law, of course, could not have a lobby, and their work was carried on by Mr.

Beach, of San Francisco, who did perfectly splendid work in presenting to the legislators their position.

I don't believe there is any class of women that need protection more than the student nurses. I know there have not been so many complaints brought to the Bureau of Labor from any other place as have come to me from the hospitals. I don't mean from the girls themselves, but the people who are in the hospitals. Patients have written me letters and telephoned me and come to me and complained of the lack of efficient care these girls have received and the long hours and overwork demanded of them. That being the case, it seems to me they should be given the protection of the law, just as women in the stores and places of that kind.

There was a great deal of hubbub about the "professional standing" of nurses. It was going to put them in the same class as labor unions. That is the sort of argument used against this bill. My only answer to that is this— that the young women who go into the nursing profession are the very finest we have. They are girls who have instilled in them the spirit of self-sacrifice; but that is no reason why they should be sacrificed. . . .

Then the cotton mills of Oakland made a hard fight on it. . . . I believe the cotton industry in Imperial is growing very rapidly, and it can't grow, it seems, unless women have longer hours. . . . [W]e asked why they did not run two eight hour shifts, if their machinery was so expensive that they would lose too much on their investment if they did not run longer, and they said they were working two shifts of fifteen hours—altogether fifteen hours and a half—and nobody understood why they didn't pay them the sixteen hours. Then, all of a sudden, it occurred to me. They said: "We don't work after 10 o'clock at night." I asked them: 'Is the reason because the majority of your employees are minors'; and they said: "Yes, madam, that is the reason." That means child labor and that is what is in the cotton mills; and we could not afford to let those children be exploited. . . .

It is by reason of such things we are interested in politics. . . .

Woman's business in politics is to keep alive the ideals and not to forget them.

Mary S. Gibson Explains Why Progressive Women Should Uplift Immigrant Women, 1914

The burning question in America today is that of the immigrant who may arrive by way of the Panama Canal. Every wild rumor as to hordes buying tickets on the installment plan is given more or less credence.

The printing press supplies a greedy public with books, magazines and newspapers dealing with the subject of immigration.

Those who think that America must still be the refuge for the world, and those who are sure that restriction is the only salvation of the commonwealth, are equally interested in what the future holds. . . .

California, with its three ports, is filled with mixed emotions of hope and fear. Governor Johnson has appointed a Commission of Immigration and Housing to consider matters affecting immigrants and for the care, protection and welfare of immigrants.

The State waits with bated breath for the opening of the canal with its stately ships, steerage laden with picturesque immigrants—but is gaily unconscious of the stranger now within her gates. California already has an immigration problem of considerable proportions, which she has neither solved nor seriously acknowledged. Her larger cities have undeniable slums, poverty and unemployment, and yet she looks forward with some degree of equanimity to a possibly overwhelming tide of humanity dependent upon her powers of assimilation! . . .

The whole question of immigration, for the immigrant and for the State, resolves itself into the one vital problem of the family, the establishment and the maintenance of the Home—the home which depends upon employment at a living wage, comfortable and reasonable housing, education and protection. . . .

California is distinguished as the State in which the alien who applies for his citizenship papers is given the address of a school where he may learn English and citizenship—as the State that has put its school houses into the hands of its citizens to be used as civic centers—as the State where playgrounds are developed to meet the social needs of the neighborhood.

In the foreign quarters our splendid teachers are doing real immigration work, doing it in crowded and ill-arranged quarters and at high pressure; striving devotedly, intelligently and determinedly to make Americans out of the swarming little aliens, and developing themselves into a new type of social expert—the expert who knows his case ten months in the year.

And the result of this magnificent effort?

The answer is unpleasant but as it is the truth we have no choice but to accept it.

Suddenly we discover that in our zeal to Americanize the foreign children we are destroying parental discipline. . . .

"Obedience to parents seems to be dying out . . ." says a Boston charity visitor. . . .

"Through the knowledge of our speech and ways, the children have a great advantage in their efforts to slip the parental leash. The bad boy tells his father that whipping "doesn't go" in this country. Reversing the natural order, the child becomes the fount of knowledge and the parent hangs on the lips of his precocious offspring. If the policeman inquires about some escapade or the truant officer gives warning, it is the scamp himself who must interpret between parent and officer."

"Still the child is not always to blame. 'Often the homes are so crowded and dirty,' says a probation officer, 'that no boy can go right.' The Slavs save so greedily that their children become disgusted with the wretched home conditions, and sleep out."

"Our immigrants," says a Superintendent of Charities, "often come here with no standards whatever. In their homes we find no sheets on the beds, no slips on the pillows, no cloth on the table, and no towels except old rags. Even in the mud floor cabins of the poorest negroes of the South you find sheets, pillow slips and towels, for by serving for, and associating with the whites, the blacks have gained standards. But many of the foreigners have no means of getting our home standards after they are here. No one shows them. They can't see into American homes and no Americans associate with them."

These instances, which could be extended indefinitely, in no way militate against the education of children—they merely point a new field of endeavor and a readjustment of our forces. A new and decisive step to be taken for the preservation of the American home, so long as immigration is stimulated by steamship agents, labor contractors and land owners, so long as the Federal government allows more or less free entrance to immigrants, just so long must we—the people—accept the responsibility of their education and protection.

And this education and protection, to be efficient, must begin at the root—with the young parents who for various reasons have come to cast their lot with us hoping for a new freedom and added opportunity.

Statistics show that 38.4 per cent, or over one-third of the alien population of America, ranges in age from 20 to 45 years.

For the men there is the opportunity of contact with his fellows, the assimilation of the unions which unite them upon an economic basis, and the political call for naturalization which beckons to the evening school and social center. For the young men and women in industry there is opportunity, but there is another group especially appealing to the women of America—the group composed of mothers busy tending their broods of children, living under the handicap of ignorance of our language and our ways. Who has not been touched by the sight of these shy creatures in their foreign clothes, painfully trying to purchase necessities for their families? These women do not go to evening schools because the babies must be tended, because they have no American clothes, because they do not learn as readily as the children who laugh at their mistakes, or because their husbands hold old-world notions regarding their women folk.

At a disadvantage with their own children, these women often lose confidence in themselves and shrink into either hopelessness or hardness, while the more yielding follow meekly in the circumscribed paths of usefulness marked out by the children. This reversal of relations is pitiful for the immigrant mother and fraught with imminent peril to the child and to the state. . . .

The home educator course works from the bottom up and is now imperatively needed to meet the splendid effort of our public schools—to round out and complete our educational system. . . .

The condition and position of the immigrant woman is of peculiar significance to the women of California, because by law the woman becomes a citizen upon the naturalization of her husband. Upon the women, brave enough and strong enough to win their own political emancipation, rests the responsibility of the education and protection of these alien women; and to so establish and sustain the mother in her own domain, is to protect the state from delinquent children and an ignorant vote.

Is there not some way by which this magnificent organization of womanhood can concentrate efforts upon this great problem of education, make the necessary demonstration by which it can prevent delinquency, by which it can carry hope and courage and opportunity to the helpless immigrant woman, and thus make the most important possible contribution to the public welfare of the state of California?

 E S S A Y S

Gerald Woods, in the first essay, analyzes the moral righteousness characteristic of the progressive reformers' "crusade against the disreputable pleasures" and reveals the different ways in which San Francisco and Los Angeles approached such problems. In doing so, he tries to present a nuanced interpretation of the larger progressive social and political movement. Such an interpretation, he argues, must incorporate considerations of religion and ethnicity as well as political philosophy. Woods received a doctorate in history from UCLA and is at present an independent consultant on criminal justice. He is the author of *The Police in Los Angeles: Reform and Professionalization* (1993).

Gayle Gullett, who wrote the second essay, teaches history at Arizona State University. By focusing on several progressive women activists, especially Mary S. Gibson, who provided leadership for the Americanization movement, she demonstrates how gender, ethnicity, race, and conceptions of nationhood were intertwined in the progressives' worldview. She exposes how middle-class female reformers used the idea that different segments of society were interdependent to promote their own class interests. Although progressive women were the main focus of her study, Gullett also notes the power of immigrant women, who were by no means unquestioning *tabulae rasae* on which American values and behavior could be inscribed. Gullett interprets their low rate of participation in the reformers' educational programs as a form of resistance against the progressives' efforts to erase immigrant cultures from American society.

Progressive Efforts to Banish Vice

GERALD WOODS

The men and women who created the progressive movement in California and led it to signal victories included people of diverse races, creeds, and colors. The leaders, however, were white, generally born in California or the midwestern states, more likely to be Republican than Democrat, and more likely to be Protestant than any other religion or sect. California progressive leaders tended to be comparatively young—in their thirties and forties—and comparatively successful. Newspaper owners and editors were well represented, as were lawyers, realtors, bankers, doctors, and other professionals. The large majority of leaders had at least one university degree. As a group they were independent, democratic, somewhat nativist, somewhat anti-labor, generally opposed to monopolies, and committed to free enterprise.

Their . . . motivation was . . . to reform the political and social institutions of their society. . . .

The ills the progressives set out to cure were of old origin. The struggle to reform the nation had been under way since at least the 1880s, when most of those who became progressives were still in school. Benjamin Parke DeWitt observed in 1915 that "although differences in name, in the specific reforms advocated, and in the emphasis placed upon them, have obscured the identity of the movement, the underlying purposes and ideals of the progressive elements of all parties for the past quarter of a century have been essentially the same." DeWitt then pointed out common interests endorsed by the Democratic, Republican, Progressive, Socialist, and Prohibition parties.

One characteristic of the progressives about which most historians could agree was their abiding antipathy toward saloons, prostitution, gambling, slot machines, horse races, prizefights, dancing (especially in nightclubs where black men played jazz music), and liaisons between black or Asian men and white women. In this regard, Spencer Olin notes that "this penchant for probity, this moral absolutism, was part and parcel of the progressive mind." George Mowry points out the "middle-class Christian respectability" implicit in the closing of saloons and gambling halls in Los Angeles at the turn of the century.

Both comments are accurate but say little about motivation. Benjamin DeWitt stated the case from the progressive perspective: "if the American city fails, it will fail not because of the work its people do or the places in which they live, but because of the pleasures which they seek. It is vice, high living, and deterioration of moral fibre more than anything else that destroys cities and democracies." For DeWitt, nothing less was at stake than the soul of America.

In California, the crusade against the disreputable pleasures was a tale of three cities. San Francisco and Los Angeles, the north and the south, proudly embodied the poles, respectively, of civic vice and civic virtue. Sacramento, specifically the state legislature, was a relatively neutral ground where proponents of "personal liberty" did battle with neo-puritans to preserve the lurid entertainments that for decades had characterized West Coast cities. In Washington, D.C., progressives in the Congress also warred against evil and won some significant victories.

During the progressive heyday, from 1909 through 1918, a variety of sumptuary laws were passed. At the national level, these included the Mann Act, directed at the transport of women across state lines for immoral purposes; more restrictive immigration regulations and anti-"white slavery" agreements with European governments, to reduce the remarkable migration of foreign prostitutes into the United States; and national wartime prohibition, the Eighteenth Amendment to the U.S. Constitution, and the Volstead Act, intended to close the saloons and end forever the consumption of beverage alcohol by Americans.

In 1909, the state assembly, described by the *San Francisco Chronicle* as "a legislature of progressive cranks," narrowly passed the Anti-Race Track Gambling Act. The act forbade "wagering or pool selling or bookmaking in any way, shape, form or place." The Local Option Law, allowing prohibition by local option, followed in 1911. This act was known generally as the Gandier Ordinance, after Daniel M. Gandier, legislative superintendent of the Anti-Saloon League. By 1913, nearly one thousand saloons had been closed through the introduction of local prohibition. About half the state went dry. The Red Light Abatement Act, aimed mainly at the owners of properties where brothels were operated, was passed in 1913. It allowed for the padlocking of such premises, thereby denying rental income to the owners.

The progressives did not win easily. . . . Once the laws were in place, however, the state legislature was out of the picture. Local governments could enforce the statutes or ignore them. Hichborn complained in 1915 that, despite the regulations, gambling was wide open during the great San Francisco Exposition. Saloons and brothels also flourished. It had ever been thus in the City by the Bay.

San Francisco had an unsavory municipal government (a "California Tammany") and a wicked demimonde. Brash San Franciscans viewed their town as "the future seat and center of the world's commerce . . . that advertised the notorious Barbary Coast to the world as a symbol of its anti-Puritan tradition." And tradition it had! In the 1880s, the city supported an estimated two thousand saloons and brothels in the Chinatown, Barbary Coast, and tenderloin districts. San Francisco's bawdy reputation was nationwide, and numerous books described the fun to be had in the city that took "uncommon pride in its past sins, real or imagined." Crusades for moral purity might come and go, but, as one prostitute told a reporter, "the police wink at us." When the police did make arrests, judges often dismissed the cases. . . .

In 1913, a reform crusade briefly closed the Barbary Coast and the tenderloin. They soon were back in operation. Herbert Asbury noted that the election of Mayor James Rolph and a new Board of Supervisors put an end to "an unfriendly, if not actively hostile" municipal administration. There were then an estimated 2,800 legal and 2,500 illegal saloons. From 1913 to 1917, "Sunny Jim" Rolph, mayor of San Francisco, and Madam Tessie Wall, the city's most notorious brothel keeper, rode together through the vice districts at the head of an annual parade organized by the entrepreneurs of pleasure. This could not have happened in Los Angeles.

Rolph favored "personal liberty" and had no identifiable interest in moral reform, progressive style. In 1917, however, an anti-vice crusade led by the Reverend Paul Smith, a Methodist from Boston, caused the Barbary Coast and the tenderloin to be shut down. Vice entrepreneurs and defenders of personal liberty argued that the spirited city had been wide open for sixty-nine years but could not carry the day. Although vice operation continued, the two most famous districts never were the same.

Douglas Henry Daniels has pointed out that "a long-established reputation as a pleasure or sin city permitted night life to thrive without gangland violence." Even during the Prohibition Era, when gangs in Los Angeles and other major cities warred for control of the liquor traffic, San Francisco remained relatively calm. Although there was plenty of graft for police and politicians, there were few scandals.

The depredations of Boss Abe Ruef and Mayor Schmitz, during the first decade of the twentieth century, are well known. It was revealed during the trials that Ruef and Schmitz shared in the profits derived from vice. Yet—significantly—the ill-gotten gain was not what the fuss was about, and alone would not have been a likely cause for throwing the rascals out. Charles Rudebaugh, a newspaper reporter, observed that "everyone knew and boasted" that the city was open and that the police took bribes. The mayor's discussing the situation in public, however, was considered bad for the municipal reputation. A private investigator was brought in to gather evidence of misconduct. The investigator took pains afterward to point out that he had been given no mandate to close illegal businesses, because the citizens of San Francisco wanted them open. The issue was the extortion of bribes from vice operators by policemen.

Reformers in San Francisco described themselves as progressives at least as early as 1896. Some of them favored moral reform of the city, including suppression of the vice districts. Associations of Protestants, Catholics, and Jews campaigned against the "adult entertainment" industry for decades. Black and Chinese residents also struggled to suppress open vice in their neighborhoods. Eventually, over a period of four decades, they succeeded. In the short term, they failed. Local-option prohibition was soundly defeated. Legislation such as the Red Light Abatement Act was seldom used. Police would not arrest. Judges would not convict. Vice, per se, apparently was not a serious issue for a majority of voters. As long as the vice districts remained quiet, the tradition of benign neglect could be maintained.

The story was very different in Los Angeles. As with San Francisco, rapid growth in population followed the discovery of gold. Los Angeles became "the toughest town in the West," home to all the traditional frontier amusements. During the 1850s, with a population of fewer than six thousand residents, the city supported about four hundred premises providing gambling, alcohol, and prostitution.

By the 1870s, native-born Protestants had become the dominant political force in Los Angeles. They later boasted that the town contained more churches in relation to population than any other city in the United States. The new middle class exhibited a strong interest in law enforcement and in control of vice operations. They found the town marshals ill-equipped to provide the safe streets and moral order to which they aspired. In 1876, the marshals were replaced by the newly formed Los Angeles Police Department. Thereafter, the police force usually was at the center of local politics, either because it could not be controlled by the municipal government or because it was involved in the protection of illegal enterprises.

At the same time that the LAPD was created, the Los Angeles Common Council issued ordinances limiting the location of vice premises, the type of "personal service" permitted, and the times at which such entertainments could be provided. At first, the ordinances merely forbade vice operations within prescribed boundaries in the central business and residential areas. Later, the council established a legal vice district but soon withdrew the law. An anti-prostitution act forbidding single women to reside on the ground floor of any dwelling was overturned by the state Supreme court. The council also forbade gambling and introduced early-closing hours and Sunday closing for saloons. Consequently, the purveyors of traditional pleasures suddenly made illicit by the council were compelled to bribe the police or the politicians, or both, if they wished to stay in business.

Despite their largely unsuccessful efforts to reform the city, the reformers believed that they might be more successful if the police were removed from politics. (The workings of politics dictated short careers for police chiefs: between 1877 and 1889, at least sixteen men held the post.) To that end, progressives set out to reform the city charter. The Los Angeles city charter was rewritten or revised in 1889, 1902, 1909, 1911, and 1925. In each case, control of the police was a major element. In 1889, the first police commission was established, replacing a council committee, to deal with appointments, promotions, dismissals, and general policy. True to their faith in nonpartisanship, the progressives first tried dividing authority between Republican and Democratic councilmen, who each appointed two members to the commission; the mayor also served but could not be chairman. Depoliticizing lines of authority over the police failed because all the commissioners were political partisans, and their decisions concerning the police force were partisan decisions.

In 1902, progressive voters ratified the initiative, referendum, and recall; established a municipal civil service; and revised the rules governing the police commission and the police. All police jobs were classified except the positions of police chief and secretary to the police chief. Physical and mental entrance standards and competitive promotional examinations were certified. Salaries were mandated by the charter and could not be reduced by the council. The charter further required that any order having to do with the police must be sent directly to the chief for action. The mayor became chairman of the police commission and could remove other commissioners with consent of the council. By these measures, the progressives hoped to raise the caliber and establish the independence of the individual officer, and place day-to-day control of the department in the chief's hands. The mayor, as chief executive officer, was given greater responsibility for the overall management of the police force.

The charter amendments of 1902 outlawed gambling and prostitution within the city limits. Before these amendments were passed, commercial vice had prospered in "the segregated zone"; indeed, directories were printed that identified brothels by address and the name of the madam, often including words of praise for the comely damsels who "assisted" her. Then two churchmen found "the Ballarino," a building of many narrow cells or "cribs," designed for prostitution. Their anti-vice crusade closed the place and brought calumny upon the police force. Afterward, the progressives won a great victory at the polls.

Whether knowledgeable progressives, hoping to gain political support, guided the two ministers to the Ballarino is not known. What is clear is that the anti-vice crusade became the standard election tactic in Los Angeles for half a century afterward. That vice should be the most volatile political issue over a period of five decades spoke volumes about the electorate, although concerns about vice were not entirely misguided. Despite the will of the voting majority, scandal after scandal occurred. Progressives routinely elected "reform" candidates who abandoned reform after the election.

Between 1904 and 1909, the voters rejected, in one way or another, three mayors accused of misconduct involving liquor and prostitution operations. . . . Five police chiefs left in disgrace.

Until about 1905, there was still some frontier-style joie de vivre apparent in Los Angeles, but it was soon to disappear. In 1908, the district attorney closed down the brothel of Pearl Morton, the city's best-known madam. The same year, Mayor Arthur Harper boasted that he did not protect vice, he condoned it, notwithstanding the laws against gambling, prostitution, and after-hours saloons. The Municipal League, formed in 1901 by Charles Dwight Willard, then initiated a recall campaign. Other reform clubs joined in, including John R. Haynes's Direct Legislation League, Edward A. Dickson's City Club, and Meyer Lissner's good government organization.

These groups formed the vanguard of the Lincoln-Roosevelt League, which became a powerful, statewide organization. The progressives could depend also on the Anti-Saloon League, the Anti-Race Track Gambling League, the Sunday Rest League, and the League of Justice. . . .

Between 1900 and 1909, Los Angeles's population tripled, to 300,000 residents. Most of the newcomers apparently were native Protestants of progressive sentiments. In the 1909 election, the progressives won all twenty-three elective offices. Subsequently, charter amendments were approved that abolished the ward system and installed nonpartisan election laws. These laws, in effect, eliminated the municipal Democratic party. The great victory of 1911 also initiated the destruction of the movement for political reform, since it witnessed the progressive/conservative coalition built to thwart the challenge from the left. By 1915, although control of the city remained in the hands of Protestant Republicans, the reform coalition was in ruins. With it went the integrity of the police force.

For the six years between 1909 and 1915, nevertheless, vice had been virtually suppressed. In this effort, the police had been aided by a platoon of ministers sworn in as special constables and by the Morals Efficiency League, also staffed by clergymen. Artistic censorship had been introduced, not only for motion pictures but for dance and drama as well. Isadora Duncan had been forbidden to dance. Eugene O'Neill's play *Desire under the Elms* was not allowed to open. Racetrack gambling and prizefighting had been abolished. To ensure the conviction of prostitutes, a local ordinance forbade sexual relations between persons not married to one another. . . .

The moral reformers who provided the voting strength of the progressive movement supported a new mid-teens coalition, led mainly by Protestant ministers. They continued the struggle to suppress vice. The various groups were vociferous and determined. They "raided" dance halls and roadhouses, and sometimes had them closed. They held tumultuous press conferences, often in the offices of the mayor or the police commission. They attacked mayors and got police chiefs ousted. They were influential on voting day . . . and they forced restrictions on anyone whose idea of fun differed from their own.

In the early 1920s, reformers persuaded the police commission to restrict the conduct of dancers. Dancing with the cheek or head touching one's partner was forbidden. The male could place his hand only on his partner's back, between shoulder and waist. The female could place her hand only in her partner's left hand. No music "suggestive of bodily contortions" could be played. Moreover, women were forbidden to smoke in any room or place adjacent to a ballroom or dance academy. One minister led a campaign against a female candidate for the school board because the woman smoked tobacco. The candidate promised to quit if elected, but the reformers were adamant. She was defeated.

For twenty-five years, the second wave of reformers campaigned for civic purity. They constantly harassed the police by publicly identifying premises where various illegal enterprises were operated. They held press conferences and large church meetings. They wrote pamphlets. They sat in court to find out which judges convicted vice operators and which ones did not. They voted overwhelmingly for charter revisions to reform the police department. Nevertheless, vice operations continued.

The success of these reformers was minimal because the police department was again at the beck and call of officials who owed their support to one or another corrupt interest. The ministerial associations and federations of laity lacked the cohesion and efficiency of the good government organizations. More important, perhaps, they lacked the financial support of philanthropic progressives such as Meyer Lissner and E. T. Earl. Political campaigns required money, but civil service regulations curtailed patronage, nonpartisan election laws vitiated precinct organizations, and abolition of vice eliminated the most generous contributors.

The electoral victories of 1902–1915 proved that the numerous and potentially all-powerful reformers could not be ignored. They could be circumvented, nevertheless. Every political candidate of the time styled himself or herself a progressive. Since the reformers would not or could not finance a municipal slate of preferred candidates, they were compelled to support the most promising of those who stood for office. Consequently, the venal politicians and purveyors of vice, the so-called underworld combination, regained influence by financing ostensible reformers who, once in office, cooperated with corrupt interests, especially by manipulating the police department. The department operated as a sort of licensing and inspection bureau for organized vice operations. Those approved by the combination were protected; independents were put out of business.

The market for disreputable pleasures grew enormously after 1910. The number of transient males—the most likely "consumers"—increased substantially with the opening of the Panama Canal, the construction of the Los Angeles harbor, and the onset of World War I. The city had a seaport, a naval station, and an army camp. New industries attracted more workers. "Factories in the fields" employed many laborers. The large, continuing migration to the area required thousands of tradesmen to construct houses and services. Transients aside, the population rose from 100,000 in 1900 to 576,000 in 1920, and to 1.3 million in 1930.

Concurrently, local prohibition in 1916, followed by the Eighteenth Amendment, created a law enforcement crisis of unprecedented proportions. Opportunities for graft exceeded anything previously known. The number of police officers and other officials eager to share in the bonanza increased as profits increased. With the vice lords ascendant, the reformers concerned themselves almost entirely with moral issues. . . .

On the surface, the similarities between San Francisco and Los Angeles were quite marked. Both had manufacturers' associations opposed to organized labor. Both had men's and women's service clubs devoted to economic prosperity and the improvement of public morals. Both accepted municipal socialism with respect to public utilities. Both engaged in successful struggles for charter reform. Both were bumptious, rapidly growing, polyglot communities dominated by white, native-born Republicans. Both were progressive. Both had stringent anti-vice laws, flourishing tenderloin districts protected by the police and politicians, and crusading religious leaders opposed to commercial vice.

Why, then, did the two cities diverge so widely where "adult pastimes" were concerned? The reason seems to be that the differences between the two cities, though fewer than the similarities, were far more significant. The simplest but most cogent explanation combines religion and ethnicity: San Francisco was a Catholic and Irish city; Los Angeles was a Protestant and evangelical midwestern city, "the capital of Iowa" moved west.

Catholic churchgoers outnumbered Protestant churchgoers in San Francisco by about a five-to-one margin. Most came from countries where the consumption of wine or beer was a part of the national way of life, or they were descended from immigrants from such countries. These people generally opposed restrictions on personal behavior. The politically active and astute Irish dominated municipal politics. Block and precinct headquarters usually were located in saloons.

The Protestants of San Francisco did favor measures for moral reform and would have passed them if they could. . . . [T]here were Catholic anti-vice crusaders and Catholic progressives in San Francisco. But no temperance campaign ever succeeded there. . . . The city was "wet" during the entire period of national prohibition. Los Angeles voters, on the other hand, voted for local prohibition in 1916 and approved other laws intended to suppress gambling and sexual promiscuity.

In retrospect, it is easy to ridicule the progressives' belief that one can reform a community by changing its laws. In truth, progressives believed more in good people than in good laws. They believed that police officers of good moral character, intelligent, educated, well trained, well paid, with tenure of office and adequate pensions, could and would enforce good laws and rid their communities of moral blight.

This ideal, never completely realized, still sustains civic reformers, as well it should. In Los Angeles, when honorable men and women held municipal office, the police enforced the laws, protected commercial vice was virtually eliminated, and the disreputable pleasures were reduced to an acceptable level. Charters, no matter how well drafted, could not achieve those goals.

The nonpartisan public service is an enduring legacy of the progressive movement. The police in particular have responded to the drive to professionalize every human vocation. Intelligence tests, mental health examinations, educational requirements, competitive promotional examinations, educational requirements, competitive promotional examinations that favor candidates with advanced education, physical health and strength regulations, even requirements to employ females and members of ethnic minorities—all these things are in the progressive tradition. When the ideal of impartial public service is violated, it is a matter of personal choice, not the failure of an institution or a law.

Fortunately for their place in history, the California progressives were more than puritanical moralists, although without their religious zeal their movement might have been less significant. . . . The progressives saw that their society was sick, and they moved to cure it with laws prohibiting certain kinds of personal, political, and economic conduct. They succeeded to a limited degree in every area, and their inheritors have generally followed the same path.

Women Progressives and Immigrant Women

GAYLE GULLETT

California women won the vote in 1911 and fundamentally changed the status of their citizenship. Over the next few years women reformers searched for ways to further transform their citizenship. They wanted to go beyond enfranchisement and acquire more political power, thereby enhancing both their membership and their position within the American polity. They sought to gain political equity in their state by influencing public policy, with their first serious attempt to do so occurring in 1913 in a campaign focusing on sexual mores. In that campaign they won legal and political victories, but not equality. Two years later in 1915 California women enthusiastically entered a different effort to redefine the meaning of U.S. citizenship, the Americanization movement, an aggressive attempt by businessmen, patriotic groups, settlement workers, and educators to acculturate immigrants. . . .

The suffragists belonged to a loose network bound by a sense of identity they called "organized womanhood." This designation reflected their belief that all women shared the same basic concerns of home and morality and their faith that gender solidarity would enable a diverse coalition of women's groups to form a single movement. Organized womanhood functioned as a separate movement and as part of the coalition known as California progressivism. Many of these women were deeply involved in the state's politics as progressives. . . .

Organized women joined the Americanization movement because the fundamental question of that campaign, defining American citizenship, merged with the basic issue they sought to resolve: how to transform women's citizenship. Americanization illustrates how women reformers combined ideologies of gender, class, and ethnicity to construct a new model of citizenship and thus answer a question posed by both social movements: Who is an American citizen? Women reformers rejected women's traditional citizenship status that relied upon the male head of household to speak for all the female members of the family; instead, the activists called for a full and independent citizenship for women that included the ability of women to speak for themselves, shape state policy, and change American nationalism.

Who is an American citizen? Women progressives in the Americanization movement responded that women, immigrant as well as native-born, qualified but not equally among themselves nor in the same way as men. Women activists extended citizenship to immigrant women, an important democratic advance. But the reformers' efforts were at least partially self-serving; they demanded that the newcomers learn from them how to become acceptable women citizens by remaking their homes into American homes. Organized women thus created a political role for themselves as managers of other women's homes. This role gave the reformers a voice over some policy issues but they gained it at the expense of immigrant women who were seen as needing uplift and not able to provide it for themselves. Furthermore, women's citizenship continued to be linked to the home and, consequently, it differed from that of men. Women progressives thus placed themselves, white, middle-class, native-born, at the center of their model for the female citizen and made the citizenship of all women distinct from that of men.

Organized women began supporting Americanization efforts in the 1890s but their numbers increased appreciably after 1915 when the California Daughters of the American Revolution, the national DAR, the California Federation of Women's Clubs (an organization that represented the largest number of women's civic groups in the state), and the national General Federation of Women's Clubs joined the campaign. . . .

According to the activists, American values could not take root unless immigrant wives and mothers taught them in the immigrant home; moreover, that instruction could not effectively occur unless women reformers had first instructed immigrant women. Women progressives perceived Americanization as crucial to the nation's well being and dependent upon women's political activism. The Americanization campaign, they concluded, offered them a vehicle for sponsoring legislation, managing programs, and even holding office—in short, for achieving full citizenship.

Progressive women viewed Americanization in this manner partly because they, along with the progressive men who joined the Americanization crusade, belonged to that part of the progressive coalition whose political objective was building an interdependent society. They envisioned society as consisting of unequal parts that must hold together if those parts and society itself were to survive. They saw their political mission as creating social cohesion through responsible political actions that they defined as those efforts that maintained a productive capitalist system. Such a system allowed for unequal class divisions but also permitted reforms protecting society from the worst hazards of unregulated capitalism. They thus avidly supported capitalism yet they abandoned the old notions of laissez faire and sought political means to bind society together—to achieve an interdependent society.

Progressives viewed Americanization as a tool to integrate immigrant workers into this interdependent society. Their means were to be "education and protection": reformers themselves teaching immigrants the values appropriate to a capitalist economy while protecting them from the most oppressive injustices of industrial capitalism. The ultimate goal of Americanization was to transform rural peasants of dubious national loyalties into contented and reasonably rewarded American workers who accepted the elite leadership of American society. This was the key, progressives felt, to building a harmonious society. These middle-class reformers used the language of interdependency to protect their own class interests.

The women who participated in the Americanization campaign shared with their male colleagues the goal of interdependency but the women described themselves, their means of achieving this goal, and the goal itself in gender specific language. We are, they announced, patriots who engage in "home defense." This definition of patriotism revealed two legacies from the antebellum women's movement. One of them defined patriotism in terms of gender. From the beginning of the nineteenth century women reformers believed that "home defense," or building a family environment supportive of the social order, was women's distinctive political responsibility. By the 1840s Americans commonly accepted that women's defense of the home might well require them to perform public tasks outside the home, such as charity work. Women of the progressive era enlarged this notion of domesticity by contending that women's "home" duties required the transformation of the immigrant family, and this necessitated women's inclusion in the Americanization campaign. By using domesticity to justify their participation in the Americanization movement, women both expanded and limited their political role in the movement.

The second legacy from the antebellum women's movement involved the interrelationship of class and gender. Early nineteenth-century female charity workers attributed the poverty of workers' homes to the moral lapses of the workers themselves; the charity workers also believed their own affluence came from the morality they taught in their homes. Because of these assumptions, the women saw their patriotic duty clearly: they must teach all women how to serve as moral guardians of the home. If women throughout the United States followed the example of elite women, America would become a morally united, prosperous nation without class conflict.

Middle-class women reformers during the progressive era intended their message for all Americans, not just the newly arrived immigrants. . . . [T]hey gave themselves . . . the responsibility for teaching the "right" values to citizens and foreigners [alike].

At first, these reformers debated sharply over the best means to achieve national unity, with businessmen and those belonging to ultra-patriotic organizations stressing the need to acculturate immigrants immediately and completely into American society, and by force if necessary. Others, especially social and settlement workers, urged a slower approach, one addressed to creating an interdependant [*sic*] society based on Anglo-American values that the immigrants themselves would help shape. In time, these two views merged, with the latter position virtually disappearing after World War I. . . .

The settlement house movement deeply influenced reformers in California, leading to the development in the 1890s of two significant settlements, the College Settlement in Los Angeles and the San Francisco Settlement. Both closely modeled themselves after Hull House in Chicago and offered Americanization programs for immigrants. Both expressed their ultimate goal in terms of "nation-building" or building a social consensus that crossed class and ethnic lines. The College Settlement, managed completely by women, was dedicated "to help[ing] the privileged and the unprivileged to a better understanding of their mutual obligations." In San Francisco, where men and women shared management responsibilities, the settlement had a similar goal: "to serve as a medium among the different social elements of the city for bringing about a more intelligent and systematic understanding of their mutual obligations."

In 1912 Simon Lubin heard Jane Addams and Frances Kellor, two renowned settlement workers, present the plank regarding immigrants to the national Progressive party. Lubin, who had served in social settlements himself, was impressed with the women's presentation, particularly with their advocacy for state agencies concerned with immigrants. He persuaded California Progressive Governor Hiram Johnson to create in 1913 a state Commission on Immigration and Housing.

The Commission's education programs, especially its home teacher program that sent female public school teachers into immigrant homes, won the praise of Americanization advocates across the nation. These programs were the creation of Mary Gibson, a Los Angeles school teacher, the widow of a banker, and nearly sixty when she joined the Commission in 1913. She came with thirty years of service in women's civic activities and more recent experience in partisan politics. . . .

Gibson's appointment to the Commission of Immigration put her in a political world where women's role remained uncertain. . . . [M]any male progressives felt uncomfortable with women in politics, a discomfort illustrated by the limited support the men gave to the fight for women's suffrage. Male progressives pushed the California legislature of 1911 to pass a constitutional amendment giving women the vote so the issue would come before the male electorate; after that, male reformers generally gave women's suffrage a minimum amount of attention. It passed in 1911 because of women's efforts. . . .

Sensing this equivocal support from male reformers, Gibson enlisted organized womanhood to promote her Americanization program. She created a place in government where women wrote, directed, and carried out policy. Immigrant wives must be Americanized, she told her superior, Commissioner Lubin. The most efficient means of doing that was by sending women teachers into immigrant homes. Lubin agreed. Gibson wrote the California Home Teacher Act. She and the Women's Legislative Council of California, the political umbrella of the California women's movement, insured that the bill passed the state legislature. The California Daughters of the American Revolution raised funding for the first home teachers. The program's success, reasoned Gibson, would strengthen American society and thus underscore women's crucial contribution to its stability. Women would subsequently be rewarded with greater political responsibilities. "If they [women]," declared Gibson in a 1915 speech, "carry through but half their far-reaching plans [for Americanization], the women of the country will have justified themselves and their claims to suffrage a hundred-fold."

As Gibson worked to make this prediction come true, she emerged as leader of women's Americanization efforts within California. She transformed her hometown of Los Angeles into a showplace of Americanization activities. She became an officer of the California Federation of Women's Clubs in 1915 specifically to direct Americanization activities statewide and then in 1919 served a similar function as chair of the Americanization committee for the national organization, the General Federation of Women's Clubs. She lectured frequently, wrote for state and national journals, and during World War I was chair of the Americanization Department of the Women's Committee of the State Council of Defense of California.

Gibson and others caught up in the California Americanization movement worried that when the Panama Canal opened in 1915, immigrants would "flood" the state. That did not happen. During the first two decades of the twentieth century the percentage of immigrants within the total population of California remained essentially the same, twenty-five percent in 1900 and 1910 and twenty-two percent in 1920. But the immigrants' place of national origin shifted. From 1900 to 1910 England and Germany headed the list of countries sending immigrants to California, but after 1910 Italians and Mexicans began coming in increasingly larger numbers. By 1920 they constituted the majority of newcomers from abroad.

To supporters of Americanization in California, Mexicans posed the most serious challenge to the state. They were the fastest growing immigrant group, and they were perceived as coming from an especially flawed culture that hindered their ability to assimilate. The California Commission of Immigration compared "the Italian with his love of industry and frugality, whose adaptability makes him quickly assimilated," to the "Mexican with his lack of initiative, whose roving temper increases the difficulty of adjusting him." . . . Mexicans could become good American citizens but only if they were so changed they could no longer be recognized as Mexicans.

Until that transformation was achieved, they remained a danger to American society. "Unguided and unprotected," stated a leaflet distributed by the California Immigration Commission, "he [the immigrant] is liable to become a menace. The correction of these evils is no more than a matter of our own self-protection." To which Gibson added in a 1915 California Outlook article: "These [immigrant] families are with us and make up a definite part of our civilization—whether that part shall be valuable[,] or a menace to the body politic, rests with us." . . .

[A]ccording to Gibson and other advocates of Americanization programs, all immigrants needed to be socialized into their proper place in American society. In this task the idea of "interdependence" was crucial. . . . She envisioned an interdependent society as hierarchical and relying on humane yet powerful experts to achieve and maintain social harmony.

Gibson, Lubin, and the others on the Commission of Immigration and Housing saw themselves as those experts, transforming the culture of immigrants through their programs of "education and protection." Immigration presents "a series of peculiar problems," affirmed Lubin, "which require for their intelligent solution a specially created body of experts, with one general view—the protection, assistance and education of the new-comer." . . .

Gibson focused her attention on education. . . . Her most significant contribution was her home teacher program, an innovation designed to send female teachers into the immigrant home to teach the foreign mother "American" standards. . . . [T]he teachers attempted to convince foreign-born wives themselves to attend classes in English, civics, and "domestic science" or home economics. The classes were held at local schools or in neighborhood homes, while later some were moved to "cottages," small houses equipped with American-style furniture and household equipment. In 1915 there was a single home teacher in Los Angeles; three years later there were twelve salaried teachers working in nineteen of the city's school districts and offering classes in five model homes. By World War I, other cities, such as Oakland, had also adopted the program.

In seeking public support for the home teacher program, Gibson emphasized that immigrant women were a potential "menace" to American society. Because they lived a life of painful isolation, either unable or unwilling to engage in a dialogue with native-born American society, foreign-born mothers, according to Gibson, did not make their homes "American homes." The result was that their children, who were more accepting of American values, developed contempt for their immigrant homes and parents, especially for their mothers, the least Americanized parent. This conflict could lead to juvenile delinquency and other problems. If the state failed to rescue immigrant women and restore family order, warned Gibson, it faced "imminent peril" and would have to "pay the penalty of social disorder." . . .

[I]mmigrant women became the object of such concern because they served as "linchpins" in maintaining immigrant culture. Immigrant wives and mothers stood at the center of immigrant culture, creating homes that honored the values of pre-industrial societies, values that stressed that individuals should place the well-being of the family over personal advancement. Immigrant family survival often rested upon family cooperation, and the person who taught, managed, and encouraged cooperation was the immigrant mother. These women were strong, intelligent, resourceful, in command of family resources, and integrated into their communities. This reality contrasted sharply with the view of Gibson and other Americanization advocates who saw immigrant women as isolated, unable to control their children, and a potential "menace" to American society. . . .

Gibson and her colleagues believed that immigrant mothers who became inculcated with American values would be crucial in the assimilation of their families, especially as they were persuaded to de-emphasize group cooperation in favor of individual ambition. To reformers the development of individualism was at the heart of the Americanization education program, for they believed that once immigrants began pursuing their own individual material interests, the economy of the country would be strengthened and the immigrant standard of living would improve. "One cannot transform a hopeless ignoramus into a good citizen," Gibson announced in a 1915 speech; "he must first be instilled with ambition." . . .

For "the making" of ambitious people, Americanization proponents stressed domestic science, a required subject in the home teacher program. Domestic science . . . emphasized teaching the immigrant mothers "restlessness and dissatisfaction" with shoddy workmanship and poor living conditions. They should not "accept the fallen plaster, the dish-water that leaks through from the flat above and the dirty and dark hall." . . .

Another goal of domestic science was to provide immigrant wives with vocational skills, transforming them from unskilled peasant women into scientific household managers. A by-product would be relief for the chronic shortage of skilled, inexpensive household help. While reformers felt immigrant wives needed ambition, they sought to instill only the kind of ambition that would leave the newcomers in the working class, moving from unskilled to semiskilled or, at best, skilled work. . . .

Thus, the assumption undergirding the Americanization program was that only elite, native-born women could resolve the menace presented to the American social order by immigrant, working-class women. "Upon the women, brave enough and strong enough to win their own political emancipation," stated Gibson, "rests the responsibility of the education and protection of these alien women; and to so establish and sustain the mother in her own domain, is to protect the state from delinquent children and an ignorant vote." . . .

As for the Americanization campaign itself, immigrants voted with their feet overwhelmingly against it. . . . [F]ew immigrants attended night schools, an early and crucial innovation by Americanization reformers that provided lessons in English and American civics for adults. . . . [E]ven during World War I, a period of intense Americanization activities, night schools "enrolled only a quarter of a million out of a possible thirteen and three quarters million immigrants . . . [and] women constituted less than a third of this already small number." Gibson and other California reformers established the home teacher program to overcome the reluctance of immigrant women to come to night classes but the drop-out rate for the home teacher program was, at eighty percent, very high. . . . "Consistently low registrations and high drop-out rates" characterize the response of immigrant women to all Americanization programs, from night schools to settlement programs. A 1920 survey of Americanization programs in Los Angeles [showed that] 3,448 people (in a city with 122,131 foreign-born) started the program and only 322 finished it.

Immigrant women often wanted the skills—for example, facility in the English language—taught in Americanization classes but they could gain these through their ethnic communities, churches, and labor organizations. Since they utilized the services of other social welfare agencies, bringing their infants to well-baby clinics and asking social workers to intervene in cases of family violence, one wonders why they rejected Americanization efforts. Perhaps they did so because the impulse behind the efforts was a fear of immigrant culture, a fear that meant that the programs, no matter how humanely conceived, were permeated with the idea that immigrant culture was basically illegitimate and something that would and should eventually disappear in the United States.

This negativity toward immigrant culture became especially pronounced during the years following the war when the Red Scare heightened fears of foreign ideas. For Americanization advocates it surfaced in the way they established themselves as arbiters or "gatekeepers" over what aspects of immigrant culture were socially acceptable. A dramatic example was the concept of immigrant cultural "gifts" which Gibson vigorously promoted after the war, although the concept was popular among Americanization reformers since the beginning of the century. In 1921 Gibson persuaded clubwomen to hold a "Homeland Exhibit of Art and Crafts" in southern California that featured the arts, songs, and dances of the foreign-born. Such an exhibit, she explained, would teach both immigrants and native-born the value of creating a new national consensus shared by all citizens.

The pageant at the Homeland Exhibit, however, like similar events presented by settlement workers and teachers in neighborhood schools, failed to offer a message of pluralism. Instead, these pageants functioned as Americanization rituals in which immigrants presented themselves in native costume to native-born officials who symbolically decided whether to accept them and their arts into American society. . . . They decided which immigrant gifts to accept and the meaning of those gifts for the larger society.

Also contributing to immigrant disenchantment with Americanization programs was an increasing element of coercion in their implementation. During and immediately after the Red Scare many states passed coercive Americanization legislation. California, along with Idaho and Utah, made attendance at Americanization classes compulsory for immigrants. Neither Lubin nor Gibson favored such forced indoctrination, yet both participated in its implementation as members of the California State Americanization Committee. Lubin openly expressed misgivings about his participation but Gibson did not. She looked upon the mandatory programs as an opportunity for "constructive publicity" of the Commission's Americanization efforts.

Some native-born citizens responded to the Red Scare by declaring that the foreign-born could never become "100 percent" Americans, a nativist sentiment that no doubt encouraged many immigrants to avoid Americanization programs. In California, the Red Scare and the 100 percent campaign fostered an anti-Japanese hysteria that swelled into a movement that demanded the expulsion of the Japanese from the state for racial as well as cultural reasons. Before the war, women reformers expressed more toleration or, at least, less active hostility toward Japanese immigrants. In 1913 most of the women's civic organizations had remained silent and officially uncommitted when the Progressives waged a campaign against Japanese land ownership; some women defended the rights of the Japanese. Japanese women attended home teacher programs where they received high marks.

But in 1919 several women's organizations backed the exclusion of Japanese from the state; these included groups with a long history of support for Americanization. The California Federation of Women's Clubs passed a resolution for Japanese exclusion in 1920, and its president, Adella Tuttle Schloss, became one of the vice-presidents of the Japanese Exclusion League of California. The willingness of the state's organized women to join the Japanese Exclusion League was linked to the women's participation in the Americanization campaign. That campaign had made them more politically active and more receptive to racial nationalism than they had been previously. . . .

The California women who supported Americanization did so because they perceived their primary political task as maintaining "interdependence"—social order, unity and peace. They would gain full citizenship; all Americans would accept their proper place and responsibilities; and the result would be social harmony. Americanization, they thought, provided a means to transform America: housekeepers would become patriots, and immigrants, citizens.

 FURTHER READING

Walton Bean, *Boss Ruef's San Francisco: The Story of the Union Labor Party, Big Business, and the Graft Prosecution* (1951; paperback edition, 1952)
Mansel G. Blackford, *The Politics of Business in California, 1890–1920* (1977)

Jacqueline R. Braitman, "A California Stateswoman: The Public Career of Katherine Philips Edson," *California History* LXV (June 1986): 82–95, 151–52

Thomas R. Clark, "Labor and Progressivism 'South of the Slot': The Voting Behavior of the San Francisco Working Class, 1912–1916," *California History* LXVI (September 1987): 196–207, 234–36

Thomas E. Cronin, *Direct Democracy: The Politics of Initiative, Referendum, and Recall* (1989)

Roger Daniels, *The Politics of Prejudice: The Anti-Japanese Movement in California and the Struggle for Japanese Exclusion* (1962)

William Deverell and Tom Sitton, eds., *California Progressivism Revisited* (1994)

Philip J. Ethington, *The Public City: The Political Construction of Urban Life in San Francisco, 1850–1900* (1994)

James C. Findley, "Cross-Filing and the Progressive Movement in California Politics," *Western Political Quarterly* XXII (September 1959): 699–711

Noralee Frankel and Nancy S. Dye, eds., *Gender, Class, Race, and Reform in the Progressive Era* (1991)

Mary S. Gibson, *Caroline M. Severance, Pioneer* (1925)

Franklin Hichborn, "The Party, the Machine, and the Vote: The Story of Cross-Filing in California," *California Historical Society Quarterly* XXXVIII (December 1959): 349–57 and ibid. XXXIX (March 1960): 19–34

Mary A. Hill, *Charlotte Perkins Gilman: The Making of a Radical Feminist* (1980)

Norris C. Hundley, Jr., "Katherine Philips Edson and the Fight for the California Minimum Wage, 1912–1923," *Pacific Historical Review* XXIX (August 1960): 271–86

William Issel and Robert W. Cherny, *San Francisco, 1865–1932: Politics, Power, and Urban Development* (1986)

Gloria Ricci Lothrop, "Strength Made Stronger: The Role of Women in Southern California Philanthropy," *Journal of San Diego History* LXXI (Summer/Fall 1989): 143–94

Richard Coke Lower, *A Bloc of One: The Political Career of Hiram W. Johnson* (1993)

Terrence J. McDonald, *The Parameters of Urban Fiscal Policy: Socioeconomic Change and Political Culture in San Francisco, 1860–1906* (1986)

H. Brett Melendy, "California's Cross-Filing Nightmare: The 1918 Gubernatorial Election," *Pacific Historical Review* XXXII (August 1964): 317–30

George Edwin Mowry, *The California Progressives* (1951)

Spencer C. Olin, *California's Prodigal Sons: Hiram Johnson and the Progressives, 1911–1917* (1968)

Keith W. Olson, *Biography of a Progressive, Franklin K. Lane, 1864–1921* (1979)

Jackson K. Putnam, "The Persistence of Progressivism in the 1920s," *Pacific Historical Review* XXXV (November 1966): 395–411

Michael Paul Rogin and John L. Shover, *Political Change in California: Critical Elections and Social Movements, 1890–1966* (1970)

Ronald Schaffer, "The Problem of Consciousness in the Woman Suffrage Movement: A California Perspective," *Pacific Historical Review* XLV (November 1976): 469–93

Gary Scharnhorst, "Making Her Fame: Charlotte Perkins Gilman in California," *California History* LXIV (Summer 1985): 192–201, 242–43

Tom Sitton, *John Randolph Haynes, California Progressive* (1992)

Jean M. Smith, "The Voting Women of San Diego, 1920," *Journal of San Diego History* XXVI (Spring 1980): 133–54

Frank W. Van Nuys, "A Progressive Confronts the Race Question: Chester Rowell, the California Alien Land Act of 1913, and the Contradictions of Early Twentieth-Century Racial Thought," *California History* LXXIII (Spring 1994): 2–13, 84–85

CHAPTER
9

Hollywood and the California Dream, 1910s–1930s

California is, to be sure, a geographic entity. At the same time it has also been an idea—"a place in the mind," as James Houston puts it. The preceding eight chapters have examined the material aspects of California's history; in this one, the focus will be on how California has been imagined and creatively portrayed.

Myths, legends, and symbols have long been integral elements in the state's history. Even the name California *comes from a work of fiction—a fifteenth-century Spanish novel,* Las Sergas de Esplandían *by Garcí Ordóñez de Montalvo. In this story, there dwelled a queen named Califia on an island full of gold and precious stones. It is likely that some of the first Spanish and Portuguese explorers to arrive in California had heard that tale. If so, then before any Europeans ever set eyes on the western shores of the North American continent, their mind's eye might already have beheld a wondrous, resplendent realm, an El Dorado that came to be called California.*

This Edenic myth has persisted and has gone through several metamorphoses. The discovery of gold in 1848, and the in-rush of people from around the world in 1849 and the early 1850s, was certainly a prophecy fulfilled. But the gold rush affected mainly northern California. The counties south of the Tehachapi Mountains remained pastoral and sparsely populated—the "cow counties," they were called. For a few decades after the gold rush, Los Angeles, San Diego, and San Bernardino (the last founded by Mormons) remained sleepy little towns compared to San Francisco, which had become a cosmopolitan city virtually overnight.

People did not flock to southern California until the late 1880s, when railroad companies actively promoted immigration. When a second transcontinental railroad—the Atchison, Topeka and Santa Fe—reached Los Angeles in 1887, it engaged in a rate war with the Southern Pacific (heir to the Central Pacific, the first transcontinental railroad) to lure settlers to southern California in order to sell them some of the vast acreage that the railroad companies owned. Fares dropped to a small fraction of what they

*had been, which enabled middle-class and working-class people from all
over the country to buy train tickets to southern California. Streams of Midwesterners arrived, fueling a brief real estate boom in the late 1880s. Sixty
new towns were established before the boom collapsed in 1889. But the discovery of oil in Los Angeles in 1892 started a new boom, enabling southern
California to continue its spectacular growth.*

In addition to the railroads, the Los Angeles Times *and the Los Angeles Merchants and Manufacturers Association played key roles in promoting
the southland. They supported writers who crafted a new image for southern California as a Mediterranean paradise where health-seekers could
relax under sunny skies, cooled by gentle sea breezes amidst palm trees,
orange groves, and flowers, with time marked by the tolling of Spanish
mission bells.*

*By the second decade of the twentieth century, the film industry had
become the most important vehicle for disseminating images of the California dream—a glamorous version of the American Dream. Of particular
importance was Hollywood, the "film colony" where movie stars lived and
played. Ordinary people became acquainted with the stars' opulent lifestyle
through stories and photographs in fan magazines. The existence of Hollywood as a residential community "proved" that the kind of life depicted on
the silver screen could be found in reality. Films eventually became the most
popular form of mass entertainment because movie tickets were cheap compared to the cost of tickets for the opera or for plays and because the plots
appealed to the public's desire for romance and escape. By conveying the
message that less sexually restrictive behavior made life more fun, the movies
and their stars exerted considerable influence on the morals of the nation. At
the same time, filmmakers were eager to prove they were not depraved and
certain films with "fallen women" heroines represented their attempt to join
the moral crusade spearheaded by progressive reformers.*

*Southern California's position as the world capital of the mass media
and of popular culture has continued to the present day. Also with us still
are heated debates over how explicitly violence, sex, and criminal activities
should be shown on screen.*

*In reading the documents and essays in this chapter, consider how the
glittering images created by Hollywood square with reality. Pay special
attention to the second essay, which discusses the discrepancy between the
stories in certain films and what was actually happening in society during
the early decades of the twentieth century.*

D O C U M E N T S

Today's movie audiences take computer-generated special effects and death-
defying stunts so much for granted that it may be difficult for them to imagine
what filmmakers in the early days of cinema had to do to create extraordinary
scenes. The director Cecil B. de Mille, a master at his craft, was a pioneer in
making epic films with a cast of thousands. In the first document, he reveals
how he made the sets for certain scenes in several of his classic films.

Making movies has always been expensive. Until films proved they could
pay for themselves, bankers were unwilling to finance movie production. A. H.

Giannini, a surgeon-turned-banker whose brother, A. P. Giannini, founded the Bank of Italy, which eventually merged with several other banks to become the Bank of America, was an exception. Because of Giannini's willingness to take risks, California has played a crucial role in developing the film industry. Not only are the major studios and Hollywood situated there, but one of the first two banks willing to lend money to producers was a California institution. In the second document, Giannini discusses why he supported the film industry.

The very success of movies, however, led critics to ask why they were so popular. One answer was disturbing: movies encouraged their audiences to act with abandon. Harmon B. Stephens, who wrote the third document and taught at the University of Tennessee, describes a segment from a 1920s film that offended his sense of propriety. Judging by the standards of the 1990s, his concerns sound almost amusing.

In the fourth document, Ruth Suckow analyzes why certain actors and actresses, even when they lacked artistic talent, became gods and goddesses of the silver screen. Considered a protégée of H. L. Mencken, Suckow published her writings regularly in such periodicals as *The American Mercury, Century,* and *Harper's.* She also wrote several novels, the best known of which is *The Folks.*

The fifth document is drawn from the novel *The Day of the Locust* (1939), by Nathanael West. It is considered by some critics to be the finest piece of fiction ever written about Hollywood, a work that strips Hollywood of its glamour. In a sardonic yet humorous manner, West depicts the bungling manner in which celluloid fantasies are fabricated. West wrote four novels and more than twenty screenplays before he died at the age of thirty-seven in an automobile accident.

Cecil B. de Mille Reveals How He Creates Special Effects, 1927

Assuming now that the scenario is perfected—though it seldom is—the director next calls in the art director. The term "art director" is sometimes a bit misleading. He is the man who designs the sets or has them designed. He is the head of that department.

We will say we have a great scene called for—the vision of temporal power in "The King of Kings," which Satan shows to Jesus. The question of how to visualize the power of the world, how to show it, how to do it, is put up to the director. That is the kind of proposition the director gets. In the handling of it he calls to his aid his art director, his technical man, his trick man, stunt man, miniature man, and glass man.

For instance, in the scene I have just mentioned (the vision of temporal power), we change the temple into a vision of Rome; and, because it is an imaginative thing, we need to show Rome even more magnificent than it was—in other words, a hundred Romes piled one on top of another. To go out and build anything of this sort would, of course, be an utter impossibility. It would take as long as it did to build Rome itself and cost a good deal more, because wages are higher now than they were then. So we take our miniature man, our glass man, our art director, our carpenter, and we say we are going to use a foreground of five hundred or a thousand feet in this.

Then we build the actual set for five hundred feet. From that point on we make a miniature which is matched by very clever camera work to the real set. Finally we have a large sheet of glass on which we paint the background. The lower portion of the glass is kept clear, so as to permit the real set and the miniature to be seen through it; and above that—because it is supposedly far in the background—we have painted by the finest artist we can get, the imaginary Rome. The real thing is in the foreground; the miniature just above it, showing the roofs of the great city of Rome cleverly blended with what we have built, and then this glass picture in front of that, but really giving the effect of a far-distant horizon. . . . In that way these great scenes are made possible.

Do not get the idea that that is not an expensive process. The making of the miniature and the matching must be very carefully done, because it must not be detected. Some of you may have seen the picture called "The Ten Commandments." In that we were given the problem of opening and closing the Red Sea. That was what the director was told to do. He could not ask how, because nobody could tell him. Nobody had opened and closed the Red Sea before, except on one memorable occasion, but we nevertheless had to duplicate that. It was done with fourteen exposures on the film. I am not going to enlarge on these technical points, but I want to give you a little of what I mean.

There were fourteen pictures or exposures on the opening and closing of the Red Sea. The effect was gained by a mixture of the real sea and very clever motion picture trick work. The wave which engulfed Pharaoh's army was obtained by building two tanks holding 60,000 gallons of water each, designed to drop at the same moment into a large curved piece of steel, so that when it threw this wave into an immense curve, the two volumes of water met at the top and in that way we got a wave that was enormous. The camera was almost underneath it. That was done before we started in with our people at all. . . .

The problems that confront a director are very interesting. Sometimes they come suddenly and unexpectedly and must be met right on the spot. To show you the quick thought that a man must have, let us take the case of the opening of the Red Sea about which I spoke a moment ago. Those of you who may have seen the picture will remember that the Children of Israel come along through the bottom of the sea for about a mile and a half. The exposure took in the walls of water on each side and it was in a curve, if you recall. The people were driving their flocks of cattle through, and, if a sheep or cow happened to run off into the side out of the line, it would run into one of the walls of water. Of course the walls of water were not there actually. They were on the second exposure of film, but if the flocks had wandered off at all you would have been treated to the sight of a herd of sheep apparently strolling into the Pacific Ocean. Therefore, we had to build a fence that exactly corresponded with the lines of the divided sea, in order to keep the cattle inside of those walls of supposed water.

But the fence posts threw a shadow. When we inspected them before shooting we discovered that there were shadows of fence posts for a mile along the bottom of the Red Sea. The only thing to do was to shoot the scene of the crossing exactly at noon. There were 3,000 people and 8,000 animals in it. That was quite an undertaking. However, we had them all ready to start, when at twenty minutes before twelve some bright chap came to me and said, "Mr. de Mille, do you know the bottom of the Red Sea is dry?" Of course the sand was dry. Here we had just sent the waters apart and yet the bottom of the sea was perfectly dry. This was twenty minutes before the time set to turn the camera. The cost upon that location was $50,000 a day, and it had meant a full day just to move the animals and people out to that particular spot, which was a long way from camp. So with $50,000 at stake and twenty minutes in which to save the situation [,] I called for a quick suggestion as to how we could darken that sand for two miles. If we could get it dark and glistening we were saved. If it remained dry and white we were lost. What could we do? Somebody suggested a pump. We had some pumps there. In about eight of the twenty minutes our men had pumped water over a strip about forty feet long and when they got to the end of it the starting point was dried again. I suggested black paint. "How much black paint have we got?" The painter stepped up and said that there wasn't paint enough in California to paint that sand. . . .

We were working by the sea within forty feet of the shore line. . . . In looking desperately about and thinking "What can I do with this thing?" I saw a great kelp bed at my feet. Instantly I gave the order—"Everybody, men, women, and children, get up this kelp!" They gathered up the kelp and laid it down for a mile and a half, like rushes that we read about on medieval floors. At exactly 12.02 we had a nice wet bottom of the sea and we turned the camera. That is the kind of problem that the director is often up against and has to solve. If we had not solved that one, you can see what the consequence would have been—a tremendous loss.

I will give you another instance, a rather amusing one. I once made a picture called "Male and Female," with Thomas Meighan and Gloria Swanson. Tommy supposedly had just shot a leopard and had it hanging over his shoulder. The property man had provided a stuffed leopard, with one foot sticking out so and the tail going off at an angle. I saw it and was greatly annoyed, because I had talked with the man about it and had said specifically, "Get me a body that is limp and will hang as though the animal were just killed." So the taking of the scene had to be postponed until we could secure a proper-looking leopard. Meanwhile one of the property men came up and said, "There is a real leopard over in the zoo that has just killed a man." I said, "Get me that leopard," because I knew the animal was going to be executed anyway. Any animal that kills is treated as a murderer and summarily put to death. "Bring him over here," I ordered, "and we will kill him and Tommy can hold this dead leopard over his shoulder while he plays his impassioned love scene."

So the leopard was brought over. It proved to be a magnificent animal. I said, "We cannot kill that animal; it is too beautiful a specimen." Tommy looked a little doubtful, but I said, "I'll tell you what we'll do. Get a lot of chloroform and ether and some sponges." The property man rushed off and bought all the chloroform and ether in Hollywood, and we poured it on the sponges and put it into the leopard's cage and put something across the front. There was a terrible to-do inside the cage, a rocking back and forth and frightful noises. Pretty soon everything was quiet, and we opened the cage and found the leopard lying limp and apparently lifeless. The scene was all rehearsed and ready. We put the unconscious leopard over Tommy's shoulder and said, "All right, Tommy, go ahead." We had men with Winchester thirty-thirties all around this love scene, and it was a rather long love scene. We had to take it two or three times.

I do not know whether you gentlemen have ever had any experience with a patient coming out of ether or chloroform or a mixture of the two; but the mixture we used certainly had a strange effect. In the middle of the love scene the leopard started. He was perfectly unconscious, but perhaps you have heard human beings talk under the influence of ether. Well, this leopard talked and talked in the middle of this impassioned love scene, and Tommy, with Gloria's hand pressed to his heart, said, "Mr. deMille [*sic*], I tell you he is coming to."

A. H. Giannini Explains Why He Decided to Finance the Film Industry, 1926

Every business man, who has given any attention within the past fifteen years to the development of American industry, must have observed how the moving picture business has progressively advanced to the front rank of our national activities.

This forward march has exceeded that of many industries, and has been surpassed only by a very few. Because of persistent misrepresentations fifteen years ago, many persons were misled into the belief that the picture business would never be anything but a bad risk for the banker.

From a very modest beginning it has grown in veritable leaps and bounds, and it has now assumed dimensions of an unbelievable size. It is estimated that one and one-half billion dollars are invested in this American enterprise. . . .

The machinery equipment employed in the business, the kind of theatres in use, the poor stories, the inexperienced director, the calibre of the cast, the incompetent title-writer—all these factors were not calculated to awaken an intense interest in the public. The banker, of course, was not attracted to this business.

It was about this time that I became acquainted with some of the men of this industry living in California. These men who became my friends were active in the management of several companies and revealed to me a serviceable efficiency that arrested my attention.

At this time I was Vice-President of the Bank of Italy of California with offices in San Francisco and Los Angeles. These friends opened accounts at the bank. We were in a position to observe their ability and honesty and I became quickly convinced that they had taken hold of a serious work. They were militantly enthusiastic crusaders of the type "who chose to earn tomorrow's bread by to-day's toil."

As their business developed, they came in for financial assistance. They were asked to present statements, but as the business was new and unknown, the customary standards of credit rating could not be applied. At first purely on personal grounds small amounts were loaned. These were always promptly paid. Further and larger amounts were given and all payments were met at maturity. Learning that the Bank of Italy of California was friendly to such business, many then sought accommodations. . . .

The bank had no losses. Our loans were at times unsecured and at other times secured by an assignment of the proceeds from the positive prints. Occasionally a loan was made on the negative print, but this was a temporary expediency for a negative in the possession of the bank made it impossible to play the picture. These loans were in every instance at the current banking rate of interest. As the business enlarged, others entered and in the rapid growth, some appeared whose intentions were not so honorable. Fortunately these creatures were quickly eliminated.

In the space of seven years, the industry had so grown that it began to challenge admiration both in and out of banking circles. However, most California bankers continued to be indifferent.

Eight years ago I came to New York as the President of the East River National Bank. . . .

I likewise noted that the bankers of New York as in California were also indifferent to the business. My commitments, however, grew proportionately larger. My associates and my directors looked with a very critical eye upon my recommendations. They very kindly but very firmly suggested caution. The Bank Examiners both of the New York Clearing House and the National Banking Department made certain written and oral comments that disturbed us. As the business was new, they very properly advised care.

The steady growth of the business made heavier demands upon the bank and it was then that I turned to the leaders of the industry and sought their co-operation. I had repeatedly stated, both in private and publicly, that the men in control of this business were just as intelligent, just as industrious and just as able as the men in any other big business. The public was responding cheerfully and generously to the support of this new, but now large, enterprise. The masses approved of this form of entertainment and the producer met this demand with better pictures. The inexorable law of supply and demand determined his position.

It was then that it occurred to me to invite to sit with me on our Board of Directors one of the industry, so that I could elicit his support in my belief of the soundness of the business and for the further reason that the business would thus have a friend in court. . . .

In our desire to do constructive work, we found that a certain menace threatened many of those engaged in the business. . . . [U]surers had a menacing hold upon some of the men in the business. The few companies that succumbed were victims of this pernicious "bonus" system.

We had a friendly working relation with every large company. We found, however, that those who were unable to weather the up and down periods were in every instance wrecked to a great degree by these bonus sharks. There were always good profits in the business, but not enough to pay such excessive rates of interest. . . . These parasites are rapidly fading out of the picture and now anyone who has a good banking proposition can easily secure accommodations from any and all banks in this country. The bankers are no longer afraid. This outstanding commercial accomplishment has amazed them and the world.

The management of the various companies is in capable hands, the financial statements are no longer vague and indefinite, budget requirements are not a matter of conjecture.

All the producing companies of the first rank receive accommodations on an unsecured basis, and are given the same consideration as to amounts and rates of interest as any other high-class, legitimate business. Independent producers, so-called, may be required to lodge with the bank the guarantee of a distributing company. . . .

Within the past several years, some of the larger companies have refinanced themselves. In each instance the new stock issue was sponsored by high and reputable investment houses. . . .

A clean, wholesome business, managed by men with clear-eyed determination to render a great public service has finally and honorably come into its own. Some of the dearest and best friends I have stand at the forefront of this industry. They have made substantial contributions to a better understanding and maintained a dignity concurrent with the sense of the importance of the relation between picture and public. I recognize in them the standards by which the progress of the moving picture business is measured. They, Prometheus-like, put the fire of life into what was fifteen years ago an inert business. They have the full support of a united people and it behooves our national government to acquaint itself fully with the magnititude [*sic*] of this business. There should be no national indifference, but every effort made to foster this great industry along every line of legitimate endeavor. It appears to me that some of the European governments are manifesting, and deservedly so, more interest in this business than ours at Washington. I will leave it to others to develop this phase of the subject, but in conclusion I desire to sound a warning. The moving picture industry is of such importance that it is entitled to the attention and support of those who are seated in high places in the councils of our country.

Harmon B. Stephens Exposes How Films
Lower Moral Standards, 1926

[I]t is well to outline several points in attempting to estimate the effect of motion pictures upon conduct.

First, we must bear in mind the psychology of mental shock. The term as here used refers to sensations of surprise, offense or horror which have no immediate tragic personal consequences, and to which one may become accustomed. It is not difficult to discover persons who are so hardened to vice and indecency that the most startling perversions make little impression upon them. . . . Much of the division of opinion as to the danger of certain pictures is due to the fact that some people are more accustomed to indecency than others. No one would argue that getting accustomed to a bad smell makes it desirable, or that getting used to seeing dirty milk bottles makes them safe. Many of the most dangerous influences never produce violent shock. Their effect is so gradually cumulative that the evil is not recognized till it is almost beyond repair.

The hope and yet the despair of humanity is that social groups never consciously encourage what is recognized as evil, yet they are constantly becoming so accustomed to one or more evils that they cannot be aroused in time to prevent great injury.

A second point relates to the relative influence upon conduct of the several mediums of expression. The writer received the following statement from a noted psychologist:

"On a scale measuring motivation of conduct, a given situation would probably rate lowest in print, next higher in still-pictures, next highest in motion pictures, and highest if reproduced in actual life." . . .

It seems reasonable to assume that the motion picture comes nearer to reproducing real life situations than any other medium of expression. . . .

A third point of importance is that, according to the estimate of one producer, eighty per cent of the box office revenue is derived from what may be called family audiences. It has thus become almost impossible to separate adolescents from adults; they all receive the same fare. Comedies which the children cry for are put on the same bill with features suitable only for adults. . . .

[In 1926] a feature film called *Up in Mabel's Room* was witnessed at Madison, Wis. This photoplay relates the complications brought about by what a theatre lobby advertisement described as a "cavorting chemise." At one point a certain Garry has been intruded upon in his bachelor apartment by Mabel, from whom he is supposed to have been divorced, and he is opposed to any reconciliation. Phyllis, Garry's fiancée, has decided to come and say good night (after a cabaret party) and Mabel wishes to break up the engagement.

Now comes a five minute sequence as follows: The butler announces that Garry's betrothed, Phyllis, wishes to come in to see him. Garry hustles Mabel behind a screen in his apartment. Phyllis enters as though in anticipation of a good night kiss. Mabel tosses her jacket over the screen. Garry tries to explain this to Phyllis. Then a close-up is shown of Mabel behind the screen removing her shoes, which she sets out in front of the screen. Garry explains to Phyllis that they belonged to his sister and were to be used as ash trays (*e.g.* of some of the comedy titles!). Then a close-up is shown of Mabel behind the screen stooping as though removing her stockings. Then the stockings are thrown over the screen, then a ladies under vest, then a pair of lacey little French panties. Garry now hustles the dismayed and astonished Phyllis out of the apartment and returns to face the screen at a distance of 15 feet or so. Mabel appears peeking from behind the screen, just her head, bare arm and shoulder, apparently naked, and calls "Ooo-ooh, Garry!" He is shocked and turns bashfully away. Again she calls, "Oh, Garry, come here!"

Garry refuses to even turn toward her, so she comes out from behind the screen, fully dressed save for her shoes. As she approaches he covers his eyes with his hands, supposing her to be naked. She turns him about so that he faces her, but he still keeps his hands tightly over his eyes, bashfully shocked. She pulls his hands away but he still keeps his eyes closed; then opens at her insistence, and sees he was fooled. He insists that she leave the apartment; she calmly goes over and starts replacing her underwear in a little vanity satchel, shaking out the French panties and holding them spread out in front of her bosom as she does so. This explains how she could throw such things over the screen and still be dressed. But the sequence was deliberately handled so as to make the audience believe she had actually disrobed.

The accuracy of this description was attested by a second observer who read it after witnessing the picture. This is but one of several questionable sequences in the same picture. At a Sunday matinée performance the shrill laughter of children completely drowned out the hilarity of adults. Young high school fellows were there with their girl friends.

The picture was produced by a member organization of the Motion Picture Producers and Distributors of America, which association, through Mr. Hays, has for several years been assuring the public that member producing companies were no longer permitting questionable scenes.

The main title of the picture bore the legend, "Passed by the National Board of Review."

The writer has recently witnessed other photoplays produced by member companies of the Motion Picture Producers and Distributors of America which carried sequences equally questionable—sequences which some young college fellows referred to as "the hottest yet." . . .

In a short article it is possible to consider only a few aspects of the relation between changing moral standards and the motion picture. The highly important matter of sensational exploitation has barely been mentioned. It is a fine thing to have our attention called to wholesome entertainment. For that we should be grateful. It is another thing to have the most risqué aspects of a picture, suitable only for adults, if for anyone, paraded before the eyes of the young on billboards, in leaflets distributed from door to door, in the family newspaper, and on the photoplay screen as an announcement of future entertainment, often in connection with a wholesome photoplay to which parents have been especially urged to take their children.

But enough has been presented to suggest that the motion picture has effected and will continue to vitally effect the moral conduct particularly of the young. . . .

Ruth Suckow Analyzes the Appeal of Hollywood Gods and Goddesses, 1936

The immense influence of Hollywood in our national life has lately passed the point where it was matter for comment (frequently for denunciation) and seems to be accepted as matter of fact. Manners, clothes, speech, tastes, all are affected by the actors and actresses of the motion picture screen as they never were by the popular figures of the stage or by any of our popular idols.

Robert Edmond Jones, I believe, once wrote of the motion picture stars as a new race of gods and goddesses comparable in their symbolic nature and the worship accorded them to the pagan deities of Greece and Rome. The fan magazines frequently, and even matter-of-factly, refer to the feminine stars as "goddesses," while at the same time trying to prove that these shining ones are just like the rest of us.

Just why do the figures of the screen loom so large in our day? A few, a very few, of the great motion picture figures have also been great actors; but it is not through superlative excellence in their profession that they have been raised to mythical heights. It often works the other way. To be an artist is a drawback. It would seem at times that this nation, losing the stern Puritan orthodoxy which it brought with it to the new continent, yet still crude and young in the mass, has turned to the worship of these picture gods, real and yet unreal, common as life and yet larger than life, known in minuter detail than next-door neighbors and yet shiningly remote, because they have come to represent certain national ideals reduced to the lowest common denominator. For that is what the screen does—it reduces while it magnifies, grinds down what it exalts into the typical.

The stories of The Stars, told over and over in those curious Hollywood addenda, the fan magazines, follow the national fairy tale: the overnight rise to fame and material wealth, to social opulence, with Sex and Beauty in headline type, and all turned out in mass quantities with great technical smoothness and ingenuity by machinery. These stories—for the screen dramas and supposedly "real" biographies have been hopelessly mixed—reveal an amazing combination of small-town familiarities, front-page magnification, and "glamorous" remoteness. The present status of the motion picture art as an art—at least in Hollywood terms—is reflected in this naïve mixing of the personal with the objective. . . .

The early gods of the screen rose out of the good old Westerns, which almost form a mythology in themselves. . . .

But the really great gods of the screen, those who step from airplanes and automobiles into mobs of palpitating women, represent unmistakably some feminine ideal of a perfect lover. Of *the* perfect lover. It took some time for this idea to flower in any single image. . . . [T]he idea of "the perfect lover" really took on definition with the appearance of Rudolph Valentino as The Sheik.

It was a very ancient ideal which Valentino so completely personified (although he gave it a distinctly contemporary aspect) and one that has proved troublesome to the hard-working males of America from the very start: that of the handsome foreigner, the suave and accomplished Latin lover with a lot of time on his hands, the other man, the eternal gigolo. The appearance of the image was perfectly timed. It came at the very hour when the fevers that followed . . . World War [I] were hottest, when women were wild to go dancing, and were all scrambling to put on sophistication. The sloe eyes, the smooth approach, the insinuating touch, led them all astray, like the call of the Pied Piper. . . .

The story of the dimming of the Valentino image and the rising of the Gable star is very much on the order of a popular novel . . . in which the plain American six-foot hero wins in the end over the more romantic (but ah, how much less sterling!) foreign prince. There is nothing foreign or morbid about the "appeal" of Clark Gable. It is native American. It goes with popcorn, horseshoe games, and B.V.D.'s. No preliminary publicity campaign was required to put over this hero. The girls themselves picked him out of his obscurity as a minor screen "heavy." Producers, still blinded doubtless by the glory of Valentino, had popularized Gable at first as "a menace"—the term was a hang-over from the over-wrought days of the Valentino craze—as a he-man cave-man lover, whose first great popular action on the screen was to give the heroine a sock on the jaw. But the girls were right when they discovered the handsome ice-man, or laundry man, or whatever the role was, and demanded that he be placed among The Stars. . . .

For surely that face—ears, eyes, dimples and all—is the face of the good-looking fellow in the next block. It is essentially a small-town face, although its owner has learned to slick back his hair and wear evening clothes. It bears the unmistakable look of the native good fellow—a Mason, an Elk, who might stand for a popular athletic coach, or be chosen as Scout Master to take the children on a camping trip. Although now groomed and made familiar with night clubs, as the movies require, this is the same fellow who used to bring his girl a box of candy every Saturday night. And Clark Gable is almost as popular with masculine as with feminine fans; for in his person, or in his screen image, the ordinary American—whether business man or garage mechanic—long famous as a good husband and a poor lover, and a big child all his days, receives the accolade from the women. . . .

In picture mythology the goddesses have always outnumbered the gods. The very fact that their chances for stardom are greater, however, makes their artistic opportunities less. More even than handsome actors, they are forced into the strict mold of accepted charm. They must all seem worthy to be loved; each be a version of "As You Desire Me." Even the most talented soon loses her appeal as an actress and becomes interesting chiefly for what she reveals and typifies. She appears as the embodiment of some ideal already loosely present in contemporary life and consciousness.

Of the early screen heroines only Mary Pickford has remained in the magnitude of a goddess. . . . The name has the same sort of familiarity as the trade mark upon any famous commercial product. What the name sums up forever is the image of a child-woman with golden curls.

It was fitting that the early days of this new art-industry should have this child-woman as its heroine. It was a pre-war ideal which Mary Pickford represented. Present for years in the national consciousness, personified in all the sweetest child heroines from Elsie Dinsmore to Pollyanna, her pretty face gave it concrete finality. This Mary Pickford image was the visible representation of those sunny mottoes and shibboleths, of the posy-framed "Smile, Just Smile" and "Be Glad" which characterized the early fair days of the century. America's Sweetheart was the embodiment of the nation's sexual and spiritual childhood. It has been said truly that a major turning point in national history was reached on the day when Mary Pickford cut her curls.

Miss Pickford at last outgrew the part. The part itself was outgrown. A smaller but also authentic goddess then more briefly ruled the screen. She was Clara Bow, the Brooklyn Bonfire.

The era of which Clara Bow was the popular symbol was known in literature as the era of the Lost Generation. But to motion-picture audiences it went by the name of the Flapper Age, the age of Flaming Youth. In this version its ideals, reduced to the lowest common denominator, became nothing more than Sex Appeal. . . .

The image was still that of a child, but of a bad child, not a good child—although of course with the proverbial movie heart of gold. The early innocence was dispelled. The Brooklyn Bonfire appealed to sailors on leave, to boys just out of the army. The child had learned the facts of life. The golden hair had turned to fiery red, the eyes were knowing, the curls were cut and tousled. The childish form had taken on seductive curves. The childish legs were provocatively shapely. (The mental age had not risen in any perceptible degree.) The child had reached the dawn of a precocious adolescence. She was running wild. . . .

All during this brief bright reign another star had been rising. It still shines with an enigmatic luster no one has quite defined. The image of Greta Garbo is the first among the goddesses of the screen with enough subtlety to puzzle anyone; and perhaps to this degree it may be taken to signify the first dawn of a coming age of the picture art-industry.

Perhaps more influence has been exerted by the personality of Greta Garbo herself than by those of earlier stars—in some ways an individuality marked to the degree of bizarre eccentricity. Nevertheless, the picture image is a representative one. Nor is it truly adult. For this goddess' strange charm analyzed proves to be that of adolescence—not the precociously and voluptuously maturing childishness of Clara Bow, but adolescence all the same, strangely childlike, still more strangely mature. The tall figure has an awkwardness sometimes crudely coltish, sometimes divinely odd with its queer off-grace. The long swinging bob of soft light hair, a variation of which is still the favorite coiffure of youth in spite of the hairdressers' efforts to supersede it, is that of a girl just past childhood. . . .

[T]he peculiar charm and power of this beauty taken as the symbol of "allure" are not those of womanhood but of neurotic adolescence crystallized and held spellbound. . . . [Garbo's] face holds intact the "mysterious" entity of emotional youth, mysterious because not yet yielded. It is a self-centered loveliness. . . .

It was altogether fitting that this more subtle quality of charm should have a foreign flavor; that America's Post-War Sweetheart should bring the conscious "allure" of the Old World. The image came into popularity along with awareness of "civilized" sophistication which was so much an outgrowth of the mingling of the Old World and the New. . . . Feminine charms were no longer open, but artful—touched with the peculiar glow of decadence in which magic lies. The luminous goddess of this day was no longer a figure of bounding health, but anaemic and almost emaciated, pale, introspective, at once adolescently boyish and ultra-female. America's new sweetheart was distinctly a neurotic girl.

Greta Garbo was the first great popular introvert heroine of a nation of blithe extroverts; and in that shift from earlier and simpler ideals lay the galvanizing shock of change, and perhaps of self-development. This image was the final reduction to the lowest common denominator—glorified of course for screen purposes—of a heroine who had appeared long ago in literature, disturbingly and variously, as the heroine of the Brontë novels, of Russian fiction, of the plays of Ibsen. She had come late to these shores but, arriving in lovely and distinguished form, had overturned the feminine ideal of the nation. The It Girl was popularly transformed into the Glamorous One. . . .

How truly are these images, in spite of their worship, the gods of America? How much are they actually and literally "build-ups"? And do they, taken all over the world to represent America and "Americanization" in the deepest sense, represent it at all? How much of this mythology is real and how much is bogus, like any over-advertised commercial product?

Examine these images and the bogus element becomes apparent at once. To create them Hollywood has misused rather than used the true power of photography. Look at the faces of the goddesses in the huge close-ups. Artificiality is so much taken for granted that it is almost accepted as a picture convention—the bleached hair, the painted eyebrows, the false eyelashes, the made-to-order mouth, the shining teeth—these are not faces but masks, created to conceal rather than to reveal. The process can be seen in the history of almost any European star brought over and "glorified" for the American screen. . . .

[L]et us look into the literature that has been built up round them; those curious contemporary documents, the fan magazines. These are all made to pattern. All are addressed to "the fans" in order to bring them into personal touch with their gods and goddesses. The personal note runs throughout—runs riot. It is in the editorials, intimate and flattering, addressed to "you and you and you," with a chummy air which says, this is *your* magazine, run only for *you,* to bring you news of *your* idols—for we, the writers, and you, the readers, are all common folk together basking in the light of these shining beings. They go into the homes of the deities, leading the readers by the hand, showing them the living rooms, the swimming pools, the playrooms, the kitchens, placing them at the tables (set for guests, menus included), almost in the beds of The Stars. . . .

But right along with this glorification goes that jeering reduction to the bottom level which runs through American journalism. The fan articles present a curious mixture of adulation and a touchy sense that these deities are no better than the rest of us. The deities are examined first to see if they are "regular"—that is, if they are going to play ball according to Hollywood rules. The first rule is, of course—tell all. You are ours, so open up. A desire to stick to professional instead of personal issues becomes "high-hat," a sign that the actor thinks himself too good to tell. Thus, one magazine spoke of the "vulgar taste" of an actress who refused to "come across" with the intimacies of her marriage. If actors hold out for the conditions under which they can do their best work they are damned with the other bludgeon adjective, "temperamental." . . .

[T]hese images which Hollywood has presented have at least the raw value of revealing where the lowest reach of the lowest common denominator seems to lie. That is how they must be read—as a broad typification, half genuine and half imposed, creative only in the tremendous influence which they exert.

With the Hollywood set-up as it is today, we cannot ask for very much else. The stories that Hollywood permits can only scrape the gaudy and tawdry surface of American life and legend. The images of its gods and goddesses are now magnified out of all proportion to their genuine value and significance. So far, American motion pictures, in spite of the skill that goes into their making, form an unconscious social document rather than an art.

Nathanael West Satirizes Hollywood Movie Sets, 1939

He asked a studio policeman where the company was shooting and was told on the back lot. He started toward it at once. A platoon of cuirassiers, big men mounted on gigantic horses, went by. He knew that they must be headed for the same set and followed them. They broke into a gallop and he was soon outdistanced.

The sun was very hot. His eyes and throat were choked with the dust thrown up by the horses' hooves and his head throbbed. The only bit of shade he could find was under an ocean liner made of painted canvas with real life boats hanging from its davits. He stood in its narrow shadow for a while, then went on toward a great forty-foot papier mâché sphinx that loomed up in the distance. He had to cross a desert to reach it, a desert that was continually being made larger by a fleet of trucks dumping white sand. He had gone only a few feet when a man with a megaphone ordered him off.

He skirted the desert, making a wide turn to the right, and came to a Western street with a plank sidewalk. On the porch of the "Last Chance Saloon" was a rocking chair. He sat down on it and lit a cigarette.

From there he could see a jungle compound with a water buffalo tethered to the side of a conical grass hut. Every few seconds the animal groaned musically. Suddenly an Arab charged by on a white stallion. He shouted at the man, but got no answer. A little while later he saw a truck with a load of snow and several malamute dogs. He shouted again. The driver shouted something back, but didn't stop.

Throwing away his cigarette, he went through the swinging doors of the saloon. There was no back to the building and he found himself in a Paris street. He followed it to its end, coming out in a Romanesque courtyard. He heard voices a short distance away and went toward them. On a lawn of fiber, a group of men and women in riding costume were picnicking. They were eating cardboard food in front of a cellophane waterfall. He started toward them to ask his way, but was stopped by a man who scowled and held up a sign—"Quiet, Please, We're Shooting." When Tod took another step forward, the man shook his fist threateningly.

Next he came to a small pond with large celluloid swans floating on it. Across one end was a bridge with a sign that read, "To Kamp Komfit." He crossed the bridge and followed a little path that ended at a Greek temple dedicated to Eros. The god himself lay face downward in a pile of old newspapers and bottles.

From the steps of the temple, he could see in the distance a road lined with Lombardy poplars. It was the one on which he had lost the cuirassiers. He pushed his way through a tangle of briars, old flats and iron junk, skirting the skeleton of a Zeppelin, a bamboo stockade, an adobe fort, the wooden horse of Troy, a flight of baroque palace stairs that started in a bed of weeds and ended against the branches of an oak, part of the Fourteenth Street Elevated station, a Dutch windmill, the bones of a dinosaur, the upper half of the Merrimac, a corner of a Mayan temple, until he finally reached the road.

He was out of breath. He sat down under one of the poplars on a rock made of brown plaster and took off his jacket. There was a cool breeze blowing and he soon felt more comfortable. . . .

A hundred yards from where Tod was sitting a man in a derby hat leaned drowsily against the gilded poop of a Venetian barque and peeled an apple. Still farther on, a char-woman on a stepladder was scrubbing with soap and water the face of a Buddha thirty feet high.

He left the road and climbed across the spine of the hill to look down on the other side. From there he could see a ten-acre field of cockleburs spotted with clumps of sunflowers and wild gum. In the center of the field was a gigantic pile of sets, flats and props. While he watched, a ten-ton truck added another load to it. This was the final dumping ground. He thought of Janvier's "Sargasso Sea." Just as that imaginary body of water was a history of civilization in the form of a marine junkyard, the studio lot was one in the form of a dream dump. A Sargasso of the imagination! And the dump grew continually, for there wasn't a dream afloat somewhere which wouldn't sooner or later turn up on it, having first been made photographic by plaster, canvas, lath and paint. Many boats sink and never reach the Sargasso, but no dream ever entirely disappears. Somewhere it troubles some unfortunate person and some day, when that person has been sufficiently troubled, it will be reproduced on the lot.

When he saw a red glare in the sky and heard the rumble of cannon, he knew it must be Waterloo. From around a bend in the road trotted several cavalry regiments. They wore casques and chest armor of black cardboard and carried long horse pistols in their saddle holsters. They were Victor Hugo's soldiers. He had worked on some of the drawings for their uniforms himself, following carefully the descriptions in "Les Miserables."

He went in the direction they took. Before long he was passed by the men of Lefebvre-Desnouttes, followed by a regiment of gendarmes d'élite, several companies of chasseurs of the guard and a flying detachment of Rimbaud's lancers.

They must be moving up for the disastrous attack on La Haite Santée. . . .

The sound of cannon was becoming louder all the time and the red fan in the sky more intense. He could smell the sweet, pungent odor of blank powder. It might be over before he could get there. He started to run. When he topped a rise after a sharp bend in the road, he found a great plain below him covered with early nineteenth-century troops, wearing all the gay and elaborate uniforms that used to please him so much when he was a child and spent long hours looking at the soldiers in an old dictionary. At the far end of the field, he could see an enormous hump around which the English and their allies were gathered. It was Mont St. Jean and they were getting ready to defend it gallantly. It wasn't quite finished, however, and swarmed with grips, property men, set dressers, carpenters and painters.

Tod stood near a eucalyptus tree to watch, concealing himself behind a sign that read, "'Waterloo'—A Charles H. Grotenstein Production." Nearby a youth in a carefully torn horse guard's uniform was being rehearsed in his lines by one of the assistant directors.

"Vive l'Empereur!" the young man shouted, then clutched his breast and fell forward dead. The assistant director was a hard man to please and made him do it over and over again.

In the center of the plain, the battle was going ahead briskly. Things looked tough for the British and their allies. The Prince of Orange commanding the center, Hill the right and Picton the left wing, were being pressed hard by the veteran French. The desperate and intrepid Prince was in an especially bad spot. Tod heard him cry hoarsely above the din of battle, shouting to the Hollande-Belgians, "Nassau! Brunswick! Never retreat!" Nevertheless, the retreat began. Hill, too, fell back. The French killed General Picton with a ball through the head and he returned to his dressing room. Alten was put to the sword and also retired. The colors of the Lunenberg battalion, borne by a prince of the family of Deux-Ponts, were captured by a famous child star in the uniform of a Parisian drummer boy. The Scotch Grays were destroyed and went to change into another uniform. Ponsonby's heavy dragoons were also cut to ribbons. Mr. Grotenstein would have a large bill to pay at the Western Costume Company.

Neither Napoleon nor Wellington was to be seen. In Wellington's absence, one of the assistant directors, a Mr. Crane, was in command of the allies. He reinforced his center with one of Chasse's brigades and one of Wincke's. He supported these with infantry from Brunswick, Welsh foot, Devon yeomanry and Hanoverian light horse with oblong leather caps and flowing plumes of horsehair.

For the French, a man in a checked cap ordered Milhaud's cuirassiers to carry Mont St. Jean. With their sabers in their teeth and their pistols in their hands, they charged. It was a fearful sight.

The man in the checked cap was making a fatal error. Mont St. Jean was unfinished. The paint was not yet dry and all the struts were not in place. Because of the thickness of the cannon smoke, he had failed to see that the hill was still being worked on by property men, grips and carpenters.

It was the classic mistake, Tod realized, the same one Napoleon had made. Then it had been wrong for a different reason. The Emperor had ordered the cuirassiers to charge Mont St. Jean not knowing that a deep ditch was hidden at its foot to trap his heavy cavalry. The result had been disaster for the French; the beginning of the end.

This time the same mistake had a different outcome. Waterloo instead of being the end of the Grand Army, resulted in a draw. Neither side won, and it would have to be fought over again the next day. Big losses, however, were sustained by the insurance company in workmen's compensation. The man in the checked cap was sent to the dog house by Mr. Grotenstein just as Napoleon was sent to St. Helena.

When the front rank of Milhaud's heavy division started up the slope of Mont St. Jean, the hill collapsed. The noise was terrific. Nails screamed with agony as they pulled out of joists. The sound of ripping canvas was like that of little children whimpering. Lath and scantling snapped as though they were brittle bones. The whole hill folded like an enormous umbrella and covered Napoleon's army with painted cloth.

It turned into a rout. The victors of Bersina, Leipsic, Austerlitz, fled like schoolboys who had broken a pane of glass. "Sauve qui peut!" they cried, or, rather "Scram!"

The armies of England and her allies were too deep in scenery to flee. They had to wait for the carpenters and ambulances to come up. The men of the gallant Seventy-Fifth Highlanders were lifted out of the wreck with block and tackle. They were carted off by the stretcher-bearers, still clinging bravely to their claymores.

 E S S A Y S

Many books have been written about the film industry, as the bibliography for this chapter indicates. Few of these studies, however, have examined the relationship between the movies and the changing contours of American society and culture. The most insightful analysis of this relationship is found in *Screening Out the Past* by Lary May, a historian at the University of Minnesota. In the first essay, drawn from this book, May evaluates earlier explanations as to why an industry that had originated on the East Coast eventually found a home in southern California. He concludes that neither the state's famed weather and scenery nor the desire of early filmmakers to escape the control of Thomas A. Edison (inventor of the movie camera) was as important as California's lifestyle—a way of life emphasizing the pursuit of physical and psychological well-being through leisure, material acquisition, and freedom from constraint.

In the second essay, Leslie Fishbein of Rutgers University discusses how, despite its intent to depict social realism and to inculcate morality, the film industry's products bore little relationship to reality. In films about prostitutes and the sexually liberated young women known as "flappers," didactic messages about the ultimate rewards of feminine chastity coexisted with demonstrations of how "modern" women could survive and enjoy themselves in "wicked" cities. Thus, Hollywood's moral crusade was shot through with ambiguities. Be sure to compare this essay to the second essay in Chapter 8 to see how women reformers and Hollywood filmmakers perceived the social status and moral standing of women.

Hollywood and the California Dream

LARY MAY

[By the 1920s,] the motion picture had become a major urban institution for the middle class. And the sheer number and size of movie houses reflected the overwhelming popularity of the mature movie industry. In New York City, ninety-seven nickelodeons held licenses in 1900. All observers agreed that they were located either in the cheap business sections or in the poorer amusement centers, and usually frequented by men. Nine years later there were 400, including several "store fronts" which were hastily converted shops showing "flickers" on a screen. Seating capacity was limited to 400. By 1912, movies could show to a 1,000-plus audience, and more luxurious, classically designed theaters began to spread up and down main thoroughfares, catering to men and women of all classes. Over the next fifteen years, the number of cinemas grew to over eight hundred, averaging 1,200 seats each, or one for every six people in the entire metropolis. . . .

[T]his expansion reflected the creation of America's first *mass* amusement—but it was clearly geared toward middle-class aspirations. . . . [T]he 1908 patrons were workers; by 1912 25 percent of the audience was clerical and 5 percent was business class of both sexes. . . . [H]igh school and college graduates went most often, although they comprised only one fourth of the population in 1920. Likewise, people with higher incomes went more often than workers or farmers; and those under thirty-five comprised the bulk of the audience. Men and women attended in equal numbers; but females were the ones who read the fan magazines, wrote letters to their idols, and knew the film plots by heart. . . .

[M]oviegoing was unquestionably an urban phenomenon. The theaters were overwhelmingly situated in cities, at a time when half the nation's population lived in rural areas. There were 28,000 theaters in 1928; and over half of them were in the industrial centers of New York, Illinois, Pennsylvania, Ohio, and California. The major cities in these states contained most of the large luxury cinemas. San Francisco, New York, Chicago, and Los Angeles each had from five to eight hundred theaters, averaging over 1,000 seats each, or one for every five to seven people. These movie houses stayed open seven days a week, twelve hours a day, while those in the small towns were only open on weekends. . . .

In twentieth-century America, . . . movies and mass culture were key elements in the transition from nineteenth-century values of strict behavior toward greater moral experimentation. As the economy consolidated, the leisure arena preserved a sense of freedom and mobility. Both on the screen and in the theater, moviegoers tasted the life of the rich as it was brought within reach of the masses, breaking down the class divisions of the past. Here was a revitalized frontier of freedom, where Americans might sanction formerly forbidden pleasures through democratized consumption. . . .

[T]his experience did not end when the patrons exited [the movie theaters]. They could see that the message of the movie and its palace was alive and well in the last great component of the motion picture universe: Hollywood. . . .

To grasp the significance of this West Coast creation, we have to first confront earlier explanations of why the movie industry came to Southern California. A generation of film scholars have offered two basic reasons. One was that the climate was ideal for film making. In this region, Mediterranean balmy weather made it possible to film outdoors all year round, without the hindrance of snow or rain. Moreover, the area included deserts, mountains, and seashore, all near by. The second argument claims that, to escape Edison's trust, independents moved to the far end of the continent where they could flee quickly into Mexico if confronted with court subpoenas or demands for their pirated cameras.

Yet on examination, neither of these factors can explain the move. Film makers had survived Eastern weather for over twenty years, going to Florida, the Caribbean, or other winter filming locations including California, if sunny weather was required. . . . More recent scholars offer an alternative to these views by pointing out that economic factors pushed the industry westward. Though this is certainly part of the reason, it still does not explain why it took so long for moviemakers to see their interests in moving from east to west. No, something else was happening in Los Angeles besides escaping winters, trusts, and high costs.

To fathom this problem, we must realize that Hollywood emerged relatively late—over twenty years after Edison invented the [movie] camera, and over a decade and a half after the movies acquired a mass market. In retrospect, it is also clear that the West Coast production site would become more than merely a place to make films. Fan magazines, newspapers, and movies themselves would spotlight the comings and goings of movie stars—a life-style that was dramatically different from that of the nineteenth or even early twentieth century. Shortly before there was a Hollywood, this imagery had just begun to be projected on the nation's screens, catering to the tastes of the newly found middle-class audience adjusting to the corporate order and a new morality. The new code generated the promise that if immigrants, as well as those rebelling from Victorianism, had money and white skin, the consumer ideal would be available to them. Another related phenomenon was the audience's demand to see this cultural mixing made real. It was not enough to see it on the screen, or to touch it in the movie house. Stars had to make the happy ending an extension of their own lives, for fans had to see that their idols could make it a reality. Was it not possible, then, that profits could be enhanced by creating a modern utopia where the dream could come off the screen and into real life? . . .

As Americans turned toward leisure, it was appropriate that the film industry moved to Los Angeles. Other Western and Southern cities grew at the same pace, had an agreeable political environment, land, climate and labor situation; indeed, winter studios had been established in these places. Yet only Los Angeles offered the vision of a new West. This was crucial for the image the movies wanted to create. For ever since the mid-nineteenth century the frontier symbolized freedom from the hierarchical, industrial East. In both political and popular literature, the West appeared to hold the promise of a future democracy without greed or class enmity. Yet at a time when the dream of independence seemed to be receding in the wake of a rising corporate order and class conflict, anxious Americans might look to Los Angeles, the farthest point on the frontier, to recreate the vision of a virgin land. Here was a city with no physical remains of an Anglo-Saxon tradition, where individuals could once again be free of Eastern difficulties. As Frank Fenton wrote in *A Place in the Sun,*

> This was a lovely makeshift city. Even the trees and plants did not belong here. They came, like the people, from far places, some familiar, some exotic, all wanderers of one sort or another seeking peace or fortune or the last frontier, or a thousand dreams of escape.

In the Mediterranean climate, the twentieth century quest for freedom from the past now took a romantic turn. Ever since the late nineteenth century, Americans coming into the area were struck by three things: the Spanish heritage, the climate, and the lack of industry. In this wide expanse of vacant land, evidences of the Spanish were visible all around. Besides the Mexican population, and the proximity of that Latin country, the Spanish-style architecture of haciendas and missions spread a romantic aura over the landscape. When this was coupled with the mild weather, and proximity to beaches, mountains, and desert, the city offered a powerful drawing card to potential settlers. With no heavy manufacturing center or tenements, the population was less densely settled than in Eastern urban centers. Planners encouraged this through zoning and developing outlying tracts and linking them together with streetcar lines. In the unique urban-suburban mixture that resulted, developers lined the streets with imported palm trees. Boosters were careful to point out, however, that this romance and fair climate was "mediterranean"—the center of a sophisticated civilization—not "tropical" like savage lands. As one of the city's major designers expressed it, Los Angeles should not be dissipating, but "natural—for here nature and the trees are the thing. It should invite family outings, lovemaking, and a forgetfulness that cities are at hand." . . .

Little wonder that movie makers were drawn to this "man made, giant improvisation." If "there was never a region so unlikely to become a vast metropolitan area as Southern California," as its most perceptive historian, Carey McWilliams, noted, what better place for the movies? Besides the economic and political environment, it seemed an ideal locale where creative imaginations could flourish. Adolph Zukor led the way when in 1913 he brought his Famous Players in Famous Plays to Los Angeles. In his company was William de Mille, a noted Broadway producer and playwright who was captivated by the traditional imagery of the West. As de Mille crossed the Rockies, he found himself becoming "younger," for in the "new state" of California men could still escape the hierarchy and traditions of the East. In addition to "choosing one's inheritance," de Mille also saw that amid the sunshine and beauty, one could find a new life of freedom. Charles Chaplin, fresh from the slums of London in 1913, was even more enthralled. Los Angeles appeared truly the "land of the future, a paradise of sunshine, orange groves, vineyards, and palm trees. I was embued with it." Still another could link this new frontier to the old imagery, and see it now open to the children of immigrants like himself. As Jesse Lasky read a western tale on a train going to the land of sunshine, he wrote,

> I became again a child at my grandfather's knee. . . . And every time I glanced out of the train window at the rolling prairies, the mountains, the desert, I saw the vast panorama of sky and earth forming a backdrop for those heroic souls whose first wagon train actually took much of the same route three quarters of a century before . . . a migration but for which I myself would not have been born in my beloved California. Superimposing the past on the present . . . was an emotional, almost mystical experience.

Film moguls brought this "mystical" atmosphere directly into their new studios, which differed dramatically from the ascetic and mundane production sites of the East. In New York, Chicago, Philadelphia, and Long Island, the studios sat primarily in downtown business sections or manufacturing areas. Producers used cheaply made warehouses and factories which were barren looking and almost indistinguishable from the surrounding commercial or industrial enterprises. . . . In contrast . . . the modern corporate studios in Los Angeles created an atmosphere where moral experimentation could blossom.

Perhaps the best example of this was Universal City, built in 1913 by Carl Laemmle, the theater owner and former clothing salesman from Chicago. Surrounded by the hills and palm trees of the San Fernando Valley, the white, Spanish-styled studio buildings glowed in the sun. Touching base with romanticism, the administration building followed the Spanish revival style. Yet it reflected a new America. Appropriately, Laemmle called his weekly column in the 1915 trade journal the "Melting Pot," for he glorified the Universal stars who rose up the ladder of success, shed their ethnic or Victorian pasts, and assumed a modern, healthy personality. . . .

Assembly line techniques and specialization encouraged high production, and yielded seventy films a year. Much of this work was routine; however, there were high compensations. Studios capitalized in the millions offered salaries for top executives and stars ranging between $100,000 and $900,000 yearly. Opulent dressing rooms and offices mirrored one's rank in the organizational hierarchy. In spite of labor strikes in the late teens and early twenties, which the city of Los Angeles helped the studios to quell, executives claimed that all employees had life, health, and retirement insurance. In addition, as early as 1914, Universal provided a veritable leisure paradise for its workers in the plant itself, complete with a free gymnasium, tennis courts, a steam room, and pool—with equal access, presumably, for all.

More than most industries, the studio also had a personnel turnover which suggested that the "new life" was open to youth and talent. Clearly, the studios existed in the corporate world, but they blended modern and traditional business styles. In other firms, upward mobility by no means ceased; but here, fame and success could happen quickly, without long apprenticeship or professional training. Film relied heavily on imagination, rather than heavy investments in elaborate machinery or scientific processes. After all, it took only a story, talent, and a camera to make a movie. But without the personal touch in advertising and selling, there could be no profits. Since the product also had to be in touch with the latest tastes and psychological needs, it was an ideal place for individuals to make it on their own ideas and talents. Then, with the children of immigrants in power, movie making appeared to offer a place where all newcomers could rise on ability, without having to face discriminatory employers or a rigid seniority system. Precisely because a volatile market encouraged mobility in the midst of bureaucratic hierarchy, one noted observer could describe the modern movie industry in nineteenth-century terms:

> the gold rush was probably the only other set up where so many people could hit the jack pot and the skids together. It has become a modern industry without losing that crazy feeling of a boom town.

Yet this boom town opened to a much wider group of aspirants than the older variety. For above all, Hollywood was an urban mobility ideal which had a much broader base than the traditional Protestant middle classes. Coming into the Los Angeles studios to create a modern life to spread to the nation's cities were a new breed of people. . . . [M]ost of the movie creators came from those places where the film audience was largest. Over two-thirds of the American film makers were born in the 1890s in metropolitan areas, compared to less than one-third of their non-movie peers.

Over half of the writers, directors, editors, and players came from urban centers containing over 100,000 people in 1890, at a time when there were only twenty-eight such areas in the entire nation. The majority of the remainder came from Canadian or European cities. Thus, with five-sixths of the movie people coming from cities when most of the nation was still rural, they had a head start on their audience, and were ideally qualified to create, propagate, and live a vision of modern urban life. . . .

[T]his was a young cosmopolitan group. With the Jewish moguls on top, and a large ethnic component among the rank and file, the creative personnel were already one step removed from the Victorian restraints holding earlier film makers. As the middle-class audience groped for ways to absorb foreign exoticism and youth, this collection of people was well suited to serve these needs as well. Those who created the aura—producers, directors, cinematographers, and set designers—came largely from European or Canadian backgrounds. . . . Those who provided the models—actors and actresses—were overwhelmingly young. Two-thirds of them were under thirty-five. Moreover, three-fourths of the industry's female performers were under twenty-five. This suggests that the youth cult so necessary for uplifting "foreign" elements concentrated most heavily on women, who were responsible for making sensuality innocent. . . .

The industry's employees looked to Los Angeles for a vision of the new life, which included foreign touches filtered through an ever-widening Anglo-Saxon lens. One way to gauge this is to look at the writers who actually formulated the stories. Over 90 percent of them were born in America and had either higher education or journalism experience. This suggests an affluent group, since less than 10 percent of the population during the teens went to college, and publishing was not usually a commoner's trade. This was also the group most likely to include morally emancipated women, a factor also reflected in the industry. During the twenties, women comprised from one-third to one-half of the screen writers. Although their numbers declined sharply in the following decades, they held prominent and influential positions during the early Hollywood heyday. In 1920, the forty top female writers were of middle class Anglo-Saxon stock. None were of poor or worker origin. Like their male counterparts, most were college educated or had publishing backgrounds. Maturing in the Victorian twilight, they were captivated by urban life. From the memoirs of several, we can see that they were in the vanguard of moral experimentation, forging into dress reform, new sexual styles, and consumption. It is no accident that these forty females created over seventy percent of the stories written by women. Their plots overwhelmingly revolved around heroines like themselves. . . .

The movie personnel were thus well prepared to participate in one of the most striking features of modern filmdom. When the large contingent of urbanites, youthful players, foreigners, and women scenarists left studios like Universal, they went home to "Hollywood." Before 1916, Hollywood had been nothing more than a sleepy community of orange groves. But after the industry moved west, it came to symbolize the fruits of the screen and the Los Angeles paradise. It was not the locale of the studios; rather it was an almost mythic place where the movie folk spent money on personal expression. This consumption encouraged individual creativity and freedom, while it also served as a mark of success. A shrewd observer of the industry, producer William de Mille, saw that the movie people's "conspicuous consumption" gave status to an often routine job, and reflected on the "company that paid you." As huge sums of money rolled in, the stars—who after all did not make a tangible product—used spending to validate their almost magical success. Mary Pickford saw her vast salary increases as the way to prove that she really had made it. Charles Chaplin had similar emotions, but also envisaged extravagance as an exciting break from bourgeois restraints. He recalled that in 1914,

> I was reconciled to wealth, but not to the use of it. The money I earned was legendary, a symbol in figures, for I had never actually seen it. I therefore had to do something to prove I had it. So I procured a secretary, a valet, a car, a chauffeur. Walking by the showroom one day, I noticed a seven passenger Locomobile . . . the transaction was simple; it meant writing my name on a piece of paper. So I said wrap it up.

Because the consumption allure was the key to the Hollywood image, the star's life took on more than a private importance. In contrast to earlier stage personalities, film idols presented national models as leisure experts. As early as 1915, fan magazines showed how the star's domain reflected the Southern California style. In a city that contained few monuments or buildings reflecting the nineteenth-century Anglo-Saxon culture, there seemed to be a release from the restraint of tradition. Amid a virgin land of constant romance, it was easier to create a life-style frowned upon in the East. . . . Freed from any nearby reminders of social responsibility, in areas cleansed through vice crusades, the stars could create a new, uplifted life without the inhibitions of the past. Usually homes drew on styles of European, African, or Asian aristocracy, reflecting not only high culture, but the quest for a more exotic life. Before the [First World] War, they were stately and classical. Always they were opulent, and mirrored cultivation and success.

A double-barreled aspiration came from this model. To the ambitious Anglo-Saxon urbanite, it suggested that achievement might yield a release from Victorian asceticism. To the equally ambitious person of immigrant stock, it suggested that upward mobility was no longer aimed toward a temperate Anglo-Saxon norm. Rather, here was a cosmopolitan eclecticism, though still dominated by American values, fit for the new order. . . .

[O]ne reason why ordinary people could identify with the stars' life was that the stars did not have the authority the industrial titans had. True, Hollywood was a "society" community setting the pace for modern life. Yet, in replacing the industrial titans of New York or Chicago, or the local gentry, as the nation's new aristocracy, the movie folk could be universally loved because they were not socially powerful: they were purely a status group. Unlike politicians or manufacturers, they did not hold authority over large groups of employees or constituents. Studio executives did manage large firms and were involved in politics; but they were not in the limelight. The force of the stars as popular idols lay in their leisure, rather than work lives. Much of their mystique was that they presumably rose from meager beginnings to become models of success. Yet on their jobs, they had no control over fellow employees; they, too, had to answer to the boss. Nor did they hold political clout. During the first four decades of the century, none of the industry's rank and file served on a Los Angeles school board, or held civic office or commission. Power would have been antithetical to their image as playful, friendly people.

More importantly, the stars offered a number of solutions to modern problems and a reformulation of dominant myths for the twentieth century. When combined with the Hollywood life, the total added up to a clear mosaic. For one thing, it showed Americans how to adjust to the corporate order. Starting as early as the mid-teens, Hollywood became an institution which offered viable proof that the new economy could be a blessing rather than a burden. In the long periods of prosperity during the late nineteenth and early twentieth centuries, a number of businessmen, reformers, and intellectuals believed that America's "excess production" would have to be exported abroad. Behind this was the quest for a larger market. Yet a potentially large market existed internally, provided the purchasing power of the masses could be expanded. Rarely was this course followed, in part due to fears of traditionalists like Josiah Strong, who believed that unleashing abundance could destroy Victorian principles as well as the work ethic of the laboring classes. For should the workers gain the luxury that was beyond their grasp, presumably they would have no further motivation to toil. But through the late teens, Hollywood showed how this scarcity psychology could be overcome, and consumption become a positive force. Rather than luxury eroding the achievement drive, or a society based on open opportunity, it flowed into rising expectations. For as success took on new rewards, as the stars became consumption idols, excess production had a purpose. Farsighted manufacturers like the film moguls could make large profits by stimulating the purchasing power of the prosperous. In this way luxuries became necessities. Abundance, therefore, would not undercut a class order based on competition or civic concerns; rather, it would give it a different emphasis.

At the same time, Hollywood kept alive a key cultural myth. As the nineteenth century drew to a close, many Americans realized that the frontier was gone, and perhaps with it went one of the main utopian aspirations in American life. For nearly a century, people had kept alive the hope that sectional divisions, or class conflicts created by industrialization, might be eased by the existence of a safety valve. On the far frontier, people could start out anew and establish an egalitarian order, free from the hierarchies of Europe and the East. Presumably this would serve as a model for the future and set the tone for all of America. In the late nineteenth century, however, the rise of big business and the influx of "new immigrants" intensified conflicts that had already been present. Heightening the sense of chaos was women's increasing restlessness concerning their place in society, and the emergence of an industrial elite with unprecedented power. The need for an outlet seemed even more urgent than before. Yet now the frontier was conquered, and the promise of an egalitarian order seemed to vanish. Americans at the turn of the century asked themselves: would men and women be able to find personal fulfillment in a conflict-ridden, hierarchical society that had spread all over the continent?

A partial answer to this bubbled up from the masses and poured out of the popular culture. Initially, it seemed that the moral revolution would subvert the home and class order even further. Yet the motion picture firms growing up after 1914 soon showed the way out of this dilemma, without returning to Victorianism. It was not just that they catered to audience needs. After 1914, the film industry itself was part of the corporate order, and film makers created a style to ease the pressures of the era that they were also feeling. . . . [T]he Victorian synthesis gave way to a less puritanical culture more amenable to non-Anglo Saxons, provided they had white skin. Consumption on a mass level showed that resentment of the rich could be lessened, and that women could find happiness in an expanded home. The mobility ideal of the stars, theater palaces, and Hollywood thus offered a new twist on the traditional success ethic: men and women would work for money to buy the trappings of the good life. With this reborn West, the Hollywood frontier promised to solve some of the major public problems facing reformers, and thus set the stage for the culmination of the consumer culture in the twenties.

Hollywood Joins the Moral Crusade, 1910–1930

LESLIE FISHBEIN

Many critics have labeled Hollywood a "dream factory," claiming that its filmmakers purvey escapism and mindless entertainment. However, an examination of films produced during the first three decades of the twentieth century that treat "fallen women," and particularly the prostitute, reveal that such films often advanced claims to social realism and were instructive and moralistic in nature. Ironically, these films bore little relationship to reality despite their claims. Instead they reflected deeply held cultural myths whose vitality was sustained by desire rather than truth.

During the late nineteenth century, social-purity crusaders attempted to end prostitution and to redeem American society by ridding it of sin and corruption. These reformers naively believed that women could lead a successful crusade to elevate men to a single standard of sexual purity, namely, the ideal of premarital chastity and marital fidelity that society had imposed upon women far more rigidly than upon men. In the early twentieth century, purity reformers came to demand that the state intervene to end "white slavery" and that the segregated vice districts long tolerated by city police

From Robert B. Toplin, ed., *Hollywood as Mirror: Changing Views of "Outsiders" and "Enemies" in American Movies,* Reprinted with permission of Greenwood Publishing Group, Inc., Westport, CT. Copyright © 1993 by Greenwood Press.

be shut down in the interest of urban reform. Purity reform thus served as a means whereby city dwellers could reaffirm their confidence in traditional morality, now buttressed by the police power of the state, in an era in which the power of religion to enforce morality had waned in an increasingly secular society.

The antiprostitution crusade derived its energy from the cultural crisis that accompanied the transformation of the United States after the closing of the frontier in 1890 through the end of World War I from a largely rural-minded society characterized by its adherence to the Protestant work ethic and a rigid standard of personal morality to a predominantly urban society oriented toward consumption, a secular way of life, and moral relativism. This response to prostitution revealed popular confusion and bewilderment with respect to modernization and to the growing acceptance of cosmopolitan values, as American purity crusaders rejected the European approach of tolerating prostitution as an inevitable social evil and regulating it for sanitary purposes. American reformers instead clung nostalgically to traditional moral values in the belief that all moral values were prescribed by God, and, therefore, absolute and eternal. The antiprostitution crusade allowed people who were discontent with modernization and urbanization to vent their diverse frustrations by targeting a single socially acceptable issue. . . .

The first films to treat prostitution . . . tended to emphasize themes of seduction, coercion, and betrayal deriving from public paranoia over white slavery. The[y] . . . reflected the assumption of the cult of true womanhood with its celebration of feminine purity, piety, passivity, and domesticity, championing the virtues of traditional womanhood in an era in which the contradictions in the cult were becoming increasingly apparent and in which a new concept of womanhood, more economically independent, less sexually reticent, was emerging. . . . Despite the fact that American filmmakers paid tribute to the cult's virtues, presumably championing feminine innocence, they simultaneously produced films that served as warnings to the ignorant, films whose purpose was to sophisticate the innocent by acquainting them with the perils of urban vice, thereby protecting the purity of women by ending their innocence via filmic enlightenment. . . .

The only redemption possible for women who have been tempted or seduced is rescue by timely male intervention prior to ravishment. In D. W. Griffith's *The Musketeers of Pig Alley* (1912), a film whose claim to authenticity was grounded in its affinity to contemporary journalistic exposés of police corruption and urban gang life and in its use of actual locations in New York slums, the Little Lady, played by Lillian Gish, is restored to the sanctity and security of family life with her struggling musician husband when Snapper, a young streetwise hoodlum, prevents her from taking a drugged drink preferred [*sic*] by a dance-hall panderer. In *The Salvation of Nance O'Shaughnessy* (1914) an unsophisticated East Side working girl seeking relief from boredom in a local dance hall innocently falls prey to the snares of traffickers in vice until rescued from temptation by Sandy McCarthy, a fellow Celt, "pureminded and fresh from the country," who floors the evil proprietor of the adjoining bar and guides Nance to the purity of the outside air where they pledge to wed each other. These films assumed that true women were not sufficiently shrewd or observant to resist sexual slavery. The films also implied that respectable women were ignorant of the hazards associated with the saloon and the cabaret, that it was their innocence that imperiled them. Hence there was a need for films that would instruct them regarding the dangers to the unwary. . . .

The American film industry responded to the popular panic over prostitution that followed in the wake of the urban vice commission reports in the early 1910s by creating its own distinctive genre, a spate of white slavery films with lurid titles intended to reflect the grim realities revealed by the reports: *Port of Missing Women, The Lure of New York, Smashing the Vice Trust, The Thorns of the Great White Way*, and *The Serpent of the Slums*. . . .

Because the filmic medium has an inherent need to dramatize and simplify a complex social problem, filmmakers perpetuated the stereotypes of prostitution already accepted by purity reformers and vice commissions, thereby reducing prostitution to white slavery rather than examining the problem in socioeconomic terms. Reformers welcomed such films because movies reached a wider audience than fiction or the legitimate stage and lacked the drawbacks of these alternative media: the opportunities for unguided introspection offered to adolescents by literature and the possibilities of exceedingly graphic representations of sexual material upon the stage. By invoking the endorsement by civic and religious leaders of the films' socially uplifting aims, interjecting moralizing remarks, and claiming to base themselves on the truths revealed by the vice commission reports, these films were able to evade censorship and to present sexually suggestive material without fear of incurring public wrath.

These white slavery films shared the assumptions of middle-class reformers that prostitution involved the corruption or coercion of innocent women by evil men who thereby spread urban vices across the nation. The films also argued that white slavery's primary victims were country lasses and immigrant girls and that the working-class saloon in immigrant districts and ethnic support of political corruption, symbolized by the boss rule of Tammany Hall, shared responsibility for the sullying of national purity by urban vice. In fact, Ruth . . . Rosen notes that most prostitutes tended to come from urban areas or small towns rather than from rural settings. Although *The Inside of the White Slave Traffic* shows an immigrant wom[a]n receiving her education in vice and *Traffic in Souls* depicts two Swedish girls duped into entering the parlor house because they believe it to be a Swedish employment agency, Rosen states that foreign-born women were underrepresented in the prostitution population, in part because "new immigrants" sought to recreate in America the strict family and community controls that had existed in their native lands. The film that pioneered the genre and achieved immense popular success, *Traffic in Souls,* claimed to have been based on the long-awaited report on prostitution by the Bureau of Social Hygiene, *Commercialized Prostitution in New York City*. In fact, the report made only incidental mention of white slavery and instead provoked controversy by linking extensive prostitution inextricably with rampant police corruption. Robert C. Allen has noted: "Far from being based on the report, *Traffic in Souls* actually contradicts it. White slavery is seen in the film as a highly efficient business enterprise of immense proportions, and it is the police, led by the incorruptible Officer Burke, who expose the slavers and save Mary's sister." The film posited a problem—an international white-slave syndicate—of immense proportions and offered as a solution only individual rescue, a response that was clearly both inadequate and inappropriate. More fundamentally, white slavery films assumed that only coercion or duplicity could impel a wom[a]n to enter prostitution, but Rosen demonstrates that "the vast majority of women who practiced prostitution were not dragged, drugged, or clubbed into involuntary servitude," that for most women it represented a bleak choice among rather unpalatable alternatives.

If the earliest films did not accurately reflect social reality, or even the conclusions of the vice commission reports in their distorted perspective of that reality, the films did echo the values and concerns of purity crusaders, sharing their fundamental distrust of the modern urban culture in which a new womanhood was emerging. Films like *The Downward Path* and *The Fate of the Artist's Model* imply that the respectable American home had proven inadequate to the task of protecting the chastity of its daughters. . . .

The white slavery tracts and the films based upon them embodied many of the contradictions of the Progressive Era. They served to humanize the prostitute, to elicit public sympathy for her as a victim of socioeconomic forces beyond her control rather than as a sinner, but, though these polemics defended the dignity of womanhood, they simultaneously portrayed women as helpless and passive dupes of men. . . .

The white-slave narratives and the films based upon them idealized the morality of the country and characterized the city as evil and degrading, yet they simultaneously provided information about the city and guidance in mastering its perils that would aid the very migration of young women to the city that these works so feared and denounced. These early films claimed to be exposés of sordid social reality and to be instructive and moralistic in nature, yet clearly their cultural function was not to objectively describe reality, but rather to create socially meaningful myths about prostitution.

In the late 1910s and early 1920s the prevailing cultural myths shifted as the United States definitely became an urban nation . . . and witnessed a sexual revolution and the emergence of a new womanhood symbolized by the flapper. . . . America's growing cosmopolitanism was accomplished by a revolution in manners and morals. . . . However, the sexual revolt associated with the flapper was more symbolic than real. Among college women, for example, sexual intercourse could be condoned when the couple planned to wed, thereby implicitly invoking love and the seriousness of their commitment to sanction sexual activity. Although respectable young women might be sexually active, thus blurring the once rigid distinction from the fallen, this sexual activity was hardly promiscuous. Instead, it was oriented toward the most traditional of goals, marriage and motherhood.

In this milieu a new genre of films treating prostitution began to emerge. Instead of viewing fallen women simply as passive victims of male lust and greed, creatures doomed from their first lapse from virtue, these new films argued that fallen women could be redeemed. These films reflected the greater freedom in manners and morals claimed by the "new woman" of the prewar period. . . .

[T]hese new films revealed that prostitutes and mistresses could be noble creatures despite their sexual lapses. No longer were these films sentimental and rather formulaic melodramas, parables intended to instruct the unwary; instead, by the early 1920s it was possible to produce occasional films of genuine moral complexity. In 1923 Charles Chaplin wrote and directed *A Woman of Paris,* the tale of an innocent country girl who becomes a wealthy Parisian mistress after she mistakenly believes that her sweetheart John has abandoned her on the eve of their elopement. Marie becomes the kept woman of Pierre Revel, the wealthiest man in Paris; as a reviewer in *Exceptional Photoplays* noted, their relationship is portrayed as involving authentic affection and mutual respect. By making Marie's fall the product of mishap rather than of treachery or choice, by granting her dignity even as she lives in sin, and by showing her worthy of redemption because her love for John is as genuine as that of his own mother, Chaplin created a film that raised more moral issues than it sought to resolve.

Just as Marie is redeemed by the purity of her love in *A Woman of Paris,* so too is the heroine saved in the 1923 film version of Eugene O'Neill's *Anna Christie,* starring Blanche Sweet. Abandoned by her father because he is enthralled by "that old devil sea," raped by a demented cousin in the country home of relatives to whom her father has sent her for her own protection, Anna is thrust into a life of prostitution in order to survive. Like *A Woman of Paris, Anna Christie* shunned moral absolutism in its tale of a harlot's progress. The Ince Studio publicity release gushingly explained the film's startling sophistication: "The age which has produced flappers, social and political revolutions, gland rejuvenation, radios, the jazz craze and world-wide unrest no longer can be coddled with fairy tales." Moreover, the studio claimed that this "picture of a modern Magdalene . . . tells a story of retribution and redemption without moralizing." The bittersweet ending does permit a former prostitute to find solace in marriage with a seaman like her father. While Anna is redeemed by Mat's willingness to wed her with full knowledge of her previous life, the fact that in a drunken stuper [*sic*] Mat has signed on a cruise on the *Londonderry* bound for Cape Town means that Anna's marriage will commence with the same abandonment that had plagued her mother's and that her child's fate may be the same as her own. *Anna Christie* thus blends fatalism and optimism, determinism and free will in its portrait of one prostitute's progress.

The films of the 1920s often blur the sharp distinction between true women and their fallen sisters that had characterized the cult of true womanhood. During the Victorian era a woman's fall from honor had been viewed as an irrevocable one and all women could be characterized as either pure or fallen. But during the 1920s film and literature created heroines who fit neither category, who were sexually active without being entirely corrupt. . . .

In sharp contrast to the helpless younger sister in *Traffic in Souls* who needs a heroic policeman to rescue her from the parlor house, in *Barriers of the Law* (1924) Rita manages to escape from a whorehouse in which she has been trapped under mob orders, despite the fact that the madam brutally stripped off her dress, by the simple expedient of wearing a kimono when she flees. Rita weds the district attorney investigating the Redding organization and resists attempts to blackmail her husband through exposure of her lurid past by infiltrating the Redding organization and investigating it herself. *Romance of the Underworld* (1928) similarly emphasizes the autonomy of its heroine, Judith Andrews, a B-girl played by Mary Astor, who escapes her sordid past by working her way up from the speakeasy through laundry and lunchroom to become a secretary and wed her boss. Although she does need the aid of a sympathetic police detective to escape a police dragnet around the speakeasy and to preserve her marriage against a blackmail threat, Judy has the resolve to break with her past and is willing to accept menial work in order to obtain respectable employment. Moreover, the film portrays her as a tender mother and loving wife, not merely alluding to her redemption but demonstrating that it has worked.

The 1920s saw a flood of optimistic films regarding redemption of the prostitute. The 1924 remake of *Tess of the D'Urbervilles*, in deference to public opinion, substituted a happy ending in which the governor of the jail dramatically interrupts the preliminaries to Tess's hanging to bring her a last-minute pardon because the public had rejected earlier releases that had included the novel's final scene, with the black flag hoisted above the jail to symbolize Tess's execution. In *Sal of Singapore* (1929) sailors kidnap a dizzy blonde harlot out of a waterfront dive to play mother to an abandoned infant. Her natural talents as a mother cause the ship's skipper to fall in love with her and to rescue her from suicide in the chill waters off the San Francisco pier. While *Sal of Singapore* demonstrated that even a common harlot might be fit for motherhood, *The Street of Forgotten Women* (1927) implied that a fallen woman might be worthy of marriage as well. Despite preserving many of the conventions of the white slavery film, it broke fundamentally with the earlier genre in that the heroine, Grace, a rich man's flapper daughter whose foolish aspirations for theatrical success have led to her rape and incarceration in a notorious house on Hester Street owned by her father, is rescued by Ken, the social worker who loves her; restored to her father, now repentant of his previous complicity in vice; and granted the comfort of Ken's undying affection. Whereas the white slavery films involved rescue before ravishment, here even a fallen woman can be redeemed. Similarly *The Red Kimono* (1925), a film produced by Dorothy Davenport as an exposé of white slavery, implies that even a harlot who has been driven to murder to avenge her degradation and betrayal may expiate her sins by patriotic service as a nurse's helper during the war, thereby proving herself fit to wed the man she loves. The film, thus, is an explicit plea for Christian toleration of modern Magdalenes, pointing to one who "won her redemption and found love and happiness" and asking that the countless others be allowed to share her joyous fate.

The irony that underlies these films promising redemption, marriage, and motherhood to fallen women is that their release coincided with the declining status of the prostitute; their optimism disguised the far more pessimistic nature of social reality. The Progressive vice crusades of the 1910s had served to eradicate tolerated urban red light districts, thereby scattering prostitution elsewhere in the city or dispersing it to surrounding communities. . . . The dispersion of prostitution resulted in far more capricious law enforcement and increased criminal control as prostitution tended to become associated with new "tenderloin" areas or speakeasies that afforded criminal syndicates substantial profits from the combined sale of women and liquor during Prohibition. . . . Thus, the Progressive purity crusaders, fearful of the city because of its association with immigrant crime and vice, in seeking to protect women from urban vice managed instead to further victimize the very women they were seeking to redeem by creating the conditions that allowed prostitution to fall into the control of organized crime.

Given this harsh social reality, how can one account for the increasing number of optimistic films treating fallen womanhood in the late 1910s and the 1920s? As the United States became officially an urban nation by the time of the 1920 census; as immigration diminished during World War I, only to face further legislative restrictions in the 1920s; as the sexual revolution lessened the distinction between true women and their fallen sisters; as the use of condoms became more widespread as a measure to prevent venereal disease; as women wage-earners moved increasingly out of the factories and into less exploitative white-collar work, films no longer needed to reflect the general cultural anxiety that accompanied modernization, and the antiprostitution crusade lost much of its symbolic significance. The blurring of the distinction between true women and their fallen sisters on the screen reflected a similar ambiguity in real life. Adolescents engaged in far more premarital sexual exploration than would have been considered permissible for their Victorian counterparts. Among college coeds the question became not whether to pet but rather the degree of the activity, for now petting was not proof of moral degradation but essential to popularity. The result was increased sexual activity among the young of even the "best," most respectable families, not to mention their less-affluent high school peers. The constant public exposure to lovemaking on screen, augmented by the sense of security in numbers, led to the relaxation of the Victorian ban upon public displays of affection. The sexual revolution and the rise of the flapper meant that it was no longer assumed that a single lapse consigned a woman to doom nor that nonmarital sexual activity was confined largely to the prostitute class. The fact that screen prostitutes were allowed marriage and motherhood reflected the preoccupations of the flapper, for whom the liberalization of sexual mores served merely as a preliminary to traditional marriage and family life.

The final films of the three decades share a belief in the fallen woman as redeemer of individual men, and at times of society in general. The fallen woman seemed remarkably devoid of the hypocrisy that characterized her respectable counterparts and bourgeois society in general. She thus served as an implicit social critic of the society that condemned her, demonstrating its inadequacy by her own superior humanity. In *The Docks of New York* (1928) a rowdy stoker, played by George Bancroft, is redeemed from a life of carousing and debauchery by saving a harlot from suicide, participating in a mock marriage with her that reveals her true affection and domesticity, and then returning to save her from being jailed for an offense he had committed and vowing to wed her. Thus, in this pre-depression film unconcerned with issues of class, a harlot's love has transformed a wastrel into a man ready to accept domesticity and responsibility. The depression-era films include an attack on the decadent nature of affluent society. *The Silver Horde* (1930) depicts a former prostitute who secretly backs a young but self-doubting and disillusioned adventurer in his scheme to open a salmon factory in Alaska against the opposition of a ruthless businessman. Although the young man had arrived in Alaska without funds and ready to quit, the reformed prostitute inspires him to fight and proves far more loyal than his wealthy but weak and insipid fiancée, whom he ultimately spurns so that he can wed the woman who truly had been his inspiration, begging her forgiveness for his condemnation as he asks her to marry.

These final films share a strong future orientation, a common derision of wealth and the status quo, and a belief in the vitality of common people like prostitutes and party girls. The films seem to respond to the disillusionment with affluence and with the prevailing socioeconomic order that accompanied the Great Depression. No longer a passive victim of male lust, the prostitute now could be portrayed as exercising autonomy and control over her own destiny; instead of being redeemed by a man, she now could be portrayed as a redeemer herself. The 1930 version of *The Sea Wolf,* based on the Jack London novel, depicts a remarkably self-possessed prostitute, Lorna Marsh, who spurns Wolf Larsen, the brutal skipper of *The Ghost,* for a despondent wastrel, Allen Rand, a wealthy but aimless man. Lorna is distinguished from previous screen prostitutes by her blatant assertion of personal autonomy. When Wolf demands that she come with him, she replies firmly: "I pick the men I want, and I don't want you." After Larsen's crew shanghais Allen, Lorna follows him aboard ship to protect him, instead exacerbating the life-and-death struggle between Wolf and the boy. Ironically it is Lorna's presence that spurs Allen to meet the challenges Wolf flings at him, to triumph in the final struggle, and to take the helm and steer himself and Lorna back home on the abandoned ship. While Allen may set their course in the final frames, it is significant that it was the compassion and support of a harlot that gave him the courage not merely to survive, but to triumph.

As the 1930s began the fallen woman had been transformed from society's victim to, at times, its implicit critic, a woman with a finer and more humane sense of virtue than that practiced by those who scorned her. In *Ladies of Leisure* (1930) party girl Kay Arnold, played by Barbara Stanwyck, becomes the model for an affluent but aimless artist, Jerry Strong. She inspires him to repudiate a life of sterile luxury and respectability; but when he casts off his wealthy fiancée in order to wed Kay, the party girl heeds his mother's pleas to renounce him, as Jerry's friends never could forgive her sordid past. In despair, Kay decides to accompany Jerry's dissolute friend Standish on a booze-filled cruise to Havana. Unable to resume her former life and unaware of a cable from Jerry assuring her of his continued love, Kay plunges overboard. But, instead of being consigned to doom as the women in the earliest films had been, Kay is picked up by a tug and restored to Jerry's loving embrace. Her redemption has renewed her hope: "Jerry—there isn't—any ceiling. I see the stars—and happiness." In *Ladies of Leisure* K[a]y may literally have been saved from death, but her presence saves Jerry from aimless existence; in inspiring him to paint and to take charge of his own life, Kay becomes redeemer as well as redeemed. Moreover, her spunkiness, honesty, and sense of purpose contrast favorably with the pointless drifting of elite society. Kay's very presence is an implicit criticism of an affluent culture gone awry. Whereas the earliest films had condemned any violation of social norms, *Ladies of Leisure* argues that society itself was too corrupt to condemn the fallen woman.

Ironically these films portraying the fallen woman as redeemer were released in an era in which the prostitute's lot had reached a new nadir. Prostitution did not decrease during the depression despite increased unemployment. . . . By the 1930s organized crime dominated prostitution . . . The grimness of the prostitute's lot left little room for optimism; the machinations of the mob left her even less room for the autonomy of her filmic counterparts.

If prostitution had reached a new nadir by 1930, why were fallen women portrayed as redeemers on the silver screen? Because prostitution no longer was the burning social issue that it had been in the Progressive Era, it became possible to transform the prostitute from a victim of society to a tool of social criticism. Standing outside the law, branded as a deviant, the fallen wom[a]n had no hypocritical vested interest in defending the status quo. Her honesty, guaranteed by the fact that, having nothing, she had nothing to lose, the prostitute was ideally suited to serve as critic of an elite society run amok.

If the image of the fallen woman in film had shifted dramatically in the first three decades of the twentieth century, from victims of male lust and greed to women capable of being redeemed, and ultimately to redeemers of men and society themselves, that transformation bore an inverse relationship to reality. Despite claims to social realism and to didactic aims, filmmakers readily abandoned realism in service of their true end: to use the prostitute as a mythic figure through whom the deepest conflicts of American culture could be resolved. If in reality the prostitute served her client's sexual needs, her screen counterpart served our culture's mythic and metaphoric ones.

FURTHER READING

Jerome Charyn, *Movieland: Hollywood and the Great American Dream Culture* (1989)

Warren Craig, *The Great Songwriters of Hollywood* (1980)

Bernard F. Dick, *Radical Innocence: A Critical Study of the Hollywood Ten* (1989)

"Envisioning California," special issue of *California History* LXVIII (Winter 1989/90)

David Fahey and Linda Rich, *Masters of Starlight: Photographers in Hollywood* (1987)

Robert R. Faulkner, *Music on Demand: Composers and Careers in the Hollywood Film Industry* (1983)

Lawrence Ferlinghetti and Nancy J. Peters, *Literary San Francisco* (1980)

Lizzie Francke, *Script Girls: Women Screenwriters in Hollywood* (1994)

Albert R. Fulton, *Motion Pictures: The Development of an Art from Silent Films to the Age of Television* (1960)

Neal Gabler, *An Empire of Their Own: How the Jews Invented Hollywood* (1988)

Douglas Gomery, *The Hollywood Studio System* (1986)

Richard Griffith and Arthur Mayer, *The Movies: A Sixty-Year Story of the World of Hollywood and Its Effect on America from the Pre-Nickelodeon Days to the Present* (1957; rev. and updated ed., 1981)

Ian Hamilton, *Writers in Hollywood, 1915–1951* (1990)

Gerald Haslam, ed., *Many Californias* (1991)

International Museum of Photography at George Eastman House, *Dream Merchants: Making and Selling Films in Hollywood's Golden Age* (1989)

Lewis Jacobs, *The Rise of the American Film: A Critical History* (1968)

Arthur Knight, *The Liveliest Art* (1957; rev. ed., 1978)

W. Robert LaVine, *In a Glamorous Fashion: The Fabulous Years of Hollywood Costume Design* (1980)

Leonard J. Leff, *The Dame in the Kimono: Hollywood, Censorship, and the Production Code from the 1920s to the 1960s* (1990)

Edward Maeder et al., *Hollywood and History: Costume Design in Film* (1987)

Stoddard Martin, *California Writers* (1984)

Gerald Mast, *A Short History of the Movies* (1976)

Lary May, *Screening Out the Past: The Birth of Mass Culture and the Motion Picture Industry* (1980)

Hortense Powdermaker, *Hollywood, the Dream Factory* (1950)

Lawrence Clark Powell, *Land of Fiction* (1952)

Lawrence Clark Powell, *California Classics: The Creative Literature of the Golden State* (1971)

Naima Prevots, *Dancing in the Sun: Hollywood Choreographers, 1915–1937* (1987)

Jorga Prover, *No One Knows Their Names: Screenwriters in Hollywood* (1994)

Lionel Rolfe, *Literary Los Angeles* (1981)

Leo C. Rosten, *Hollywood: The Movie Colony, the Movie Makers* (1941; 1970)

Thomas Schatz, *The Genesis of the System: Hollywood Filmmaking in the Studio Era* (1988)

Robert Sklar, *Movie-Made America: A Social History of the Movies* (1975)

Kevin Starr, *Americans and the California Dream, 1850–1915* (1973)
Kevin Starr, *Inventing the Dream: California through the Progressive Era* (1985)
Kevin Starr, *Material Dreams: Southern California through the 1920s* (1990)
Franklin Walker, *San Francisco's Literary Frontier* (1939)
Franklin Walker, *A Literary History of Southern California* (1950)
Richard Webb, ed., *Hollywood: Legend and Reality* (1986)
David Wyatt, *The Fall into Eden* (1987)

Farmworker Struggles in the 1930s

The defining event of the 1930s was, of course, the Great Depression. Californians shared the miseries suffered by the rest of the nation: by 1932 farm income in the state had fallen to less than half of what it had been in 1929; by 1934 more than a fifth of all Californians were dependent on public relief for survival. Tens of thousands of retirees in southern California became destitute because their savings and investments were wiped out.

Californians proposed all kinds of utopian schemes to deal with their grim situation. Francis E. Townsend, a doctor in Long Beach—a city housing 40,000 retirees from the state of Iowa alone—attracted many followers with his proposal that Congress give each retiree two hundred dollars a month with the proviso that he or she spend the entire sum the following month. The Townsend Plan found adherents outside of California as well. Another pension plan, called "Ham and Eggs," suggested issuing thirty one-dollar scrips every Thursday to unemployed persons over the age of fifty— pieces of paper that could be redeemed for money from the state at year's end. Despite its peculiarity, the Ham and Eggs initiative appeared on the 1938 ballot and received support from over a million voters.

Upton Sinclair, author of dozens of muckraking books, switched his affiliation from the Socialist party to the Democratic party to run for governor in 1934. He won the Democratic nomination with 52 percent of the vote. He presented his platform in a short novel entitled I, Governor of California, and How I Ended Poverty: A True Story of the Future *(1933). The End Poverty in California (EPIC) campaign called for the abolition of the regressive sales tax, for the state acquisition of farmland and factories where the unemployed could work in cooperatives, and for a monthly pension of fifty dollars to each needy person above the age of sixty. Alarmed by Sinclair's success, however, Democratic party stalwarts abandoned their own nominee shortly after the primary election, while Republicans denigrated him as a communist, an atheist, and an advocate of free love. Sinclair nevertheless managed to garner 38 percent of the vote compared to the 49 percent captured by Frank Merriam, the winner.*

Another manifestation of hard times was labor strife. Bolstered by new national laws, organized labor felt encouraged to use strikes to improve the lot of workers. In May 1934 longshoremen and other maritime workers on San Francisco's waterfront, under the leadership of Harry Bridges, went on strike. When violent confrontations with the police broke out, Governor Frank Merriam called out the National Guard. In response, workers in other industries called a general strike. Tens of thousands of employees walked off their jobs for four full days.

Equally dramatic were the strikes that erupted in the most important farming areas: the Santa Clara, San Joaquin, and Imperial valleys and the Los Angeles basin. This chapter focuses on three strikes in the Imperial Valley, where the reaction of farm owners was especially repressive and where class antagonism was suffused with racial animus.

Family farming in California has never been as important as so-called agribusiness. The most important agricultural production has been carried out on large tracts of land, often owned by absentee landlords, with the crops cultivated and harvested by migrant farmworkers. "Factories in the field" is the apt phrase that Carey McWilliams coined to characterize this industrial pattern of production.

Since the days of the Spanish missions, the backbreaking work in California agriculture has been performed by people of color: first the California Indians, then the Californios, followed by the Chinese, Japanese, Indians (from India), Koreans, Filipinos, and Mexicanos (a term that includes both Mexican immigrants and Americans of Mexican ancestry).

Due to their migratory existence, grinding poverty, and, often, alien status (with the threat of deportation ever present), California's farmworkers have encountered enormous difficulties in organizing labor unions. Even more important, the power of agribusiness has been formidable; legal statutes and law enforcement officers have usually supported the growers. By branding union organizers and farmworker leaders as "agitators" and "communists," the farm owners have also had ideology on their side.

For all these reasons, agriculture, though a cornerstone of California's prosperity, has been debased by oppressive working conditions. Only sporadically have these extreme conditions entered the public consciousness. The farmworkers' strikes that took place during the Great Depression were one such occasion.

The two essays at the end of the chapter offer contrasting perspectives of the Imperial Valley strikes. One account emphasizes the role of Anglo Communist organizers as the primary shapers of events; the other focuses on the role and experiences of the Mexicanos. In reading the documents and the two essays, try to discern what really happened and who played the more significant role in organizing the strikes. Also ask why historians might choose to portray historic events from two such different perspectives.

 D O C U M E N T S

The first document, drawn from a report published by the California Department of Industrial Relations, describes the labor contracting system in California agriculture. It is followed by a short segment from Carlos Bulosan's celebrated work, *America Is in the Heart* (1943). Though touted as Bulosan's "personal history," the book is not an autobiography per se but a group portrait of Filipino immigrants, many of whom worked as migrant farm laborers from the mid-1920s until the early 1970s.

The third document is an episode from an even more famous work, *The Grapes of Wrath* (1939) by John Steinbeck. Like Carey McWilliams's *Factories in the Field* (also 1939), it called attention to the miserable life of migrant farmworkers and refugees from the Dust Bowl. The influx of so many poverty-stricken white people elicited official concern, for the first time in California history, for the farmworkers' plight.

The fourth document, written by James Rorty, a journalist thrown out of the Imperial Valley because he tried to investigate conditions there, offers an eyewitness account of social upheavals in the early 1930s.

The fifth and sixth documents, both penned by farm owners, reveal two diametrically opposite attitudes toward the strikes. Frank Stokes, a citrus grower in Covina, argues that his fellow citrus growers should sympathize with the desire of farmworkers to unionize since the growers themselves had organized and benefited from marketing cooperatives. In contrast, Ralph H. Taylor, executive secretary of the Agricultural Council of California in 1938, expresses great vehemence toward labor organizers, calling them mobsters and communists. He urges his fellow farm owners to do whatever is necessary to protect themselves against both labor agitators and the insecure market conditions facing California's growers.

The California Department of Industrial Relations Evaluates Agricultural Labor Contracts, 1930

Filipinos are hired to work in agricultural pursuits through labor contractors. These contractors are usually themselves Filipinos with whom the growers enter into agreements to plant or harvest their crops. This labor contracting system is generally used in the harvesting of many California crops. When Mexicans are employed the contractor is usually a Mexican, but Mexican contractors sometimes hire both Mexicans and Filipinos to perform the labor required, and Filipino contractors hire Filipinos and sometimes also Mexicans. The labor contractor may also be a Japanese, a Chinese, or a Hindu, depending upon the kind of crop, the location of the work, and the preference of the grower. In the picking of melons, in Imperial County, for instance, the contractor is likely to be a Mexican because of the preponderance of Mexican labor in the county.

In all agricultural labor contracts, which have come to the attention of the Division of Labor Statistics and Law Enforcement of the Department of Industrial Relations, the growers reserve the absolute right to dictate to the contractor as to how many laborers should be hired in the harvesting of their crops. At times the growers prefer to have the contractor employ a mixture of laborers of various races, speaking diverse languages and not accustomed to mingling with each other. This practice is intended to avoid labor troubles which might result from having a homogeneous group of laborers of the same race or nationality. Laborers speaking different languages and accustomed to diverse standards of living and habits are not as likely to arrive at a mutual understanding which would lead to strikes or other labor troubles during harvesting seasons, when work interruptions would result in serious financial losses to the growers.

The principal points generally embodied in agricultural labor contracts are these:

1. The labor contractor, who is usually as poor as the laborers whom he hires, undertakes to furnish a sufficient number of men to harvest the crop. The grower, or the owner, when the grower is also the owner of the land, is the sole judge as to the adequacy and competence of the men employed.

2. The grower reserves the right to cause the discharge of laborers whom he considers imcompetent, and reserves the further right of demanding that additional laborers be hired when, in his judgment, they are needed properly to execute the provisions of the contract relative to the harvesting of the crop in a workmanlike manner, which the contractor undertakes to do.

3. The contract specifies how and when the harvesting work shall be done, and the grower is the sole judge as to whether the contract is being complied with in this respect. If, in the judgment of the grower, the contractor is not properly carrying out his part of the contract, the grower reserves the right at any time to terminate the contract and to secure another contractor to complete the terms of the contract. The grower also reserves the right, in lieu of terminating the contract and discharging the contractor, to hire additional workers to perform the labor required at the expense of the contractor.

4. The grower, or the owner, undertakes to furnish the contractor with a cook house and sleeping quarters for the laborers employed by the contractors.

5. The contract stipulates the price per box, per crate, or per hundredweight, to be paid to the contractor weekly, semimonthly, or monthly, usually depending upon the custom prevailing in the locality where the harvesting is carried on.

6. The contract generally provides that a certain proportion of the moneys due to the contractors shall be withheld by the grower until the end of the season as a guarantee that the contractor will fully comply with all provisions of the contract.

7. The contract also provides that the contractor, not the grower, shall be liable under the California Workmen's Compensation, Insurance and Safety Act for all injuries sustained by the laborers employed by the contractor in the harvesting of the crop.

8. The grower undertakes to furnish the contractor with a cook house and bunk houses for the contractor's laborers, and the contractor undertakes to keep the cook house and living quarters in good and sanitary condition.

9. There is frequently a supplementary understanding, written or oral, under which the grower undertakes to pay to the contractor a certain amount of money for his services as contractor and foreman.

Since, under the agricultural labor contract described, the labor contractor is considered the employer of the laborers cultivating and harvesting the grower's crop, the grower makes payments to the contractor, who pays the laborers' wages. The growers find this system very convenient because it makes it unnecessary for them to keep the laborers on their pay rolls and to pay them separately.

This system has frequently resulted in wage losses to the laborers employed in the harvesting of crops. Since the labor contractor is very seldom bonded, and is usually a financially irresponsible man, his workers are dependent entirely upon his honesty in getting their wages. It happens, not infrequently, that the labor contractor absconds with the pay roll entrusted to him by the grower, especially towards the end of the harvesting season when the contractor receives the final payment, which is biggest because it contains the money withheld by the grower as a guarantee of the fulfillment of the contract. In such instances the laborers flock to the offices of the Division of Labor Statistics and Law Enforcement of the Department of Industrial Relations to file wage claims under the California laws pertaining to payment of wages. But since the grower, who is the financially responsible person, can not be held liable for the wages which the contractor owes to *his* laborers, the Division of Labor Statistics and Law Enforcement finds it most difficult to collect the unpaid wages, even when the contractor is apprehended.

A good many of the laborers filing such wage claims are Filipinos employed in the harvesting of various agricultural crops of the state. Only one large packing company is known to bond its labor contractors in the sum of $1,000 to $2,000 to safeguard the interests of the laborers harvesting the crops. But even this bond would prove only a partial safeguard for the reason that the amount of money with which the contractor is likely to disappear may be much in excess of the amount of the bond.

To do away with frequent defalcations of contractors and thereby to safeguard the wages of the agricultural workers in Imperial County, the Department of Industrial Relations, with the cooperation of the growers, managed to revise the terms of the labor contract used in the harvesting of melons and other crops in the Imperial Valley, so as to make the growers responsible for the wages of the laborers employed by their labor contractors.

Carlos Bulosan Describes the Harsh Existence of Filipino Migrant Farmworkers

I began to be afraid, riding alone in the freight train. I wanted suddenly to go back to Stockton and look for a job in the tomato fields, but the train was already traveling fast. I was in flight again, away from an unknown terror that seemed to follow me everywhere. Dark flight into another place, toward other enemies. But there was a clear sky and the night was ablaze with stars. I could still see the faint haze of Stockton's lights in the distance, a halo arching above it and fading into a backdrop of darkness.

In the early morning the train stopped a few miles from Niles, in the midst of a wide grape field. The grapes had been harvested and the bare vines were falling to the ground. The apricot trees were leafless. Three railroad detectives jumped out of a car and ran toward the boxcars. I ran to the vineyard and hid behind a smudge pot, waiting for the next train from Stockton. A few bunches of grapes still hung on the vines, so I filled my pockets and ran for the tracks when the train came. It was a freight and it stopped to pick up carloads of grapes; when it started moving again the empties were full of men.

I crawled to a corner of a car and fell asleep. When I awakened the train was already in San Jose. I jumped outside and found several hoboes drinking cans of beer. I sat and watched them sitting solemnly, as though there were no more life in the world. They talked as though there were no more happiness left, as though life had died and would not live again. I could not converse with them, and this barrier made me a stranger. I wanted to know them and to be a part of their life. I wondered what I had in common with them beside the fact that we were all on the road rolling to unknown destinations. . . .

José and I traveled by freight train to the south. We were told, when we reached the little desert town of Calipatria, that local whites were hunting Filipinos at night with shotguns. A countryman offered to take us in his loading truck to Brawley, but we decided it was too dangerous. We walked to Holtville where we found a Japanese farmer who hired us to pick winter peas.

It was cold at night and when morning came the fog was so thick it was tangible. But it was a safe place and it was far from the surveillance of vigilantes. Then from nearby El Centro, the center of Filipino population in the Imperial Valley, news came that a Filipino labor organizer had been found dead in a ditch.

I wanted to leave Holtville, but José insisted that we work through the season. I worked but made myself inconspicuous. At night I slept with a long knife under my pillow. My ears became sensitive to sounds and even my sense of smell was sharpened. I knew when rabbits were mating between the rows of peas. I knew when night birds were feasting in the melon patches.

John Steinbeck Portrays Social Pressures
in Rural California, 1939

They turned off the highway and walked down a graveled road, through a small kitchen orchard; and behind the trees they came to a small white farm house, a few shade trees, and a barn; behind the barn a vineyard and a field of cotton. As the three men walked past the house a screen door banged, and a stocky sunburned man came down the back steps. He wore a paper sun helmet, and he rolled up his sleeves as he came across the yard. His heavy sunburned eyebrows were drawn down in a scowl. His cheeks were sunburned a beef red.

"Mornin', Mr. Thomas," Timothy said.

"Morning." The man spoke irritably.

Timothy said, "This here's Tom Joad. We wondered if you could see your way to put him on?"

Thomas scowled at Tom. And then he laughed shortly, and his brows still scowled. "Oh, sure! I'll put him on. I'll put everybody on. Maybe I'll get a hundred men on."

"We jus' thought—" Timothy began apologetically.

Thomas interrupted him. "Yes, I been thinkin' too." He swung around and faced them. "I've got some things to tell you. I been paying you thirty cents an hour—that right?"

"Why, sure, Mr. Thomas—but—"

"And I been getting thirty cents' worth of work."

His heavy hard hands clasped each other.

"We try to give a good day of work."

"Well, goddamn it, this morning you're getting twenty-five cents an hour, and you take it or leave it." The redness of his face deepened with anger.

Timothy said, "We've give you good work. You said so yourself."

"I know it. But it seems like I ain't hiring my own men any more." He swallowed. "Look," he said. "I got sixty-five acres here. Did you ever hear of the Farmers' Association?"

"Why, sure."

"Well, I belong to it. We had a meeting last night. Now, do you know who runs the Farmers' Association? I'll tell you. The Bank of the West. That bank owns most of this valley, and it's got paper on everything it don't own. So last night the member from the bank told me, he said, 'You're paying thirty cents an hour. You'd better cut it down to twenty-five.' I said, 'I've got good men. They're worth thirty.' And he says, 'It isn't that,' he says. 'The wage is twenty-five now. If you pay thirty, it'll only cause unrest. And by the way,' he says, 'you going to need the usual amount for a crop loan next year?'" Thomas stopped. His breath was panting through his lips. "You see? The rate is twenty-five cents—and like it."

"We done good work," Timothy said helplessly.

"Ain't you got it yet? Mr. Bank hires two thousand men an' I hire three. I've got paper to meet. Now if you can figure some way out, by Christ, I'll take it! They got me."

Timothy shook his head. "I don't know what to say."

"You wait here." Thomas walked quickly to the house. The door slammed after him. In a moment he was back, and he carried a newspaper in his hand. "Did you see this? Here, I'll read it: 'Citizens, angered at red agitators, burn squatters' camp. Last night a band of citizens, infuriated at the agitation going on in a local squatters' camp, burned the tents to the ground and warned agitators to get out of the county.'"

Tom began, "Why, I—" and then he closed his mouth and was silent.

Thomas folded the paper carefully and put it in his pocket. He had himself in control again. He said quietly, "Those men were sent out by the

Association. Now I'm giving 'em away. And if they ever find out I told, I won't have a farm next year."

"I jus' don't know what to say," Timothy said. "If they was agitators, I can see why they was mad."

Thomas said, "I watched it a long time. There's always red agitators just before a pay cut. Always. Goddamn it, they got me trapped. Now, what are you going to do? Twenty-five cents?"

Timothy looked at the ground. "I'll work," he said.

"Me too," said Wilkie.

Tom said, "Seems like I walked into somepin. Sure, I'll work. I got to work. ["]

Thomas pulled a bandanna out of his hip pocket and wiped his mouth and chin. "I don't know how long it can go on. I don't know how you men can feed a family on what you get now."

"We can while we work," Wilkie said. "It's when we don't git work."

Thomas looked at his watch. "Well, let's go out and dig some ditch. By God," he said, "I'm a-gonna tell you. You fellas live in that government camp, don't you?"

Timothy stiffened. "Yes, sir."

"And you have dances every Saturday night?"

Wilkie smiled. "We sure do."

"Well, look out next Saturday night."

Suddenly Timothy straightened. He stepped close. "What you mean? I belong to the Central Committee. I got to know."

Thomas look apprehensive. "Don't you ever tell I told."

"What is it?" Timothy demanded.

"Well, the Association don't like the government camps. Can't get a deputy in there. The people make their own laws, I hear, and you can't arrest a man without a warrant. Now if there was a big fight and maybe shooting—a bunch of deputies could go in and clean out the camp."

Timothy had changed. His shoulders were straight and his eyes cold. "What you mean?"

"Don't you ever tell where you heard," Thomas said uneasily. "There's going to be a fight in the camp Saturday night. And there's going to be deputies ready to go in."

Tom demanded, "Why for God's sake? Those folks ain't bothering nobody."

"I'll tell you why," Thomas said. "Those folks in the camp are getting used to being treated like humans. When they go back to the squatters' camps they'll be hard to handle." He wiped his face again. "Go on out to work now. Jesus, I hope I haven't talked myself out of my farm. But I like you people."

Timothy stepped in front of him and put out a hard lean hand, and Thomas took it. "Nobody won't know who tol'. We thank you. They won't be no fight."

"Go on to work," Thomas said. "And it's twenty-five cents an hour."

"We'll take it,' Wilkie said, "from you."

Thomas walked away toward the house. "I'll be out in a piece," he said. "You men get to work." The screen door slammed behind him.

James Rorty Reports on Conditions in the Imperial Valley, 1935

What happens in the Imperial Valley in California—the strikes, killings, arrests, kidnappings, beatings—is both shocking and interesting, as I can personally testify. But what is more interesting is why these things happen—why "law and order" has broken down, why there is no prospect of peace in the valley, and why thus far neither the state nor the federal government has been able to do much about it.

I visited the valley during the last week of February, while a strike of the lettuce packers and trimmers was in progress. Eager for information, I asked questions of everybody I could get hold of—for the brief period of less than three days. Then the blow fell. I was a very aggrieved reporter when the sheriff's deputies, after keeping me incommunicado overnight in the El Centro jail, escorted me across the line into Arizona. . . . I was a hundred miles the other side of the California border before I could even send a telegram. But here is the essential pattern as I saw it. It is not unique. Conditions are as bad or worse in Arizona, Colorado, and southern Texas.

The major crops in the valley are lettuce, cantaloupe, and peas—all grown "out of season" with respect to Eastern markets, all highly perishable, all produced on irrigated desert land lying from 50 to 150 feet below sea level. The conditions of production are industrial rather than agricultural in the older sense. Ninety per cent of the crops in the valley are grown or financed by a small group of large shipper-growers. Through a prorating agreement the lettuce acreage in the Imperial Valley, which was approximately 30,000 acres in 1933, was reduced for the 1934–35 season to 16,789 acres. Of this acreage only 3,510 acres are tilled by so-called "independent" growers—whose independence, incidentally, is qualified by the fact that the big shipper-growers to whom most of them sell control the facilities for packing and shipping, and hence can more or less set the price paid to growers. The same situation is found in the other major crops.

Labor in this industrialized agriculture divides into two categories: the shed workers and the field or "stoop" labor. The former, in general, are 100 per cent American fruit tramps. Many of them have a semi-permanent employee status with respect to the large shipper-growers and move from one area to another as the crops mature. Since the depression, however, the number of these migratory workers has been greatly increased by the accession of all sorts of destitute and dispossessed people—industrial and white-collar workers from the cities, whole families of dispossessed sharecroppers from Oklahoma, Texas, and the deep South.

The field workers, or "stoop labor," are chiefly Mexicans. In the report made by Will J. French, J. L. Leonard, and Simon J. Lubin to the National Labor Board a year ago, it was estimated that there were then in the valley about 15,000 Mexicans, 3,000 Filipinos, and smaller groups of Japanese,

Negroes, and Hindus. Since then there has been a considerable "repatriation" of Mexicans, for whom there was no employment. But to compensate for this there has been a fairly constant movement of Mexicans across the border, as well as a steady influx of migrants from the East into the valley. So that whereas there were in January, 1934, between 4,000 and 5,000 unemployed in the valley, plus their women and children, the number had increased rather than decreased a year later when I was there. John R. Lestner, the deputy labor commissioner in El Centro, estimated that with opportunities for employment for from 5,000 to 7,000 stoop laborers, there are now in the valley from 8,000 to 10,000 Mexicans plus 5,000 Filipinos. In 1932 the hourly scale for stoop labor dropped to as low as 10 cents; this year it was 25 and 30 cents, but despite the efforts of the labor commissioner to enforce the state law, the workers continue to be exploited by the labor contractors, who sell them at so much a head to the growers.

The three-men-to-one-job surplus of stoop labor is fully matched by the surplus of shed workers. It was this surplus, together with the strong-arm methods of the growers, that broke the strike of lettuce packers and trimmers this year. The shed owners simply went out on the highway and picked up migratory workers, with the result that by the end of the strike about a thousand new packers and trimmers had been added to the labor pool.

All this labor is heavily subsidized by relief. Both for stoop labor and shed labor the wage scale is so low and employment so intermittent that only at the peaks of the harvest seasons do the workers make subsistence wages. . . .

During the peak of the lettuce harvest men and in some cases women, although this is against the law, are worked under the frantic speed-up of the split-bench system from four in the morning until ten at night. Hence the demand of the Fruit and Vegetable Workers' Union of California for the ending of the split-bench system (a combination of piece work for the packers and hourly wages for the trimmers which speeds up both), for time and a third for all work over ten hours a day, and for the privilege of hiring a "booster" or substitute to relieve a packer or trimmer when he is about to drop in his tracks.

To complete the picture of this below-sea-level, sweated, overpopulated, 130-degrees-Fahrenheit Eden it is only necessary to add that, with the exception of the banks and individuals—including Harry Chandler of the Los Angeles *Times*—who own the land and lease it to the shipper-growers, nobody has been consistently making money in the valley since 1930. The Labor Board report states that "in spite of all economies, and with wages during 1933 as low as $12\frac{1}{2}$ and 15 cents per hour, the shippers point out that they have lost an average of $3,500,000 per year for the past four years." . . .

Off-season lettuce is grown all the way from Florida to California. The industry has yielded huge profits in the past, but its economics are extremely fragile and also subject to fantastic forms of racketeering. The shipper-growers have an organization—the Western Growers' Protective Association—but as far as I could learn from its secretary, C. B. Moore, its activities are restricted to fighting adverse legislation and breaking strikes. Mr. Moore stated flatly that the association is not interested in marketing: that was left to the individual responsibility of the grower or shipper-grower. The result is a sort of chronic chaos; the price, set by commission merchants in the Eastern and Middle Western markets, varies from day to day. If you are a shipper-grower, you load and "roll" your cars, and then attempt to divert them while they are on the road to whatever market seems to offer the best price at the moment. Since all or most of the growers in all the producing areas are doing this, markets are frequently glutted, hundreds of tons of lettuce are spoiled and dumped; other huge quantities of lettuce wither and blow away in the fields; racketeers flourish. A favorite device of the less scrupulous commission merchants is to buy a given crop of lettuce, for which the grower pays the cost of harvesting, trimming, and packing. The commission merchant then reports that as the Kansas City market was glutted, he sent it to Chicago, which was also glutted by the time it got there; then it went to Baltimore, and by that time it had spoiled. Maybe it was and maybe it wasn't. The grower loses in any case. Everybody I talked to in the valley agreed that the small independent grower, the man who cultivates forty acres or less, practically always loses. His condition is little better than that of the fruit tramps and the stoop labor; which makes the suggested remedy of subsistence homesteads as a device for anchoring the floating labor seem highly questionable.

Is it any wonder that law and order and human decency have gone completely to pot in the valley, that we are presented with a matured and functioning vigilante terror directed not only against Communists but against labor marching under whatever banner? . . . [T]he barons of El Centro . . . hired gunmen as strike-breakers and the sheriff deputized them. They broke the strike.

Grower Frank Stokes Defends Mexican Farmworkers' Efforts to Organize, 1936

California citrus-fruit growers have joined the legions of the exploiters of labor. They have taken over at the same time the whole vicious machinery of vigilantes, strike-breakers, night riders, tear gas, and prejudiced newspapers. This appears strange considering that there was a time when these citrus-fruit growers themselves were so sorely oppressed that they were driven to create one of the first, and certainly one of the greatest, cooperative organizations ever formed by tillers of the soil. Because they were being exploited and robbed by brokers and shippers, the California citrus farmers were forced to organize or perish. Their object was to obtain a greater return for their sweat and labor. Yet now they are determined that others shall not be permitted to organize for the same purpose.

Oppression was the father and desperation the mother of the California Fruit Growers' Exchange. It has become a mighty organization with 13,500 grower members. There are in California approximately 309,000 citrus-growing acres valued at close to $618,000,000, and more than 75 per cent of this acreage and value are represented in the exchange. Its headquarters are in the new Sun-Kist building, which it owns, in the city of Los Angeles. All this is the result of the banding together of an exploited group of citrus-fruit growers. It is this group which recently crushed ruthlessly an attempt by Mexican workers to organize a union of citrus-fruit pickers.

The Mexican is to agricultural California what the Negro is to the medieval South. His treatment by the vegetable growers of the Imperial Valley is well known. What has happened to him in the San Joaquin has likewise been told. But for a time at least it appeared that the "citrus belt" was different. Then came the strike of the Mexican fruit pickers in Orange County. In its wake came the vigilantes, the night riders, the strike-breakers, the reporters whose job it was to "slant" all stories in favor of packers and grove owners. There followed the State Motor Patrol, which for the first time in the history of strike disorders in California set up a portable radio broadcasting station "in a secret place" in the strike area "to direct law-and-order activities." And special deputy badges blossomed as thick as Roosevelt buttons in the recent campaign.

Sheriff Jackson declared bravely: "It was the strikers themselves who drew first blood so from now on we will meet them on that basis." "This is no fight," said he, "between orchardists and pickers. It is a fight between the entire population of Orange County and a bunch of Communists." However, dozens and dozens of non-Communist Mexican fruit pickers were jailed; 116 were arrested en masse while traveling in automobiles along the highway. They were charged with riot and placed under bail of $500 each. Twice their preliminary hearing was delayed on motion of the district attorney. After fifteen days in jail the hearing was finally held—and the state's witnesses were able to identify only one person as having taken part in trouble occurring on the Charles Wagner ranch. Judge Ames of the Superior Court ordered the release of all but the one identified prisoner and severely criticized the authorities for holding the Mexicans in jail for so long a time when they must have known it would not be possible to identify even a small proportion of the prisoners.

For weeks during the strike newspaper stories described the brave stand taken by "law-abiding citizens." These stories were adorned with such headlines as "Vigilantes Battle Citrus Strikers in War on Reds." During all this time, so far as I know, only one paper—the Los Angeles *Evening News*—defended the fruit pickers. . . .

These Mexicans were asking for a well-deserved wage increase and free transportation to and from the widely scattered groves; they also asked that tools be furnished by the employers. Finally they asked recognition of their newly formed union. Recognition of the Mexican laboring man's union, his cooperative organization formed in order that he might obtain a little more for his commodity, which is labor—here was the crucial point. The growers and packers agreed to furnish tools; they agreed to furnish transportation to and from the groves. They even agreed to a slight wage increase, which still left the workers underpaid. But recognition of the Mexican workers' union? Never!

I have been an orange grower and a member of the California Fruit Growers' Exchange for twenty years. I have also had connections with other types of ranching less efficiently organized or not organized at all. Only in the citrus business is the producer free of all selling worries. My job is merely to grow the fruit. The exchange picks it, packs it, pools it, according to grade, with the fruit of other members, ships it, sells it, and sends me the proceeds. I have often borrowed money from my packing house, secured by my crop, thereby saving interest at the bank. Through the Fruit Growers' Supply Company (owned and operated by the associations within the exchange system) I can buy automobile tires or radios, shotguns or fertilizer, generally at a very substantial discount. I can pay for it at the end of the season.

The Fruit Growers' Supply Company provides other benefits. Because the company owns vast acres of timber and its lumber mill at Susanville, my fruit is shipped in containers furnished at cost. More than one hundred million feet of lumber are required each year for the making of exhange box shook. Cooperation even extends to the maintenance of a group of pest-control experts whose services are free to exchange members. In many other ways the citrus-fruit growers of California have profited by coopera-tion. I irrigate my orchard with water delivered by a non-profit combination of growers. My trees are sprayed or fumigated by a non-profit partnership. Because of cooperation I can sleep through the winter nights or until a voice on the telephone informs me that my thermometers have dropped to the danger point.

One would think that California citrus people, at least those belonging to the exchange, would not be adverse to organization by others. . . . [M]ore than three-fourths of all citrus growers are steadfast cooperators. If these cooperators had raised their voices to protest against the unjust treatment of the Mexicans, the affair might have ended with honor to us all.

The fact is, however, that Jack Prizer, manager of an exchange packing house in Orange County and a member of the exchange board of directors . . . was one of those most active in crushing the strike. . . .

I have said that the Mexicans are to agricultural California what the Negro is to the medieval South, exploited and despised. Before the day of the CCC camps Spanish was the language most frequently heard on every mountain fire-line; and those Spanish-speaking people were taken to the fires by force, even though the burning mountains, with their high peaks stopping rain clouds and their dense brush storing water, were vastly more important to white men than to Mexicans. Towns and cities, farms and orchards, valley springs and deep sunk wells, all depend upon those mountains.

Not only in the fields are the Mexican people exploited. Not only as earners but as buyers they are looked upon as legitimate prey—for old washing machines that will not clean clothes, for old automobiles that wheeze and let down, for woolen blankets made of cotton, for last season's shop-worn wearing apparel. Gathered in villages composed of rough board shanties or drifting with the seasons from the vegetable fields of the Imperial Valley to the grape vineyards of the San Joaquin, wherever they go it is the same old, pathetic story. Cheap labor!

Usually these people are patient and yielding. But occasionally a leader appears—he is always said to be a Communist—and then they rise up in their righteous wrath and strike. They struck in the Imperial Valley and they lost. They struck in the glorious land north of the Tehachapi—and again they lost. They lost because of tear-gas bombs, special deputies, and unfriendly newspapers. Lastly, they struck in Orange County. And once more they have lost.

Ralph H. Taylor Rallies California's Growers to Protect Their Interests, 1938

The time has come for blunt talk in California's farm labor crisis!

More to the point, the time has come for united decisive action!

California, today, is the No. 1 Farm State in the United States. It has more efficient production than any other State in the Nation. It has pioneered the way in cooperative marketing, expanding its markets, selling its products in the four corners of the world. It has enforced rigid standards to insure better quality; it has made the word "California" a quality trademark in far-distant trading places. More than any other industry, agriculture has BUILT CALIFORNIA! And it has paid the highest farm wages in the country; carried far more than its proportionate share of the State's tax load; overcome seemingly insurmountable difficulties to win its rightful place in the sun!

Those elemental facts are known to every Californian; they are attested by government records. California agriculture, with all its difficulties—despite the fact that it is still struggling with problems of crop surpluses, battling freezes and transporting its commodities thousands of miles to reach its major markets—is tops in agriculture.

It is tops because tens of thousands of industrious farmers have worked from sunup to sundown, regardless of weather, regardless of years without profit, regardless of every manner of discouragement, to achieve a reasonadle [sic] measure of security.

The question that now confronts California agriculture is simply and bluntly this: "Shall agriculture abdicate and give over its plant to the domination of 'beef squads' and city labor bosses—drunk with power and determined to rule or ruin?"

In short, "Shall the California farming industry submit to a labor dictatorship?"

Shall agriculture admit: "We've licked the weather; we've licked the depression; we've licked plant pests and diseases, but we can't lick Harry Bridges; we can't say 'NO' to Dave Beck and his hired mobsters?"

Such are the questions which California agriculture—every branch of it; every individual farmer—must answer! And the answer, in this writer's opinion, will soon be forthcoming.

At the outset, in this discussion, it is important that a few basic questions should be briefly stated and tersely answered. Here they are:

Question: "Why is agriculture opposed to 'the closed shop'?" . . .

Answer: "Because 'the closed shop,' as labor leaders admit, is but the forerunner to 'the union hiring hall.'"

Question: "Why is agriculture opposed to 'the union hiring hall'?"

Answer: "Because it would deny farmers the right to hire their own men and run their own properties. If the Dave Becks and Harry Bridges and all their sub-chiefs and organizers are competent to operate farms, they should buy them—and pay their own losses!"

Question: "How can agriculture combat labor leader domination when the union organizers single out one branch at a time?"

Answer: "By a union of farmers, willing to back up every individual farmer and every branch of the industry with money and concerted assistance."

California agriculture is not opposed to decent living conditions; it favors the best wages that can be paid to agricultural workers. It has proved that over a period of years and it will continue to prove it. It has no conflict with its workers. But it is determined to fight the efforts of the city labor bosses to browbeat and exploit farm workers in an effort to expand their sphere of influence. If agriculture is to remain California's basic industry—building California—it must be conducted by farmers, not by the Bridges and Becks!

The newspaper headlines read:

"Beck and Bridges Battle for Control of Shipping!"

There's another headline, too—a more recent one. It reads:

"1937 STRIKE LOSSES COST AMERICA FIVE BILLION DOLLARS!"

Scan the headlines in the cities; any day's headlines. Then ask yourself: "Can agriculture afford to submit?"

Thugs who seize factories and plants, who hold up the United States mails, who fire on police and terrorize peaceful workers unwilling to accept their dictation, are also capable of setting fire to grain fields, firing on produce-laden trucks and calling strikes at peak harvest seasons—if they once get control of farm labor and are balked in their demands for exorbitant wage scales! And even if all demands should be met, which would mean bankruptcy for tens of thousands of farmers, farm crops may still rot in the fields while the C.I.O. and the A.F. of L. engage in a ruinous battle for supremacy—while Lewis or Green, Bridges or Beck seeks to become the American Stalin or Mussolini!

Can agriculture afford it?

There is only one answer to that question. Agriculture CAN'T afford it! But how, you may ask, can agriculture prevent it? Labor union organizers already have served notice that they propose to brand farm produce as "hot cargo" in San Francisco, Chicago, New York and all principal markets when their demands are rejected. And "hot cargo" means that no union teamster would dare to haul such produce; no union store would dare to handle it; no union member would dare to buy it.

This is a serious threat, as California turkey growers—who were given their choice of ruin or union dictation, shortly before Christmas—know from experience.

But agriculture has two possible defenses against such "rule or ruin" practices. Each, however, requires a united industry, ready to pool its funds and resources and to act as a unit to fight off disaster.

Agriculture might, for example, capitulate—invite the "beef squads" and the organizers to come in and take over; it might make Dave Beck president of the Farm Bureau and Harry Bridges head of the Grange; it might grant the five-day week and double pay for overtime; gladly pay all wage scales demanded. Then it might sit back and LET FOOD PRICES SOAR UNTIL THE GENERAL PUBLIC STEPPED IN to demand an end to it. That, of course, would invite national disaster; it might well end in a Fascist dictatorship.

But agriculture wants no part of Fascism; nor does it want Communism, with its reign of terror like that experienced in Soviet Russia.

There is, then, another defense—a drastic, but thoroughly American defense against injustice. IF LABOR DESPOTS, DRUNK WITH POWER, DECLARE CALIFORNIA FARM PRODUCTS "HOT CARGO," THEN— as has been proposed by several organizations—AGRICULTURE MIGHT BOYCOTT ANY CITY WHICH PERMITS THE "HOT CARGO" EMBARGO. It could go still further and BOYCOTT ALL UNION LABEL GOODS, OR AT LEAST THOSE OF THE OFFENDING UNIONS. It might say to its home-town merchants, who know its problems, "So long as you handle the goods manufactured by members of that union, which is seeking to destroy our business, we must trade elsewhere." It might say to San Francisco—if San Francisco "beef squads" are terrorizing rural areas— "We are exceedingly sorry, but until our workers are safe from intimidation and our trucks are safe on your city streets, we must trade in some other city." It might say to public officials who fail to maintain law and order, "Sorry, but we're voting for the other fellow!"

E S S A Y S

The authors of the two essays in this chapter discuss exactly the same events, but they highlight different protagonists. Cletus E. Daniel, a labor historian at Cornell University, emphasizes, in the first essay, the important role that white labor organizers played. The essay is excerpted from his highly praised study *Bitter Harvest: A History of California Farmworkers, 1870–1941*(1981). Though Daniel recognizes that the vast majority of the farmworkers who went on strike were Mexicanos, he relegates them to the background of the story. Their actions are said to be "completely unplanned, and thus devoid of . . . strategical and tactical considerations." When Daniel gives the Mexicanos any credit at all, he attributes their militance to "a slow process of acculturation."

In contrast, Devra Anne Weber, who teaches history at the University of California, Riverside, points out how the radical tradition born of the Mexican Revolution influenced the Mexicano farmworkers who went on strike in the

Imperial Valley. She shows that the membership in the mutual assistance organizations in the Mexicano community overlapped that of the labor unions they established. Writing about the events from a Mexicano perspective, Weber depicts the strikers as people with the ability to assess and to deal with the harsh conditions they faced—in short, as agents in the making of their own history.

Communist Organizers in the Imperial Valley

CLETUS E. DANIEL

Since low wages, irregular employment, harsh and abusive working conditions, and an utterly degraded standard of living had been the prevailing facts of the California farmworker's life for decades, the rise of an agricultural labor movement in the state at the beginning of the 1930s was due to more than a simple desire among workers to alleviate particularly oppressive features of their generally desperate economic situation. Rather, it was the product of a gradual realization among Mexican workers, who comprised a majority of the farm-labor force, that only through organization were they likely to mitigate their endemic powerlessness. Whatever other purposes it was destined to serve, the emergence of a militant disposition among Mexican farmworkers shattered the employers' comforting stereotype of the amiable and accommodating if somewhat dim-witted and disease-prone peon consigned by the infallible logic of nature to precisely that station which best served the interests of California's industrialized agriculture. This "new" Mexican was a product less of a dramatic transformation than of a slow process of acculturation. . . .

Mexican farmworkers had provided most of the labor power necessary to the operation of the Imperial Valley's highly industrialized agriculture almost from the beginning of the century, when massive irrigation efforts transformed the region from a barren desert into a fertile garden of unexcelled productive capacity. By the late 1920s the Imperial Valley was one of the leading vegetable- and melon-growing areas in the country. And with its large-scale production, absentee corporate ownership, labor-intensive crops, and seasonal reliance on an army of nonwhite immigrants, the valley's agriculture represented industrialized farming in its most extreme and unalloyed form.

For those employed on the valley's farms, mainly Mexicans and a large minority of Filipinos by the late 1920s, conditions were as oppressive as those faced by farmworkers anywhere in America. Until 1928 the discontent of the valley's farmworkers had usually remained submerged, although sporadic labor troubles had appeared often enough to give farm employers in the region some reason for concern. On the eve of the cantaloupe harvest in the early spring of 1928, Mexican farmworkers, in apparent response to the upsurge of interest in unionization among their countrymen in other parts of Southern California, formed the Workers Union of the Imperial Valley (La Unión de Trabajadores del Valle Imperial). With the assistance of Carlos Ariza, the Mexican vice-consul at Calexico, and the support of local mutual-aid societies, the union succeeded in attracting a membership of roughly 1,200 workers by early May. The union acted immediately to bring about improvements in wages and working conditions, but its respectful overtures to area melon growers were rejected out of hand. The union's leadership had apparently not contemplated any action so direct and forceful as a strike, but a few dozen rank-and-file militants rejected their leaders' conciliatory posture and struck several farms just as the harvest was getting under way. Employers and local authorities joined forces to smash the strike almost immediately, but not without suffering the unsettling realization that Mexican farmworkers might not be the docile, uncomplaining beasts of burden that they had so confidently described them as being for more than a decade.

Despite its brevity, and the fact that only a relative handful of the Imperial Valley's farmworkers were directly involved, the 1928 cantaloupe workers' strike was significant in that it revealed both a militant spirit and a firm expectation among Mexican laborers that their new union ought to be a fighting organization rather than simply another mutual-aid society. The strike also disclosed, however, that the new unionism among Mexican farmworkers was not without serious defects. The strike was completely unplanned, and thus devoid of the strategical and tactical considerations that might have enhanced its effectiveness. While the strikers deserved high marks for their militancy and courage, especially in light of the violent antiunionism they confronted, those laudable characteristics counted for little in the absence of an equally impressive measure of leadership. The other major weakness revealed by the strike was that the pronounced ethnic consciousness of the Mexican unionists, which derived as much from irremediable cultural differences as from a conscious choice, isolated them almost entirely from the non-Mexican farmworkers in the valley. This was particularly damaging to the potential success of farm unionism in the Imperial Valley because it tended to increase the estrangement of the large minority of Filipino workers in the region from the Mexican majority. And given the reputation for militancy and radicalism enjoyed by Filipino workers, it appears likely that had their cooperation been solicited, the strike would have posed a much more formidable challenge to farm employers.

The task of uniting the farmworkers and giving effective organizational focus to the palpable discontent that surged through their ranks in the Imperial Valley during 1928, as well as in California generally throughout the 1930s, was fraught with problems of staggering complexity. Both the A.F. of L. [American Federation of Labor] and the IWW [Industrial Workers of the World] had proved unequal to the challenge of organizing California's agricultural proletariat and abolishing its historic powerlessness, the former because of a lack of will and the latter because of a lack of coherent vision. Toward the end of 1929 the Communist Party of the United States, having proclaimed itself the new best hope of America's toiling masses, resolved to try its hand at accomplishing that task. And though they, too, were destined to fail in the end, in the early 1930s the Communists did provide the forceful leadership that was conspicuously absent in earlier organizing efforts among the state's farmworkers. Once fully joined, this volatile combination of farmworker militancy and radical leadership produced one of the most turbulent and eventful chapters in the history of agricultural unionism in the United States. . . .

On the first day of 1930, Mexican and Filipino farm laborers, increasingly dissatisfied with declining wages and the miserable working conditions in the lettuce fields of the Imperial Valley, walked off their jobs at several farms in the vicinity of Brawley. Within a few days what had started as a spontaneous, uncoordinated protest among a few hundred workers had become a full-fledged strike involving an estimated 5,000 field laborers. Because most of the Mexican workers, who constituted the majority of the strikers, belonged to the Mexican Mutual Aid Society of the Imperial Valley, the quasi-union that had succeeded the Workers Union of the Imperial Valley following the cantaloupe pickers' strike in 1928, that organization reluctantly assumed leadership of the strike. . . .

As they had done two years before, growers mobilized their forces, which included city, county, state, and federal authorities, in order to crush the strike before it had time to gain real momentum. Imperial County Sheriff Charles Gillett, an enthusiastic enforcer of the growers' antilabor program, immediately set about his strikebreaking task by insisting that no strike existed. . . .

With strikers getting little effective leadership from the cautious Mexican Mutual Aid Society, with intimidating threats being made by immigration officials, and with the ubiquitous Sheriff Gillett appearing throughout the valley to break up strikers' meetings and arbitrarily arrest all "troublemakers," the strike seemed destined to collapse as rapidly as it had begun. But the sudden appearance in the region of three energetic, if not particularly knowledgeable, Communist organizers from the TUUL [Trade Union Unity League] quickly altered the strike's course. . . .

Upon arriving in the town of Brawley, in the heart of the strike region, the three men made contact with local sympathizers and hastily formed a branch of the Agricultural Workers Industrial League [AWIL]. . . .

After several quiet days of preliminary organizational work, . . . [they] finally surfaced to conduct the AWIL's strike agitation among a wider circle of workers, including Filipino laborers. Making effective use of their mimeograph machine, the organizers soon flooded the strike region with a variety of handbills and leaflets imploring workers both to support the ongoing strike and to join the AWIL. To promote the latter goal an attractive list of AWIL strike demands was drawn up and widely distributed throughout the valley. Included among the twelve demands on the rather ambitious list were a minimum hourly wage of 50 cents for all workers, with higher pay for more difficult or skilled work; a guarantee of at least four hours' pay any time workers were called to the fields; an eight-hour day with time and a half for overtime and double time for Sundays and holidays; abolition of the labor contracting system; recognition of the AWIL; no work for children under sixteen; no discrimination on the basis of race, sex, or union membership; improved housing provided by employers; and the establishment of a hiring hall under the exclusive control of the AWIL—in effect, a closed shop.

Although it is clear that Communist organizers sought to establish the AWIL as the only farmworker union in the Imperial Valley, it is equally clear that they saw the necessity of building the union's appeal around fundamental issues involving wages and working conditions, and not around abstract ideological arguments that had little meaning to these deprived workers. . . .

By revealing their presence in the valley, . . . AWIL organizers . . . provoked vigorous counteractions by growers and their supporters. Moreover, those intent on breaking the lettuce workers' strike were now able to proceed in the name of selfless Americanism rather than in the less noble and altruistic cause of simple antiunionism. . . .

In response to the growing clamor for all-out repression of radical "agitators" in the valley, arrests of strikers mounted rapidly. An especially vigorous manhunt was launched to apprehend AWIL organizers once their activities came to light, and on January 12 the inevitable arrests were made. The three were charged with vagrancy and placed in separate jails, where each was interrogated and roughly treated over several days. The efforts of authorities were particularly directed toward forcing the men to confess that they had planned to blow up lettuce sheds in the valley. Despite much mistreatment, each steadfastly denied the existence of such a plan. . . .

Without relief from the outside, strikers with families to feed, and most Mexican workers fell into that category, had no choice but to return to work. . . .

At the same time that they called off the lettuce strike, however, AWIL organizers announced that they would launch a second strike in late spring, when the valley's cantaloupe harvest was due to begin. While admitting that the lettuce strike had failed, they insisted that the invaluable experience that had been gained from that encounter would virtually guarantee the success of the projected cantaloupe workers' struggle. . . .

Filipino farmworkers, whom Communist organizers had come to consider the most militant element in the Imperial Valley's agricultural labor force, were the earliest and most enthusiastic supports of the AWIL's strike agitation, although large numbers of Mexican laborers also unhesitatingly lent themselves to the new venture. AWIL organizers had hoped that white workers, too, could be persuaded to join their ranks. . . .

From the beginning, however, the striking shed workers made it plain that they wanted nothing to do with the AWIL. . . .

The failure of AWIL organizers to recruit white shed workers was viewed as only a minor setback, and did not affect efforts to rally support for the melon strike. During March, AWIL organizers, operating out of a shack in Brawley which served as the league's official headquarters, moved from town to town throughout the valley, organizing and conducting mass meetings among Mexican and Filipino workers. . . .

Because the AWIL made little or no effort to keep its strike plans confidential, wide publicity attended the activities of Communist organizers during the entire period of their agitation. The responses of growers, authorities, and most valley citizens to sensational local newspaper reports of prestrike doings were predictably hostile. Any threat to the region's multimillion-dollar melon crop was viewed as a threat to the personal well-being of every citizen in the valley. That Communists were behind the agitation provided an additional, if essentially superfluous, justification for prompt and untempered suppression. . . .

The strategy that authorities ultimately adopted to combat the AWIL menace was one that initially generated no publicity. In response to intense pressure from the major farm employers in the region, Imperial County District Attorney Elmer Heald finally decided to crush the farmworker movement by using the state's well-tested criminal syndicalism law against the Communist leadership of the AWIL. With the expert assistance of Captain William Hynes of the Los Angeles Police Department's notoriously antilabor "Red Squad," Heald secured the services of three professional labor spies. The three were instructed to infiltrate the AWIL, to gain the confidence of Communist organizers in the valley, and then to collect evidence that would facilitate the criminal syndicalism prosecutions that Heald intended. . . .

The inevitable showdown between the AWIL and antiunion forces came in mid-April. Late in March the AWIL had announced that a conference of all agricultural workers in the Imperial Valley would be held on April 20 in El Centro. At that conference, AWIL spokesmen advised, final preparations for the cantaloupe strike would be made and the first steps taken to form a "national industrial union in agriculture." On the evening of April 14, while preliminary meetings were being held in various parts of the valley, city, county, and state law-enforcement officials began a massive roundup of AWIL leaders and militant farmworkers. Meetings were raided throughout the valley, as were the several AWIL offices that had been established. Scores of workers were arrested, and what authorities described as "incriminating" evidence was seized. . . . The initial charge lodged against those arrested was conspiracy to destroy the Imperial Valley's cantaloupe crop. Bail was fixed at the prohibitively high figure of $40,000 per man, although the normal bail for such charges in the rest of the state ranged from $500 to $3,000. After much effort, the International Labor Defense finally persuaded the presiding judge to reduce the bail, but $15,000 was as low as he would go.

Most of the arrested workers were released within a few days. Only those identified by District Attorney Heald's undercover agents as leaders of the farmworker agitation remained in custody. . . .

With the arrest of the AWIL's most active organizers, agitation for the cantaloupe strike quickly died out. . . .

During the six weeks between the arrests of AWIL leaders and the start of their trial, Communists in the southern part of the state were forced to abandon their organizational efforts in favor of legal defense work on behalf of the eleven men finally selected by District Attorney Heald to stand trial in El Centro. . . .

The El Centro trial began on May 26. . . .

The only testimony offered in evidence against the defendants came from the three professional labor spies in Heald's employ. In succession, each took the stand to testify that the defendants had conspired to destroy the valley's melon crop, and had counseled farmworkers to use violence and terrorism in accomplishing that goal. In addition, each informer dutifully testified that the defendants had intimated that their ultimate goal in promoting a strike was to effect the destruction of capitalism and the overthrow of the government of the United States. To complete the prosecution's case, Heald sought to convince the jury that proof of membership in the Communist Party, as in the IWW, was enough in itself to justify conviction of the defendants under the state's criminal syndicalism law. . . .

Though they believed from the start that a fair trial was impossible under prevailing circumstances, defense attorneys endeavored nonetheless to refute the state's charges. Individually and collectively, the defendants denied the prosecution's allegations that they had conspired to destroy the valley's melon crop or that they had advocated the use of sabotage and terrorism by valley farmworkers. The charges made by Heald's "hirelings" were, defense attorneys argued, fabricated in every detail, products of a crude conspiracy by growers and authorities to deny farmworkers their right to organize and strike for better wages and working conditions. The highly emotional but irrelevant issues of communism and violent revolution, the defense insisted, were merely part of a tired subterfuge introduced by growers and their cohorts to conceal the true nature of the economic struggle going on in the valley. . . .

Late in the afternoon of June 30 the Imperial Valley criminal syndicalism cases went to the jury. After little more than an hour of deliberation, the jury filed back into the courtroom to announce that the defendants had been found guilty on all counts. Conviction on each count carried a penalty of from one to fourteen years in prison. The five veteran Communists among the defendants were given prison sentences of three to forty-two years each. The single Filipino defendant received a somewhat less severe sentence of two to twenty-eight years. For the three Mexican defendants, none of whom was a citizen of the United States, sentencing was held in abeyance pending the issuance of deportation orders. . . .

If the Imperial Valley struggle succeeded in generating vigorous legal and political activities in defense of agricultural unionism in California, it failed to provide an equally forceful stimulus for further organizational efforts among farmworkers . . . [partly due to] its inability to put effective new organizers into the field to replace those eliminated by the El Centro prosecutions. . . .

The decision by the Communist Party leaders . . . [in 1933] to return to the Imperial Valley . . . was prompted less by a desire to settle old scores than by their feeling that the region was especially ripe for organization. Wages had been as low as 10 cents per hour during 1933, and working and living conditions, which had long been recognized as the worst in the state, had become unspeakable by 1933. And, the fact that many of the Mexican and Filipino workers assembling in the valley for the winter lettuce harvest were veterans of earlier . . . strikes helped to convince party and union leaders that the prospects for organization there had never been brighter. . . . [Two Communist organizers, twenty-five-year-old] Stanley Hancock . . . [and nineteen-year-old] Dorothy Ray . . . took up the challenge armed with little more than high enthusiasm and a keen sense of revolutionary purpose. . . .

The antiunion campaign of Imperial Valley growers and shippers began even before organizers had entered the region. In late October, . . . valley employers took steps to block the organization of their workers by the CAWIU [Cannery and Agricultural Workers Industrial Union]. Their initial strategy, ironically, was to impede authentic organization by encouraging the revival of the Unión de Trabajadores del Valle Imperial, the short-lived Mexican union that had been active during the 1928 cantaloupe harvest. With the cooperation of Joaquín Terrazas, the Mexican consul in the valley, employers arranged a meeting with leaders of the newly resurrected union for the purpose of establishing wages and working conditions for the coming lettuce harvest. Out of the meeting, which involved no genuine bargaining, came an unwritten agreement by employers that the wage for field labor would be increased from the prevailing level of roughly 15 cents per hour to 22.5 cents per hour, and that a minimum of five hours' pay would be guaranteed to lettuce workers whenever they were called to work. Employers further agreed that once lettuce prices were established for the 1934 harvest season, they would hold a second meeting with the workers to discuss the possibility of a further increase in wages.

If employers hoped that their actions would guarantee labor peace, they were soon disappointed. On November 13 lettuce workers belonging to the Mexican union staged a one-day strike to protest several growers' refusal to honor the working agreement reached only two weeks before. Protests of a less disruptive nature continued into December. In response to the workers' protests, representatives of the Western Growers Protective Association, the dominant employers' organization in the valley, acknowledged that there had been innumerable violations of the working agreement, but insisted that they were powerless to do anything about the situation.

The refusal of lettuce growers to comply with the provisions of the working agreement undoubtedly facilitated the organizational drive that CAWIU organizers finally launched during the last week of November. Claiming that employers had conspired with Joaquín Terrazas to turn the Mexican union into a weak company union that could be easily manipulated, Communist organizers invited lettuce workers in the valley to join a "fighting union" that would win them higher wages and better conditions through uncompromising struggle. The response of Mexican workers was particularly strong in the vicinity of Brawley, and quickly resulted in the formation of a large and influential Communist-led opposition group within the Mexican union. During the latter part of December this group put increasing pressure on leaders of the Mexican union to demand substantially higher wages and improved working conditions before the lettuce harvest reached its peak.

In keeping with the understanding they had reached with growers' representatives at the November 1 meeting, leaders of the Mexican union asked employers in late December to meet with them to negotiate a new working agreement. Somewhat reluctantly, growers agreed to a meeting on January 2. At the meeting Mexican leaders frankly advised growers' representatives that unless the wage for lettuce fieldwork was raised to 35 cents per hour, Communist agitators would capture complete control of their union's membership. Spokesmen for the growers replied that existing economic conditions would not permit a wage increase of any kind, and insisted that lettuce workers were bound by the existing agreement to work for 22.5 cents an hour. Feeling that they had lost face, leaders of the Mexican union promptly stepped aside to allow the CAWIU to become the exclusive representative of Mexican farmworkers in the valley.

Communist organizers immediately seized the opportunity provided by the Mexican union's abrupt retreat. . . .

When the strike call went out on the morning of January 8, an estimated 3,000 farmworkers, many of whom were probably already unemployed, responded. On the following day another 2,000 or so workers joined the strike. . . .

The methods used to persuade workers to return to the fields consisted for the most part of unrestrained physical violence and arbitrary arrest. The use of violent strikebreaking tactics was common to most of the agricultural strikes in California during the early 1930s, but nowhere did farm employers and local authorities bring so much enthusiasm to their strikebreaking activities or pursue a course of violence and terror as single-mindedly and purposefully as in the Imperial Valley. . . .

The special enthusiasm with which the valley law-enforcement officers carried out their strikebreaking duties is partially attributable to a natural desire to serve the needs of the farm employers who controlled the economic and political life of the region. However, . . . the attitudes of law-enforcement officials were also shaped by important personal considerations. . . . [M]ost of the officials of the area . . . [were] themselves growers. . . .

As strikers persisted in their efforts to hold daily strike meetings, authorities' strikebreaking tactics became even more ferocious. On the evening of January 12 several hundred strikers and their families gathered for a meeting at Azteca Hall in Brawley, the strike headquarters. While the meeting was in progress a large force of police, deputy sheriffs, highway patrolmen, and deputized growers surrounded the hall, presumably to serve arrest warrants on several Communist organizers inside. Claiming that the large crowd of strikers was interfering with the execution of his duty, the Brawley police chief gave the signal for a barrage of tear gas to be fired into the hall. Once this had been done, authorities barred the doors from the outside, forcing the men, women, and children inside to break out every window in the building in order to escape the effects of the gas. When the hall had been cleared, authorities entered and destroyed every typewriter, duplicating machine, and other piece of equipment they could find, including appliances in a kitchen that had been used to feed strikers and their families. The arrest warrants for strike leaders, who clambered out a window to escape the choking gas along with everyone else, were not served.

Following the Azteca Hall attack, the lettuce strike rapidly lost its effectiveness. . . . Hundreds of strikers were taken into custody by local authorities, but most were later released without being charged with a crime. Of the dozens who were formally arrested, most were charged with vagrancy or disturbing the peace. Bail ranged between $500 and $1,800 per person. . . .

By January 18 the combined efforts of police terror and inadequate preliminary organization had so greatly reduced the impact of the lettuce strike that CAWIU leaders were forced to call it off. . . .

Communists considered the rural proletariat in California an especially vulnerable group. Farm laborers were, beyond any question, among the most disadvantaged workers in the United States. They spent their lives in a maze of abject poverty seemingly without avenues of escape. In the eyes of society, they were at once indispensable and despised. They were the essential reason for the prosperity of California's industrialized agriculture but were the state's least prosperous workers. Yet in indulging the impression that California farmworkers were, because of their demeaned status, likely to be amenable to anticapitalist political remedies, Communist planners fell victim to their own intellectual myopia. For unlike Communists, who necessarily looked to a fixed ideology to make sense of the volatile economic conditions of the early 1930s, farmworkers seeking to identify the principal cause of their economic suffering did not conclude that capitalism had failed them. Most farmworkers . . . concluded that they were desperately poor because they did not receive enough money for their labor. And, in the absence of a political consciousness that might have afforded them a less provincial understanding of their plight, the solution that suggested itself to California farmworkers was not the disestablishment of capitalism, but higher wages.

Mexicano Farmworkers on Strike

DEVRA ANNE WEBER

The period from 1928 to 1934 saw the organization of perhaps the first permanent Mexican agricultural unions in the United States. . . . [C]onscious

Excerpts from Devra Weber, "The Organizing of Mexicano Agricultural Workers: Imperial Valley, and Los Angeles, 1928–1934: An Oral History Approach," *Aztlan*, 3, no. 2, 1972: pp. 307–326. Copyright © 1972 by Devra Weber.

links existed with earlier, often radical, organizing which had originated in México. It was a time of intense organizing in the face of . . . a flooded labor market which had grown with the onslaught of the depression, a repatriation movement, and the growing power of the Associated Farmers. . . .

A general background of the Mexican workers' communities and organizations of the period is useful for understanding individual organizing efforts and the similarity of these efforts.

First, a primary source of agricultural labor in the Imperial Valley and Los Angeles remained Mexican between 1928 and 1934 in spite of the repatriation movement. . . . Among the 54,000 inhabitants of the Imperial Valley in 1927, 20,000 or one third of the population, were Mexicans. In 1934 the Mexican population was estimated conservatively at between 15,000 and 20,000. The maintenance of the population was due in part to the Valley's proximity to México. In 1930 there were approximately 80,562 Mexicans in Los Angeles. A heavy Mexican population remained in spite of massive repatriation drives. . . .

Second, most of the Mexican agricultural workers and strikers were residents of the communities, not migrants. The common misconception that Mexican agricultural workers were migrants profoundly affected official treatment of the Mexican. As a migrant the Mexican was not eligible for social services. . . . The high incidence of residency had important implications. Residency enabled organizations and leadership to develop, allowed for a continuity in organizing, and provided a purpose for organizing to better future conditions.

Third, Mexicans shared a common identity as workers and as Mexicans. In the ordinary working-class communities merchants and industrial workers had strong social and economic ties with the agricultural laborers. As a result, in both areas the Mexican communities overwhelmingly supported the agricultural workers' organizations and strike efforts. . . .

Fourth, . . . Mexican workers' mutual aid societies, mutualistas, were the most important community organizations. Mutualistas provided unemployment insurance, medical insurance, funeral care, and legal aid. They were the hub of Mexican social and political activity. Aid and benefits were extended to all members of the community. Earlier, the mutualistas had helped lead labor strikes. In 1928 they functioned as labor unions. The mutualistas and the unions were separate organizations but used common buildings, had common leadership, and boasted a common membership. . . .

Fifth, Mexican labor leadership arose out of the Mexican community and the mutualistas. The misconception that the union and strike leadership was Anglo, not Mexican, is rooted in an ignorance of the Mexican's political and organizational heritage.

Radical and militant thought was exhibited in the strikes and radical Anglos were often present. Many scholars and journalists . . . [therefore] concluded that it was . . . Anglo radicals who led the strikes, and that the radical ideas in the Mexican community were born out of the American stream of radical thought and introduced by Anglo organizers. In fact, the radical thought which existed in the communities originated in México from the Mexican labor movement and the Mexican revolution. . . .

The existence of Mexican ideologies and patterns of organizing is pivotal to understanding the strikes. . . . [I]n México[, m]utualistas had emerged in the 1870s and 1880s. Allegedly social organizations, they were the only legal arena for labor organizing under the Díaz dictatorship. From 1900 to 1910 these organizations flourished as membership climbed to 80,000, and they embraced a diversity of political ideologies. . . .

In Mexican workers' communities in both countries, workers' self help organizations became increasingly involved in labor organizing in a repressive atmosphere. . . . In both . . . [countries] mutualista membership represented a variety of frequently divergent political ideologies. Anarchist syndicalist thought was a force in both cases. Similarities suggest that workers applied their knowledge and organizational experience gained in México to the workers' organizations in the United States.

The United States Mexican community of the 1910s was radical. Mexican sociopolitical clubs, largely anarchistic in character, were the primary political organizations of Mexicans. These were headquartered in Los Angeles. Most Mexicans who voted in 1914 voted for the Socialist Party. . . .

Ricardo Flores Magón had the most powerful influence on Mexican radical thought and organizing in the United States. In 1904 he and his brother had fled to the United States after the seizure of their press and threatened imprisonment. . . . [He then] organized the United States based Mexican Liberal Party (MLP).

The purpose of the Mexican Liberal Party was, according to Flores Magón, "to conquer land and liberty for all. Its ideals are anarchist communist."

> Capital, Authority, the Clergy. Here we have the somber trinity which makes this earth a paradise for those who have succeeded by cunning, violence, and crime, in getting into their claws what the sweat, the blood, the tears and the sacrifices of thousands of generations of toilers produced; and a hell for those who, with arm and brain till the soil, set the machinery in motion, build the houses, and transport the products; the result being that humanity is divided into two classes whose interests are diametrically opposed—the capitalist class and the working class. Between these two social classes there cannot be any bond of friendship or fraternity.

Officials of the Mexican Liberal Party estimated the 1914 membership to be 6,000, although many more sympathized with the aims of the Party. In Los Angeles alone, the Party newspaper, *Regeneración,* had a circulation of 10,500 and was the most widely read newspaper in the Mexican community. All of the five Mexican papers in Los Angeles at the time were anarchistic or revolutionary. . . .

Although Flores Magón himself was concerned primarily with events in México, his thought and organizing were perhaps most influential in the United States. . . . The Mexican Liberal Party worked closely with its ally, the IWW, in early organizational efforts.

The close cooperation between the IWW and the MLP was a precedent for later Mexican cooperation with the Trade Union Unity League (TUUL) and the Cannery and Agricultural Workers Industrial Union (CAWIU). . . . The Mexican radical tradition was still strong in the 1930s in the rural and urban areas [of California]. . . .

The more conservative faction in organizing from 1928 to 1934 had Mexican precedents as well. The Mexican source for the philosophy of some of these forces was the Confederación Regional Obrera Mexicana (CROM). CROM formation and development in 1918 had marked the end of a strong anarchist syndicalist influence in the Mexican labor movement. . . . [T]he more conservative faction gave lip service to radical ideals, but preferred to organize within and with the present economic and social structure. . . .

In each strike the Mexican union encompassed radical and more moderate factions; the radical faction was allied with or cooperated with an Anglo radical union, the more moderate faction worked with the Mexican consul. . . . [S]ometimes the [Mexican] consul opposed the growers, often he tried to work with them. . . .

Mexicans had been employed in the Imperial Valley since the earliest days of United States rule. They worked on the railroads, on the ranches, in irrigation work and in agriculture, which they dominated during and after World War I. The 20,000 Mexicans, a third of the valley's population, were centered around the towns of Brawley and El Centro. About half lived on the ranches outside these towns.

As early as 1927 [economist] Paul Taylor . . . noted, "[The resident] group is vastly more important numerically than the group which crosses the line for seasonal work in the valley and returns to México when the season ends; and of infinitely greater social significance to the United States, for these are becoming a permanent part of the culture of the valley." . . .

Isolated from other ethnic groups, Mexicans had their own social organizations. . . . [T]he mutualistas were the most important. . . . The two dollar monthly dues were paid by a fluctuating membership of from forty to 125 people, depending on the season. Mutualista facilities and aid were extended to all members of the Mexican community. The most prominent of these societies were the Benito Juárez Mutual Aid Society of El Centro, founded in 1919, and the Miguel Hidalgo Mutual Aid Society of Brawley, founded in 1922. . . .

[M]utualista membership was comprised of laborers, along with a handful of labor contractors and others who had small jobs or businesses in the community. . . . [T]here was no evidence of class distinctions. Out of these mutualistas emerged early strike groups, labor unions, and strike leaders.

The major power and source of employment in the Valley was agriculture, and the seventy-four huge grower-shippers who owned the land. The large agricultural industry was characterized by absentee ownership, tenant farming, and general instability and impermanence. Ninety percent of the crops were grown or financed by these farming industrialists. This situation was not exceptional: California agriculture had been characterized by massive holdings and concentrated ownership since the days of the Spanish land grants, which had often been passed on intact to Anglo owners. The Times-Mirror Company, with 8,000 acres and the Southern Pacific Railroad Company, with 42,000 acres, were the major land holders in the area.

The dairy cattle industry thrived here, as did a variety of orchid [*sic*] and garden crops. The most important money crops were peas, lettuce, and melons. . . .

The work force was primarily Mexican, although Filipino labor predominated in some crops. Anglos worked in the dairies, the canneries, in the packing sheds, or drove heavy machinery. . . . In April 1928, a proposal was made for the formation of La Unión de Trabajadores del Valle Imperial, the Imperial Valley Worker's [*sic*] Union. . . .

Mutualistas joined to form the union and mutualista leaders became leaders of the union. No formal links existed between the unions and the mutualistas, but the informal connections were strong. Mutualista halls were union meeting places, and union and mutualistas often boasted a common membership.

The union admitted all Latins, but membership was primarily Mexican. . . . In 1928 the union claimed 2,746 members. The entire community had a financial stake in agriculture and was interested in promoting a union to better conditions. . . .

The melon strike began inauspiciously in May, 1928. Growers were preparing agreements with contractors as usual, when the newly formed union sent a polite request to growers and the Chamber of Commerce for increased wages and improved working conditions. They requested fifteen cents a crate or seventy-five cents an hour; picking sacks and ice water for drinking were to be supplied by the growers along with sanitary facilities and accident indemnities. The few growers who paid attention to the letter refused the request. Many growers had already signed at thirteen cents a crate and felt the requested seventy-five cents an hour to be exhorbitant [*sic*].

No formal strike was declared, but in an action unsanctioned by the union, cantaloupe pickers in the Brawley-Westmoreland area, refused to work for less than union demands. It appears that the union [had] lost control of these striking members and [Mexican] Consul [Carlos] Ariza, incensed by their action, refused any further connection with the union. Arguments and scuffles ensued between striking and working laborers, and on May 7 strikers who refused to leave the ranches were arrested. . . .

Unsigned circulars, presumably written by the growers, threatened and cajoled the striking workers and stated they should be grateful to the growers for fighting immigration restrictions. . . . Deportation was threatened as well as importation of scab workers. . . . Arrests continued. . . .

The strike was not settled, but soon subsided, perhaps because of arrests and intimidation. By May 14 most workers were back in the fields. Major issues of the strike remained: Housing was not improved, no proper insurance was instigated, no safeguards were erected against defaulting contractors, and no mechanism had been devised to insure just wages for the work performed.

Rumors continued among the Anglos that the sheriff had quelled a dangerous "red strike," stirred by agents from México City . . . [but t]he Mexican union itself was not communistic, anarchistic, or even remarkably radical or militant. . . . Due in large part to the diversity of union membership, no clear-cut philosophy emerged from the union. . . .

In the strike of 1930 Anglo radicals entered the Valley. . . . Class conscious Anglo unions had been in the Valley before, but they had been absent since the decline of the IWW after World War I. In January, 1930, the Trade Union Unity League [*sic*] (TUUL), admittedly a communist organization, entered the Imperial Valley attempting to gain control of the labor situation, and enlist membership among the workers. . . . [A] spontaneous strike in the lettuce fields . . . had been provoked by the wage reductions brought on by the depression. Strikers' demands were similar to those of 1928[:] . . . an increase in wages, improvement in housing conditions, and an adjustment of grievances. The TUUL organizers formed the Agricultural Worker's Union, headquartered in Brawley, through which they tried to organize field and picking workers together in an industrial type union. . . .

[T]he TUUL was more radical, more class conscious, and more militant than the Mexican labor union. . . . [It] enrolled a large number of heretofore unorganized migratory Filipino workers, primarily single men who lived outside the town on the ranches. Among the Mexicans, the Asociación Mexicana del Valle Imperial was still strong. Some Mexicans who disagreed with . . . [their own] union . . . made alliances with the TUUL. . . .

Despite ideological differences the Mexican union and the TUUL worked together on the strike committee and ideological differences were discussed in the strike meetings. . . .

[T]he [1930] lettuce strike [also] ended after a short time as the strikers returned to the fields with no improvements made. The Mexican union collapsed. . . .

In April, a TUUL meeting was broken up by Brawley Sheriff Gillette [*sic*] and those attending the meeting were arrested. Nine were tried and convicted of violating the Criminal Syndicalism Act which declared illegal any organization that "advocates and teaches the change of industrial ownership and control of effecting any political change through the commission of crime and sabotage or unlawful acts of force and violence or unlawful methods of terrorism." . . . The TUUL collapsed after these convictions, but the relationship between radical Anglo organizations, Mexican radicals, and the Mexican union and the community emerged again in 1934. . . .

By the Fall of 1931, the economic decline heralded by the 1929 stock market crash had descended into the Great Depression. . . . Midwestern farmers and laborers out of work joined the migrant force as hundreds of Anglos poured into the California fields, many entering in the Imperial Valley and working their way north. The new influx of labor heightened competition and lowered wages. Mexican labor became expendable and in 1930 massive repatriation drives were launched, sending people of Mexican descent, citizen and noncitizen, back to México. [However, t]he Valley was too hot for many Anglos to stay long in the fields, and Mexican deportations here were minimal, although a constant threat. Mexicans again organized to strike for better wages and conditions. Conditions had not improved since the 1930 strike. The 1934 strike was to be longer, and the repression more brutal.

In October, 1933, the Mexican Mutual Aid Association was revived in Brawley. On November 1, the union met with growers to stave off a possible strike in the lettuce fields, agreeing on a wage rate of twenty-two and one-half cents an hour, a guaranteed five hours of work a day, and an opportunity to review the agreement in January, 1934, if the market for lettuce had improved. Claiming the growers had broken the agreement, a strike was called thirteen days later. . . .

In late December a group of strikers in the union sent a delegation to Los Angeles to ask help from the allegedly communist organization, the Cannery and Agricultural Workers Industrial Union (CAWIU). Frank Nieto, a member of the strike committee, headed the delegation which brought back to the Valley Stanley Hancock and the young [nineteen-year-old] Dorothy Ray Healy. Arriving January 1, they met with local leaders at the Azteca Hall in Brawley used by the union, two doors up on a dusty street from the Miguel Hidalgo Society. . . .

On January 2, the growers refused to grant an increase in pay to thirty-five cents an hour because, the workers felt, of market drops. Leaflets had been issued twenty-four hours before announcing a union meeting in Brawley for the night of January 2. According to Dorothy Ray Healy, several thousand jammed the small hall. A strike committee was elected and subcommittees created, each headed by a strike committee member, to care for publicity, picketing, welfare distribution, and other needs. . . .

A strike call on January 8 triggered violent grower reaction. On January 9, a Brawley cavalcade of cars leaving for a mass meeting in El Centro was broken up by city, county, and state law officers using tear gas. Arrests followed, numbering upward of eighty-seven. On January 12 a mass meeting in Azteca Hall was broken up by a body of gun-wielding law officers using tear gas bombs, one of which killed a child. Two deaths resulted and numerous arrests were [made].

The struggle in the Valley became a focal point of interest. Reporters, lawyers, and a federal investigator, General [Pelham D.] Glassford, filed into the desert to record the violation of the workers' civil rights by the growers and law enforcement officers. . . .

On February 19, the strike was crushed when the shacks of some strikers were burned, and 2,000 strikers evicted. The Azteca Hall raid and arrests helped halt the strikes, yet evidence of unrest was still apparent. Well stocked jails became schools for future labor organizers. At least thirty of those imprisoned were actively making plans for future strikes. Feelings of solidarity were growing among Anglo and Filipino workers, and Mexicans continued to organize under new leadership. General tension and agitation continued.

Mexican radicals . . . were active in the strike efforts of 1934 and held positions of leadership. Dorothy Ray Healy remembers the Mexicans to be more politically aware than the CAWIU representatives, a fact she contributes [*sic*] to their revolutionary heritage. . . . Guillermo Martínez remembers that the works of [Ricardo] Flores Magón were circulated and were influential in the community. . . .

Names of the leaders who were Marxists, socialists, or anarchist syndicalists emerge in interviews: Gonzalo Quinn, Frank Nieto, Smiley Rincón who later died in the Spanish Civil War, Alejandro Murieta, Rivera, and Gutiérrez. Nieto and Murrieta [*sic*] were on the strike committee and had allegedly been influenced by the writings of Magón.

Contrary to claims that the CAWIU took over and controlled the strike, the two young representatives of the CAWIU worked closely and amicably with the union and community organizers, except for the group led by the Mexican Consul, Joaquín Terrazas. Following grower refusal of terms, it appears that the more militant members of the Mexican union gained a large following, became the more influential power in the union, and called in the CAWIU. . . . Dorothy Ray Healy says that the CAWIU organizers followed the dictates of the Mexicans who better understood the community. Decisions were made by Mexicans in large strike meetings.

Although working together on the strike committee, sharp conflict still existed between the radicals, now allied with the CAWIU, and the members of the Mexican union supported by the Mexican consul in Caléxico, Joaquín Terrazas. The consul's role in this strike was important. Terrazas was the most powerful Mexican in the Valley. He had access to the press and the growers. He had a degree of prestige within the Mexican community and within the Anglo community as a representative of the Mexicans. As a result, his participation and opinion were often interpreted inaccurately as representative of the desires and opinions of the whole Mexican community. . . .

Carey McWilliams in *The Nation* stated that the growers favored or even induced Consul Terrazas to reorganize the union. This became the organization which Dorothy Ray Healy described as a company union, a union the growers felt to be "legitimate and without communist tendencies." There were reports that workers were being forced to join this union.

On March 28, the faction of the union supported by Terrazas met with the growers. In an agreement signed by union President Augustín Duarte, the growers gave job preference to the resident members of the Mexican union supported by Terrazas. The contract guaranteed water furnished by the growers, a pay scale of twenty-five to thirty-five cents an hour and thirteen cents per picked crate, and the establishment of a grievance committee. The growers agreed to give protection from communist agitators.

The contract indicates that the faction Terrazas supported made the agreement in the name of the union but without the total support of the union. . . .

It was this faction of the union which, with grower encouragement[,] was misinterpreted by those outside the community as representing the whole of the Mexican union. . . . As a result the role and the tenor of the Mexican union has been misinterpreted.

Strikes were to come again to the Valley, but none so large. The growers had succeeded in maintaining power and in jailing or deporting much of the strike leadership.

 # FURTHER READING

Francisco E. Balderama, *In Defense of La Raza: The Los Angeles Mexican Consulate and the Mexican Community, 1929–1936* (1982)

Clarke A. Chambers, *California Farm Organizations: A Historical Study of the Grange, the Farm Bureau, and the Associated Farmers, 1929–1949* (1952)

Sucheng Chan, *The Bittersweet Soil: The Chinese in California Agriculture, 1860–1910* (1986)

Cletus E. Daniel, *Bitter Harvest: A History of California Farmworkers, 1870–1941* (1981)

William F. Dunne, *The Great San Francisco General Strike* (1934)

Paul Eliel, *The Waterfront and General Strikes, San Francisco, 1934* (1934)

H. E. Erdman, "The Development and Significance of California Cooperatives, 1900–1915," *Agricultural History* XXXII (July 1958): 179–84

Lloyd S. Fisher, *The Harvest Labor Market in California* (1953)

Mario Gamio, *The Mexican Immigrant: His Life-Story* (1931; 1969)

J. D. Gaydowski, "The Genesis of the Townsend Plan," *Southern California Quarterly* LII (December 1970): 365–82

Gilbert G. Gonzalez, *Labor and Community: Mexican Citrus Worker Villages in a Southern California County, 1900–1950* (1994)

James N. Gregory, *American Exodus: The Dust Bowl Migration and Okie Culture in California* (1989)

Abraham Hoffman, *Unwanted Mexican Americans in the Great Depression: Repatriation Pressures, 1929–1939* (1974)

Abraham Holtzman, *The Townsend Movement* (1963)

Claude B. Hutchinson, ed., *California Agriculture* (1946)

Lawrence J. Jelinek, *Harvest Empire: A History of California Agriculture* (1979; 2nd ed., 1982)

Stephen Johnson, Gerald Haslam, and Robert Dawson, *The Great Central Valley: California's Heartland* (1993)

John Kagel, "The Day the City Stopped," *California History* LXIII (Summer 1984): 212–23

Charles E. Larsen, "The Epic Campaign of 1934," *Pacific Historical Review* XXVII (May 1958): 127–48

Bruno Lasker, *Filipino Immigration to Continental United States and to Hawaii* (1931; 1969)

Leonard Leader, "Upton Sinclair's EPIC Switch: A Dilemma for American Socialists," *Southern California Quarterly* LXII (Winter 1980): 361–85

Richard Lowitt, *The New Deal and the West* (1984)

Carey McWilliams, *Factories in the Field: The Story of Migratory Farm Labor in California* (1939)

Carey McWilliams, *North from Mexico: The Spanish-Speaking People of the United States* (1948; 1968)

Linda C. Majka and Theo J. Majka, *Farm Workers, Agribusiness, and the State* (1982)

Greg Mitchell, *The Campaign of the Century: Upton Sinclair's Race for Governor of California and the Birth of Media Politics* (1992)

William H. Mullins, *The Depression and the Urban West Coast, 1929–1933* (1991)

Bruce Nelson, *Workers on the Waterfront: Seamen, Longshoremen, and Unionism in the 1930s* (1988)

William L. Preston, *Vanishing Landscapes: Land and Life in the Tulare Lake Basin* (1981)

Jackson K. Putnam, *Old-Age Politics in California* (1970)

Mike Quinn, *The Big Strike* (1949)

Ricardo Romo, *East Los Angeles: History of a Barrio* (1983)

Vicki L. Ruiz, *Cannery Women, Cannery Lives: Mexican Women, Unionization, and the California Food Processing Industry, 1930–1950* (1987)

Ann Foley Scheuring, ed., *A Guidebook to California Agriculture* (1983)

Harvey Schwartz, *The March Inland: Origins of the ILWU Warehouse Division, 1934–1938* (1978)

Harvey Schwartz, "Harry Bridges and the Scholars: Looking at History's Verdict," *California History* LIX (Spring 1980): 66–79

Walter J. Stein, *California and the Dust Bowl Migration* (1973)

Ronald Tobey and Charles Wetherell, "The Citrus Industry and the Revolution of Corporate Capitalism in Southern California, 1887–1944," *California History* LXXIV (Spring 1995): 6–21, 129–31

Tom Zimmerman, "Ham and Eggs Everybody!" *Southern California Quarterly* LXII (Spring 1980): 1–48

The Impact of World War II
on California's Economy

*Despite the New Deal's many programs, full recovery from the Great
Depression had not yet been achieved by the end of the 1930s. In California,
total personal income in 1939 stood at the same level as it had in 1930,
while per capita income was below that figure. After Adolf Hitler invaded
Poland in September 1939, however, the U.S. economy received a tremendous boost as it started filling orders from America's European allies for
ships, airplanes, weapons, and ammunition. By the time the United States
entered the war, after Japan's December 1941 bombing of Pearl Harbor,
economic recovery was well on the way.*

*California benefited more than any other state from the mobilization for
war. Fully 10 percent of all federal funds were spent in the state. Defense
industries sprang up and numerous new military installations were built.
California's fine weather and its geography both proved to be assets. The
clear, blue skies of virtually rainless southern California were ideal for testing airplanes. The dry sands of the state's deserts provided the right terrain
for training troops and testing tanks headed for military engagement in
North Africa. The shipyards fronting the Pacific facilitated naval operations.
California's long coastline offered many beaches where troops could practice
amphibious landings. Units destined for the Pacific theater all shipped out
from Pacific Coast and particularly California ports.*

*Entrepreneurs such as Henry J. Kaiser, Donald Douglas, John K.
Northrop, and the Loughead brothers Allan and Malcolm (who changed
their name to Lockheed to avoid mispronunciation) expanded their existing
plants and established new ones to mass-produce all kinds of ships and airplanes under defense contracts. Production facilities operated around the
clock, staffed by three shifts of workers. The production process became so
streamlined that a Liberty ship (a type of mass-produced cargo ship widely
used during World War II) could be completed in twenty-five days. Similar
freighters had taken more than 250 days to build before the war. To manufacture steel for the ships he was building, Henry Kaiser in 1942 opened the
first integrated blast furnace and steel-rolling mill in California.*

California's scientists also played a crucial role in war production. Scientists at the California Institute of Technology developed new designs in rocketry and established the world-famous Jet Propulsion Laboratory. Professors at the University of California did the research that enabled the United States to build the first atomic bomb. Engineers at Stanford University nurtured the nascent electronics industry (see Chapter 14).

As a result of this wartime boom, the total personal income of Californians more than tripled in five short years. Tens of thousands of people from other parts of the country flooded into the state to fill the new jobs that became available, causing severe shortages in housing, transportation, educational facilities, and many other necessities. Instead of widespread unemployment, a labor shortage now characterized many California industries. At their zenith in 1943 the aircraft and shipbuilding industries each employed over a quarter million workers, many of whom had migrated into the state.

Wartime growth helped consolidate a pattern of urban development that historian Roger W. Lotchin has called the "metropolitan-military complex." In a provocative book, Fortress California, 1910–1961: From Warfare to Welfare (1992), Lotchin argues that the major partnership in California has not been between industries and the military (as implied in the term military-industrial complex) but has, rather, been one in which municipalities and the military have worked in tandem as the engine of the state's economic development.

This pattern first emerged during World War I—in a period when the U.S. Navy dreamed of a Pacific empire—and became increasingly entrenched during the interwar years. World War II and the cold war increased the impact of military spending on California's economic health to such an extent that when several large military bases were scheduled for closing in the early 1990s, cries of desperation filled the air.

Some historians, notably Gerald D. Nash in the first essay in this chapter, view the boom years of World War II as a watershed in California history, a period of tremendous growth in which California finally shook off a subordinate relationship with the East and became a leader among American states. Other historians, such as Paul Rhode in this chapter's second essay, argue that the basic change actually occurred around 1900 and that the period of greatest growth was the 1920s. As you read the documents and essays, ask whether the World War II years were, in fact, as crucial as Nash maintains, or simply a part of a trend that began decades earlier.

 ## D O C U M E N T S

The first document, excerpted from a report prepared by the Bureau of Labor Statistics in the U.S. Department of Labor, points out that California's plants did not make entire airplanes but, rather, assembled them by combining engines and propellers manufactured elsewhere in the nation with bodies fabricated in California. In addition to citing many statistics, the report praises employers and employees in California's aircraft industry for their efforts to maintain industrial peace.

The second document consists of vignettes published in Fore'N'Aft, the employee magazine produced by the Kaiser shipyards. It offers a glimpse of the competitive spirit among shipyard workers who enthusiastically committed themselves to buttressing the "home front."

An exceptionally high percentage of the workers in the shipyards and airframe manufacturing plants were women. Marye Stumph, the narrator in the third document, was one among thousands of women who had migrated to California in search of a better life. Her story was recorded by Sherna B. Gluck, who teaches women's studies at California State University, Long Beach, and directs the Oral History Program there, as part of the research done for the 1980 documentary film *Rosie the Riveter.*

By 1944, a series of defeats suffered by Japan signaled the war's imminent end. Accordingly, defense industries began to cut back on production and many workers, especially women, were laid off. Industrial leaders nonetheless remained hopeful that the stupendous transformations that had occurred during the war would continue to prime California's economic pump in the postwar period. The fourth document, written by Worth Hale in 1946, summarizes the industrialists' optimistic assessment of California's economic prospects after the war.

The U.S. Bureau of Labor Statistics Reports on California's Airframe Industry, 1945

California is the principal airplane-producing State in the Nation; during the war approximately 20 percent of its manufacturing labor force was engaged in one phase or another of aeronautical production. The State provided aircraft not only to this country's Army, Navy, and commercial airlines, but to many foreign nations as well. The gamut of models is complete, including bombers, fighters, transports and trainers. . . . California accounted for 33 percent of total airframe weight accepted when production reached its peak in early 1944.

California's aircraft are produced in the southern part of the State, with concentration in the Los Angeles and San Diego areas. Strict interpretation requires use of the term "airframe" rather than "aircraft" when referring to California, since the State's only producer of aero-engines ceased to be a prime contractor in mid-1943, and at no time were propellers made in the State. In June 1945 there were seven facilities in the Los Angeles area and two in the San Diego area which may be properly termed airframe plants. Most of these had established "feeder plants" in the surrounding areas— shops specializing in a small phase of the production job which, upon completion, is forwarded to the main plant for installation. This technique was resorted to in order to increase production floor space, but more important, to utilize areas where labor was still available. In this way workers could be employed who ordinarily would not have been engaged in airplane manufacture. The airframe facilities and their feeders have been supplemented by plants producing subassemblies, instruments, and parts—all combining to make up the aircraft community. However, local suppliers provided only a fractional part of total requirements. All types of items—engines, propellers, subcontractor assemblies, parts, instruments, accessories—from all sections of the country funneled through the airframe plants, and the handling of these, together with their own fabrication and assembly operations, placed upon them the burden of a coordination job of first magnitude.

At the beginning of 1940, California airframe plants employed approximately 30,000 workers, but by the end of the year this figure more than doubled, reaching 70,200. . . . In 1941 employment again more than doubled. By the time of the Pearl Harbor attack, therefore, 151,500 persons were at work in these plants—5 times the early 1940 figure.

The year 1942 witnessed a 67-percent gain, which brought total employment to 254,400 by December. . . . Major expansion had been accomplished by that time, even though the peak was not reached until mid-1943. This is evident from the monthly net gain in employment. During 1940 the net monthly increase averaged 3,650 workers. The corresponding figure for 1941 was 6,800, but the maximum average increase was reached in 1942 with 8,600. The all-time record for any one month occurred in December 1942, when the number at work increased from the previous month by 16,900. . . . California's July 1943 airframe employment was 280,300, almost 10 times the number at work when expansion began. For the 3 succeeding months, the airframe labor force approximated 275,000. It should be noted that these figures refer to prime contracting plants only, and do not include a considerable volume of California employment in plants making aircraft parts and subassemblies.

The decline in aircraft employment in California followed the same general pattern experienced by the industry in other areas, though it started a few months earlier. A decrease was registered each month, beginning in November 1943 and extending throughout 1944. More than 97,000 persons were off the pay rolls by December 1944, when employment was down to 182,700 or two-thirds of the peak level. The downward trend was temporarily halted in January 1945. However, the decline began again in February and continued moderately through April. The 18,000 drop in May was a direct result of cutbacks which became operative with VE-day [Victory-over-Europe-day] and by the end of June the State's airframe employment was down to 142,200. Following VJ-day [Victory-over-Japan-day], aircraft employment dropped precipitously as military contracts were canceled or reduced. California aircraft employment declined from 136,700 in July to 93,200 at the end of August, a reduction of about a third.

Because of the concentration of the State's airframe facilities in only two labor markets, the areas affected were under extreme pressure soon after the outbreak of the war. Contracts for an unprecedented number of airplanes to be delivered as quickly as possible resulted in a scramble for manpower by the airframe plants themselves. The competition was accentuated by needs of neighboring establishments, both aeronautical and nonaeronautical. . . .

The enormous growth of California's airframe employment would have been impossible had it not been for the extensive recruitment and training of women workers. Faced with the manpower squeeze earlier than the rest of the industry, the California plants hired women workers sooner and in larger numbers than anywhere else. There were fewer than 10,000 women workers in California airframe plants in 1942, . . . but by June 1943 the employment of women reached peak when 120,700 (12 times as many) were at work. From January 1943 until VE-day 40 percent or more of the State's airframe employment consisted of women. . . . Until June 1945 total employment of women workers was proportionately higher in California than elsewhere. The State also had one large facility in which, throughout 1943 and 1944, there were more women workers than men.

While employment of women in California airframe plants was still at the 40-percent level in April 1945, their number was down to 69,400. By June their employment had dropped to 52,300, or 37 percent of total. Thus until VE-day, women maintained their relative position, with their number declining only in proportion to the general decrease in employment. A sharp drop in the proportion of women employees occurred after the Japanese surrender, as increasing lay-offs brought the number of women down to 30.8 percent of the total. . . .

California's contribution to industrial peace is also noteworthy. Management in the airframe plants was aware of the potential difficulties inherent in the complete lack of uniformity existing in wages paid for seemingly identical jobs. Consequently, in the early part of 1941 an intercompany committee was formed to study the problem of standardization of jobs and job titles. The success of the committee's work can be measured by the fact that 1,154 job titles were reduced to 116. . . . The standardization ultimately became known as the Southern California Aircraft Industry System (SCAI plan). When the National War Labor Board assumed responsibility for wage stabilization in the fall of 1942, it appointed a special committee to examine wage rates in California airframe plants, preparatory to its program of wage stabilization for the entire airframe industry. The SCAI plan was accepted by the committee and then by the National War Labor Board as the basis for airframe wage stabilization. The results of the California investigation, which was limited to 8 companies, served as a pattern for the entire industry, and, together with subsequent wage orders, eliminated troublesome inequalities. To the cooperative spirit of California labor and management and the Government in harmoniously reaching an early solution of wage differences goes the credit for removing what might have developed into a major obstacle to the aircraft program.

Kaiser Shipyard Workers Fight on the Home Front, 1943

After thousands of Yard Three people answered the call of a committee of their own co-workers, pledged General Eisenhower that they would open a real Second Front on the home front, things began to happen. Second Front subcommittees were formed all over the yard . . . all the way from the warehouse to the plate shop. It was on a Saturday morning we heard of the invasion of Sicily. Saturday, Sunday and Monday of the previous week, production had been running at a typical level. Saturday, Sunday and Monday after the announcement of the second front in Europe, weld footage per man was up 3.7 per cent—not 20 per cent yet, as pledged—but on the way.

Steel erection for the period after the formation of the Second Front Committee was, at last report, 9.7 per cent higher. The number of rivets driven was greater . . . much greater. Morale all along the line looked better; certainly among Yard Three workmen, and probably among our invading soldiers, many of whom heard Yard Three's message via OWI broadcasts.

One of the Pacific Coast's most powerful organized labor groups went on record this month as being enthusiastically in favor of the "Second Front on the Home Front" movement, which was begun voluntarily last month as the encouraging answer of Yard Three's workers to Gen. Eisenhower's forces invading Europe via Sicily.

The Bay Cities Metal Trades Council's newspaper, *American Labor Citizen,* reported the Yard Three pledge to "do our damndest to step up production by 20 per cent or more" under the head, "THE SPIRIT OF THE AFL."

Said the Council newspaper, "When the thousands of AFL workers at Richmond Shipyard Number Three voluntarily signed a pledge to increase production of ships of war by 20 per cent, they launched a movement which promises to sweep throughout the entire shipbuilding industry of the Nation."

Men and women working in another Bay Area shipyard thought so, too. As reported in the *Citizen,* "The challenge embodied in the action of the Richmond workers brought almost immediate response from the thousands of shipyard workers at Marinship in Sausalito, who went even further in extending the challenge into a competitive race between themselves, the Richmond workers and the shipyard employees at Kaiser's Swan Island yard in Washington, and to the Alabama Dry Dock Company."

They drew up the following challenge: "We, the workers of Marinship, hereby challenge the workers of the above-named yards to a competitive production race for the period ending October 31, 1943—results to be judged by the Maritime Commission."

A Second Front Leader in Yard Three who had been contacted by the Marinship group, told Fore 'N' Aft: "We are in a good position in this contest. Men and management are both promising cooperation in our drive; we are all squared away to step production up."

Marye Stumph Recalls Her Work Experiences in an Aircraft Factory

December of 1940, why, I finally got to California. I'd been saving my money until I got my fare saved up. I sent the kids out during the summer and they came out on the train by themselves. Then I went out on the bus in December. . . .

I started looking for a job right away, but there wasn't anything. So I found this Grau Business School, where I could have classes in the morning and then we worked in the afternoon addressing envelopes. That paid our tuition. . . .

The owner of the business school told us that we could go down to Third and Olive where they were training people for the defense plant. It was part of the Long Beach City College system. Well, naturally, I was interested in most any job because I wanted to get my family back together. It wasn't that I was particularly thinking about defense. That was just what came along. So I went down there right away. They were teaching us to work with simple wiring and pliers, things for electrical subassembly— which I never used when I did get out there.

I don't think I was even there six weeks when the foreman of the sub-assembly section at Vultee came down there and picked out some people to interview. It was July when I went to work. I started at 62.5 cents an hour. I thought I'd hit the mother lode!

That was the first time I'd ever worn slacks. I felt kind of funny because I didn't really have the figure for slacks. I was pretty buxom. Of course, we got quite used to it, and later I wore them all the time, even on my day off. We didn't have to wear safety shoes; most everybody wore leather oxfords. If you worked with any of the machinery, you were supposed to wear a hair net, and if you were working around welding, you wore goggles.

I had worked in factories and it wasn't too strange to me. I kind of stood around, and they decided where they wanted people to work. The planes that Vultee put out, they weren't these big bombers; they were like two-seater planes. All the names started with "V" like in Vultee. They had a training plane called the Vanguard and, later on, a dive bomber called the Vengeance.

Anyway, I went into subassembly. They had these "skins": sheets of aluminum about four feet by eight feet. These were riveted on to the sides of the plane. But they had to be cleaned. They had two tanks, one a rinse tank with clear water and one with a real strong acid. We wore big heavy rubber gloves that came way up our arms. We dipped these skins in this acid and we had to take a cloth and swab it around. Then we'd rinse them in the clear tank and stand them up on the floor and dry them with an air hose. Then they were taken over to the spot-weld machines.

After a few days I was kind of in charge of the tanks, and when they'd have a few girls in other departments who'd run out of work and be at loose ends, they'd send them over to work with me. That job seemed to be a place where they put new people, and then they'd gradually go off to other jobs as they showed an aptitude for certain things.

After a while, the supervisor wanted me to go on the spot-welding machine. It was a big, tall machine and you just sat there and ran the pieces together and the hot iron would just come down and hit it. It just welded in a little spot, like a needle. It wasn't anything that anybody couldn't do, but the men got all up in arms. They didn't want any women on there and they all protested. So I didn't get on the spot-welding machine.

I liked anything mechanical like that and I would have liked spot welding, but it didn't break my heart because I didn't. Later, I heard that there was a vacancy over in the machine shop. That sounded interesting to me, so I just asked if I could have a chance over there. Everybody that went into the machine shop started out with burring, scraping the rough edges off of parts.

Then they started me out on a Harding lathe, which was a little, small lathe. I guess maybe the whole thing was about five foot. They didn't do too many operations on those; it was more like cutting rods to a certain length, which was very simple. I worked for a few months on that and on the drill press, and then I got a chance to go on one of the big lathes, the number three—the number fives were the big ones. I really liked that.

By that time, the war had started and a lot of the men started leaving and there were a lot of women. In fact, practically all those men on spot welding had to go into the service and they put women on the machines. Right in my own department, they never did put women on the really big, number five lathes. The men seemed to be professional machinists; they had a lot of experience and were able to do their own set-ups. Class A machinists were still men. The women got to be Class B machinists, which was as much as we expected to be. We weren't making a career of it like men. We were doing what was there to do. . . .

I didn't actually think too much about the future. Oh, occasionally I did worry about what I'd do when the war ended. I could have enjoyed an assembler job. I could have just gone on and made a career out of that. But I didn't think that there was anything like that available for women. It was just an emergency that they hired women in, and I didn't figure that there was enough chance finding anything to bother trying to keep in that line.

It just ended overnight. My daughter had been visiting her aunt for the summer down in New Mexico, and I had taken a week's vacation and gone down to bring her back. The war ended while I was down there. By the time I got back, I had a telegram saying that the job was over. A ten-word telegram.

Industrial Leaders Assess the West's
Postwar Economic Prospects, 1946

Aviation—Its Future Largely Depends on Government

Financially this industry is in magnificent shape and ready for whatever developments may occur. Broadly speaking, the future depends on . . . the government. What it will demand of aviation will be determined by everything from ultimate disposition of the atom bomb, possible merger of the armed forces, and the new policy of national defense.

Labor-wise, . . . firms find . . . they have no way of estimating their future labor needs in terms of quality or quantity. There is a distinct shortage of special skills such as design engineers.

From the production standpoint, manufacturers of passenger planes are enjoying substantial orders. [A c]omplicating factor is that producers heretofore not engaged in this type of work are prepared to take substantial losses to break into the market.

[The f]uture of private flying and cargo planes suffers from lack of a decisive government policy. No one knows whether the government will keep, sell or give away the countless millions of dollars worth of surplus planes which hang over the market.

Although tenuous, the future of the aircraft industry is being measured by speculators in terms of all-time highs in the quotations of their securities.

Steel—Leaders of Industry Point to an Urgent Market

Prospective volume is excellent in all categories of products for at least a year. Further than that no one knows. Some believe that demand will continue for several years. The answer lies in how fast labor works and how much production per man-hour is obtained.

While an extended period of maximum operations can be anticipated, steel men remind themselves that the backlog of orders is not inexhaustible. Processors can sell all the products they can make, but to do so they require steel and labor—neither of which can be obtained in sufficient quantity— not to mention prices.

Faced by imminent prospects of an industry-wide strike, the mills admit they are behind the 8-ball. The pipeline from mill to consumer is just about dry. . . .

Building products show a tremendous demand in spite of the complications of labor, costs and rentals. Paradoxically the demand is heavy and yet there is relatively little building going on. . . .

Shipping—Wholly in the Hands of Government Policy

The next twelve months for this industry's future lies almost wholly in the hands of government. What happens to shipping depends almost entirely on the outcome of the Ship Sales Bill. This legislation is not satisfactory to the industry in its present shape. Foreign competition is, was, and always will be an item of paramount importance to the industry, and present plans for disposal of surplus American bottoms may create a greater competition than existed in the past. . . .

The bulk of war-built vessels are inappropriate for American trade. C-1s, C-2s and C-3s can be readily adapted with additional deeptanks and reefers, but Liberties and Victories are definitely not suitable. The C-4, with its funnel aft, is a good round-the-world vessel and the CP-3 is a good ship, but suitable bottoms are not available in quantity sufficient for the volume of commerce.

Reconversion is not taking place as rapidly as had been anticipated. . . .

Utilities—Officials Look to Great Expansions

Expansion and capital investments totaling $200 million may be anticipated in this industry, depending on the condition of the manpower, materials and housing markets. . . .

Water companies project considerable volume of . . . deferred maintenance . . . and have the money available.

Pacific Tel. & Tel. is launching a huge construction and installation program which alone will amount to $100 million in 1946, and no better index to prospective population trends and business conditions could be asked. . . .

Per capita power consumption reached an all-time high during the war and although base loads already show some signs of recession, individual consumption is expected to continue at a high rate, especially when new appliances return to the market. . . .

Pulp and Paper—An Optimistic Future, According to Experts

All categories of paper are expected to continue scarce throughout the product range, with special emphasis on processed lines such as citrus tissue, towels and waxed paper. Newsprint is tight and will continue so. . . .

Plant is reported to have come through the war in excellent shape. . . .

Contrary to the record of many other industries, this one saw no wartime expansion, no new mills, little increase in productive capacity, and no new machinery. . . .

Not a large consumer of labor, except in newsprint, this business is in a relatively happy position laborwise.

Financially the industry is in extraordinarily healthy condition.

Railroads—Big Rehabilitation Looming, Say Railroad Heads

The tremendously improved financial condition of the railroads is perhaps the outstanding aspect of this industry. . . .

Congestion is expected to continue until April at least . . . .

Passenger miles will fall from three times pre-war years, but are expected to continue at a level higher than 1929, the previous peak. Freight will naturally be off from the trebled war-time totals. . . .

Revenues are expected to decline at a relatively faster rate than tonnage itself, due to the changing nature of freight and consequent lower tariffs. . . .

Packing—Food Executives Expect Plenty of Demand

Packers' finances are in the best condition of any period in their entire history.

. . . Considerable expansion has taken place in productive capacity and all plants have been operating at full capacity. Hinged so closely to general economic conditions, the business could swing either way violently—

downward if strikes persist, with resultant unemployment and dissipation of savings. On the other hand, the shelves of the nation could be bare by the end of the year if the armed forces fail to disgorge their stocks. . . .

Sugar will continue to be scarce . . .

Considerable mechanization has taken place . . . during the war, to such an extent that those not mechanized will find themselves under compulsion to do so.

Labor is expected to be a continuing and major problem.

Prices are expected to continue at a high level. . . .

Oil—Oil Men Say Demand May Exceed Supply

Estimates for the coming year in the oil industry range from high to extremely optimistic. . . .

On the obvious and favorable side of the ledger stand the insatiable demands from all consuming categories. . . . Continued mechanization of farms will make the agricultural market one of increasing importance. Demand is almost overwhelming.

Facilities, greatly expanded during war years, are adequate to handle the increased volume. However, the industry is uncertain about the time element due to the shortage of construction materials and manpower.

Labor and wages are an unknown quantity. . . .

Increased industrial activity will require a greater concentration on industrial fuels and lubricants; . . .

Chemicals and by-products will command increasing attention in the industry this year, with long-range prospects of the offspring swallowing the parent. This applies particularly to the well-integrated companies.

Barring labor pains, prospects for the industry appear extremely favorable.

 E S S A Y S

Gerald D. Nash, a historian at the University of New Mexico, Albuquerque, has forcefully argued that World War II finally enabled the American West to discard its colonial relationship to the East. The changes that occurred were both quantitative and qualitative. In Nash's view, the mushrooming defense industries, the cutting-edge scientific research, and the immigration of a diverse population all turned the American West into a dynamic pacesetter for the nation. In the first essay, drawn from two of Nash's books, *World War II and the West: Reshaping the Economy* (1990) and *The American West Transformed: The Impact of the Second World War* (1985), Nash chronicles the West's frenetic efforts to find workers not only for the manufacturing industries but also for agriculture.

Nash's thesis has been widely accepted, but Paul Rhode, an economic historian at the University of North Carolina, Chapel Hill, offers an effective rebuttal to Nash in the second essay. Rhode uses voluminous and detailed statistics (not reproduced here) to substantiate his thesis that the war years did not represent the fundamental discontinuity in California's economic history that Nash has claimed. Rather, according to Rhode, the state's most significant growth occurred *before* the Great Depression. The economy's performance during the war years seemed more spectacular than it really was only because the Depression had lasted so long.

World War II Transforms California's Economy

GERALD D. NASH

World War II left an indelible imprint on the economy of the American West. No other event in the twentieth century had such far-flung influence. Domestic mobilization diversified the western economy, as yet underdeveloped in comparison with the older and more heavily industrialized Northeast and Middle West. In four short years it accomplished a reshaping of the region's economic life that would have taken more than forty years in peacetime. . . . [F]ederal expenditures in wartime provided the capital they had lacked for so many decades. Government funds now helped to boost manufactures, even if a significant portion went directly into the aircraft and shipbuilding industries and into the expansion of many kinds of military installations. The federal government also created new industries such as aluminum, magnesium, and synthetic rubber production. At the same time it built a vast new scientific complex for the West, establishing major new laboratories at Los Alamos, New Mexico, and Hanford, Washington, and the future Jet Propulsion Laboratory at Pasadena, California. The Office of Scientific Research and Development also awarded numerous contracts to western universities for special projects. These facilities did much to spawn new technologically oriented industries in the region.

Such a reshaping of the economy spurred other changes. It encouraged an influx of new settlers, particularly to the Pacific Coast and the Southwest, and did much to stimulate expansion of service industries and financial institutions. And the unprecedented growth of the armed forces increased the federal presence in the western economy. Scores of new military installations, whether storage facilities, arsenals, airfields, or testing and training centers, added another dimension to the economic life of the area. Proximity to the Pacific theater of war contributed to the growing importance of the West in the broader context of national security policies. And as the Orient assumed greater prominence in American diplomacy, the trans-Mississippi West acquired a new geopolitical importance.

The result of such changes was a diversification of the western economy on an unprecedented scale. In 1940 the West was still characterized by a colonial economy. The region's primary emphasis was on the extraction of raw materials to be sent for processing to the older East, where the region also secured its manufactured goods. Agriculture, livestock, and mining were the major industries of this underdeveloped area that constituted

Reprinted from *World War II and the West: Reshaping the Economy,* by Gerald D. Nash, by permission of the University of Nebraska Press. Copyright © 1990 by University of Nebraska Press. Gerald D. Nash, *The American West Transformed: The Impact of the Second World War.* Copyright © 1985 by Indiana University Press. Excerpted by permission of Indiana University Press.

America's "Third World." But the forces unleashed by World War II wrought momentous changes by 1945. The West emerged from the conflict with a more developed and diversified economy. In addition to raw materials, the region now boasted expanded manufacturing facilities, rapidly growing service establishments, and pioneering technologically oriented industries such as aeronautics, electronics, and atomic energy development. The presence of recently established science and engineering operations now gave the West a cutting edge that was to make it an economic pacesetter in the postwar decades. In four short years westerners had undertaken an impressive reshaping of their erstwhile colonial economy. . . .

How did westerners accomplish this mighty leap, this reshaping of their economy in the course of World War II? The process was complex, but the main engines of restructuring were the federal government and private enterprise. The federal investment in the West between 1940 and 1945 was large, about $40 billion. These dollars flowed westward through government contracts for thousands of goods, but primarily for ships and planes. Federal largesse also affected the West through the establishment of a vast network of military installations such as army camps and supply depots. The presence of more than three million military personnel did much to boost the region's service industries. And since most of the new science installations in the West were federally owned and operated, they brought additional public money into the area.

If Washington provided a substantial portion of the new investment capital that sparked the reshaping of the West, private enterprise—individuals and corporations—did much of the actual work. That meant big business had a major role in the process while small business played only an auxiliary part. Their respective functions in reshaping the region's economic life led to chronic disagreements during the war years. When peace came, big business emerged with its influence enhanced.

The range of federal expenditures in the West was wide: vast purchases from business and agriculture; wage and salary payments to civilians as well as to military personnel; investments in new manufacturing facilities; disbursements for public projects such as dams, roads, and highways; and transfer payments, subsidies, and grants. In addition, benefit payments to farmers, social welfare recipients, and large-scale conservation and reclamation projects also contributed to the flow. Federal spending was not only important for its immediate, direct impact, however. It was also significant because in 1940 it triggered the rejuvenation of a depression-wracked economy. Consequently it had what economists designate as a multiplier effect. Federal funds revitalized many spheres of the economy and accelerated the general pace of economic activity, in classical Keynesian terms.

California was not a typical western state, but it starkly reflected the significant impact of federal spending as revealed in selected economic indicators. The value of its manufactures tripled during the war, increasing three times as rapidly as the national average. Personal income of Californians doubled in the war years, as did also their per capita income. California's share of federal revenues also rose sharply, from $15.1 billion in

1942 to $50.2 billion in 1945. Federal spending in California ballooned from $1.3 billion in 1940 to $8.5 billion five years later. Personal income climbed so rapidly because the federal government contributed fully 45 percent of the state's personal income during the war years, compared with only 8.5 percent a decade earlier. The wages the federal government disbursed in the state also mushroomed, from $216 million in 1940 to $2.1 billion in 1945—a tenfold increase. Perhaps the effect of federal expenditures in other western states was not quite so dramatic as in California. It is true that most did not receive the large-scale aircraft and shipbuilding contracts that went to the Pacific Coast states. Still not a single western state was left untouched by the sudden increase of federal spending. . . .

The economic expansion prompted by the war triggered a spectacular population boom in the West. Of course, the region was no stranger to population booms. Throughout much of its history, western settlement had been characterized by spurts rather than by a pattern of gradual and steady population growth, beginning with the gold and silver rushes of the 1850s and 1860s. The decade after the First World War witnessed another major surge of people pouring into the West, particularly into urban areas. But the depression of the 1930s brought this expansion to a halt. . . . As by 1941 mobilization created new job opportunities, these served as a magnet for Americans in every part of the United States and created yet another wave of migration. . . .

The flow of people into these areas provided an enormous impetus to the expansion of their service industries—banks, food establishments, health care services, and schools. Although strained to the limit by the influx of newcomers, western communities welcomed the vast reservoir of new job opportunities. At the same time the unprecedented expansion of federal installations in the West also created thousands of new civilian openings. As land had served as a magnet for western migrants in the later nineteenth century, so wartime mobilization set into motion another major population expansion movement in the trans-Mississippi West. Indeed, it could be said that the entire American West became a giant boom town in the World War II era.

Within the region, however, population gains were uneven. Urban areas experienced the most dynamic expansion, sometimes with spectacular growth reminiscent of nineteenth-century western boom towns. . . .

Of the more than 8 million people who moved into the trans-Mississippi West in the decade after 1940 almost one-half went to the Pacific Coast. California gained three and a half million individuals, leading to a population surge from 6,907,000 in 1940 to 10,586,000 in 1950. The state's growth rate continued to be significantly higher than in the nineteenth century. And 72.2 percent of that growth was due to in-migration. Elsewhere, the population increase was not as spectacular. . . .

This wave of western migrants shared certain common characteristics. In contrast to the nineteenth century, when many migrants hailed from east of the Mississippi River, this migration had a substantial proportion of men and women born and raised in western states. As a group they tended to be youthful (under 30) and not highly skilled, and the vast majority came from urban rather than rural or farm backgrounds. Culturally, they were geared to city life. Significant also was the influx of racial and ethnic minorities, particularly blacks, Mexican-Americans, and Indians (from reservations to the cities).

The urban origins of this migration helps to explain why the newcomers gravitated to metropolitan areas. . . .

The war [also] accelerated the growth of suburbs in western metropolitan areas. That trend had already been noticeable before 1940 in the more heavily congested eastern cities. In this as in other demographic patterns, the West was already emerging as a pace-setter for the nation. California was far ahead of other states in spawning suburban areas which emerged after the First World War. By 1950 31.1 percent of California's population lived in suburbs—compared to a national average of 13.9 percent. . . .

Another striking characteristic of the World War II migration was its racial and ethnic diversity. In a not-untypical Oakland shipyard one could find Slavs, Russians, Portuguese, Germans, Irish, Chinese, Greeks, Italians, and large numbers of Okies among the milling throng of workers. But perhaps most remarkable of all was the increase in the number of black Americans. In 1940 they had constituted 1.8 percent of the population in California. By 1950 this had increased to 4.4 percent. The trend was similar in Washington, Oregon, Arizona, New Mexico, and Colorado. New job opportunities and a network of friends and relatives brought more than 250,000 blacks westward, most from the rural South. In addition, the number of Mexicans who visited the United States after 1942 to alleviate desperate labor shortages in the West came to constitute about half a million people. Precise statistics are difficult to determine because of the high rate of illegal immigration. The westward movement also affected Native Americans. From reservations in Oklahoma, New Mexico, Arizona, Utah, and other states, about 25,000 Indians moved to take up war jobs on the Pacific Coast, also establishing an Indian urban enclave in Los Angeles.

One of the most significant changes in the western labor force during World War II was the large-scale infusion of women. In the aircraft and shipbuilding industries on the Pacific Coast at various times they constituted at least one-third, and sometimes more, of the active workers. The role of women in the West during the war is a subject so vast, and so important, that it merits detailed book-length studies in its own right. No brief mention can do it justice, except to call attention to the need for intensive study. . . .

As the pace of mobilization increased in 1940 and 1941, severe labor shortages developed in the new war production centers. Until Pearl Harbor, the residue of unemployed left by the depression provided a pool of workers upon which employers with defense contracts could draw. But by the middle of 1942 the available local labor supply in most areas of the West was being exhausted. It was then that war contractors embarked on a frantic search for workers, whether skilled or unskilled. The shortage was most pronounced in the urban centers of the Pacific Coast, but was also evident in Phoenix, Denver, and many smaller cities. As Frank Roney of the War Manpower Commission said on September 9, 1943: "The entire West Coast economy is completely dominated by critical war industries. The economy of the West Coast centers around . . . aircraft, shipbuilding and repair, military installations of all types, non-ferrous mining, logging and lumbering, high value agriculture, and fishing. . . . That means that all major production areas on the West Coast today are . . . now facing a serious labor shortage."

By 1943 the depletion of the available labor pool was threatening to disrupt production. The situation was critical and led U.S. Senator Sheridan Downey of California to inaugurate an investigation into the problem. He estimated in January 1943 that California would need at least 123,000 additional shipyard workers and another 55,000 individuals to work in the expanding aircraft industry. Anxious to promote the industrial expansion of his state, Downey hoped that the federal government might inaugurate a program to encourage available labor outside of California to migrate there. But as Americans elsewhere heard of congested housing and living conditions, they were increasingly loath to relocate on the West Coast. Downey hoped to change the then-current California image.

The lack of housing on the Pacific Coast was a major impediment to the recruitment of new workers. "Housing is almost non-existent in most of the major areas of the West Coast at the present time," noted Frank Roney, "despite the fact that programs of housing developed for the West Coast have been the largest of any equivalent area in the country." Donald W. Douglas, the president of Douglas Aircraft Company, stated even more bluntly that the major obstacle to increased production at his plants was the housing shortage. In his estimation, it could be remedied only with federal aid. . . .

Transportation problems also contributed to the labor shortage on the Pacific Coast. As Senator Robert Reynolds (N.C.), chairman of the Senate Committee on Military Affairs, complained, in California, Oregon, and Washington workers had greater difficulties in getting to and from their plants than in the East because of the distances involved. In the San Francisco Bay Area, for example, it took many workers more than two hours to travel from San Francisco to the Richmond shipyards in the East Bay. In Los Angeles major factories were located on the periphery of the city—accessible only by automobile. The average worker in the California shipyards . . . traveled to and from work at least 52 miles daily. Many labor problems that slowed production, such as absenteeism and fatigue, were largely due to commuting difficulties. . . .

Related to housing and transportation bottlenecks were inadequate service facilities for thousands of newcomers. For many, mundane shopping became a nightmare. After working full shifts workers were often forced to stand in line for hours in grocery stores, frequently distant from factory or home. More often than not the supply of scarce food items was exhausted by the time they were able to do their shopping. . . .

The profusion of federal agencies attempting to deal with production bottlenecks was often more of a hindrance than a help. The Office of War Mobilization and Economic Stabilization, the Coordinator of Defense Housing, the National Housing Agency and the War Manpower Commission were only a few of the governmental bodies that attempted to deal with western production problems from Washington. Far distant from these western localities, and often working at cross purposes, they were not particularly effective in improving working conditions in the frenzied activity on the Pacific Coast.

By July 1943 the serious disruptions of production schedules in shipyards and aircraft factories alarmed President Roosevelt. In an effort to unsnarl the morass of conflicting federal programs, on April 9, 1943, he created, by Executive Order, the Committee for Congested Production Areas in the Executive Office of the White House. Its primary function was to cut through red tape and overlapping jurisdictions of the many war agencies involved in the mobilization effort in order to achieve the primary objective—increased production. Since a Congressional committee was already investigating glaring inefficiencies of federal agencies in important production areas, Roosevelt's move was undoubtedly also designed to forestall political criticism.

At the same time the Office of War Mobilization headed by James F. Byrnes also attempted to remedy the situation by preparing a West Coast Manpower Plan. . . . [T]he program was designed to meet an estimate of the War Manpower Commission for 500,000 additional workers required in the three Pacific states in 1943 if production quotas set by the War Production Board were to be met. . . .

The severe labor shortage in the West affected not only the new factories producing war materials but agribusiness as well. Already in 1942 crop losses due to labor shortages were considerable. W. E. Spencer, chairman of the Agricultural Producers Labor Committee of the California Citrus Growers Association, estimated that 50 percent of that year's crop would rot for lack of harvesting help. At least 21,000 additional workers were needed, he claimed, if 75,000 carloads of citrus fruit were not to be lost.

Several factors contributed to this farm labor shortage. Obviously, the wartime draft was denuding rural areas of their traditional labor supply. Moreover, the lure of higher paying jobs in urban industries drew many workers from the farming regions of the nation. With a lessening of racial discrimination due to the increasing labor shortage, minorities such as blacks and Mexican-Americans pursued more lucrative job opportunities in industry. And in contrast to the depression years when farmers had decreased production in the face of shrinking markets, the enormous wartime demands now found farmers seeking bumper crops.

Throughout 1942 various farm organizations mobilized their members to demand government help. . . .

Many farm operators blamed the federal government for their labor shortage. Some of the large citrus growers in California and Arizona placed direct responsibility on the U.S. Employment Service for their plight.

Instead of referring applicants to farms, they noted, the Service sent them to industrial establishments. . . .

[O]ther influences contributed to the increasing seriousness of the farm labor shortage. . . . Removal of all Japanese-Americans to internment camps left a major gap; they had been a vitally important factor in vegetable and fruit production. . . . [W]hile western farmers were beset with a shrinking agricultural labor force, they also had to contend with an increasingly serious farm machinery and equipment shortage. To curtail the use of steel, for example, the War Production Board on October 20, 1942, issued its Limitation Order L-170, severely restricting the production of farm machinery. This constituted a heavy blow to western farmers, who were more heavily mechanized than those in other regions. . . .

During 1942 many farmers in California, Oregon, Washington, Colorado, and Arizona recruited students, women, retired people, and moonlighting white collar workers to help bring in their harvests. In the fruit-growing areas of the Pacific Northwest this auxiliary force worked well, in part because farmers had resorted to similar expedients in prewar days. But in other types of specialized farming such an ad hoc labor force did not prove to be very practical. . . .

By June of 1942 much of this discontent had crystallized into a proposal, supported by many western farmers, for the importation of Mexican farm labor. Governor Culbert Olson of California yielded to the pressure when on June 15, 1942, he sent an urgent telegram to Secretary of Agriculture Claude R. Wickard, Secretary of Labor Frances Perkins, and Secretary of State Cordell Hull. "Without substantial numbers of Mexicans," the Governor pleaded, "the situation is certain to be disastrous to the entire Victory program." . . .

Throughout the spring and summer of 1942 representatives of Mexico met with State Department officials to negotiate a formal agreement for the importation of Mexican labor. The Mexicans still remembered their World War I experience when more than 150,000 of their nationals had gone to work in western states as farm laborers. They had encountered miserable working conditions and less than adequate housing and sanitation facilities. They had usually received substandard wages; sometimes the promises of work did not materialize; and they were chronically threatened by deportation. Thus the Mexican representatives were cautious. On the other hand, State Department negotiators were subject to increasing pressure from agricultural interests. In addition to California and Arizona agribusiness, the beet sugar producers in western states like Colorado, Idaho, and Montana were among the most eager for Mexican labor, and it was in response to their requests that in April 1942 the Immigration and Naturalization Service established an interagency committee to investigate the possibility of importing *braceros.* . . .

Th[e] *bracero* agreement of 1942 provided the basis for the importation of Mexican labor into the United States during the next five years. In the United States the Department of Agriculture had major responsibility for recruiting workers, using the U.S. Employment Service. In Mexico a bureau of migrant labor in the Ministry of Foreign Affairs was in charge of selecting workers. Mexicans in the United States were not subject to military service, and were guaranteed transportation, living expenses, and repatriation. To mollify U.S. labor unions the arrangement provided that Mexicans would not be used to displace American workers or to reduce wage rates. Negotiation of contracts between individual *braceros* and American employers were to be handled by the Farm Security Administration. Thus, the United States government now became an employer of *braceros,* in a modern version of the seventeenth-century practice of indentured servitude.

Contracts were to be made for a six-month period and were renewable. The United States was to pay all transportation costs. Although the federal government was authorized to seek reimbursement from employers, in practice it absorbed these costs. *Braceros* were assured of the same wage levels that prevailed for Americans, and to be offered similar conditions of housing, food, and health care. . . .

In view of the pressing need for farm labor in the United States American farmers lost little time in making the agreement operational. More than 4,000 Mexican workers came to the United States during the second half of 1942, 53,000 more in 1943, and 62,000 in 1944. Of a total of 309,538 wartime farm workers imported into the United States between 1942 and 1947, 219,000 were Mexican. Others came from the Bahamas, Barbados, Jamaica, Canada, and elsewhere. California used one-half of this work force while the remainder was scattered in the other western states.

An Economic Historian Challenges the Nash Thesis

PAUL RHODE

In a series of influential studies, Gerald Nash has explored the impact of the Second World War on the social and economic development of the West. He has argued that the war transformed the American West from a mordant, economic colony of the East into a dynamic, pacesetting society. The driving forces of this transformation were expanding employment in military-related activities; government-financed investments in military installations and manufacturing capacity, especially in the basic metal industries; and rapid population growth. According to his seminal work, the war effort condensed four decades of development into four short years.

This paper challenges Nash's thesis concerning the crucial role of the war in transforming the economy of California, the largest state in the West. In 1940, its income and population were as large, or larger, than the rest of the West combined. And much of the war activity, especially aircraft pro-

Copyright © 1994 by Pacific Coast Branch, American Historical Association. Excerpted from *Pacific Historical Review,* 63, August 1994, pp. 363–364, 367, 370–374, 376–379, 381–382, 384–392, by permission of the publisher and the author, Professor of Economics, University of North Carolina, Chapel Hill.

duction and shipbuilding, was concentrated in the urban areas of the state. Thus, California's experience is central to Nash's interpretation of the impact of the war on the West.

Based on a long-term perspective on California's economic development, I raise the following serious objections to the Nash thesis. First . . . [California's] income, population, and employment in manufacturing were growing robustly over the 1900 to 1940 period . . . [so] that by the eve of the war, urban California already possessed its own internal dynamic of development. Second, based on an examination of measures of economic and social performance circa 1940, I reject the notion that California was a "backward" region, part of an American "Third World." Third, this paper argues that the wartime expansion was, in large part, the result of California's existing dynamism and that the growth of the aircraft and shipbuilding industries was rooted in the state's past economic achievements. Fourth, it notes the wartime boom was transitory and highly unbalanced and that the postwar conversion experience was potentially highly problematic. Growth during the immediate postwar years was similar in form to early expansions in the state. The construction boom, the growth of trade and services, and the inflow of branch manufacturing plants of national firms resembled the experience of the 1920s. Fifth, I argue that the new basic metals sector, created by the wartime investments, contributed less to the postwar expansion than many contemporaries had anticipated. The establishment of these new industries did not provide the essential foundation for the region's subsequent manufacturing growth or, more particularly, for its emergence as an international leader in high technology. Sixth, the paper shows that the war led to increased specialization of California's economic structure, not greater diversification as Nash asserts.

I do not deny, in any way, that the Second World War had a major impact on California, accelerating its growth. But a study of [the] state's economic history over the twentieth century leads me to reject the view that the war pushed California from the one stage of development, as part of a dependent colonial region, to another stage, as a dynamic pacesetter. My research suggests that the Nash thesis greatly overstates the discontinuity and understates the continuity in California's development experience. . . .

Nash asserts that the economic changes wrought by the war were greater than would have occurred in forty years of peacetime. In order to assess this claim for California, it is helpful to have a long-run perspective on the state's growth relative to other regions and the country as a whole. . . .

California's growth from 1940 to 1945 is highly impressive if viewed in the short run, but less so if considered as a part of a medium or long term period. The five-year period following 1945 essentially consolidated the gains achieved during the war, and the preceding decade was one of depression. Comparing growth across decades reveals that the 1920s were a more robust period than the 1940s. The twenty-year time spans that include the war also appear far from exceptional. By 1940, California was already experiencing an accelerated per capita income growth, population expansion at rates two-to-three times the national averages, and significantly more rapid total income growth. . . .

There is a break in the region's growth, but it did not happen around 1940. Rather, . . . the "discontinuity" in California's growth, if indeed there was one, occurred around the turn of the century. Before 1900, the state's income share was declining and its population share was growing only very slowly. Between 1900 and 1960, the shares were steadily climbing higher. Growth during the war decade does not dominate the expansion of the previous forty years. . . .

Taking a long-run perspective also reveals the substantial growth of California's manufacturing sector over the twentieth century. . . . Again, growth during the war period was impressive; the number of production workers in the state's manufacturing sector doubled between 1939 and 1947. Yet it is a gross exaggeration to claim that the 1940s expansion dominated growth over the previous forty-year period because manufacturing employment in the state had increased nearly fourfold since 1899. Of course, growth was slow during the 1930s, but it was still positive in contrast to national trends. Between 1929 and 1939, manufacturing employment actually increased in California whereas it declined nationwide. Considering the 1899–1939 period as a whole, California's share of total production workers in the United States doubled.

By the late 1930s, California's cities, with Los Angeles in the lead, was already emerging as the nation's second industrial core. The southland metropolis could boast it was the nation's leading producer of aircraft and the second leading producer of automobiles and rubber tires. For the region's aircraft industry, the real breakthrough occurred in the early 1930s. The Pacific Coast firms were in the vanguard of the "airframe revolution," designing and producing streamlined, all metal, cantilevered monoplanes— the first modern airliners. The key aircraft embodying the new technologies were Boeing's 247 and Douglas's DC-2 and DC-3. Each of these planes incorporated the revolutionary aerodynamic ideas of California-based John Northrop, the nation's most prominent design innovator. Douglas came to dominate the entire commercial market by the mid-1930s. But Douglas was not alone; its traditional rivals, Lockheed and Boeing, also grew in the late 1930s. In addition, North American and Consolidated moved to the West in order to be closer to the new technologies and pools of engineering talent and venture capital. By 1939, the Pacific Coast was the center of airframe production with the California industry employing roughly half of the workers nationally. This provided the foundation for the Pacific Coast aircraft industry's major role during the Second World War.

Aircraft is normally considered a military-oriented industry. It is worth noting, however, that the Pacific Coast industry achieved its aircraft leadership based on its success with planes designed and built to serve the western, commercial market. And this success was itself based on technological innovations of the small cluster of aviation engineers and entrepreneurs. On its way to global leadership, the Pacific Coast industry had to overcome the locational inertia caused by agglomeration economies in eastern input markets. Ironically, the boom and bust cycle characterizing aircraft demand probably contributed to the industry's eventual concentration in southern California by preventing the eastern centers of production from solidifying the advantages of their earlier start.

Urban California's emergence as a center of automobile and tire production was a part of a larger process—the spread of branch plants. From the 1910s on, national firms often found it advantageous to establish western factories in order to save on transportation costs and to serve better the growing local market. Among the hundreds of firms setting up California plants were Ford, Chevrolet, Goodyear, and Procter & Gamble. . . . There was an intense upswing in the second half of the 1920s and a smaller boom in the late 1930s. . . . [O]ver twenty percent of California manufacturing employment in 1939 was employed in branch plants. By [the] end of the 1930s, the pattern was already set for the influx of branch plants of the late 1940s and early 1950s.

Nash characterizes the West on the eve of the Second World War as America's "Third World." It would, perhaps, be hard to find a less apt description of California. By almost any relevant measure, California in 1940 was among the more "advanced" regions of the most "advanced" economy in the world. . . .

In 1940, per capita income in California stood more than forty percent above the national average. Only Delaware, Connecticut, and Nevada ranked higher. The state was among the most urbanized in the nation, with over seventy percent of its population living in towns and cities. The extractive or primary sector, far from dominating the state's economy, was less important than it was nationally. Only about thirteen percent of California's labor force was employed in extractive activities compared with twenty-one percent nationally. In terms of the importance of the extractive sector, California ranked in the same class as Illinois, Ohio, Pennsylvania, and Michigan. The extractive sector's share of California's earnings was close to the U.S. average of around eleven percent, but this should be taken as a sign of progress, rather than of backwardness. California's extractive workers generated much higher earnings than did such workers in the country as a whole. Extraction was not a low-income sector in California as it was elsewhere. A similar picture emerges if we examine educational attainment or the degree of innovativeness (as measured by the number of patents per person). The state stood significantly above the national average. Long before World War II, California had ceased to be a "backward" region.

What, then, was the impact of the Second World War? There is no question that the war led to an intense boom in the state, ending a decade of slower growth during the worldwide depression. The federal government called on urban California's production capabilities in aircraft, shipbuilding, and other military activities, stimulating rapid expansion in industrial output and employment. Between June 1940 and September 1945, the federal government spent $16.4 billion on major war supply contracts in California. With nine percent of the national total, the state ranked third, behind only New York and Michigan. Within the state, the metropolitan areas received all but a negligible share of the contracts; Los Angeles County itself accounted for almost 58 percent of the total. The San Francisco Bay area received about 24 percent, and San Diego 12 percent. Most of this money went to purchase aircraft (about 54 percent) and ships (about 30 percent); ordinance [*sic*], communication equipment, and other goods accounted for far less.

In addition to purchasing war supplies, the federal government also invested heavily in military and industrial projects in California. Between June 1940 and September 1945, it spent about $1.5 billion on military installations and over one billion on manufacturing facilities in the state. The sum invested in industrial capacity was about six percent of the national total, placing California behind New York, Texas, Ohio, Michigan, Pennsylvania, and Illinois. The state's private sector invested about $475 million in industrial expansion over this period. . . . The bulk of the federal money, more than $400 million, went to the shipbuilding sector. Aircraft, chemicals, and iron and steel received smaller, but still hefty sums. Private sector investments were concentrated in chemicals and aircraft.

The wartime boom led to a forty percent increase in employment in the state between 1940 and 1944. This expansion of job opportunities resulted in dramatic reductions in unemployment, substantial increases in labor force participation, especially of women, and significant inflows of population. The California jobless rate, which stood at over twelve percent in 1940, fell to less than one percent in 1944. Migration surged as job seekers, who had been unwelcome in the late 1930s, were now actively recruited. . . .

California's per capita income rose over the war period. Between 1940 and 1943, the rate of growth in the state paralleled the national increase and its relative income remained constant at 140 percent of the national average. After 1943, California's relative income began to fall, reaching about 125 percent of the national average by 1950. . . . Nonetheless, the leading attraction of California was probably not the rising relative wages, but the expanding number of jobs in an economy long characterized by high wages. . . .

Between 1940 and the peak in 1943, manufacturing employment rose from 320,000 to 896,000. Gains in aircraft and shipbuilding accounted for four-fifths of this increase. The number of aircraft workers increased from 41,000 to 237,000, while shipbuilding workers increased from 7,000 to 274,000 over this period. By way of contrast, many nondefense industries experienced little growth. Indeed, several sectors, including printing, lumber, and automobile manufacturing actually suffered employment declines during the war. . . .

The wartime boom was intense, yet it did not result in a complete or balanced transformation of the economy. There were serious problems during the war with overcrowded housing and schools and serious questions after the war concerning whether the region would retain the industries and residents that it had gained. Without question, World War II generated powerful forces of change, but by focusing on its "four short years," Nash's treatment neglects the crucial challenges of solidifying the region's growth in the immediate postwar period.

In contrast to his observation that the West emerged from the war with a new self-confidence, the actual picture was far more mixed. As the contemporary press noted, the prevailing opinion varied from deep pessimism that the depressed conditions would soon return to optimism that the "West was on its way." . . .

As we now know, the predictions of moderate optimists proved true and conversion was easier than many, or most, anticipated. But this was itself largely due to the incomplete nature of the wartime boom. The boom had increased population, but wartime conditions had slowed economic adjustments needed to meet the enlarged civilian demands. Civilian construction during the war virtually stopped. As a result of the increased population and pent-up demand generated during the war, the state enjoyed a vigorous residential construction boom in the late 1940s. The number of building jobs increased by over 100,000, or by nearly sixty-five percent, between 1945 and 1948. Even larger and more immediate changes occurred in the trade and service sectors, which had grown little during the war. Almost 400,000 new jobs were created in these sectors during the same period, picking up much of the slack from the decline in the war industries.

In addition, there was a significant expansion of nonmilitary manufacturing in the postwar period as firms, led by branches of eastern-based corporations, established new plants in the West or expanded existing facilities in order to supply the greatly enlarged local market. . . . New branches, local start-up firms, and expanding existing enterprises all kept California's industrial investment boom going after the war. The California State Chamber of Commerce, which tracked new factory start-ups and plant expansions, estimated that in the four years from 1945 to 1948, $1,069,000,000 of private capital was invested in California manufacturing facilities. This was divided fairly evenly between some 3,270 new factories ($487 million was invested) and 3,160 plant expansions ($582 million invested).

These figures are not directly comparable to the investments during the war period. The price level was higher in the postwar period. For example, the national implicit price deflator for nonresidential fixed investment increased about twenty-seven percent between 1941–1944 and 1945–1948. As a consequence, the real value of the later investment was lower. But several countervailing factors suggest that the postwar investments contributed more to the civilian economy. The wartime investments were concentrated in activities such as shipbuilding with limited peacetime economic value. The projects were often located in areas based on national security as opposed to economic reasons, and they were frequently constructed on a stepped-up time schedule at higher cost. These considerations are reflected in the sales prices that the federal government received after the war for its surplus plants. The War Assets Administration sold off the plants for, on average, less than half of the estimated cost of construction.

According to many contemporary observers, the most important wartime addition to the region's industrial capacity was the new basic metals sector. Prevailing opinion during the immediate postwar period embraced what might be termed "basic metals thinking," the idea that steel and other basic metals were strategic building blocks of full industrialization. As Robert Elliott, a prominent Pacific Coast business observer put it, steel was the "mother of industry." In this view, the West's key "war winnings" were the new integrated steel plants at Fontana, California, and Geneva, Utah, operated by Kaiser and U.S. Steel, respectively. And the crucial question of the postwar period, as Fortune magazine's 1945 survey of the Pacific Coast noted, was "whether the mills would continue to operate?" Government and business leaders devoted considerable energy and attention to this question. Both mills stayed open, run by the firms that served as wartime managers, but they made a much smaller direct contribution to the region's industrialization than contemporaries anticipated.

California never developed into a center of production of either primary or fabricated metals. In 1958, the fraction of the state's production workers in manufacturing employed in the . . . primary metals industries . . . was only 4.2 percent, down from 4.7 percent in 1939, and the share in . . . fabricated metals . . . was only 7.4 percent, up from 7 percent in 1939. In sum, there was little overall change. Even the growth of machinery (excluding electrical equipment) was relatively small. The share of . . . nonelectrical machinery . . . increased only by about two percentage points from 4.7 percent in 1939 to 6.6 percent in 1958. The key changes were in electrical and transportation equipment, particularly aircraft. The driving forces behind growth in these sectors were technological innovation and military demand, not improved access to metals.

The new steel industry failed to live up to the expectations of the "basic metals thinking" for a number of reasons. First, the mills were initially designed for a product mix concentrating on heavy steel plate suitable for building ships, but not for many industrial applications. Much of the output in the early postwar years went to construction projects such as oil pipelines. In contrast to the national picture, construction demand in the West greatly exceeded industrial demand for iron and steel. Second, the establishment of the western mills did not lead to a significantly lower price structure until Kaiser's 1962 move to equalize prices. In 1947, Kaiser had deviated from the eastern structure by *raising* his prices during a gray-market period of steel shortages. Third, by the early 1960s, imported steel from Europe and Japan began to compete seriously with the western mills. Finally and probably most importantly, the contemporary observers were simply wrong about the direction the economy was taking. The "basic metals thinking" may have been appropriate for a U.S. region industrializing fifty years earlier, but it was anachronistic by 1947.

Although World War II vastly increased employment and fostered a new metals sector, it did not lead to measurable diversification or rapid structural change in the California economy. Most of the wartime employment increases were in aircraft and shipbuilding. In fact, the manufacturing sector and the entire labor force became more specialized, not more diversified. . . .

[D]ata . . . [for] civilian employment . . . for 1940 and 1943 to 1948 . . . clearly indicate that the California economy became more specialized during the war, contrary to Nash's frequent assertions about the experience of the West. As war production wound down after 1943, diversification did increase, but the economy was only marginally less specialized at the end of the 1940s than it was at the beginning. The longer-term census data indicate that the trend over the 1930 to 1960 period was toward greater specialization. Thus, arguments linking the war with diversification seem far off the mark for California.

The war's long-run impact on the structure of the California economy also appears limited. In order to examine this issue, it is useful to analyze changes in the employment shares in manufacturing and the labor force as a whole. . . . Between 1939 and 1947, natural resource-based industries declined in importance from about fifty percent of employment to about forty percent and the durable goods share in employment rose from forty-five percent to about fifty-five percent. Equally significant shifts occurred in the 1950s, so this did not represent a one-time change resulting from the war. . . .

[T]he distribution of the California labor force by major industrial category from 1930 to 1960 . . . [shows that t]he distribution in 1950 is remarkably close to that in 1940. . . . The recognition that the war did not fundamentally alter the region's economic structure is not new. As the San Francisco Federal Reserve Bank noted in 1949, "the distribution of workers among major industry groups is now not markedly different than before the war. Little trace remains of the wartime pattern of employment. . . ." In summary, an evaluation of the quantitative evidence on diversification and structural change simply does not jibe with sweeping assertions about the region's transformation.

The Second World War changed urban California. It would be hard to find a region anywhere in the world that did not feel the war's effects. Assessing the impact of the war is especially difficult because it came on the heels of the Great Depression. The more rapid than normal growth of the early 1940s appears extraordinarily dramatic in comparison with the slower growth of the 1930s. Based on a study of the region's economic history over the twentieth century, this paper rejects the view that the Second World War single-handedly pushed California from one stage of development, as a mordant, dependent region, to another stage, as a pacesetting, developed economy. It argues, instead, that by 1940 the state possessed an internal dynamic of development and that the wartime expansion was the result of this economic dynamism, not its cause. The Second World War did not make urban California an advanced, pacesetting region. It already was one.

F U R T H E R   R E A D I N G

Arthur P. Allen and Betty V. Schneider, *Industrial Relations in the California Aircraft Industry* (1956)

Katherine Archibald, *Wartime Shipyard: A Study in Social Disunity* (1947)

David L. Clark, *The Aerospace Industry as the Primary Factor in the Industrial Development of Southern California* (1976)

Arlene Elliott, "The Rise of Aeronautics in California, 1849–1940," *Southern California Quarterly* LII (March 1970): 1–32

"Fortress California at War: San Francisco, Los Angeles, Oakland, and San Diego, 1941–45," a special issue of *Pacific Historical Review* LXIII (August 1984)

Mark S. Foster, "Giant of the West: Henry J. Kaiser and Regional Industrialization, 1930–1950," *Business History Review* LIX (Spring 1985): 15–30

Mark S. Foster, *Henry J. Kaiser: Builder in the Modern American West* (1987)

Ewall T. Grether, *The Steel and Steel-Using Industries of California: Prewar Development, Wartime Adjustments, and Long-run Outlook* (1946)

George H. Hildebrand, *The Pacific Coast Maritime Shipping Industry, 1930–1948* (1954)

Forest G. Hill, "An Analysis of Regional Economic Development: The Case of California," *Land Economics* XXXI (February 1955): 1–12

Clayton Koppes, *JPL and the American Space Program: The Jet Propulsion Laboratory, 1936–1976* (1982)

Frederick C. Lane, *Ships for Victory: A History of Shipbuilding under the U.S. Maritime Commission in World War II* (1951)

Roger W. Lotchin, *Fortress California, 1910–1961: From Warfare to Welfare* (1992)

Seymour Melman, *The Permanent War Economy: American Capitalism in Decline* (1985)

Gerald D. Nash, *The American West Transformed: The Impact of the Second World War* (1985)

Gerald D. Nash, *World War II and the West: Reshaping the Economy* (1990)

James J. Parsons, "California Manufacturing," *Geographical Review* XXXIX (April 1949): 229–41

John B. Rae, *Climb to Greatness: The American Aircraft Industry, 1920–1960* (1968)

Martin Schiesl, "City Planning and the Federal Government in World War II: The Los Angeles Experience," *California History* LXII (May 1979): 127–40

William A. Schoneberger and Paul Sonnenburg, *California Wings* (1987)

Harold G. Vatter, *The U.S. Economy in World War II* (1988)

"War Comes to San Diego," a special issue of *Journal of San Diego History* XXXIX (Winter/Spring 1993)

Gerald T. White, *Billions for Defense: Government Financing by the Defense Plant Corporation during World War II* (1982)

Charles Wollenberg, *Marinship at War: Shipbuilding and Social Change in Wartime Sausalito* (1990)

The Changing Lives of Women

and Minorities, 1940s–1950s

World War II has been called a watershed in California history not only
because of the rapid economic transformation that occurred but also because
social relationships among the various segments of the state's population
changed in notable ways. Members of several groups experienced significant
shifts in their socioeconomic status, some for the better, others for the worse.

Due to the great demand for labor, women of all ethnic backgrounds,
African Americans, Mexicanos, Native Americans, Chinese Americans, and
Filipino Americans all found openings in industries that had formerly
barred them. Not only did they earn more money, but they also broke down
many discriminatory barriers. At the same time, significant numbers of
these groups joined the U.S. armed forces and were perceived as patriotic
Americans for the first time. Laws and court decisions that had hitherto prevented Asian immigrants from acquiring U.S. citizenship through naturalization were brushed aside; American citizenship was conferred upon
hundreds of foreign-born Asians residing in the United States so that they
could be inducted into the armed services.

In contrast, people of Japanese ancestry were singled out for harsh treatment, even though two thirds of them had been born in the United States
and hence had always been American citizens. Both the Issei (first-
generation Japanese immigrants) and Nisei (second-generation Japanese
Americans) were rounded up and sent to hastily erected camps in remote
inland areas. Allowed to take only what they could carry in their two
hands, they left behind homes, farms, shops, and other possessions. They
were never charged with any crime, nor were they ever accused of a single
instance of sabotage.

Two concepts were used to justify this violation of an entire group's civil
rights: "military necessity" and "protective custody." To ensure the military
security of the Pacific Coast, it was supposedly necessary to lock up all persons of Japanese ancestry. The argument for "protective custody" arose several months later in order, it was said, to protect them from a hostile public.

At the time, the internment of Japanese Americans was widely accepted and few questioned its constitutionality. Leaders in all branches of the federal government participated in the decision and its implementation. Various interest groups that had long opposed the Japanese presence and a number of influential journalists also clamored for the removal and imprisonment of the Japanese Americans. The incarceration of Japanese Americans was the culmination of almost a century of anti-Asian activities in California. Thus Californians did not flinch at the wholesale incarceration of Japanese Americans.

Despite their shoddy treatment at the hands of the government and their fellow citizens, more than 23,000 Nisei joined the U.S. Army when their eligibility for the draft was reinstated. Serving in segregated units, they made significant contributions to winning the war in both the European and Pacific theaters.

As a result of their incarceration, Japanese Americans suffered downward mobility. Having lost almost everything they had owned, aging Issei in the postwar years became gardeners and domestic servants. Many Nisei veterans, however, were able to use the GI Bill to get an education while working at whatever jobs were available. It took Japanese Americans two decades to make a "comeback." But they succeeded so well that by the mid-1960s scholars and journalists were calling them the "successful" or "model minority."

The trajectory followed by women and by African Americans differed from that of Japanese Americans. These two groups improved their economic well-being during the war but found it difficult to hold on to their gains in the postwar period. For European American women, the housing boom of the postwar years softened the regression that many experienced. Moving into appliance-filled, single-family homes in new suburbs, many women felt they had no right to complain about anything.

African Americans, however, could not rely on the "cushion" of homeownership. Having been disproportionately concentrated in shipyards and other defense industries, African Americans in California suffered a higher rate of unemployment than did the general population when those industries contracted at war's end. Discriminatory hiring practices in private firms after the war made it nearly impossible for blacks to find good jobs in the private sector. Even so, a large proportion of those who migrated to California during the war chose to stay. In San Francisco, the number of African Americans more than tripled during the war. In Richmond across the bay, where Kaiser's main shipyard was located, the increase was even more dramatic. In the state as a whole, African Americans, who had comprised less than 1.8 percent of the population in 1940, stood at 4.3 percent in 1950.

Tens of thousands of Mexican farmworkers who entered the United States during the war under the bracero program also increased the number of Mexicanos in California. The most notable incidents involving this group during the war years were blatant police harassment in connection with the "Sleepy Lagoon" murder trial and the six days of "zoot suit" riots. Both incidents reminded Mexicanos that though they were sorely needed to perform the backbreaking labor that European American workers shunned, they were nonetheless not welcome.

In reading the selections in this chapter, try to identify the changing patterns of economic and social discrimination against women and minorities.

What societal attitudes and government practices fostered discrimination? What reduced it? How was it different from the discrimination practiced before the war? How did the various groups react to discrimination during and after the war? How did it affect their lives?

 D O C U M E N T S

Charles Kikuchi, author of the first document, was incarcerated in an assembly center at the Tanforan Race Track in San Mateo County where he and his family had to live in a converted horse stall. Kikuchi, who had been a graduate student at the University of California, Berkeley, kept a diary of life in this American concentration camp. In the excerpt selected here, he notes the differential impact of the internment on various segments of the Japanese American community.

The second document contains two poems, the first written by Toyo Suyemoto Kawakami, one of the first Nisei women to see her poetry in print, and the second by Lawson Fusao Inada, a Sansei (third-generation Japanese American). Inada was the first Japanese American to have an entire book of poems published; *Before the War: Poems as They Happened* appeared in 1971. Inada is presently professor of English at Southern Oregon State College.

Fanny Christina Hill, narrator of the third document, is one of the many African American women who found work in the airframe manufacturing industry. Unlike many European American women dismissed from their jobs at the end of the war, Hill was terminated but later called back to work at the same company. She recounts how she dealt with the discrimination that black workers experienced. Her story was recorded by Sherna B. Gluck as part of the *Rosie the Riveter* oral history project.

The fourth document is drawn from an article in *This Week,* the weekly magazine of the *San Francisco Chronicle* at that time. The author, Willard Waller, was associate professor of sociology at Barnard College in New York City when his article appeared in 1945. Without mincing words, Waller tells women it is their patriotic duty to produce babies now that the war is over. This article is representative of the dozens that were published in the late 1940s and early 1950s to persuade women that it would be desirable to return to prewar patterns in the sexual division of labor.

Charles Kikuchi Observes Life in an American Concentration Camp, 1942

May 4, 1942 Monday

There are such varied reactions to the whole thing: some are content and thankful; others gush "sank you" but are full of complaints within their own circles. Still others are bolder and come right out with it. We thought that we would not have any dinner tonight because the cooks went on strike. They really are overworked—preparing 3000 meals. . . . The waiters also joined the strike because they only have 1000 dishes to feed 3000 people and they really have to get them out in a rush. I saw one Issei dishwasher slap a Nisei girl because she complained that the cups were so dirty. Their nerves are on edge in the cooking division because they are the target for many complaints when it really is not their fault. They are going to open up the new messhalls for sure tomorrow so a great deal of the overload rush will be cut down. The electricians are also griped because they have to replace so many fuses. The wiring system in the stables is very poor and with all the extra lights needed, the system has broken down. Because of the cold, many of the people use cooking heaters to keep warm with. They brought in 50 kerosene heaters today for the aged, ill, and the babies, but this is by no means sufficient. . . .

May 7, 1942 Thursday

There are all different types of Japanese in camp. Many of the young Nisei are quite Americanized and have nice personalities. They smile easily and are not inhibited in their actions. They have taken things in stride and their sole concern is to meet the other sex, have dances so that they can jitterbug, get a job to make money for "cokes," and have fun in general. Many are using the evacuation to break away from the strict control of parental rule.

Other Nisei think more in terms of the future. They want to continue their education in some sort of "career" study and be successes. The background which they come from is very noticeable: their parents were better educated and had businesses. . . .

Made me feel sort of sorry for Pop tonight. He has his three electric clippers hung up on the wall and Tom has built him a barrel chair for the barber seat. It's a bit pathetic when he so tenderly cleans off the clippers after using them; oiling, brushing, and wrapping them up so carefully. He probably realizes that he no longer controls the family group and rarely exerts himself so that there is little family conflict as far as he is concerned. What a difference from about 15 years ago when I was a kid. He used to be a perfect terror and dictator. . . .

Mom is taking things in stride. I have a suspicion that she rather enjoys the whole thing. It certainly is a change from her former humdrum life. She dyed her hair today, and Pop made some comment that she shouldn't try to act so young. One thing about these stables is that it does cut down the amount of "nagging" because people can overhear everything that is said.

May 8, 1942 Friday

. . . The question came up as to what were we fighting for. All of us agreed that Fascism was not the answer, but there was a difference of opinions on whether an Allied victory would be any solution to the whole mess. Jimmy thinks that it offered the most potentialities and hope for the world. Would the solution include only the white races, or will we be in a position to tackle the problem of India, China, and the other millions of "exploited" peoples? If not, our efforts will not have accomplished their purposes. The problem is so immense that it staggers the imagination.

Two Poems About the Camps

Barracks Home

TOYO SUYEMOTO KAWAKAMI

This is our barracks, squatting on the ground,
Tar-papered shack, partitioned into rooms
By sheetrock walls, transmitting every sound
Of neighbors' gossip or the sweep of brooms
The open door welcomes the refugees,
And now at last there is no need to roam
Afar: here space enlarges memories
Beyond the bounds of camp and this new home.

The floor is carpeted with dust, wind-borne
Dry alkali, patterned by insect feet.
What peace can such a place as this impart?
We can but sense, bewildered and forlorn,
That time, disrupted by the war from neat
Routines, must now adjust within the heart.

Mud

LAWSON FUSAO INADA

Mud in the barracks—
a muddy room, a chamber pot.

Mud in the moats
around each barracks group.

Mud on the shoes
trudging to the mess hall.

Mud in the swamp
where the men chopped wood.

Mud on the guts
under a loaded wagon—

crushed in the mud by the wheel.

Fanny Christina Hill Fights Discrimination Against Black Workers in the Aircraft Industry

I decided I wanted to make more money, and I went to a little small town—
Tyler, Texas. . . . [T]he only thing I could do there for a living was domes-
tic work and it didn't pay very much. So I definitely didn't like it. . . . [So]
I left Tyler. . . . [S]omeone told me, "Well, why don't you try California?"

So then I got Los Angeles in my mind. I was twenty and I saved my money till I was twenty-one. In August 1940, I came here. . . .

Los Angeles was a large city but I adjusted to it real well. It didn't take me long to find a way about it. I knew how to get around, and I knew how to stay out of danger and not take too many chances. I read the *Eagle* and I still get the *Sentinel* once in a while. [The *California Eagle* and the Los Angeles *Sentinel* were local black newspapers.] I have to get it to keep up with what the black people are doing. I used to read those papers when I was a child back home. . . .

I told my sister, "Well, I better get me a good job around here working in a hotel or motel or something. I want to get me a good job so when the war is over, I'll have it." And she said, "No, you just come on out and go in the war plants and work and maybe you'll make enough money where you won't have to work in the hotels or motels." . . .

When I went . . . [to the aircraft manufacturing company] the man didn't hire me. They had a school down here on Figueroa and he told me to go to the school. . . .

I stayed at the school for about four weeks. They only taught you shooting and bucking rivets and how to drill the holes and to file. You had to use a hammer for certain things. After a couple of whiles, you worked on the real thing. But you were supervised so you didn't make a mess.

When we went into the plant, it wasn't too much different than down at the school. It was the same amount of noise; it was the same routine. One difference was there was just so many more people, and when you went in the door you had a badge to show and they looked at your lunch. I had gotten accustomed to a lot of people and I knew if it was a lot of people, it always meant something was going on. I got carried away: "As long as there's a lot of people here, I'll be making money." That was all I could ever see.

I was a good student, if I do say so myself. But I have found out through life, sometimes even if you're good, you just don't get the breaks if the color's not right. I could see where they made a difference in placing you in certain jobs. They had fifteen or twenty departments, but all the Negroes went to Department 17 because there was nothing but shooting and bucking rivets. You stood on one side of the panel and your partner stood on this side, and he would shoot the rivets with a gun and you'd buck them with the bar. That was about the size of it. I just didn't like it. I didn't think I could stay there with all this shooting and a'bucking and a'jumping and a'bumping. I stayed in it about two or three weeks and then I just decided I did *not* like that. I went and told my foreman and he didn't do anything about it, so I decided I'd leave.

While I was standing out on the railroad track, I ran into somebody else out there fussing also. I went over to the union and they told me what to do. I went back inside and they sent me to another department where you did bench work and I liked that much better. You had a little small jig that you would work on and you just drilled out holes. Sometimes you would rout them or you would scribe them and then you'd cut them with a cutters.

I must have stayed there nearly a year, and then they put me over in another department, "Plastics." It was the tail section of the B-Bomber, the Billy Mitchell Bomber. I put a little part in the gun-sight. You had a little ratchet set and you would screw it in there. Then I cleaned the top of the glass off and put a piece of paper over it to seal it off to go to the next section. I worked over there until the end of the war. Well, not quite the end, because I got pregnant, and while I was off having the baby the war was over. . . .

[T]hey laid off a lot of people, most of them, because the war was over. It didn't bother me much—not thinking about it jobwise. I was just glad that the war was over. I didn't feel bad because my husband had a job and he also was eligible to go to school with his GI bill. So I really didn't have too many plans. . . .

When North American called me back, was I a happy soul! . . . That was a dollar an hour. So, from sixty cents an hour, when I first hired in there, up to one dollar. That wasn't traveling fast, but it was better than anything else because you had hours to work by and you had benefits and you come home at night with your family. So it was a good deal. . . .

But they'd always give that Negro man the worst part of everything. See, the jobs have already been tested and tried out before they ever get into the department, and they know what's good about them and what's bad about them. They always managed to give the worst one to the Negro. The only reason why the women fared better was they just couldn't give the woman [sic] as tough a job that they gave the men. But sometimes they did. . . .

There were some departments, they didn't even allow a black person to walk through there let alone work in there. Some of the white people did not want to work with the Negro. They had arguments right there. Sometimes they would get fired and walk on out the door, but it was one more white person gone. I think even to this very day in certain places they still don't want to work with the Negro. I don't know what their story is, but if they would try then they might not knock it.

But they did everything they could to keep you separated. They just did not like for a Negro and a white person to get together and talk. . . .

And they'd keep you from advancing. They always manage to give the Negroes the worst end of the deal. I happened to fall into that when they get ready to transfer you from one department to the next. That was the only thing that I ever ran into that I had to holler to the union about. And once I filed a complaint downtown with the Equal Opportunity. . . .

They had a good little system going. All the colored girls had more seniority in production than the whites because the average white woman did not come back after the war. They thought like I thought: that I have a husband now and I don't have to work and this was just only for the war and blah, blah, blah. But they didn't realize they was going to need the money. The average Negro was glad to come back because it meant more money than they was making before. So we always had more seniority in production than the white woman.

All the colored women in production, they was just one step behind the other. I had three months more than one, the next one had three months more than me, and that's the way it went. So they had a way of putting us all in Blueprint. We all had twenty years by the time you got in Blueprint and stayed a little while. Here come another one. He'd bump you out and then you went out the door, because they couldn't find nothing else for you to do—so they said. They just kept doing it and I could see myself: "Well, hell, I'm going to be the next one to go out the door!"

So I found some reason to file a grievance. I tried to get several other girls: "Let's get together and go downtown and file a grievance" [a discrimination complaint with the Equal Opportunities Employment Commission]. I only got two girls to go with me. That made three of us. I think we came out on top, because we all kept our jobs and then they stopped sending them to Blueprint, bumping each other like that. So, yeah, we've had to fight to stay there.

Willard Waller Announces the Postwar Battle of the Sexes, 1945

When our soldiers get through fighting Germans and Japs [*sic*], they will have to fight their own women. For the next war is the war of the sexes. Founded upon the oldest antagonism in the world, this ancient conflict sometimes smoulders but it never dies. It is not a savage war but a very important one, because our future depends upon its outcome.

During the war years, American women have forged steadily ahead in industry, politics and education, but the soldiers probably will put an end to all that when they return. Several soldiers, wounded on widely separated war fronts, recently spoke their opinions about women working after the war, in no uncertain terms. They, speaking for themselves, said woman's place is in the home.

Tech. Sgt. John A. Price, who was wounded in the European theater, is married and has a little girl. "After the war," he says, "women will be needed in the home. They're needed to rear children to become good citizens. Our civilization needs homes, and the woman is the foundation of a good home."

Now convalescing in Halloran General Hospital is Cpl. Fred Bienstock, who says: "I'm married. My wife's working now, but we want to start a family as soon as possible. You can't have a family when the wife is working. I want her to quit, and let me do the supporting. Anyway, there aren't going to be too many jobs and the men ought to get 'em. And something else: If a woman isn't married, she certainly isn't going to be unless she quits her job—or is willing to quit."

Wounded in the Middle East, Cpl. Otto Makovy declared, "I'm not married. But when I am, I'll insist on doing all the supporting and my wife's staying home. That's a woman's place. Another thing it seems to me that we won't have to worry so much about juvenile delinquency if there's somebody in the home looking after the kids.

Rattling in this fashion seems to be our ancestral burden. There was discord in Eden and at all times since.

Always the two halves of the human race have struggled for supremacy. Especially in the period following a major war are men and women at loggerheads. War brings about a temporary revolution in the relations of the two sexes. One might say the women get out of hand. This happened in World War I, and, before that, in our Civil and Revolutionary Wars. But after this war the women will probably put up a stronger fight for supremacy because this war's changes have merely climaxed generations of feministic progress.

Three Phases

The battles in the coming war on women will be three: the battle for jobs, the battle of the birth rate, and the battle of personal ascendancy. But may God help the men, the women and the United States of America if the men lose. At least for the next generation, the patriarchal family must be restored and strengthened. Women must bear and rear children; husbands must support them.

First will come the battle of jobs. Because we must have jobs for returning veterans as well as for millions of displaced war workers, many millions of women are certain to be forced out of industry. We hear a lot of easy talk about 60,000,000 postwar jobs, but such a figure is more a possibility than a probability. Even today, at the peak of our war effort, we have, as of August, 1944, somewhat less than 54,000,000 employed in civilian pursuits. An estimate of about 55,000,000 postwar jobs, therefore, seems generous. Even if, by some miracle, there are 60,000,000 jobs, there will be a great surplus of labor when the veterans return. That means there will be some millions of men, with families, tramping the streets and looking for jobs. This group will exert pressure on the jobs of 18,460,000 women now employed. Many of these women, of course, will marry or return to already established homes.

If we are intelligent, we can make use of the postwar displacement of women by men to put more men in certain fields where they are now lacking. More men are needed in the teaching profession, which has become increasingly feminized since women got their first real foothold during the Civil War. The public schools could absorb at least 250,000 men. Other fields, such as social work, would also be the better for a strong infusion of masculinity.

However the affair is managed, millions of women must give up their jobs. There is other work for them to do, woman's work. Here will arise the second battle, that of the birth rate. For our nation must have more babies or become a second-rate power. Estimates of the populations of 1970, based upon prewar birth rates, show the future strength of nations in the clearest possible perspective. In 1970 Russia may have 250,000,000 people, possibly many more. Japan, unless checked, may have 100,000,000. India's youthful population may reach 500,000,000.

In 1970 the United States may have a rapidly aging population of about 160,000,000. It may have difficulty in keeping its position as a major power. Russia may have twice as many men of military age, and twice as many women to propagate the next generation. Other nations encourage reproduction by every device that the ingenuity of lawmakers can invent, but our country, unable to face the facts of life, continues to give every advantage and preferment to the unmarried and the childless.

If we are to have an adequate birth rate, we must hear less talk about women's rights and more about their duty to the race. The plain fact is, women do not produce children under the conditions of freedom and equality that have existed in the United States since the last war. The birth rate among educated, emancipated women is very low indeed, since few women manage to compete with men and, at the same time, produce their due number of children. Usually the career of a brilliant woman is bought at the cost of an empty nursery. The price is too high, even if the contribution is great.

Threat to the Nation

The facts behind these statements? Consider the birth rate among college-educated women, who have failed for generations to produce enough children to maintain their own numbers. Or consider a small sample of 100 married women listed in "Who's Who." Sixty-nine of these distinguished women are childless; the other 31 have borne a total of 70 children; only eight members of the group have contributed three or more members to the next generation. To keep up their proportion, these women should have borne 300 children instead of 70.

The failure of able women to reproduce is a serious threat to the nation, because both quantity and quality of the population are important. If the reproduction of people with superior capacities stops but a single generation, the race can never be the same again. We cannot afford sex equality if it entails biological degeneration. Therefore, we must exert pressure, offer every inducement to favor reproduction, especially of the fit.

Now surely some old-fashioned feminist will say that a woman is the mistress of her own body; the nation has no right to force her to bear children. Well, a man is the master of his body too, but hardly anyone questions the right of the nation to force him to expose his body to the risks of war. A woman's ownership of her body should be subordinate to her obligation as the trustee of the race.

There is yet a third battle, that of personal ascendancy. In vulgar language, men and women must fight it out to see who is going to wear the pants. Here men should gain at least a partial victory. Both men and women will be happier so, for even women are rarely wholehearted feminists. But whether the women like it or not they will have to give some ground. Men are certain to gain some victories, if only because they are so few and women like living alone even less than men. And young men who have fought a war are not likely to accept petticoat domination.

It will be better for the men, and the women too, if the men do not go down in defeat. For nobody loves a henpecked man, not even the woman who henpecks him. To illustrate, let me tell about a really henpecked man whom I once knew. Shortly after his marriage, his wife forced him to give up smoking. Occasionally he would visit his bachelor friends, and sometimes smoke a cigarette. After such a spree he would carefully gargle with a deodorizing mouthwash. "Juanita would give me hell," he explained, "if she smelled smoke on my breath." On his rare evening away from home he played cribbage, but his wife always scolded him if he lost. One evening he played with Jones and lost a dollar. He gave Jones a dollar and a half. His conversation with his wife was as follows: "Well, where have you been? "Uh— playing cribbage with Jones." "And how much did you lose this time?" "Jones owes me fifty cents." The moral of that story is: Nobody feels sorry for such a poor devil, but is contemptuous of him, resents him a poor example of his sex. His wife resents him most of all. A man living with a modern woman faces hard choices.

It is not so easy, as once it was, to kill the cat on the first day, but it is necessary to keep on trying. The woman of today is so constituted that she cannot help trying to dominate her husband, and if she fails she will resent that, but if she succeeds she will be forever embittered. Therefore a husband will do just as well to give up trying to please his wife in all things and to be content with pleasing himself in many matters.

In the struggle for domination, the simplest, most straightforward methods are probably best for the man. A man should not try to convince his wife that he is more intelligent than she is, because very likely that is not true. It is better just to tell her plainly that he is going to be the boss, and then she will be very angry and will threaten to leave him and will love him to distraction.

And that is why the men must win the postwar battle of the sexes. They cannot afford defeat; the women cannot afford victory.

 ## E S S A Y S

The first essay is excerpted from *Asian Americans: An Interpretive History* by Sucheng Chan, professor of Asian American Studies at the University of California, Santa Barbara. There is a voluminous literature on how 112,000 persons of Japanese ancestry living in the Pacific Coast states were removed from their homes and incarcerated at the beginning of World War II. Chan's account of what happened is one of the most succinct available.

Albert S. Broussard, author of the second essay, directed the San Francisco Black Oral History Project and is presently professor of history at Texas A&M University. He has also served as president of the Oral History Association. His book, *Black San Francisco: The Struggle for Racial Equality in the West, 1900–1954* (1993), from which the second essay is drawn, offers the most detailed analysis available of the African American community in San Francisco during the first half of the twentieth century.

The third essay comes from *California Women: A History* (1987) by Joan M. Jensen, professor of history and women's studies at New Mexico State University, Las Cruces, and Gloria Ricci Lothrop, professor of history and women's studies at California State University, Northridge. The essay reminds us how the status of women has often remained ambiguous even during periods when it was supposed to be improving.

The Incarceration of Japanese Americans During World War II

SUCHENG CHAN

As soon as the United States declared war on Japan, following the latter's bombing of the American naval base at Pearl Harbor in Hawaii on 7 December 1941, more than 40,000 Japanese living on the Pacific Coast, along with their 70,000 American-born children—who were U.S. citizens—were removed from their homes and incarcerated. . . . [T]he FBI pick[ed] up more than 1,700 enemy aliens, including 736 Japanese, along the Pacific Coast on the very day that war was declared. (There were about a quarter million enemy aliens living in the western states at this time: 114,000 Italians, 97,000 Germans, and 40,000 Japanese.) Four days later, the FBI had 1,370 Japanese under detention. The number rose to over 2,000 on the mainland by March 1942—about half the total enemy aliens arrested. In addition, the bureau also picked up almost 900 Japanese in Hawaii who were detained in army-run camps in the islands until they were transferred to Justice Department camps on the mainland. One little-known fact is that Japanese in other parts of the Americas, especially Peru, were also arrested and sent for incarceration in the United States.

The individuals rounded up were officers of various community organizations, Japanese language school teachers, Shinto and Buddhist priests and priestesses, newspaper editors, and other identifiable leaders. They were arrested under a blanket presidential warrant (which did not specify any grounds for the arrests) and taken to camps run by the Immigration and Naturalization Service in Lordsburg and Santa Fe, New Mexico; Crystal City and Seagoville, Texas; Livingston, Louisiana; Fort Missoula, Montana; and Fort Lincoln, North Dakota.

Meanwhile, General John L. DeWitt, commander of the Western Defense Command headquartered at the Presidio in San Francisco, sought permission from the Justice Department to enter "all alien homes" without warrants in order to search for and seize contraband. The U.S. attorney general refused to grant authorization for such warrantless searches, but on 29 December 1941 the Justice Department itself ordered all enemy aliens in seven western states to surrender their radios, shortwave sets, cameras, binoculars, and any weapons they possessed. During these initial weeks of the war, enemy aliens of Japanese, German, and Italian ancestry were

---

Excerpted with permission of Twayne Publishers, an imprint of Simon & Schuster Macmillan, from *Asian Americans: An Interpretive History* by Sucheng Chan. Copyright © 1991 by Sucheng Chan.

treated alike, but shortly afterward, the Japanese, together with their American-born children, were singled out for discriminatory treatment. . . .

[T]he Justice Department announced in late January that enemy aliens would be excluded from 86 prohibited zones in California—all of them chosen by DeWitt. These included areas around San Francisco Bay, the Los Angeles airport, several other airports, railroad stations, power plants, dams, gasworks, and the like. All enemy aliens were told they had to leave these localities no later than 24 February. A second proclamation specified 7 prohibited areas in Washington and 24 in Oregon. During the first part of February, some 10,000 enemy aliens—8,000 of them Japanese—left their homes in the prohibited areas. In addition, the entire coastal strip from the Oregon border to a point 50 miles north of Los Angeles and extending 30 to 150 miles inland was declared a restricted zone, in which enemy aliens had to abide by travel restrictions and a curfew. Meanwhile, on 14 January 1942 the president authorized a compulsory registration program for all enemy aliens.

Apparently at this stage DeWitt felt that the steps being taken would be sufficient safeguard against espionage and sabotage, so he did not yet advocate mass evacuation. The attorney general and secretary of war also were not convinced such a drastic measure was necessary or practical. However, the latter's subordinates—the assistant secretary of war and the provost marshal general and his assistant—wanted all persons of Japanese ancestry, including Nisei citizens, moved out of the Pacific Coast and interned inland.

The War Department officials' effort to realize their goal was aided by politicians and nativists who launched a campaign in mid-January to get persons of Japanese ancestry incarcerated. On 16 January California congressman Leland Ford sent identical letters to the secretary of war and the attorney general to urge that "all Japanese, whether citizens or not, be placed in inland concentration camps." Ford made the same proposal on the floor of the Congress four days later. Then the entire congressional delegation from Washington, Oregon, and California, as well as the Native Sons of the Golden West, the California Joint Immigration Committee (a private organization, despite its name), and other anti-Japanese groups asked Roosevelt to remove "all persons of Japanese lineage . . . *aliens and citizens alike*" [italics added] from the West Coast.

The report of a committee headed by Supreme Court Justice Owen J. Roberts to investigate the destruction of Pearl Harbor, which was released in late January, also helped to fuel hostility against persons of Japanese ancestry in the United States. The Roberts report blamed the islands' army and navy commanders for the lack of preparedness that made possible Japan's attack and charged that the enemy had been greatly aided by an alleged espionage network involving many American citizens of Japanese ancestry and centered at the Japanese consulate in Honolulu. No evidence has ever been offered for these charges, which were based entirely on racist rumors.

The conclusions of the Roberts Report no doubt unnerved DeWitt, who soon drafted a statement (referred to as his "Final Recommendation") calling for the removal of all persons of Japanese ancestry on racial grounds. The Japanese were "an enemy race," declared the document, whose "racial affinities [were] not severed by migration" and whose "racial strains" remained "undiluted" even among members of the second and third generations. Therefore, because the army had no ready means to separate out the disloyal from the loyal, all persons of Japanese ancestry, regardless of their citizenship status, must be removed from the coast.

At this point a number of journalists called national attention to the issue. Walter Lippmann, the highly influential columnist, published a column on 12 February entitled "The Fifth Column on the Coast," in which he deplored the unwillingness of the federal government to remove enemy aliens from what he called a "combat zone." He declared that there was "plenty of room elsewhere" for suspect persons to exercise their rights. Lippmann's column was carried in hundreds of newspapers. Another journalist, Westbrook Pegler, wrote, "The Japanese in California should be under armed guard to the last man and woman right now—and to hell with habeas corpus until the danger is over."

Upon receiving DeWitt's "Final Recommendation," the army's chief of staff immediately approved it, as did all the civilian heads of the War Department. They drafted an executive order for President Roosevelt's signature that would give the army complete power to remove Japanese aliens and citizens alike from the Pacific Coast. The draft was presented to Roosevelt on the afternoon of 19 February. He signed it as Executive Order 9066 the same evening, authorizing the secretary of war to designate military areas "from which any and all persons may be excluded as deemed necessary or desirable." The next day, the secretary appointed DeWitt to carry out the order as he saw fit. . . .

Under the authority granted him by Executive Order 9066, at the beginning of March DeWitt proclaimed the western halves of Washington, Oregon, California, and the southern half of Arizona as Military Areas 1 and 2, from which enemy aliens of German, Italian, and Japanese ancestry, as well as all persons of Japanese ancestry, should prepare to remove themselves. In an accompanying press release, he explained that the Japanese were scheduled to leave first. As it turned out, the Italians and most Germans were never ordered to move. A week before DeWitt's first proclamation, all persons of Japanese ancestry had already been evicted from Terminal Island (off San Pedro, California) by order of the U.S. Navy. On 16 March DeWitt designated Idaho, Montana, Nevada, and Utah as Military Areas 3, 4, 5, and 6. The following week, he ordered all persons of Japanese ancestry to leave Bainbridge Island, near Seattle, Washington. To allow DeWitt to enforce his orders with criminal penalties, on 19 March Congress passed Public Law 503 by voice votes, following only a half hour's debate in the House of Representatives and an hour's discussion in the Senate. Again, without hesitation, Roosevelt signed the bill into law two days later.

During March more than 3,000 persons moved from the prohibited to the restricted zones of California, while almost 5,000 left Washington, Oregon, and California altogether. Then suddenly on 27 March DeWitt announced voluntary moves would no longer be allowed. Thereafter, the Wartime Civil Control Authority (WCCA)—a unit created within the Western Defense Command to take charge of civilian affairs—took over the forced evacuation of more than 100,000 persons of Japanese ancestry. The WCCA asked several other federal agencies to help: the Federal Security Agency was responsible for social services, the U.S. Employment Service was to help evacuees find new jobs, the Farm Security Administration was to oversee the transfer of farms owned or leased by Japanese to other operators, while the Federal Reserve Bank was to aid evacuees in disposing of their property.

None of these bureaucracies, however, was able to aid the Japanese very much. Stripped of its leadership, its liquid assets frozen, the entire community was in a state of shock. Given no more than a week to sell, store, or otherwise dispose of their property, people sold their possessions at great loss. Each family was told to take bedding and linen, toilet articles, clothes, kitchen utensils, and whatever other personal effects they could hand carry. Nothing else was allowed, and people could not even send packages to themselves through the mail. The JACL [Japanese American Citizens League] urged everyone to cooperate, so with the exception of several individuals who defied the evacuation orders, there was virtually no resistance. People quietly stood in long lines, wore tags around their necks showing the numbers assigned their families, tried to keep their children from crying, allowed themselves to be examined by medical personnel and searched by soldiers, and traveled on buses and trains (often with the blinds drawn down the windows) to unknown destinations.

Before mass evacuation got very far, it turned into an internment program, because officials in ten inland western states declared in early April that they would not welcome any Japanese. The state officials agreed to allow the federal government to move the latter into their territories only if it placed the evacuees into guarded camps and guaranteed they would be "deported" after the war ended. Under such hostile conditions, virtually all persons of Japanese ancestry were uprooted from their homes in Military Areas 1 and 2 between April and August. Because incarceration was now the goal, many people had to move twice—first to temporary assembly centers and then to more permanent so-called relocation centers. Left behind were about 800 hospital patients too sick to travel, children in orphanages, and inmates of prisons and insane asylums, and around 600 non-Japanese spouses and mixed-blood children.

Sixteen assembly centers were set up at fairgrounds, race tracks, and other facilities able to hold 5,000 persons apiece. These were located at Puyallup, Washington; Portland, Oregon; Marysville, Sacramento, Tanforan, Stockton, Turlock, Salinas, Merced, Pinedale, Fresno, Tulare, Santa Anita, Manzanar, and Pomona, California; and Mayer, Arizona. The Army Corps of Engineers also built relocation centers on federal land in desolate places: Tule Lake and Manzanar, California; Minidoka, Idaho; Heart Mountain, Wyoming; Topaz, Utah; Poston and Gila River, Arizona; Amache, Colorado; and Rohwer and Jerome, Arkansas. The smallest housed 8,000 persons, the largest 20,000, with 10,000 being the average capacity. The last batch of evacuees moved from an assembly to a relocation center at the beginning of November. . . .

Japanese residents in Alaska were also uprooted. After the United States entered the war, the Alaska Defense Command was incorporated into the Western Defense Command and Alaska was designated as a combat zone. All persons of "Japanese race of greater than half blood"—fewer than 200 persons—were excluded from certain military areas and removed to the United States.

Though Hawaii was in much greater danger of being attacked and martial law was declared immediately following the bombing of Pearl Harbor, no mass evacuation of the 150,000 Japanese took place there, because to have removed them, when they comprised 37 percent of the islands' total population and an even larger proportion of its skilled labor force, would have disrupted the islands' economy too much and would, moreover, have tied up too many ships.

Once the Japanese were in the relocation camps, the War Relocation Authority (WRA), created by Roosevelt on 18 March 1942, took over supervision of the internees, though the army retained control over the camps. In addition to the civil servants who staffed it, the WRA hired Nisei to assist in a variety of capacities. Regardless of the degree of skill needed in a job, however, internees received wages ranging from only $12 to $19 a month. WRA officials especially favored members of the JACL, some of whom informed on their fellow internees in order to curry favor for themselves.

Camps were divided into blocks, each with fourteen barracks subdivided into apartments. Hastily constructed with green lumber and tar paper and unfinished on the inside, the barracks developed cracks in their walls when the lumber began to dry. Since the camps were located in semideserts, sand seeped through the cracks into the apartments whenever the wind blew. Summers were blistering hot, while winters were freezing cold. An average apartment housing a family of four to six persons measured 20 feet by 25 feet, was heated by a single stove, and was furnished only with army cots and straw mattresses. Internees used communal bathrooms with no partitions—a fact that caused some of the women great discomfort. They ate in mess halls in shifts. Complaints about food were rampant. To make their living conditions more tolerable, the more enterprising internees scrounged for scrap lumber and whatever else they could find, with which they constructed makeshift furniture.

Even more troubling than the poor food and unpleasant physical environment was the fact that the internees' families started to disintegrate, . . . The status and authority of the Issei [Japanese immigrant] fathers, whose average age was 55 in 1942, began to erode once they lost their role as breadwinners. The older Nisei [second-generation Japanese Americans], especially those earning salaries or who were block leaders, on the other hand, all of a sudden acquired independence and power. The younger children often preferred to eat meals with their friends rather than with their families and ran around the camps out of their parents' sight and control. More important, WRA policy with regard to education and social life helped to widen the cultural gulf between the Issei parents and their Nisei children: Japanese language schools and the practice of Shintoism were forbidden, while Euro-American teachers and WRA staff in the camps assiduously promoted Americanization. Political judgment and official policy now served to underpin the intense and almost desperate desire of Nisei to be accepted as Americans.

Internees were allowed to leave the camps only under very limited conditions. During 1942 some 9,000 evacuees left camp for short periods to help harvest crops. A National Japanese American Student Relocation Council aided about 250 college students whose studies had been interrupted to enroll in midwestern institutions for the fall term of 1942. In time, the council placed several thousand Nisei students, but only in colleges and universities where no war-related research was being done. And of the eligible institutions of higher learning, not all were willing to accept Japanese American students. . . .

Within a few months of being moved into the camps, some internees began to show resentment against their lot. . . . [S]ome held demonstrations and engaged in strikes to protest the more repressive aspects of camp life. These incidents reflected the deep divisions within the internee population—divisions based on both social and political differences. The most fundamental cleavage was between Kibei [Japanese Americans born in the U.S. but educated in Japan] and Issei, who were proud of their Japanese heritage and who deeply resented the injustice of their incarceration, on the one hand, and, on the other, Nisei—particularly leaders of the JACL—who wanted so badly to be accepted as Americans that they acted as the U.S. government's most ardent apologists.

A second set of responses developed in reaction to the army's decision to allow Nisei to serve. These ranged from outright refusal to register to eager acceptance of the chance to prove their loyalty in blood. . . .

[The U.S. Army decided] at the beginning of 1943 to induct Americans of Japanese ancestry into an all-Japanese combat team. Internees found the procedures set up to screen individuals for this purpose to be especially objectionable. The WRA, which had been trying to work out for some time a more efficient system for leave clearance, now combined efforts with the army to devise a questionnaire to separate the "loyal" from the "disloyal." Between early February and late March, all American citizens of Japanese ancestry and aliens over age seventeen, except those who had already requested repatriation to Japan, were required to fill out a Selective Service questionnaire as well as a WRA questionnaire. Both contained two "loyalty" questions.

Both questionnaires asked male citizens, "Are you willing to serve in the armed forces of the United States on combat duty, wherever ordered?"

and, "Will you swear unqualified allegiance to the United States of America and faithfully defend the United States from any or all attacks by foreign or domestic forces, and forswear any form of allegiance or obedience to the Japanese Emperor or any other foreign government, power or organization?" The WRA form for female citizens and aliens of both sexes inquired, "If the opportunity presents itself and you are found qualified, would you be willing to volunteer for the Army Nurse Corps or the W.A.C.?" while the second question was similar to that answered by male citizens. However, as soon as officials started helping people to fill out these forms, they realized that the second question, as worded, was inappropriate for aliens, who would become stateless persons if they forswore allegiance to Japan. So on the forms for aliens, officials hastily changed the question to read, "Will you swear to abide by the laws of the United States and to take no action which would in any way interfere with the war effort of the United States?" Those who wished to enlist had to fill out yet additional forms. At first, the army accepted only citizens. Several months later, it announced it would also take "loyal" aliens and make it possible for them to apply for citizenship, the existing naturalization laws [that barred Asian immigrants from becoming U.S. citizens through naturalization] notwithstanding.

The registration drive created real dilemmas for the camps' residents and split many families further apart. Answering yes to the question about forswearing allegiance to the Japanese emperor implied that one held such allegiance in the first place. A vast majority of the Nisei felt no attachment to Japan whatsoever and refused to be so impugned. On the other hand, by answering yes to both questions they became eligible for the draft. Many individuals resented being asked to serve a country whose government had imprisoned them and their families in concentration camps. Especially offensive was the fact that should they be inducted, they would be placed in a segregated unit. Some worried about what would happen to their aged parents, who had now been stripped of their possessions and had few remaining means of survival. Many Issei begged or cajoled their American-born children to answer no to both questions, as a means to keep their families together in a time of extreme uncertainty. . . .

Altogether, 78,000 individuals were required to register—20,000 of them male Nisei between the ages of 17 and 37 subject to the draft. Over 4,000 of the latter refused to answer the two questions or gave negative or qualified answers. The percentage of internees registering and the proportion of affirmative versus negative answers varied considerably in the different camps, depending on how the WRA officials and army representatives dealt with the situation, as well as on the internal political dynamics among the internees at particular camps. . . .

As news of the resistance to registration leaked out, hostile public reaction developed, calling for punishment of the "disloyals." In July 1943 Congress passed a bill enabling the WRA to segregate them. Since the largest contingent of such persons was at Tule Lake, it was designated as the segregation center. Five categories of individuals were placed into Tule Lake:

aliens who had requested repatriation to Japan; American citizens who desired to renounce their citizenship—even though there existed no procedure for doing so until July 1944—and requested expatriation to Japan; "disloyals" answering no; persons held in Justice Department camps who wished to join their families; and "old Tuleans" who did not wish to move yet one more time. There were about 6,000 persons in the last category, many of them people with large families containing small children. In September more than 6,000 "loyal" Tuleans moved out to other centers, while 12,000 "disloyal" persons from the other nine centers (both figures include family members) moved in. Thus Tule Lake now had 18,000 inhabitants cramped into facilities meant for 12,000. . . .

Given the poor internee showing during registration, when only 1,200 Nisei volunteered for service (triple that number had been expected), the Selective Service reintroduced the draft for Japanese Americans at the beginning of 1944. To its surprise, this effort also met with resistance, especially at the camp in Heart Mountain, Wyoming. Led by the Heart Mountain Fair Play Committee, formed by Kiyoshi Okamoto, a Nisei from Hawaii, and encouraged by the editorials of James Omura, editor of the *Rocky Shimpo*, a Japanese newspaper published in Denver, dozens of Nisei defied the draft orders. . . .

In contrast to these various kinds of resisters, many Nisei eagerly grasped the chance offered by military service to prove their loyalty—in blood, if necessary—to the country of their birth. Approximately 25,000 Nisei served in the military during the war. The first and least-publicized group was trained at the Army's Military Intelligence Service Language School (MISLS). Established in November with temporary headquarters in San Francisco, this institution was moved first to Camp Savage and then to Fort Snelling in Minnesota. It trained 6,000 individuals, 3,700 of whom saw service in combat zones. To their dismay, MISLS instructors discovered that few Nisei knew Japanese well enough to translate and decode captured documents or to interpret for and interrogate prisoners. Ironically, it was the mistrusted Japan-educated Kibei who proved most valuable. Large numbers of MISLS graduates—working for the U.S. Army, Navy, and Marines, as well as within units of Allied forces—were stationed in Australia, India, Burma, China, and Hawaii. A few also served in the Pentagon in Washington, D.C. These men followed Allied troops into New Guinea, the Marianas, the Philippines, and Okinawa—all of which had been occupied by Japanese forces—to interrogate captured Japanese soldiers and to translate Japanese-language documents.

Another group of Nisei who saw military service was the One Hundredth Battalion, made up largely of individuals expelled from the Hawaii Territorial Guard soon after Pearl Harbor. Although the War Department wanted to discharge the Hawaiian Nisei, the commanding general in Hawaii chose to retain them. He placed them into a separate battalion, which was sent to Camp McCoy, Wisconsin, and Camp Shelby, Mississippi, for training. The battalion departed for North Africa in September 1943. From there they proceeded to Italy, where they were joined by the third group of Nisei recruited for combat duty—the 442nd Regimental Combat Team, whose members came out of the mainland concentration camps and were trained at Camp Shelby. In June 1944 the 100th formally merged with the 442nd in central Italy, whence it proceeded to France. Its bloodiest engagement came when it was sent to save a "lost" battalion of Texans near Bruyeres, during which the 442nd suffered 800 casualties in a week. The total casualties at the end of this campaign numbered above 2,000, with 140 dead.

The 442nd gained fame as the most decorated unit of its size during World War II. It received seven Presidential Distinguished Unit Citations, while its members earned more than 18,000 individual decorations, including a Congressional Medal of Honor, 47 Distinguished Service Crosses, 350 Silver Stars, 810 Bronze Stars, and more than 3,600 Purple Hearts. But it paid dearly in lives for such honor, suffering almost 9,500 casualties (300 percent of its original strength), including 600 killed. In all, 18,000 Nisei served in this unit during the war. Their exploits, publicized in newsreels and newspaper headlines, did a great deal to reduce, though not to erase, the prejudice against Japanese Americans, as President Harry S Truman himself noted when he added the Presidential Unit banner to their regimental colors.

During the same period that these visible forms of protest took place, a number of individuals fought a quieter but equally significant battle. Minoru Yasui, Gordon Hirabayashi, and Fred Korematsu challenged [in court] the constitutionality of the curfew and evacuation orders, while Mitsuye Endo questioned the WRA's right to keep her under custody. . . .

In all four test cases, the justices [of the U.S. Supreme Court] rested their decisions on the narrowest legal grounds and failed to address the fundamental constitutional issues raised by the internment for a number of reasons. . . . For one thing, the government's lawyers concealed from the Supreme Court important analyses done by the FBI and the Federal Communications Commission—based on these agencies' own investigations—that General DeWitt's claims of Japanese American espionage and sabotage activities were simply unfounded. At the same time, the national board of the ACLU, whose lawyers played important roles in the four cases, made a policy decision not to attack the constitutionality of Executive Order 9066 out of loyalty to Franklin Delano Roosevelt. Finally, conflicts within various agencies of the federal government itself, and the sense of institutional loyalty certain individuals felt towards their agencies, forced some of them to acquiesce to decisions that their own consciences deplored.

A final form of resistance available to Japanese Americans was renunciation of their American citizenship. . . .

The Justice Department received over 6,000 applications for renunciation, almost 5,600 of which it approved. As war drew to a close, however, many of these individuals wrote the Justice Department asking to withdraw their petitions. After the war ended, San Francisco lawyer Wayne Collins . . . filed two suits on behalf of 4,322 renunciants in an effort to regain their citizenship, arguing that they had acted under duress and coercion. The federal district court in San Francisco issued a temporary injunction to stop their deportation and in April 1948 canceled their renunciation and declared them U.S. citizens. The federal government appealed but eventually decided to rescind the outstanding orders against the 302 renunciants still being held in its internment camps, whereupon Collins petitioned for a dismissal of the unsettled suits on the grounds that the cancellation had rendered the issue moot. His petition was granted, but the renunciants did not regain their citizenship.

At war's end in August 1945, 44,000 persons of Japanese ancestry were still in camp, even though the federal government had revoked the mass exclusion orders in December 1944. This population was so large because the dispossessed people had no place to go and were fearful of the hostile outside world. But they were forcibly pushed back into a society that did not want them. Those lucky enough to have children or other relatives who had resettled in the Midwest or the East Coast joined them, while less fortunate ones received nothing more than train fare to the locations where they had lived before the war. Those who still owned property found their homes dilapidated and vandalized, their farms, orchards, and vineyards choked with weeds, their personal belongings stolen or destroyed. Others with nothing left were sheltered for a time by churches and a few social agencies as they looked for ways to eke out a living. Issei men, now in their sixties, found work as gardeners and janitors; their wives toiled as domestic servants. Despite such harsh circumstances, these old pioneers picked up the broken pieces of their lives and carried on as their children struggled to join postwar mainstream America.

Changes in the Status of African American Workers in the 1940s and 1950s

ALBERT S. BROUSSARD

Black San Franciscans established the state's earliest black schools, press, churches, political conventions, protest organizations, and benevolent societies. They were also the most prominent figures in the struggle for civil rights throughout the state during the nineteenth and early twentieth centuries. . . .

San Francisco . . . possessed a mystique as a racially tolerant and progressive city toward blacks. Few white San Franciscans admitted that any form of racial discrimination existed in their city before 1940. . . . Unlike many midwestern and eastern cities, San Francisco whites did not restrict blacks to well-defined communities as they did in many cities, including Los Angeles. The majority of San Francisco's segregation laws were abolished by 1900, and blacks were permitted to frequent most places of public accommodation, ride public transportation, and attend the public schools on an integrated basis. Not one black was ever lynched in San Francisco,

Reprinted from *Black San Francisco: The Struggle for Racial Equality in the West, 1900–1954* by Albert S. Broussard. Copyright © 1993 by the University Press of Kansas. Used by permission of the publisher.

and there are few recorded instances of interracial violence between blacks and whites. Nor did San Francisco ever experience race riots before the 1960s, like many northern and southern cities that exploded during the World War I era and in the early 1920s. Thus San Francisco's race relations did not conform to the rigid pattern that developed in many twentieth-century urban centers. . . .

Prior to the 1940s, it did not contain a large industrial black working class like Chicago, Cleveland, Detroit, Pittsburgh, or Milwaukee, although the number of blacks in industrial jobs did increase steadily after 1910. Black workers were slower to gain industrial jobs in San Francisco than their counterparts in other cities, however, and the vast majority of black workers remained outside organized labor until the 1940s. San Francisco's black population also remained relatively small between 1900 and 1940, at a time when many northern and southern cities experienced sizable increases in their black communities. . . .

The Second World War was a watershed for many black San Franciscans, because it provided, for the first time, jobs in semiskilled, skilled, and white-collar occupations in sizable numbers. The war also shifted the major patterns of black and white migration from the North to the Sunbelt states. Black migration, in particular, increased dramatically throughout the entire San Francisco Bay Area, as high-paying industrial jobs became available in Bay Area shipyards and defense industries. San Francisco's black population increased more than 600 percent between 1940 and 1945 alone, as black southern migrants sought economic opportunity, better schools for their children, and freedom from racial violence. The war also accelerated the campaign for racial equality that black San Franciscans had been waging for more than four decades. As black leaders joined with white leaders to form interracial organizations, racial discrimination was under greater assault than ever before, and by 1954, blacks faced fewer barriers in their quest for full equality. . . .

Hearing the cries of the federal government, business, and industry to support the war effort, both at home and abroad, blacks aspired to participate fully in the mainstream economic opportunities of the era. Black workers sought and demanded employment in the traditional areas open to nonwhite workers, but they pursued, with equal fervor, nontraditional employment avenues in both the skilled and semiskilled sectors. Blacks' entrance into new sections of the labor market was supported by a presidential executive order, a federal Wartime Commission, the prodding of black leadership, and the efforts of the California CIO, whose racial policies toward the admittance of blacks to organized labor were far more egalitarian that [*sic*] the AFL's. It would restructure black employment patterns throughout the Bay Area. . . .

The California CIO was . . . vigilant during World War II in monitoring the conditions of black workers in the defense industry and suggesting more effective ways to integrate black workers into the burgeoning labor force. The CIO organized a minorities committee in the early 1940s specifically for this purpose, headed by the black labor leader Matt Crawford.

. . . [B]lack workers were . . . slow to gain a foothold in the war industries, but as the manpower shortage . . . intensified, the area of acceptance . . . steadily enlarged.

Within two years of the United States' entrance into the war, that proverbial foothold had been attained in many critical wartime industries. Blacks could find employment in the aircraft, construction, iron and steel, and shipbuilding industries. . . .

The Bay Area's shipyards, in particular, hired black workers in large numbers. As shipyards like the Kaiser companies frantically attempted to meet their hiring schedules and honor their defense contracts, workers of all races were in demand. The number of black shipbuilders varied from locality to locality and precise figures are impossible to ascertain. However, several reliable organizations, such as the California CIO and the Bay Area Council against Discrimination (BACAD), a local civil rights organization, estimated that 15 to 16 thousand blacks worked in Bay Area shipyards in 1943, a figure that exceeded the 1940 black populations of San Francisco and Oakland combined. The United States Fair Employment Practices Committee (FEPC) corroborated the progressive employment practices in Bay Area shipyards. The FEPC stated unequivocally in its *Final Report* that by September 1945, "more than twenty-six percent of the Negro working force were engaged in shipbuilding or ship repair. Another twenty-five percent were employed in servicing water transportation, which was largely government work." These two industries alone, concluded the report, accounted for approximately 12,000 black workers. . . .

At the start of World War II, the range of employment opportunities for black females in San Francisco was no different than in most northern or southern cities. However, with the coming of the war, the expansion of defense industries, and the president's executive order to prod them to greater achievement, black women gradually began to break the familiar mold of menial work. To be sure, the war produced rising expectations in black females because they took the initiative to apply for white-collar and skilled employment as well as unskilled jobs. Given the low percentages of black women in white-collar, skilled, and professional positions before the war, employers were uneasy about the prospect of integrating their female work force. . . .

Determined, many black females pushed their claims for employment. Most were rebuffed in their quest for white-collar respectability and career advancement, as was a black woman who responded to an advertisement for an operator, but was turned down with the familiar claim that no positions were available. Another black female attempted to circumvent the racial classification section on her application by writing in "American." The interviewer, apparently in no mood for deception or for black females, told her candidly, "That won't do," and refused to hire her. . . .

Black women not only complained that they were denied employment opportunities, but that they were forced to bear the added indignity of employers inviting white women to apply for positions that they had been denied. One black female college graduate with fifteen years teaching

experience was denied employment as a secretary, a position that was frequently difficult for black women to obtain. Another black woman
lamented, "They were hiring girls, but not my color of skin." . . .

The opposition to hiring black women can be explained on several levels. Many employers had not hired blacks of any gender, so black women
were at the same competitive disadvantage as their black male counterparts.
But black females generally faced an even bigger obstacle. They had made
less progress in breaking the cycle of domestic service and menial labor
than white females or black males. Consequently, black women were type-
cast by the general working population and major employers—they were
seen as suitable only for menial labor. It was one thing to hire a black
woman to scrub a toilet, yet quite another, as several employers indicated
in their refusal to hire black women, for black women to share toilet facilities with white women.

A more common argument against hiring black women was the charge
that the morale of white women would suffer if black women were hired.
No doubt, many white women felt a bit apprehensive at the prospect of
black women sharing the same offices and becoming, in effect, economic
equals. Some white women took refuge in the monopoly they had held on
secretarial and white-collar privileges at the expense of black women—that
was evident from the stern opposition of their employers and personnel
directors to hiring black females. But many employers probably hid behind
the excuse that hiring blacks would cause poor morale or mass walkouts. If
these predicted walkouts ever occurred in any industry in the Bay Area,
they were never reported.

Finally, companies balked at hiring black women because they did not
wish to establish a precedent within their industry. This was the fear of one
employer, who stated that "no [San Francisco] envelope manufacturing
companies had as yet employed colored girls and that he would not be the
first to do so." Other black women must have felt bitterly disgusted after
they were referred to jobs by either the Civil Service Commission or the
United States Employment Service and [were] politely rejected or told that
there was no opening. Why else would the Civil Service Commission have
"sent me to the job?" a black female asked in her complaint to the FEPC's
Regional Office. "I feel that there was an opening," she wrote, "and that
refusing to employ me was based on racial prejudice." Even though labor
shortages continued to plague Bay Area businesses and industries throughout the war, black females, like their male counterparts, encountered resistance in their attempts to find jobs in the private sector. Black women
gradually penetrated some of the barriers prohibiting their progress, but the
walls of employment segregation eroded even more slowly for them. Their
dreams of occupational advancement continued to be frustrated by employers who resented their race as well as their gender. . . .

Most black leaders believed that the ILWU [International Longshoremen's and Warehousemen's Union] was the most progressive union in
the Bay Area. Matt Crawford estimated that the ILWU's San Francisco
local alone contained 800 black members. The local's president, Richard

Lynden, claimed that the ILWU "is perhaps the most significant labor union in the Bay Area, insofar as progressive and democratic practices regarding the Negro worker is concerned." Given this relatively large black membership, his claim appears valid. . . .

The ILWU's status as the largest CIO-affiliated union in the San Francisco Bay Area offered advantages for black workers. The union did not enact quotas limiting the number of black workers. In fact, the ILWU's black membership was a respectable one-third of the union's total. . . .

As a result of the ILWU's egalitarian policies, a small but influential cadre of black leadership gradually developed within their respective Bay Area locals. Oakland, not San Francisco, boasted the largest number of black union members and, accordingly, elected several blacks to supervisory positions. . . .

Even though the ILWU could claim the largest black membership of any union in the Bay Area, its record in upgrading black workers was dismal. Almost nothing had been accomplished in this area since the integration of blacks into the union during the mid-1930s. "We have not done anything in upgrading in the plants where we hold jurisdiction for any of the minorities," Lynden said. Since blacks were the newest members of the union and held the least seniority, they were least likely to be promoted. The ILWU's policy was that "seniority shall be the basis of upgrading." Although Lynden and union officials were concerned about upgrading blacks and promised action, little progress was achieved. But as far as blacks were concerned, the ILWU stood head and shoulders above other Bay Area locals in virtually every respect, even though the union acknowledged that there was still room for improvement. The ILWU was as close to a "model" union as black San Franciscans were likely to find during the years of the Second World War.

The ILWU was not the only union to underutilize black workers. . . . The barriers to upward mobility for blacks within most Bay Area companies were formidable. The typical black worker could expect only a minimum of advancement beyond the entry level, and supervisory positions were virtually impossible for blacks to obtain . . . because of the common conviction that white workers would not serve under Negroes. . . .

The majority of black workers[, however,] were affiliated not with the CIO unions, but with the unions of the AFL. . . . Both the CIO and the AFL . . . had clauses in their constitutions "prohibiting discrimination on the grounds of race or color." While the CIO proudly but cautiously "carried its non-discrimination principle into a positive program for the acceptance of racial groups," the dominant AFL had "not enforced its anti-discrimination policy upon its affiliated unions." In effect, the AFL left the enforcement of its nondiscrimination clause to the respective locals.

This discretionary power on the part of the AFL locals was repeatedly abused. Some locals did not admit blacks under any circumstances, either before or during the war. . . .

The most flagrant abuses of the locals' discretionary power did not involve excluding blacks outright, but denying them membership in the parent union. To perpetuate their inferior social and economic position, black laborers were shuttled into separate Jim Crow auxiliaries. The largest industrial craft union in the San Francisco Bay Area, the International Brotherhood of Boilermakers, adopted this policy, which was uniform throughout the union's locals. . . .

Since the shipyards employed the majority of black defense-industry workers in the Bay Area, bypassing the separate black auxiliary union was difficult. The leading shipyards, Kaiser and Moore Drydock, had contracts with these unions obligating them to hire only union laborers or workers with union clearance. Some companies occasionally hired blacks without union clearance, though when they did, they risked the ire of union officials. Still other companies hired blacks, but demanded that they obtain union clearance before commencing their work. Thus, being hired was no guarantee of a job—the union would first have to grant clearance, as some Afro-Americans learned to their dismay. . . .

The auxiliary unions came under sharp attack from both black and white leaders, but none was more scathing than the attack of Joseph James, the San Francisco NAACP's branch president. . . . Like many black workers, James obtained employment in 1942 at Marinship, one of the largest Bay Area shipyards. In a matter of months, he had advanced from a welder's helper to journeyman. Despite his own advancement, James protested the segregated auxiliary arrangement and worked toward its abolition.

James organized a broad coalition of interracial opposition against the auxiliary. . . . He . . . spearheaded an interracial committee composed of black shipyard workers and civic leaders to protest the segregated auxiliary union directly. . . .

He called the auxiliary a "Jim Crow fake union." In denouncing it, he drew a familiar parallel between Hitler's racism in Europe and American racism at home. Moreover, he argued that the auxiliary union policy was divisive to the labor movement in general. Both black and white workers, he insisted, stood a much better chance of persevering during the postwar era if they were closely associated with the parent union. . . .

James initiated a series of lawsuits against the Boilermakers in an attempt to eradicate the segregated auxiliary structure. . . . [His] legal action was successful. . . . [He] was supported by several civil rights organizations and succeeded in allying the national office of the NAACP as well as the San Francisco branch with his cause. . . .

The Marin [County] Superior Court . . . ruled that the Boilermakers' arrangement of "discriminating against and segregating Negroes into auxiliaries is contrary to public policy of the State of California." Accordingly, the Superior Court prohibited the union from laying off workers who refused to pay dues and barred the union from requiring blacks to join segregated auxiliaries as a condition of employment. In short, the court ruled that the Boilermakers must "admit Negroes as members on the same terms and conditions as white persons" if they wished to "retain closed shop privileges."

Union leaders felt that the Marin Superior Court had overstepped its authority and promptly appealed the decision to the California Supreme Court. In a decision, *James* v. *Marinship,* that both surprised and jolted Boilermakers' officials, the California Supreme Court upheld the Marin Superior Court's decision. In the court's view, "the fundamental question in this case is whether a closed union coupled with a closed shop is a legitimate objective of organized labor. . . . In our opinion an arbitrarily closed or partially closed union is incompatible with a closed shop." The court also found the "discriminatory practices involved in this case contrary to the public policy of the United States and the State." It cited Executive Order 9346, which declared that "it is the policy of the United States to encourage full participation in the war effort of all persons regardless of race, creed, color or national origin, that there should be no discrimination in the employment of any person in war industries because of such." Hence, the court ruled that blacks "must be admitted to membership under the same terms and conditions applicable to non-Negroes unless the union and the employer refrain from enforcing the closed shop agreement against them." The decision was unanimous. . . .

Postwar employment progress proceeded slowly for black San Franciscans. To be sure, blacks had made impressive wartime employment gains, but many areas remained restricted because of race. . . . Black workers had a particularly difficult time making the transition from defense employment to permanent employment in the private sector, and black women continued to face even greater obstacles because of their gender. Yet black workers slowly began to integrate many businesses and corporations that had hired few blacks either before or during the war. Moreover, black professionals would be hired to teach in the San Francisco Unified School District for the first time since the nineteenth century. San Francisco, despite its unwillingness to eradicate all racial barriers in employment, would be far more open and integrated on the eve of the historic 1954 *Brown* v. *the Board of Education of Topeka, Kansas* decision than at any previous time in the city's history.

Instead of a large postwar out-migration, San Francisco's black population continued to grow between 1945 and 1950. The 1950 federal census reported 43,460 blacks in San Francisco, a staggering 904 percent increase from the 1940 population. . . .

As early as 1944, black migrants had shown an inclination to remain in the Bay Area, when a northern California industry survey revealed that only 15 percent of black workers expected to return home at the war's end. One-third of white workers surveyed indicated a desire to return to their former location. Though the survey did not reveal the black workers' reasons for wishing to remain in California, it is likely that the majority of black migrants believed they had found a better life for themselves and their children in California. Two-thirds of the black newcomers had migrated from southern states, where postwar economic opportunities were few, where segregation was sanctioned by state law, and where fear and racial violence had been an integral part of their world. Those memories were probably uppermost in their minds.

Several additional factors stimulated the black community's postwar growth. Unlike the pre–World War II years, when black workers made only marginal progress in semiskilled and skilled jobs, blacks made relatively significant gains in organized labor between 1941 and 1950. . . .

Black occupational advances also occurred more frequently in white-collar, civil service, and professional jobs. Before 1940, blacks had either been excluded from these areas or employed in them sparingly. Yet according to the San Francisco Urban League, black workers gradually began to penetrate the private sector as clerks, stenographers, office personnel, and secretaries. Some banks, insurance companies, and corporations, such as the Pacific Gas and Electricity Company (PG&E) and Pacific Telephone and Telegraph (PT&T), were also lifting the racial veil that had excluded blacks from many white-collar jobs.

The occupational gains by Bay Area black females, though less dramatic than those made by black men, were nonetheless significant. . . . Although black females still worked at the lowest occupational levels, important strides had been made in many areas. . . . [A] larger percentage of black women than ever before were employed as unskilled and semi-skilled laborers, clerks, secretaries, managers, and professionals.

Black professionals, both male and female, also found fewer obstacles in their path during the 1940s. Blacks were more likely to gain employment as managers, proprietors, and professional workers than ever before. The San Francisco Unified School District had hired its first black teacher, Josephine Cole, in 1944, and several others, along with a black principal, would follow. Cole's breakthrough was an important achievement for black San Franciscans, for San Francisco had lagged behind Oakland, Los Angeles, Portland, and Seattle in hiring black teachers. . . .

Black San Franciscans' perceptions of postwar economic opportunities were often skewed by the tremendous demand for black employment that existed during World War II. Since most blacks were wartime migrants and had not competed with whites for employment under normal circumstances, they underestimated employment discrimination in San Francisco. Thus, the rapid layoffs and the high black unemployment rate that followed the armistice were a rude awakening for many blacks. Bay Area shipyards reduced their work forces to a fraction of the peak wartime levels. The Kaiser shipyards alone, which employed more than 47,000 workers in late 1944, employed less than 9,000 by the spring of 1946.

The reduction of the wartime labor force was catastrophic for black workers. Throughout the Bay Area, black workers suffered a disproportionately high unemployment rate between 1945 and 1950. As early as 1946, 20 percent of all persons receiving unemployment insurance were nonwhites, primarily blacks, though blacks accounted for only 5 percent of the Bay Area's population. A year later the California State Employment Service reported that the black unemployment rate was 30 percent. Similarly, a 1948 sample of the Bay Area's black labor force revealed that black males had an unemployment rate twice as high as the statewide level. The unemployment rate for black women, however, was six times as great as the statewide level. . . .

Several factors contributed to the high black unemployment rate in San Francisco and throughout the Bay Area. Black workers had been less diversified in their employment than white workers during World War II. More than half of all blacks worked in either shipbuilding or government employment, and the precipitous declines in these two sectors resulted in widespread joblessness for many blacks. . . .

Black San Franciscans were faced with a paradox during the postwar years. On the one hand, a broader spectrum of jobs was open to them than ever before. On the other hand, employment discrimination was widespread in both the public and private sectors, preventing them, in effect, from gaining access to these jobs. . . .

[M]any large private businesses . . . hired no blacks or nonwhites whatsoever by 1951. Many other employers hired blacks in minuscule numbers. . . .

Blacks were also denied the opportunity to train and acquire skills for many positions. Some secretarial training schools felt that black applicants would be wasting their time, since it would be difficult to place a skilled black secretary. "We don't have no rule against accepting Negroes," reported one secretarial school. But the manager "doesn't want to place a burden on the [black] student by taking her money and finding she can't place her." . . .

Nor were black domestic and service workers protected from employment bias. "It is also a fact that with respect to employment of custodial service workers in hotels and apartment houses that our union hiring halls are every day asked to dispatch persons of a particular national group because the employer has certain policies," testified Richard Liebes, research director for the Building Service Employers Union in San Francisco. . . .

Aspiring black teachers also found that placement offices were of little help in light of the resistance of many school districts to hiring blacks. Some college placement services simply refused to refer prospective black teachers to school districts that had not hired Afro-Americans in the past. As late as 1954, San Francisco State College referred black teachers seeking employment only to school districts "where they know they will be hired." . . .

Black workers also lagged behind white workers and other nonwhite races in median income in San Francisco and throughout the state. The median income for blacks in California was $1,575 in 1949, compared with $2,234 for whites and $1,695 for other nonwhite races. . . .

As a result, black San Franciscans lagged behind the employment gains of black workers in midwestern and eastern cities, where black workers were employed in higher percentages in the automobile industry and as semiskilled factory operatives.

Women's Wartime and Postwar Experiences

JOAN M. JENSEN AND GLORIA RICCI LOTHROP

During World War II one of the films made in Hollywood was called *Rosie the Riveter.* Rosie is a young, attractive Anglo woman who works as a riveter during the day and romances two young men at night—one working class, the other middle class. Finally, after many laughs, Rosie chooses the working-class man who joins the U.S. Marine Corps and goes off to war amid chorus girls clad in red, white, and blue.

The movie Rosie was Hollywood's version of the Rosie created by the United States government to encourage women to go to work while young men went into the military. The war, and the work of women in it, was a watershed for women. . . . [They] rushed to tools and machines rather than to arms. They cut down trees, planted crops, typed for military and civilian bureaucracies, piloted planes, . . . drove tractors and ambulances. Curtiss Wright Company sent eight hundred women engineering trainees to college, and Standard Oil hired women chemists for the first time. Women became electricians, steamfitters, and welders. In San Francisco, one of the ten cities most affected by the war, female workers increased from 138,000 to 275,000. But the greatest gain in female employment was in the burgeoning California aircraft industry.

The female work force assembled in the swollen defense industry of southern California, particularly in Los Angeles, was central to war work. Nationwide, women constituted thirty percent of aircraft workers, but in Los Angeles they were forty-two percent. By 1944, over 62,000 women, about ten percent of the female labor force, worked in the Los Angeles aircraft industry. At the end of the war, the percentage of women holding better-paying defense jobs plummeted from the wartime peak of forty-three percent to nine percent. Most women who had been in the work force before the war returned to the type of work they had done previously, and, for the most part, to gender-segregated and low-paying jobs. As many as a third of the women who returned to duties at home soon opted to continue their outside work or to return to the work force after a short period. By 1950, the proportion of women in defense work had increased to fourteen percent, and thereafter, even with a drop in 1963, women remained approximately sixteen percent of the aircraft industry. Los Angeles defense work veterans also took clerical jobs as manufacturing and other business activity expanded with the establishment of corporate centers in southern California. . . .

[T]heir experiences of being part of an integrated work force, in jobs highly valued by society and at higher wages than they could have expected in traditional jobs, altered their self-esteem and lives. Marguerite Hoffman, who had been a seamstress, observed, "You know, I learned to stand up for myself working with men all those years at Douglas." . . .

From Joan M. Jensen and Gloria Ricci Lothrop, *California Women: A History.* (San Francisco: Boyd and Fraser, 1987), pp. 105–113, 117–121, 123–125. Reprinted by permission.

Aircraft work seemed to affect women in different ways, however. . . . Probably older women were affected more drastically than younger women. Former housewives used the confidence gained on the job to challenge the husbands who had been making choices about their lives. Older single women, with or without children, found the opportunities opened new hopes for future job stability. . . .

Those least affected by their work experience seemed to be young single women. They viewed themselves as future wives and mothers, not as workers. Rose Echeverría, who entered the aircraft industry just out of high school, recalled "happiness was getting married to a winner, to a hero, to the conqueror." These women willingly left their jobs and accepted the ideology that nothing had changed. Some older women shared these feelings, but the skills learned at nontraditional jobs were retained. Many engaged in construction activities in their own homes, and at least one became the neighborhood handywoman.

For thousands of California women of Japanese heritage, the wartime experience was vastly different. . . . Incarceration . . . meant broken homes and families. Many fathers like Ruth . . . [Azawa's] who had studied martial arts or who for some other reason were suspect were imprisoned separately. Kimiko Kitamaya [sic] . . . remembered the effect of imprisonment on her family. "The family unit had been very strong until that time," she said. "It broke down a little bit in camps because the younger kids were running around and being very independent. So the family unit that we always considered as very strong, slowly disintegrated."

Incarceration was probably hardest on those daughters who were already making their way successfully in the Anglo culture. Kitayama never got over the apprehension she had when the time to be relocated came: "It was a horrible feeling to go[.]" . . . Although postwar developments hastened the integration of the Japanese Americans when they returned to California, for many the fear they had experienced could never be erased. . . .

Although Chinese women did not undergo disruption equal to that of the Japanese, the war also changed their lives. Many Chinese had moved back and forth between China and the United States during the 1920s and 1930s, thus keeping alive the Chinese culture, but war ended these family sojourns. They also recalled having to carry identification cards during World War II because Californians could not distinguish Chinese from Japanese, and they risked physical harm as well as discrimination if they ventured abroad without them. . . .

With the end of the war, Japanese Americans returned to an unsettled future. Internment and the war hastened the integration of nisei [second-generation Japanese Americans] into California society. Prejudice was very strong against them in farming areas, and housing was difficult to obtain anywhere. The Quakers' California Council for Civic Unity . . . helped returning Japanese obtain shelter by purchasing houses and then selling them to the Japanese. In 1952, the California law barring aliens from land ownership was challenged successfully in court when Haruye [sic] Masaoka brought suit to retain title to her small Pasadena lot. (*Haruya*

Masaoka et al. v. *State of California*). Masaoka had been cited in the *Congressional Record* as one of two mothers having five sons in combat simultaneously in World War II. A few nisei women joined the Democratic party in the late 1940s, often gaining experience through the Democratic women's clubs. . . .

Black women were as profoundly affected by World War II as the Asian women, but for different reasons. Because the war came at the end of two decades of organizing in California, black women used their skills to pressure labor unions into removing some of their job disabilities. For black women, the "double V" meant not only victory abroad but victory at home against discrimination for gender and race. . . . In Los Angeles, the Negro Victory Committee threatened to organize blacks to march on the United States Employment Services to demand the hiring of black women in the aircraft industry and to march on the board of education unless there was an expansion of school programs in the black community. For black women, World War II also put a cap on the percentage who did housework for wages. From a prewar high of fifty-five percent in 1940, the proportion of employed black women in domestic service declined to forty percent in 1950. . . . Not only did black women emerge from the war to new jobs, they also entered an incipient civil rights movement that gained momentum in the 1950s and culminated with the entry of some black women into political offices in the 1970s.

The majority of black women remained clustered in urban areas of California, particularly in Los Angeles, where most wartime migrants settled. Following the war, blacks joined in mass organizing efforts to dismantle the discriminatory laws of California that ranged from antimiscegenation statutes and racially restrictive covenants to exclusion of social workers from local professional organizations. In 1945, black coalitions pressured the legislature into enacting a fair employment law.

Black and white women also joined in political coalitions to work for continuation of state child-care services after the war ended. With the support of Governor Earl Warren they got the state to extend child care to May 1948. . . .

Building on the women's mass mobilization, the NAACP formed a statewide coalition in 1953 to lobby for a Fair Employment Practices Act. Although a bill to establish fair employment as a policy had passed in 1945 with the support of Governor Warren, no bill to implement the policy had yet been authorized. . . . In 1959, . . . the legislature [finally] passed a bill creating the first Fair Employment Commission, which put California in the forefront of civil rights issues. The success was due not only to new representatives with different attitudes and to mass mobilization, but also to the volunteer work of women within the [political] parties. . . .

World War II left a mixed domestic legacy for women. It probably affected most directly middle-aged housewives whose husbands were in the military. Regardless of their previous domestic arrangements, these women now assumed greater or total responsibility for family management. During World War II, the government mailed allotment checks directly to wives of men overseas so that many women now had management and control of household budgets for the first time. They disciplined children; arranged for their education; maintained houses, apartments, and yards; and developed their own female and male support networks. . . . Women emerged from the war with increased abilities to handle households.

They also emerged with experience at serial wage labor—that is, combining periods of work at home with periods of work in industry. Because defense industries often ran twenty-four hours a day and because women were permitted to work fifty-four- to sixty-hour weeks, women staggered their work. Day care was unstable, erratic, and often unavailable. . . . In 1943, Los Angeles schools reopened for the summer so that women could continue work while hundreds of private arrangements helped women cope with complex scheduling. Shortages of civilian commodities also made difficult the woman's home-front tasks. A woman working sixty hours a week simply could not afford to wait in long lines for scarce items. Sick children, dirty houses, empty refrigerators, unmended clothes meant that women had to move in and out of the work force to maintain their homes. . . . Young men and women being raised in these female-headed households had the opportunity to grow up with maternal rather than paternal authority. Many of these families settled, sometimes uncomfortably, back into traditional patterns of male familial dominance [after the war]. For others, however, the pattern could never be resumed. Some servicemen returned restless and determined to move elsewhere in the country to better their economic chances. Some returned expecting to continue the multiple sexual relations in which they had engaged overseas. Some returned willing to negotiate greater sexual freedom with their wives. Still others returned physically and mentally ill, totally unable to resume the habits of male dominance around which they had patterned their prewar lives. . . .

Because over 300,000 service personnel elected to take their discharges in California and thousands of the veterans' families soon joined them, many California families reflected these postwar tensions. Families newly arrived in California to work in defense industries also had to adjust to postwar conditions. . . . For housewives with young families . . . acres of new suburbs beckoned. As the [end of the] war released manpower and material for home construction, Californians turned thousands of acres of agricultural land into residential suburbs. Whole communities, such as Burlingame and West Covina, appeared abruptly as agricultural acres were transformed into street after street of small low-cost tract homes. . . .

For women who moved to the suburbs there were few jobs of any significance except unpaid housework and child care. In these economic wastelands, California women created a baby boom that was to stagger state institutions for decades to come as the children moved successively through education and employment and produced their own children in a second baby boom. The new suburbs became isolated islands inhabited by young women and children during most of the week. There were also few social institutions except churches and grocery stores, seldom any public transportation, and only one family car that the husband usually used to drive to work. . . . Married women were soon demanding their own access to the new suburban lifelines. Installment credit and new shopping centers allowed the suburbanites to purchase the results of their combined household and marketplace productivity. While Californians did not differ significantly in their consumer purchases from the rest of the country, they did make more of them. California exceeded the nation in the purchase of all household appliances.

Suburban living was what most of these women wanted—houses where children (but not themselves) could have their own rooms, and where there were green lawns, tidy households, and other women who shared similar lifestyles and problems. . . . *The Ladies' Home Journal* of the 1950s showed ebullient women in their appliance-filled homes busily ironing, washing, baking, and cleaning, while Dr. Benjamin Spock's columns advised them on childbirth, breastfeeding, child rearing, and volunteer work.

Television and radio assured men as well as women that this was indeed what they had been fighting for. . . .

Women of all cultures flooded into both the public and private colleges during the 1950s. As undergraduates, they received the same education as men except that most crowded into schools of education, the arts, and the humanities. . . .

Despite the growing number of female undergraduates, college administrations and faculty remained male dominated. The proportion of women faculty declined as the faculties enlarged. . . . There were few live role models for nontraditional occupations in most colleges . . . since departments hired faculty women primarily in feminized fields such as social welfare, home economics, and education. Colleges also gave women little support for continuing in graduate school or excelling in their fields of expertise. Most male faculty members advised young women that they had to choose either a career or marriage and a family. In the society of the 1950s, choosing a career as a single person was tantamount to becoming a social outcast. The percentage of women who did not marry was the lowest in history and childless marriages were not in fashion. Educated women had few ways to use their training. . . .

Volunteerism became the ideal for women in the 1950s. . . . [But it] did not last long. . . . By 1956, women in a majority of . . . [middle-class] families had to work to provide the education and consumer items they wanted for their families. By 1960, almost one in every three civilian workers in California was a woman, and fifty-seven percent of these were married and living with their husbands.

 F U R T H E R   R E A D I N G

Alison R. Bernstein, *American Indians and World War II: Toward a New Era in Indian Affairs* (1991)

Alfred S. Broussard, "Strange Territory, Familiar Leadership: The Impact of World War II on San Francisco's Black Community," *California History* LXV (March 1986): 18–25, 71–73

Albert S. Broussard, *Black San Francisco: The Struggle for Racial Equality in the West, 1900–1954* (1993)

Commission on Wartime Relocation and Internment of Civilians, *Personal Justice Denied* (1982)

Lawrence P. Crouchett, Lonnie G. Bunch III, and Martha Kendall Winnacker, *Visions toward Tomorrow: The History of the East Bay African American Community, 1852–1977* (1989)

Roger Daniels, *Concentration Camps USA: Japanese Americans and World War II* (1971)

Roger Daniels, *Prisoners Without Trial: Japanese Americans in World War II* (1993)

Roger Daniels, Sandra C. Taylor, and Harry H. L. Kitano, eds., *Japanese Americans: From Relocation to Redress* (1986; rev. paperback ed., 1991)

Ernesto Galarza, *Merchants of Labor: The Mexican Bracero Story* (1964; 1978)

Mario T. Garcia, "Americans All: The Mexican-American Generation and the Politics of Wartime Los Angeles, 1941–1945," *Social Science Quarterly* LXV (June 1984): 278–89

Sherna B. Gluck, "What Did 'Rosie' Really Think? Continuity, Change, and Subjective Experience: Lessons from Oral History," *Southwest Economics & Society* VI (Fall 1983): 56–63

Sherna B. Gluck, *Rosie the Riveter Revisited: Women, the War, and Social Change* (1987)

Kimberley A. Hall, "Women in Wartime: The San Diego Experience, 1941–1945," *Journal of San Diego History* XXXIX (Fall 1993): 261–79

Susan M. Hartmann, *The Home Front and Beyond: American Women in the 1940s* (1982)

Tom Holm, "Fighting a White Man's War: The Extent and Legacy of American Indian Participation in World War II," *Journal of Ethnic Studies* IX (1981): 69–81

Yuji Ichioka, ed., *Views from Within: The Japanese American Evacuation and Resettlement Study* (1989)

Peter Irons, *Justice at War: The Story of the Japanese American Internment Cases* (1983)

Thomas James, *Exile Within: The Schooling of Japanese Americans, 1942–1945* (1987)

Marilynn S. Johnson, *The Second Gold Rush: Oakland and the East Bay in World War II* (1993)

Eugenia Kaledin, *Mothers and More: American Women in the 1950s* (1984)

Christina M. Lim and Sheldon H. Lim, *In the Shadow of the Tiger: The 407th Air Service Squadron, 14th Air Service Group, 14th Air Force, World War II* (1993)

Valerie Matsumoto, *Farming the Home Place: A Japanese American Community in California, 1919–1982* (1993)

Mauricio Mazon, *The Zoot-Suit Riots: The Psychology of Symbolic Annihilation* (1984)

Raul Morin, *Among the Valiant: Mexican Americans in World War II and Korea* (1963; repr., 1966)

Sandra C. Taylor, "Leaving the Concentration Camps: Japanese Americans and Resettlement in the Intermountain West," *Pacific Historical Review* LX (May 1991): 169–94

Sandra C. Taylor, *Jewel of the Desert: Japanese American Internment at Topaz* (1993)

Jacobus tenBroek, Edward N. Barnhart, and Floyd W. Matson, *Prejudice, War and the Constitution: Causes and Consequences of the Evacuation of the Japanese Americans in World War II* (1954)

Dorothy S. Thomas and Richard Nishimoto, *The Spoilage: Japanese-American Evacuation and Resettlement during World War II* (1946; repr., 1969)

Michi Weglyn, *Years of Infamy: The Untold Story of America's Concentration Camps* (1976)

Robert Wenkert, *An Historical Digest of Negro-White Relations in Richmond, California* (1967)

Charles Wollenberg, "James vs. Marinship: Trouble in the New Black Frontier," *California History* LX (Fall 1981): 262–79

CHAPTER

13

Politics and Protest,

1960s–1970s

The decade of the 1960s is now remembered as an era of myriad protest movements. In fact, a lot of other things were going on besides the civil rights movement, the student movement, the counterculture movement, the antiwar movement, the black power, brown power, red power, and yellow power movements, and the feminist movement. California was home to many of these movements, but it was also the place where conservatism was revived and liberalism was transformed.

The roots of these developments lay in the 1950s, a decade symbolized by the organization man in the gray flannel suit. Despite unprecedented prosperity in the postwar years, many people felt bored and harbored a vague sense that something was missing from their lives. This personal anomie developed in the larger context of the cold war, which intensified after U.S. troops fought against Chinese and North Korean Communist forces during the Korean War (1950–1953). Enmity between the United States and the Communist bloc had domestic repercussions: Americans lived through political witch hunts, ever fearful that they or someone they knew might be called a spy or a traitor. While Senator Joseph McCarthy of Wisconsin was busy accusing movie stars, diplomats, and others of being Communists through the hearings of the House Un-American Activities Committee (HUAC), the California legislature in 1947 set up its own version of HUAC: a California Senate Un-American Activities Committee chaired by Senator Jack B. Tenney. The Tenney committee succeeded in ruining the reputations of many individuals before it was abolished in 1949. A second Un-American Activities Committee was soon formed, however, and it functioned until the 1970s.

Despite the prevalent anticommunist hysteria of the late 1940s and early 1950s, California was led, paradoxically, by three liberal governors: Republicans Earl Warren and Goodwin Knight and Democrat Edmund "Pat" Brown. Warren, a leading liberal of the Republican party, left the governorship in 1953 to become chief justice of the U.S. Supreme Court. His successor Goodwin Knight built a closer rapport with organized labor than had any other Republican governor in California history, including Hiram Johnson.

When Brown defeated a conservative publisher in the 1958 governor's race, modern liberalism was consolidated. A large number of Democrats won office the same year, enabling Democrats to control the state legislature for many years thereafter.

The social movements of the 1960s, therefore, were more a protest against the repressive social atmosphere of the 1950s than against the liberal politics that dominated California during the same period. Though each protest movement had its own perspective, they all shared certain features. Young people comprised a large part of the active membership. Many participants believed that the "Establishment" was morally bankrupt, so its authority should be questioned and even defied. International events raised the political consciousness of many participants. Youthful American activists echoed the slogans shouted by China's Red Guards, felt a sense of solidarity with student protesters in France, and supported Vietnamese peasants who were fighting U.S. troops.

Partly in reaction to these leftist protest movements of young Americans, a conservative trend reemerged in mainstream politics. Even though Pat Brown was again elected governor in 1962, a conservative won the post of state superintendent of education. Two years later, the actor George Murphy, a conservative, was elected to one of California's U.S. Senate seats. In 1966 another Hollywood conservative, Ronald Reagan, trounced incumbent governor Pat Brown with a margin of almost one million votes. Reagan had stressed three issues during his campaign: morality, spending and taxes, and the negative impact of "professional" politicians. He denounced administrators at the University of California, Berkeley, for their inability to quell student protests.

In response to the rising tide of conservatism led by Reagan, some younger politicians, primarily Democrats, began espousing a "new liberalism." Jerry Brown, son of Pat Brown, articulated this philosophy better than anyone else. Like conservatives, he questioned the ability of government to solve all social problems. Without abandoning long-standing liberal support of such programs as Social Security and Medicare, he called for reduced public spending and asked people to lower their expectations in what he called an "era of limits." He won the governorship in 1974 and served two four-year terms. Sometimes derided as "Governor Moonbeams," he supported environmental concerns and lived simply in a modest apartment instead of in the governor's mansion in Sacramento.

Throughout these turbulent years, the tides of leftist protest and political response swirled through the daily headlines. In reading the selections, try to assess how the protesters and the guardians of traditional government interacted with each other. To what extent did the protest movements build on each other, each group encouraging new groups to articulate their grievances? To what extent did the conflicting sides carry the seeds of their own demise?

DOCUMENTS

The first document is by Mario Savio, a philosophy major who emerged as a leader in the Free Speech Movement at the University of California, Berkeley, in 1964. Savio points out that the civil rights movement had greatly influenced the student activists at Berkeley and articulated his dissatisfaction with the kind of education that he thought the university's president, Clark Kerr, was promoting. The second document is a speech given by Ronald Reagan at the Cow Palace in San Francisco in 1966, during which he assailed the "morality gap" at Berkeley.

The remaining five documents offer glimpses of how various protest groups viewed the world in the late 1960s. In the third document, Bobby Seale, cofounder of the Black Panther party, emphasizes that the party was waging a class, and not a race, struggle. According to historian Gerald Horne in *Fire This Time: The Watts Uprising and the 1960s* (1995), the black nationalism that emerged after the dissolution of the integrated civil rights movement split into two camps: cultural nationalism and "revolutionary" political nationalism. The latter was exemplified by the Black Panther party.

The fourth document is part of a long manifesto that Chicano students proclaimed during a conference at the University of California, Santa Barbara, in 1969. The authors explain why they have decided to call themselves *Chicanos;* they reject the goal of assimilation and affirm their roots in the Chicano community.

The fifth document voices Asian American students' quest for identity and political power. Like the black and Chicano authors of the two preceding documents, members of the Asian American Political Alliance (who participated in the Third World Strike at Berkeley in 1969) place their desire for social change within a larger global context. In addition to fighting racism, the AAPA also opposes capitalism and imperialism.

The sixth statement is a proclamation by Native Americans from various tribes who occupied Alcatraz Island in the middle of San Francisco Bay in November 1969. They sarcastically remind white Americans how European immigrants took Manhattan Island from the Indians three centuries ago and then list ten ways in which Alcatraz Island resembles an Indian reservation.

The final document reveals how a feminist consciousness was forged out of the anger that many women felt toward their radical but sexist "brothers" in the male-dominated protest movements of the 1960s. The two authors, who were working as secretaries at the University of California, Berkeley, graphically describe the humiliation they daily experienced.

Mario Savio Defends the Free Speech Movement at Berkeley, 1965

[T]he order banning student politics on campus was an ideal locus of fierce protest. It combined an act of bureaucratic violence against the students themselves with open attack on student participation in the Bay Area civil rights movement. The seemingly inexhaustible energy which the Berkeley students had so long devoted to the struggle for Negro rights was now turned squarely on the vast, faceless University administration. This is what gave the Free Speech Movement its initial impetus.

But the new restrictions were not aimed so much at curtailing activity which would result in civil rights work in the South as at halting the very active participation of students in the civil rights movement in the Bay Area. The University was apparently under considerable pressure to "crackdown" on the student activists from the right-wing in California business and politics. . . .

The liberal University of California administration would have relished the opportunity to show off in the national academic community a public university enjoying complete political and academic freedom **and** academic excellence. And if student politics had been restricted either to precinct work for the Democrats and Republicans, or to advocacy (by public meetings and distribution of literature) of various forms of wholesale societal change, then I don't believe there would have been the crisis there was. . . . [S]ectarian "revolutionary" **talk** can be tolerated because it is harmless. The radical student activists, however, are a mean threat to privilege. Because the students were advocating consequential actions[,] because . . . these [were] radical **acts,** the administration's restrictive ruling was necessary. . . .

The Free Speech Movement demanded no more—nor less—than full First Amendment rights of advocacy on campus as well as off: that, therefore, only the courts have power to determine and punish abuses of freedom of speech. The Berkeley Division of the Academic Senate endorsed this position on December 8, 1964 by declaring against **all** University regulation of the content of speech or advocacy—by a vote of 824 to 115.

Probably the most meaningful opportunity for political involvement for students with any political awareness is in the civil rights movement. Indeed, there appears to be little else in American life today which can claim the allegiance of men. Therefore, the action of the administration, which seemed to the students to be directed at the civil rights movement, was felt as a form of emasculation, or attempted emasculation. . . . The student response to this "routine directive" was outraged protest. . . .

We found we were being denied the very possibility of "being a student"—unquestionably a **right.** We found we were severed from our proper roles: students denied the meaningful work one must do in order to be a student. Instead we were faced with a situation in which the pseudo-student role we were playing was tailor-made to further the interests of those who own the University, those vast corporations in whose interest the University is managed. . . .

[T]he schools have become training camps—and proving grounds—rather than places where people acquire education. They become factories to produce technicians rather than places to live student lives. And this perversion develops great resentment on the part of the students. Resentment against being subjected to standard production techniques of speedup and regimentation; against a tendency to quantify education—virtually a contradiction in terms. Education is measured in units, in numbers of lectures attended, in numbers of pages devoted to papers, number of pages read. This mirrors the gross and vulgar quantification in the society at large—the

real world—where everything must be reduced to a lowest common denominator, the dollar bill. In our campus play-world we use play money, course units. . . .

It is significant that the President of the University of California should be the foremost ideologist of this "Brave New World" conception of education. President Clark Kerr dreamed up the frightening metaphors: "the knowledge industry," "the multiversity," which has as many faces as it has publics, be they industries of various kinds, or the Federal Government, especially the Pentagon and the AEC [Atomic Energy Commission]. He also invented the title "the captain of bureaucracy," which he is, by analogy with earlier captains of industry. He is the person directly charged with steering the mighty ship along the often perilous course of service to its many publics in government and industry. Not to **the** public, but to its many publics, the Kerrian whore is unlawfully joined.

Those disciplines with a ready market in industry and government are favored and fostered: the natural sciences, engineering, mathematics, and the social sciences when these serve the braintrusting propaganda purposes of "liberal" government. The humanities naturally suffer, so that what should be the substance of undergraduate education suffers. The emphasis is given to research instead of to teaching undergraduates. Teaching graduate students is less effected [*sic*] by this prostitution since such teaching is intimately bound to research. But the undergraduate has become the new dispossessed; the heart has been taken from his education—no less so for science students—for the humanities are no longer accorded the central role they deserve in the university.

And of course there are whole areas which never see the light in undergraduate instruction. Who takes undergraduate courses in the history of the labor movement, for example? Certainly no one at the University of California. Likewise, American Negro history is a rarity and is still more rarely taken seriously. To be taken at all seriously it would have to be seen as central to all American history.

In a healthy university an undergraduate would have time to do 'nothing.' To read what he wants to read, maybe to sit on a hill behind the campus all alone or with a friend, to 'waste time' alone, dreaming in the Eucalyptus Grove. But the university, after the manner of a pesky social director, sees to it the student's time is kept filled with anti-intellectual harassment: those three crdits [*sic*] in each three unit course, those meaningless units themselves. The notion that one can somehow reduce Introductory Quantum Mechanics and Philosophy of Kant to some kind of lowest common denominator (three units a piece) is totally irrational, and reflects the irrationality of a society which tries to girdle the natural rhythms of growth and learning by reduction to quantitative terms, much as it attempts to market the natural impulses of sex.

From my experience, I should say the result is at best a kind of intellectual cacaphony [*sic*]. There are little attractions in various places, philosophy in one corner, physics in another, maybe a bit of mathematics every now and again, some political science—nothing bearing any relationship to anything else. . . . It is easy to see that there should be real resentment on the part of the students. But it is resentment whose causes are, as we have seen, very difficult for the student to perceive readily. That is why what occurred last semester gained its initial impetus from the very different involvements of what are mostly middle-class students in the struggles of the Negro people. Thus, it was both the irrationality of society, that denies to Negroes the life of men, and the irrationality of the University, that denies to youth the life of students, which caused last semester's rebellion.

Ronald Reagan Denounces the Morality Gap at Berkeley, 1966

There has been a leadership gap and a morality and decency gap at the University of California at Berkeley where a small minority of beatniks, radicals and filthy speech advocates have brought such shame to and such a loss of confidence in a great University that applications for enrollment were down 21% in 1967 and are expected to decline even further.

You have read about the report of the Senate Subcommittee on Un-American Activities—its charges that the campus has become a rallying point for Communists and a center of sexual misconduct. Some incidents in this report are so bad, so contrary to our standards of decent human behavior that I cannot recite them to you in detail.

But there is clear evidence of the sort of things that should not be permitted on a university campus.

The report tells us that many of those attending were clearly of high-school age. The hall was entirely dark except for the light from two movie screens. On these screens the nude torsos of men and women were portrayed from time to time in suggestive positions and movements.

Three rock and roll bands played simultaneously. The smell of marijuana was thick throughout the hall. There were signs that some of those present had taken dope. There were indications of other happenings that cannot be mentioned here.

How could this happen on the campus of a great University? It happened because those responsible abdicated their responsibilities.

The dance was only called to a halt when janitors finally cut off the power in the gymnasium forcing those attending to leave.

And this certainly is not the only sign of a leadership gap on the campus.

It began when so-called "free-speech advocates," who in truth have no appreciation of freedom, were allowed to assault and humiliate an officer of the law. This was the moment when the ringleaders should have been taken by the scruff of the neck and thrown off of the campus—permanently.

It continued through the filthy speech movement, through activities of the Vietnam Day Committee and all this has been allowed to go on in the name of academic freedom.

What in Heaven's name does academic freedom have to do with rioting, with anarchy, with attempts to destroy the primary purpose of the University which is to educate our young people?

These charges must neither be swept away under the rug by a timid administration or by public apologists for the University. The public has a right to know from open hearings whether the situation at Berkeley is as the report says.

The citizens who pay the taxes that support the University also have a right to know that, if the situation is as the report says, that those responsible will be fired, that the University will be cleaned up and restored to its position as a major institution of learning and research.

For this reason I today have called on the State Legislature to hold public hearings into the charges of Communism and blatant sexual misbehavior on the campus. I have sent personal wires to Senator Hugh Burns, the President Pro Tem of the Senate and to Assembly Speaker Jesse Unruh urging that they hold joint public hearings.

Only in this way can we get at the facts. Only this way can we find who is responsible for the degradation of a great University.

Only this way can we determine what steps must be taken to restore the University to its position, steps that might go even beyond what I have already suggested.

Yes, there are things that can be done at the University even if a hearing is never held. This administration could make changes. It could demand that the faculty jurisdictions be limited to academic matters.

It could demand that the administrators be told that it is their job to administer the University properly and if they don't we will find someone who will.

The faculty could also be given a code of conduct that would force them to serve as examples of good behavior and decency for the young people in their charge.

When those who advocate an open mind keep it open at both ends with no thought process in the middle, the open mind becomes a hose for any idea that comes along. If scholars are to be recognized as having a right to press their particular value judgments, perhaps the time has come also for institutions of higher learning to assert themselves as positive forces in the battles for men's minds.

This could mean they would insist upon mature, responsible conduct and respect for the individual from their faculty members and might even call on them to be proponents of those ethical and moral standards demanded by the great majority of our society.

These things could be done and should be done. The people not only have a right to know what is going on at their universities, they have a right to expect the best from those responsible for it.

Bobby Seale Explains What the Black
Panther Party Stands For, 1968

We, the Black Panther Party, see ourselves as a nation within a nation, but not for any racist reasons. We see it as a necessity for us to progress as human beings and live on the face of this earth along with other people. We do not fight racism with racism. We fight racism with solidarity. We do not fight exploitative capitalism with black capitalism. We fight capitalism with basic socialism. And we do not fight imperialism with more imperialism. We fight imperialism with proletarian internationalism. These principles are very functional for the Party. They're very practical, humanistic, and necessary. They should be understood by the masses of the people.

We don't use our guns, we have never used our guns to go into the white community to shoot up white people. We only defend ourselves against anybody, be they black, blue, green, or red, who attacks us unjustly and tries to murder us and kill us for implementing our programs. All in all, I think people can see from our past practice, that ours is not a racist organization but a very progressive revolutionary party.

Those who want to obscure the struggle with ethnic differences are the ones who are aiding and maintaining the exploitation of the masses of the people: poor whites, poor blacks, browns, red Indians, poor Chinese and Japanese, and the workers at large.

Racism and ethnic differences allow the power structure to exploit the masses of workers in this country, because that's the key by which they maintain their control. To divide the people and conquer them is the objective of the power structure. It's the ruling class, the very small minority, the few avaricious, demagogic hogs and rats who control and infest the government. The ruling class and their running dogs, their lackeys, their bootlickers, their Toms and their black racists, their cultural nationalists— they're all the running dogs of the ruling class. These are the ones who help to maintain and aid the power structure by perpetuating their racist attitudes and using racism as a means to divide the people. But it's really the small, minority ruling class that is dominating, exploiting, and oppressing the working and laboring people.

All of us are laboring-class people, employed or unemployed, and our unity has got to be based on the practical necessities of life, liberty, and the pursuit of happiness, if that means anything to anybody. It's got to be based on the practical things like the survival of people and people's right to self-determination, to iron out the problems that exist. So in essence it is not at all a race struggle. We're rapidly educating people to this. In our view it is a class struggle between the massive proletarian working class and the small, minority ruling class. Working-class people of all colors must unite against the exploitative, oppressive ruling class. So let me emphasize again—we believe our fight is a class struggle and not a race struggle.

Manifesto of the Chicano Student Conference, 1969

For all peoples, as with individuals, the time comes when they must reckon with their history. For the Chicano the present is a time of renaissance, of *renacimiento.* Our people and our community, *el barrio* and *la colonia,* are expressing a new consciousness and a new resolve. Recognizing the historical tasks confronting our people and fully aware of the cost of human progress, we pledge our will to move. We will move forward toward our destiny as a people. We will move against those forces which have denied us freedom of expression and human dignity. Throughout history the quest for cultural expression and freedom has taken the form of a struggle. Our struggle, tempered by the lessons of the American past, is an historical reality.

For decades Mexican people in the United States struggled to realize the 'American Dream'. And some—a few—have. But the cost, the ultimate cost of assimilation, required turning away from *el barrio* and *la colonia.* In the meantime, due to the racist structure of this society, to our essentially different life style, and to the socio-economic functions assigned to our community by Anglo-American society—as suppliers of cheap labor and a dumping ground for the small-time capitalist entrepreneur—the *barrio* and *colonia* remained exploited, impoverished, and marginal.

As a result, the self-determination of our community is now the only acceptable mandate for social and political action; it is the essence of Chicano commitment. Culturally, the word *Chicano,* in the past a pejorative and class-bound adjective, has now become the root idea of a new cultural identity for our people. It also reveals a growing solidarity and the development of a common social praxis. The widespread use of the term *Chicano* today signals a rebirth of pride and confidence. *Chicanismo* simply embodies an ancient truth: that man is never closer to his true self as when he is close to his community.

Chicanismo draws its faith and strength from two main sources: from the just struggle of our people and from an objective analysis of our community's strategic needs. We recognize that without a strategic use of education, an education that places value on what we value, we will not realize our destiny. Chicanos recognize the central importance of institutions of higher learning to modern progress, in this case, to the development of our community. But we go further: we believe that higher education must contribute to the information of a complete man who truly values life and freedom.

The destiny of our people will be fulfilled. To that end, we pledge our efforts and take as our credo what José Vasconcelos once said at a time of crisis and hope: 'At this moment we do not come to work for the university, but to demand that the university work for our people.'

Declaration of the Asian American
Political Alliance, 1969

The Asian American Political Alliance is people. It is a people's alliance to effect social and political changes. We believe that the American society is historically racist and one which has systematically employed social discrimination and economic imperialism, both domestically and internationally, exploiting all non-white people in the process of building up their affluent society.

They did so at the expense of all of us. Uncontrolled capitalism has pushed all of the non-white people into a social position so that only manual jobs with subhuman pay are open to them. Consequently, we have been psychologically so conditioned by the blue-eye-blond-hair standard that many of us have lost our perspective. We can only survive if "we know our place"—shut up and accept what we are given. We resent this kind of domination and we are determined to change it.

The goal of AAPA is political education and advancement of the movement among Asian people, so that they may make all decisions that affect their own lives, in a society that never asks people to do so. AAPA is not an isolated group, and should never profess to be such. Its only legitimacy and value is in the effects it has on many people, not just a small group of people. In the same vein, AAPA is not meant to isolate Asians from other people; it is unhealthy as well as unwise to do such a thing. AAPA must constantly expand and grow, and reach out to other people and groups. At the same time, AAPA must meet the needs of its own members and deal with its own problems.

In the past political organizations have tended to subject themselves to rigid, traditional levels of structure in which a few make the decisions, present them to the body, and the body can vote either "yes" or "no." This hierarchistic organization, however, is only a manifestation of the elite control, primidal [*sic* (pyramidal)] structure mentality in which you are not capable of making your own decisions, an idea drilled into you from the foundations of this society.

AAPA is only what the people make it. We have adopted a structure which better fits the needs and goals of our alliance, not a structure to which we have to adjust ourselves. Furthermore, there is no membership in AAPA in the strict sense of the word. There are workers who for common interests join together with one or more people to intensify the effectiveness of an action.

Indians of All Tribes Occupy Alcatraz Island, 1969

Proclamation
To the Great White Father and All His People

We, the native Americans, re-claim the land known as Alcatraz Island in the name of all American Indians by right of discovery. We wish to be fair and honorable in our dealings with the Caucasian inhabitants of this land, and hereby offer the following treaty:

We will purchase said Alcatraz Island for twenty-four dollars (24) in glass beads and red cloth, a precedent set by the white man's purchase of a similar island about 300 years ago. We know that $24 in trade goods for these 16 acres is more than was paid when Manhattan Island was sold, but we know that land values have risen over the years. Our offer of $1.24 per acre is greater than the 47 cents per acre the white men are now paying the California Indians for their land.

We will give to the inhabitants of this island a portion of the land for their own to be held in trust by the American Indian Affairs and by the bureau of Caucasian Affairs to hold in perpetuity—for as long as the sun shall rise and the rivers go down to the sea. We will further guide the inhabitants in the proper way of living. We will offer them our religion, our education, our life-ways, in order to help them achieve our level of civilization and thus raise them and all their white brothers up from their savage and unhappy state. We offer this treaty in good faith and wish to be fair and honorable in our dealings with all white men.

We feel that this so-called Alcatraz is more th[a]n suitable for an Indian reservation, as determined by the white man's own standards. By this we mean that this place resembles most Indian reservations in that:

1. It is isolated from modern facilities, and without adequate means of transportation.
2. It has no fresh running water.
3. It has inadequate sanitation facilities.
4. There are no oil or mineral rights.
5. There is no industry and so unemployment is very great.
6. There are no health care facilities.
7. The soil is rocky and non-productive; and the land does not support game.
8. There are no educational facilities.
9. The population has always exceeded the land base.
10. The population has always been held as prisoners and kept dependent upon others.

Further, it would be fitting and symbolic that ships from all over the world, entering the Golden Gate, would first see Indian land, and thus be reminded of the true history of this nation. This tiny island would be a symbol of the great lands once ruled by free and noble Indians.

What use will we make of this land?

Since the San Francisco Indian Center burned down, there is no place for Indians to assemble and carry on tribal life here in the white man's city. Therefore, we plan to develop on this island several Indian institutions:

1. A CENTER FOR NATIVE AMERICAN STUDIES will be developed which will educate them to the skills and knowledge relevant to improve the lives and spirits of all Indian peoples. Attached to this center will be traveling universities, managed by Indians, which will go to

the Indian Reservations, learning those necessary and relevant materials now about [*sic*].

2. AN AMERICAN INDIAN SPIRITUAL CENTER which will practice our ancient tribal religious and sacred healing ceremonies. Our cultural arts will be featured and our young people trained in music, dance, and healing rituals.

3. AN INDIAN CENTER OF ECOLOGY which will train and support our young people in scientific research and practice to restore our lands and waters to their pure and natural state. We will work to de-pollute the air and waters of the Bay Area. We will seek to restore fish and animal life to the area and to revitalize sea life which has been threatened by the white man's way. We will set up facilities to desalt sea water for human benefit.

4. A GREAT INDIAN TRAINING SCHOOL will be developed to teach our people how to make a living in the world, improve our standard of living, and to end hunger and unemployment among all our people. This training school will include a center for Indian arts and crafts, and an Indian restaurant serving native foods, which will restore Indian culinary arts. This center will display Indian arts and offer Indian foods to the public, so that all may know of the beauty and spirit of the traditional INDIAN ways.

Some of the present buildings will be taken over to develop an AMERICAN INDIAN MUSEUM, which will depict our native food & other cultural contributions we have given to the world. Another part of the museum will present some of the things the white man has given to the Indians in return for the land and life he took: disease, alcohol, poverty and cultural decimation (As symbolized by old tin cans, barbed wire, rubber tires, plastic containers, etc). Part of the museum will remain a dungeon to symbolize both those Indian captives who were incarcerated for challenging white authority, and those who were imprisoned on reservations. The museum will show the noble and the tragic events of Indian history, including the broken treaties, the documentary of the Trail of Tears, the Massacre of Wounded Knee, as well as the victory over Yellow Hair Custer and his army.

In the name of all Indians, therefore, we re-claim this island for our Indian nations, for all these reasons. We feel this claim is just and proper, and that this land should rightfully be granted to us for as long as the rivers shall run and the sun shall shine.

Signed,

Indians Of All Tribes
November 1969
San Francisco, California

Why Secretaries in Academia Are Fed Up, 1971

We [Carol Hatch and Margaret Henderson] are secretaries in one of the hippest departments of that radical and hip school, the University of California at Berkeley. To many students and some other secretaries our office looks like a "liberated area." There is no front counter barricading off the work area. Students, dogs, and faculty wander in and out. The secretaries seem to control what is going on and do not seem easily intimidated. They wear pants and have posters above their desks. A conservative faculty member once complained that the office looked more like the office of an underground newspaper than a University office. But the liberated image does not change the nature of our work: boring, painful, degrading.

The women in our office have consciously tried to achieve workers' control, and we've tried to wage that struggle collectively. After each small gain from collective action or resistance, the basic structure of the situation always closed suffocatingly around us. We found out that behind the easy friendliness between faculty and secretaries existed a master-servant relationship, we found out there was no way to institutionalize change within a structure where we had no decision-making power, we found within ourselves an anger that we'd anesthetized ourselves to in other "more oppressive" offices. . . .

As in most jobs available to women in this society, the role of a secretary is the role of a servant. When she works in the University, she is provided as a service to the faculty or administration. Along with square feet of office space and number of bookcases, amount of secretarial servant-time is a status symbol for the professor or administrator.

Secretarial work can be divided roughly into two categories: tasks that save time for the master and tasks that bolster the prestige of the master and maintain status boundaries between master and servant. Being paid very little to perform alienating tasks that save someone else's very well paid (and more enjoyably spent) time is bad enough. Worse yet, much of our work falls into the second category: boundary maintenance rituals. A few examples: pushing the buttons on a self-service Xerox machine while the faculty member stands by waiting for his copy to be handed to him; having a faculty member return a letter which you have typed and he has signed so that you can fold it and put in [*sic*] into its envelope for him while he stands in front of your desk; being bugged on the intercom by an administrator who gives you a phone number which you are to dial as he waits at his desk. You dial the number, state the formula: "One moment, Mr. Administrator would like to speak to you," place the call on hold, buzz the administrator on the inter-com and tell him that his call is ready. (Some administrators are not even able to pick up the receiver by themselves and the compleat secretary is expected to hand him the receiver after dialing the number.)

Secretaries have often been particularly conned as workers, by the pretense that they are not servants, by being called white collar workers, by being forced to dress as if they spent their day in leisure and by having been socialized to identify themselves primarily by some other role (e.g., wife, pre-wife, student, or student-wife). Secretaries, socialized as women to please men and to internalize the goals and desires of men, are particularly vulnerable to identifying with the policies and aims of the men they work for more than with their own interests and needs. This absence of class consciousness, absence of women's consciousness and the illusory sense of privilege vis-a-vis other workers has contributed in the past to the lack of unionization and struggle on the part of secretaries. When rising women's consciousness and rising workers' consciousness cause this line of internalized control to break down, when the masters' orders are no longer automatically accepted as rational and reasonable requests and when the masters perceive that they are not admired and loved as they previously believed, all hell breaks loose. . . .

A secretary . . . must risk the sudden termination of her means of livelihood each time she decides to resist or refuse any one of the numerous humiliations which occur each day. Not only is there risk involved, but if a secretary allows herself to notice even half the insults she endures, she will be suffering from extreme adrenal exhaustion by noon. Raised consciousness brings raw nerve endings and as we have allowed ourselves to notice and react to more and more incidents, we find ourselves almost continually in an exhausting state of rage. And that rage is often impossible to act out. . . .

What makes it particularly difficult to handle all this anger is that we are always in public. Ironically, the very conditions that make our work situation more human—a loose, casual, open office—means that we work with complete lack of privacy. The only time we can meet together with any semblance of privacy is at noon when we can use the meeting room. And even then, as often as not, we are interrupted by a faculty member strolling casually through our meeting. He would never walk through a meeting of faculty, a seminar, or a meeting of students, but he considers our meeting unworthy of the same courtesy or he simply fails to perceive us as a meeting (just a group of "the girls" eating lunch together). And if we can't meet in private, we can hardly work out a common strategy.

Another problem that our constant public exposure poses is that we are very noticeable when we aren't at our desks, and the faculty want their servants visible at all times. If our work should take us anywhere out of the main office (to the mimeo machine, for example), we are assumed to be on some endless break. . . .

At this point, our mood is schizophrenic. We feel both strong and powerless. Individually and as a group we have grown surly, mean, raucous, and uppity. We also feel hopelessly crazy most of the time. Realization that the craziness is socially induced does not make us feel any more sane. Realization that we can change only bits and pieces of the insane conditions in which we are forced to earn our living makes us more surly, mean, raucous, and uppity. If we sometimes feel that the difficulties of working collectively are not worth the gains we make, we also sometimes feel that the process of organizing ourselves, of dealing with the problems of collective action, is the only non-alienating work we can do.

E S S A Y S

The two essays in this chapter contrast the two kinds of politics that enlivened California in the 1960s: the tumultuous protest movements that caught a great deal of media attention and the conservative trend spearheaded by Ronald Reagan after he was elected governor.

W. J. Rorabaugh, professor of history at the University of Washington, is author of *Berkeley at War: The 1960s* (1989), from which the first essay is drawn. In addition to the student movement at Berkeley, the book also analyzes the black power movement, the antiwar movement, and the counterculture movement in the San Francisco Bay Area.

The second essay comes from journalist Lou Cannon's biography of Ronald Reagan. In the segments excerpted here, Cannon examines Reagan's running battle against the institutions of higher learning in California, his dismissal of University of California president Clark Kerr, and the governor's effort to reform the tax system and the welfare system. It was Reagan who first drew a distinction between "tax payers" and "tax takers"—a distinction that Governor Pete Wilson has echoed in more recent years in attempting to trim various social programs.

Berkeley in the 1960s

W. J. RORABAUGH

In the sixties Berkeley was a city at war. Students revolted against the University of California, blacks demanded their rights, radicals surged into prominence, and a counterculture of major proportions blossomed. White, black, red, and green—these movements coincided, fed into one another, and reacted against each other in myriad and sometimes surprising ways. The decade began with President John Fitzgerald Kennedy's Camelot; it ended amid chaos. Berkeley, no less than the country, went through a crisis. On the surface this crisis revolved around turmoil generated by quite specific social issues; it was, at that level, a social crisis.

The underlying issue, however, was one of power. During the sixties, *conservatives* hated communism, both abroad and at home, rejected socialism, distrusted all government, disliked labor unions, and abhorred the high level of domestic government spending that was called the welfare state; they admired Barry Goldwater and, later, Ronald Reagan. Berkeley's conservatives, who had long held power in the city, refused to compromise and became paranoid reactionaries. *Liberals* also hated communism and rejected socialism, but they trusted the government, liked labor unions, and favored the welfare state; they admired Franklin Roosevelt, Adlai Stevenson, and, to a lesser extent, John Kennedy. The city's liberals built an unstable, biracial political coalition, used government programs to maintain their power, and ultimately lacked principle. *Radicals* hated anticommunism more than communism, usually accepted some elements of socialism, were ambivalent about government, liked labor unions, and favored either an expanded welfare state or a drastic reconstruction of society; they admired (in varying degrees) Martin Luther King, Jr., Malcolm X, Fidel Castro, Che Guevara, Mao Tse-tung, or themselves. In Berkeley white radicals and black militants angrily tried to seize control and, failing that, were determined to make it impossible for anyone else to hold power. . . .

College students, young blacks, members of the New Left, and hippies believed that power should flow from the bottom up rather than from the top down. This is an important point, and it suggests that the history of the decade needs to focus on those at the bottom. Historians, however, have written few local studies, and those who have concentrated on the national picture, overly influenced by events at 1600 Pennsylvania Avenue, on CBS News, or in the *New York Times,* have found society to be unraveling. In reality, it was only centralized authority that was in decline. At the local level, those on the bottom saw less a disintegration of society than a rebirth of community spirit and individual liberty in opposition to a corrupt, bureaucratic social order. It is the emergence of this latter vision and its implications for the exercise of power in American society that is the most profound legacy of the sixties. . . .

By 1964 the world's premier example of a multiversity was the University of California, and the University's crown jewel was its campus at Berkeley. No other campus had such close ties to the government, such a heavy emphasis upon government-sponsored research, or such a neglect of undergraduates. Students were alienated and ripe for revolt. The revolt began in September 1964, when the administration suddenly banned political activists from passing out literature, soliciting funds, or organizing support from card tables set up at the edge of campus. This ban led the activists, largely civil rights workers, to attack the new rules and, following the administration's reprisals, to demand that all sorts of political activity be permitted throughout the campus. The activist students called themselves the Free Speech Movement (FSM). They rallied wide support from alienated students and, after the largest sit-in and mass arrest in California history, gathered overwhelming faculty support. In December 1964 the FSM triumphed. It was to be the greatest success of the student movement during the 1960s. . . .

When the University opened . . . [in] September [1964], activists looked forward to recruitment and fund-raising. Over the summer thirty to sixty students had worked for civil rights in Mississippi, and they returned to campus with renewed dedication and determination. These activists, including Mario Savio and Art Goldberg, were dumbfounded in mid-September when the University suddenly issued new rules that banned tables from the edge of Bancroft and Telegraph, where they had been placed in growing numbers for two or three years. When the activists sought an explanation for the change, they could get no answers. The dean of students, Katherine A. Towle, talked with the activists but declared her own lack of power, while those who held the power refused to talk. . . .

The activists . . . knew what they wanted. Although their specific demands changed over time, they demanded an end to the regulation of political activity on campus. This was called free speech. . . . [They] identified the issue as a traditional American right in order to appeal to large numbers of students, . . . some of the activist leaders were battle-tested veterans of the civil rights movement. "A student who has been chased by the KKK in Mississippi," observed one student, "is not easily scared by academic bureaucrats. . . ." They knew when to advance, when to retreat, how to use crowds, how to use the media, how to intimidate, and how to negotiate. The activists understood their ultimate weapon, the sit-in, and were prepared to use it. Although the leaders were not close to one another, they spoke a common language gained through a common experience. . . . Finally, activist leaders knew how to maintain discipline over their troops. Mass psychology, song, theater, and other techniques long favored among revivalists and street politicians accompanied innovative mass meetings at which people freely spoke and at which collective decisions were made by a kind of consensus that came to be called participatory democracy. Through these techniques and by focusing on the simplicity of the demand for free speech, activists created an environment within which followers were disciplined. They created an army. In contrast, [University of California President Clark] Kerr badgered his beleaguered bureaucracy until it could barely function.

Throughout September 1964 skirmishes continued as defiant activists set up tables and were cited by irritated deans. The angry students escalated the conflict by moving their tables to Sproul Plaza. This protest led to a mill-in inside Sproul Hall and the summary "indefinite suspension" of eight students—Mario Savio, Art Goldberg, Mark Bravo, Sandor Fuchs, David Goines, Donald Hatch, Brian Turner, and Elizabeth Gardner (Mrs. Sydney Stapleton). Finally, on October 1, University police went to the plaza to arrest a former student, Jack Weinberg, who was manning a CORE table. The police drove a car onto the plaza to take Weinberg to be booked, and as Weinberg got into the car, someone shouted, "Sit down." Suddenly, several hundred students surrounded the car. The police did not know what to do, because they had never encountered such massive defiance. Kerr's bureaucracy became paralyzed. This event launched the Free Speech Movement. Participants later recalled the spontaneity of the sit-down, the thrill of power over the police, and the feeling that something important was happening. For thirty-two hours Weinberg sat in the back of the police car. Although students came and went, there were always at least several hundred surrounding the car. . . . During the night students who disapproved of the sit-down—many from nearby fraternities—molested the protesters by tossing lighted cigarettes and garbage into the crowd. The activists responded by singing civil rights songs.

During the sit-down the demonstrators used the roof of the police car (with police permission) as a podium to speak to the crowd. People aired all sorts of views, and the discussion moved from the rules banning political activity to analyses of the University's governance. Students expressed their powerlessness, which contrasted with the power that they held over the immobilized police car. So many people stood on the car's roof that it sagged; the FSM later took up a collection and paid the $455.01 damage. Several times a twenty-one year old junior, Mario Savio, removed his shoes to climb atop the car, and when he spoke, his words seemed especially to energize the crowd. He became a celebrity and was identified by the crowd as the leader of the activists. From then on Savio battled Kerr. . . .

[Savio's] power came from his ability to articulate a tone that expressed the frustrations and anxieties of his generation. While others were as angry as Savio, they found it impossible to articulate their anger. Savio had the gift, perhaps the result of his Catholic education, to discourse rationally. Even as he did so, there was an undertone of anger. This powerful projection of personality contrasted with his private conversation, which was often marred by stuttering, hesitancy, and coldness. Self-doubts and inhibitions dissolved when Savio spoke to a crowd. . . .

Much of Savio's appeal came from his ability to blend alienation, sexuality, and politics. . . . Students, said Savio, were oppressed by "the organized sadism of the power structure." The University forced students to suppress their "creative impulses." What was the result? He declared, "The University is well structured, well tooled, to turn out people with all the sharp edges worn off. . . ." In other words, the University emasculated students. Indeed, taking away the right to place tables at the edge of campus had been an act of "emasculation, or attempted emasculation." By talking about politics in this fashion, Savio guaranteed an audience. Few students cared about political rights, but many felt alienated, and no males wanted to be emasculated. . . . [N]o student could accept the administration's position without risking a perceived loss of his own sexual potency. After the Free Speech Movement was over, Savio was asked what had been most important in leading him to oppose the administration. Without hesitation he answered, "Balls."

While the police car was trapped, Kerr's bureaucrats dithered, and the activists came to realize that they could extract concessions from Kerr in exchange for quietly ending the sit-down. Both sides picked negotiators. . . . For the first time, some faculty members became involved, and they encouraged both the administration and the activists to accept a compromise. Kerr's terms appeared to be generous. Jack Weinberg, still in the police car, was to be booked and then released with the University not pressing charges. The eight students suspended summarily by the administration for activities prior to the sit-down were to face discipline before a faculty committee. Another committee, to be composed of administrators, faculty members, and students appointed by the administration, was to negotiate permanent rules for political activity on campus. . . . After much internal debate . . . the student leaders accepted Kerr's offer. Savio then returned to the police car to announce the settlement. He invited everyone to rise up and go home quietly. To many, the crisis appeared to be over. . . .

[But d]uring October and November the pact of October 2 unraveled. One irritant involved a final resolution of the discipline for the eight students suspended prior to the capture of the police car. The activists, who distrusted the administration, had rejected the normal disciplinary process because it forced them to submit their cases either to the very deans who had cited them or to a faculty committee controlled by the administration. The activists believed that the pact of October 2 required Kerr to send the disciplinary cases to an *independent* faculty committee appointed by the faculty senate. . . . Kerr insisted on sending the cases to a faculty committee that he controlled, . . . [but] Kerr finally yielded and let the faculty senate name an ad hoc committee to consider these cases. . . .

Meanwhile, the second committee formed as a result of the October 2 pact also bogged down. . . . The activist students on the committee rejected an administration proposal for limited political rights on campus, while an activist counterproposal that rights be based on the first amendment to the U.S. Constitution got no support from faculty members or administrators. The activists, in the end, rejected a faculty compromise. . . .

[N]either side was prepared to settle because each believed that it could get more later. Kerr, convinced that in time support for the activists would decline, calculated that in the end the administration could grant limited political rights that would satisfy the administration, the faculty, and a majority of students. Kerr did not understand the FSM strategy, which was to continue agitation to build wide student support. The agitation, however, had to be controlled so that escalation only took place after a mass student base had been prepared. . . .

In order to gain student support, the FSM began to hold rallies almost every day at noon on the steps of Sproul Hall. Large numbers of students passed through the plaza, and sunny days brought a large audience. As many as five thousand students sometimes attended. These events both bolstered the confidence of the FSM leaders, whose self-doubts were reduced by mass approval, and ratified and legitimated the FSM demands. Not surprisingly, some administrators proposed eliminating the rallies, but such an act would have driven moderate students into solidarity with the most hotheaded activists. . . .

During rallies the FSM leaders often led mass singing of civil rights songs or union songs from the 1930s. The FSM also created its own songs, published a songbook, and made recordings, which provided a major source of funds. Most songs expressed alienation. . . .

While students sang, administrators quarreled among themselves. Some urged new disciplinary action; others opposed it. . . . When the Regents finally met to discuss the issue, the FSM organized a march of several thousand students from Sather Gate across campus to a rally in front of University Hall, where the Regents met. . . .

Just as matters were quieting down, Kerr intervened maladroitly. In late November 1964, with the disciplinary cases settled amid bitterness and the political rules committee suspended, Kerr decided, perhaps under pressure from certain Regents, to punish the FSM leaders for their role in the events immediately preceding and surrounding the capture of the police car. Kerr's grant of amnesty in the pact of October 2 had excluded the events that took place during the actual seizure and holding of the car. . . . Four activist leaders—Savio, Art Goldberg, Jackie Goldberg, and Brian Turner—were singled out, and it appears that Kerr intended to suspend Savio and Art Goldberg on the grounds that on October 1 and 2 they had violated the terms of the retroactive probation that had been recommended by . . . [the] faculty committee and imposed . . . in late November. "They are trying to pick off our leaders one by one," said Steve Weissman, an FSM spokesman. Kerr's petty act rallied both the faculty and large numbers of otherwise uninvolved students to the FSM cause. The activists, in a spirit of rage, decided to confront Kerr with their ultimate weapon.

From the beginning the activists had considered a sit-in. . . . One of the most important functions of sit-ins was to win converts. Friends would join, and then friends of friends, and the feeling of camaraderie experienced in the sit-in gave the movement what it needed most: bodies. The fellowship of a sit-in promised a vast expansion of the activist population on campus and the beginnings of an activist community. Berkeley would have not dozens of activists but hundreds, possibly even thousands. . . . [I]f a sit-in brought police, and the FSM leaders calculated that Kerr was not shrewd enough to avoid this outcome, then the bringing of police onto campus could generate benefits. The presence of police would both demonstrate Kerr's failure to manage the University and generate publicity that would bring sympathizers to Berkeley. Above all, the faculty could not tolerate the University run as a police state. Thus, a large sit-in would demonstrate widespread support for the FSM and push the faculty to act. The activists set a trap to humiliate Kerr and to bring the faculty to the rescue of the FSM. . . .

[F]aced with one of the largest sit-ins in history, Kerr was pushed toward a decision he did not want to make. Painfully aware of the faculty's disdain for the use of police on campus, a disdain enhanced by the large number of European war refugees on the faculty, Kerr did not want to be remembered for using police to make arrests. So he kept his role in the unfolding events secret. . . . Throughout the crisis Kerr had consulted with the chairman of the Regents, Edward Carter, and Carter in turn had frequently talked by phone with Governor Pat Brown. The liberal Democratic governor had long been an admirer and supporter of Kerr's. . . .

The governor . . . issued the order to arrest the protesters. Brown, a former prosecutor and attorney general, did not need to be persuaded of the virtue of law and order. His action, however, and his high visibility were politically unwise. The arrests enraged the protesters . . . and failed to appease those Californians who came to consider Brown as part of the problem of Berkeley's disgrace. . . .

[T]he police came. The FSM leaders had urged students under arrest to refuse to walk in order to force policemen to carry them from the building. The police obliged, although not necessarily in the gentlest manner. While females who refused to walk were taken down the elevator, males were

tossed from officer to officer and hurled down the terrazzo stairs. . . .
[D]espite the 367 police officers who took part, the building was not
cleared and the last of 773 arrests made until 4 p.m. on the afternoon of
December 3. It was the largest mass arrest in California's history. . . .

During 1966 the idea of Black Power swept through the nation's black
communities. The word "Negro" began to disappear, and "black" came into
common usage. The Negro had been polite and obsequious; the black was
angry and proud. . . .

[I]n Berkeley . . . [n]either Malcolm X nor [Martin Luther] King[, Jr.,]
had been local heroes, and both the SCLC [Southern Christian Leadership
Conference] and the SNCC [Student Nonviolent Coordinating Committee]
seemed far away. The black-white liberal coalition that had come to power
in Berkeley had given blacks more influence than in any other mostly white
city in the country. In 1965 the coalition had won a smashing victory and
swept all four council seats for a six to three majority. . . . In 1966, however, the coalition began to disintegrate. The war in Vietnam split white liberals, while the race issue split blacks. . . .

Politics aside, Berkeley was unusual in its commitment to biracial ventures. The city YWCA had been integrated for years, and the ad hoc com-
mittees to end job discrimination had been biracial. A local biracial theater
company had taken a militant black position. . . .

Here was the paradox: the strength of the liberal coalition and the biracial community ventures in Berkeley made it difficult for blacks to articulate a position of Black Power. Power in Berkeley was destined to be shared
through a coalition rather than through any claim to exclusive use of power.
Yet the black need to escape the suffocation of white benevolence was just
as great in Berkeley as in the rest of black America. . . . The result was that
black extremism in Berkeley took a peculiar form. At one and the same
time, black militants had to articulate a sense of black autonomy that res-
onated with the Black Power rhetoric of Stokely Carmichael while acced-
ing to the pattern of biracial cooperation that had become a hallmark of
Berkeley politics since 1961. The movement would have to be both
autonomous and nonracist.

Such a movement did emerge in the Berkeley-Oakland area. It was
called the Black Panther party, and while it achieved national fame, it
largely remained a local institution. Its leaders were a group of young
blacks who had grown up in the Berkeley-Oakland ghetto. Caught up in
Carmichael's demand for autonomy, they retained a faith in cooperation
with white people (or at least certain white people). . . . The Panthers came
to this position not from an optimistic assessment of society but from a
shallow Marxism that led them to envision themselves as black revolutionaries. Being revolutionaries, they considered it their duty to cooperate with
other revolutionaries, regardless of race. Radical ideology enabled the Panthers at one and the same time to call for black self-determination and to
urge black-white cooperation. It was an ironic use of revolutionary
ideology.

Two students at Merritt College, a largely black junior college then located in North Oakland, founded the Panthers. One was Bobby Seale, who had been born in 1936 in Texas, but who had grown up in Berkeley's Codornices Village. . . .

While at Merritt, Seale met Huey P. Newton. . . . Born in 1942 in Louisiana, Newton had grown up in Oakland. . . . Newton . . . spent much time on the street, where he had a reputation for being tough. . . . Although Newton's formal education was poor . . . he had enrolled at Merritt and started to read on his own. . . . Seale introduced Newton to the work of the radical black author Frantz Fanon. Fanon's attack upon the French exploitation of the colony of Algeria struck a sympathetic chord with the two young blacks. They noted parallels between French exploitation of the Algerians and white exploitation of American blacks; they began to think of white America as the mother country and the black ghetto as a colony. . . .

The Panthers knew how to attract attention. They wore black trousers, black leather jackets, and black berets that vaguely suggested a Castro connection, and they carried firearms in the streets. In 1966 California law provided it was legal to carry unloaded weapons openly in public places. At a time when race riots were occurring in almost every black ghetto in the country, the Panthers' arms alarmed not only whites but also the police. . . . When the police harassed the Panthers by stopping their cars frequently for traffic violations, the Panthers responded by harassing the police. Whenever a patrol car entered the Oakland-Berkeley ghetto, it was tailed by the Panthers, who had their own communications system. After Don Mulford, the conservative Republican who represented the Berkeley hills in the legislature, introduced a bill regulating guns, the Panthers decided to lobby the legislature. On May 2, 1967, they drove to Sacramento in a caravan, marched with their unloaded weapons into the capitol, and after getting lost inside the building, accidentally walked onto the floor of the Assembly bearing their arms. The legislators were frightened, the media became hysterical, and the Panthers, some of whom were arrested, never again lacked publicity. . . .

As the Panthers grew in numbers, the leaders became somewhat distant from their followers. Newton and Seale gave speeches, wrote party propaganda, and mediated disputes, but they never succeeded in building a structured organization. A number of Panthers were caught in robberies, and some thought the Panthers nothing more than a crime gang. . . .

The [Panthers'] most important recruit was Eldridge Cleaver, who had lived more than half his thirty-one years in California prisons. While in prison the former resident of Los Angeles had become a Black Muslim and, like Malcolm X, had broken with the Muslims. He had also written a startling account of his desire to rape white women. When published in 1968, *Soul on Ice* topped the best-seller list. . . .

On October 28, 1967, Huey Newton was stopped late at night by a policeman on an Oakland street. Exactly what happened next is unclear, but there was a shootout; one white officer was killed, while Newton went to the hospital with a bullet wound. He soon faced a murder charge, which pushed the Panthers onto the front pages day after day. When the prosecutor asked for the death penalty, some blacks recalled the racist southern justice of their own childhoods. . . . In the black community declarations of support for Newton became a badge of racial honor. Many blacks who had previously ignored the Panthers joined the Newton defense effort. . . .

On September 8, 1968, the jury rejected the murder charge and convicted Newton of involuntary manslaughter. . . .

In the fall of 1968, a group of students at the University invited Cleaver to teach a course on racism. They did so under the auspices of the University's Board of Educational Development, which had been established after the Free Speech Movement to generate innovative and experimental courses. When the appointment was announced, the public, Governor Ronald Reagan, and the Regents fumed. Although Chancellor [Roger] Heyns privately lamented that Cleaver had been invited to teach, he defended the appointment to the Regents. By one vote the angry Regents allowed Cleaver to give a single lecture in a hastily reconstructed course. An enraged Cleaver then barnstormed the state's campuses. He seemed to get a particular thrill out of cursing the governor. . . . [B]efore the school term ended, Eldridge Cleaver's parole had been revoked, and he jumped bail and fled to Algeria. . . .

In early 1969 . . . militant black students at San Francisco State College struck over the issue of a black studies program on that campus. Support for the strike spread to the Berkeley campus, where militant black students joined militant Chicanos, Asians, and native [sic] Americans to form the Third World Liberation Front (TWLF). The TWLF presented the administration at Berkeley with a list of demands, which included the establishment of student-controlled minority programs. "The real issue," said the TWLF, "is the right of people to determine their own destinies." The administration could not accept the demands, and they were presented in such a way that no acceptance was anticipated. . . .

TWLF leaders then joined white radicals to declare a student strike. As the strike began, one of the University's main lecture halls, Wheeler Auditorium, burned. The fire turned many students against the strike, which drew little support from whites on campus. . . . [The] militants blocked entry to campus at Sather Gate with a closely formed picket line, threats, and blows. The University advised students to enter campus elsewhere. Plainclothesmen beat the TWLF pickets with blackjacks. . . . On February 27, police severely beat Ysidro Macias, a key Chicano leader, and the next day the National Guard arrived. Although this strike . . . failed, the ill-will that it left behind cannot be overestimated. The University administration felt besieged, minority students were frustrated, and everyone was weary.

By the end of the decade both race relations and society were in disarray. . . . Except for school desegregation, the liberal program [had] failed. Its failure disillusioned many blacks, who drew away from white paternalism and toward black autonomy. For blacks the decade had combined hope with frustration. . . . But soaring hope invites great disappointment, and the decade ended with Malcolm X and Martin Luther King, Jr., dead, with a number of black leaders exiled or imprisoned, with young blacks trapped in the ghetto, and with white Americans increasingly distracted from black problems by the war in Vietnam.

Ronald Reagan as Governor

LOU CANNON

Many of the first campus rallies in favor of civil rights and against the Vietnam War which typified the 1960s took place in California. The state also was a spawning ground for the conservationist and antinuclear movements and the United Farm Workers, and a major recruiting area for the John Birch Society. In California, celebrities like Reagan and George Murphy could become politicians, and politicians like Jerry Brown could become celebrities. In California, an unknown and overweight Texas sharecropper's son like Jesse Unruh became the power-wielding speaker of the state Assembly. For all its people and problems and urban sprawl, California remained an outpost of the western frontier where nothing seemed impossible and everything could be achieved. California was the wave of the future.

Reagan saw the coming wave and rode the edge of the conservative counterrevolution which swept across the nation. The movement had economic reasons for being, as Americans became disenchanted with government growth, runaway inflation and rising taxes. But its deeper causes were social. In the 1960s middle class Americans looked around them at urban disorders, rising black militancy and antidraft protests spurred by the Vietnam War and did not like what they saw. Middle class parents who had striven to put their children through college particularly did not like what they thought was happening at the University of California's best-known campus at Berkeley. In 1965 [*sic*], a part-time student named Mario Savio led the Free Speech Movement into protesting a ban on distribution of political material at the university's Sather Gate entrance. When the university persisted in its restrictions, the protests grew, degenerated into a "filthy speech" movement, and were finally and reluctantly put down by force on orders of Governor Pat Brown. Later, as violence rocked campuses across the country, including California, the UC demonstrations of 1965 [*sic*] would seem quite tame. But Americans at the time of the first Berkeley demonstrations were accustomed to quiet, orderly campuses and angry at those who disrupted this order.

Reagan's audience roared with approval when he promised to "clean up the mess at Berkeley" where, he said, had occurred "sexual orgies so vile I cannot describe them to you." After being rebuffed by the chairman of the state Senate Subcommittee on Un-American Activities in his demand for an investigation, Reagan promised in his campaign to name a commission headed by former Central Intelligence Agency Director John J. McCone to "investigate the charges of communism and blatant sexual misbehavior on the Berkeley campus." Nothing came of the investigation, but it set the tone for a running battle between Reagan and the state's higher education establishment which continued during most of Reagan's first term. On December 3, 1966, a month after his election, Reagan issued a warning to dissidents, "Observe the rules or get out." An unknown admirer made a bronze-and-walnut plaque of these words and sent it to Reagan. The governor liked his own admonition so much that he hung the plaque on the cloth-upholstered wall above the entrance to his office.

From the first day of his governorship, Reagan and higher education saw each other as the enemy. On inauguration day, Reagan's inept finance director, Gordon Smith, prematurely disclosed the governor's plan to impose a $400-a-year tuition at the university and a $200-a-year tuition at state colleges in addition to the 10 percent budget cuts. The higher education establishment, overcome by suspicion and hostility, interpreted these proposals as punitive and reacted with denunciations nearly as extreme as Reagan's had been of the UC demonstrators. In the meantime, reports circulated within both administration and academic circles that UC President Clark Kerr would soon be fired. Kerr, a former professor and labor mediator of distinction whose administrative skills had been questioned even by some of his supporters, was at the center of the Berkeley controversies. One of his favorite sayings was, "The university is not engaged in making ideas safe for students; it is engaged in making students safe for ideas." Kerr was assailed on the right by such foes of "permissiveness" as state Superintendent of Public Instruction Max Rafferty, a member, as was the governor, of the university Board of Regents, and on the left by radicals like Savio, who blamed Kerr for the impersonality of what he called "the multiversity." Several of the regents had been critics of Kerr since 1964, and others considered him too politically damaged to negotiate with Reagan over the university budget. A majority wanted his resignation.

Kerr talked it over with the chairman of the regents, Theodore Meyer, and the vice-chairman, Dorothy B. Chandler, both of whom asked him to resign. Kerr refused and instead sought a vote from the full Board of Regents. The action surprised Reagan, who was so preoccupied with his budget problems that he wanted to postpone any decision on the university presidency. Reagan told me in 1968 that he thought Kerr had "outlived his usefulness," but that he didn't want to instigate a move to fire him. Kerr did that himself, by asking for what was in effect a vote of confidence. On the motion of Laurence J. Kennedy, Jr., an appointee of Governor Brown, the regents voted 14–8 to dismiss Kerr with Reagan supporting the majority. "We had tuition and the budget on our hands, and I would have preferred to wait until June or so," said Reagan afterwards. "But you can't turn around and give a man a vote of confidence in January and then fire him five months later."

Kerr's dismissal occurred on January 21, 18 days after Reagan took office. Reagan's low-key maneuvering on this issue and his unwillingness to take the lead in firing Kerr was one of the first clues that he would be a governor more restrained in his practice than he had been in his rhetoric. Another clue came a month later when Reagan offered only token resistance to the regents' decision to postpone consideration of the tuition. In his dealings with the university and state colleges, Reagan from the outset looked for ways in which he could prevail by compromise. He cultivated those willing to defer to the administration, notably the flexible Glenn Dumke, chancellor of the state colleges. Secure in his public support for a firm stand against campus dissidents, Reagan believed he could afford a strategy of delay and compromise. Usually his more militant, or thoughtless, adversaries played into his hands with some disorderly protest that made Reagan a sure winner on television. Even as a novice governor, Reagan understood that rational objections tended to be drowned out by irrational ones on the nightly news. . . .

On August 4, 1970, Governor Reagan sent a confidential memo to his cabinet and senior staff which revealed his true feelings about those who depended on the state of California for their well-being. Announcing a study of the state's public assistance and education programs, Reagan wrote: "This study will place heavy emphasis on the tax-payer as opposed to the tax-taker; on the truly needy as opposed to the lazy unemployable; on the student as opposed to educational frills; on basic needs as opposed to unmanageable enrichment programs; on measurable results as opposed to blind faith that an educator can do no wrong." The memo, drafted for Reagan by Edwin Meese, was the governor's call to action for the welfare reform legislation that would become the dominant issue of his second term. Looking beyond the coming election, it called for recommendations by January 1971 that would propose administrative remedies, suggest a long-range legislative program, pinpoint problems with the federal government and make local government more accountable. "I am determined to reduce these programs to essential services at a cost the tax-payers can afford to pay," Reagan concluded the memo. "This is our NUMBER ONE priority. We must bring all our resources to bear in this endeavor. Therefore, I am asking you to make available your best employees including directors for this all-out war on the tax-taker. If we fail, no one ever again will be able to try. We must succeed."

Such apocalyptic rhetoric might have been suited for a commando raid or, at best, a meeting of the Young Republicans; its presence in a cabinet memorandum reflected Reagan's growing realization in the final year of his first term that he was a long way from accomplishing the bold goals of his inaugural message. As the memo recognized, the Reagan administration had braked the growth of government in some areas but had failed to do anything about welfare and educational costs, "which are virtually out of our realm of authority because of outmoded constitutional and statutory requirements and federal laws and regulations." By any standard, after nearly four years in office, Reagan's achievements were modest ones. After his initial fling at across-the-board budget cutting, he had become a fairly orthodox governor who had restored funds for higher education and provided money for a community mental health treatment program. . . . All in all, Reagan's record as governor had been moderate and responsible but undistinguished. He had failed, after the 1967 tax bill, to get his most cherished programs through the legislature. He was running for reelection as much on the record of not having done the terrible things predicted by his opponents as on the record of what he had actually accomplished. . . .

The elections of 1970 were a setback for the Nixon administration and the Republican Party, but a ratification for Reagan. The governor won a second term with 3,439,664 votes and 52.9 percent of the total to Unruh's 2,938,607 votes and 45.1 percent. Candidates for the left-wing Peace and Freedom Party and the right-wing American Independent Party almost evenly divided the other 2 percent of the vote. But Reagan's reelection, along with Rockefeller's unprecedented fourth-term victory in New York, was one of the few big races that Republicans could cheer about. Agnew's purge attempt had failed, with Republicans gaining only two Senate seats and losing nine in the House. Except for California and New York, the gubernatorial races were even more disastrous for the Republicans than they had been for the Democrats four years earlier. The GOP lost eleven state houses. In California, John V. Tunney defeated Senator Murphy by a margin exceeding Reagan's. And Reed's fears about a Democratic comeback in blue-collar districts proved justified. Democrats picked up three seats in the Assembly and two in the Senate, winning control of both houses. The Democratic gains were most conspicuous in working class precincts, where Reagan ran ahead of the GOP ticket but less strongly than in 1966. There had been a Reagan victory but not a Republican one.

Reagan's mandate was reduced, but his sense of purpose was keener and his goals more focused in his second term. Instead of waging a vague war on government programs of all kinds, Reagan now proposed a focused battle for what he saw as welfare reform. . . .

The California Welfare Reform Act is Reagan's proudest achievement in the eight years of his governorship. By almost any yardstick—liberal, conservative, or managerial—the law has been a success. It is easier to administer than the law it replaced, and it pays AFDC recipients more money. However, many who applaud the results of the legislation also believe that Reagan ascribes to it wonder cures which never occurred. The welfare reform bill tightened eligibility in several ways and reduced the number of hours an unemployed father could work and still have his family eligible for aid. Household furnishings were for the first time counted as assets. A complex and confusing "needs standard" was simplified into a uniform statewide schedule which varied only according to family size. A one-year residency requirement, long advocated by Reagan, was written into the law despite warnings that is was probably unconstitutional. Antifraud measures included a state cross-check between county welfare records and employer earnings records and financial incentives to counties to recover support payments from absent fathers. . . .

Though Reagan had signed more than forty bills providing stiffer sentences for criminals or other intended improvements in the criminal justice system, California had not become a safer place to live by the time Reagan left office in 1974. In eight years the homicide rate had doubled, and the rate of armed robberies had increased even more. Law enforcement is, of course, primarily a local responsibility. The same cannot be said for taxes, which increased under Reagan as they had never increased in California before. On the campaign trail Reagan boasted of returning $5.7 billion in taxes, including $4 billion in property-tax relief, to Californians. He never said that these taxes came from Reagan-sponsored tax increases that were the largest, up to that time, in California history. Under Reagan the state budget increased from $4.6 billion annually to $10.2 billion. The operations portion of the budget, over which the governor has the most control, went from $2.2 billion to $3.5 billion. State taxes per $100 of personal income, a measure which adjusts both for population and price changes, increased from $6.64 to $7.62.

At the same time Reagan had done much to control the growth of state government. "Reagan was not so much an underachiever as he was an over-committer," observed Judson Clark of California Research, who served as a top aide to Democratic Speaker Unruh and Republican Speaker Monagan. "He did some important things, but not as much as he said he would do and not as much as he said he did." One of the things Reagan did do was slow the growth of the state work force, which had increased nearly 50 percent during the Brown years. The growth was less than half of this during the Reagan administration, rising from 158,400 to 192,400 positions. If higher education, where Reagan's control was indirect, is excluded, the growth was 7 percent (from 108,090 to 115,090) at a time when government work forces in other states were growing rapidly. If the $4 billion in direct property-tax relief is subtracted from the Reagan budgets, they increased only slightly more than inflation.

Ultimately, the judgment of the Reagan administration has to rest on something other than statistics, which can be cited to infinite purpose both by the governor's critics and by his defenders. Reagan came to office an utter novice, proclaiming a conservative gospel which his adversaries confidently predicted was too simpleminded and backward-looking for a modern democratic state. He went through a long learning period at taxpayers' expense during which California's much maligned and highly professional state government bureaucracy did the actual governing. But Reagan did not abandon his ideals or his beliefs that government had become too little the servant and too much the master. Instead, he learned and accommodated and compromised and found ways of doing things which accomplished parts of his purpose. He found good people to work for him, and by trials and errors learned the limits of what he could delegate and what he could not. In his second term he finally came down out of the announcer's booth and onto the political playing field where men sweat and work and sell judgeships and write laws. He did all right in this world, which was not all that different from the one he had known in Dixon. "He had certain assets," said Moretti. "He had a philosophy he was willing to pursue, to enunciate, that he was willing to attempt to push. Even if you disagreed with that philosophy, the fact that he had one and that he stood up for it was something.

And he was a strong personality. . . . He had an enduring desire to leave something behind that was really material which he could point to as a change. He wanted to improve where he had been."

FURTHER READING

Gene Anthony, *The Summer of Love* (1980)
John Constantinus Bollens and G. Robert Williams, *Jerry Brown: In a Plain Brown Wrapper* (1978)
Bill Boyarsky, *Ronald Reagan, His Life and Rise to the Presidency* (1981)
Edmund Gerald Brown and Bill Brown, *Reagan, the Political Chameleon* (1976)
Lou Cannon, *Ronnie and Jesse: A Political Odyssey* (1969)
Lou Cannon, *President Reagan: The Role of a Lifetime* (1991)
Jack Citrin, *California and the American Tax Revolt: Proposition 13 Five Years Later* (1984)
Eldridge Cleaver, *Soul on Ice* (1968)
Stephen Cornell, *The Return of the Native: American Indian Political Resurgence* (1988)
Eric Cummins, *The Rise and Fall of California's Radical Prison Movement* (1994)
Royce D. Delmatier et al., *The Rumble of California Politics, 1848–1970* (1970)
Adam Fortunate Eagle, *Alcatraz! Alcatraz! The Indian Occupation of 1969–1971* (1992)
Yen Le Espiritu, *Asian American Panethnicity: Bridging Institutions and Identities* (1992)
Philip S. Foner, ed., *The Black Panthers Speak* (1970)
Todd Gitlin, *The Sixties: Years of Hope, Days of Rage* (1987; repr., 1989; rev. trade ed., 1993)
David Lance Goines, *The Free Speech Movement: Coming of Age in the 1960s* (1993)
Juan Gomez-Quinones, *Chicano Politics: Reality and Promise, 1940–1990* (1990)
Gladwin Hill, *Dancing Bear: An Inside Look at California Politics* (1968)
Gerald Horne, *Fire This Time: The Watts Uprising and the 1960s* (1995)
Andrew Jamison and Ron Eyeman, *Seeds of the Sixties* (1994)
Howard Jarvis, with Robert Pack, *I'm Mad as Hell: The Exclusive Story of the Tax Revolt and Its Leader* (1979)
John Kirlin and Jeffrey Chapman, *California State Finance and Proposition 13* (1979)
Mary Ellen Leary, *Phantom Politics: Campaigning in California* (1977)
Joseph Lewis, *What Makes Reagan Run: A Political Profile* (1968)
Seymour M. Lipset and Sheldon S. Wolin, eds., *The Berkeley Student Revolt* (1965)
J. D. Lorenz, *Jerry Brown, the Man on the White Horse* (1978)
Gene Marine, *The Black Panthers* (1969)
Howard Brett Melendy and Benjamin F. Gilbert, *The Governors of California: Peter H. Burnett to Edmund G. Brown* (1965)
Timothy Miller, *The Hippies and American Values* (1991)
Carlos Muñoz, Jr., *Youth, Identity, Power: The Chicano Movement* (1989)
Huey P. Newton, *Revolutionary Suicide* (1973)
Robert Pack, *Jerry Brown, the Philosopher-Prince* (1978)
Hugh Pearson, *The Shadow of the Panther: Huey Newton and the Price of Black Power in America* (1994)
Jackson K. Putnam, *Modern California Politics* (1984)
Roger Rapoport, *California Dreaming: The Political Odyssey of Pat & Jerry Brown* (1982)
Ronald Reagan and Richard G. Hubler, *Where's the Rest of Me?* (1965)
W. J. Rorabaugh, *Berkeley at War: The 1960s* (1989)

Theodore Roszak, *The Making of a Counter Culture* (1969)
Ed Salzman, *Jerry Brown, High Priest and Low Politician: An Analysis of Governor Edmund G. Brown, Jr. as a Candidate for Office and as California's Chief Executive for the First Two Years of His Term* (1976)
Orville Schell, *Brown* (1978)
Bobby Seale, *Seize the Time: The Story of the Black Panther Party and Huey P. Newton* (1968; ed., 1970)
William Wei, *The Asian American Movement* (1993)
Lewis Yabonsky, *The Hippie Trip* (1968)

C H A P T E R
14

The Rise of
Information Capitalism

The arrival of the microelectronics and semiconductor industries in California (or, more specifically, in Santa Clara County, later dubbed "the Silicon
Valley") after World War II signaled a dramatic transformation of the
state's economy away from its traditional manufacturing base. Of crucial
importance to this economic restructuring was the role of the military as a
major consumer of electronics, communications systems, and synthetic materials. Massive amounts of federal spending during and after the war greatly
stimulated high-technology production. The original computers, it is worth
remembering, were designed for military applications.

At the center of this historic economic transformation is the "information sector," which includes both information technology (hardware) and
the use of advanced information systems (software). In this important new
sector, the processing and distribution of information are central and time-
consuming activities, providing employment for millions of people nationwide. These information-oriented occupations are extremely diverse and
include managers, lawyers, accountants, computer programmers, realtors,
stockbrokers, clerks, and teachers. As early as 1950, this information sector
accounted for more employment in the United States than either manufacturing or services, and by the late 1960s information-oriented activities produced more than 46 percent of the country's national income.

As we try to understand these dramatic economic and social changes in
California, the concept of "information capitalism"—indicating a new stage
of economic development beyond industrial manufacturing—is especially
useful. The concept refers to new forms of organization in which computeri-
zation and data-intensive techniques serve as key resources. It refers, as well,
to the legions of information providers who work with the "tools"—word
processors, databases, spreadsheets—that actually process and distribute
information. These forms of organization and these "knowledge" workers
are found in all sectors of the California economy— agriculture, manufacturing, and services—not merely in the so-called high-technology industries.

To be sure, the computer industry at the core of this new information sector was first developed in prestigious universities on the East Coast, not in California, and in such large companies there as IBM, Digital Equipment, Prime Computer, and Wang. In the early years of the information age, California computer companies such as National Semiconductors, Intel, and Advanced Micro Devices made the silicon chips that went into computers elsewhere. Until the late 1970s, the only viable minicomputer makers in California were Hewlett-Packard and Tandem, considered by most knowledgeable observers to be second tier when compared with their East Coast counterparts.

That all changed in 1977 with the founding of Apple Computer. In the decade that followed, California entered the computing world's major leagues, as billion-dollar-a-year Apple was soon joined by other companies, including Sun Microsystems and Seagate Technology. Later, California-based clone-making companies such as AST Research and Wyse Technology cut heavily into IBM's market share. By the late 1970s, the Silicon Valley had surpassed Route 128 in Massachusetts to become the leading center of semiconductor production and the most important software-development region in the United States. Other areas in California, such as Orange County, were also emerging as major innovation and production sites of information capitalism.

These profound economic and technological developments have had important political and spatial reverberations. In political terms, for example, they have forced a reevaluation of the relationship between state government and private markets. Computer technology has also had a direct impact on the political process itself (see the fourth document in this chapter). Spatially, information capitalism has reshaped the structure of daily work by making it possible (through the use of mobile technologies such as car phones and portable computers) for workers to communicate with their managers and customers from "virtual offices," rather than from traditional offices in urban centers. Another spatial consequence of information capitalism—the increasing mobility of capital and information technology on a global scale—is discussed in this chapter's third essay.

It is difficult to discern the consequences of a major societal transformation while it is still going on. In the case of information capitalism, with its tremendous political, economic, spatial, and social effects, the rate of change over the past twenty years has accelerated so rapidly that historians can do little more than study changes in specific areas. The essays in this chapter focus on the impact of information capitalism in specific geographic areas: its effects on business culture and on the family in Silicon Valley and its political ramifications in Orange County. From these perspectives and others, future historians should be able to develop a synthesis, a general interpretation, of the impact of information capitalism and the way it is changing our lives.

 D O C U M E N T S

The first document lists the leading California computer companies at the end of the 1980s. The jobs provided by these companies differ greatly from those in California's traditional agricultural and manufacturing industries, which had previously dominated the state's economy. In the second document, Art Garcia, a feature writer for a leading California business journal, provides an upbeat, optimistic assessment of the information age. In 1985 one of the most important "information capitalists," Steven Jobs, cofounder (with Stephen Wozniak) of Apple Computer, bitterly resigned his position in a power struggle with Apple's president. Jobs's all-important role in creating a California computer giant is described by a staff writer from the *Los Angeles Times* in the third document.

The computer technologies so essential to information capitalism also directly influence the political process. Faith Alchorn, formerly an intern for the monthly *California Journal,* describes a particular software program designed for campaign management and assesses the role of information technology in Art Agnos's campaign for mayor of San Francisco. In the chapter's final document, Duane Spilsbury, a freelance writer and former journalism professor at California State University, Sacramento, describes yet another impact of information technology: the reshaping of work under information capitalism in the form of "telecommuting," that is, the use of nonterritorial, virtual offices characterized by one observer as "the most radical redefinition of the workplace since the Industrial Revolution."

California Computer Companies, 1989

		1988 REVENUES ($MILLIONS)	FOUR-YEAR % GROWTH
CHIP COMPANIES			
Intel	Santa Clara	2,875.0	77
National Semiconductor	Santa Clara	2,469.7	49
Advanced Micro Devices	Sunnyvale	1,125.9	–
LSI Logic	Milpitas	378.9	349
Anthem Electronics	San Jose	264.6	34[#]
Chips and Technologies	San Jose	141.5	1,012*
Cypress Semiconductor	San Jose	135.3	4,067
Silicon Systems Inc	Tustin	120.8	48[#]
Xicor	Milpitas	90.1	39[#]
Microsemi	Santa Ana	83.7	47*
Western Microtech, Inc.	Saratoga	73.4	41[#]
Linear Technology	Milpitas	51.3	612
HARDWARE COMPANIES			
Hewlett-Packard *systems*	Palo Alto	9,831.0	22[#]
Apple Computers *personal computers*	Cupertino	4,071.4	53[#]
Amdahl *computers*	Sunnyvale	1,801.8	20[#]
Tandem Computers *computer products*	Cupertino	1,300.0	26[#]
Seagate Technology *disk drives*	Scotts Valley	1,265.9	268
Wyse Technology *monitors*	San Jose	456.6	609
AST Research *add-on boards*	Irvine	412.7	547
Micropolis Corp *computer products*	Chatsworth	353.1	23[#]
Tandon Corp *computer products*	Moorpark	314.0	16[#]
Applied Magnetics *computer components*	Goleta	293.0	38[#]
Everex Systems *personal computers*	Fremont	266.7	69[#]
Conner Peripherals *disk drives*	San Jose	256.6	127[#]

SOFTWARE COMPANIES		1988 REVENUES ($MILLIONS)	FOUR-YEAR % GROWTH
Micro D Inc.	Santa Ana	553.4	57[#]
Ashton-Tate	Torrance	267.3	522
Informix	Menlo Park	103.5	121[*]
Telos Corp	Santa Monica	100.8	23[#]
Adobe	Mountain View	83.5	3,679
Borland International	Scotts Valley	81.6	7,179
Autodesk	Sausalito	79.3	6,566
Software Publishing	Mountain View	73.1	179
Boole & Babbage	Sunnyvale	56.7	28[*]
Micropro Int'l Corp	San Rafael	42.5	3[#]
MacNeal-Schwendler	Los Angeles	39.9	21[*]
Broderbund Software	San Rafael	24.3[@]	139
DISTRIBUTION COMPANIES			
Computerland	Pleasanton	2,040.0	n/a
Businessland	San Jose	871.6	872
Softsel Computer Products	Inglewood	465.0	190

one-year growth   * two-year growth   @ fiscal 1986

Art Garcia Describes California's New Economic Frontier, 1984

If man doesn't blow up his planet first, the 1980s and 1990s will see an explosion of new technologies that will make marvelous changes in the way we work, live and play. The boom is well under way with miracle machines and systems leading the transition from an industrial to an information society.

But the next new wave the world rides to a truly high-tech society will be marked not by revolution but evolution. "Just the advent of the microprocessor and cheap computer power has opened up tons of opportunities—and we've barely begun to scratch the surface," says Robert Johnson, principal in Southern California Ventures, an Irvine venture capital firm.

Silicon chips fired the growth of Silicon Valley, but the game has broadened and the stakes have fattened. Outside California, high-tech centers are blossoming beyond the familiar clusters along Route 128 in Massachusetts and in the Research Triangle in North Carolina. Tennessee is readying development of a "technology corridor," and similar centers are sprouting in Texas, Michigan, Minnesota, Arizona, Colorado, Washington and Georgia. Internationally, the United States is in a neck-and-neck race with Japan to develop a "fifth generation" computer and "super-computer." . . . Britain, France, even tiny Israel, are also giving chase in the technology sweepstakes.

The U.S. Commerce Department reports that more than two-thirds of this nation's workers currently are employed in information-based jobs, evidence of the shift from an industrial to an informational society. Only about a third of the U.S. work force is on manufacturing sector payrolls.

William Miller, president and chief executive of SRI International in Menlo Park, suggests California is the "best precursor or model" for the coming information society. "It's not a perfect model, but it may be the best one we have." . . .

All of the state's base industries—information services, agriculture, aerospace, forest products, electronics, financial services, various retail and wholesale services—have a huge component of electronics and information technologies. . . .

"In aerospace, for example, the California manufacturers concentrate on the high-technology end of the aerospace business. . . . Agriculture is increasingly becoming a high-technology business, . . . with sophisticated farming operations relying as much on computers as on fertilizers and pesticides."

Each year from 1973 to 1980, California added nearly a half million net new jobs to its work force, which in 1980 totaled around 10 million out of a population of about 22 million. Of the half million new jobs, approximately 60 percent were created directly or indirectly by the new technologies.

"Interestingly, few of them were created in the electronics-computer-telecommunications industry," says Miller. "There are no more than 300,000 to 400,000 jobs in that industry, depending on how broadly you define it. It grew very rapidly during this period, but the total number of jobs still remained relatively small.

"Where did the job growth come? In the industries using the new information technologies," Miller says—what he calls "the ripple effect." The California model, he adds, is evidence the information technologies are "job-creating, not job-destroying." . . .

Paul Shay, corporate communications vice president at SRI International, is co-authoring with William Miller a book titled "The American Renaissance," due out later this year. In it, he pinpoints five emerging technologies he predicts will be driving forces in the next decade: new materials, factory and office automation, biotechnology, and health and medical technologies.

Behind the drive are new values as well as new technologies. "People are much more inclined to be entrepreneurial, to take risks, to do their own thing," Shay contends. "It's the opposite of the man-in-the-gray-flannel-suit syndrome. People want to be creative, are willing to take risks."

Shay believes the dynamism in the United States will come from smaller companies, "not our giants. And that's been true since 1970. The work force is now 103 million people in this country, up from 70 million in 1970. The 'Fortune 500' companies as a group actually lost jobs. People are using new technologies to offer new services."

Donald Woutat Ponders the Resignation of
Steven Jobs from Apple Computer, 1985

It's been said about Steven P. Jobs that he would have made a good king of France. It's too bad the position has been eliminated, because the 30-year-old co-founder of Apple Computer is suddenly available.

Jobs' bitter resignation Tuesday from the chairmanship of Apple marks the unofficial end of a brief era of technology in which the mercurial young entrepreneur—perhaps more than anyone else—managed to personalize the computer, make it affordable and persuade millions of ordinary folks that they needed it.

The rich tale of Apple Computer, founded in 1976 by loner Jobs and his nerdy high school chum, Stephen Wozniak, has become as familiar to baby boomers as Horatio Alger stories were to an earlier generation. And Apple's overnight transformation into a $2-billion company that couldn't be properly managed by a computer hacker or a temperamental marketing genius is a classic example of the metamorphosis of business.

Through it all strode Jobs, a complex college dropout variously described as brilliant, arrogant, private, egotistical, and an extraordinary pitchman who was totally consumed by his creation. He is said to command an almost religious devotion among the youthful electronic zealots who developed the computers that, in what might have been Jobs' niftiest idea of all, were called Apple.

The Apple label somehow managed to link the computer—a cold and fearsome machine in the minds of many—to such Woodstock-generation values as environmentalism, friendliness and other non-threatening and distinctively non-corporate ideas. . . .

The adopted son of a machinist, Jobs grew up in what was becoming the Silicon Valley and attended high school in Cupertino. With Wozniak and others, he tinkered with electronics and, among other things, made a device that enabled phone users to bypass Ma Bell and make free long-distance calls. He later dropped out of Reed College in Oregon, flirted with Far Eastern religions, worked for Atari and tried communal living and vegetarianism. . . .

In 1975, while working for Atari, the company that pioneered video games, he frequented meetings of the local Homebrew Computer Club. Wozniak, who had quit UC Berkeley, was a serious club member who was developing a computer that was to become the Apple I.

By most accounts a second-rate technician, Jobs knew a good idea when he saw it, and the seed for Apple was planted. And it was to become a press agent's dream that the new partners financed the prototype of their new computer with proceeds from the sale of Jobs' Volkswagen bus, the unofficial vehicle of the "flower children."

They began calling on venture capitalists and approached Regis McKenna, a powerful Silicon Valley public relations man, for help. McKenna made the most of the entrepreneurs' unlikely backgrounds, and

Jobs' beard, sandals, and blue jeans became part of the rapidly evolving Apple image. . . .

Jobs . . . led Apple on its dizzying path to success. Faster than any company before it, Apple cracked the Fortune 500 within five years. Largely on the strength of its Apple II computer, the company in December, 1980, went public in one of Wall Street's most successful new stock offerings. It raised $1 billion—the stock price started the day at $12 and ended it at $20—and about 100 millionaires were instantly created. Jobs himself was suddenly worth about $150 million. . . .

In the end, Jobs couldn't adapt to being kicked upstairs. A power struggle over the direction of the company last May left him with the chairman's title but no operating responsibilities. He failed in a reported effort to overthrow [Apple's President John] Scully at the time, then further angered the board last week by raiding five talented Apple executives for a new computer venture of his own.

By Wednesday night he was holed up with associates at his sprawling new home in a wooded area behind Stanford University, too busy, he said, to discuss his plans.

Faith Alchorn Ties Information Technology to Political Campaigns, 1988

Television, and the ability to craft a candidate's image through 15- and 30-second television commercials, helped rush political campaigning into the electronic age. Still, the campaigns themselves remained intensely human, requiring hundreds of volunteers contributing thousands of hours of work.

But as election tactics became more and more sophisticated and campaign laws more complex, only the largest and best-financed campaigns could bring enough volunteers on board or afford the cost of enough paid workers to keep track of polls, voter preferences, contributors, expenses, ad infinitum. Also, the larger the campaign, the more unwieldy its operations. More and more time was spent managing the details at the expense of intangible human contact with voters.

Enter, the personal computer.

Personal computers—those ubiquitous little boxes crammed with microchips, wires and a touch of black magic—are revolutionizing every facet of life, allowing fewer people to accomplish more work. Word-processing programs make editing faster; accounting programs turn even the sloppiest mathematician into a near-competent CPA; database programs store, sort and regurgitate a zillion bits of information.

Given the wide-spread use of computer technology, it was inevitable that high-tech would eventually seep into the political arena. As a result, an inexpensive personal computer, and its attendant software, has given even the smallest campaign management tools that were once too costly.

Computer software, designed specifically for campaign management, has put personal computers to work on many jobs that would otherwise be done by hand or by paying oodles of campaign bucks for a few hours of time on someone else's huge mainframe computer. A number of software packages on the market perform a variety of functions and make it possible to tailor a system to the needs of a particular campaign.

Say, the campaign that recently elected Art Agnos as mayor of San Francisco. Agnos, a former Democratic assemblyman, began the race as a decided underdog to Supervisor John Molinari. But Agnos eventually won a landslide victory and credits a large part of the victory to the use of campaign software.

"This was a difficult campaign," Agnos wrote the software manufacturer. "Our strategy was to contact thousands of voters, coordinate the activities of hundreds of volunteers and track all of the fund-raising solicitations, all on time and accurately. Software made it possible for us to meet our objective and timetable promptly and economically."

According to C. J. Maupin, Agnos' deputy campaign manager, the staff at first tried to use a standard database, but "the program got overloaded." The staff then contacted a company that had created software specifically designed to run a campaign.

"We had over 20,000 names of volunteers, contributors, people who had (Agnos) signs on their houses," said Maupin. "The software allowed us to sort them by name, address, zip code, precinct number, neighborhood. The program was able to identify who had house signs, who was a precinct captain, an area coordinator. It helped identify donors and gave the amount of their donations."

The possibilities for identifying voters and volunteers were endless, added Maupin. For example, the campaign could ask the computer to print a list of every donor from a particular neighborhood who donated more than $100 and also put an Agnos sign on his or her front lawn.

"(The software) allowed us to manage human resources," said Maupin. "It allowed us to be very precise when assigning people to do things for the campaign, and with our recruiting volunteers for the campaign." . . .

What the software does is increase a campaign's efficiency. It allows volunteers, who would otherwise be processing information manually, to press the flesh and promote their candidate among the public. Even though the mechanics of running a campaign may become increasingly technological, the fundamental importance of person-to-person contact with the voter remains.

Duane Spilsbury Reports on Telecommuting, 1989

Jim Drinkard is a State of California telecommuter. He is paid to stay out of the office and work at home.

Rather than driving 10 miles daily to his P Street office in downtown Sacramento, Drinkard operates with a laptop personal computer and a modem unit in his suburban home.

He travels about six days a month as a property appraiser for General Services. "My job goes into my suitcase," he says, and then he comes home to finish the paper work.

Drinkard is one of 150 state employees from 14 different agencies and departments who have been engaged in the California Telecommuting Pilot Project since January 1988. The purpose: to see if the state can benefit from energy savings and air-quality improvement by reducing the number of commuter trips. . . .

[T]he main premise is to transport ideas and information, rather than people.

"The basic telecommunications tool is the telephone, and it has been for a long time, . . . [b]ut the real technological developments that make the idea of working at home feasible are the transportable personal computer, the modem hookup which allows the computer to have electronic access to the telephone and the reasonably priced fax machine which provides quick transmission of printed materials." . . .

Drinkard considers telecommuting "a great program. I feel more in control of my life, and at the same time I feel like I'm a more trusted and respected employee. I feel happier, and I'm sure my production has gone up."

Yet there are some disadvantages, according to Drinkard. "I feel more cut off from my co-workers, and it's harder to keep abreast of the activities and scuttlebutt in the office. I try to keep up by telephone, and if I get lonesome for a human voice in the room, I go into the office to work."

Patty Smith, a 28-year-old staff services analyst with the Franchise Tax Board, finds telecommuting helpful in her personal life. Her job—tracking legislative bills that could have an economic or policy impact on the Franchise Tax Board—is now accomplished at a work station in her home in Placerville, about 30 miles east of Sacramento.

Mother of an infant and a six-year-old daughter, Smith had planned to take a year's maternity leave from state service. Instead, her boss, Alan Hunter, the tax board's chief deputy director, assigned her to the telecommuting project for the final year of the study. (Hunter's own administrative aide for budgeting does most of her work from her home in Auburn.)

"It was a great opportunity for me," Smith says. "My day starts at 5 a.m., and by 9 I have put in half a day's work. This spring I was able to be a parent volunteer in Brittany's class at school. I've never been able to do that before." . . .

The idea of working at home is, of course, nothing new. Self-employed consultants, independent salespersons, free-lance writers and editors have been working out of home offices for decades. A survey last fall in *U.S. News and World Report* said about 14 million Americans work at home eight or more hours per week, up 18 percent since 1986.

The fastest-growing category of telecommuters are those who work for American corporations, according to *Time*. Their numbers have grown to 600,000 in the past five years. . . .

For some, telecommuting will require adjustments. Appraiser Drinkard says one of his colleagues flatly refused an invitation to participate in the project. "He apparently felt he wouldn't have the self-discipline to work at home," says Drinkard.

Traditional employee-employer relations will need revision, too. Eight employees of the American General Group Insurance Co., in Houston—all female veteran insurance claim processors—sued the firm for $1 million in punitive damages, saying the company pressured them into working 16-hour days by misrepresenting the arrangements they would have as home workers. The suit was settled out of court for nominal damages.

Karen Nussbaum, executive director of 9-to-5, a national association of working women, lamented recently about what telecommuting has become for many women who are "working unreasonably long hours without over-time pay, doing computerized piecework in electronic sweatshops."

Dave Fleming takes a more optimistic view: "Telecommuting is one significant solution to what I call the '8-to-5 worktime,' which we have been stuck with since the Industrial Age began. . . . The modern trend is toward management by results, not by surveillance."

 E S S A Y S

Silicon Valley is the computer and microelectronics capital of the United States. Between 1960 and 1980, 400,000 new jobs were created in this region; by 1980 Silicon Valley was creating roughly 20 percent of all high-technology and information-oriented jobs in the United States. In the first essay, AnnaLee Saxenian, a member of the Department of City and Regional Planning at the University of California, Berkeley, describes the origins of Silicon Valley, its subsequent development, and the unusual business culture that emerged there. Her larger scholarly project, from which this essay is drawn, is a formal comparison of two leading technology regions: Silicon Valley and Route 128 in Massachusetts.

In the second essay, Judith Stacey, a sociologist at the University of California, Davis, explores the "unsettling conditions" of work and family life in what she calls the "postindustrial society" in contemporary California. After extensive ethnographic research among residents of the Silicon Valley, she reaches a number of disquieting conclusions about how the major industry in that region has influenced working conditions and family life.

In the third essay, Spencer Olin, a historian at the University of California, Irvine, focuses on a rival center of information capitalism: Orange County, adjoining Los Angeles County. Building on his coauthored volume, *Postsuburban California: The Transformation of Orange County Since World War II* (1991; paperback ed., 1995), Olin analyzes the political impact of the vast economic and technological changes wrought by the new system. The increasing mobility of capital within a global market economy, as it becomes easier to shift investment from domestic to foreign sites, has increased corporate power at the expense of local government's capacity to control regional development. In Orange County, as elsewhere, this tension between "placeless power and powerless places" has resulted in the rise of popular struggles over growth and the quality of life, which Olin calls "the politics of locality."

The Origins and Business Culture of Silicon Valley

ANNALEE SAXENIAN

Silicon Valley's origins are typically traced to the founding of the Hewlett-Packard Company (HP) in 1937. The small Palo Alto garage where two Stanford graduate students started an electronics instrumentation business has become a Silicon Valley landmark. The legend surrounding the company's origins captures the key elements of the region's ascent, particularly the distinctive role played by Stanford University and the value placed on entrepreneurship.

Frederick Terman, who moved to Stanford to become an electrical engineering professor after his graduation from MIT [Massachusetts Institute of Technology], encouraged his graduate students William Hewlett and David Packard to commercialize an audio-oscillator that Hewlett had designed while working on his master's thesis. In fact, he lent Hewlett and Packard $538 to start producing the machine, he helped them find work to finance their initial experiments, and he arranged a loan from a Palo Alto bank which allowed them to begin commercial production. This episode foreshadowed Stanford's active role in the Silicon Valley economy.

HP's fortunes, like those of many of its East Coast counterparts, were shaped by the war [World War II]. Although the firm's first major sale was a contract for eight audio-oscillators for the Walt Disney studios, HP took off during the war. Military contracts for its electronic measuring devices and receivers that were used to detect and analyze enemy radar signals boosted sales from $37,000 in 1941 to over $750,000 in 1945. Yet these were minuscule sums relative to those garnered by the established East Coast producers such as Raytheon. With only 130 employees, HP was dwarfed by GE, RCA, Westinghouse, and Raytheon, each of which employed thousands.

A small cluster of prewar technology firms—many actively encouraged and supported by Stanford's Terman—grew up alongside HP to provide a foundation for the region's emerging electronics industry. Charles Litton, a Stanford graduate, founded Litton Engineering Laboratories in 1932 to produce glass vacuum tubes. During the war it was the nation's leading source of glass-forming machinery, and subsequently it became Litton Industries, a major manufacturer of military electronics systems. When brothers Sigurd and Russell Varian invented the klystron, a flexible microwave receiver and transmitter, at Stanford in the late 1930s, the university gave them $100 of materials and free use of its physics laboratory in exchange for a 50 percent interest in any resulting patents for applications of the technology. Their klystron tube became central to U.S. antiaircraft and antisubmarine radar during the war, and in 1948 the brothers formed Varian Associates, which became a major electronic instrumentation manufacturer.

The early commercial successes of firms such as HP, Litton, and Varian consolidated Northern California's position as an emerging center of electronics production. There were, to be sure, antecedents. A handful of fledgling hydroelectric power and electrical firms had located in the Bay Area in the early twentieth century. However, the scale of industrial activity was insignificant compared to that of the Boston area at the time. In fact, some of the region's leading companies moved east during the 1930s when radio became a national medium.

As it had for Boston, the Second World War marked a turning point for the Santa Clara Valley. The war attracted large numbers of people in war-related industries in the San Francisco Bay area. Santa Clara County was well positioned to take advantage of this growth; it was convenient to military installations and industrial centers in Richmond, Oakland, and San Francisco, the gateway to the Pacific theater. The Moffett Field Naval Air Station alone drew thousands of military personnel. Local industry, from vegetable canneries to electronics companies, geared up for war production.

While the military demand dramatically improved the fortunes of Northern California firms, the government awarded the majority of the wartime military electronics contracts to large East Coast companies. The West Coast Electronics Manufacturers Association (WCEMA) was formed in 1943 in response to an announcement by the War Production Board of a drastic cutback in the contracts to West Coast firms. The twenty-five California electronics manufacturers (thirteen from the north, twelve from the south) that formed this forerunner of the American Electronics Association sought to promote their industry, particularly by lobbying for a share of the defense contracts that were going to eastern companies.

After the war, Terman intensified his efforts to promote the development of the region's base of technology and industry. He left his faculty position at Stanford in the early 1940s to take up a wartime post as director of Harvard's Radio Research Laboratory, and returned to Stanford in 1946 as Dean of Engineering. Terman's experience in the East had exposed him to military electronics research and convinced him of the weaknesses of West Coast industry and universities. Not only was there little industry on the San Francisco peninsula, but, in Terman's words: "Stanford emerged from World War II as an underprivileged institution. It had not been significantly involved in any of the exciting engineering and scientific activities associated with the war." Impressed by the technological dynamism of the Boston area and determined to stop the loss of his best students to the East, Terman dedicated himself to developing Stanford and local business in tandem. . . .

Although the region's industrial base remained small relative to its East Coast counterpart throughout the 1950s, it grew rapidly. WCEMA moved its headquarters from Los Angeles to Palo Alto in 1964 in recognition of the emerging center of technical activity in Northern California. By the late 1960s Santa Clara County was recognized as a center of aerospace and electronics activity. Its most explosive growth, however, was driven by the emergence of an industry that had not even existed until 1951.

The Santa Clara Valley was dubbed Silicon Valley in the early 1970s after the main ingredient in the semiconductor. The industry had taken root in California with the location of Shockley Transistor in Palo Alto in 1955. By 1970 it was the largest and most dynamic sector of the regional economy and Santa Clara had established itself as the nation's leading center of semiconductor innovation and production, surpassing even the early industry cluster around Route 128 [in Massachusetts]. . . .

Military and aerospace markets accounted for a diminishing share of the semiconductor business as the growth of the computer industry fueled demand for transistors and integrated circuits. Government purchases, which had accounted for half of total semiconductor shipments during the 1960s, dropped to only 12 percent in 1972, and continued to fall throughout the decade. Silicon Valley, never as dependent on defense markets as Route 128, thus managed to achieve a gradual transition to commercial production during the 1960s and 1970s.

Venture capital replaced the military as the leading source of financing for Silicon Valley start-ups by the early 1970s. Independent investors, encouraged by the favorable tax treatment of investments in small businesses, established SBICs [Small Business Investment Corporations] and partnerships in California during the 1950s and 1960s. The growth of the venture capital business mirrored that of the local semiconductor industry, as successful entrepreneurs chose to reinvest their earnings in promising new companies. By 1974 the region was home to more than 150 active venture capitalists. Stanford University—in marked contrast to MIT—also regularly invested a portion of its endowment in venture activities. . . .

The early entrepreneurs of Silicon Valley saw themselves as the pioneers of a new industry in a new region. They were at once forging a new industrial settlement in the West and advancing the development of a revolutionary new technology, semiconductor electronics. The shared challenges of exploring uncharted technological terrain shaped their view of themselves and their emerging community.

This collective identity was strengthened by the homogeneity of Silicon Valley's founders. Virtually all were white men; most were in their early twenties. Many had studied engineering at Stanford or MIT, and most had no industrial experience. None had roots in the region; a surprising number of the community's major figures had grown up in small towns in the Midwest and shared a distrust for established East Coast institutions and attitudes. They repeatedly expressed their opposition to "established" or "old-line" industry and the "Eastern establishment."

As newcomers to a region that lacked prior industrial traditions, Silicon Valley's pioneers had the freedom to experiment with institutions and organizational forms as well as with technology. Having left behind families, friends, and established communities, these young men were unusually open to risk-taking and experimentation. . . .

Silicon Valley was quickly distinguished by unusually high levels of job-hopping. During the 1970s, average annual employee turnover exceeded 35 percent in local electronics firms and was as high as 59 percent in small firms. It was rare for a technical professional in Silicon Valley to have a career in a single company. An anthropologist studying the career paths of the region's computer professionals concluded that job tenures in Silicon Valley averaged two years. One engineer explained: "Two or three years is about max (at a job) for the Valley because there's always something more interesting across the street. You don't see someone staying twenty years at a job here. If they've been in a small company with 200 to 300 people for 10 or 11 years you tend to wonder about them. We see those types coming in from the East Coast." . . .

Although many Silicon Valley entrepreneurs became millionaires, most appear to have been motivated less by money than by the challenge of independently pursuing a new technological opportunity. The culture of the Valley accorded the highest regard to those who started firms; status was defined less by economic success than by technological achievement. The elegantly designed chip, the breakthrough manufacturing process, or the ingenious application was admired as much as the trappings of wealth—and the emerging electronics industry offered manifold opportunities for such accomplishments.

The region's culture encouraged risk and accepted failure. An entrepreneur who moved to Silicon Valley from Route 128 to start a computer company describes this culture: "Start-ups here tend to move very fast. The culture of the Valley is a culture of change: the peer pressures and social pressures support risk-taking and people changing jobs a lot. The velocity of information is very high—much higher than the rest of the country. Rapid change is the norm. That's exactly what's needed for start-ups." The founder of a semiconductor equipment and fabrication consulting business based in Silicon Valley reports that it took him only six days to finance his company. This was possible in part because of professional networks that extended back to his days at Fairchild [Semiconductor Corporation], and in part because of the willingness of the region's venture capitalists to move very rapidly on promising opportunities.

Not only was risk-taking glorified, but failure was socially acceptable. There was a shared understanding that anyone could be a successful entrepreneur: there were no boundaries of age, status, or social stratum that precluded the possibility of a new beginning; and there was little embarrassment or shame associated with business failure. In fact, the list of individuals who failed, even repeatedly, only to succeed later, was well known within the region.

New ventures were typically started by engineers who had acquired operating experience and technical skills working in other firms in the region. The archetypical Silicon Valley start-up was formed by a group of friends and/or former colleagues with an innovative idea that they could not realize in their current workplace. They drew up a business plan, sought funding and advice from local venture capitalists (often former engineers and entrepreneurs themselves), and relied on an expanding circle of university researchers, consultants, and specialized suppliers for additional assistance in starting the new enterprise. . . .

Without fully recognizing the consequences, Silicon Valley's pioneers were creating the foundations of a decentralized industrial system that blurred the boundaries between social life and work, between firms, between firms and local institutions, and between managers and workers. This model, though hardly universal even in Silicon Valley, has influenced the organization and workplace practices in many other industries faced with rapid changes in markets and technology.

Paradoxically, however, while the region's engineers saw themselves as different from the rest of American business, they failed to recognize the importance of the networks they had created. Silicon Valley's entrepreneurs failed to recognize the connection between the institutions they had built and their commercial success. They saw themselves as the world did, as a new breed of technological pioneers, and they viewed their successes as independent of the region and its relationships.

What appeared to both the actors and the outside world to be the outcome of individual entrepreneurial achievement and competitive markets was in fact the result of a complex, highly social process rooted in an industrial community. While they competed fiercely, Silicon Valley's producers were embedded in, and inseparable from, these social and technical networks.

Lacking a language to describe this unusual mix of cooperation and competition, they saw themselves through the lens of American individualism. They attributed their spectacular growth and unchallenged dominance of world markets to individual technical prowess and entrepreneurial risk-taking. Just as the vocabulary of rugged individualism, entrepreneurship, and free markets blinded Silicon Valley's engineers to the institutional and social underpinnings of their industrial strength, it also left them unable to ensure their own survival. Assuming that the dynamism of free markets would be self-perpetuating and self-governing, they saw no need to attend to the institutional foundations of their vitality. This lack of self-understanding would lead them to make choices that would threaten the long-term dynamism of the industrial region they had created.

Women, Families, and Work in the Information Industry

JUDITH STACEY

During the 1960s and 1970s, while many urban industrial areas in the United States began to decline, Santa Clara County enjoyed spectacular economic growth. Between 1960 and 1975 county employment grew by 156 percent, three times the national rate, as local manufacturing jobs increased to 130,000 and auxiliary employment in construction and services expanded apace. The electronics industry provided jobs for almost one

---

Excerpts from *Brave New Families: Stories of Domestic Upheaval in Late Twentieth Century America* by Judith Stacey. Copyright © 1990 by Judith Stacey. Reprinted by permission of Basic Books, a division of HarperCollins Publishers, Inc.

of every three county workers, and it generated most of the construction and service needs that employed the majority of the rest. In those heady days, the media and even some scholars portrayed the Silicon Valley as a true-life American fairy tale, and few were the voices raised, or heard, in dissent. The Mecca of the new technological entrepreneurs, its worshippers proclaimed, was a sunny land where factories resembled college campuses, where skilled, safe, and challenging work was replacing the monotonous, degrading, dangerous labors of the now-declining industries, and where American technical know-how and entrepreneurial spirit once again would rescue the flagging U.S. economy and better the lives of all.

An unusually high proportion (25 percent) of the electronics industry did consist of the most highly educated and highly paid salaried employees in any U.S. industry—engineers and professionals employed in research and design. Along with those heralded health clubs and fitness tracks, they were offered exceptional challenges and economic opportunities. As in "traditional" industries, however, the vast majority of these most privileged employees were white men (89 percent males, 89 percent non-Hispanic whites). During those start-up years in the 1950s and 1960s the industry also employed white men in most of its production jobs where they too enjoyed unusual opportunities. Even those with very limited schooling could advance into technical ranks, particularly those whom the military had first trained in mechanics before depositing them conveniently in nearby bases.

But as the electronics industry matured, it feminized (and minoritized) its work force, turning increasingly to female, ethnic minority, and recent migrant workers to fill production positions that offered far fewer advancement opportunities. By the late 1970s the industry's occupational structure was crudely stratified by gender as well as by race and ethnicity. White men were at the top, white women and ethnic minorities at the bottom. Almost half the employees were assembly workers and operatives; three-fourths of these were women, and 40 percent were minorities. Two groups of workers made up the middle: the moderately well-paid technicians and craft workers, also primarily Anglo males but into whose ranks women and Asians were making some inroads, and the clerical work force composed overwhelmingly of Anglo women. These middle-income jobs were declining, however; in Silicon Valley as elsewhere in postindustrial America, growth of new jobs is at the top and the bottom. The preferred labor pool for the bottom continued to grow here during the 1980s as the proportion of nonwhite county residents increased dramatically.

The popular media image of egalitarian and innovative work relations symbolized by engineers in blue jeans at computers in open cubicles masks the startlingly unequal, far-from-innovative working conditions with which the industry's production workers contend. Electronics remains the only nonunionized major industry in the United States, and its production workers earn lower wages and endure greater risks and hardships than do their counterparts in most "traditional" industries. In 1981, for example, electronics workers earned an average wage only 57 percent of that paid to auto and steel workers, despite the mandatory wage concessions extracted from the latter. Ironically, the "clean rooms" in which many electronics workers toil are filled with highly toxic solvents. Almost half of the occupational illness cases reported among semiconductor workers involve systemic poisoning from toxic materials, and the rate of occupational illness in electronics production in California is three times as great as in other manufacturing occupations. Many electronics firms operate around the clock and require production workers to accept night and weekend shifts as well as long and highly irregular schedules. Yet they offer workers no job security and subject them to frequent, sudden layoffs and forced vacations.

In 1974 the first major slump in the electronics industry signaled its inherent volatility. Dependent on defense contracts and highly turbulent global market conditions, the industry's boom-bust cycle and the high failure rate of firms promised recurrent unemployment. Corporate strategists began to ship many production jobs to cheaper labor areas in the United States and abroad and to replace "permanent" workers with a flexible fleet of what soon became the highest concentration of "temporary" workers in the nation—workers, that is, who lack all employee benefits.

By . . . 1984, "Silicon Valley fever" had begun to subside as most county residents directly or indirectly suffered ill effects of the electronics industry's previously concealed "downside." Increasing numbers of residents were out of work, and the entry-level work available promised few prospects for a family wage. Local unemployment rates rose in the 1980s, escalating sharply during the industry's severe prolonged slump in 1984 and 1985. Even after that recession had bottomed out, untrained, entry-level workers found that their best employment prospects were not in the electronics industry but as hotel housekeepers and security guards.

Employed and unemployed alike suffered from the industry's destruction of their once-bucolic environment. As cancer rates and birth defects in the county rose alarmingly, outraged residents discovered that their water supplies had been contaminated by more than one hundred industrial chemicals that were known or suspected to be carcinogens, mutagens, or teratogens. Air pollution and nightmarish traffic, predictable products of the region's decades of untrammeled, unplanned development, destroyed the celebrated quality of life that had once enticed so many to the fabled region. And yet the cost of living rose as sharply as the quality of life declined. This was not an anomaly; rather, as urban analyst Annalee [*sic*] Saxenian has demonstrated, it is a case of chickens fed by the industry's stratified employment policies now come home to roost. The skewed salaries that the industry paid its sizable professional and managerial elite raised local housing costs to among the highest in the nation, beyond the reach of its underpaid, often underemployed production workers. The local media began to treat its audiences to the embarrassing spectacle of mounting homelessness in the land of affluence. Most of the new homeless, moreover, were family units.

Local and national media became more consistently preoccupied with the escalating narcotics problems of the postindustrial era, and here too the

Silicon Valley gave cause for grave alarm. Illegal drug use in the county seat cost its residents $500 million annually, and the region gained an unenviable reputation as the state capital for the use of PCP, a potent animal tranquilizer that induces behavior so violent that local police identify it as "the single highest cause of officer injury in this department." The federal Drug Enforcement Agency identified Silicon Valley as "one of the biggest cocaine users in the United States." Drug dealing offered an irresistible occupational alternative to mounting legions of unemployed youth. Indeed the electronics industry offered many workers on-the-job training in drug dependency, as foremen and coworkers distributed drugs to sustain workers through the monotony and stress of lengthy shifts and speedups. More than 35 percent of the electronics employees surveyed by the *San Jose Mercury News* in 1985 acknowledged using illicit drugs on the job. In 1988 the county Board of Supervisors and the San Jose City Council approved higher bail and longer jail sentences for dealers as they passed a resolution introduced by a coalition of local church groups stating that "drugs represent a severe health epidemic which is destroying the lives of our families and the future of our community."

Such regional maladies may have failed to shake the faith of some high-tech devotees, . . . but in the 1980s more people declared themselves eager to leave than to enter the South Bay futureland. Population growth in Santa Clara County slowed considerably after 1980, falling below California rates. As the decade neared its close, a Bay area poll found the once-glorified Silicon Valley to be the least popular county in the region. Almost half the county residents queried claimed they would prefer to live somewhere else. It was a twist of cruel irony, therefore, when in 1989 Hewlett-Packard—the area's preeminent high-tech firm, credited by many with creating the Silicon Valley—cited the region's spiraling cost of living as the basis for its decision to move 10 percent of its computer manufacturing operations to a less-populated California valley.

While the changing character of work in the Silicon Valley commanded global attention, most outside observers overlooked concurrent gender and family changes that preoccupied many residents. In earlier, self-congratulatory days, before the national political climate made feminism seem a derogatory term, local public officials liked to describe San Jose, the county seat, as a feminist capital. The city elected a feminist mayor and hosted the statewide National Organization of Women convention in 1974. Santa Clara soon became one of the few counties in the nation that could boast of having elected a female majority to its Board of Supervisors. In 1981 high levels of feminist activism made San Jose the site of the nation's first successful strike for a comparable worth standard of pay for city employees. And, according to sociologist Karen Hossfeld, young working-class women who vehemently rejected a feminist identity took for granted women's rights to political and economic equality and to control their own sexuality.

It should come as no surprise, therefore, that during these postindustrializing decades the Silicon Valley has also been the site of a significant degree of family turbulence. Much of the data on local family changes represent an exaggeration of . . . national trends. . . . For example, while the national divorce rate was doubling after 1960, in Santa Clara County it nearly tripled. By 1977 more county residents filed divorce papers than registered marriages. By 1980 the divorce rate in the county seat ranked ninth among U.S. metropolitan areas, higher than Los Angeles or San Francisco. Likewise the percentage of "nonfamily households" grew faster in the Silicon Valley than in the nation, and abortion rates were one and one-half times the national figures. And although the percentage of single-parent households was not quite as high as it was in the nation as a whole, the rate of increase was more rapid. The high marriage casualty rate among workaholic engineers was dubbed "the silicon syndrome." County social workers and residents . . . shared an alarmist view of the fate of family life in their locale summarized in the opening lines of a feature article in a local university magazine: "There is an endangered species in Silicon Valley, one so precious that when it disappears Silicon Valley will die with it. This endangered species is the family. And sometimes it seems as if every institution in this valley—political, corporate, and social—is hellbent on driving it into extinction."

These concurrent changes in occupational, gender, and family patterns make the Silicon Valley a propitious site for exploring the ways in which "ordinary" working people have been remaking their families in the wake of postindustrial and feminist challenges. The Silicon Valley is by no means a typical or "representative" U.S. location, but precisely because national postindustrial work and family transformations were more condensed, rapid, and exaggerated there than elsewhere, they should be easier to perceive. Yet most popular and scholarly literature about white working-class people portrays them as the most traditional, as the last bastion, that is, of the modern family. Relatively privileged members of the white working class are widely regarded as the bulwark of the Reagan revolution and the constituency least sympathetic to feminism and family reforms. Those whose hold on the accoutrements of the American Dream is so recent and tenuous, it is thought, have the strongest incentives to defend it. Curiously, however, few scholars have published book-length, in-depth studies of such families in recent years.

Conventional images of progressive, middle-class families embracing egalitarian changes in gender and work patterns that "traditional"—that is to say, "modern"—working-class families resentfully resist fail to recognize the complexity, fluidity, and unresolved character of contemporary gender, class, and family arrangements. Only ethnographic research . . . can capture this complexity sufficiently to dispel distortions in the popular clichés. Based on such research, *Brave New Families* narrates stories about working-class gender relations and kinship strategies that are as creative, flexible, and postmodern as those among the most innovative strata of the middle classes. Indeed, working people . . . have served as the unrecognized pioneers of the postmodern family revolution. . . .

Recent books with such titles as *Falling from Grace* and *Fear of Falling* convey widespread suffering and anxiety among once-settled, middle-class Americans. And Americans, as historian Linda Gordon noted, recurrently frame social anxieties in familial terms. Sociologists may attempt to reassure an anxious populace that family life is "here to stay," but, as political analyst Andrew Hacker once observed, "it is hardly news that families are not what they used to be." The modern family system has lost the cultural and statistical dominance it long enjoyed, and no new family order has arisen to supplant it. The postmodern family is a site of disorder instead, a contested domain.

The passionate public response to the Moynihan report of the 1960s signaled a prolonged era of national conflict and confusion over which gender and kinship relationships are to count as "families" in postindustrial America. And in this family quarrel, gender and sexual politics occupy pride of place. Which relationships between and among women and men will receive legal recognition, social legitimacy, institutional and cultural support? In the postmodern period, a truly democratic gender and kinship order, one that does not favor male authority, heterosexuality, a particular division of labor, or a singular household or parenting arrangement became thinkable for the first time in history. And during the past several decades, family visionaries and reformers have been organizing struggles to bring it to fruition. They have met, however, with fierce resistance, and, as feminists have learned with great pain, it is not men alone who resist.

Why do many people of both genders recoil from the prospect of a fully democratic family regime? While there are multiple motives, including theological ones, this book suggests compelling sociological sources of popular ambivalence about family reform. Not only would a democratic kinship system threaten vested gender and class interests, but even under the most benevolent of social orders, it promises also to bring its own kind of costs. A fully voluntary marriage system, as this century's experience with divorce rates indicates, . . . institutionalizes conjugal and thus parental instability. A normless gender order, one in which parenting arrangements, sexuality, and the distribution of work, responsibility, and resources all are negotiable and constantly renegotiable, can also invite considerable conflict and insecurity. These inescapable "burdens of freedom" have been magnified monstrously, however, under the far-from-benevolent social conditions of this turbulent, conservative period.

Many men, African-American men most of all, have suffered from postindustrialization and the eroding modern family order, while, thanks to feminism, numerous women, particularly white, middle-class ones have achieved substantial gains. The resilient gender inequality of the transitional period, however, places the vast majority of women at disproportionate risk. In exchange for subordination and domestic service, the modern family promised women a number of customary protections and privileges, principal among these, lifelong support from a male breadwinner. Scarcely had working-class women . . . achieved access to this "patriarchal bargain," however, before it collapsed in a postindustrial deluge. With few social protections provided to replace the precarious "private" ones that the modern family once offered, many women have found good cause to mistrust the terms postmodern conditions appear to offer in its place. Women have been adding the burdens and benefits of paid labor to their historic domestic responsibilities, but men seem less eager to share the responsibilities and rewards of child rearing and housework. Moreover, as feminists have demonstrated in depressing detail, women have suffered numerous unexpected, and disturbing, consequences of egalitarian family reforms, such as no-fault divorce, joint custody provisions, shared parenting, and sexual liberation. Consequently, as Deirdre English, former editor of *Mother Jones* once observed, many women have come to "fear that feminism will free men first."

The insecure and undemocratic character of postmodern family life fuels nostalgia for the fading modern family, now recast as the "traditional" family. Capitalizing on this nostalgia, a vigorous, antifeminist "profamily" movement was able to score impressive political victories in the 1980s. It successfully, if incorrectly, identified feminism as the primary cause of the demise of the modern family, rather than the mopping-up operation for postindustrial transformations that were long underway. Defining the ERA and abortion rights as threats to the family, it placed feminists in the same defensive posture that housewives had come to assume. And partly because the profamily movement could draw on the volunteer labors of the disproportionate numbers of housewives it attracted to its political ranks, the backlash movement was able to achieve political visibility and victories far in excess of its numerical strength. Former President Reagan assured this movement a profound and lasting political legacy by rewarding its contribution to his "revolution" with antifeminist appointments to the Supreme Court and the federal judiciary who promise to inhibit the progress of democratic family reform well into the twenty-first century.

Many feminists . . . were caught off guard by the retreat from feminist activism and the resurgence of profamilialism that characterized the 1980s. During the 1970s family instability seemed to swell the ranks of the women's liberation movement. Feminist ideology, disseminated not only by the media but in flourishing grass-roots community activities and women's reentry programs, served women . . . well to ease the exit from, or the reform of, unhappy modern marriages. Even older women in successful long-term marriages . . . employed feminist principles to improve their relationships. Second-wave feminism also supported women's efforts to develop independent work lives and career goals. With high divorce rates and women's paid work continuing throughout the eighties, feminist activism and family reforms might have been expected to progress apace.

Yet optimistic projections like these did not reckon with the ravages of postindustrialism. Neither feminism nor the other progressive family reform movements have been as useful in addressing the structural inequalities of postindustrial occupational structure or the individualist, fast-track culture that makes all too difficult the formation of stable intimate relations on a democratic, or any other basis. In these circumstances, many have sought support for troubled family relationships from organized religion, particularly from fundamentalist varieties.

The unsettling conditions of postindustrial society and the global economy seem to have intensified cravings for security and spirituality. The ensuing retreat from rationalism and secularism has fueled an unanticipated resurgence of fundamentalist religious revivalism worldwide. It has been challenging and painful for feminists to understand why women even more than men are drawn to such movements. Why do women who have been exposed to feminist ideas voluntarily embrace an ideology of male headship and female submission, often attempting . . . to convert their more secular husbands? For, at least in postindustrial America, although male supremacy is alive and well, participation in a formally patriarchal marriage is a woman's choice. The social and material conditions that underwrote the modern family—the family many fundamentalists erroneously portray as the biblical family—are long gone. As a recent ethnography of a fundamentalist community notes, no fundamentalist husband today can dominate a wife who does not choose to submit. . . .

Freed from the restrictions and protections of the modern family system, women remain institutionally disadvantaged. From that position, however, we make our own choices and develop our own strategies, including patriarchal marriage and religious orthodoxy. Although the nominal ideologies of contemporary revivalist religious movements are patriarchal, many, like Global Ministries, enable women actively to reshape family life in postmodern and postfeminist directions. Generated partly as a backlash against feminism, postfeminist evangelical gender ideology also selectively incorporates many feminist family reforms. There are parallel tendencies within revivalist Orthodox Judaism. "There's nothing in Judaism that says men and women can't share household responsibilities, that a man can't change a baby, or that a woman can't work," an Orthodox rabbi . . . reassures his class of recent converts, the majority of whom are single women. Although we may feel troubled by its character, secular and religious feminists alike, I believe, can take credit for the extraordinary impact our ideological influence has had on even this most unlikely of constituencies.

Globalization and the Politics of Locality in Orange County

SPENCER C. OLIN

For the past several decades, the American economy has been experiencing both internal restructuring and globalization. That is to say, the economy has been transformed domestically away from its manufacturing base toward the service and information sectors, while being integrated into an international market system. In this expanding global economy, capital and

Excerpted from Spencer C. Olin, "Globalization and the Politics of Locality in Orange County, California in the Cold War Era," *Western Historical Quarterly,* 22, May 1991: pp. 143–148, 153–158, 160–161. Copyright © 1991 by Western History Association. Reprinted by permission.

technology have become increasingly mobile, sharply limiting the ability of local governments to control the use of space.

This article seeks to explain the *political* impact of such profound economic and technological transformations on relatively affluent and privileged regions whose economies are globally integrated. In such regions, the old realities of local place and local tradition have been supplanted by the new realities of footloose capital and information technology. Tensions and conflicts have emerged between proponents of the new global system and those forces seeking to preserve and protect locality. Indeed, the idea of locality has assumed a heightened political importance in contemporary America. What are these new global forces, and in what ways has insurgency against them been expressed? After some general observations, this study focuses on Orange County, California, a leading participant in such changes. In other words, it examines smaller-scale effects of large-scale changes in a local setting.

To be sure, there have been repeated instances throughout western American history of resistance to the impact of capitalist transformation on specific localities. As Rodman Paul, Michael Malone, and William Robbins, among others, have reminded us, until the Second World War the economy of the West was most accurately described in colonial terms, in the sense that its valuable resources were continually exploited and appropriated by eastern capitalists and manufacturers. This was especially true of extractive industries (gold, coal, oil, and timber) in such states as Colorado, Idaho, Montana, Oregon, Utah, and Wyoming.

In the mid-1980s, Gerald Nash joined others in claiming that the experience of World War II had fundamentally altered the American West by liberating it from its previous subservience to the East: "In World War II Americans transformed the West to a more mature stage, one in which it began to shed its colonial status. . . ." Enormous military-related expenditures by the federal government during and immediately following that war, Nash argued, helped propel the West toward increased economic self-sufficiency.

William Robbins has disputed the transformative impact of that war on the West's economy, pointing especially to the experience of much of the Intermountain West and arguing that "old relations and patterns have persisted to a remarkable degree." Michael Malone would seem to agree with this emphasis on continuity, writing in moving terms about how foreign competition devastated the western mining industry in the 1970s, thereby exemplifying "the ever increasing integration of the western economy into the global economy. . . ." In the case of Wyoming, as well, the old colonial theme remained relevant well after World War II, as the collapse of oil profits there in the 1980s caused one economist to refer to that state as "a Third World energy colony."

Not even California has been exempted from this continuing dependency on outside capital, although its status is somewhat more ambivalent. Despite its position "as the geopolitical power center of the American West," Robbins nonetheless stresses California's heavy reliance on federal defense spending beginning with the Second World War and continuing throughout the Cold War. This relationship has severely compromised any sense of economic independence. Yet, while California's economy has been heavily subsidized for many years, it also functions as a major marketplace for tributary provinces in the hinterlands of the American West. . . .

[W]ithin California, Orange County has shared elements of this ambivalent status. Like the state of which it is a part, it too has experienced many years of economic expansion. Yet, until recently it was also, to a large extent, dependent on massive federal military expenditures (a fact that is strikingly at odds with its laissez faire political culture). In political terms, furthermore, its many cities have been struggling to exercise control over their own destinies in the face of economic globalization. We need to understand Orange County, therefore, in its national and international contexts, to determine the extent to which "old relations and patterns" have persisted or changed.

The aforementioned internal economic restructuring of the United States in recent decades has involved what many economists and urban geographers refer to as "sectoral recomposition." The industrial sector (including manufacturing, mining, and agriculture), for example, recently has been surpassed by the services category (including retail trade, health care, and producer services such as finance, real estate, and computer software). Due largely to declines in such key industrial areas as the automobile and steel industries, civilian aircraft construction, and the construction materials industry, the overall contributions of manufacturing to the total production of goods and services in the United States dropped from 30 percent in 1960 to 24 percent in 1980. Such changes, in turn, have had dramatic spatial consequences, accelerating the internal migration of capital and population from the manufacturing centers of the Northeast and Midwest to the South and Southwest, including most especially California.

One major cause of this profound economic restructuring is the growing importance of the military as a consumer of manufacturing output. Military requirements have resulted in increasing government domination of America's innovative process in the form of federal funding for research and development. The bulk of these expenditures is allocated for electronics, new synthetic materials, and sophisticated communications systems, the production of which, for military purposes, has provided the basic impetus for the postwar high-tech revolution. In the years since World War II, those industrial firms receiving Department of Defense contracts have located primarily in the suburban areas of southern and western states, not in the industrial heartland of America.

Such military-related suburbs have come to constitute a kind of high-tech, intensive defense perimeter within the United States. According to Ann Markusen, a leading student of this process, the defense perimeter "encompasses much of the Intermountain West as well as the Pacific Coast. . . ." Regionally, the Pacific region garnered most military expenditures per capita from the 1960s through the 1980s. And within this Pacific region,

California, in 1988, received more military/defense payroll and pension dollars than any other state.

In sum, massive military expenditures have spurred a major spatial shift in manufacturing production to the so-called defense perimeter. In this manner, the federal government, by means of its military budget and locational preferences, has promoted uneven regional development. In 1987, for example, the gap between the nation's richest and poorest regions continued to widen. Metropolitan regions in the defense perimeter (such as San Jose and Anaheim-Santa Ana in California) ranked in the top ten in per capita personal income, while the lowest-ranked regions were concentrated in the oil-producing states, primarily Texas.

At the center of these processes of economic structuring and spatial shifts is the information sector, which includes both information technologies (the hardware part) and the use of advanced information systems (the software part). The spatial consequences of these information technologies and systems deserve more attention from historians than they have received. Introduction of these new technologies in manufacturing and service sectors, for example, directly affects where businesses choose to locate—since it reduces the need for spatial proximity. Because of improved communication, according to Lionel Nicol, "economic activities that are functionally interdependent can operate efficiently despite increasing spatial dispersion. . . ."

Urban geographers Jeffrey Henderson and Manuel Castells claim that these new telecommunication technologies "are the electronic highways of the information age, equivalent to the role played by the railway systems in the process of industrialization." What is needed, according to some observers, is a "regional economics of information" designed to assess the relationship between existing information technologies and systems, on the one hand, and the economic development of regions, on the other. As two British students of this process, John Goddard and Andrew Gillespie, conclude, developments in the information economy "are likely, without policy intervention, to exacerbate geographical divisions and to make worse geographical disparities in economic well-being. . . ." The wealth of regions now largely depends on the wealth of information within those regions.

As mentioned, a leading participant in all of these processes—economic restructuring, the militarization of production, spatial transformation, the presence of information technologies and systems, and the internationalization of its regional economy—is Orange County in southern California. During the Cold War era, that county evolved rapidly from a predominantly agricultural area into, first, an industrial region and bedroom adjunct to Los Angeles and, currently, into a sprawling metropolis consisting of twenty-eight separate municipalities with a dynamic, diversified regional economy. During that era, as well, its population multiplied by a factor of ten, from two hundred thousand in 1950 to more than two million by 1987.

Beginning in the 1950s and 1960s, then, Orange County became an increasingly important component of a larger southern California region comprised of Los Angeles, Ventura, San Bernardino, Riverside, and Orange counties. During the Cold War era, this larger region was one of the major industrial metropolises in the world. Orange County's economy has become more and more powerful, exceeding $64 billion in 1989 and now ranking as this nation's tenth largest county economy. Indeed, as urban geographer Allen Scott has concluded in an empirically rich economic analysis of the region, Orange County's "extraordinarily powerful engines of growth have driven it forward to become one of the most important and highly developed production centers in the American industrial system today." . . .

Some regions historically dependent on military spending have made a successful transition to more diversified economic activity. Such is the case with Orange County, which has epitomized the shift from an industrial goods- to a service- and information-orientation. As we have seen, manufacturing, largely in aerospace-defense, was the key to Orange County's transformation, in the 1960s, from an agricultural to an industrial economy. As the 1970s progressed, however, gains in the aerospace-defense industry were matched, and even surpassed, by less cyclical and more stable areas. In 1973, for example, the major employment growth sectors were finance, insurance, real estate, trade, and services, and there was also continued expansion in state and local government employment. According to Allen Scott, while communications equipment was still the major industrial employer in the late 1970s and early 1980s, its relative weight in the overall Orange County economy had sharply declined. After the mid-1970s, therefore, the region's labor force worked primarily in the information sector, composed of those occupations in which the processing and distribution of information is a central and time-consuming activity. Indeed, it can be argued that Orange County exemplified a new stage of economic development referred to by some as "information capitalism."

Furthermore, by the late 1970s, as international trade assumed major importance in Orange County, its economy became more tightly integrated into the global market system. Nearly 25 percent of county-based firms were, by then, involved in overseas commerce and a large proportion were controlled from outside the region. By means of information technologies, they were tied into a wide-ranging international network of linkages and subcontract relations. . . .

A heavy stream of federal expenditures, foreign investments, and global economic ventures by banking, financial, and multinational corporations thus helped shape the economic and spatial organization of Orange County during the years after World War II. These economic changes also transformed the county's political life. The decade of the 1980s, especially, witnessed intense conflicts between multinational growth strategies, on the one hand, and local forces seeking to increase their political clout and preserve the "quality of life," on the other. There were, in other words, increasing tensions between the global nature of contemporary economic life and the more restricted territorial concerns of local politicians and social activists.

In Orange County, as in other relatively affluent, economically advanced regions, therefore, the new political dynamics of the late twentieth century emerged from the growing contradiction between what Henderson and Castells refer to as "placeless power and powerless places." Not only are we now faced with the increased mobility of capital, but also with the diminished capacity of government to control the forces of development. This has led one observer to conclude that "the cities of the world have been reduced to disposable commodities in an increasingly globalized economy characterized by a fluid movement of capital seeking profit."

The lobbying organization most actively representing the interests of global capital in Orange County during much of the Cold War era has been the Industrial League of Orange County (ILOC). Formed in 1970 as the Greater Irvine Industrial League, it was designed from the outset to promote coordination among representatives of national and international capital and to present a unified position with regard to such growth-related issues as transportation, water, and waste disposal. Because the interests of the organization's member firms soon grew to be much broader than merely the Irvine area, the Greater Irvine Industrial League went countywide and, in 1982, was renamed the Industrial League of Orange County. Within five years, its membership had grown to 800 companies that employed more than 130,000 workers.

The industrial league's composition and focus were different from those of local chambers of commerce, which were usually comprised of owners and middle-level managers of small firms. The ILOC was controlled by senior-level executives and chief executive officers of the county's major corporations. Furthermore, its interests and goals were predominantly regional and statewide, not municipal. Accordingly, it directed its lobbying efforts at the county board of supervisors, the state legislature, and various state agencies, not at local city councils. In so doing it brought to bear the power and prestige of the large firms that comprised its core, such as the Irvine Company, the Fluor Corporation, First International Bank, and the aerospace-defense giants Rockwell International, Northrop, and Hughes Aircraft.

This impressive exercise of political power by representatives of military-related industries and international corporations, and a growing sense of powerlessness at the local level, led, during the 1980s, to a counterreaction in the form of widespread grass roots activism. Numerous organizations arose throughout the Orange County region seeking to reclaim space and to recapture political control of their respective localities. These grass roots efforts are perhaps best illustrated by local battles over growth and economic development. But they include, as well, other activities designed to defend the quality of everyday life from perceived deterioration. To that end, social activists placed on the public agenda such issues as arms control, the family, child care, the improvement of ethnic and race relations, greater equity in rates of taxation, the availability of affordable housing, and environmental protection.

As in so many other metropolitan regions in the United States, local government in Orange County was ineffective in dealing with such matters, largely because of its preoccupation with the twin challenges of uncoordinated development and growth management. Growth, inasmuch as it was tied primarily (although not exclusively) to the needs of large corporations, appeared to many as destructive of the locality's general well-being. The major political issue in Orange County during the 1980s was whether powerful growth networks could be constrained by the political process. On behalf of their notions regarding the quality of life those Orange County citizens seeking to retain some degree of local autonomy and control over the pace and scope of growth coalesced to wage an intense struggle over locality. It had become apparent to many, in other words, that if regional limits on growth were not promoted and constructed from the bottom up, such growth would most certainly be imposed by more powerful interests from the top down.

What made such resistance difficult was the impressive power mobilized by the region's new global capitalists (bankers, financiers, and owners and managers of Orange County's largest corporations) when joined, in a larger growth network, with the small handful of individuals, families, and corporations that owned nearly all of the remaining developable land in the southern portion of the county. This development oligopoly had the financial resources, the organization, and the staying power that the grass roots lacked, despite mounting evidence, in the 1980s, of surging sentiment throughout the county in favor of slower growth.

To counteract the slow growth forces, Orange County builders, by the end of 1987, had amassed a $250,000 legal-defense fund. This fund was designed to pay for legal challenges to a Citizens' Sensible Growth and Traffic Control Initiative known as Measure A, which would have made new development contingent on adequate roads and the availability of other public services. Declaring the urgent need to become proactive, such large landholders as Anthony Moiso, president of the Rancho Santa Margarita Company, Donald Bren of the Irvine Company, and Harvey Stearns of the Mission Viejo Company closed ranks with other developers and with the Southern California Building Association to design a less restrictive initiative measure.

In the bitter political struggle that occupied most of Orange County's attention for the next six months, opponents of Measure A mounted an extremely well-financed attack (California's most expensive progrowth/slow growth campaign to that date), spending more than $2.5 million, as against only $106,000 by its supporters. The ultimate defeat of the initiative in June 1988 was due, in large measure, to an intensive five-week campaign conducted by political consultant Lynn Wessell. Wessell effectively used information technologies (such as computerized demographic analyses and telecommunication banks) as well as more traditional methods (such as 3,100 door-to-door campaigners). Targeting five large central and north county cities—Anaheim, Fullerton, Garden Grove, Orange, and Santa Ana—Wessell's organization was instrumental in converting public opinion that was once four-to-one in favor of the initiative into a 56 to 44 defeat. In this instance, the struggle over locality had been won decisively by the Orange County growth network, which clearly had not been constrained by the political process. . . .

As the 1990s began, therefore, those engaged in popular struggles over growth, economic development, and the quality of life in Orange County—in short, those engaged in the "politics of locality"—were reassessing their strategies and tactics. Whatever analyses and decisions are made in the future, it is in precisely those relatively wealthy and privileged regions such as Orange County that the most strident struggles are likely to be waged. For, as urban sociologists John Logan and Harvey Molotch have pointed out, it is affluent professionals who at present most clearly recognize "the life style damage of the continuing press for intensified land use."

Global society is still in its infancy. Its future shape will depend, in large measure, on the kinds of actions taken by those municipalities and metropolitan regions most directly affected by the process of globalization. "Global consciousness and a global ethic are being forced upon this generation by new technological, ecological, and political realities," argues Richard Knight, an informed observer of the integration of cities into the world economy. "Global imperatives are forcing citizens to act more responsibly both locally and globally. . . ." Orange County, California, it would seem, offers a paradigmatic example of the operation and local impact of these global imperatives. While the Cold War era apparently has ended, in Orange County the struggle over locality continues. The local state—there and elsewhere—appears to many to be worth fighting for, precisely because it is so often the setting for political conflicts that cannot be resolved at the national level. Furthermore, it constitutes an important object of inquiry for scholars seeking to understand those political factors mediating the local effects of global economic change.

 FURTHER READING

Manuel Castells, *The Informational City: Information Technology, Economic Restructuring and the Urban-Regional Process* (1989)

Bradley Cleveland, "A Polarization of the Workforce," *Bay Area Business* (August 1985): 20–23

John M. Findlay, *Magic Lands: Western Cityscapes and American Culture After 1940* (1992)

Peter Hall and Ann Markusen, eds., *Silicon Landscapes* (1985)

Dirk Hanson, *The New Alchemists: Silicon Valley and the Microelectronics Revolution* (1982)

Rob Kling, Spencer Olin, and Mark Poster, eds., *Postsuburban California: The Transformation of Orange County Since World War II* (1991; paperback ed., 1995)

David Lyon, *The Information Society: Issues and Illusions* (1988)

Marc Uri Porat, *The Information Economy* (1977)

Mark Poster, *The Mode of Information: Poststructuralism and Social Context* (1990)

Robert W. Preer, *The Emergence of Technopolis: Knowledge-Intensive Technologies and Regional Development* (1992)

T. R. Reid, *The Chip* (1985)

AnnaLee Saxenian, *Regional Advantage: Culture and Competition in Silicon Valley and Route 128* (1994)

Allen John Scott, *Metropolis: From the Division of Labor to Urban Form* (1988)

John Sculley, *Odyssey: Pepsi to Apple—A Journey of Adventure, Ideas, and the Future* (1987)

Judith Stacey, *Brave New Families: Stories of Domestic Upheaval in Late Twentieth Century America* (1990)

Shoshana Zuboff, *In the Age of the Smart Machine: The Future of Work and Power* (1988)

The Environment and the Quality of Life Since 1960

California's rich natural environment made possible the high quality of life once enjoyed by Californians. The profit-maximizing manner in which that environment has been exploited, however, is now a prime cause of the state's declining quality of life. Although struggles to preserve California's land and water began in the nineteenth century, only in recent decades have most Californians become aware of the connection between the state's amazing economic growth and its deteriorating environment.

The state's five most important industries are agribusiness, aerospace, other defense industries, electronics, and petroleum and petrochemicals. Although these industries create great corporate and personal wealth, they also, unfortunately, are the state's major producers of chemical waste— much of it toxic.

California agriculture is the single largest consumer of pesticides in the world. While pesticides have made it possible for California agriculture to achieve extraordinarily high yields by controlling rodents and other pests, they harm the environment through both "point source contamination" and "non-point source contamination." The former occurs when pesticides are spilled before field application or when water used to rinse out pesticide-application equipment runs into the ground. The latter comes from the infiltration of pesticides into the soil, groundwater, and air after they have been applied to crops. In other words, pesticide residues are found not only on the food we eat but also in the water we drink, the air we breathe, and on the skin of farmworkers who apply them in the fields.

The aerospace and defense industries likewise use a wide range of toxic materials, including organic solvents, strong acids and bases, cyanides, toxic metals, radioactive materials, and poisonous gases. When these materials are disposed of as waste, they, like pesticides, contaminate the soil and groundwater. Even when they are put into underground tanks, leaks can and do occur.

In the electronics industry, in addition, poisonous gases such as phosgene and arsine are sometimes used, as well as toxic metals. All of these, when

421

dumped, become hazardous wastes. Thus, though the electronics industry is visually "clean," with no belching smokestacks, it is, in fact, hardly clean at all.

The petroleum and petrochemical industries, though not as important as the defense and electronics industries in terms of providing jobs and income in California, also create many kinds of chemical waste. With varying degrees of toxicity, they contaminate California's air, soil, and water supplies.

Though California has been a leader in monitoring hazardous waste management facilities, the great variety and large volume of waste produced pose a continuing risk. Little attention is paid to particular disposal sites until leaks or other problems occur, so California's efforts in hazardous and toxic waste management are mostly directed toward cleanups rather than to the prevention of contamination.

A second, equally troubling paradox is the fact that the very things that have enabled so many to live so well—the high incidence of home owner-ship, the widespread use of cars, and easy access to scenic spots and recre-ational facilities—are simultaneously the causes of the state's urban sprawl, traffic congestion, air pollution, and scarcity of water. Urban sprawl began with the construction boom after World War II. While providing much-needed housing, the new suburbs destroyed irreversibly some of the state's best farmland. In addition, the burgeoning urban population in southern California has shifted the distribution of the state's water resources. Dozens of dams, reservoirs, and the California Aqueduct were built to control the flow of rivers and to transport water from northern and central California to the southland. These efforts have increased the salinity of waterways and of the soil in the Sacramento–San Joaquin Delta and around San Francisco Bay, resulting in measurable harm to wildlife and in lower crop yields in one of the state's most productive agricultural regions. Even worse, Califor-nians have been using so much more water than nature provides that the state's water table is falling rapidly. Insufficiently replenished by surface flows, many parts of the state are experiencing soil subsidence. Meanwhile, many aquifers have been irreversibly contaminated by toxic waste. Finally, the water scarcity will get worse as Arizona claims its full share of the water from the Colorado River—water that California has been relying on and taking for granted for decades.

The air we breathe in many localities may also be endangering human health. Although great progress has been made in reducing smog in the Los Angeles basin in the last three decades, other parts of the state, particularly the Central Valley, now experience severe air pollution. Despite this, Califor-nians' long love affair with the automobile continues.

Not everyone is convinced that California's natural environment is in serious danger or that diminished environmental quality poses a hazard to humans. The last document in this chapter, for example, decries the excesses of "environmental doomsters." The author of the second essay feels that bad air may be ugly and a nuisance but that government clean-air standards are far too strict. The other documents and essays offer a variety of perspec-tives in support of the environmental movement. In reading the selections, try to assess which approaches seem most compelling and most reasonable— keeping in mind, however, that a reasonable compromise may not be the most valid approach.

DOCUMENTS

The first document, which deplores urban sprawl, comes from a slim volume, *California, Going, Going . . .* , (1962), one of the first warning bells sounded by California's "second-wave" environmental movement. Its authors, Samuel E. Wood and Alfred Heller, are the founders of California Tomorrow, a think tank dedicated to publicizing the state's environmental problems and to evaluating public policies and planning efforts related to the environment.

The authors of the second and third documents, who were also associated with California Tomorrow, describe the problems of water and air pollution. Frank M. Stead, a consultant in environmental management, worked for the California Department of Public Health. Richard Reinhardt is a writer who penned *California 2000: The Next Frontier* (1982), which takes stock of California's multifaceted environmental problems in an integrated, rather than piecemeal, manner.

The fourth document, on pesticides, is drawn from a report by the California Committee for Economic Development chaired by Leo McCarthy, the state's lieutenant governor at the time. Although the report did not state so explicitly, its apparent aim was to demonstrate that environmental pollution would undermine California's prosperity.

The fifth document points out that environmental problems have social dimensions. Its author, Carl Anthony, an architect and community activist who cofounded the Earth Island Institute's Urban Habitat Program, tries to persuade his fellow African Americans to get involved in efforts to protect the environment because minority communities are often affected by pollution and toxic waste to a far greater degree than are white communities.

The last document debunks the environmental movement as a scam. Ron Bailey, its author, has written articles about science for Forbes magazine and has produced programs for PBS, the Public Broadcasting System.

Samuel E. Wood and Alfred Heller
Oppose Urban Sprawl, 1961

[A]t the western shore of the American continent there lies a temperate land of unlimited beauty and unlimited bounty, which may be shared by all who choose to follow the sunset. . . .

[T]oday . . . we still sing in praise of the golden state, notwithstanding the smog, the water pollution, the crowded roads, the dirty blighted cities, the disappearing open space. . . .

[H]owever, . . . how polluted can a bright land become, and still be bright? The answer to that question is being written right now, across the surface of this chaotically growing state.

Californians are beginning to recognize that the great asset of their state, the very goose that has laid and will lay the golden eggs of their pleasures and profits, is their golden land. This land, our bright land—the charm of its open spaces, the vitality of its soils—is the true economic base of our state, its attraction as a place to live.

Within the past decade, at all levels of government, there have been efforts to control the development and the uses of California land, in order to conserve it and protect it from unnecessary encroachments of new towns, new people, new roads, new sewage—to protect it, that is, from *us*. Plans have been laid, laws and policies made. . . .

In spite of all efforts to the contrary, California's unique bright land is increasingly defiled by badly located freeways and housing subdivisions and industries that needlessly destroy beautiful scenery and entomb agricultural land; by reservoirs and aqueducts that unwittingly encourage the growth of mislocated communities; by waste products; by cars and jeeps and cycles that preempt our very living and breathing space. . . . How long before the bright lands are dead lands?

With every daily increase of 1,500 people in California, 375 acres of open farmland come under the blade of the bulldozer, to be used for subdivisions, roads, industry, public and private facilities. This amounts to 140,000 acres annually. At this rate, we can expect three million acres of bright open land to disappear by 1980, under the searing progress of growth. . . .

The character and quality of such urban sprawl is readily recognized: neon bright strip cities along main traveled roads; housing tracts in profusion; clogged roads and billboard alleys; a chaotic mixture of supermarkets, used-car lots, and pizza parlors; the asphalt plain of parking spaces; instead of parks, gray-looking fields forlornly waiting to be subdivided. These are the qualities of most of our new urban areas—of our *slurbs*—our sloppy, sleazy, slovenly, slipshod semi-cities. . . .

A typical example of the scattered, checkerboard character of California's slurban expansion may be seen in what happened in Santa Clara County—along El Camino Real, and throughout the rich orchard lands— despite the county's planning program, which has become recognized as one of [*sic*] best in the state.

If all the land put into urban use in Santa Clara between 1947 and 1956 had been placed in one parcel, that parcel would have consisted of about 26 square miles. But development in Santa Clara County was so disorderly that there existed in 1956 not a single square mile in a 200-square-mile area that had not been invaded by one subdivision or more. The result was that all 200 square miles were in effect held hostage for eventual development.

This situation is more or less duplicated up and down the state. The effect is that much of our land is being driven out of farm production and present or eventual recreational use, and the costs of services in slurban areas have risen beyond the ability of people to pay for them.

Only one-sixth of the state's land is suited for intensive agriculture. Of these sixteen million acres only about five million have top-rated soils, but it is these very lands in the fertile San Joaquin Valley, the Los Angeles Basin and the Santa Clara Valley that are receiving the major impact of slurban growth. . . .

There is no question that California is growing and will grow. The question is, shall we have slurbs, or shall we plan to have attractive communities that can grow in an orderly way while showing the utmost respect for the beauty and fertility of our landscape? If present trends continue, we shall have slurbs. . . .

Of all the creatures of our society, the automobile, which allows us to move from slurb to slurb, from home to job, from job to shopping center and back home again—the automobile is most like a locust, a plague on the bright land.

Almost every family in California needs or wants one or two or more cars. The car has been accepted as the *sine qua non* of transportation. People want cars. Cars need space. People try to see to it that cars get the space they need, in the form of roads and parking areas and garages and driveways.

That is why the state legislature in 1959 approved a 20-year plan for a statewide freeway-expressway system consisting of 12,400 miles of controlled access highways to cost $10.5 billion. That mileage is the distance between California and Afghanistan. The system will use up almost one-half million acres of California land. The 17 million cars in California in 1980 will consume over two million acres of land for parking, for driveways and garages, for roads, highways and freeways. Thus in 20 years 2 percent of all the land in California will be signed, sealed and delivered to the exclusive use of cars.

Still the freeways are crowded. Plans are being revised and will continue to be revised. Even more of the bright land will disappear, for the number of cars and trucks is increasing faster than we can provide road space for safe and economical movement. . . .

The freeways are dumping so many people into downtown areas that more and more land is being used for parking space. In the Los Angeles central business district one-third of the buildable land is devoted to parking. And some of the parking areas are multi-level garages. Even now California's major downtown areas are unable to handle the traffic dumped into them by existing freeways. What will the situation be by 1980?

It is small wonder that people are pushing out into the open bright lands of California, building their slurbs and shopping centers, and forsaking the old worn-out, traffic-glutted downtown areas. We can expect, too, that as present slurban centers become glutted with traffic, people will abandon them, and push out once again into the bright land, driving their cars, on new freeways, in search of new parking, new slurbs, new lives under smoggy skies.

Frank M. Stead Assesses California Water Pollution, 1968

As California embarked upon its second great period of development under the impetus of World War II, unmistakable signs began to appear that the waters of the state were threatened by pollution. First to show was pollution of the saltwater bays. Santa Monica Bay became so polluted by sewage that the State Board of Public Health in 1941 quarantined 14 miles of the West's most popular beach.

In the San Francisco Bay Area, the discharge into the bay of raw sewage by all of the cities produced unsightliness and intense odors. The proud citizens of the Bay Area tolerated these conditions until the taunts of the visitors to the International Exposition at Treasure Island exceeded their endurance and finally they demanded action.

Furthermore, the groundwaters of the state were showing signs of irreversible damage. . . .

Management of sewage and industrial wastes alone will not preserve water quality in California. The basic problem of water quality in the long run is rising mineral content. The greatest use of water is for irrigation. In the irrigation process, evaporation directly from the ground surface and through the leaves of plants concentrates a large share of the minerals originally present in the applied water in the top layers of the soil. If the soil is flushed by deliberate overirrigation so that the water not used by the crops percolates downward through the soil (as was done early in the Imperial Valley), the drainage water contains not only these standard minerals, but also salts dissolved from the soil itself.

The underground aquifers in the coastal plains all terminate in the ocean, and if ground-water levels are lowered, salt water moves into these aquifers unless "hydraulic dams" (ground-water mounds produced by injecting water through wells) are maintained.

Finally, the principal water-resource system of the sate—namely, the Sacramento and San Joaquin river system—is directly connected to the ocean through San Francisco Bay, and here tidal action will serve as a gigantic pump to thrust a wedge of heavy salt water far up into the delta itself, unless fresh water is used to hold back this threatening salt-water flood. So it should be clear that a program dealing only with sewage and industrial waste cannot do the big job. . . .

The California Water Plan has two basic and fundamental flaws: it is, in reality, only "half a system," and it ruthlessly transforms the ecology of vast areas of the state.

The California Water Plan provides the facilities to bring water into the San Joaquin Valley and the Southern California coastal areas, but provides no parallel facilities to remove waste water, and these basins are devoid of natural rivers to remove water pollution without polluting the groundwaters. Each form of "use" (agricultural, domestic and industrial) actually consumes only a small portion of the water and converts the remainder into "waste water," which contains not only the chemicals present before the "use" but also a great *increment* of chemicals as a result of the use. This increment ranges from about 200 ppm (parts of chemical per million parts of water) in domestic sewage, to several thousand ppm in agricultural drainage, and in the case of industrial waste waters may amount to tens of thousands of ppm. Unless these increments of chemical loadings are removed in some way, the chemical content of the surface and groundwaters of the basin will increase until the water becomes unusable. This phenomenon is already occurring in parts of Ventura and Orange counties where groundwater is so highly mineralized it approaches the point of unusability, for either agriculture or domestic use. It is the threat of the same situation in the San Joaquin Valley that has prompted the proposal for the San Luis Drain, which if constructed will carry the valley's polluting wastes into the delta and San Francisco Bay systems.

But the State Water Plan contains no *comprehensive* statewide system for removal of the chemical loadings in waste waters, and because of this fatal flaw must be considered as but "half a system."

In regard to ecological damage, not only does the State Water Plan write off the delta as expendable, but it threatens to eliminate one of the most valuable estuaries in the world—the San Francisco Bay system. An estuary is not a bay, filled with saltwater from the ocean, but a transition zone between saltwater and freshwater. The gradations of salinity in such a zone support a wide, interdependent spectrum of biologic forms, as well as the necessary means for anadromous fish (striped bass, salmon, steelhead, etc.) to go from the sea to freshwater spawning grounds. The "disconnecting" of the San Francisco Bay from the Sacramento and San Joaquin rivers that is implicit in the peripheral canal plan (which will detour the Sacramento River around the delta) will convert San Francisco Bay into an ocean-water cul-de-sac.

An even greater tragedy will result in the North Coastal area if the full California Water Plan is carried out, because here centuries-old wild river environments will be virtually dried up in their lower reaches and in their upper reaches be filled with a tame succession of end-to-end reservoirs whose water levels fluctuate, leaving broad muddy strips around their shrunken shorelines in dry seasons (or dry years).

But two new sources of supply are available near points of need. The first is high-quality water reclaimed from waste water. . . .

The techniques of reclaiming water from domestic sewage have been demonstrated in Southern California at both Santee in San Diego County and Whittier Narrows in Los Angeles County. . . .

Agricultural drainage represents a different problem. Reclamation of the water calls for demineralization as well as removal of organic materials. Two methods of demineralization, electrodialysis and reverse osmosis, are being currently tested at Coalinga. The costs are relatively high, but much lower than the present cost of distillation.

But even with waste-water reclamation, we still fall far short of meeting our ultimate needs unless an entirely new and massive water source is found. That source of course is the ocean itself, the only source upon which at this time we can responsibly stake our future.

The technology of seawater conversion is well known. The costs at the present time are admittedly high ($1.00 per 1,000 gallons), but by no means out of the range of economic feasibility for urban areas, and these costs are sure to come down dramatically.

So there is a way out of the dilemma.

Richard Reinhardt Looks at Air
Pollution Problems, 1982

In California, particularly, it is impossible to think about the future without considering the possibility of "running out" of fresh air. In such regions as the Los Angeles basin, the Central Valley, and the southern lobe of San Francisco Bay, where geographic and atmospheric barriers trap the air in great inverted bowls, there already are what might be called periodic shortages of clean air. Can these areas endure the exhaust fumes exhaled by a still greater population, more numerous cars and trucks, and continuing industrial development? Can there be health without clean air? Is clean air worth its cost? Is *anything* worth the cost of poisoned air?

If air pollution were merely a nuisance—an unesthetic, eye-stinging, foul-smelling cloud over the business district on certain autumn days—it might not deserve much attention. Unfortunately, there is evidence that air pollution has lasting consequences. It is an increasingly severe hazard to the health of humans and their agriculture, and to Earth's forests and watersheds.

Moreover, air pollution typifies a whole class of environmental hazards that are either new, or increasingly lethal. These factors appear to be displacing disease-causing organisms as the greatest threats to human health.

Measured by the standards of the world, and of the past, California is a relatively healthy place. The number of deaths due to infectious diseases has fallen dramatically, as it has throughout the United States, since the beginning of this century.

At the same time, however, the rate of chronic diseases has risen sharply. Four of the five leading causes of death in California (heart disease, cancer, stroke, and cirrhosis of the liver) are attributable, in some respect, to the way of life or the environment of the victim; and the other leading cause of death—accidents—clearly is related to our system of high-speed highway transportation. Our technological society is creating new killers to replace the killers it has conquered. The World Health Organization has estimated that as many as eight of ten cancers are precipitated by environmental factors: carcinogens in the atmosphere, workplace, and the food supply, as well as by overall stress. . . .

Air pollution, though probably not the most dangerous part of . . . [the] "hazardous waste stream," is the most visible and ubiquitous manifestation of it. Approximately 85 percent of Californians live in areas where bad air is a constant or at least an occasional threat. Not only lung cancer, emphysema, asthma, and other respiratory diseases, but also heart disease and diseases of the nervous system, are believed to be caused or exacerbated by exposure to polluted air.

Of the many reasons (economic, esthetic, spiritual) for minimizing pollution, none makes more immediate sense than preventing illness. However, many Californians don't understand the connection between maintaining environmental standards and maintaining public health.

Environmental hazards, unlike acute illnesses, are slow to reveal their effects, and the origins of environmentally related illnesses are extremely difficult to pinpoint. So it seems almost necessary to overlook the gradual deterioration of one's health, to accept as "normal" the poisonous influences of impure air, degraded water, adulterated foods, nervous tension. . . .

Looking ahead toward several decades of growth in California, one can anticipate an increasing output of toxic wastes, much of which will wind up in the air we breathe. Yet, . . . there are strong political pressures to weaken or even abandon the clean air standards established by the state and federal governments. "Nonattainment," a bureaucratic term for failure, is in effect becoming an acceptable goal. Clearly, if life in California is to remain endurable for the next two decades and beyond, the standards for maintaining air quality and other environmental values should not be lowered but raised.

A Government Commission Discusses the Dangers of Pesticides, 1988

California applies about 25% of the pesticides used each year in the entire world, or more than 1.5 billion pounds. In terms of sheer volume, pesticide production and use is more important for California than for any other state.

Agricultural chemicals provide positive benefits when they are used judiciously. But is [sic] must be remembered that unlike other chemicals, these poisons are made specifically for release into the environment. Through food consumption and home use, pesticides and other agricultural chemical [sic] directly reach a far broader segment of the population on a daily basis than do most industrial chemicals.

A recent study by senior EPA [Environmental Protection Agency] officials ranked the severity of 31 environmental problems. In terms of cancer risk, the report identified pesticide residues on food as third. In relation to a broad range of non-cancer health effects that the study ranked as high, medium or low in risk, pesticide residues were included in the high risk grouping. Even though the individual risk of disease from pesticide residues is relatively low compared to something like cigarette smoking, the net result is still very large because these residues affect virtually every American.

Pesticide food residues remain a major issue of concern, both for fresh produce and processed foods. With regard to produce, a 1984 study by the Natural Resources Defense Council found that despite state and federal programs to test produce for pesticide residues, 44% of produce randomly sampled in San Francisco contained detectable levels of 19 pesticides. . . .

The situation is even worse for processed food testing. In 1984, in the wake of revelations of high levels of fumigant ethylene dibromide (EDB) in cake and muffin mixes, the State Legislature passed a law requiring establishment of a state program to test processed foods for pesticide residues. Four years later, that program still is not in place. . . .

Every pesticide is made up of both active and "inert" ingredients. The active ingredients, which can make up less than a few percent of the volume, act as the pesticide. "Inert" ingredients are the chemical fillers that can make up as much as 99% of the liquid.

EPA has been extremely slow to develop health data for the 600 active ingredients now in use in thousands of different formulations. But although "inert" ingredients sometimes are extremely toxic, only active ingredients are regulated. Some of these fillers are restricted as active ingredients, but when used as fillers for another pesticide they escape regulation. Federal law actually prohibits manufacturers from listing the non-active ingredients on the container of a product sold for home use. Inactive ingredients have included such known hazards as DDT, vinyl chloride, xylene, pentachlorophenol, and benzene. Legal action was necessary to force pesticide manufacturers to substantially reduce the use of DDT as a filler.

The EPA agrees that unregulated ingredients are a problem, and has slowly begun testing pesticides to determine what chemicals are used as inert ingredients. Of the 1,200 substances used as inert ingredients, roughly 100 are hazardous or chemically similar to chemicals known to be hazardous, 200 are generally recognized as safe, and the health effects of the remaining 900 are largely unknown. . . .

While use of agricultural chemicals undoubtedly contributes to California's high food productivity, it is important to ensure that pesticides work for us, not against us. In addition to environmental and health damage from pesticide exposure, there is increasing evidence pesticides are not doing their job. Insect and weed resistance continues to grow, resulting in greater volumes and increased toxicity to achieve the same result. With the introduction of newer pesticides, the onset of resistance comes more rapidly. Insects need shorter and shorter periods to adjust to each new chemical. Some insects appear capable of resisting virtually all pesticides. With decreasing effectiveness, pesticides become an increasingly expensive component of food production.

This pesticide spiral is incompatible with development of an agricultural system that is sustainable for the long-term. Benefits and costs of pesticide use must be put to a sober comparison. In addition to killing the targeted pest, pesticides also kill beneficial insects, worms and other organisms that help maintain the fertility of the soil. Since some pesticides are applied strictly to make produce look good, we may well ask if the benefit is worth the cost. . . .

There are some positive changes occurring among growers, consumers and food marketers in terms of agricultural chemicals. Growers are discovering the advantages of Integrated Pest Management, which provides techniques for growing food crops with far lower pesticide use. An increasing number of California consumers are demanding food that is grown without pesticides, or without certain more dangerous pesticides.

Carl Anthony Outlines Why African Americans Should Be Environmentalists, 1990

African Americans could benefit from expanding their vision to include greater environmental awareness. . . .

Environmental organizations in the United States should also modify recruitment efforts in order to expand their constituency to include African Americans and members of other minority groups as participants in shaping and building public support for environmental policies. With the exception of limited collaboration between environmentalists and Native American groups, as well as anti-toxics campaigns, there has been little communication between environmentalists and non-European minority groups in the US. Critical issues—such as population control, limiting human intervention in the ecosystem, or rebuilding our cities in balance with nature—have been discussed almost entirely from a European and often elitist perspective.

Environmental organizations have taught us to appreciate and respect the diversity of non-human species and to recognize the fundamental interdependency of human and non-human life on the planet. Thus far, however, the environmental movement, despite its highlighting of crises in underdeveloped countries, has tended to be racially exclusive, expressing the point of view of the middle- and upper-income strata of European ethnic groups in developed countries. It has reproduced within its ranks prevailing patterns of social relations. Until recently, there has been little concern for the environmental needs and rights of historically disadvantaged groups in developed countries. . . .

The principle of social justice, however, must be at the heart of any effort aimed at bringing African Americans into the mainstream of environmental organizations in the United States. Such a vision must offer a real alternative to a view of the tropical rainforest as an inviolate preserve or a private laboratory for multinational pharmaceutical companies, ignoring the needs of indigenous populations. While recognizing limits to growth, it must avoid misuse of environmental information as a way of rationalizing the economic status quo. It must not misuse concern for endangered species as a way of diluting our responsibility to meet basic needs for human health care, food and shelter. It cannot manipulate terms so that the legitimate need for population control becomes a code word for preserving racial dominance and purity.

Environmental protection must be understood as intimately connected to efforts to eradicate injustice. . . .

The American inner-city was once a wilderness. Today, islands, estuaries, forests, and riparian habitats that once existed in these locations have been replaced by asphalt, concrete, barbed wire fences, boarded-up stores, crack houses, abandoned factories, landfills and pollution. After generations of isolation and manipulation, the people who live in these places rarely remember what it once was—or speculate on what it might become.

Isolation of African Americans from stewardship of the environment has deep historic roots. . . . The African American population migrated to the cities to escape the four centuries of exploitation on the plantations, crop farms and in the coal mines of the South. . . .

For two decades, the central city cores have been shrinking in population as those more fortunate have been fleeing to the suburbs in search of a better life. Suburban flight, in turn, exacerbates the destruction of fragile agricultural lands. Can we afford a new round of urban expansion and abandonment as America's African American population—after twelve generations of exploitation and oppression—seeks to realize its legitimate aspirations as a part of the American Dream? Can we ignore the underclass trapped in American ghettos while claiming to speak for reconciliation of economic growth with environmental integrity? If we are to restore the cities, we must invest in the future of the people who live there. . . .

[I]nvestment in education and social organization of the existing inner-city population is needed if this population is to have a stake in the outcome. Restoration of such inner-city neighborhoods should be a high priority for environmentalists. . . .

In order to meet responsibilities for citizenship, African Americans must have opportunities and learn to play a greater role in formulating environmental policies which affect all members of the community. We must find new ways to bridge the gap between environmental advocates and African American communities.

Ronald Bailey Denounces the "Eco-Scam," 1993

Doom haunts the end of the twentieth century. Millenarian predictions of impending global disaster are heard on every side. The fast-approaching year 2000—the end of the Second Millennium A.D.—is the benchmark date for all kinds of dire predictions, prophecies, and fears. *Fin-de-millennium* blues also afflict the intellectual and policy elites, and, increasingly, the citizenries of the industrialized nations. . . .

Modern ecological millenarians, impatient with waiting for the flash of a thermonuclear doom, now claim there is a "global environmental crisis" threatening not just humanity, but all life on earth. A cadre of professional "apocalypse abusers" frightens the public with lurid scenarios of a devastated earth, overrun by starving hordes of humanity, raped of its precious nonrenewable resources, poisoned by pesticides, pollution, and genetically engineered plagues, and baked by greenhouse warming. The new millenarians no longer expect a wrathful God to end the world in a rain of fire or overwhelming deluge. Instead humanity will die by its own hand. . . .

Environmental millenarians, like their medieval forebears, declare that humanity can only avert total ruin if society repents and quickly adopts their sweeping proposals for radical social restructuring and economic redistribution. . . .

Environmental doomsters believe themselves uniquely capable of seeing the impending catastrophe while the rest of humanity remains stubbornly blind to the danger. "Ecologists are the saved" who believe that they "are better able to plan man, space, and the environment than existing institutions," concludes historian Anna Bramwell. . . .

A sizable portion of the contemporary environmental movement has goals far beyond merely preserving wilderness, protecting endangered species, recycling garbage, or even trying to prevent global climate change. American "Green" political activists are building "support for a political outlook that merges ecological and social activism, with a strong emphasis on participatory democracy and political and economic decentralization. The Greens have helped sustain a hopeful alternative voice in a period characterized by a distinct shortage of idealism on the left." . . .

The environmental movement's widening social justice agenda includes not only preventing the construction of incinerators and nuclear power plants, fighting over landfill sites and recycling campaigns, but also opposing the Persian Gulf War, supporting native treaty rights, and organizing the inner city poor to demand more public housing. . . .

An increasingly influential wing of the modern environmental movement consists of the adherents of the religio-mystical worldview known as "deep ecology." Deep ecologists are even more radically egalitarian than those environmentalists whose roots are in a social justice tradition. They urge us to shun a narrow ethical focus on humanity and adopt a "biocentric" view which treats humans and all other species as morally identical. "Man is no more important than any other species," concludes Earth First! founder Dave Foreman.

Calling for "greater environmental humility," many deep ecologists are frankly antihuman. Foreman says, "We are a cancer on nature." And the highly regarded "ecotheologian" Reverend Thomas Berry doesn't mince words either: "We are an affliction of the world, its demonic presence. We are the violation of Earth's most sacred aspects." . . . This strong antihuman and anticivilization inclination has caused some friction between "deep ecologists" and environmentalists who stem from the more human-centered social justice tradition. . . .

There are more than 450 national organizations, and countless ones at the local level, promoting environmentalism. While certainly not all of these organizations are radical, they all share an institutional imperative to find and publicize an endless series of crises and disasters, since without calamities to combat, they have no reason to exist. Consequently, many of these groups have become quite skilled at mass-marketing doom.

Leading environmental organizations, including the Sierra Club, Greenpeace, the National Wildlife Federation, and the Natural Resources Defense Council, pulled in more than $400 million from a contributor base of nearly four million in 1990. Four hundred million dollars is ten times the amount of money that Republican and Democratic parties *together* raised in 1990. . . .

Since the 1960s the United States has adopted scores of new environmental laws and thousands of environmental regulations. Some have been beneficial and necessary. But environmental regulation has been expensive, costing the economy $123 billion in 1991, with the price tag rising to $171 billion annually by the year 2000. The Environmental Protection Agency's budget has jumped 31 percent since 1989, while its staff swelled by 23 percent. . . .

Another disturbing and disheartening aspect of the rise of radical environmentalism is the growing pressure on scientists to manipulate research findings in order to attract funding. "It is well known that Congress has a short attention span—so short that it often appears capable of dealing only with crises. Because everyone else is crying 'crisis,' responsible scientists are forced to join the chorus or risk losing their research programs," avers Harvard University researcher Peter Rogers. He adds that the phony crisis atmosphere engendered by this dismal process causes environmentalists, politicians, and citizen's [sic] groups to demand immediate action, which is not what most scientists had in mind at all. . . .

Unfortunately, not only do scientists have an incentive to cry "crisis," so too do the environmental advocacy groups need crises. Without them, how could advocacy groups justify their pleas for donations? . . . The media also have a strong incentive to report "crises"—they must sell newspapers and airtime after all. So there it is—an iron triangle of scientists pleading for research funds, interest groups who need crises to justify their existence, and a press that needs to sell papers. It's no wonder people are frightened.

 E S S A Y S

The author of the first essay, Tim Palmer, a landscape architect who has worked as a planner, became a full-time writer in 1980. He has produced eight books, including *California's Threatened Environment: Restoring the Dream* (1993), an anthology on various aspects of California's current environmental problems, from which the first essay is drawn.

The second essay is by Dixie Lee Ray, at one time a professor of zoology at the University of Washington. During her long career, she also headed the U.S. Atomic Energy Commission, served as governor of Washington (1977–1981), and received many awards, including the United Nations Peace Prize. Before her death in 1994, Ray, along with antigreen organizers Ron Arnold and Chuck Cushman, spearheaded a Wise Use movement that calls for the abolition of all government environmental regulations and demands the unregulated use of natural resources—including oil, gas, other minerals and metals, timber, and rangeland—whether they be publicly or privately owned. Many American and foreign corporations, tired of being monitored and irked at the high cost of reducing pollution, have become active in the Wise Use movement. Support for the movement has come, as well, from the National Rifle Association, the Heritage Foundation, the American Farm Bureau Federation, and the Unification Church of Korean evangelist Sun Myung Moon.

The third essay is by Robert D. Bullard, professor of sociology at the University of California, Riverside. The author of *Dumping in Dixie: Race, Class, and Environmental Quality* (1990) and *Confronting Environmental Racism* (1993), he is an authority on issues related to environmental racism and justice.

California's Threatened Environment

TIM PALMER

The abundance of California's natural world and the life-giving qualities of its environment are why this land was settled and why many millions of people have come here. With the gold that was hauled away and the water that now runs short, the abundance has mostly disappeared, and the qualities that created California's reputation as a paradise on earth are stretched thin or reduced to wreckage. Yet the boom persists, and the dreams of fruitful fields, safe homes for our children, and strikingly beautiful landscapes persist as well, fed by the remains of a resounding spaciousness that our ancestors knew. It is this combination of what has been lost and what remains, of the threats and the dreams, that has led California to have the strongest environmental movement in America. . . .

Beyond our own concerns, California is of interest—even if begrudgingly—to the rest of the country. One of the many clichés is its role as a trendsetter. More important, the many-faceted front of environmental protection on these western shores articulates choices; we are a laboratory seething with experiments. We may have more problems than anyone else, but we have more people working on them, and those elsewhere can watch with interest and criticism—not necessarily with a willingness to follow but a willingness to learn.

The *1991–1992 Green Index* ranked California first among all states for its environmental policies but nineteenth for its environmental conditions. The state scored first for renewable energy but emerged abysmally in forty-ninth place for municipal solid waste generated and sustainable farming practices, and in forty-eighth place for violations of air quality standards. Tragically, one of the lessons California provides best is what *not* to do. . . .

It is certain that the coming years will bring unprecedented change, leaving environmental impoverishment in its wake. . . . To hope for improvement in the face of an extreme growth in the state's population— 26 percent in ten years—might be credited to ignorance, denial, or deliberate conniving of vested interests. The environment cannot absorb 834,000 more people in 1990 and the population of another San Francisco *every year* and not feel the pain. The future has never looked worse for people dedicated to quality of life, broadly defined as health for all people and for the fundamental systems of life support—air, water, soil, and the whole community of creatures on earth.

Nine of the nation's twenty worst air quality regions are in California. The water quality of the Sacramento–San Joaquin Delta is threatened, though it is the source of domestic supply for 20 million people. More than 50,000 acres of farmland are lost to land developers each year, and many more are ruined by nonsustainable irrigation practices. Every second, 1.5 tons of solid waste are generated. California uses 10 percent of all pesticides in the world, and doctors report nearly 3,000 cases of worker poisonings a year in the state. More than 1,200 species of animals and plants are of "special concern," many of them facing the threat of extinction. At the same time—and this is one of the centrally significant dynamics as California approaches its 150th year of statehood—the possibilities to act and institute change for environmental improvement may never be better. . . .

California, the proverbial land of extremes, really is. Here are the oldest, the largest, and the tallest living things on earth. The Delta is the largest wetland on the West Coast. Lake Tahoe is America's largest mountain lake. The middle elevations of the Sierra were called the greatest conifer forest on earth by John Muir. Mount Whitney is the highest point in forty-nine states, and Death Valley is the lowest in all fifty.

But the extremes and the extraordinary that exist today are only a token of what was, and much of the fraction that remains is under siege. The Central Valley wetlands were the finest on the Pacific Flyway for ducks and geese. The population of grizzly bears that foraged in places such as the San Francisco peninsula were probably more hale and hearty than any other group of the great bears. The population of American Indians was the densest, supported by the labor of gathering healthy food in an incomparably rich homeland. But little of that exists today.

Look, for example, at the official symbols of the state. The grizzly went extinct in the 1920s, before it was designated the official state animal. Logging has reduced old-growth stands of the state tree, the redwood, to 15 percent of their original range and much of that is unprotected and may be cut. The state bird, the California quail, does well but depends heavily on oak forests, which are in alarming decline with little regeneration of keystone species—the valley and blue oaks. The state fish, the golden trout, thrives in only a few streams in the southern Sierra, and the major one is now inundated by hordes of visitors served by an unnecessarily improved road to the backcountry. The state reptile, the endangered desert tortoise, is perhaps the best indicator species of the health of the desert and has declined in some areas by 80 percent in ten short years.

Splendor certainly remains and brings joy and wonder to Californians and visitors from all over the world, but in many places the splendor is only a remnant—effective as a tourist draw, which accounts for the state's largest industry, but woefully inadequate as an ecosystem to support the vibrant assemblage of life that was once California.

Many of the changes are obvious: urban hills are not only peppered with homes and carved with roads, but some are just plain gone, bulldozed into ravines to eliminate the double nuisance of hill and valley so that banal flats can accommodate shopping centers. But not all of the environment reflects a transformation as dramatic as asphalt, dams, and bombing ranges in the desert. Obscured from sight, a wholesale rearrangement of the ecology goes unnoticed but is all-important to this one-time Eden. The native grasses—virtually all of them—are gone because of cattle and exotic grass imports, and therefore gopher populations explode on the new exotic grasses. And, without predators to keep the gophers in check, many oak trees cannot grow past the seedling stage, and so, because of the cows, grasses, gophers, and a lack of oaks, deer herds dwindle, mudslides are more plentiful without the latticework of oak roots, and groundwater is more scarce.

Lowlands, whose cultivated swirls or patchworks of crops may please the eye from the height of an airplane, once constituted the finest waterfowl habitat there was, and while one might see a duck now and then and conclude that California is a good place for them, waterfowl visit and live here in a tiny fraction of the numbers they used to.

Moving uphill to the conifer forests, stands of second growth sport healthy trees—sometimes—but grown in plantations like rows of soybeans wetted in herbicides, they cease to provide the diversity, sustenance, and shelter that are the very essence of a true forest.

Urban air lies in a haze that sometimes makes pretty sunsets, and people get acclimatized to the daytime dreariness; but ozone is killing pine trees in the Sierra, diminishing crops in the Central Valley, and leading to public health problems of epidemic proportions.

Rivers look clean and no longer smell like sewage, but most of the salmon are gone. In short, environmental quality has plummeted, sometimes in news-making of oil-spill scale but more often in incremental changes, unnoticed, such as the temperature of water in the proverbial frog pond that was warmed one degree each day so that the frogs, unaware, failed to jump out of the pond, then belatedly realized that they had waited too long and now *couldn't* jump.

It seems that the plunder of almost everything in California's natural world is up in the 80 percent or 90 percent bracket: Pacific Flyway wetlands, 96 percent gone; native grasslands, 99 percent gone; wilderness, 80 percent gone; riparian woodlands, 89 percent gone; salmon and steelhead, 90 percent to 100 percent gone; valley oaks, 98 percent gone; and all major rivers but one dammed at least once. On the increase are people and cars. These kinds of statistics get tiresome but might be worth thinking about when one is confronted by the seductive, comfortable, and peace-making argument that we still need to compromise for environmental quality.

No one says that the development of California is not serving a purpose or that just about everybody here isn't enjoying at least some of the harvest of the economic machine. The state is home to more people than all the rest of the western United States, and its economy is larger than the economies of all but six nations. The needs and desires of its residents and the opportunities afforded them are real. But so much of what has happened to modern-day California seems to represent people's real needs gone berserk or, at least, gone shortsighted. Water that has been dammed and diverted goes to grow needed crops by family farmers, and that may well justify the subsidy and the trade-offs. But why can't we just leave it at that, instead of subsidizing waste and destruction? Is it wise public policy that huge quantities of water were developed with enormous taxpayer subsidies, destroying dozens of rivers and ecosystems, and that the subsidized water is used to grow crops such as cotton, which the government in many years pays farmers not to grow, and in the process produces toxic air and toxic drainage that causes new ducklings in national wildlife refuges to have such problems as one leg or no beak, and then, that the same water could flow on down to endanger the Delta, from which 20 million people drink, and could even threaten San Francisco Bay? We know all of this; yet this type of thing continues to go on. We are like arsonists striking matches to the environmental equivalent of our own homes of warmth and security, with only the vague realization that we will be living in the streets, as will our children and grandchildren. How did we, as a society, get to this point?

Closer to home, perhaps, are myriad examples of freeways built at great public expense that tore out neighborhoods and led to more commuters, to further suburban sprawl, and thus to more cars and more freeways, with the resulting pollution that makes both Californians and the global climate sick. Flood-prone areas are developed, displacing farms from the richest soil and exacerbating the need for expensive flood control levees or dams, which lend a sense of security and lead to more flood plain development, which, when a big enough storm comes, will be flooded anyway and require millions in disaster relief that common sense could have avoided. A lot of non-flood-prone land is available.

There is nothing particularly new about these observations. But if they're so familiar, why doesn't anything change? Why do we, as voters, as elected officials, and as a society continue to make short-sighted decisions regarding the environment? The California Environmental Quality Act states: "It is the policy of the state to . . . ensure that the long-term protection of the environment shall be the guiding criterion in public decisions." With all respect to many organizations, individuals, and officials, we have made decisions for reform—a long list could be cited and would be more impressive than reforms made in any other state—but the list of continuing or worsening ailments is longer. The problems are growing faster than the solutions, and like the bucket-carrying brooms in *The Sorcerer's Apprentice,* they seem to multiply uncontrollably from the tools originally designed to make life easier.

Inherent in any discussion of the environment and the future is a raft of concerns regarding social equity. Does environmental protection limit the ability of disadvantaged people to improve their economic status? Does it conflict with human needs and with the ideal of opportunity for all? To the disenfranchised, the issue will not be the environment in its often-perceived though inaccurate sense of saving specimens of nature. The issue will be enfranchisement, including jobs, infrastructure improvements, basic services, and the health of the neighborhood and workplace.

But the poor suffer most from an inefficient and grossly polluting transportation system in which a person without a car can't hold down a job because of inadequate public transit. Polluted waters most afflict the people who live at the lower urban ends of rivers or who depend on questionable supplies for drinking, rural or urban. The foulest pockets of air pollution and the dumping of toxic wastes take place in neighborhoods of people who are the least able to move away or gain control over their living places. Recreation and open space needs are felt severely in urban centers and among people who are not able to escape for a weekend at Mammoth, Monterey, or Mendocino. Farmworkers are emphatically on the front line of injury from improper pesticide use. The disadvantaged and the disenfranchised are the foremost victims of environmental abuse and may stand to gain the most by reform.

Beyond the public health and living space issues, some argue that endangered species, fish and wildlife, scenic rivers, and wilderness are elitist pursuits. Yet these are public resources, the enjoyment of them is often available for free, and they are more accessible to disadvantaged people than are many of the higher-touted fruits of our society—expensive cars or motorboats, for example. Additionally, "wild land" concerns have been eclipsed within the environmental movement itself by public health and global issues of life support, and furthermore, much environmental protection that may appear to deal with purely recreational or aesthetic pursuits is essential to other fundamental needs. Without sustained growth in forests, there will be fewer long-term jobs in rural logging communities, and housing costs will increase. Without watershed protection, water quality for cities and farms will be ruined and food costs will escalate. Without a rich and biologically diverse environment, entire ecosystems fall apart and lead to climatic changes, burdensome to all and threatening to life.

The three leading causes of death—heart disease, cancer, and stroke—are attributable at least in part to the environment of the victim. This relationship may even be more significant for people who have urgent problems with health care availability and insurance and who are unable to escape the toxins to which their neighborhoods are shackled.

Perhaps recognizing these linkages, the Latino districts of Los Angeles voted in 1990 in favor of the "Big Green" environmental measure, though it lost statewide. The Black Congressional Caucus in Washington, D.C., has one of the best environmental voting records.

One might argue that people's basic needs should be provided as a societal priority. Environmental goals need not conflict with this priority because it is often not the basic needs of food, shelter, health care, and education that cause the worst problems. While everyone must bear the burden of change from an exploitive and wasteful society to one that respects both the earth and human dignity, it is ironically the people who are the most able to change, to choose, to influence, and to reform who contribute most to the sapping of California's environmental wealth. Commuters who drive alone for dozens or even hundreds of miles a day dump carbon into the atmosphere at a far higher rate than people who ride buses because they don't own cars. Suburban housing that preempts the finest farmland is rarely bought by poor people.

The issue of subsidies falls in the midst of the social equity quandary. Taxpayer subsidies—nearly everyone's burden—permitted the damming of many rivers and the resulting extinction of various salmon runs; the building of freeways while ignoring public transit; the clear-cutting of national forests that often earns the government even less money than the government spends to sell the timber; and the grazing on public lands that returns less than it costs and, for a pittance of beef, destroys more wildlife habitat than any other single endeavor of humans in the West. These subsidies are paid by everybody who pays taxes, but too often the lion's share of benefits goes to an influential few who are adept at making their good fortune appear to be everyone's.

Looking to the future of California, the state's resources could be shared more equitably and the disenfranchised groups might partake more fully in the mainstream of society. But if everybody were to live the way the upper middle class now lives, environmental destruction would be exacerbated, much as if Third World countries were to consume as much energy per capita as Americans do—a scenario of global disaster far worse than even the current threat of global warming. It is inconceivable that our Third World neighbors or the underclass at home will take a dominant society seriously as it calls for environmental protection until it sees that particular society acting responsibly with the preponderance of wealth that it holds and controls. Rather than more people creating more consumption, waste, and pollution in pursuit of the materialistic American dream, people who have realized the goal of financial wealth could lower their standard of consumption—not to be confused with standard of living. For example, people who now drive to work could take improved public transit instead of everybody commuting in cars. . . .

Otherwise, the only social equity for anyone may be the ironic and tragic equity of environmental impoverishment for all.

Natural Ways to Reduce Urban Air Pollution

DIXIE LEE RAY

Air pollution in populated areas has two facets. One is smog, in which ozone is implicated. The other is a more general decline in air quality, doubtless determined by large numbers of people and all their activities crowded into relatively small areas. In addition, when cities are built, the original vegetation is replaced by buildings and paved streets, with the result that the heat balance is altered. Incoming sunlight is absorbed and reflected differently from asphalt and building materials than from green leafy surfaces, and so cities are always warmer than neighboring areas. Cities, therefore, constitute "heat islands," and this, in turn, alters patterns of air circulation and the dispersion of pollutants.

City air has higher concentrations of sulfur and nitrogen oxides, various hydrocarbons and other organic compounds, particulates such as soot and dust, and carbon monoxide than does the surrounding countryside. It is these five components, plus lead, that were targeted in the 1970 Clean Air

Act as the prime constituents of air pollution. To control them, strict ambient air quality standards were established, and deadlines were set for meeting them. How well have they worked?

There has been considerable progress. And for that we can be thankful, because the air we breathe is pretty important to all of us. Naturally, we want it to be clean, free from hazardous substances, and we like it to smell good or not to smell at all. Actions taken during the past two decades have succeeded in removing the heavy load of industrial pollutants that used to flow unchecked from the smokestacks of factories. Particulates, other than those that are extremely minute (10 microns or less) or come from volcanoes, wind, or sand storms, forest fires, and other natural events, have been brought under control. The sulfur oxides have been significantly reduced, but less progress has been achieved in the effort to cut back on levels of hydrocarbons, nitrogen oxides, carbon monoxide, and the formation of ground-level ozone. These are the remaining substances of interest.

Automobiles and buses—the internal combustion and diesel engines— are major contributors to these pesky pollutants. Nevertheless, there has been an improvement here, too. Today's cars produce 96 percent less hydrocarbon and carbon monoxide, and 76 percent less nitrogen oxide than those built 20 years ago. The removal of lead from gasoline has resulted in an 80 percent reduction. All this is a real achievement—but the air quality standards set by the EPA have not been met. The deadlines have been extended several times, and still many communities are declared to be "non-attainment" areas. How come?

After a 20-year effort and the expenditure of $30 billion, surely it is time for a critical review of the clean air programs. We need to ask, for instance: Is there a good justification, a solid base of scientific facts for the presumed relation between air pollutants and human health? Are the programs to reduce pollutants realistic and cost-effective? What benefits have been achieved?

But instead of analyzing what we've learned and determining whether continuation of programs already under way is justified, government regulation has merely bred more regulation. The 1990 Clean Air Act amendments, for example, mandate spending an additional $12 billion per year. For what benefit?

In a recent review of the municipal ozone-smog problem submitted early in 1992, the National Academy of Sciences reported that "billions of dollars invested at refineries and gasoline stations and in the hardware of cars to reduce organic emissions . . . have been misdirected because efforts to reduce nitrogen oxides have been neglected. . . . Smog is so poorly understood that much of the nation's effort to control it may [also] be misdirected."

This startling comment from America's most prestigious science organization compels attention, since there has been intensive research on air pollution, smog formation, and human health for more than two decades. What has been learned? . . .

[T]he belief that air pollution, as defined for purposes of regulation and control, has an adverse effect on public health is well established in the public mind. Yet many careful studies, dating back to the 1960s, do not find such a relationship. In an analysis and critical review of the possible association between general urban air pollution and lung cancer, a member of the California Air Resources Board, John R. Goldsmith, reported in 1968:

> If such a relationship exists, a number of consequences should follow which have not been observed:
>
> 1. The urban factor should be largest in those countries where there is the heaviest urban population. It is not.
> 2. Assuming that the larger the city, the greater the population exposure will be to air pollution, then the urban factor should increase regularly with city population. It does not, at least in the United States.
> 3. If exposure to urban pollution causes an augmentation in lung cancer, then the rates should be higher in lifetime urban residents than in migrants to urban areas. They are not.
> 4. Correlations of lung cancer rates with measured pollution should be found by studies in the United Kingdom, where both lung cancer rates are high and pollution is great. A positive correlation is found with population density, but not with pollution.
> 5. If the urban factor were community air pollution, it should affect women at least as much as men. It does not.
>
> There may be other explanations of the urban factor (greater smoking, occupational exposure, population density, infections), but the evidence presently available that it is air pollution *does not confirm the suspicion of causality* which previously existed.

Despite evidence to the contrary, the "suspicion of causality" still exists—and it is still without proof. But what about carbon monoxide and ozone; aren't these two constituents of air pollution known to be toxic?

The answer for carbon monoxide (CO), of course, is "yes"—but at concentrations far beyond the levels set by the EPA's air quality standards, which require ambient air to have no more than nine parts per million of CO. But that doesn't tell the whole story about the EPA's standards. If only one CO monitor shows more than that amount for eight hours on any one day, then the EPA regulators consider the whole city to be a "nonattainment" area for the entire year.

The physiological effects of breathing carbon monoxide are well known; they can be fatal, if enough CO is inhaled. Carbon monoxide combines irreversibly with the hemoglobin of red blood cells and thus effectively blocks the oxygen-carrying capacity of blood, which, of course, is essential for life. Fortunately, the human blood stream contains a large number of red cells, and it takes quite a bit of CO to saturate them. At 20 percent carboxy hemoglobin—which is equivalent to saturation at about 120 ppm CO—some impairment of activities occurs, but little performance degradation is observable at 10 percent saturation, equivalent to CO at 60 ppm. At 8 percent saturation—equivalent to 48 ppm CO—there is no convincing evidence of adverse effects. The permissible standard of 9 ppm CO can, therefore, be considered very conservative. This level is based on a

1967 study by Beard and Wertheim which claimed impairment of time-interval discrimination after human subjects were exposed for 90 minutes to 50 ppm of CO. Their results have not been accepted, and even the authors recognize the shortcomings of their research. They have been unable to verify or repeat their results. Nevertheless, the EPA's air quality standards and non-attainment rules are based on this flawed study. It costs cities many millions of dollars.

Now, what about ground level ozone? It has long been claimed that breathing air with detectable levels of ozone is hazardous to our health. Ralph Nader's Public Interest Research Group has warned, "Lung damage from ozone-polluted air is a risk faced by roughly three out of five Americans." How great a risk from how much ozone is not made clear by Mr. Nader, but, doubtless, many people believe that some harm is involved. . . .

[W]here does smog-related ground-level ozone come from? It has long been known that ozone forms under the influence of high temperatures, 90 degrees Fahrenheit or above, bright sunshine, the presence of hydrocarbons, and low wind speed or temperature inversion. True enough, but, as usual, the conventional wisdom is an oversimplification. *Both* hydrocarbons and nitrogen oxides are required, but it is the ratio between these two chemicals that is crucial. This ratio cannot be controlled by law, no matter how stringent the regulations are, because nature intervenes.

In some places like Atlanta, Georgia; Baton Rouge, Louisiana; Tampa-St. Petersburg, Florida; and the entire Los Angeles basin, the natural production of hydrocarbons from trees and other vegetation far exceeds what we humans can be held responsible for. Nitrogen oxides also come from both natural and human sources. . . .

[L]iving plants emit from two to four times as much hydrocarbon as man produces. Moreover, vegetation releases its organic emissions preferentially on hot summer days that are favorable for ozone formation. Of course, if the naturally occurring hydrocarbons were produced by human activity, they would be classified as "air pollutants." Since they form in nature, they are ignored. In the rarefied atmosphere of bureaucracy, where computer models and simulations take the place of human brains, natural phenomena apparently don't count.

No matter, the possible health effects of elevated levels of ozone have been studied intensively for more than 20 years without finding problems beyond some temporary respiratory and eye irritation. Only among persons with pre-existing breathing problems—asthma, for example—does ozone appear to be harmful since it will trigger an attack. Even this can be avoided by refraining from vigorous exercise or other heavy physical activity during a smog episode. The EPA's own five-volume ozone review, published in 1986, concludes that no long- or short-term impacts on human health have been discovered or demonstrated.

The National Ambient Air Quality Standard, required by the 1970 Clean Air Act, sets the limit for ozone concentration at 0.120 ppm. Ozone monitoring devices are maintained at several hundred locations around the country. If even one monitor registers ozone concentration over 0.124 ppm for one hour or more, that whole region is declared to exceed the standard for that day. Four such instances in any three-year period results in that region being declared an ozone non-attainment region.

Throughout the nation, 85 percent of all ozone exposures above 0.120 ppm are in California, and 82 percent occur in the Los Angeles Basin.

If elevated ozone causes health problems, we would expect to find the evidence in Los Angeles. The residents of that city have been exposed to air that has exceeded the EPA standards for ozone from between 100 to 200 days a year for at least 40 years. Where are the respiratory invalids? Where are the smog victims' bodies? Despite intensive research, health statistics for Los Angeles fail to show any distinction between the health of the residents of Los Angeles and any other American city.

If every human being, all automobiles, and all industry were to be removed from the Los Angeles Basin, it would still fail to meet EPA ozone standards on most days, due entirely to natural conditions and weather.

Throughout the nation, human-influenced ozone levels have dropped by 74 percent since 1985. Today California is the only state with an important ozone regulatory problem. But especially since most of California's ozone is produced by nature, why should taxpayers throughout the U.S. continue to pay $10 to $15 billion per year for fractional further reductions that have dubious benefit?

The EPA'a already strict rules about "non-attainment" have been made even more draconian by the 1990 Clean Air Act requirements. . . .

The EPA's regulations are counterproductive because auto fleet turnover is the only proven means of significantly reducing ozone pollution. Ten percent of America's cars are responsible for 50 percent of all emissions, and most of those cars are pre-1981 vehicles without catalytic converters and other emissions control devices. Regulations that increase the costs of new cars will simply delay the turnover of the auto fleet and unnecessarily postpone further improvements in air quality.

[The EPA's] rhetoric aside, America has made great strides in smog abatement over the past decade. Temperature-adjusted data indicate that ozone pollution outside California has been reduced by 74 percent since 1985.

Today only three urban areas outside California have serious or severe ozone non-attainment problems. Another 25 areas, which suffer only marginal to moderate smog problems, show every sign of achieving attainment within two to five years without the additional onerous regulatory controls spelled out in the 1990 amendments to the Clean Air Act.

Any major ozone-smog problem in America is confined to the state of California, particularly the Los Angeles Basin. It is ridiculous to treat all America as if it faced the problems California does and to impose on the entire nation massive economic costs that are ultimately unnecessary and counter-productive.

In pursuit of greater budgets, increased regulatory authority, and the political benefits of front-page coverage, the EPA has perpetrated a fraud on the American people. The agency's refusal to acknowledge that the 1988 data on ozone were an aberration and its failure to publicize preliminary 1991 data in a timely manner could cost the economy $26 billion a year.

The result can only be continued economic stagnation, higher unemployment, and reduced international competitiveness. Three-quarters of the cost of the EPA's ozone non-attainment program is a total waste of money. Even under optimistic assumptions, the costs of the program outweigh any possible benefits by a factor of from 9 to 48.

But nobody likes dirty air, even if illness can't be attributed to it. Isn't there some additional way of improving urban air quality without all the new, expensive regulations? Indeed there is—by using the same phenomenon that nature does: photosynthesis.

By planting lots of green growing plants downtown, we could bring to cities a breath of fresh air. . . .

Suppose that in addition to city parks and parkways, tree-lined streets, and the occasional tubs with flowers (all at ground level), we were to make use of every building as a planting site. Roof gardens should abound. Most building roofs are sufficiently strong to support plantings, especially around the periphery, and water is generally available to serve air-conditioning systems. With plantings suspended from parapets and cornices, we could greatly augment the ground level plantings and make our buildings look better, too—bringing back memories of the hanging gardens of Babylon.

By judicious selection of species that use carbon monoxide, as well as carbon dioxide, such as Alder and English ivy, in addition to hardy species of leafy plants that consume quantities of carbon dioxide, the composition of urban air could be beneficially affected. Plants also absorb other air pollutants, including sulfur, nitrogen, and organic compounds and particulates. Since city temperatures are several degrees warmer that outlying areas, temperature moderation becomes another worthy goal achievable with green plants. And, finally, plantings on such a large scale would render the cities far more pleasant to the eye, ear, and nose of residents and tourists alike.

Another important advantage—a political one—should be mentioned. Such a plan would not only bring the positive results mentioned; it would prove to everyone that we can better reach the goal sought through natural means and voluntary cooperation than we have done thus far with punitive legislation, which hasn't done the job and whose enforcement grows continually more expensive.

Environmental Racism and Justice

ROBERT D. BULLARD

Despite the many federal laws, mandates, and directives by the federal government to eliminate discrimination in housing, education, and employment, government rarely addresses discriminatory environmental practices. People of color (African Americans, Latino Americans, Asian Americans, and Native Americans) are disproportionately affected by industrial toxins, dirty air and drinking water, and the location of noxious facilities such as municipal landfills, incinerators, and hazardous-waste treatment, storage, and disposal facilities.

All communities are not created equal. Some are subjected to all kinds of environmental assaults. Many differences in environmental quality between communities of color and white communities result from institutional racism. Institutional racism influences local land use, enforcement of environmental regulations, industrial facility siting, economic vulnerability, and where people of color live, work, and play. Environmental racism is just as real as the racism that exists in housing, employment, and education. . . .

People-of-color communities have borne a disproportionate burden of this nation's air, water, and waste problems as well as the siting of sewer treatment plants; municipal landfills; incinerators; hazardous-waste treatment, storage, and disposal facilities; and other noxious plants. Residents of many of these same communities live in housing contaminated with lead, whose problems are further complicated by hospital closures and inaccessible health clinics. . . .

Environmental racism disadvantages people of color while providing advantages (i.e., privileges) for whites. A form of illegal exaction forces people of color to pay costs of environmental benefits for the public at large. Determining who pays and who benefits from our current urban and industrial policies is central to an analysis of environmental racism. Exclusionary zoning and unequal protection have created environmental sacrifice zones where residents pay with their health. Racial barriers in housing limit mobility options available to people of color.

Racism influences every social and economic strata [*sic*] of people of color. . . . [E]nvironmental inequities do not result solely from differences in social class. In the United States, race interpenetrates class and creates special health and environmental vulnerabilities. People of color are exposed to greater environmental hazards in their neighborhoods and on the job than are their white counterparts. Studies find elevated exposure levels by race, even when social class is held constant. For example, research indicates race to be independent of class in the distribution of air pollution, contaminated fish consumption, location of municipal landfill and incinerators, abandoned toxic-waste dumps, and lead poisoning in children.

From Robert D. Bullard, "Anatomy of Environmental Racism," in Richard Hofrichter, ed., *Toxic Struggles: The Theory and Practice of Environmental Justice.* (Philadelphia: New Society, 1993). Reprinted by permission of New Society Publishers, a Division of New Society Education Foundation, Inc.

Lead poisoning is a classic example of an environmental health problem that disproportionately affects children of color at every class level. Lead affects between three and four million children in the United States— most of whom are African American and Latino Americans who live in urban areas. Among children five years old and younger, the percentage of African American children who have excessive levels of lead in their blood far exceeds the percentage of whites who do at all income levels.

The federal Agency for Toxic Substances Disease Registry (ATSDR) found that, for families earning less than $6,000, 68 percent of African American children had lead poisoning, compared with 36 percent for white children. In families with income exceeding $15,000, more than 38 percent of African American children suffer from lead poisoning, compared with 12 percent of whites. Even when income is held constant, African American children are two to three times more likely than their white counterparts to suffer from lead poisoning.

People of color do not have the same opportunities as whites to escape unhealthy physical environments. Most environmental-justice activists challenge an environmental ethic that allows individuals, workers, and communities to accept health risks others can avoid by virtue of their skin color. . . . African Americans, no matter what their educational or occupational achievement or income level, experience greater environmental threats because of their race.

Institutional barriers such as housing discrimination, redlining by banks, and residential segregation prevent African Americans from buying their way out of health-threatening physical environments. The ability of an individual to escape a health-threatening physical environment usually correlates with income. However, racial barriers complicate this process for millions of African Americans. An African American who has an income of $50,000 is as residentially segregated as an African American on welfare.

Some communities, located on the "wrong side of the tracks," receive different treatment in the delivery of public services, including environmental protection. In the heavily populated South Coast air basin of Los Angeles, for example, over 71 percent of African Americans and 50 percent of Latino Americans reside in areas with the most polluted air, while only 34 percent of whites live in highly polluted areas. . . .

In Los Angeles . . . the mostly African American South Central Los Angeles and Latino American East Los Angeles neighborhoods were targets for municipal solid-waste and hazardous-waste incinerators, respectively. . . .

The now riot-torn South Central Los Angeles . . . has suffered from years of systematic neglect, infrastructure decay, high unemployment, poverty, and heavy industrial use.

The South Central Los Angeles neighborhoods suffer from a double whammy of poverty and pollution. A recent article in the *San Francisco Examiner* described the ZIP code in which South Central Los Angeles lies (90058) as the "dirtiest" in the state. The 1990 population in the ZIP code is 59 percent African American and 38 percent Latino American.

Abandoned toxic-waste sites, freeways, smokestacks, and waste water pipes from polluting industries saturate the one-square-mile area. The neighborhood is a haven for nonresidential activities. More than eighteen industrial firms in 1989 discharged more than 33 million pounds of waste chemicals in this ZIP code.

Why has South Central Los Angeles become the dumping ground of the city? Local government decisions are in part responsible. Trying to solve them, the city (under a contract with the EPA) developed a plan to build three waste-to-energy incinerators. Odgen-Martin was selected to build the incinerators dubbed LANCER (Los Angeles Energy Recovery). The first of the three incinerators, LANCER 1, was slated to be built in South Central Los Angeles.

Proponents of LANCER 1 attempted to speed the project through and locate it in South Central, as one way to blunt public opposition when LANCER 2 and 3, planned for the wealthier and mostly white Westside and San Fernando Valley came up for review. City officials reasoned that they would be hard-pressed to justify killing LANCER 2 and 3, if LANCER 1 was up and running. City council members, however, underestimated the organizing skills of South Central Los Angeles residents.

After learning about the incinerator project in 1984, residents organized themselves in a group called Concerned Citizens of South Central Los Angeles, most of whom were African American women. Local activists from Concerned Citizens were able to form alliances with several national and grass-roots environmental groups, as well as with public-interest law groups to block construction of the city-initiated municipal solid-waste incinerator. Concerned Citizens was assisted by Greenpeace, the Citizen's [sic] Clearinghouse for Hazardous Waste, the Center for Law in the Public Interest, the National Health Law Program, the Institute for Local Self-Reliance, the California Alliance in defense of Residential Environments (CARE), and a group called Not Yet New York. Opponents applied pressure on city officials, including Mayor Tom Bradley. In 1987, the mayor and the Los Angeles city council killed the LANCER project—a project that had included a commitment of $12 million.

Just as Los Angeles' largest African American community was selected for the city's first state-of-the-art municipal solid-waste incinerator, the state's first state-of-the-art hazardous-waste incinerator was slated to be built near East Los Angeles, the city's largest Latino American community. Officials of the California Thermal Treatment Services (CTTS) planned the hazardous-waste incinerator for Vernon, an industrial suburb that has only 96 people. Estimates indicated that the incinerator would burn about 22,500 tons of hazardous waste per year.

Several East Los Angeles neighborhoods, made up mostly of Latino Americans, are located only a mile and downwind from the proposed hazardous-waste incinerator site. The Vernon incinerator was intended to be the "vanguard of the entire state program for disposal of hazardous waste." Residents of East Los Angeles questioned the selection of their community as host for the state's first hazardous-waste incinerator. Opponents of the incinerator saw the project as just another case of industry dumping on the Latino American community.

Mothers of East Los Angeles (MELA) led the opposition to the Vernon incinerator. MELA consisted of Latino American women who had originally organized against the state's plan to locate a prison in East Los Angeles.

MELA targeted the South Coast Air Quality [M]anagement District (AQMD), the California Department of Health Services (DHS), and the Environmental Protection Agency (EPA)—agencies responsible for awarding permits for the hazardous waste incinerator. MELA, like its South Central Los Angeles counterpart, was also able to garner allies to oppose the government-sanctioned hazardous-waste incinerator. MELA and its allies pressured CTTS through a lawsuit and the passage of a more stringent California state law requiring environmental impact reporting on hazardous-waste incinerators.

In 1988, as CTTS was about to start construction on the project, AQMD decided that the company should conduct environmental studies and redesign the original plans because of the new, more stringent state clean-air regulations. CTTS challenged the AQMD's decision up to the state supreme court and lost. In May, 1991, CTTS decided to withdraw because the lawsuits threatened to drive the costs beyond the $4 million the company had already spent on the project. The incinerator was not built.

The other California community slated for a state-of-the-art hazardous-waste incinerator is Kettleman City, a rural farm-worker community of about twelve hundred residents. Because of their work, residents are exposed to dangerous pesticides. Moreover, the city is home to a Chemical Waste Management hazardous-waste landfill, California's largest hazardous-waste landfill.

In 1991, the California Rural Legal Assistance Foundation, a public-interest law group, filed a class-action lawsuit, *El Pueblo Para el Aire y Agua Limpio* (*People for Clean Air and Water*) v. *County of Kings*. The lawsuit challenged the environmental-impact report in its use of English as the only language used to communicate risks to local residents when 40 percent of the residents speak only Spanish, and for its operating hazardous-waste incinerators in mostly minority communities. In 1992, a Superior Court judge overturned the Kings County board's approval of the incinerator, citing its impact on air quality and agriculture. . . .

A new form of grass-roots environmental activism has emerged in the United States that emphasizes securing environmental justice for communities of color. Knowing that environmental racism is a major barrier to achieving environmental and economic justice for people of color, grass-roots activists have not limited their attacks to noxious facility siting and toxic contamination issues. Instead they have begun to seek change in destructive industrial production processes, wasteful consumptive behavior, urban land use and transportation, spatial housing patterns and residential segregation, redlining, and other environmental problems that threaten public safety.

People-of-color groups have begun to build a national movement for environmental justice. However, a national policy is needed to address environmental problems that disproportionately affect people-of-color, working class, and low-income communities. All communities deserve to be protected from the ravages of pollution. No one segment of society should have to bear a disparate burden of the rest of society's environmental problems.

Finally, pushing "risky" technologies and "dirty" industries off on a people as a form of economic development is not a solution to the under-development in impoverished Third World-like communities in this country and in similar communities around the world. Social-justice and equity goals must be incorporated into all levels of environmental decision making and policy formulation.

 F U R T H E R   R E A D I N G

David R. Brower, "Restoring Hetch Hetchy," *Earth Island Journal* (Fall 1987): 24–25

Ted K. Bradshaw and Edward J. Blakely, *The Rural Community in the Advanced Industrial Society* (1980)

William Bronson, *How to Kill a Golden State* (1968)

Robert D. Bullard, *Confronting Environmental Racism* (1993)

Raymond F. Dasmann, *The Destruction of California* (1965)

Raymond F. Dasmann, *California's Changing Environment* (1981; 2nd ed., 1988)

Harry Dennis, *Water and Power: The Peripheral Canal and Its Alternatives* (1981)

David E. Dowall, *The Suburban Squeeze* (1986)

Harrison C. Dunning, "Dam Fights and Water Policy in California: 1969–1989," *Journal of the West* XXIX (July 1990): 14–27

Robert Easton, *Black Tide: The Santa Barbara Oil Spill and Its Consequences* (1972)

Ernest A. Englebert, ed., *Competition for California Water* (1982)

Robert C. Fellmuth, *The Politics of Land: Ralph Nader's Study Group Report on Land Use in California* (1973)

Bernard J. Frieden, *The Environmental Hustle* (1979)

Harold Gilliam, *Between the Devil and the Deep Blue Bay: The Struggle to Save San Francisco Bay* (1969)

Robert Gottlieb, *Forcing the Spring: The Transformation of the American Environmental Movement* (1993)

Charles A. Gulick, *The Fight for San Francisco Bay: The First Ten Years* (1971)

Garrett Hardin, *Living within Limits: Ecology, Economics, and Population Taboos* (1993)

John Hart, ed., *The New Book of California Tomorrow: Reflections and Projections for the Golden State* (1985)

Robert G. Healy, ed., *Protecting the Golden Shore: Lessons from the California Coastal Commission* (1978)

David Helvarg, *The War against the Greens: The "Wise Use" Movement, the New Right, and Anti-Environmental Violence* (1994)

Richard Hofrichter, ed., *Toxic Struggles: The Theory and Practice of Environmental Justice* (1993)

Jennifer K. Hollon, *Solar Energy for California's Residential Sector* (1980)

W. Turrentine Jackson and Alan M. Paterson, *The Sacramento-San Joaquin Delta and the Evolution and Implementation of Water Policy: An Historical Perspective* (1977)

Yvonne Olson Jacobson, *Passing Farms, Enduring Values: California's Santa Clara Valley* (1985)

James E. Krier and Edmund Ursin, *Pollution and Policy: A Case Essay on California and Federal Experience with Motor Vehicle Air Pollution, 1940–1975* (1977)

Martin W. Lewis, *Green Delusions: An Environmental Critique of Radical Environmentalism* (1992)

Richard G. Lillard, *Eden in Jeopardy: Man's Prodigal Meddling with His Environment—The Southern California Experience* (1966)

Ronald F. Lockmann, *Guarding the Forests of Southern California* (1981)

Leo McCarthy, *Poisoning Prosperity: The Impact of Toxics on California's Economy: Report by the California Commission for Economic Development* (1985)

Leo McCarthy, *Poisoning Prosperity II: Chemical Exposures vs. Public Health: Report to the California Commission for Economic Development* (1988)

Rice Odell, *The Saving of San Francisco Bay: A Report on Citizen Action and Regional Planning* (1972)

Tim Palmer, ed., *California's Threatened Environment: Restoring the Dream* (1993)

Sandra Postel, *Last Oasis: Facing Water Scarcity* (1992)

Richard Reinhardt, *California 2000: The Next Frontier* (1982)

Robert W. Righter, "Wind Energy in California: A New Bonanza," *California History* LXXIII (Summer 1994): 142–55, 174–75

Jim Robbins, *Last Refuge: The Environmental Showdown in the American West* (1994)

Alfred Runte, *Yosemite: The Embattled Wilderness* (1991)

Ed Salzmann, ed., *California Environment and Energy: Text and Readings on Contemporary Issues* (1980)

Susan R. Schrepfer, *The Fight to Save the Redwoods: A History of Environmental Reform, 1917–1978* (1983)

Susan R. Schrepfer, "The Nuclear Crucible: Diablo Canyon and the Transformation of the Sierra Club, 1965–1985," *California History* LXXI (Summer 1992): 212–37, 291–94

Mel Scott, *The Future of San Francisco Bay* (1963)

Stanley Scott, ed., *Coastal Conservation: Essays on Experiments in Governance* (1981)

Fred Setterberg and Lonny Shavelson, *Toxic Nation: The Fight to Save Our Communities from Chemical Contamination* (1993)

Lenny Siegel, "High Tech Pollution," *Sierra Club Bulletin* LXIX (December 1984): 58–64

Al Sokolow, "Urbanizing California's Farmland," *California Journal* XXI (November 1990): 535–38

Douglas H. Strong, *Tahoe: An Environmental History* (1984)

Samuel J. Walker, "Reactor at the Fault: The Bodega Bay Nuclear Power Plant Controversy, 1958–1964—A Case Study in the Politics of Technology," *Pacific Historical Review* LIX (August 1990): 323–48

Charles F. Wilkinson, "Crossing the Next Meridian: Sustaining the Lands, Waters, and Human Spirit in the West," *Environment* XXXII (December 1990): 14–20, 32–34

Samuel E. Wood and Alfred Heller, *California, Going, Going . . .* , (1962)

Charles Zurhorst, *The Conservation Fraud* (1970)

Racial and Class Tensions, 1960s–1990s

Two events occurred in 1965 that would have profound effects on the state of California in the years to come. On the evening of August 11, the California Highway Patrol arrested an intoxicated African-American driver near but not in the section of Los Angeles known as Watts. This incident spiraled into six days of civil unrest that ended with thirty-four persons dead, more than a thousand injured, almost four thousand arrested, and more than $40 million in property damage. Some observers called the civil unrest a riot, underlining the unlawful behavior of those involved, while others called it an insurrection, a rebellion, or an uprising, to make the point that they thought the actions were justified given the centuries of oppression that black Americans had suffered. In the aftermath, numerous studies were done to identify underlying causes and to propose solutions. Some commentators warned that if the appalling conditions faced by African Americans in Los Angeles and other large cities were not ameliorated, similar disorders might occur again.

Almost twenty-seven years later, on April 29, 1992, another conflagration engulfed Los Angeles when four Los Angeles Police Department officers were acquitted for their brutal beating of African-American motorist Rodney King. This eruption was more complex in terms of race, more destructive in terms of human and property losses, and more dispersed in geographic area. Fifty-two people died, almost 2,400 were injured, and more than 16,000 were arrested. Of those 16,000, many were Latinos, who were subsequently deported. Estimates of property damage ran as high as $1 billion. While certain aspects of the 1992 civil unrest, now called "America's first multiethnic riot," seem similar to those of 1965, there are also notable differences.

The differences result from the second event in 1965—a quiet episode that occurred three thousand miles away in Washington, D.C.—that also had momentous, though unanticipated, consequences for California. On October 3, Congress amended the nation's immigration laws. Under the new laws, Asians were permitted, for the first time in more than forty years, to enter the United States in sizable numbers as immigrants. Each country in the Eastern Hemisphere was allowed to send a maximum of up to 20,000 immigrants per year, with a hemispheric ceiling of 170,000. The cap for the Western Hemisphere was 120,000. In addition, the spouses, minor children, and parents of U.S. citizens could enter without being counted as part of the allotted quotas. For the first time, aspiring Asian immigrants could compete for slots on the same footing as Europeans.

Since 1965 more than five million Asians have arrived in the United States. Today, a diverse range of Asians comprise approximately half of the total number of immigrants entering the United States each year. The post–1965 Asian population has further swelled with the influx of well over a million refugees from Vietnam, Cambodia, and Laos after the governments of those countries became Communist in 1975.

The Latino-ancestry population has also become more diverse in this same period. Though still dominated by persons of Mexican ancestry, California is now home to large numbers of people from El Salvador, Nicaragua, Guatemala, and other Central and South American countries. Immigrants and refugees have also hailed from various countries in the Middle East. At the same time, the composition of immigrants from Europe has changed. After the former Soviet Union relaxed its emigration controls, tens of thousands of Soviet Jews settled in the United States.

The 1990 census showed that California was the nation's most ethnically diverse state. California now has the country's largest number and highest percentage of Asians (9.6 percent of California's population), the largest percentage of Latino Americans (25.8 percent of Californians), and the second largest number of African Americans (2.2 million, second only to New York's 2.9 million), as well as the second largest number of Native Americans (242,164, second only to Oklahoma's 252,420).

Diversity exists not only in terms of race and ethnicity but also in terms of class. Individuals from many socioeconomic backgrounds are found in every ethnic group. Well-to-do professionals and business entrepreneurs live the good life, while their poorer compatriots toil for less-than-minimum wage in garment factories, hotels, and restaurants, and as road construction crews, groundskeepers, and janitors.

Racial, ethnic, and class antagonisms abound, but neighbors usually manage to get along or at least to tolerate one another. Tensions flare and fights erupt when drug dealers or ethnically-exclusive youth gangs infringe on each other's turf. Police officers who treat all young men of color as though they were criminals only add fuel to the fire.

In the quarter century following World War II, when the California economy was booming, African American workers in Los Angeles could find reasonably well paid blue-collar jobs in heavy industry. But by the late 1980s and early 1990s, such jobs had virtually disappeared due to three processes—global restructuring, deindustrialization, and demilitarization.

The first two processes are closely related. Global restructuring refers to the fact that nearly half the goods sold in the United States are now made in newly industrializing Asian nations or in Latin America to take advantage of lower labor costs. The result is fewer manufacturing jobs left in the United States. Deindustrialization refers to the decline of manufacturing coupled with the rise of the service sector. The services offered are not just for consumers but also for businesses. They include banking and other financial operations, insurance, brokerage, advertising, information processing, *building maintenance, transportation, health care, recreation, education, and law enforcement. To find jobs in the professionalized service sector, one must have a good education. Minority youths who drop out of high school are not employable in this fast-growing sector of the economy. Both the youths and the adults who lost their jobs in manufacturing often end up relying on public assistance for survival.*

The third process, demilitarization, has hit California especially hard. With the disintegration of the Communist bloc, many U.S. military bases have closed. The ripple effects of base closures have been traumatic. Local economies supported by the salaries of military personnel have suffered, and defense contracts have plummeted.

These larger forces that originate outside California, together with the widening racial and class polarization within the state, do not augur well for California's future. That polarization was dramatically revealed once again by the acquittal of O. J. Simpson, a well-known African American charged with murder. The jurors' verdict prompted intense emotions ranging from joy to outrage, responses that split largely along racial lines.

The massive civil disorders that erupted in Los Angeles in the 1960s and the 1990s have been analyzed in depth by newspaper reporters, sociologists, politicians, criminologists, psychologists, historians, and others. The disorders are especially troubling because they signal serious social divisions throughout the state, not just in Los Angeles. While differences in socioeconomic opportunity available to the various classes of society form the crux of the problems, they are exacerbated by differences in race and ethnic background. Nearly everyone agrees that unless the problems are successfully addressed, civil unrest is likely to spread and erupt again and again. The selections in this chapter offer several perspectives on the causes of the problems, but the real challenge lies in finding solutions.

DOCUMENTS

The first document is excerpted from the report on the Watts riot made by the Governor's Commission on the Los Angeles Riots. Appointed by Governor "Pat" Brown in 1965, the commission was chaired by John McCone, former director of the U.S. Central Intelligence Agency. Brown named McCone to this post because he hoped McCone's impeccable conservative credentials would help to squelch accusations that Democrats were too "soft" on crime and on African Americans.

The second document, by David Rieff, a senior fellow at the World Policy Institute, was written before the events of 1992. Rieff notes how the demographic composition of Los Angeles made immigrants highly conscious of their racial origins. Race unfortunately did become a salient feature of the 1992 eruptions and of the O. J. Simpson trial.

The next five documents present different perspectives on the 1992 events. Mwatabu S. Okantah, poet, performance artist, and author of the third document, powerfully protests the Rodney King beating. Armando Navarro, professor of ethnic studies at the University of California, Riverside, provides a Latino perspective in the fourth document. The fifth document is by Eui-Young Yu, professor of sociology and director of the Center for Korean American and Korean Studies at California State University, Los Angeles. He offers a Korean view of events. The sixth document is excerpted from a speech by Patrick Buchanan, a conservative Republican candidate for president in 1992 and 1996. John Bryant, in the seventh document, encourages business executives to treat minorities fairly. Himself a product of the black community in Los Angéles, today he heads Operation Hope, Inc., an organization working to funnel loans and investments into the black communities of Los Angeles.

The last two documents appeared in response to the "not guilty" verdict in the O. J. Simpson trial. In the eighth document, Lynell George and David Ferrell, staff writers for the *Los Angeles Times,* discuss how race relations in Los Angeles are complicated by the very features that have distinguished the city from other large metropolitan areas in the nation. The ninth document is by George Regas, rector emeritus of All Saints Church in Pasadena, who offers his vision of how racial healing can be achieved. Sermonic in tone, Regas emphasizes the importance of human understanding and love but ignores the larger structural forces that divide one group from another.

The McCone Commission Analyzes the Watts Riot, 1965

The rioting in Los Angeles in the late, hot summer of 1965 took six days to run its full grievous course. In hindsight, the tinder-igniting incident is seen to have been the arrest of a drunken Negro youth about whose dangerous driving another Negro complained to the Caucasian motorcycle officer who made the arrest. The arrest occurred under rather ordinary circumstances, near but not in the district known as Watts, at seven o'clock on the evening of 11 August, a Wednesday. The crisis ended in the afternoon of 17 August, a Tuesday, on Governor Brown's order to lift the curfew which had been imposed the Saturday before in an extensive area just south of the heart of the City.

In the ugliest interval, which lasted from Thursday through Saturday, perhaps as many as 10,000 Negroes took to the streets in marauding bands. They looted stores, set fires, beat up white passersby whom they hauled from stopped cars, many of which were turned upside down and burned, exchanged shots with law enforcement officers, and stoned and shot at firemen. The rioters seemed to have been caught up in an insensate rage of destruction. By Friday, the disorder spread to adjoining areas, and ultimately an area covering 46.5 square miles had to be controlled with the aid of military authority before public order was restored.

The entire Negro population of Los Angeles County, about two thirds of whom live in this area, numbers more than 650,000. Observers estimate that only about two per cent were involved in the disorder. Nevertheless, this violent fraction, however minor, has given the face of community relations in Los Angeles a sinister cast.

When the spasm passed, thirty-four persons were dead, and the wounded and hurt numbered 1,032 more. Property damage was about $40,000,000. Arrested for one crime or another were 3,952 persons, women as well as men, including over 500 youths under eighteen. The lawlessness in this one segment of the metropolitan area had terrified the entire county and its 6,000,000 citizens. . . .

While the Negro districts of Los Angeles are not urban gems, neither are they slums. Watts, for example, is a community consisting mostly of one[-] and two-story houses, a third of which are owned by the occupants. In the riot area, most streets are wide and usually quite clean; there are trees, parks, and playgrounds. A Negro in Los Angeles has long been able to sit where he wants in a bus or a movie house, to shop where he wishes, to vote, and to use public facilities without discrimination. The opportunity to succeed is probably unequaled in any other major American city.

Yet the riot did happen here, and there are special circumstances here which explain in part why it did. Perhaps the people of Los Angeles should have seen trouble gathering under the surface calm. In the last quarter century, the Negro population here has exploded. While the County's population has trebled, the Negro population has increased almost tenfold from 75,000 in 1940 to 650,000 in 1965. Much of the increase came through migration from Southern states and many arrived with the anticipation that this dynamic city would somehow spell the end of life's endless problems. To those who have come with high hopes and great expectations and see the success of others so close at hand, failure brings a special measure of frustration and disillusionment. . . .

When the rioting came to Los Angeles, it was not a race riot in the usual sense. What happened was an explosion—a formless, quite senseless, all but hopeless violent protest—engaged in by a few but bringing great distress to all.

Nor was the rioting exclusively a projection of the Negro problem. It is part of an American problem which involves Negroes but which equally concerns other disadvantaged groups. In this report, our major conclusions and recommendations regarding the Negro problem in Los Angeles apply with equal force to the Mexican-Americans, a community which is almost equal in size to the Negro community and whose circumstances are similarly disadvantageous and demand equally urgent treatment. That the Mexican-American community did not riot is to its credit; it should not be to its disadvantage.

In examining the sickness in the center of our city, what has depressed and stunned us most is the dull, devastating spiral of failure that awaits the average disadvantaged child in the urban core. His home life all too often fails to give him the incentive and the elementary experience with words and ideas which prepares most children for school. Unprepared and unready, he may not learn to read or write at all; and because he shares his problem with 30 or more in the same classroom, even the efforts of the most dedicated teachers are unavailing. . . .

Frustrated and disillusioned, the child becomes a discipline problem. Often he leaves school, sometimes before the end of junior high school. (About two-thirds of those who enter the three high schools in the center of the curfew area do not graduate.) He slips into the ranks of the permanent jobless, illiterate and untrained, unemployed and unemployable. All the talk about the millions which the government is spending to aid him raise his expectations but the benefits seldom reach him.

Reflecting this spiral of failure, unemployment in the disadvantaged areas runs two to three times the county average, and the employment available is too often intermittent. A family whose breadwinner is chronically out of work is almost invariably a disintegrating family. Crime rates soar and welfare rolls increase, even faster than the population. . . .

Yet, however powerful their grievances, the rioters had no legal or moral justification for the wounds they inflicted. Many crimes, a great many felonies, were committed. Even more dismaying, as we studied the record, was the large number of brutal exhortations to violence which were uttered by Negroes. Rather than making proposals, they laid down ultimatums with the alternative being violence. All this nullified the admirable efforts of hundreds, if not thousands, both Negro and white, to quiet the situation and restore order.

What can be done to prevent a recurrence of the nightmare of August? It stands to reason that what we and other cities have been doing, costly as it all has been, is not enough. Improving the conditions of Negro life will demand adjustments on a scale unknown to any great society. . . .

[However, t]he consequences of inaction, indifference, and inadequacy, we can all be sure now, would be far costlier in the long run than the cost of correction. If the city were to elect to stand aside, the walls of segregation would rise even higher. The disadvantaged community would become more and more estranged and the risk of violence would rise. The cost of police protection would increase, and yet would never be adequate. Unemployment would climb; welfare costs would mount apace. And the preachers of division and demagoguery would have a matchless opportunity to tear our nation asunder.

As a Commission, we are seriously concerned that the existing breach, if allowed to persist, could in time split our society irretrievably. So serious and so explosive is the situation that, unless it is checked, the August riots may seem in comparison to be only a curtain-raiser for what could blow up one day in the future.

Our recommendations will concern many areas where improvement can be made but three we consider to be of highest priority and greatest importance.

1. Because idleness brings a harvest of distressing problems, employment for those in the Negro community who are unemployed and able to work is a first priority. Our metropolitan area employs upwards of three millions of men and women in industry and in the service trades, and we face a shortage of skilled and semi-skilled workers as our economy expands. We recommend that our robust community take immediate steps to relieve the lack of job opportunity for Negroes by cooperative programs for employment and training, participated in by the Negro community, by governmental agencies, by employers and by organized labor.

2. In education, we recommend a new and costly approach to educating the Negro child who has been deprived of the early training that customarily starts at infancy and who because of early deficiencies advances through school on a basis of age rather than scholastic attainment. What is clearly

needed and what we recommend is an emergency program designed to raise the level of scholastic attainment of those who would otherwise fall behind. This requires pre-school education, intensive instruction in small classes, remedial courses and other special treatment. The cost will be great but until the level of scholastic achievement of the disadvantaged child is raised, we cannot expect to overcome the existing spiral of failure.

3. We recommend that law enforcement agencies place greater emphasis on their responsibilities for crime prevention as an essential element of the law enforcement task, and that they institute improved means for handling citizen complaints and community relationships.

The road to the improvement of the condition of the disadvantaged Negro which lies through education and employment is hard and long, but there is no shorter route. The avenue of violence and lawlessness leads to a dead end. To travel the long and difficult road will require courageous leadership and determined participation by all parts of our community, but no task in our times is more important. Of what shall it avail our nation if we can place a man on the moon but cannot cure the sickness in our cities?

David Rieff Sees Los Angeles as the Capital of the Third World, 1991

[T]he more you looked, the more inadequate a notion like diversity became as a frame for thinking about what was going on in Southern California. . . . Anglo Californians, accustomed as they were to thinking of the world in terms of whites and "minorities," and having in general only the shakiest grasp of the particular characteristics of the countries the immigrants were arriving from, fell easily into the habit of thinking of their new neighbors as Hispanics, Asians, or Middle Easterners. What was more interesting, though, was that the immigrants themselves were coming to accept a similar self-conception. This was an enormous transformation in consciousness, and one that was neither as automatic nor as easily accomplished as it might have appeared to be on the surface.

For the immigrants had not turned up in Los Angeles with any such ideas in their heads, far from it, nor had their initial experiences of life in the region done much more than replicate, however luxurious some of the settings, the sense they had had of life back home. This was part economic necessity—the fact that immigrants, even if they worked for Anglos, otherwise relied on their fellow countrymen in almost every material aspect of life from shopping to finding a job—part language barrier, and since the familiar tastes and customs in the alien world of Los Angeles (alienness being also in the eye of the beholder) were a consolation, it was tempting to stay in the ethnic ghetto.

In the first generation, they did. If you went to a Salvadoran restaurant patronized by people just in from the South, you *were* in El Salvador, at least until, blinking, you walked out into the mini-mall parking lot and found yourself—that was what it felt like—back in L.A. The same held true in a Korean bar on Olympic Boulevard, an Iranian coffee shop in Westwood, or an Ethiopian diner on Washington Boulevard. And in these places, people tended to talk about their own national identities as if they had never made the trip to the United States. . . .

In their insularity, it was possible for Anglos to assume that since they thought of themselves as Americans, and the Europeans they met usually described themselves as coming from France, Germany, or Italy . . . , such broad categories had always predominated. In fact, it had only been a few generations since Americans had described themselves as Missourians and Oregonians, Yankees and Southerners. . . . [W]here this increasing sense of generalization was taking hold was not in the Third World at all, but right there in Los Angeles, California, U.S.A. . . .

[I]n the space of three generations or less, the immigrants would move from being part of subgroups within their own countries of origin to becoming American minority groups. It was a trajectory as confusing, if not more so, to the people within the immigrant communities themselves as it was to Anglo and black L.A. In Salvador, you were not Hispanic, you were a Salvadoran. In Asia, you were not an Asian, you were Chinese. And yet in Los Angeles, these deepest of selves were simply subsumed in the broader context of a new, overarching Hispanicity or Asianness.

Paradoxically, in leaving their homelands in the Third World to go to L.A., the immigrants had in fact joined the Third World for, in many cases, the first time in their lives. Because the term "Third World" really only made sense in America, or some other rich country; that is, as an antonym to some other world, the white world, say. What else bound such diverse places as Mexico, El Salvador, the Philippines, South Korea, Hong Kong, and Iran, which were so unlike one another in terms of language, culture, history, and national character, if not the weight of some enormous counterdistinction that made even these intricate questions seem secondary? The answer, of course, was that just such a supervening category did exist, in Los Angeles as everywhere else in America, and it was race. . . .

[T]he idea of the Third World was the inescapable legacy of European imperialism, a system that had divided peoples—colonizers and colonized—along the cruel dichotomous lines of white and nonwhite. That was an inheritance no part of the world could so easily shrug off, least of all the United States, whose great national tragedy had always been race, just as Europe's had been class. Americans might prefer the euphemisms of "majority" and "minority," but the meaning was the same. And where else could the immigrants themselves fall, once they had arrived, but into this oldest of American fault lines, even if, ironically, the whole idea of a white majority and a nonwhite minority was rapidly becoming a statistical as well as a metaphysical illusion?

If anything, what was surprising about Los Angeles, and what made it so different, so very much more hopeful, than other cities and other regions in the United States, was that for all the prevailing myopia there were many voices there calling for the country's long racial civil war to end—even if this meant, as it were, going over to the nonwhite side. That old Angeleno disdain for the past had conferred a kind of freedom. It permitted clear-

we live in your house.
we are strangers.
we see you in the workplace.
we are invisible.
we die in your wars.
we kill for you.
we make you laugh.
we sing, we dance for you.
you do not see us.
you see us
only when we wreak havoc
in your streets,
framed nightly on your tv screens,
you see us only
when we leap
out of your wildest dreams.

we saw them beat him.
you say
you just don't understand.
you have eyes.
you refuse to see.
to see us,
you have to look into our lives,
into that darkening
 terror
mirror reflecting
your deeply
deep felt
why:

you don't understand.
you live in fear.
you have not
 listened.
you
turned
a deaf ear . . .

Armando Navarro Offers a Latino Perspective
on the 1992 Civil Disorders, 1993

The eruption was but the calm before the storm. The frustration and anger that exploded on April 29, 1992, remains [*sic*]. Unless major economic and political changes take place and race and ethnic relations improve, Los Angeles will be subject to further "balkanization" that will continue to pit ethnic and racial groups against each other. . . .

The nation and California's economy are plagued by increasing poverty, unemployment, the exodus of industry, and social problems. From the federal to the state to the local level, government is increasingly incapable of fiscally meeting the exigencies of the urban crisis. The inability of these governmental entities to act in bringing about change to areas such as SCLA [South Central Los Angeles] is heightening the people's level of frustration and discontent. This pervasive economic crisis is fostering conflict and tensions among not only ethnic and racial groups, but among the "have-nots," "have-little-want-more," and the "have-it-all-want-more" socioeconomic classes. American society today is becoming increasingly class-stratified. . . .

The lack of commitment by the federal government is shown by its failure to provide adequate assistance relief via the Federal Emergency Management Agency to victims. According to the *Los Angeles Times,* "denial rates for nearly all Federal grant and loan programs are running at fifty percent or higher, leaving many victims and their advocates with a sense that the aid process is not working." At the local level, even efforts initiated by Rebuild L.A. were being scaled down in 1993. . . . To date, there is no governmental entity at any level that is designed or equipped to effectively deal with the consequences of . . . such events as the eruption of SCLA.

Without the federal government stepping in and developing a comprehensive "Urban Marshall Plan" that can produce jobs, improve schools, build adequate housing, clean up crime and drugs, provide health care, and involve the people in the reconstruction of their cities, the eruption of SCLA portends worse crises. . . .

The consequences of the eruption for Latinos are even worse. SCLA is becoming heavily Latino. By the twenty-first century, Latinos will be the largest ethnic group in the city and comprise over 50 percent of its population. Peace in Central America will more than likely slow the exodus of immigrants. However, the exodus from Mexico will continue, regardless of the condition of the Mexican economy. . . . This translates to the possibility of Latinos in SCLA being relegated to a quasi-"South African syndrome" status, where Latinos will constitute the majority of the population, yet the non-Latino minority will control the economic and political power. . . . The immigrant bashing has intensified to a fever pitch where in California, both Republican and Democrat, federal and state officials have proposed scores of restrictive and racist immigration policies directed at the Latino immigrant. . . .

In order to avoid this negative scenario, Latinos must put aside their differences and forge powerful alliances among themselves that are based on popular participation. Politicians need to be held accountable via the power of an organized , politicized, and registered populace. To accomplish this, massive political education efforts must be initiated to convince the thousands of legal immigrants to become naturalized citizens and to vote. The same must be done for the United States native-born Latinos who reside in SCLA.

The most powerful weapon the people have with which to obviate a South African syndrome is the formation of powerful grass-roots organizations led by individuals indigenous to SCLA. . . . Latinos in SCLA must design economic, political, and social developmental plans that will with time empower them and give them control of their own *barrio* economies, political structures, and social institutions. Self-sufficiency and self-reliance in these times of economic crisis must guide the actions of these plans.

Concomitantly, if Latinos are to avoid another disruption, they must seek to form coalitions with other ethnic and social groups. Inter-ethnic coalition-building is a must. Latinos must be willing to share economic and political power. Other groups must be willing to do the same. The Latino's growing population has value both politically in the vote and economically in the form of purchasing power. Hence, accords must be reached so that the rifts and conflicts are mitigated and a more united development process is realized that is beneficial to all.

Eui-Young Yu Offers a Korean American Perspective on the Los Angeles Civil Disorders, 1992

Korean-Americans are shocked and dismayed. We are shocked because we did not know that what happened in Los Angeles last week could happen in this country. We came to this country with a dream to build a new and better life; waking up in early morning hours, putting in 14 hours a day, going to bed at midnight, six to seven days a week, without a vacation for years so that we could send our kids to college to fulfill that dream. We built our homes, our businesses and our town with tears and toil. We transformed a rundown section of the center city into the booming Koreatown, full of life, enthusiasm and hope.

Last week, we saw our lifelong dreams ransacked and burned down for no reason. We saw a complete destruction of humanity. Was there no ethic, no morality, no responsibility, no human dignity among those people who looted and burned our property, livelihood and dreams? We saw children, teen-agers, men, women and the elderly turn into mobs. Some people said it was class warfare. But these children are too young to be class-conscious. Some others said it was a race war. But we saw all colors among the looters, and the burned-down shops had no color.

Where were our mayor, our police chief, our governor, our President when innocent citizens and shopkeepers were under siege on the TV screen for hours and hours and days and days? Our leaders are out of touch. Get out of your limousines, take the RTD and ride through the Koreatown and South-Central. Live with the real people.

It was a total breakdown of humanity, civility, the system. We are all responsible, you and I. It was our system that failed. The system failed to protect us, did not educate our children right, did not provide help when needed. The system left us in anarchy for three horrifying days.

By Wednesday evening, we knew the mobs would soon reach Koreatown. Desperate calls for help to city authorities were not answered. Koreatown leaders thought they had many friends in City Hall as they gave generously to their campaign coffers. At the time of crisis, no one provided us with police protection. We had to stand alone in times of danger. Don't talk about the National Guard being held up because of an ammunition delay. That is ridiculous. Some veteran groups wanted to arm themselves in order to defend the town. Community leaders pleaded not to, that it would not be a right thing to do. Police handcuffed some armed defenders face down on the ground, while letting looters go.

On TV screens the scenes of armed Koreans defending their property were shown again and again. Some of them were seen aiming at would-be attackers. The attacking mobs were not shown. Why? The defenders were portrayed by the mainstream media, particularly KABC, as gun-toting hoodlums. They just wanted to scare away the mobs. While Koreans were desperately calling for help, hosts and guests on TV talk shows were framing the black/Korean conflict as the main cause of the riot. Like our leaders, editors and reporters of the mainstream media are out of touch, insensitive and seemingly uncaring.

We feel under siege by police, news media and mobs, and have never felt so betrayed, helpless and lonely.

The three-day madness in Los Angeles has nothing to do with us Korean-Americans. It was a violent explosion of anger accumulated over centuries of frustration, helplessness and alienation of the people of color in this country. The Los Angeles experience of the past several days shows that our system, one based on the dominant Eurocentric ideology—one that puts Eurocentric civilization above all others—is not working. From the experience of the 1965 Watts riot, many learned minds predicted a repeat unless the pre-riot conditions improved drastically. The dominant ideology said that there was nothing wrong with the system. The explosion was waiting. The conditions will not improve unless the dominant group opens its mind and treats the people of color and their institutions and culture as equal and decent.

It is unfair for the media and public officials to shift the focus of the current jolt to the black/Korean issue. Many Koreans got hurt because they happened to be near the scene of the explosions. Yes, there are problems between Koreans and blacks, and we need to improve our relationship and learn to live together in peace. But these mobs were not targeting us alone. The media never show the total picture.

We are equally shocked by the verdict on the Rodney King beating and stand in unity with the black community on the issue. Something is very wrong with the judicial system as far as justice for the people of color is concerned. Many of us feel that justice was not served in Soon Ja Du's verdict, either. We understand the anger and frustration expressed by the black community on these events.

But we also want you to know that since Jan. 1, 1990, at least 25 Korean-American merchants have been killed by non-Korean gunmen. Most of the merchants had been held up at gunpoint more than once.

We have no apologies to looters and arsonists who have mutilated our property and town. We do not apologize for years of hard work. Violence will not bring the needed change. We must educate our children to grow [up] to be decent and responsible human beings and we must organize ourselves better, or we will not be able to change the status quo.

We have survived extreme oppression ourselves. We have survived the colonial atrocities, World War II and the Korean War. We will not leave Koreatown. We will rise again and rebuild the city. They took away our property but we still have our hopes and dreams. This time we want to rise with all groups, and together make this city a better place to live for all of us.

Patrick J. Buchanan Condemns the "Barbarism" of the Mob, 1992

Last Monday in Los Angeles, I went to Koreatown to visit the devastated zone. As I came upon a shop, gutted and burned, a man came up beside me. "This was my business," he said, and he told me what happened:

On Thursday afternoon, 24 hours after the riot began, no police were around. And the mob came. The man was on the roof watching when the firebombs came through his front window. "I couldn't do anything," he said. So he ran. "My whole life was here in this laundry," he told me. "I started it 12 years ago; I built it up to 19 workers; now, it's all gone. I came to America in 1968, I am an American citizen. But I have no insurance, and only $2,000 left in the bank. What am I going to do?"

Then, that evening, I watched on television, as some of those who had been in the thick of the rioting laughed in exultation and triumph at how the Koreans had gotten what they deserved.

Theirs was the authentic laughter of the barbarian from time immemorial, after some church or synagogue is burned or looted, after they have brutalized and beaten. From Brown Shirts to Red Guards, the mocking laughter is always the same. Friends, make no mistake, what we saw in Los Angeles was evil exultant and triumphant and we no longer saw it as through a glass darkly, but face to face.

In Los Angeles, government failed in its first duty, to protect the property and lives of its citizens. And those who lacked the courage to move against that mob, or to condemn its evil deeds unequivocally, are guilty of moral appeasement. . . .

As America's imperial troops guard frontiers all over the world, our own frontiers are open, and the barbarian is inside the gates. And you do not deal with the Vandals and Visigoths who are pillaging your cities by expanding the Head Start and food stamp programs. . . .

It is folly to think you can engender character in men and women by taking away from them their duty and responsibility as parents and citizens to feed, clothe, house, educate, and nurture their own children and obey society's laws like everyone else.

But where did the mob come from?

Well, it came out of public schools from which God and the Ten Commandments and the Bible were long ago expelled. It came out of corner drug stores where pornography is everywhere on the magazine rack. It came out of movie theaters and away from TV sets where macho violence is romanticized. It came out of rock concerts where rap music celebrates raw lust and cop-killing. It came out of churches that long ago gave themselves up to social action, and it came out of families that never existed.

If they didn't know any better, perhaps they were never taught any better. When the Rodney King verdict came down, and the rage boiled, these young men had no answer within themselves to the questions: Why not? Why not riot, loot and burn? Why not settle scores with the Koreans? Why not lynch somebody—and get even for Rodney King?

For decades, secularists have preached a New Age gospel, with its governing axiom: There are no absolute values in the universe; there are no fixed and objective standards of right and wrong. There is no God. . . . Every man lives by his own moral code. Do your own thing.

And the mob took them at their word, and did its own thing.

For 30 years, we have watched, one by one, as the conscience-forming and character-forming institutions—family, home, school and church—collapsed. When the mob came out into the street, it discovered that society's external defenses as well—the police—were gone. So, for 38 hours, the city was theirs. While we conservatives and traditionalists were fighting and winning the Cold War against Communism, we were losing the cultural war for the soul of America. And we can see our defeat in the smoking ruins of Los Angeles, in the laughter of the mob, in the moral absolution already being granted the lynchers and the looters.

In the wake of Los Angeles, everyone has a "solution" to the "problem." And these solutions come from earnest and well-intentioned men and women. But, invariably, they advance economic or political ideas to solve what are at root moral questions. Social programs and enterprise zones may be excellent ideas—but they are not relevant to the crisis at hand. They are not going to stop a mob on a rampage; they are not going to convert evil men into good men. They do not reach the human heart. . . .

Can anyone believe this Lost Generation, steeped in drugs, crime, immorality and hate, is going to be converted to decency by an offer of jobs at the minimum wage? . . .

America is the greatest country on earth; our history is one of glory and greatness, of tragedy and hope. We must not let them take it away. . . .

[W]e must take back our cities, and take back our culture and take back our country.

God bless America.

John Bryant Encourages Corporate America to Invest in Minority Communities, 1995

As founder of Operation HOPE Inc., I find myself in the business of showing financial institutions that it is in their enlightened best interest to lend and invest in neglected minority and underserved communities.

I have found that some institutions do a good job naturally, but most need a helping hand; some occasionally need a firm nudge. The lead pitch from me is not one of charity, but market viability. But no matter how I select my words, nor sound the statistics, sometimes the person on the other side of the desk only hears "handouts," "government mandates" or "bad loans."

We hear what we want to hear; it's what we don't know that kills us. This is why Congress in 1977 passed the Community Reinvestment Act, or CRA.

Basically, CRA means new markets. CRA is not some kind of weird loan guarantee for a person who shouldn't be extended credit, but is simply an invitation to sit down and have a rational chat with a person who normally would probably not give you the time of day. It is a foot in the door, period. . . .

My principal audience is Caucasian, and even when they want to, they often simply don't get it. . . .

I recognize that America has taken a prolonged and painful economic haircut, and that tolerance and compassion are luxuries of a democracy with a solid middle class. But at this most tenuous time in our history, the most fragile time of our history, with the emergence of a society that is increasingly of color, this is no time to be promoting indifference, intolerance, a lack of inclusion. This is no time to divide and conquer.

As unpopular as it may be, that's why I resist the attacks on what is traditionally known as affirmative action. All these laws are intended to do is say, "Look, obviously you haven't been able to do it naturally, so we are going to create an environment where you must do it legally. . . . But we are not asking you to hire incompetents who can't do the job. At the end of the day, if you can show that the people are not qualified, you don't have to hire them at all."

Merit is not one-dimensional. How you approach things and how you get to things can be unique and different, and that process needs to be respected. If I want to do business in Korea, then I sure better know something about the cultures and customs of Koreans. If you want to do business in South-Central Los Angeles, you had better understand how to deal with the fact that there is a resurgence in cultural identity, and the fact that the community that I grew up in doesn't trust white people, or the mainstream systems created by white people. They don't trust financial institutions, they don't trust government, so the basic system has broken down. There is no identifiable infrastructure. But there is a market!

So there are different rules and different ways and different customs in different communities. The value of diversity is being able to tap into that knowledge base. And diversity should be factored into our assessment of merit. . . .

What I am saying to corporate America is: Practice affirmative action, because ultimately it is in your vested best interest as a business to do it. Do not lie to me and suggest that discrimination does not exist in 1995 and that there does not need to be another system that allows me fair and equal unencumbered access to the market place. Do not put that lie in front of me.

We cannot afford to play politics with this issue. This is not about being a Democrat or a Republican. This is about being good Americans, committed to a universal moral law. We need to have an honest debate—if you want to remove affirmative action, fine, but replace it with something better. But don't stand up and lie to me.

I am not asking anyone to think like me. I am not asking anyone to be an advocate for African Americans and minorities. I will take care of myself. But I am passionately pleading with you, please do not stand in my way. Please do not create an environment where hate and anger are easy. Please do not create an environment where you might have race riots and where our racial relationships are tinged even further.

The same people who are saying that we don't need affirmative action have benefited directly from it. Now that they are at the top of the ladder, they kick it away, and say, "I don't need it." Everybody needs somebody. Nobody made it alone. . . .

[Y]ou have got to get people who don't have hope a reason to become hopeful. Self-esteem is not natural, it's nurtured.

If you believe in what we, and others like us, are doing, find a middle ground, find a way, find something that works and don't just end it; mend it.

Lynell George and David Ferrell Analyze the Staggering Racial Complexity of Los Angeles, 1995

The high-flown public image of Los Angeles sprang up as if by magic: a searchlight-swept Hollywood facade, obscuring the nastier blemishes— frustration, anger, urban strife—which periodically threatened to mar the veneer.

Then came Watts, and Rodney G. King, and now O. J. Simpson, and the city's racial rapport teeters, the factions staunchly divided. A place once viewed as idyllic and tolerant, a palm-lined paradise, has come to be seen as quite the opposite—a worst-case example.

"In many ways, L.A. symbolizes the racism in this country like probably no other city," said Richard G. Majors, a senior researcher at the Urban Institute in Washington, D.C. "It's become the poster city for racism in America."

The truth is, Los Angeles has never been the perfect melting pot, with equal opportunity for all—nor is it the most racist of major urban hubs. It is, instead, a fast-changing metropolis where race relations are complicated by many of the same traits that lent the city its distinctive character: its newness, its wealth, its sprawling landscape, even its snaking system of freeways.

L.A.'s racial complexity is staggering. . . . [V]arious subgroups form an array of micro-cities divided by class, race, ethnicity and religion. As some neighborhoods merge, others secede from one another.

"You have neighborhoods changing ethnically literally overnight, displacing people—and displaced people never feel good," said Fernando Guerra, director of the Center for the Study of Los Angeles at Loyola Marymount University. "And it's not only a Latino, black, white thing: You can see it in Monterey Park, which went from being white to increasingly Latino, to now increasingly Asian, and you hear Latinos talking about

Asians the way blacks talk about Latinos, and the way whites talk about blacks."

Situations arise that seldom, if ever, exist anywhere else in the world, demonstrating time and again the vexing nature of racial problems in Los Angeles.

On a single street in South-Central a few years ago, four cultures came together, clashing like mismatched gears. The home-owners were mostly black, living side by side with newly arrived Latino immigrants who occupied several large apartment houses. At each end of the block was a family-owned convenience store—one run by Koreans, the other by Vietnamese.

The blacks thought the Latinos were ruining the neighborhood: growing corn in their front yards, working on junker cars in the street. The Asian store owners refused to allow schoolchildren to place fund-raising signs in their shop windows. Language and cultural barriers prevented anyone from talking, so the anger smoldered until some blacks began moving out; others mounted a "Don't move, improve" campaign. . . .

It used to be . . . that most neighborhoods had individuals—typically older men and women—who would step in and mediate . . . problems. But cultural tensions in Los Angeles have ratcheted up so far, become so entwined with violence and crime, that would-be peacemakers have retreated to the safety of their homes. . . .

Newcomers are often startled by the intricacy of Los Angeles' racial dynamics, especially after arriving from less-fragmented cities where racial issues involve only two or three groups. . . .

One thing people learn is that Los Angeles' sprawling size makes it a highly contradictory place. There are communities—Culver City, Pasadena, Silver Lake—where racial mixing is rich, and usually amicable. And then there are communities entirely cut off from one another, either by freeways or hillsides or by sheer distance. In some segregated white enclaves, the appearance of minorities causes unease. They are watched with suspicion, followed through stores, discouraged in subtle ways from ever coming back.

"You're not treated very well," said social worker Mike Neely, who said huge segments of the black community thus never venture to beaches, art galleries or trendy hangouts. . . .

For many, the easiest answer to L.A.'s racial tensions is to avoid contact with other groups. . . .

The great labyrinth of freeways, one of the hallmarks of L.A. life, also complicates racial relations, setting Los Angeles apart from other cities because of the great distances that people travel in the insular confines of a car. Freeway driving prevents even the most superficial interaction with other racial groups. A subway commuter in Manhattan might encounter scores of blacks, Latinos and Asians in a single five-mile trip to the office; but a white commuter from Sherman Oaks might drive 40 minutes Downtown, day in, day out, for years, and never really see people of other races except at work, or possibly the gas station.

A Times poll in 1992 found that 35% of the city's white population has never been in South-Central or Watts. And thus many have no idea that those communities are filled with stucco homes, churches, furniture stores, palm trees and families working and raising their children.

Instead, many whites tend to see those areas as a featureless shadow land, a danger zone that symbolizes black rage, gangs, drive-by shootings and welfare mothers. In the resulting climate of distrust, racial biases harden; there is less interest in bridging differences, erasing stereotypes. . . .

More than any other single dynamic, the tension between the black community and the police represents the city's most enduring and defining racial problem. How it came to be that way involves not only the profound social problems of the city core but also the geographic and social forces that shaped Los Angeles.

Whites dominated the city's early growth, seeking out the beaches and claiming many communities just inland of those—or near Downtown—by placing restrictions on property: *"Said property shall not at any time be lived upon by any person whose blood is not entirely that of the Caucasian race,"* one typical deed read. Racial minorities were excluded from Inglewood, Glendale, Culver City and Mid-Wilshire.

Blacks found homes in inland communities, which merged during the heavy migrations of the 1940s and '50s into one of the nation's largest predominantly black centers, an area spanning close to 50 square miles. In it were doctors['] offices, corner grocers, clubs—everything. There was little reason for blacks to venture outside. . . .

There were also plenty of industrial jobs—until the big factories began to close. Bethlehem Steel, Firestone, Goodyear. In the four-year period ending in 1982, 75,000 manufacturing jobs disappeared in greater Los Angeles. . . .

Economic decline heightened racial tensions. To struggling blacks, whites represented the financial power-brokers who closed up those factories and who kept blacks from gaining work elsewhere. Eventually, the Latinos who immigrated by the thousands to South-Central came to be seen as competition for the jobs that were left. Koreans were resented for owning stores that blacks could not afford for lack of loans or personal assets.

Social problems also grew out of the economic despair—notably drug dealing and gang warfare. In cracking down, LAPD officers sometimes resorted to excessive force, using race as a means to identify "crimnals." . . .

L.A.'s fascination with wealth—mansions, Rolls-Royces—further complicates the picture. . . .

L.A. thrives as a center for sports, film and music—all fields in which minorities have excelled. That influence opens doors for blacks and other groups in Los Angeles. . . .

Yet the percentage of minorities who achieve entree into those elite circles is still small . . . racial relations here suffer because of the yawning chasm between rich and poor. That gulf creates enormous frustration, . . . especially in a city where every facet of life is chronicled by the mass media. . . .

Ads and TV series tout the lifestyles of the rich and famous. . . . And all the while, TV and radio newscasts create the impression that gangsters, drugs and violence run rampant throughout all communities of color. . . .

Racial issues are allowed to fester; even the language of discussion— "riots," "minorities"—has become a minefield of potential conflict.

"We're so sensitive, so raw," said [Christopher] McCauley, the city human relations executive. "People are afraid that if they voice a concern, they'll cross a social border—and the consequences will be hellish."

Instead, they do nothing—usually. But there are exceptions, people who are sufficiently concerned by the complexity of the problem that they are breaking out of old habits, trying new things, being very L.A. in that respect. . . .

[They learn] that there are still vast racial differences, but that there is a healing power in being able to listen.

George Regas Advocates a Shared Moral Vision, 1995

More than any other event in the last 20 years, the Simpson trial forces all of us to look into the chasm of race and see unmistakably its breadth and depth. We are so deeply polarized that no verdict could reconcile our feelings. We have pretended race isn't an issue for the last 20 years, but the Simpson trial shoves it right into our eyes. . . .

Outraged feelings from both sides have been expressed and the divide between us is profound. But it would be the ultimate outrage if we let this brutal murder and trial drive us further apart. The jury is still out on whether we are committed to healing the racial chasm. I would suggest some ways toward racial healing.

First, we must understand our differences. The trial didn't create this division among African Americans and white Americans—it only brought it dramatically to the surface. Healing will come only if there are places where blacks and whites take the risks to be frank and candid about race. . . .

We won't heal the division by living in segregated worlds and never sharing honestly with each other.

Second, a culture must be created that allows us to see that one person's gain means the advancement of us all. Over the last 15 years, the concept of the common good has been tragically corrupted. . . . We can never eradicate racism that corrodes the soul of the nation unless we affirm our membership in that one human family, brothers and sisters, all sacred. I believe this is the central issue of our time. Our lives and destinies are wrapped up together. . . .

What an incredible gift to families raising children in these troubled days if we could create a moral vision for America where the affluent are tied to the poor, the secure ones are bound together with the homeless and the well-being of my children and grandchildren is dependent on the health of all children. If a nation could not survive half-slave and half-free, no nation will be blessed if it is half-rich and half-impoverished.

There is something decadent about a city or a nation that denies this human solidarity. There is something corrupting about the assumption that a few have the right to good health, dignified jobs, fine education and decent housing—while others live in misery. It is my deepest conviction that any hope of racial healing is found in this renewed commitment to the common good and creating a culture in which this texture is unmistakably clear.

Third, we must find a new way to love. The primary quality of divine love is its inclusive and universal dimension. So many today in churches and legislatures take pride in their exclusive claims and promote a message that divides the nation. . . .

Suspicion, fear and hatred of the "other"—the one not like me—is the fundamental disease of the world today. This disease of the heart is the source of every genocide, every holocaust, every ethnic cleansing, every gay bashing, every urban riot, every skinhead outbreak. And today's political climate is playing this card of hate.

Our hope is in setting our faces against the tide of this disease, and building communities of inclusive love. . . .

The spirit of Martin Luther King Jr. transformed this nation and he believed love was the only alternative to hatred and racism. Some would say he sounds sentimental before the raw emotions of race today. Yet Dr. King looked at those horrific walls of segregation and believed love put into action, love appealing to human goodness, could bring that wall tumbling down.

Racial healing is hugely complex, but if we could find ways to love we could, in Martin's words, "inject new meaning and dignity into the veins of civilization." It is our overwhelming responsibility. . . .

Will we learn before it is too late? Of all Michelangelo's powerful figures, none is more poignant than the man in the Last Judgment being dragged down to hell by demons, his hand over one eye and in the other eye a look of dire recognition. He understood, but too late. That's our story in America. Michelangelo was right: Hell is truth seen too late.

  E S S A Y S

The authors of the first essay are all professors of sociology at the University of California, Los Angeles. As scholars committed to promoting the well-being of all minority communities, they carefully avoid depicting the events of 1992 as conflicts between various minority groups. Instead, they strive to ensure that their readers understand the larger context in which the 1992 civil disorders took place. Especially enlightening is their analysis of how the demographic composition of South Central Los Angeles has changed in the last few decades and their discussion of how the "social safety net" has been dismantled. They end the essay with recommendations on what needs to be done.

Sumi K. Cho, author of the second essay, is a Korean American and one of the first individuals to receive a Ph.D. in ethnic studies from the University of California, Berkeley. She is presently a professor of political science at the University of Oregon. Cho believes that Korean grocer Soon Ja Du's killing of the African American teenager, Latasha Harlins, was wrong, but she questions "why the individual actions of one store owner are attributed to an entire race." She urges scholars to go beyond a black-white dichotomy when they analyze American race relations and points out that many of the tensions between Korean Americans and African Americans arise out of class antagonisms rather than racial or cultural differences.

The Causes of the 1992 Los Angeles Civil Disorders

MELVIN L. OLIVER, JAMES H. JOHNSON, JR., AND WALTER C. FARRELL, JR.

In this essay, we reflect on the Los Angeles civil disorder of 1992 from an urban political economy perspective. It is our contention that the course and magnitude of changes in the urban political economy of American cities in general, and Los Angeles in particular, were crucial in bringing to the forefront the contradictions underlying the Los Angeles urban rebellion. . . . [W]e situate the civil unrest within the broader context of the recent demographic, social, and economic changes occurring in the Los Angeles milieu. The object of this analysis is to ground the rebellion in the context of a political system that is frayed at the edges in its attempt to integrate new voices into the body politic and, at the same time, is incapable of bringing into the economic mainstream significant portions of the African-American community (traditionally one of the most economically marginal segments of American society). . . .

The recent civil unrest in Los Angeles was the worst such event in recent U.S. history. None of the major civil disorders of the 1960s, including the Watts rebellion of 1965, required a level of emergency response or exacted a toll—in terms of loss of life, injuries, and property damage and loss—comparable to the Los Angeles rebellion of 1992. . . . The burning, looting, and violence that ensued following the rendering of a not-guilty verdict in the police-brutality trial required the deployment of not only the full forces of the Los Angeles Police Department (LAPD) and the Los Angeles County Sheriff's Department, but also 10,000 National Guardsmen and 3,500 military personnel. . . . The Fire Department received 5,537 structure fire calls and responded to an estimated 500 fires. An estimated 4,000 businesses were destroyed. Fifty-two died and 2,383 people were injured, including 20 law-enforcement and fire personnel. Property damage and loss have been estimated at between $785 million and $1 billion. . . .

In contrast to the civil disorders of the 1960s, this was a multiethnic rebellion. . . . It has been estimated that 1,200 of the 16,000 plus arrested were illegal aliens, roughly 40% of whom were handed over to the INS officials for immediate deportation. . . . Also in contrast to the civil disorders of the 1960s, the burning and looting were neither random nor limited to a

Excerpted from *Reading Rodney King, Reading Urban Uprising*, Robert Gooding-Williams, ed. (1993), by permission of the publisher, Routledge: New York and London.

single neighborhood; rather, the response was targeted, systematic, and widespread, encompassing most of the legal city. This fact has led us to purposefully and consistently refer to the civil unrest as a rebellion as opposed to a riot. . . .

The videotaped beating of Mr. Rodney King was only the most recent case in which there were serious questions about whether LAPD officers used excessive force to subdue or arrest a black citizen. For several years, the City of Los Angeles has had to pay out millions of taxpayers' dollars to settle the complaints and lawsuits of citizens who were victims of LAPD abuse. Moreover, the black citizens of the city of Los Angeles have been disproportionately victimized by the LAPD's use of the choke hold, a tactic employed to subdue individuals who are perceived to be uncooperative. During the 1980s, 18 citizens of Los Angeles died as a result of LAPD officers' use of the choke hold; 16 of them reportedly were black.

Accordingly, the not-guilty verdict rendered in the police-brutality trial was also only the most recent in a series of cases in which the decisions emanating from the criminal-justice system were widely perceived in the black community to be grossly unjust. This decision came closely on the heels of another controversial verdict in the Latasha Harlins case. A videotape revealed that Ms. Harlins—an honor student at a local high school—was fatally shot in the back of the head by a Korean shopkeeper following an altercation over a carton of orange juice. The shopkeeper received a six month suspended sentence and was ordered to do six months of community service.

These and related events have occurred in the midst of drastic demographic change in South Central Los Angeles. Over the last two decades, the community has been transformed from a predominantly black to a mixed black and Latino area. . . . Today, nearly one-half of the South Central Los Angeles population is Latino. In addition, there also has been an ethnic succession in the local business environment, characterized by the exodus of many of the Jewish shopkeepers and a substantial influx of small, family-run Korean businesses. This ethnic succession in both the residential environment and the business community has not been particularly smooth. The three ethnic groups—blacks, Latinos, and Koreans—have found themselves in conflict and competition with one another over jobs, housing, and scarce public resources.

Part of this conflict stems from the fact that the Los Angeles economy has undergone a fairly drastic restructuring over the last two decades. This restructuring includes, on the one hand, the decline of traditional, highly unionized, high-wage manufacturing employment; and on the other, the growth of employment in the high-technology-manufacturing, the craft-specialty, and the advanced-service sectors of the economy. . . . South Central Los Angeles—the traditional industrial core of the city—bore the brunt of the decline in manufacturing employment, losing 70,000 high-wage, stable jobs between 1978 and 1982.

At the same time these well-paying and stable jobs were disappearing from South Central Los Angeles, local employers were seeking alternative sites for their manufacturing activities. As a consequence of these seemingly routine decisions, new employment growth nodes or "technopoles" emerged in the San Fernando Valley, in the San Gabriel Valley, and in El Segundo near the airport in Los Angeles County, as well as in nearby Orange County. . . . In addition, a number of Los Angeles–based employers established production facilities in the Mexican border towns of Tijuana, Ensenada, and Tecate. Between 1978 and 1982, over 200 Los Angeles–based firms, including Hughes Aircraft, Northrop, Rockwell, as well as a host of smaller firms, participated in this deconcentration process. Such capital flight, in conjunction with the plant closings, has essentially closed off to the residents of South Central Los Angeles access to what were formerly well-paying, unionized jobs.

It is important to note that, while new industrial spaces were being established elsewhere in Los Angeles County (and in nearby Orange County as well as along the U.S.-Mexico border), new employment opportunities were emerging within or near the traditional industrial core in South Central Los Angeles. . . . But, unlike the manufacturing jobs that disappeared from this area, the new jobs are in competitive sector industries, which rely primarily on undocumented labor and pay, at best, minimum wage.

In part as a consequence of these developments, and partly as a function of employers' openly negative attitudes toward black workers, the black-male jobless rate in some residential areas of South Central Los Angeles hovers around 50%. Whereas joblessness is the central problem for black males in South Central Los Angeles, concentration in low-paying, bad jobs in competitive sector industries is the main problem for the Latino residents of the area. Both groups share a common fate: incomes below the poverty level. . . . Whereas one group is the working poor (Latinos), the other is the jobless poor (blacks).

In addition to the adverse impact of structural changes in the local economy, South Central Los Angeles also has suffered from the failure of local institutions to devise and implement a plan to redevelop and revitalize the community. In fact, over the lat [*sic*] two decades, the local city government has consciously pursued a policy of downtown and westside redevelopment at the expense of South Central Los Angeles. . . .

Finally, the seeds of the rebellion are rooted in nearly two decades of conservative policy making and implementation at the federal level. Many policy analysts talk about the adverse impact on minorities and their communities of Democratic president Lyndon Johnson's "War on Poverty" programs of the 1960s, but we must not lose sight of the fact that Republicans have been in control of the White House for all but four (the Carter years) of the past 20 years. A number of public policies implemented during this period, and especially during the years when Mr. Reagan was president, we contend, served as sparks for the recent civil unrest. Three of these policy domains are worthy of note here.

The first pertains to the federal government's establishment of a laissez-faire business climate in order to facilitate the competitiveness of U.S. firms. Such a policy, in retrospect, appears to have facilitated the large number of plant closings in South Central Los Angeles and capital flight to the U.S./Mexico border and various Third World countries. Between 1982 and 1989 there were 131 plant closings in Los Angeles, idling 124,000 workers. Fifteen of these plants moved to Mexico or overseas.

The second involved the federal government's dismantling of the social safety net in minority communities. Perhaps most devastating for the South Central Los Angeles area has been the defunding of community-based organizations (CBOs). Historically, CBOs were part of that collectivity of social resources in the urban environment which encouraged the inner-city disadvantaged, especially disadvantaged youth, to pursue mainstream avenues of social and economic mobility and discouraged dysfunctional or antisocial behavior. In academic lingo, CBOs were effective "mediating" institutions in the inner city.

During the last decade or so, however, CBOs have become less effective as mediating institutions. The reason for this is that the federal support they received was substantially reduced. In 1980, when Mr. Reagan took office, CBOs received an estimated 48% of their funding from the federal government. As part the Reagan Administration's dismantling of the social safety net, many CBOs were forced to reduce substantially programs that benefited the most disadvantaged in the community. Inner-city youth have been most adversely affected by this defunding of community-based initiatives and other safety-net programs.

It should be noted, moreover, that the dismantled social safety net has been replaced with a criminal dragnet. That is, rather than allocate support for social programs that discourage or prevent disadvantaged youth from engaging in dysfunctional behavior, over the past decade or so, the federal government has pursued a policy of resolving the problems of the inner city through the criminal-justice system.

Given this shift in policy orientation, it should be not be surprising that, nationally, 25% of prime-working-age young black males (ages 18–35) are either in prison, in jail, on probation, or otherwise connected to the criminal-justice system. Although reliable statistics are hard to come by, the anecdotal evidence suggests that at least 25% of the young black males in South Central Los Angeles have had a brush with the law. What are the prospects of landing a job if you have a criminal record? Incarceration breeds despair and in the employment arena, it is the scarlet letter of unemployability.

Educational initiatives enacted during the late 1970s and early 1980s, which were designed to address the so-called "crisis" in American education, constitute the third policy domain. There is actually a very large body of social-science evidence which shows that such policies as tracking by ability group, grade retention, and the increasing reliance on standardized tests as the ultimate arbiter of educational success have, in fact, disenfranchised large numbers of black and brown youth. In urban school systems, they are disproportionately placed in special-education classes and are more likely than their white counterparts to be subjected to extreme disciplinary sanctions.

The effects of these policies in the Los Angeles Unified School District (LAUSD) are evident in the data on school-leaving behavior. For the Los Angeles Unified School District as a whole, 39.2% of all the students in the class of 1988 dropped out at some point during their high-school years. However, for high schools in South Central Los Angeles, the drop-out rates were substantially higher, between 63% and 79%. . . . It is important to note that the drop-out problem is not limited to the high-school population. According to data complied by LAUSD, approximately 25% of the students in the junior high schools in South Central Los Angeles dropped out during the 1987–88 academic year. . . .

Twenty years ago it was possible to drop out of school before graduation and find a well-paying job in heavy manufacturing in South Central Los Angeles. Today, however, those types of jobs are no longer available in the community, as we noted previously. Juxtaposing the adverse effects of a restructured economy and the discriminatory aspects of education reforms, what emerges is a rather substantial pool of inner-city males of color who are neither at work nor in school. These individuals are, in effect, idle; and pervious research shows us that it is this population which is most likely to be in gangs, to engage in drug trafficking, and to participate in a range of other criminal behavior. Moreover, we know that it is this population of idle, minority males that experiences the most difficulty forming and maintaining stable families, which accounts, at least in part, for the high percentage of female-headed families with incomes below the poverty level in South Central Los Angeles.

The most distinctive aspect of the Los Angeles rebellion was its multi-ethnic character. While blacks were the source of the disturbances as they broke out on the first night of the rebellion, by the second evening it was clear that the discontent that emerged initially was shared by many of the city's largest racial group, the Latino community. . . . [T]he economically depressed Latinos in Los Angeles are comprised of a working-poor population, characterized by a large and significant core of Mexican and Central American immigrants. But what is interesting is that the rebellion did not encompass the traditional Mexican-American community of East Los Angeles. Indeed, the fires and protest were silent in these communities as political leaders and local residents ardently cautioned residents against "burning your own community." Nevertheless, Latinos in South Central Los Angeles did not hesitate to participate in looting, primarily against Korean merchants. How do we explain this pattern?

One important element necessary to explain the uneven participation of Latinos in the rebellion is to place the Latino experience into the context of struggles to incorporate that community politically into the electoral system in Los Angeles city and county. With the largest Latino population outside of Mexico City, Latinos have been severely underrepresented in city and county governments. In a struggle emanating from the 1960s, Latinos, particularly Mexican Americans, have been involved in protesting this situation, in ways ranging from street-level, grass-roots activity to highly coordinated court challenges to racially biased redistricting schemes that have unfairly diluted Latino voting strength. That struggle has just recently begun to bear fruit. In the important court case *Garza et al.* v. *County of Los Angeles,* Los Angeles County was found guilty of racial bias in the redistricting process and ordered to accept an alternative redistricting plan that led to the election of Gloria Molina as the first Latino(a) to serve on the powerful five-person Los Angeles County Board of Supervisors. Recent maneuvering at the city level will ensure significant representation of Latinos on the Los Angeles City Council, but not without considerable conflict between entrenched black and Latino City Council leaders over communities that are racially mixed. Los Angeles is a city in flux politically.

While it is clear that an emerging Latino majority will assume greater political power over time, the political-empowerment process has left several portions of the Latino population behind. In particular, Mexican Americans in Los Angeles, who have a longer history there and are more likely to constitute greater portions of the voting-age-citizen population, are the key recipients of the political spoils that have come in the Latino struggle for electoral power. All the elected officials to come into power as a consequence of these struggles are Mexican, and while they articulate a "Latino" perspective on the issues, they also tend to represent a narrow "Mexican" nationalism. The growing Central American population, which is residentially based in South Central Los Angeles and not in the traditional core of East Los Angeles, has not benefited for the most part from the political empowerment of Mexicans in Los Angeles. They are recent immigrants, not able to vote, and thus have become the pawns in negotiations with the county and city over the composition of political districts. Black and white politicians now represent districts with up to 50% of the population being Latino. But because they are unable to vote, a declining black or white population of 25% to 35% can maintain control over these districts without addressing the unique need of a majority of the community. The upshot has been the political neglect of a growing community whose problems of poverty have been just as overlooked as those of the black poor.

This contrast was easily observed during the rebellion as traditional Mexican-American community leaders were either silent or negative toward the mass participation of Latinos in the rebellion. Those Latinos in South Central had little stake in the existing political and economic order while East Los Angeles was riding the crest of a successful struggle to incorporate their political demands into the electoral system. Just as the black community is divided into a middle and a working class that are connected to the system by way of their political and economic ties, the Latino community in Los Angeles is increasingly divided by income, ethnicity, and citizenship.

The second element necessary to understand the involvement of Latinos, particularly Central American and Mexican immigrants, in the rebellions is the existence of interethnic hostilities between these groups and Korean-Americans. While much is made of African-American and Korean-American conflict, little is said about an equally and potentially more volatile conflict between Latinos and Koreans. While the crux of African-

American and Korean-American conflict is based on the uneasy relationship between merchant and customer, the Latino-Korean conflict has the added dimensions of residential and workplace conflict. Latino involvement in the rebellion was most intense in Koreatown. Koreatown is an ethnic enclave demarcated by both the Korean control of businesses and a dwindling Korean residential presence. The community, in fact, is residentially mixed, with large portions of Latinos and Koreans. Latinos in this community come into contact with Koreans on multiple levels and, from all we know from current research, experience considerable hostility in each level. First, in terms of residence, Latinos complain of discrimination on the part of Korean landlords as buildings and apartments are rented according to racial background. Second, as customers in Korean establishments, Latinos complain of forms of disrespectful treatment similar to that about which black customers complain. Third, as employees in Korean small businesses, Latinos point to high levels of exploitation by their employers. Thus, in this context, it was not surprising to see the vehemence and anger that the Latino community in South Central Los Angeles expressed, especially toward the Korean community. . . .

The federal blueprint and . . . the local "Rebuild L.A." initiative headed by Mr. Peter Ueberroth . . . [are both] built on the central premise that, if the proper incentives are offered, the private sector will, in fact, play the leading role in the revitalization and redevelopment of South Central Los Angeles. We do not think this is going to happen . . . [because] the types of governmental incentives currently under consideration in Washington are not high on private businesses' locational priority lists. . . .

[W]e firmly believe that what is needed to rebuild South Central Los Angeles is a comprehensive public-works service-employment program, modeled on President Roosevelt's Works Progress Administration program of the 1930s. Jobs to rebuild the infrastructure of South Central Los Angeles can provide meaningful employment for the jobless in the community, including the hard-core disadvantaged, and can be linked to the skilled trades' apprenticeship-training programs.

To incorporate the hard-core disadvantaged into such a program would require a restructuring of the Private Industry Council's Job Training Partnership Act Program (JTPA). The program must dispense with its performance-based approach in training where funding is tied to job placement. This approach does not work for the hard-core disadvantaged because training agencies, under the current structure, have consistently engaged in creaming—recruiting the most "job-ready" segment of the inner-city population—to ensure their continued success and funding. Meanwhile, the hard-core unemployed have received scant attention and educational upgrading. . . .

Such a program would have several goals that would enhance the social and economic viability of South Central Los Angeles. First, it would create meaningful jobs that could provide the jobless with skills transferable to the private sector. Second, it would rebuild a neglected infrastructure, making South Central Los Angeles an attractive place to locate for business and commerce. Finally, and most important, by reconnecting this isolated part of the city to the major arteries of transportation, by building a physical infrastructure that could support the social and cultural life of this richly multicultural area (e.g., museums, public buildings, housing), and by enhancing the ability of community and educational institutions to educate and socialize the young, this plan would go far in providing a sustainable "public space" in the community. . . . [O]nly when South Central Los Angeles is perceived as a public space that is economically vibrant and socially attractive will the promise of this multicultural community be fulfilled. Thus far, private-sector actions and federal-government programs and proposals have done nothing to bring us nearer to reaching this goal.

The fires have been extinguished in South Central Los Angeles and other cities, but the anger and rage continue to escalate, and they are likely to reemerge over time to the extent that the underlying political and economic causes are left to fester. While political, business, and civic leaders have rushed to advance old and new strategies and solutions to this latest urban explosion, much of what is being proposed is simply disjointed and/or déjà vu.

Clearly there is a need for additional money to resolve the underlying causes of this urban despair and devastation, but money alone is not enough. Government . . . alone cannot empower poor communities. And although blacks and other people of color have a special role and obligation to rebuild their neighborhoods because they are the majority of the victims and the vandals, they cannot solely assume the burden of responsibility.

What is needed, in our view, is a reconceptualization of problem solving where we meld together, and invest with full potential, those strategies offered from liberals and conservatives, from Democrats and Republicans, and from whites and people of color. . . .

[M]inorities find themselves in the ambiguous situation of needing greater police service on the one hand and protection from the excesses of those same services on the other. This contradictory situation had kept relations between these groups at a race/class boiling point.

More police officers are desperately needed in high-crime communities that are disproportionately populated by the poor. . . . [T]his increase in police power should be deployed via a community policing program. Such an effort can serve to control minor offenses and to build trust between police and community residents. . . . In addition, the intensive recruitment of minority officers and specific, ongoing (and evaluated) diversity training will further reduce police/minority community tensions. But most important in this effort is enlightened, decisive leadership from the office of the chief. . . .

[T]he policy implication that needs to be drawn from the rebellion is that, in order to bring the poor and disenfranchised into mainstream society, in order to enhance their acceptance of personal responsibility, and in order to promote personal values consistent with those of the wider society, we must find a way to provide a comprehensive program of meaningful assistance to this population . . . [through] job training, job creation, and the removal of racial stereotypes and discrimination. . . .

[R]epresentatives of the affected ethnic and racial groups must be in key decision-making roles if these efforts are to achieve success. Citizens of color, individually and through their community, civic and religious institutions, bear a responsibility to promote positive values and lifestyles in their communities and to socialize their youth into the mainstream. But they cannot do this alone.

They cannot be held accountable for the massive plant closings, disinvestments, and exportation of jobs from our urban centers to Third World countries. There must be an equality in status, responsibility, and authority across race and class lines if we are to resolve our urban crises. Government, in a bipartisan fashion, must direct its resources to those programs determined to be successful with the poor, the poor must be permitted to participate in the design of programs for their benefit, and society at all levels must embrace personal responsibility and a commitment to race and gender equity.

How likely are these reforms to be implemented? . . . [T]he answer . . . [is] not . . . an optimistic one. However, an important consequence of the rebellion was to shake the very foundation of the taken-for-granted quality of our discourse and practice about race and class in American society. It opens up the opportunity for reassessing positions, organizing constituencies, and collectively engaging issues that have been buried from sight until now. Given these new openings, the Los Angeles urban rebellion of 1992 gives us all the opportunity to work on building a society in which "we can all get along."

Perceptions Across the Racial Divide

SUMI K. CHO

The violence and destruction that followed the Rodney King verdict again exploded the myth of a shared consensus around American justice and democracy. The blind injustice of the Simi Valley "not guilty" verdict produced a rainbow coalition of people—old, young, of all colors—who had few or no reservations about looting stores owned primarily by Koreans and Latinos. It soon became clear that the nation's professional, academic, political, and business elite were ill-equipped to deal with the complexity of issues before them, captured in the simple but straightforward plea by Rodney King: "Can we all get along?"

King's question hints at the real question confronting U.S. society: Who is the "we" that must get along? For too long, the political and academic tradition has defined U.S. race relations in terms of a Black/white binary opposition. For example, a CNN-*Time Magazine* poll taken immediately after the verdict surveyed "Americans" on their opinions regarding the

Excerpted from *Reading Rodney King, Reading Urban Uprising*, Robert Gooding-Williams, ed. (1993), by permission of the publisher, Routledge: New York and London.

verdict and the violence that followed. Yet the poll only sought the views of African Americans and whites regarding the future of race relations. The Black/white framing of race issues must give way to a fuller, more differentiated understanding of a multiracial, multiethnic society divided along the lines of race, class, gender, and other axes in order to explicate effectively the Los Angeles explosion and to contribute to the long-term empowerment of those who, for a short time, exercised the power of their own agency.

Dominating the current debate within the Black/white racial paradigm are, on the one hand, the human-capital theorists who assert that the degradation of "family values" caused the fires in L.A. . . . On the other hand, there are structuralists proposing that the U.S. adopt a "Marshall Plan" for its cities to address the institutional lockout of people of color from economic development.

While the structural explanations provide more illuminating insights than human-capital theories, they cannot fully explain the myriad of events in Los Angeles, particularly those that affected the Korean-American community. The portrayal of Asian Americans as the paragons of socioeconomic success contributed to the targeting of Korean Americans as a scapegoat by those above and below Koreans on the socioeconomic ladder during the L.A. riots. The King verdict and the failure of the U.S. economy to provide jobs and a decent standard of living for all its peoples, the ostensible root causes of the rioting, were not the fault of Korean (or Latino) shopowners. . . .

Manipulation of Korean Americans into a "model minority" contributed to their "triple scapegoating" following the King verdict. The first layer of attack came from those who targeted Korean-owned stores for looting and arson. The second layer consisted of those in positions of power who were responsible for the sacrifice of Koreatown, Pico Union, and South Central Los Angeles to ensure the safety of wealthier, whiter communities. The final scapegoating came at the hands of the media, eager to sensationalize the events by excluding Korean perspectives from coverage and stereotyping the immigrant community. These three forces combined to blame the Korean-American community for the nation's most daunting economic and sociopolitical problems.

Rodney King's spontaneous reaction seeing the varied groups of color pitted against each other in L.A. reflected a deeper understanding of the commonalities among those groups than many intellectuals and politicians have shown. "I love people of color," he declared, although almost all the mainstream edited out this statement. Further, his plea can be read as a challenge to the academic community and intellectual activists of racial and ethnic politics: "We're all stuck here for awhile. . . . Let's try to work it out."

Race-relations theorists must accept this challenge and go beyond the standard structuralist critique of institutional racism to incorporate the most difficult issues presented by the aftermath of the not-guilty verdicts in the Rodney King case. Specifically, intellectual activists must devise a new approach to understanding interethnic conflict between subordinated groups and work toward a proactive theory of social change. Such a theory would examine the structural conditions that influence patterns of conflict or cooperation between groups of color, racial ideologies and how they influence group prejudices, as well as the roles of human agency, community education, and political leadership and accountability. Such a theory should strive to explain and resolve interethnic conflicts to unite subordinated groups. . . .

The deteriorated socioeconomic conditions of neglected inner cities have led scholars to compare ghettos like South Central Los Angeles . . . to South African "bantustans" that serve solely as "holding space for blacks and browns no longer of use to the larger economy." African Americans constitute 73.9 percent of South Central's residents, and Latinos account for 22.9 percent (with a quickly growing undocumented population). Only 3.6 percent of the total land mass is zoned for industry. South Central residents lack self-determination and political-economic power. In this context, Korean Americans who open stores in the neighborhood are resented by long-deprived residents and are seen as "outsiders" exerting unfair control and power in the community. The interaction between the two racial groups is structured strictly by market relationships: one is the consumer, the other is the owner. This market structuring of group relations has influenced the "Korean/Black conflict" and contributed to the course of events following the not-guilty verdicts.

Koreans first were scapegoated by rioters of all colors who looted stores and later set them afire. . . . The most oft-stated reason for the targeting of these stores and Korean stores in general was a familiar refrain: Korean owners were rude to African American and Latino customers. One Latino interviewed on television was asked why people were looting Koreans. "Because we hate 'em. Everybody hates them," he responded.

Much has been said about the rudeness of Korean owners. Some of the major media outlets that covered the tensions between African Americans and Korean Americans attempted to reduce the conflict to "cultural differences" such as not smiling enough, not looking into another person's eyes, not placing change in a person's hands. Although Koreans wanted very badly to believe in this reductionism, one making an honest assessment must conclude that far too many Korean shopowners had accepted widespread stereotypes about African Americans as lazy, complaining criminals.

The dominant U.S. racial hierarchy and its concomitant stereotypes are transferred worldwide to every country that the United States has occupied militarily. Korean women who married American GIs and returned to the United States after the Korean War quickly discovered the social significance of marrying a white versus an African-American GI. American racial hierarchies were telegraphed back home. When Koreans immigrate to the U.S., internationalized stereotypes are reinforced by negative depictions of African Americans in U.S. films, television shows, and other popular forms of cultural production. . . .

On the other hand, many African Americans also internalize stereotypes of Korean Americans. Asian Americans walk a fine line between being seen as model minorities and callous unfair competitors. The result is a split image of success and greed that goes together with callousness and racial superiority. Distinctions between Asian ethnicities are often blurred as are distinctions between Asians and Asian Americans. "Sins of the neighbor" are passed on to Koreans in the United States. For example, when the prime minister Yasuhiro Nakasone of Japan made his blundering remarks in 1986 that "the level of intelligence in the United States is lowered by the large number of Blacks, Puerto Ricans, and Mexicans who live there," this comment was often applied generally to represent the views of all Asians, including Koreans, although Korea has a long history of colonization at the hands of the Japanese.

In rationalizing the violence that followed the verdict, African-American leaders often repeated the myth that Korean immigrants unfairly compete with aspiring entrepreneurs from the Black community because Korean Americans receive preferential treatment over African Americans for bank and government loans. . . . In reality, however, banks and government lenders uniformly reject loan applications for businesses located in poor, predominantly minority neighborhoods such as South Central Los Angeles, regardless of the applicant's color. Korean immigrants rarely receive traditional financing. Those who open liquor stores and small businesses often come over with some capital and/or borrow from family and friends. At times, groups of Koreans will act as their own financial institutions through informal rotating credit associations known as "kyes" (pronounced "keh").

Thus, the ability to open stores largely depends upon a class variable, as opposed to a racial one. . . .

Nevertheless, the politics of resentment painted Koreans as callous and greedy invaders who got easy bank loans. As this depiction ran unchecked, it became increasingly easy to consider violence against such a contemptible group. . . . When the scorching injustice of the verdict was announced, Korean-owned businesses were scapegoated as the primary target for centuries of racial injustice against African Americans—injustice that predated the bulk of Korean immigration which occurred only after the lifting of discriminatory immigration barriers in 1965. . . .

The police nonresponse to the initial outbreak of violence represented a conscious sacrificing of South Central Los Angeles and Koreatown, largely inhabited by African Americans, Chicanos, Latinos, and Korean Americans, to ensure the safety of affluent white communities. . . . When it became evident that no police would come to protect Koreatown, Koreans took up arms in self-defense against other minority groups. Rather than focus on whether these actions by the Korean community were right or wrong, one should question the allocation of police-protection resources and the absolute desertion of Koreatown and South Central L.A. by the police. . . .

When Korean Americans called the LAPD and local and state officials for assistance and protection, there was no response. It was very clear that Koreatown was on its own. In the absence of police protection, the community harnessed its resources through Radio Korea (KBLA) in Los Angeles to coordinate efforts to defend stores from attack. People from as far away as San Bernadino and Orange County came to help. Radio Korea reported on the movement of the crowds and instructed volunteers where to go. In short, the radio station and individual volunteers served as the police force for Koreatown. It is bitterly ironic that some Koreans defending stores were later arrested by police for weapon-permit violations.

In stark contrast, when looters began to work over major shopping malls such as the Fox Hills Mall in Culver City, they were quickly stopped by the police, with "merchants and residents praising [police] efforts." Likewise, the police made sure that the downtown business interests were secured. The west-side edition of the *Los Angeles Times* even boasted that the police forces in the predominantly white communities of Santa Monica, Beverly Hills, and West Hollywood "emerged remarkably unscathed by the riots." Other areas, especially communities of color such as South Central, Pico Union, and Koreatown, effectively became a "no-person's land." . . . There was no protection for these areas. Although residents paid taxes for police protection, the LAPD made a conscious choice to stay out of the neighborhoods of color that were most at risk during the postverdict rioting. . . .

Many Koreans mistakenly believed that they would be taken care of if they worked hard, did not complain, and contributed handsomely to powerful politicians such as Governor Wilson and local officials. One hard lesson to be learned from the aftermath of the King verdict and the Korean-American experience is that a model minority is expediently forgotten and dismissed if white dominance or security is threatened. . . .

The exclusion of Korean Americans and Asian Americans from mainstream media analysis allows distorted stereotypes to be perpetuated. Stereotypic media portrayals of Koreans as smiling, gun-toting vigilantes and African Americans as vandals and hoodlums trivialize complex social and economic problems. A reasoned Korean perspective would help to balance the picture of hardship and frustration felt by all communities. It would be too simplistic, however, to relegate all of the media to a monolithic mind-set in the coverage. The coverage and stereotypes varied and reflected different political perspectives.

For conservative journalists, Korean Americans were held up as hardworking, law-abiding citizens rightfully taking matters into their own hands. . . . Korean Americans, as a model minority, were depicted as the "legitimate victims" (along with Reginald Denny) and singled out in the media for praise and sympathy.

For liberal members of the media, Korean Americans were manipulated as dangerous vigilantes who were directly responsible for the plight and oppression of African Americans. Already anguished by the not-guilty verdicts of the four white police officers, liberal journalists sought to redeem themselves by providing critical coverage of Korean Americans. From this angle, Korean Americans, not white Americans, became the primary instigators of racism against African Americans. . . .

In Los Angeles, the Black/white tensions resulting from the Rodney King beating and verdict became the filter through which the Latasha Harlins killing was mediated. It is possible that the leadership organizing the African-American community around the Latasha Harlins case was viewed by the mainstream media as less visible and threatening. . . . [C]onflicts between Korean Americans and African Americans in Los Angeles may have provided a safe opportunity to portray Korean "racism," deflect attention away from white racism, while not risking the legitimization of problematic (to whites) Black leadership.

Clearly, Soon Ja Du's killing of Latasha Harlins was wrong, as was Judge Karlin's failure to incarcerate her. The point here is not to provide an excuse for what Du did, but to question why the individual actions of one store owner are attributed to an entire race. . . .

Recent books on race, such as Andrew Hacker's *Two Nations: Black and White, Separate, Hostile, Unequal,* and Studs Terkel's *Race: How Whites and Blacks Think and Feel about the American Obsession,* further embed the construction of U.S. race relations as a binary opposition. Although the theoretical framing of race relations in Black/white terms has substantial historical and contemporary grounding, the recent events in Los Angeles reveal that such an essentialism misses many of the factual complexities in contemporary, urban politics. Latinos suffered nearly one-third of the 58 casualties related to the riot. About one-third of those arrested following the verdict were Latino (mostly for curfew violations, not for looting), although the media portrayed African Americans as the primary participants. At least 1,000 of the Latinos arrested were undocumented immigrants who were immediately scheduled for deportation by the Immigration and Naturalization Service. A substantial number (estimated between 30 and 40 percent) of stores that were lost were Chicano- or Latino-owned. Over 300 Chinese businesses were looted and burned. Vietnamese-owned stores were targeted in Long Beach. Filipino-owned stores were also lost. These facts are overlooked due to the dominant racial framing of the explosion. Although Chicanos, Latinos, and Asian-Pacific Americans are the fastest-growing immigrant groups in the United States, the oppositional Black/white character of the race-relations debate excludes discussion of the colors in the middle, now inexorable parts of the Black/white spectrum. . . .

Typically, non-African American people of color are categorized as either Black or white if they are discussed at all. Native Americans, Chicanos, and Latinos are often summarily included with African Americans under the people of color rubric. The ubiquitous internalization of the model-minority myth by the general population and academics leads to the invisibility of Asian Americans in the racial landscape. . . .

Even in the so-called "Black/Korean conflict," although Koreans are necessarily included in the discussion, the conflict is viewed through the lens of Black/white relationships. In other words, how Korean relationships with African Americans are represented and interpreted often depends upon the latter group's relationship to whites. Korean Americans are instrumentalized in a larger public-relations campaign on behalf of Euro-Americans. Moreover, important class and gender dynamics become obscured by the emphasis on racial differences.

The conflict between Korean Americans and African Americans contains definite cultural differences and racial animosities. But many of the tensions may be class-, rather than racially, based, actually reflecting differences between the store-owning Korean immigrants and the African-American customers. Violence between shopkeepers and residents exists in inner cities regardless of which racial group owns the majority of the stores. . . .

Scholars of ethnic and racial politics must confront head on the challenges of racial theory for the twenty-first century. In order to do this, a serious effort must be made to incorporate the histories and the contemporary experiences of people of color between the two poles of Black and white on the racial spectrum, especially those of the new and rapidly expanding immigrant groups such as Salvadorans, Guatemalans, Vietnamese, Hmong, Mien, Palestinians, Pacific Islanders, and Koreans, among many others. Intellectual activists must grapple openly and critically with the position of each community of color within the complexities of race, ethnicity, class, and gender relations in a post-industrial society. . . . Diversity within ethnic and racial groups must be acknowledged and incorporated into theoretical analyses to avoid essentializing race and obscuring important differences and contradictions.

 F U R T H E R   R E A D I N G

Nancy Abelmann and John Lie, *Blue Dreams: Korean Americans and the Los Angeles Riots* (1995)

Bill Barich, *Big Dreams: Into the Heart of California* (1994)

Leon Bouvier, *Fifty Million Californians: Inevitable?* (1991)

Paul Bullock, ed., *Watts: The Aftermath* (1969)

Pastora San Juan Cafferty and William C. McCready, eds., *Hispanics in the United States: A New Social Agenda* (1985)

Jose Calderon, "Latinos and Ethnic Conflict in Suburbia: The Case of Monterey Park," *Latino Studies Journal II* (1990): 23–32

Edward T. Chang and Russell Leong, eds., *Los Angeles—Struggles toward Multiethnic Community* (1994)

Leo Chavez, *Shadowed Lives: Undocumented Immigrants in American Society* (1992)

Jerry Cohen and William S. Murphy, *Burn, Baby, Burn! The Los Angeles Race Riot, August, 1965* (1966)

Robert Conot, *Rivers of Blood, Years of Darkness* (1967)

Mike Davis, *City of Quartz: Excavating the Future in Los Angeles* (1990; 2d ed., 1992)

Mike Davis, "Who Killed Los Angeles? A Political Autopsy," *New Left Review* 197 (January/February 1993): 3–28, and "Who Killed Los Angeles? Part II: The Verdict Is Given," ibid., 199 (1993): 29–53

Steven P. Erie and Harold Brackman, *Paths to Political Incorporation for Latinos and Asian Pacifics in California* (1993)

Timothy P. Fong, *The First Suburban Chinatown: The Remaking of Monterey Park, California* (1994)

Lynell George, *No Crystal Stair: African Americans in the City of Angels* (1992)

Robert Gooding-Williams, *Reading Rodney King, Reading Urban Uprising* (1993)

Governor's Commission on the Los Angeles Riots, The, *Violence in the City—An End or a Beginning?* (1965)

Pierrette Hongdagneu-Sotelo, *Gendered Transitions: Mexican Experiences of Immigration* (1994)

Gerald Horne, *Fire This Time: The Watts Uprising and the 1960s* (1995)

L. C. Ikemoto, "Traces of the Master Narrative in the Story of African American/Korean American Conflict: How We Constructed 'Los Angeles,'" *Southern California Law Review* LXVI (May 1993): 1581–98

"Immigration and Economic Restructuring: The Metamorphosis of Southern California," a special issue of *California Sociologist* XII (Summer 1989)

Bryan O. Jackson and Michael B. Preston, eds., *Racial and Ethnic Politics in California* (1991)

Maria-Rosario Jackson, James H. Johnson, Jr., and Walter C. Farrell, Jr., "After the Smoke Has Cleared: An Analysis of Selected Responses to the Los Angeles Civil Unrest of 1992," *Contention: Debates in Society, Culture, and Science* IX (Spring 1994): 3–21

Joel Kotkin and Paul Grabowicz, *California, Inc.* (1982)

Leadership Education for Asian Pacifics, Asian Pacific American Public Policy Institute and University of California, Los Angeles, Asian American Studies Center, *The State of Asian Pacific America: Policy Issues to the Year 2020* (1993)

Tom Lutz, "The Management of Diversity, Culture Wars, and the Burning of Los Angeles," *American Studies in Scandinavia* [Denmark] XXV (1993): 1–26

Haki R. Madhubuti, ed., *Why L.A. Happened: Implications of the '92 Los Angeles Rebellion* (1993)

Leonard Michaels, David Reid, and Raquel Scherr, eds., *West of the West: Imagining California* (1989)

Peter A. Morrison and Ira S. Lowry, *A Riot of Color: The Demographic Setting of Civil Disturbance in Los Angeles* (1993)

Angela E. Oh, "Race Relations in Los Angeles: 'Divide and Conquer' Is Alive and Flourishing," *Southern California Law Review* LXVI (May 1993): 1647–56

Laurie Olsen, *Crossing the Schoolhouse Border: Immigrant Students and the California Public Schools* (1988)

Paul Ong, ed., *Economic Diversity: Issues and Policies* (1994)

Paul Ong, Edna Bonacich, and Lucie Cheng, eds., *The New Asian Immigration in Los Angeles and Global Restructuring* (1994)

Manuel Pastor, Jr., et al., *Latinos and the Los Angeles Uprising: The Economic Context* (1993)

Policy Analysis for California Education, *The Conditions of Children in California* (1989)

David Rieff, *Los Angeles: Capital of the Third World* (1991)

Reginald Leamon Robinson, "The Other against Itself: Deconstructing the Violent Discourse between Koreans and African Americans," *Southern California Law Review* LXVII (November 1993): 15–115

Dan Walters, *The New California: Facing the 21st Century* (1992)

Charles Wollenberg, "A Usable History for a Multicultural State," *California History* LXIV (Summer 1985): 202–09

Eui-Young Yu, ed., *Black-Korean Encounter: Toward Understanding and Alliance, Dialogue between Blacks and Korean Americans in the Aftermath of the 1992 Los Angeles Riots* (1994)

DOCUMENT SOURCES

Chapter 2 The First Californians

Map of Tribal Territories Based on Robert F. Heizer, ed. *A Collection of Ethnographic Articles on the California Indians.* Ramona, Calif.: Ballena Press, 1976, p. ii.

Indian Material Culture Santa Barbara Museum of Natural History, Photograph by William Dewey. American Museum of Natural History.

The Three Worlds of the Chumash Excerpted from Thomas C. Blackburn, ed. *December's Child: A Book of Chumash Oral Narratives Collected by J. P. Harrington.* Berkeley and Los Angeles: University of California Press, 1972, pp. 91–100. Copyright © 1972 by The Regents of the University of California. Reprinted by permission of the University of California Press.

Pablo Tac Approves of His Tribe's Conversion, 1835 From Minna and Gordon Hewes, trans. and ed. *Indian Life and Customs at Mission San Luis Rey, A Record of California Mission Life by Pablo Tac, an Indian Neophyte, Written About 1835.* San Luis Rey, Calif.: Old Mission, 1958 [originally published 1952], pp. 6–8. Reprinted by permission of the American Academy of Franciscan History.

Father Geronimo Boscana Describes the San Juan Capistrano Indians, 1832 From John P. Harrington. *A New Original Version of Boscana's Historical Account of the San Juan Capistrano Indians of Southern California.* Washington, D.C.: Smithsonian Institution, 1934, pp. 5–6, 16, 23–25, 29–30.

A *Sacramento Union* Editorial Ponders the Indians' Fate, 1855 From "Indian War," in Robert F. Heizer, ed. *The Destruction of California Indians: A collection of documents from the period 1847 to 1865 in which are described some of the things that happened to some of the Indians of California.* Lincoln and London: University of Nebraska Press, 1993 [originally published in *Sacramento Union*, February 3, 1855], pp. 35–36.

Chapter 3 The Spanish Impact on the Indians, 1769–1821

Father Luis Jayme Criticizes the Behavior of Spanish Soldiers, 1772 From Maynard Geiger, trans. and ed. *Letter of Luís Jayme, O.F.M.: San Diego, October 17, 1772.* Los Angeles: San Diego Public Library, 1970, pp. 38–42. Reprinted by permission of the San Diego Public Library, San Diego, California. Footnotes 28–31 omitted by permission.

Father Junipero Serra Reports the Destruction of the San Diego Mission, 1775 From Antonine Tibesar, O.F.M., ed. *The Writings of Junipero Serra.* Washington, D.C.: Academy of American Franciscan History, 1956, vol. II, pp. 401, 403, 405, 407. Reprinted by permission of the Academy of American Franciscan History.

Captain Alejandro Malaspina Praises the Beneficial Impact of Spanish Missions, 1792 From Donald C. Cutter. *California in 1792: A Spanish Naval Visit.* Norman: University of Oklahoma Press, 1990, pp. 128–30. Copyright © 1990 by University of Oklahoma Press. Reprinted by permission of University of Oklahoma Press.

Lorenzo Asisara Narrates the Assassination of a Priest by Santa Cruz Indians, 1812 From Edward D. Castillo, trans. and ed. "The Assassination of Padre Andrés Quintana by the Indians of Mission Santa Cruz in 1812," *California History,* 68 (Fall 1989): pp. 120–24. Reprinted by permission of the California Historical Society.

Chapter 4 Mexican California, A Study in Contrasts

A Mexican Commission Urges the Secularization of the California Missions, 1833 From "The Secularization of the Missions: A Newly Discovered California Document," *Historical Society of Southern California*, 16 (1934): pp. 68–73. Reprinted by permission of the Historical Society of Southern California.

Angustias de la Guerra Ord Defends the Virtue of Mission Priests, 1878 From Francis Price and William H. Ellison, trans. and ed. *Occurrences in Hispanic California*. Washington, D.C.: Academy of American Franciscan History, 1956, pp. 31–33. Reprinted by permission of the Academy of American Franciscan History.

Richard Henry Dana, Jr., Criticizes the Mexicans in California, 1834 From Richard Henry Dana, Jr. *Two Years Before the Mast*. New York: Modern Library, 1964 [originally published 1840], pp. 158–63.

Guadalupe Vallejo Reminisces About the Ranchero Period From Oscar Lewis, ed. *Sketches of Early California: A Collection of Personal Adventures*. San Francisco: Chronicle Books, 1971, pp. 3–5, 18, 22.

William Robert Garner Promotes the American Annexation of California, 1847 From Donald Munro Craig, ed. *Letters from California, 1846–1847*. Berkeley and Los Angeles: University of California Press, 1970, pp. 187–88. Copyright © 1970 by The Regents of the University of California. Reprinted by permission of the University of California Press.

Selected Articles from the Treaty of Guadalupe Hidalgo, 1848 From N. C. Brooks. *A Complete History of the Mexican War: Its Causes, Conduct, and Consequences*. Baltimore: Hutchinson and Seebold, 1849, pp. 541–42, 546–47.

Chapter 5 Conflicts over Land in a New State, 1850s–1870s

E. Gould Buffum Exults in Gold's Discovery, 1850 From E. Gould Buffum. *Six Months in the Gold Mines: From a Journal of Three Years of Residence in Upper and Lower California, 1847–8–9*. Philadelphia: Lea and Blanchard, 1850, pp. xiv–xvi, 107–8.

Louisa Clapp Pokes Fun at Her Experiences as a Gold "Mineress," 1851 From Carl I. Wheat, ed. *The Shirley Letters from the California Mines, 1851–1852*. New York: Alfred A. Knopf, 1961, pp. 83–85. Copyright © 1949 by Alfred A. Knopf, Inc. Reprinted by permission of the publisher.

J. D. Borthwick Observes Chinese Gold Miners, 1851 From J. D. Borthwick. *Three Years in California, 1851–1854*. Edinburgh and London: W. Blackwood and Sons, 1857, pp. 117–19.

John F. Morse Supports Traditional Agrarian Values, 1865 From *Transactions of the California State Agriculture Society During the Years 1864 and 1865*. Sacramento: State Printing Office, 1866, pp. 183–85.

Henry George Censures Land Monopoly, 1871 From Henry George. *Our Land and Land Policy*. New York: Doubleday, 1871, pp. 36–39.

Chapter 6 Disputes over Water, 1880s–1910s

Lux v. *Haggin* **Establishes the "California Doctrine," 1886** From *The Pacific Reporter*, 10 (March 25–June 3, 1886): pp. 700–1, 775.

The Wright Act Asserts Community Water Rights, 1887, 1889 From U.S. Congress, Senate, Special Committee on the Irrigation and Reclamation of Arid Lands. *Report*. 51st Cong., 1st sess. Washington, D.C.: Government Printing Office, 1890, pp. 250, 264–65.

Congress Acts: Selections from the Reclamation Act of 1902 From Appropriation Act. *U.S. Statutes at Large*, 32 (1902): part I, pp. 388–89.

John Muir Admires the Hetch Hetchy Valley, 1908 From "The Hetch Hetchy Valley," *Sierra Club Bulletin*, 6 (January 1908): pp. 211–17, 219–20.

Robert Underwood Johnson Decries Paying Too High a Price for Water, 1909 From "A High Price to Pay for Water: Apropos of the Grant of the Hetch Hetchy Valley to San Francisco for a Reservoir," *Century*, 7 (January 1909) [originally published August 1908]: pp. 69–71.

Chapter 7 Big Business and Urban Labor, 1860s–1930s

Henry George Expresses Skepticism About Railroads, 1868 From "What the Railroads Will Bring Us," *The Overland Monthly*, 1 (October 1868): pp. 297–98, 300–2.

Leland Stanford Extols the Public Benefits of Railroad Construction, 1887 From U.S. Pacific Railway Commission. *Testimony Taken by the United States Pacific Railway Commission Appointed under the Act of Congress Approved March 3, 1887, Entitled "An Act Authorizing an Investigation of the Books, Accounts, and Methods of Railroads Which Have Received Aid from the United States."* Senate Executive Doc. 51, 50th Cong., 1st sess. Washington, D.C.: Government Printing Office, 1887, pp. 2465–66.

Collis P. Huntington Shows Contempt for Congress, 1887 From U.S. Pacific Railway Commission. *Testimony Taken by the United States Pacific Railway Commission Appointed under the Act of Congress Approved March 3, 1887, Entitled "An Act Authorizing an Investigation of the Books, Accounts, and Methods of Railroads Which Have Received Aid from the United States."* Senate Executive Doc. 51, 50th Cong., 1st sess. Washington, D.C.: Government Printing Office, 1887, pp. 3698, 3700–1.

Frank Norris Excoriates the Railroad as "The Octopus," 1901 From Frank Norris. *The Octopus*. New York: Bantam, 1977 [originally published 1901], pp. 31–33, 368–69.

Denis Kearney Organizes the Workingmen's Party of California, 1877 From Ira B. Cross. *A History of the Labor Movement in California*. Berkeley and Los Angeles: University of California Press, 1935, pp. 96–97. Copyright © 1974 by The Regents of the University of California. Reprinted by permission of the University of California Press.

Henryk Sienkiewicz Appraises Chinese Labor in California, 1880 From Charles Morley, trans. with Foreword. "The Chinese in California: A Report by Henryk Sienkiewicz," *California Historical Society Quarterly*, 34, no. 4, (1955): pp. 308–9, 311. Reprinted by permission of the California Historical Society.

The American Federation of Labor Opposes Chinese Immigration, 1902 From American Federation of Labor. *Some Reasons for Chinese Exclusion—Meat vs. Rice: American Manhood Against Asiatic Coolieism—Which Shall Survive?* Washington, D.C.: American Federation of Labor, 1902, pp. 18, 35–36.

Chapter 8 California Progressives: The Ambiguities of Political and Moral Reform

Franklin Hichborn Praises Reform Governor Hiram W. Johnson, 1911 From Franklin Hichborn. *Story of the Session of the California Legislature of 1911*. San Francisco: James H. Barry, 1911, pp. 40–49.

John Randolph Haynes Advocates Direct Legislation, 1911 From John Randolph Haynes. "Direct Legislation," *Transactions of the Commonwealth Club of California*, 6 (September 1911): pp. 94–95.

Chester H. Rowell Analyzes the Problem of Japanese Immigration in California, 1914 From "The Japanese in California," *The World's Work*, 26 (June 1914): pp. 195–97, 199, 201.

Carrie Chapman Catt Argues That Home and Government Are Related, 1907
From "The Home and the Government," *The Yellow Ribbon*, 1, no. 6 (March 1907): p. 4.

Katherine Philips Edson Boasts of Women's Influence on State Legislation, 1913 From Mrs. Charles Farwell Edson. "Women's Influence on State Legislation," *The California Outlook*, 14, no. 24 (June 14, 1907): pp. 7–8, 19.

Mary S. Gibson Explains Why Progressive Women Should Uplift Immigrant Women, 1914 From "The Immigrant Woman," *The California Outlook*, 16, no. 19 (May 9, 1914): pp. 6–7.

Chapter 9 Hollywood and the California Dream, 1910s–1930s

Cecil B. de Mille Reveals How He Creates Special Effects, 1927 From "Building a Photoplay," in Joseph P. Kennedy, ed. *The Story of the Films*. Chicago and New York: A.W. Shaw Co., 1927, pp. 129–31, 145–49.

A. H. Giannini Explains Why He Decided to Finance the Film Industry, 1926 From "Financing the Production and Distribution of Motion Pictures," *The Annals of the American Academy of Political and Social Science*, 128 (November 1926): pp. 46–49.

Harmon B. Stephens Exposes How Films Lower Moral Standards, 1926 From "The Relation of the Motion Picture to Changing Moral Standards," *The American Academy of Political and Social Science*, 128 (November 1926): pp. 154–57.

Ruth Suckow Analyzes the Appeal of Hollywood Gods and Goddesses, 1936 From "Hollywood Gods and Goddesses," *Harper's Magazine*, 173 (July 1936): pp. 189–94, 198–200. Copyright © 1936 by *Harper's Magazine*. All rights reserved. Reproduced from the July issue by special permission.

Nathanael West Satirizes Hollywood Movie Sets, 1939 From *The Day of the Locust*. New York: Penguin Books, U.S.A., 1983 [originally published 1939], pp. 125–31. Copyright © 1939 by Estate of Nathanael West. Reprinted by permission of New Directions Publishing Corp.

Chapter 10 Farmworker Struggles in the 1930s

The California Department of Industrial Relations Evaluates Agricultural Labor Contracts, 1930 From State of California Department of Industrial Relations. *Facts About Filipino Immigration into California*. San Francisco: State Building, 1930, pp. 60–62.

Carlos Bulosan Describes the Harsh Existence of Filipino Migrant Farmworkers From *America Is in the Heart: A Personal History*. Seattle: University of Washington Press, 1973 [originally published 1943], pp. 119, 144. Reprinted by permission of the publisher.

John Steinbeck Portrays Social Pressures in Agricultural California, 1939 From *The Grapes of Wrath*. New York: Penguin Books, U.S.A., 1976 [originally published 1939], pp. 377–80. Copyright 1939, renewed © 1967 by John Steinbeck. Used by permission of Viking Penguin, a division of Penguin Books U.S.A., Inc.

James Rorty Reports on Conditions in the Imperial Valley, 1935 From "Lettuce—With American Dressing," *The Nation* (May 15, 1935): pp. 575–76. Reprinted with permission from *The Nation* magazine. Copyright © The Nation Company, L. P.

Grower Frank Stokes Defends Mexican Farmworkers' Efforts to Organize, 1936 From "Let the Mexicans Organize," *The Nation* (December 19, 1936): pp. 731–32. Reprinted with permission from *The Nation* magazine. Copyright © The Nation Company, L. P.

Ralph H. Taylor Rallies California's Growers to Protect Their Interests, 1938 From "The Farmer's Problem," Associated Farmers of California, Inc. *Bulletin*, 38 (January 18, 1938): pp. 2, 4.

Chapter 11 The Impact of World War II on California's Economy

The U.S. Bureau of Labor Statistics Reports on California's Airframe Industry, 1945 From U.S. Department of Labor, Bureau of Labor Statistics. "Wartime Expansion of the California Airframe Industry," *Monthly Labor Review,* 61, no. 4 (1945): pp. 721–27.

Kaiser Shipyard Workers Fight on the Home Front, 1943 From "Second Front Scoreboard," *Fore'N'Aft,* 3, no. 30 (July 30, 1943), and "Yard 3 Is Challenged!!" *Fore'N'Aft,* 3, no. 33 (August 20, 1943).

Marye Stumph Recalls Her Work Experiences in an Aircraft Factory From Sherna B. Gluck. *Rosie the Riveter Revisited: Women, the War, and Social Change.* Boston: Twayne, 1987, pp. 60–63, 65. Reprinted with the permission of Twayne Publishers, an imprint of Simon & Schuster Macmillan. Copyright © 1987 by Sherna Berger Gluck.

Industrial Leaders Assess the West's Postwar Economic Prospects, 1946 From Worth Hale. "Industry's Leaders Outline West's Industrial Prospects," *Pacific Factory* (January 1946): pp. 48–52.

Chapter 12 The Changing Lives of Women and Minorities, 1940s–1950s

Charles Kikuchi Observes Life in an American "Concentration Camp," 1942 From *The Kikuchi Diary: Chronicle from an American Concentration Camp.* Ed. John Modell. Urbana: University of Illinois Press, 1973, pp. 55, 61–63. Copyright © 1973 by the Board of Trustees of the University of Illinois. Used with permission of the University of Illinois Press.

Two Poems About the Camps From Toyo Suyemoto Kawakami. "Camp Memories: Rough and Broken Shards," in *Japanese Americans: From Relocation to Redress.* Ed. Roger Daniels, Sandra C. Taylor, and Harry H. L. Kitano. Seattle: University of Washington Press, 1991 [originally published 1986], p. 28. Copyright © 1986, 1991, by Daniels, Taylor, and Kitano. Used with permission of the University of Washington Press. From Lawson Fusao Inada. "Mud," in *Before the War: Poems as They Happened.* New York: William Morrow, 1971, p. 16.

Fanny Christina Hill Fights Discrimination Against Black Workers in the Aircraft Industry From Sherna B. Gluck. *Rosie the Riveter Revisited: Women, the War, and Social Change.* Boston: Twayne, 1987, pp. 31–32, 35–38, 41–44.

Willard Waller Announces the Postwar Battle of the Sexes, 1945 From "The Coming War on Women," *San Francisco Chronicle This Week Magazine.* February 18, 1945, pp. 4–5. © 1945 by the San Francisco Chronicle. Reprinted by permission.

Chapter 13 Politics and Protest, 1960s–1970s

Mario Savio Defends the Free Speech Movement at Berkeley, 1965 From "Berkeley Fall: The Berkeley Student Rebellion of 1964," in Mario Savio, Eugene Walker, and Raya Dunayevskaya, *The Free Speech Movement and the Negro Revolution.* Detroit: News and Letters, 1965, pp. 15–18.

Ronald Reagan Denounces The Morality Gap at Berkeley, 1966 From *The Creative Society: Some Comments on Problems Facing America.* New York: Devin-Adair Co., 1968, pp. 125–27.

Bobby Seale Explains What the Black Panther Party Stands For, 1968 From *Seize the Time: The Story of the Black Panther Party and Huey P. Newton.* New York: Vintage Books, 1968, pp. 71–72.

Manifesto of the Chicano Student Conference, 1969 From Carlos Munoz, Jr. *Youth, Identity, Power: The Chicano Movement.* London: Verso, 1989 [originally published by the Chicano Coordinating Committee on Higher Education. *El Plan de Santa Barbara, 1969*], pp. 191–92. Copyright © 1969 by the Chicano Coordinating Committee on Higher Education, Santa Barbara, California.

Declaration of the Asian American Political Alliance, 1969 From Amy Tachiki et al., eds. *Roots: An Asian American Reader.* Los Angeles: University of California, Los Angeles, Asian American Studies Center, 1971 [originally published by Asian American Political Alliance. "AAPA Perspectives," 1, no. 6 (1969)], p. 251. Reprinted by permission of Asian American Studies Center.

Indians of All Tribes Occupy Alcatraz Island, 1969 From Roger Daniels and Spencer C. Olin, eds. *Racism in California: A Reader in the History of Oppression.* New York: Macmillan Co., 1972 [originally published in *Indians of All Tribes News,* 1 (January 1970): pp. 2–3], pp. 51–53.

Why Secretaries in Academia Are Fed Up, 1971 From *The Second Wave: A Magazine of the New Feminism,* 1, no. 2 (Summer 1971) [originally published in *Every Other Weekly* (newsmagazine of *The Daily Californian*), February 17, 1971]: pp. 18–20, 23.

Chapter 14 The Rise of Information Capitalism

California Computer Companies, 1989 From *California Business,* 24 (October 1989): p. 31.

Art Garcia Describes California's New Economic Frontier, 1984 From Art Garcia. "What New Frontiers Are Californians Developing?" *California Business,* 19 (April 1984): pp. 35–36, 40.

Donald Woutat Ponders the Resignation of Steven Jobs from Apple Computer, 1985 From "Jobs' Departure from Apple End of an Era," *Los Angeles Times,* September 19, 1985. Copyright 1995, *Los Angeles Times.* Reprinted by permission.

Faith Alchorn Ties Information Technology to Political Campaigns, 1988 From "Software for the Hard Sell," *California Journal,* 19 (January 1988): pp. 33–34, 37. Reprinted by permission of *California Journal.*

Duane Spilsbury Reports on Telecommuting, 1989 From Duane Spilsbury. "Testing Telecommuting," *Golden State Report* (October 1989): pp. 13–14, 16.

Chapter 15 The Environment and the Quality of Life Since 1960

Samuel E. Wood and Alfred Heller Oppose Urban Sprawl, 1961 From John Harte, ed. *The New Book of California Tomorrow: Reflections and Projections from the Golden State.* Los Altos, Calif.: William Kaufmann, 1984 [originally published in *California Going, Going . . .,* Sacramento: California Tomorrow, 1962], pp. 32–35, 95–96. Copyright © 1994 by William Kaufmann, Inc., Los Altos, CA 94022. All rights reserved.

Frank M. Stead Assesses California Water Pollution, 1968 From John Harte, ed. *The New Book of California Tomorrow: Reflections and Projections from the Golden State.* Los Altos, Calif.: William Kaufmann, 1984, pp. 171–75. Copyright © 1994 by William Kaufmann, Inc., Los Altos, CA 94022. All rights reserved.

Richard Reinhardt Looks at Air Pollution Problems, 1982 From John Harte, ed. *The New Book of California Tomorrow: Reflections and Projections from the Golden State.* Los Altos, Calif.: William Kaufmann, 1984 [originally published in *California 2000: The Next Frontier.* San Francisco: California Tomorrow, 1982], pp. 396–98. Copyright © 1994 by William Kaufmann. Inc., Los Altos, CA 94022. All rights reserved.

A Government Commission Discusses the Dangers of Pesticides, 1988 From Leo McCarthy. *Poisoning Prosperity II: Chemical Exposures vs. Public Health: Report to the California Commission for Economic Development.* Sacramento, Calif.: California's Commission for Economic Development, 1988, pp. 23–27.

Carl Anthony Outlines Why African Americans Should Be Environmentalists, 1990 From "Why African Americans Should Be Environmentalists," *Earth Island Journal* (Winter 1990): pp. 43–44. Reprinted by permission of the publisher.

Ronald Bailey Denounces the "Eco-Scam," 1993 From *Eco-Scam: The False Prophets of Ecological Apocalypse.* New York: St. Martin's, 1993, pp. 1, 3, 7–10, 16–17, 19, 21–22. Reprinted with permission of St. Martin's Press.

Chapter 16 Racial and Class Tensions, 1960s and 1990s

The McCone Commission Analyzes the Watts Riot, 1965 From John A. McCone et al., *Violence in the City: An End or a Beginning? A Report by the Governor's Commission on the Los Angeles Riots.* Los Angeles: Governor's Commission on the Los Angeles Riots, 1965, pp. 1–9.

David Rieff Sees Los Angeles as the Capital of the Third World, 1991 From *Los Angeles: Capital of the Third World.* New York: Simon & Schuster,1991, pp. 237–40. Reprinted with the permission of Simon & Schuster. Copyright © 1991 by David Rieff.

Mwatabu S. Okantah Protests the Beating of Rodney King, 1993 From "America's poem, or 81 seconds and 56 blows," in *Why LA Happened: Implications of the '92 Los Angeles Rebellion.* Ed. Haki R. Madhubuti. Chicago: Third World Press, 1993, pp. 136–40. Copyright © 1993. Reprinted by permission of Third World Press.

Armando Navarro Offers a Latino Perspective on the 1992 Civil Disorders, 1993 From "The South Central Los Angeles Eruption: A Latino Perspective," *Amerasia Journal,* 19, no. 2 (1993): pp. 80–82. Copyright © 1993 and reprinted by permission of Asian American Studies Center, UCLA.

Eui-Young Yu Offers a Korean American Perspective on the Los Angeles Civil Disorders, 1992 From "We Saw Ourselves Burned for No Reason," *Los Angeles Times,* May 18, 1992. Copyright © 1992 by Eui-Young Yu. Reprinted by permission.

Patrick J. Buchanan Condemns the "Barbarism" of the "Mob," 1992 From "War for the Soul of America," commencement address, Liberty University, Lynch-burg, Virginia, May 9, 1992 (from an abbreviated version printed in *Los Angeles Times,* May 28, 1992). Copyright © 1992 and reprinted by permission of Tribune Media Services.

John Bryant Encourages Corporate America to Invest in Minority Communities, 1995 From "The Business of Fairness," *Los Angeles Times,* August 29, 1995. Reprinted by permission of the author.

Lynell George and David Ferrell Analyze the Staggering Racial Complexity of Los Angeles, 1995 From "L.A.'s Veneer Stripped to Show Blemishes," *Los Angeles Times,* October 10, 1995. Copyright © 1995 *Los Angeles Times.* Reprinted by permission.

George Regas Advocates a Shared Moral Vision, 1995 From "The Jury Is Still Out," *Los Angeles Times,* October 10, 1995. Copyright © 1995 by George F. Regas; William Coffin for the Michelangelo interpretation. Reprinted by permission of the author.

Major Problems in American History Series
Titles Currently Available

Boris, Lichtenstein, *Major Problems in the History of American Workers* (1991, 19925-7)

Brown, *Major Problems in the Era of the American Revolution, 1760—1791* (1992, 19755-6)

Chudacoff, *Major Problems in American Urban History* (1994, 24376-0)

Escott, Goldfield, *Major Problems in the History of the American South,* two volumes (1990)
Volume I: *The Old South* (13157-1)
Volume II: *The New South* (19924-9)

Fink, *Major Problems in the Gilded Age and the Progressive Era* (1993, 21680-1)

Griffith, *Major Problems in American History Since 1945* (1992, 19625-8)

Hall, *Major Problems in American Constitutional History,* two volumes (1992)
Volume I: *From the Colonial Era Through Reconstruction* (21209-1)
Volume II: *From 1870 to the Present* (21210-5)

Hurtado, Iverson, *Major Problems in American Indian History* (1994, 27049-0)

Kupperman, *Major Problems in American Colonial History* (1993, 19922-2)

McMahon, *Major Problems in the History of the Vietnam War* (2d ed.) (1995, 35252-7)

Merchant, *Major Problems in American Environmental History* (1993, 24993-9)

Milner, Butler, Lewis, *Major Problems in the History of the American West* (2d ed.) (1997, 41580-4)

Norton, Alexander, *Major Problems in American Women's History* (1996, 35390-6)

Paterson, Merrill, *Major Problems in American Foreign Relations* two volumes, (4th ed., 1995)
Volume I: *To 1920* (35077-X)
Volume II: *Since 1914* (35078-8)

Perman, *Major Problems in the Civil War and Reconstruction* (1991, 20148-0)

Riess, *Major Problems in American Sport History* (1997, 35380-9)

Wilentz, *Major Problems in the Early Republic, 1787—1848* (1992, 24332-9)